Research Handbook on Start-Up Incubation Ecosystems

T0295941

Edited by

Adam Novotny

Researcher, Nord University Business School, Bodø, Norway

Einar Rasmussen

Professor, Nord University Business School, Bodø, Norway

Tommy H. Clausen

Professor, Nord University Business School, Bodø, Norway

Johan Wiklund

The Al Berg Chair and Professor of Entrepreneurship, Whitman School of Management, Syracuse University, USA

Cheltenham, UK • Northampton, MA, USA

Published by
Edward Elgar Publishing Limited
The Lypiatts
15 Lansdown Road
Cheltenham
Glos GL50 2JA
UK

Edward Elgar Publishing, Inc.
William Pratt House
9 Dewey Court
Northampton
Massachusetts 01060
USA

Paperback edition 2021

A catalogue record for this book
is available from the British Library

Library of Congress Control Number: 2019951924

This book is available electronically in the **Elgar**online
Business subject collection
DOI 10.4337/9781788973533

Printed on elemental chlorine free (ECF)
recycled paper containing 30% Post-Consumer Waste

ISBN 978 1 78897 352 6 (cased)
ISBN 978 1 78897 353 3 (eBook)
ISBN 978 1 80220 166 6 (paperback)
Printed and bound in the USA

Contents

PART II START-UP SUPPORT ORGANIZATIONS

PART III UNIVERSITY-BASED SUPIEs

Contributors

B.W. Åmo, Nord University Business School, Norway

Cristiano Bellavitis, Auckland University, New Zealand

Paul Benneworth, Western Norway University of Applied Sciences, Norway; University of Twente, the Netherlands

Peter M. Bican, Friedrich-Alexander University, Germany

Anders Billström, Nord University Business School, Norway; Halmstad University, Sweden

J.J. Bragelien, Western Norway University of Applied Sciences, Norway

Marit Breivik-Meyer, Nord University Business School, Norway

Alexander Brem, Friedrich-Alexander University, Germany; University of Southern Denmark, Denmark

Espen Carlsson, Trøndelag R&D Institute, Norway

Tommy H. Clausen, Nord University Business School, Norway

Carlos M. DaSilva, School of Management – Fribourg, HEG-Fr / HES-SO, Switzerland

Matthew Good, University of Oslo, Norway

Jorunn Grande, Nord University Business School, Norway

Magnus Gulbrandsen, University of Oslo, Norway

Jens Ø. Hansen, Nordland Research Institute, Norway

Roberto Rivas Hermann, Nord University Business School, Norway

Espen J. Isaksen, Nord University Business School, Norway

Are Jensen, Nord University Business School, Norway

Alan R. Johnson, Nord University Business School, Norway; RATIO Institute, Sweden

Eva Jenny B. Jørgensen, UiT – The Arctic University of Norway, Norway

Kerul Kassel, Fielding Graduate University, CA, United States

Mirjam Knockaert, Ghent University, Belgium

Lars Kolvereid, Nord University Business School, Norway

Matteo Landoni, Università Cattolica del Sacro Cuore, Italy

Karolina Lesniak, Norwegian University of Science and Technology, Norway

Åge Mariussen, Nordland Research Institute, Norway

Katherine E. Masyn, Georgia State University, GA, United States

Alexander McKelvie, Syracuse University, NY, United States

Karim Messeghem, University of Montpellier, France

Shelley F. Mitchell, HULT International School of Business, MA, United States

Dolores Modic, Kyushu University, Japan; Nord University Business School, Norway

Nhien Nguyen, Nordland Research Institute, Norway; Norwegian University of Science and Technology, Norway

Guénola Abord-Hugon Nonet, Jönköping University, Sweden

Nadja Nordling, Tampere University, Finland

Adam Novotny, Nord University Business School, Norway; Eszterházy Károly University of Applied Sciences, Hungary

Allan O'Connor, University of South Australia, Australia

I.B. Pettersen, Western Norway University of Applied Sciences, Norway

Rhiannon Pugh, Örebro University, Sweden

Einar Rasmussen, Nord University Business School, Norway

Tiago Ratinho, IÉSEG School of Management, France; LEM-CNRS 9221, France

Sami Saarenketo, LUT University, Finland

Shruti Sardeshmukh, University of South Australia, Australia

Michael Sargent, Auckland University, New Zealand

Ronda Smith, Ball State University, IN, United States

Roger Sørheim, Norwegian University of Science and Technology, Norway

Oliver Straub, Friedrich-Alexander University, Germany

Christina Theodoraki, TBS Business School, France

Elisa Thomas, University of Stavanger Business School, Norway

Lasse Torkkeli, LUT University, Finland

E. van der Lingen, University of Pretoria, South Africa

Hannes Velt, LUT University, Finland

K. Voldsund, Western Norway University of Applied Sciences, Norway

Johan Wiklund, Syracuse University, NY, United States

Tohru Yoshioka-Kobayashi, University of Tokyo, Japan; Hitotsubashi University, Japan

Preface

While start-up firms are usually born small, many of them have the potential to revitalize the whole economy, or parts of it, and change the way we think about business, innovation, and life in general. People tend to believe that successful start-up entrepreneurs are lonely champions and start-up firms are standalone stars, but even the biggest talents are lost without a supporting environment. Applying an ecosystems perspective to study the development of innovative small firms is hence becoming increasingly popular among entrepreneurship scholars. Still, we have limited knowledge of how the interactions between the context and the firm affect the development of both.

In this handbook, we offer various empirical, literature-based, and conceptual studies that focus on how the different actors and factors in the ecosystem incubate start-ups. Similar to living organisms, the care and resources firms receive at the start of their life are crucial for their growth potential and future success. We propose a Start-up Incubation Ecosystem (SUPIE) perspective, which, in contrast to other ecosystem approaches, focuses on a more specific and perhaps more critical context that surrounds firms at the time of "hatching", when they start learning how to become independent, i.e. survive and grow by using the available resources in their proximate environment.

SUPIEs are both exciting and challenging to study. Similar to natural ecosystems, they vary significantly in size, from a group of individuals to a whole geographical region, or even more; in type, as some incubate software firms while others nurture biopharma companies; in resources, as shown by the comparison of urban and rural SUPIEs. Besides, they are also connected to and embedded in one another.

The above considerations brought alive a new aspiration at Nord University Business School, where an internationally recognized research team, led by local professors and assisted by renowned visiting scholars, have been studying the crossroads of innovation and entrepreneurship for more than three decades. The new aspiration was to gather researchers from around the world interested in understanding and further exploring SUPIEs, and to create a research handbook that sums up previous works on, offers original contributions to, and sets future directions for the study of start-ups and their environments.

In Spring 2018, we issued an open call for researchers to submit their ideas and ongoing projects with us for possible publication in a SUPIE research handbook. During the following 12 months, the proposals were evaluated, and the submitted chapters went through two rounds of blind peer review. The editors helped author-teams to align their ideas and research projects with the theme of the book. Between the two revision rounds, in November 2018, we invited contributors to Nord University in Bodø, to present their works and receive additional feedback, and at the same time network with fellow researchers. While some chapters have been withdrawn during the process, we are happy that 23 manuscripts ended up being accepted for publication. These chapters are written by 54 scholars affiliated to institutions in 15 countries including Australia, Belgium, Finland, France, Germany, Hungary, Italy, Japan, the Netherlands, New Zealand, Norway, South Africa, Sweden, Switzerland, and the United States.

The SUPIE handbook would not have been published without essential financial and human resources. First of all, we would like to thank the contributors for their interest in publishing their research with us and for actively collaborating with the editors during the review process. We express our gratitude to the Regional Research Funds for Northern Norway and Nord University for providing the funding that made this project possible. We also thank the publisher, Edward Elgar, for expressing their interest in the topic and for the kind assistance they have provided throughout the publication process.

We hope that the story of a book does not end when published, and the SUPIE research handbook becomes an important piece in the field of ecosystems approaches to entrepreneurship and innovation. The book is primarily recommended for those who would like to get acquainted with the topic and different ways of studying it. For example, PhD students may find it a good starting point before submitting their research proposal, but we believe that many other academics, researchers, practitioners, and policymakers can also benefit from the variety of chapters included.

Finally, before they start reading the book, we advise the readers to look at Figure I.1 in the introduction, which organizes the chapters according to their relationship with the primary layers of SUPIEs: individual and organizational, in addition to framework conditions. The other dimension of the figure relates to the unit of analysis, also used to structure the chapters. Accordingly, following the introduction, the studies are divided into three main groups: *Part I* deals with the start-up incubation ecosystem as a whole, its build-up and functioning; *Part II* discusses the role of start-up support organizations within SUPIEs; and *Part III* focuses on how university-based SUPIEs spin out and support start-ups.

The Editors

Introduction: Helping birds to fly: Introducing start-up incubation ecosystems

Adam Novotny, Einar Rasmussen,
Tommy H. Clausen, and Johan Wiklund

INTRODUCTION

Start-up firms play a critically important role in the development of our economy. Through the process of creative destruction (Schumpeter, 1934), the new replaces the old, and soon, a significant share of economic activity will be performed by firms that do not exist today. Start-ups create jobs, improve economies, increase social mobility, facilitate innovation, and generate other benefits (Aldrich & Ruef, 2006). They serve as engines of regional development (Fritsch & Mueller, 2004) and bring to life innovations that contribute to resolving global challenges (Fini, Rasmussen, Siegel, & Wiklund, 2018). Indeed, the promotion of entrepreneurial activity is often a key ingredient in economic and social development policies (McCann & Ortega-Argilés, 2016). However, start-ups do not occur and develop in a vacuum. Just as no man is an island, no start-up is an island. Instead, they grow in close interaction with their surrounding environments, leveraging existing resources, and engaging in exchange with other parties (Gnyawali & Fogel, 1994; Van de Ven, 1993). The types of resources and relationships established during the early years have a formative influence on the development, growth and performance of start-ups (Beckman & Burton, 2008).

More recently, the notion of an entrepreneurial ecosystem has become a famous analogy for understanding the role of the environment in entrepreneurship (Malecki, 2018; Mason & Brown, 2014). The analogy stems from the similarity between the life and development of living organisms in natural ecosystems and those of start-ups in entrepreneurial ecosystems. Living beings represent complex structures that need constant energy supplies obtained from their environment to survive and grow. Their environments constitute multi-layered systems that provide them with external energy that is passed on from one trophic level to the next (i.e., solar energy, plants, herbivores, and predators) until decomposers return nutrients to the environment. This large community of interdependent living beings, together with the nonliving components of the environment,

1

make up an ecological system or ecosystem. Similar to natural ecosystems, entrepreneurial ecosystems comprise complex and diverse networks of organizations, individuals, and other environmental components that interact to influence entrepreneurial activity and economic functioning in a particular context, region, or locality. A fundamental feature of ecosystems, either natural or entrepreneurial, is that each organism/organization must use some energy/resources that they receive from other organisms/organizations to survive.

Like organisms in natural ecosystems, innovative new firms, often referred to as start-ups, are embedded in an ecosystem which helps or hinders their access to resources and thus influences their development and impact (Spigel & Harrison, 2018; Spilling, 1996). Many initiatives have been implemented to support start-ups, such as incubators (Bergek & Norrman, 2008), accelerators (Shankar & Shepherd, 2018), outside assistants (Chrisman & McMullan, 2004) and government funding mechanisms (Rasmussen & Sørheim, 2012). These initiatives aim to provide "life energy" in the form of various resources for start-ups to survive, grow and contribute to social and economic impact. Studies often look at these support mechanisms in isolation, while their effectiveness depends on the context in which they operate (Brown, Gregson, & Mason, 2016). Different natural ecosystems, for example, a tropical evergreen forest and a desert, differ in both the numbers and types of species as well as in physical components such as vegetation, soil type, rainfall, and temperature. Such contextual differences make it hard to compare populations in different locations because the variation in species richness and abundance is influenced by indigenous environmental factors (Naeem et al., 1999). Similarly, when comparing firms in two different ecosystems, the variations in the number and success of start-ups is partly due to differences in various framework conditions, available resources, and support mechanisms. While firms in poorer ecosystems with weaker prospects for growth seem to be less successful at first sight, they may be quite effective in adjusting their goals and means to their environment. By the same token, policymakers must consider the characteristics of a particular context before setting economic goals or emulating practices of ecosystems with entirely different resource profiles. Hence, the ecosystem analogy is valuable to entrepreneurship research because it conceptually addresses the need for more knowledge on how start-ups interact with and are in turn influenced by, their environment (Audretsch, Cunningham, Kuratko, Lehmann, & Menter, 2019).

Drawing on extant entrepreneurship ecosystems literature (Acs, Stam, Audretsch, & O'Connor, 2017; Autio, Nambisan, Thomas, & Wright, 2018; Spigel, 2017; Spigel & Harrison, 2018; E. Stam, 2015; F. Stam

& Spigel, 2016), this book seeks to conceptualize, provide empirical examples, and discuss different aspects of start-up incubation ecosystems (SUPIEs), defined as *a set of interdependent actors and factors that interact in a system to provide a nurturing environment for the creation and successful development of start-ups.* The distinct value of this concept is that it directs attention to the incubation of start-ups as a critical activity and function within entrepreneurship ecosystems. As a concept, incubation has mainly been studied in conjunction with incubators (Hackett & Dilts, 2004; Mian, Lamine, & Fayolle, 2016). Incubators, however, are only one of the many elements and organizations within an ecosystem that take part in the process of incubating start-ups. Typically, start-ups receive value-adding contributions from several external actors, such as universities, Technology Transfer Offices (TTOs), investors, government agencies, other start-ups, as well as large firms. The multitude of actors involved in start-up development implies that incubation at the ecosystem level should be conceptualized in a more holistic, cooperative, collective, and distributed way. However, while scattered evidence suggests that incubation is a crucial process at the level of entrepreneurial ecosystems, we have limited insight into its nature, sources, antecedents and performance implications. The concept of SUPIE directs attention to the role ecosystems play in incubation, i.e., the formation, validation and early development of start-ups.

A better understanding of SUPIEs is vital for entrepreneurship policy, practice, and research. The existing literature provides limited knowledge on what kind of support, how much support, and in what context it is likely to result in the creation and growth of new firms with a positive impact on social and economic progress. It is difficult to emulate a thriving ecosystem such as Silicon Valley, as organizations and individuals are more comfortable to study in isolation, and the domain where their interactions take place, where resources flow from one actor to another to create value for both, is intricate and often invisible to the researcher's and policymaker's eyes.

Conceptualizing SUPIEs: How Much Help Do Birds Need to Fly?

A key idea in SUPIEs is the process of incubation. The term incubation is also an analogy from biology related to keeping an organism under optimal conditions to develop. An egg incubator is a device creating perfect conditions for eggs to hatch, and the term business incubator has become well-established to describe organizations dedicated to helping start-ups develop and grow (Bergek & Norrman, 2008; Bruneel, Ratinho, Clarysse, & Groen, 2012; Grimaldi & Grandi, 2005). The literature on incubation initially focused on the creation of sheltered environments for start-ups, often in terms of physical infrastructure below market prices (Bruneel et al., 2012). The usefulness of this approach has been questioned because such sheltered environments are not necessarily well suited to prepare start-ups for future success in the market. Incubators are increasingly offering a broader set of support services including training, coaching, networking, and access to financing (Bergek & Norrman, 2008; Bruneel et al., 2012). The broadening scope of incubation activities reflects that not all start-ups develop in the same way or need the same amount of protection and the same type of external resources to find their place as a standalone business.

The analogy of how young birds hatch and become independent in natural ecosystems can be used to illustrate the diverse incubation needs of start-ups. The early development of birds, i.e., the period from laying an egg until the young bird separates from its parents, varies a lot primarily based on the particular species. Their maturity at hatching has important implications for how their parents should care for the nestlings and what kind of environment they need to survive and grow. At the one end of the spectrum are *precocial birds*, e.g., domestic chicken, duck, or megapodes, which hatch with eyes open, covered with down, and leave the nest within a day or two after hatching. Precocial young birds require limited parental care as they can walk, run, swim, and feed self-sufficiently just a few hours after the breakout. At the other end of the spectrum are *altricial birds*, e.g., songbirds, which hatch with their eyes closed, have little or no down and are incapable of leaving the nest to join their parents whom they rely on for food. In between the two ends of the spectrum, there are several different levels of independence. For example, semi-precocial birds can leave the nest soon after hatching, but they stay at the nest and are fed by their parents for a while.

Similar to young birds, the needs of start-ups during incubation, i.e., roughly from drafting a business idea until the firm establishes itself on the market, may be very different depending on the nature of the firm. For example, academic spin-offs that commercialize new to the market technologies may be more similar to altricial chicks, as they typically have many liabilities and require more support (e.g., in the form of financial resources and business/entrepreneurial competencies) and longer incubation times before they gain sustainable returns (Rasmussen, Mosey, & Wright, 2011; Vohora, Wright, & Lockett, 2004). Scalable software start-ups, in contrast, may be more like precocial hatchlings, since they are more independent right from their birth and can develop relatively quickly, find business partners, customers, and their place in the market. Other characteristics, such as a high level of human capital among the founders (Colombo & Grilli, 2005), can also make a start-up resemble a precocial arrival. Hence, there is not one optimal type of SUPIE because new ventures have different preconditions, pursue different goals, and face various organizing problems.

There are further parallels between the birth and growth of young birds and those of start-up firms. For example, filial imprinting, a theory borrowed by entrepreneurship scholars from ethology, is typical of precocial birds and primarily occurs during the first day or first hours after hatching. Because of imprinting, young birds such as ducklings start following the first large moving object, ideally their mother (incubator organization), to minimize threats from the surrounding environment, such as adverse weather, predators (competition) and the lack of nutrition (resources). Similarly, environmental conditions at founding have been found to imprint upon a new venture in ways that affect growth and survival (Mathias, Williams, & Smith, 2015). As chicks grow and develop, they will undergo another imprinting, one that provides recognition of their species, so that they can establish proper social interactions with their kind later in life. Likewise, new ventures build legitimacy and acquire resources by conforming to their environment (Vestrum, Rasmussen, & Carter, 2017; Zimmerman & Zeitz, 2002). Moreover, the decision of birds is influenced by the breeding experience of their conspecifics when they select breeding habitats. For example, cliff-nesting seabirds tend to recruit to the previous year's most productive cliffs and to emigrate from the least productive ones (Danchin, Boulinier, & Massot, 1998). In a similar fashion, innovative start-ups tend to locate close to universities to access knowledge spillovers (Audretsch, Lehmann, & Warning, 2005).

Conceptualizing SUPIEs: How Does the Environment Help Birds to Fly?

Analogies from birdlife show that birth and survival in natural ecosystems bear many similarities with how SUPIEs are conducive to the creation and development of new ventures. The optimal conditions for firm growth are likely to depend on the type of the start-up and that of its environment, like different types of young birds need different kinds of support from their parents in different habitats. The concept of entrepreneurial ecosystems has been critiqued for drifting away from the assumptions of the original inspiration in natural ecosystems (Isenberg, 2016). In the following paragraphs, we outline five key points that can be translated from the biological analogies to the SUPIE context and then link them to the main topics discussed in the chapters. It is proposed that SUPIEs, similar to natural ecosystems, are *multilayered, spontaneous, connected, complex,* and *multipurpose.*

First, in nature, there is a healthy interdependence among organisms at different levels of the ecosystem. Each trophic level absorbs energy obtained from the level below it and also transfers some of it to the next level – this upward energy flow is often depicted in an ecological pyramid that illustrates the relative abundance of biomass among trophic levels (Trebilco, Baum, Salomon, & Dulvy, 2013). Similarly, resources from different layers of the ecosystem are of crucial importance for start-ups and the functioning of SUPIEs. While all ecosystem layers (micro, meso, and macro) contain essential elements, the chapter by *Sardeshmukh, O'Connor, and Smith*, for instance, shows that the essence of the ecosystem is the middle layer, where the interactions and interdependencies among individuals and organizations create something more than the mere sum of bilateral relationships. The intermediate ecosystem level is the domain where we can understand the relationship between the parts and the whole. Some start-ups may need a more sheltered environment initially, obtain more resources from other actors at the meso-level, while others are born with better-developed capabilities or can make better use of the resources available in their immediate microenvironment. The chapter by *Breivik-Meyer* reviews the literature on organizational sponsorship and aims to improve the understanding of the mechanisms supporting start-ups, and how they are aligned with the needs of these firms.

Second, the components valuable to start-ups in a SUPIE may be in place for reasons other than supporting the development of firms. In nature, the ultimate goal of individual organisms is to survive and reproduce, but at the same time, each is used by other organisms that also want to survive and reproduce. Red-billed oxpeckers, for example, eat everything (tick, dead skin, blood, etc.) they can collect on large African mammals, whose primary purpose is not feeding birds. The role or usefulness of the components of an ecosystem depends on the perspective taken, or the purpose and needs of the particular organism analyzed. In our case, while some actors of a SUPIE may intentionally support start-ups, like a business incubator or tax break scheme for start-up investing, most of the components and actors do not. For example, a particular new technology/ digital platform or an expanding market may provide excellent opportunities for start-ups to succeed, but they may be in place for different reasons. The chapter by *Ratinho*, for example, suggests a more holistic approach to start-up support including both the antecedents of entrepreneurial activity (e.g., entrepreneurial competence development) and policy tools that shape the broader environment not necessarily targeted at start-ups. The chapter by *Lesniak and Sørheim* provides an intriguing account of how an entrepreneurial ecosystem emerged spontaneously, as a result of bottom-up processes, rather than a product of an overall plan. Their case supports the view that ecosystems are not centrally controlled and cannot be created or designed – they can only be affected, influenced or facilitated (Isenberg, 2016). The spontaneous nature of SUPIEs is further elaborated in the chapter by *Rasmussen, Benneworth, and Gulbrandsen*, who advocate a broader understanding of why universities should be motivated to contribute to start-up incubation.

Third, the boundaries of a natural ecosystem are hard to define because adjacent ecosystems are often connected through flows of energy, materials, and organisms (Banks-Leite & Ewers, 2009). The same applies to conceptualizations of SUPIEs, where the flow of financial, human, and other resources can easily cross the boundaries of an individual ecosystem. Hence, both natural and start-up incubation ecosystems are often defined based on the interest or interpretation of the researcher. For example, a biologist may choose to study the ecosystem of a pond, forest, or mountain. Similarly, entrepreneurship researchers can also focus on smaller environments such as a group of students and professors as shown by *Lesniak and Sørheim*, and larger ones such as a town or region. Among the chapters in this book, SUPIEs are linked to, for instance, universities (chapters in *Part III*), cities (*Landoni*), and regions (*Velt, Torkkeli, & Saarenketo*). Ecosystems are always in contact with adjacent ecosystems, and their boundaries are often difficult to define, both in theory and practice. The chapters in this book illustrate this nicely. *Nguyen, Mariussen, and Hansen* scrutinize the boundaries of the SUPIE concept by comparing it to other similar theoretical approaches, such as entrepreneurial ecosystems and (regional) innovation systems. The chapter by *Landoni* indicates that there might be separate SUPIEs centred around different universities within the same city. Some ecosystems cross national borders to provide an optimal combination of resources, as shown by *Velt et al.* However, it is difficult to claim that there are national ecosystems because there is too much variation within a country to identify a standard set of ecosystem properties.

Fourth, in natural ecosystems, there is more than one type of food source for most organisms. Food chains can be so complicated, intersecting, and overlapping that they resemble a "food web" (Pimm, Lawton, & Cohen, 1991) rather than a linear sequence of organisms. This analogy implies that a broad array of different actors and factors at different levels of the ecosystem need to be included to capture the whole essence of SUPIEs. Still, studies looking at one actor or a fragment of the system are necessary to understand the role of individual SUPIE components; several chapters in this book study specific actors within a SUPIE. *Kolvereid and Isaksen* study the role of the government and banks, *Nordling, Thomas, Pugh, and Hermann* examine the contribution of multinational companies, while *Jensen, Nguyen, and Hansen* as well as *Straub, Bican, and Brem* investigate the outcomes and business models of incubators. While essential, studies of individual actors cannot be seen as representing the entire system. For example, an incubator organization is only one element of a broad range of actors and factors providing an environment for start-ups. A couple of chapters study the behaviour and characteristics of a group of support organizations. *Novotny*, for example, proposes a taxonomy for ecosystems networks, i.e., groups of actors whose resources are typically used in combination by start-ups, and suggests that the main task of the university TTO is to bridge these isolated networks and facilitate the flow of different types of resources to spin-off firms. *Theodoraki and Messeghem* show that the interactions of start-up supporting organizations are characterized by both cooperation and competition, i.e., coopetition, depending on the phase of firm development. *Bellavitis, Sargent, and DaSilva* point to the differences between the main types of start-up support organizations and suggest that nascent entrepreneurs should be guided towards particular ones that may best meet their needs and stage of development.

Finally, because of their inherent complexity and variation, it is hard to grasp the purpose and performance of ecosystems in general. Natural ecosystems have a certain level of biodiversity (species richness), productivity (rate of generation of biomass) and stability (resistance to environmental perturbations); these dimensions are in close connection with one another. Their performance or rather functioning can be quantified by measuring the magnitudes and dynamics of ecosystem processes (Naeem et al., 1999). SUPIEs can be evaluated by their ability to create and develop successful start-ups, and some chapters in this book study the performance of start-ups. *Johnson, Masyn, and McKelvie*, for instance, point out that start-ups can have different goals compared to other firms; thus, researchers assessing their performance should go beyond continuous measures such as sales and employment, and consider survival outcomes such as failure, merger, and acquisition. *Billström* draws attention to the broader, societal impact of some spin-off firms, which by diffusing innovative technologies can bring about long-term benefits for the society. Yet, similar to the success of populations and species in natural ecosystems, start-up success is also highly dependent on SUPIE processes, on the effective and efficient distribution, absorption, and recombination of resources. *Grande and Carlsson* suggest that the cooperation between supporters and start-ups is more burdensome but also more important in a rural/nature-based context than in urban/high growth industries. A rich start-up support system that includes several sources and types of resources is more likely to result in a more stable ecosystem that permanently and reliably provides new firms with the required life energy. So, in addition to productivity (high rate of start-up generation), diversity (multiple types and sources of support) and stability (resistance to external economic shocks) are also important attributes of successful SUPIEs.

OUTLINE OF THE SUPIE HANDBOOK

The chapters of the handbook are divided into three main groups: (1) holistic or multi-level approaches that try to capture the essence and/or study several layers and outcomes of SUPIEs; (2) start-up support mechanisms and organizations such as incubators, accelerators, co-working spaces, government agencies, banks, and multinational companies; and (3) university-based ecosystems and the role of universities in SUPIEs.

The chapters in *Part I* aim to understand the goal and functioning of the whole system of start-up incubation. Their methods are varied; some are conceptual or literature-based, while others build on empirical data primarily from Scandinavian countries. They cover several SUPIE elements at a time, a larger geographical area, different outcomes, or use a multi-level approach demonstrating the various dimensions of SUPIEs. The chapter by *Nguyen, Mariussen, and Hansen* studies the role of smart specialization in establishing sustainable entrepreneurial ecosystems and in connecting innovation policies with SUPIEs. The authors also contrast the different systems approaches to entrepreneurship and innovation and regard SUPIE as the core of ecosystems of various magnitudes. *Sardeshmukh et al.* develop a multi-level view of SUPIE to explain the bottom-up emergence of ecosystem resources through the "transactional configurations" between the micro (individuals) and meso (organizational forms) levels that give rise to "coalesced" attributes at the macro ecosystemic level. *Ratinho*, drawing on nascent entrepreneurial ecosystem literature also suggests that entrepreneurship support manifests itself at three domains: the institutional level shapes the environment in which entrepreneurs operate; at the organizational level start-ups obtain resources; while at the individual level they develop entrepreneurial skills. *Good and Knockaert* compare technology transfer ecosystems at eight Scandinavian universities to identify the key micro-, meso- and macro-level drivers that affect the overall organizational design of ecosystems in a university context. Geographical considerations are also important when analyzing SUPIEs. The elements and resources of a peripheral/rural SUPIE can differ from those of urban/high growth areas, which have important implications on how nature-based start-ups are (and should be) incubated in rural ecosystems (*Grande & Carlsson*). There is no limit in scale, either lower or upper, to the SUPIE concept, which can refer to environments as small as a university class (as shown by *Lesniak and Sørheim* in *Part III*) and ones that reach over national borders.

Regarding the latter, the chapter by *Velt et al.* examines the qualities of a transnational SUPIE and finds that born-global start-ups perceive less observable elements, such as talent and knowledge, as the most critical for their development. SUPIEs are complex and diverse, thus when researchers want to evaluate their performance, they have to understand the goals (potential outcomes) and nature of the firms they comprise and use descriptive and exploratory plots before applying more sophisticated multivariate statistical procedures (*Johnson et al.*).

Part II includes a literature review and empirical data from Brazil, France, New Zealand, Norway, the U.S., and several other countries, to deal with organizations engaged in start-up incubation and support. These chapters show that start-up support mechanisms are complex and support organizations are heterogeneous, and their differences are mainly based on the development phase and needs of their clients and stakeholders. The incubation (or sponsorship) process can include services related to "buffering", "bridging", and "boosting" provided by private, government, academic and non-governmental organizations, to different types of firms, at different stages of development, having different goals such as emergence, survival, and growth (*Breivik-Meyer*). Start-up development organizations are quite diverse and can be classified as (traditional and university) incubators, (traditional and corporate) accelerators, co-working spaces, or hybrid, each having different peculiarities, business logic, clientele and goals (*Bellavitis et al.*). There is an increasing need for establishing financially sustainable or self-sufficient incubators, which can cover expenses with their own revenues (*Straub et al.*). At the same time, support organizations simultaneously compete and cooperate, however, their "coopetition" strategies change during the incubation process from competition-dominated through equal to cooperation-dominated relationships (*Theodoraki & Messeghem*). In addition to financial sustainability, there is a growing need for "conscious" support organizations that place a stronger emphasis on incorporating social and environmental concerns into their business models and practices (*Kassel et al.*). The incubation process can be targeted at firms and individuals; the outcomes of the latter may manifest through founders' champion behaviour (*Jensen et al.*). This section also concerns the role of powerful SUPIE-shaping institutions, i.e., the national government, banks, and large (multinational) firms. While multinational companies appear to successfully amalgamate the interests of the local community, such as developing local business ecosystems, with their own growth and market development motives (*Nordling et al.*), government finance and good advice seem to have a weak relationship with firm births and successive outcomes, especially compared to those of banks (*Kolvereid & Isaksen*).

Finally, relying on data from Italy, Japan, Norway, and South Africa, the chapters in *Part III* present a special case of SUPIE, i.e., university-based ecosystems. The role of universities in academic entrepreneurship and SUPIEs is often associated with the activities of the Technology Transfer Office, but TTOs seem to be limitedly useful in bridging firms with non-academic/private ecosystem actors, which would be vital in integrating spin-offs into SUPIEs (*Novotny*). Individual factors also play an essential part in university-based ecosystems. Entrepreneurial academics and students can provide life energy in the form of information, role models, and inspiration for emerging SUPIEs (*Lesniak & Sørheim*). Furthermore, students' real-life entrepreneurial experience and those of their important others (*Åmo et al.*), and the principal investigators' commercialization experience (*Modic & Yoshioka-Kobayashi*) impact start-up intention and formation. Universities can encourage the internationalization of spin-offs by fostering an internationally oriented organizational culture (*Jørgensen & Novotny*) and can generate societal impacts by creating and coordinating other support organizations in the academic entrepreneurship ecosystem (*Billström*). The decisions and strategies of spin-off firms in urban SUPIEs will be shaped by both university-level and city-level factors (*Landoni*). However, even fundamental questions such as why universities support spin-offs and what these firms need are not easy to answer, as shown by *Rasmussen et al.*; the authors propose that it is wider stakeholder network benefits (at the ecosystem-level) that will make the university–firm relationship valuable for both.

Figure I.1 presents the chapters in a multi-level wheel diagram, which shows the focus of the studies (whole ecosystem, start-up support organizations, or the university) as well as the different levels of the ecosystem (individual, organizational, and framework conditions) they pertain to. The chapters in the bottom circular sector (*Part I*) are broader in scope, reach across several SUPIE dimensions and even outside of SUPIEs. The chapters on the right (*Part II*) deal with classic start-up development organizations, while the ones on the left (*Part III*) regard universities as fundamental sources of start-up activity.

TOWARDS A RESEARCH AGENDA ON SUPIEs

The chapters of this handbook provide a first important glimpse into the nature, functioning, and make-up of SUPIEs. The SUPIE concept attempts to move beyond the "nature *versus* nurture" dichotomy, i.e., the artificial juxtaposition of whether firm behaviour is determined by the environment, at firm birth or later stages, or by internal characteristics.

START-UP INCUBATION ECOSYSTEM (SUPIE)

Framework Conditions

Organizations

Individuals

University-based SUPIEs (Part III)

Start-up Support Organizations (Part II)

The Role of the University TTO in the SUPIE (Novotny)

The Key Drivers for Emergence of an EE (Lesniak & Sørheim)

Toward a Model for Universities as Incubation Ecosystems (Åmo et al.)

Individual-level Determinants of Academic Patent Licensing to Start-ups (Modic & Yoshioka-Kobayashi)

The University Ecosystem and the Internationalization of Spin-off Firms (Jørgensen & Novotny)

The Role of the University for Societal Impact of Academic Spin-offs (Billström)

Urban Universities as a Start-up Ecosystem (Landoni)

Motivating Universities to Support Spin-off Firms: Stakeholders and SUPIEs (Rasmussen et al.)

In Support of University Spin-offs – What Drives the Organizational Design of Technology-Transfer Ecosystems? (Good & Knockaert)

Organizational Sponsorship (Breivik-Meyer)

Understanding Start-up Development Organizations (Bellavitis et al.)

Distinguishing Self-sufficient Business Incubators (Straub et al.)

Incubators' Coopetition Strategy (Theodoraki & Messeghem)

Enterprise Support Organizations for Conscious and Conventional Capitalism (Kassel et al.)

Incubation and Founders' Champion Behaviour (Jensen et al.)

Multinational Companies' Roles in SUPIEs (Nordling et al.)

Outsider Support, Firm Births and Outcomes (Kolvereid & Isaksen)

A Contingency Approach to the Incubation of New Ventures in Entrepreneurial Ecosystems (Johnson et al.)

Transnational EEs: The Perspectives of Finnish and Estonian Born-global Start-ups (Velt et al.)

The Support System's Influence on Nature-based Business Start-ups in a Rural Context (Grande & Carlsson)

The Domains of Entrepreneurship Support (Ratinho)

Incubating Start-ups in EEs: A Multilevel Perspective on Entrepreneurial Resources (Sardeshmukh et al.)

The Role of Smart Specialization in Providing Regional Strategic Support for Establishing Sustainable SUPIEs (Nguyen, Mariussen, & Hansen)

Holistic Approaches to SUPIEs (Part I)

Note: some chapter titles have been shortened to better fit in the figure.

Figure I.1   The chapters of the handbook and the levels of SUPIE

We are convinced that there is much more to learn about SUPIEs. We, therefore, hope others will further examine, scrutinize, and develop our perspectives, through qualitative or quantitative methods, and conceptual development. Below we explain and discuss why other scholars should join us in such an undertaking.

The handbook, similar to existing literature, shows that entrepreneurial ecosystems consist of layers, or sub-systems, within systems. Indeed, the very concept of ecosystem, as used in the natural sciences, is flexible and can include everything from the surface of a rock to the surface of our entire planet. Arguably, this is a strength of the concept, particularly when applied to understand entrepreneurship, since new venture creation occurs in many different contexts and settings and is influenced by variables at many different levels of analysis. However, it has also been argued that the ecosystems approach to entrepreneurship is atheoretical (Spigel & Harrison, 2018). Indeed, the very flexibility of the ecosystem concept may hinder theoretical progress since it is not clear what the object of study is. In ecology, it is acknowledged that ecosystems can cover many orders of magnitude. In our view, this is a fruitful way of thinking about SUPIEs. Thus, when the key unit of analysis is a start-up venture, we argue that a SUPIE is the "innermost" ecosystem residing between the start-up venture and its external environment. The SUPIE concept directs attention to the importance of ecosystem influences in shaping the first formative period of new ventures, which have enduring implications on the survival and growth of these firms. Similar to child development, e.g., the positive relationship between early childhood nutrition and subsequent academic performance (Glewwe, Jacoby, & King, 2001), firms that do not get the necessary resources during their "prenatal" and early growth stages, will find it hard to make up for this in later development stages.

Moreover, an implication of the view of ecosystems as systems-within-systems is that SUPIEs are nested within other (types of) entrepreneurial ecosystems residing at higher levels of analysis or order of magnitudes. However, the interactions and flows between different types of ecosystems, with varying orders of magnitude, is something that we do not fully understand. This book provides examples of interactions between individuals and organizations within SUPIEs, but there is a need to understand better the interactions between different types of ecosystems, where the ecosystem is treated as the unit of analysis. What is the key role and function of SUPIEs in such a perspective? Based on the chapters in this handbook, we argue that the *raison'd etre* of SUPIEs is the generation of a variety of new start-up ventures that subsequently feed other ecosystems, at higher orders of magnitude, with much-needed energy for innovation, entrepreneurship, and business activity. The chapter by *Sardeshmukh et al.,* for instance, shows that as start-ups grow and develop into established and potentially more significant organizations, they may contribute to the emergence of new ecosystemic elements at higher levels. Thus, without well-designed SUPIEs, a vital source of ecosystem energy, i.e., start-up activity, will be missing or reduced, and as a consequence, the energy flow or "food chain" breaks, and the whole SUPIE as well as broader ecosystems that feed on SUPIEs become imbalanced and even collapse.

Accordingly, three essential research directions appear vis-à-vis understanding the role of SUPIEs in the economy. They are related to the *emergence*, *elements*, and *similarities* of different SUPIEs. First, how SUPIEs emerge as a result of bottom-up initiatives and top-down measures is not clearly understood. Policymakers around the world are trying to emulate thriving ecosystems on their home turf. To what extent this can be done successfully is still an open question. Given the prominence of entrepreneurial ecosystems to present economic policy, exploring further which policy measures work and which do not is a worthwhile endeavour. In particular, it seems necessary to examine how top-down policy best supplements bottom-up initiatives.

Second, from the contributions to this handbook, as well as in reviewing the now extensive literature on entrepreneurial ecosystems, it is clear that there is little consensus on which are the constituent elements of a SUPIE. Establishing robust typologies of such elements appears to be the first vital step to advance the literature. Once that is done, it would be possible to turn to questions related to how ecosystems function and operate, and how individuals, organizations and other elements of the ecosystem interact with each other to form a SUPIE.

Third, the richness and variety of contributions to this handbook show that not all ecosystems are created equal. There is extensive variation across them. What is specific to a particular context, such as a university-based start-up ecosystem or an urban one, and what is generic to ecosystems across contexts constitutes an important consideration. Seeing beyond specificities to focus on generalities is essential to build theories about SUPIEs. We believe that such mid-range theorizing (Hitt, Hoskisson, & Ireland, 1994) is relevant in the context of entrepreneurial ecosystems. However, the term entrepreneurial ecosystem may be too broad to be useful as a unit of theorizing. In other words, entrepreneurial ecosystems seem to be so diverse that it is challenging to establish generalizations across them. SUPIEs, on the other hand, represent a somewhat more homogeneous category that potentially offers a more useful unit of theorizing.

CONCLUDING REMARKS

In the introduction, we showed how the functioning of natural ecosystems helps us understand the challenges of firm birth and development in a particular context. Similar to natural ecosystems, SUPIEs are made up of "biotic" components (individuals and organizations), "abiotic" components (framework conditions such as start-up support programs, education and research, physical infrastructure, cultural and social norms, etc.) and interactions between these components. The concept of an incubation ecosystem is almost contradictory in that it combines the notion of a reasonably controlled environment with a clear purpose, i.e., an incubator, with a self-organizing and self-sustaining environment, i.e., an ecosystem.

However, we believe this inherent contradiction nicely illustrates the challenges faced by policymakers aiming at promoting SUPIEs. In our view, a well-functioning SUPIE cannot be designed top-down because it relies on the interplay of a large variety of actors who contribute in different ways and have different motivations. However, it seems clear that a SUPIE can be influenced and supported, just like natural ecosystems can be nurtured. The chapters in this book show that start-ups and their founders are assisted, get help, obtain resources, and interact with many individuals and organizations in their ecosystem. Moreover, different types of actors and support organizations exist, all vital for the process of incubation at the ecosystem-level. Due to this process of incubation in the ecosystem, start-ups and their founders can overcome initial challenges and establish a venture that, without this process, would not have been established, or faced stricter barriers impeding their development.

The book covers a wide array of topics that illustrate the different aspects and types of SUPIEs. However, SUPIEs have to face current global trends and Grand Challenges that will change their role and operation in the future. For example, digitalization has transformed many industries and provides new opportunities for entrepreneurship. SUPIEs conducive for digital start-ups may be different for instance, because geographical co-location is less critical. Also, digital technologies influence how start-ups interact with and get access to resources from various stakeholders. Crowdfunding and social media provide new tools that are capable of connecting a large number of stakeholders for access to resources and thereby change the nature of SUPIEs for many new ventures. Next, the issue of sustainability, for instance, related to the UN sustainable development goals, is gaining more and more attention among the public, policymakers, and industry, which creates both new demands and new opportunities for start-ups. A popular concept is related to the transition to a circular economy in which resources are not extracted, used and disposed of as waste, but remain productive through extended use and regeneration. SUPIEs aiming to support such a transition and the opportunities for start-ups emerging, will need to be different from many of the examples presented in this book. Hence, this volume represents a starting point for our understanding of SUPIEs, but there are ample opportunities for extending this work.

REFERENCES

Acs, Z. J., Stam, E., Audretsch, D. B., & O'Connor, A. (2017). The lineages of the entrepreneurial ecosystem approach. *Small Business Economics, 49*(1), 1–10.

Aldrich, H. E., & Ruef, M. (2006). *Organizations evolving* (2nd ed.). London: Sage Publications.

Audretsch, D. B., Cunningham, J. A., Kuratko, D. F., Lehmann, E. E., & Menter, M. (2019). Entrepreneurial ecosystems: economic, technological, and societal impacts. *The Journal of Technology Transfer*, *44*(2), 313–325.

Audretsch, D. B., Lehmann, E. E., & Warning, S. (2005). University spillovers and new firm location. *Research Policy*, *34*(7), 1113–1122.

Autio, E., Nambisan, S., Thomas, L. D. W., & Wright, M. (2018). Digital affordances, spatial affordances, and the genesis of entrepreneurial ecosystems. *Strategic Entrepreneurship Journal*, *12*(1), 72–95.

Banks-Leite, C., & Ewers, R. M. (2009). Ecosystem boundaries. *Els (Essential for Life Science)*. Chichester: John Wiley & Sons Ltd. doi: https://doi.org/10.1002/9780470015902.a0021232.

Beckman, C. M., & Burton, M. D. (2008). Founding the future: path dependence in the evolution of top management teams from founding to IPO. *Organization Science*, *19*(1), 3–24.

Bergek, A., & Norrman, C. (2008). Incubator best practice: a framework. *Technovation*, *28*(1–2), 20–28.

Brown, R., Gregson, G., & Mason, C. (2016). A post-mortem of regional innovation policy failure: Scotland's Intermediate Technology Initiative (ITI). *Regional Studies*, *50*(7), 1260–1272.

Bruneel, J., Ratinho, T., Clarysse, B., & Groen, A. (2012). The evolution of business incubators: comparing demand and supply of business incubation services across different incubator generations. *Technovation*, *32*(2), 110–121.

Chrisman, J. J., & McMullan, W. E. (2004). Outsider assistance as a knowledge resource for new venture survival. *Journal of Small Business Management*, *42*(3), 229–244.

Colombo, M., & Grilli, L. (2005). Founders' human capital and the growth of new technology-based firms: A competence-based view. *Research Policy*, *34*(6), 795–816.

Danchin, E., Boulinier, T., & Massot, M. (1998). Conspecific reproductive success and breeding habitat selection: implications for the study of coloniality. *Ecology*, *79*(7), 2415–2428.

Fini, R., Rasmussen, E., Siegel, D., & Wiklund, J. (2018). Rethinking the commercialization of public science: from entrepreneurial outcomes to societal impacts. *The Academy of Management Perspectives*, *32*(1), 4–20.

Fritsch, M., & Mueller, P. (2004). Effects of new business formation on regional development over time. *Regional Studies*, *38*(8), 961–975.

Glewwe, P., Jacoby, H. G., & King, E. M. (2001). Early childhood nutrition and academic achievement: a longitudinal analysis. *Journal of Public Economics*, *81*(3), 345–368.

Gnyawali, D. R., & Fogel, D. S. (1994). Environments for entrepreneurship development: key dimensions and research implications. *Entrepreneurship Theory and Practice*, *18*(4), 43–62.

Grimaldi, R., & Grandi, A. (2005). Business incubators and new venture creation: an assessment of incubating models. *Technovation*, *25*(2), 111–121.

Hackett, S. M., & Dilts, D. M. (2004). A systematic review of business incubation research. *The Journal of Technology Transfer*, *29*(1), 55–82.

Hitt, M. A., Hoskisson, R. E., & Ireland, R. D. (1994). A mid-range theory of the interactive effects of international and product diversification on innovation and performance. *Journal of Management*, *20*(2), 297–326.

Isenberg, D. J. (2016). Applying the ecosystem metaphor to entrepreneurship: uses and abuses. *The Antitrust Bulletin*, *61*(4), 564–573.

Malecki, E. J. (2018). Entrepreneurship and entrepreneurial ecosystems. *Geography Compass*, *12*(3), e12359.

Mason, C., & Brown, R. (2014). Entrepreneurial ecosystems and growth oriented entrepreneurship. *Final Report to OECD, Paris*.

Mathias, B. D., Williams, D. W., & Smith, A. R. (2015). Entrepreneurial inception: the role of imprinting in entrepreneurial action. *Journal of Business Venturing*, *30*(1), 11–28.

McCann, P., & Ortega-Argilés, R. (2016). Smart specialisation, entrepreneurship and SMEs:

issues and challenges for a results-oriented EU regional policy. *Small Business Economics*, *46*(4), 537–552.

Mian, S., Lamine, W., & Fayolle, A. (2016). Technology business incubation: an overview of the state of knowledge. *Technovation, 50–51*, 1–12.

Naeem, S., Chapin III, F., Costanza, R., Ehrlich, P. R., Golley, F. B., Hooper, D. U., . . . Sala, O. E. (1999). Biodiversity and ecosystem functioning: maintaining natural life support processes. *Issues in Ecology, 4*(11).

Pimm, S. L., Lawton, J. H., & Cohen, J. E. (1991). Food web patterns and their consequences. *Nature, 350*(6320), 669.

Rasmussen, E., Mosey, S., & Wright, M. (2011). The evolution of entrepreneurial competencies: a longitudinal study of university spin-off venture emergence. *Journal of Management Studies, 48*(6), 1314–1345.

Rasmussen, E., & Sørheim, R. (2012). How governments seek to bridge the financing gap for university spin-offs: proof-of-concept, pre-seed, and seed funding. *Technology Analysis & Strategic Management, 24*(7), 663–678.

Schumpeter, J. A. (1934). *The theory of economic development: an inquiry into profits, capital, credit, interest, and the business cycle.* Cambridge, MA: Harvard University Press.

Shankar, R. K., & Shepherd, D. A. (2018). Accelerating strategic fit or venture emergence: different paths adopted by corporate accelerators. *Journal of Business Venturing, 34*(5). doi: https://doi.org/10.1016/j.jbusvent.2018.06.004.

Spigel, B. (2017). The relational organization of entrepreneurial ecosystems. *Entrepreneurship Theory and Practice, 41*(1), 49–72.

Spigel, B., & Harrison, R. (2018). Toward a process theory of entrepreneurial ecosystems. *Strategic Entrepreneurship Journal, 12*(1), 151–168.

Spilling, O. R. (1996). The entrepreneurial system: on entrepreneurship in the context of a mega-event. *Journal of Business Research, 36*(1), 91–103.

Stam, E. (2015). Entrepreneurial ecosystems and regional policy: a sympathetic critique. *European Planning Studies, 23*(9), 1759–1769.

Stam, F., & Spigel, B. (2016). Entrepreneurial ecosystems. *USE Discussion paper series, 16*(13).

Trebilco, R., Baum, J. K., Salomon, A. K., & Dulvy, N. K. (2013). Ecosystem ecology: size-based constraints on the pyramids of life. *Trends in Ecology & Evolution, 28*(7), 423–431.

Van de Ven, A. H. (1993). The development of an infrastructure for entrepreneurship. *Journal of Business Venturing, 8*(3), 211–230.

Vestrum, I., Rasmussen, E., & Carter, S. (2017). How nascent community enterprises build legitimacy in internal and external environments. *Regional Studies, 51*(11), 1721–1734.

Vohora, A., Wright, M., & Lockett, A. (2004). Critical junctures in the development of university high-tech spinout companies. *Research Policy, 33*(1), 147–175.

Zimmerman, M. A., & Zeitz, G. J. (2002). Beyond survival: achieving new venture growth by building legitimacy. *Academy of Management Review, 27*(3), 414–431.

PART I

HOLISTIC APPROACHES TO SUPIEs

1. The role of smart specialization in providing regional strategic support for establishing sustainable start-up incubation ecosystems
Nhien Nguyen, Åge Mariussen, and Jens Ø. Hansen

INTRODUCTION

The ecosystem concept is rooted in biology, where it refers to a community of living and non-living components that interact with each other in a complex way (Acs, Stam, Audretsch, & O'Connor, 2017). The concept has been adopted by the sciences of economics and management, where it appears in several related guises, such as innovation ecosystems, business ecosystems, and entrepreneurial ecosystems (Rinkinen, 2016). The notion of a start-up incubation ecosystem, defined as a system of interdependent actors and factors which supports the creation and successful development of start-ups (Novotny, Clausen, Rasmussen, & Wiklund, 2018), is most closely connected to the entrepreneurial ecosystems approach. Since entrepreneurial ecosystems are a "critical tool for creating resilient economies based on entrepreneurial innovation" (Spigel, 2017, p.49), regional authorities are advised to build an underlying support policy for creating and strengthening these ecosystems in the interest of economic development. To understand the role of regional strategic support in establishing sustainable start-up incubation ecosystems, it is logical to draw on observations from both the entrepreneurial ecosystems literature and the literature on ecosystem-based innovation policy.

The ecosystem concept in economics and management theory can be viewed as related to biological ecosystems through the prism of emergence and complexity. Entrepreneurial ecosystems have some of the properties of complex systems as described by complexity theory (Byrne & Callaghan, 2014). According to Byrne and Callaghan (2014, pp.17–38), complexity rests on a few simple assumptions: (1) complex systems are not designed top-down but are the result of self-organization by many autonomous, interrelated decision-makers; (2) complex systems have emergent properties in the sense that they have the capacity to change in new directions; (3) in order to do so, complex systems are able to create energy, by increasing the system scale; (4) complex systems are inherently unstable; and (5) openness is an inherent feature of complex systems. Such systems also tend to be dissipative in that they interact with their environments. They are likely to experience a continual inflow and outflow of energy, matter, and information (Virkkala & Mariussen, 2019). Similarly, the entrepreneurial ecosystem concept focuses on a bottom-up approach, emphasizing the leading role of entrepreneurs (Spigel & Harrison, 2018). The system comprises several phases including creation, discovery, and exploitation of knowledge-based entrepreneurial opportunities (Qian, Acs, & Stough, 2013). However, since complex systems are open and unstable, an entrepreneurial ecosystem should be supported by an appropriately designed innovation policy in order to ensure its sustainability. In the present chapter we discuss several types of innovation policy, including smart specialization, and explain how smart specialization strategies can support entrepreneurial and start-up incubation ecosystems.

This chapter is structured as follows. We start by providing a general overview of concepts related to ecosystems in the economics and management literatures and summarizing – briefly, since other chapters in the present volume analyze the same concept in depth – the notion of an entrepreneurial ecosystem. Next we introduce several approaches to innovation policy, focusing primarily on smart specialization and ecosystem-based approaches, and examine how these relate to each other. The chapter concludes with a discussion of implications for policy design.

CO-EXISTING ECOSYSTEMS AT THE REGIONAL LEVEL

There are two general views of the term "ecosystem": *ecosystem-as-affiliation*, which views ecosystems as "communities of associated actors defined by their networks and platform affiliations", and *ecosystem-as-structure*, which sees them as "configurations of activity defined by a value proposition" (Adner, 2017, p. 40). In this chapter we adopt the ecosystem-as-structure approach, which defines an ecosystem as "the alignment structure of the multilateral set of partners that need to interact in order for a focal value proposition to materialize" (p. 42). This definition highlights the value-creating activities that determine how an ecosystem is (or should be) structured rather than placing emphasis on a focal actor and its network of affiliated entities. Therefore, the ecosystem-as-structure perspective is well suited to the context of young firms that are not yet embedded in industry networks but do have value propositions, such as start-up firms under incubation. We will also argue in this chapter that a modified version of Adner's ecosystem-as-structure approach may be a useful perspective for policymakers to adopt when designing regional innovation policy.

Proceeding from this definition of ecosystems, we understand a *start-up incubation ecosystem* as the alignment structure of the multilateral set of partners that need to interact in order to incubate new start-ups. The objective of setting up such an ecosystem is to support the survival of start-ups that have a high growth potential. A successful start-up might go through several supporting stages such as establishment, incubation, acceleration, scaling up, etc. Therefore, start-up incubation ecosystems can be placed under the umbrella of start-up ecosystems, which aim to produce high-growth start-ups. We also propose that start-up ecosystems could be placed under the umbrella of entrepreneurial ecosystems, the objective of which is to produce not only high-growth start-ups but also successful entrepreneurs (Stam, 2015). Entrepreneurial ecosystems are often studied in connection with a specific territory or geography (Spigel, 2017; Cavallo, Ghezzi, & Balocco, 2018), and important regional factors may "interactively influence the creation, discovery and exploitation of entrepreneurial opportunities" (Qian et al., 2013, p. 2). By this argument, start-up incubation ecosystems, as well as start-up ecosystems and entrepreneurial ecosystems in general, are closely connected to a specific region. Regional support thus plays a vital role in determining the success of such ecosystems.

There are other, related types of ecosystems that may co-exist at the regional level with those mentioned here, including business ecosystems and innovation ecosystems. Business ecosystems are built around "platforms that offer solutions to firms" (Rinkinen & Harmaakorpi, 2018, p. 344), and their geographical scope can be global (p. 345). Innovation ecosystems include an economic dimension as well as political and technological dimensions (Rinkinen, 2016), but their geographical scope is restricted to a region or nation. To provide an overview of the ecosystem concepts and clarify how they relate to one another, Figure 1.1 compares the different types of ecosystems. Figure 1.1 views the different systems through the lens of a modified ecosystem-as-structure perspective: while we use the terminology of Adner (2017), the value propositions in the figure do not represent particular products or services but the general potential for value creation of each type of ecosystem. The figure compares the different types of ecosystems according to (i) their degree of *geographical* scale, ranging from regional to global, and (ii) the level of direct value the ecosystem will generate if successful. Rather than being mutually exclusive, different ecosystems can co-exist in the same geographical region, with overlapping actors and activities.

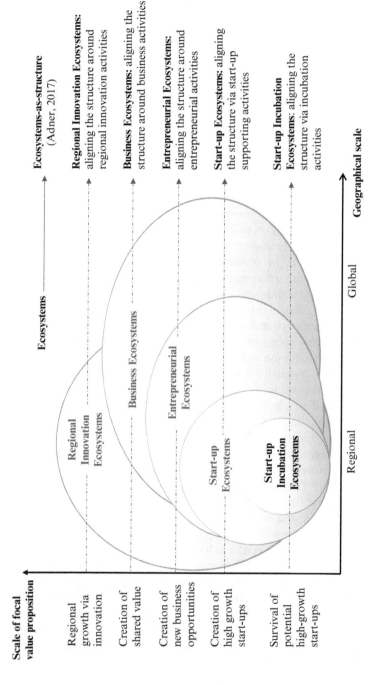

22

Source: main author.

Figure 1.1   Comparison of co-existing ecosystems in a region

Turning to the relationship between regional strategies and start-up incubation ecosystems, we argue that the creation of successful start-ups can be viewed as a sub-goal connected to the greater goal of the regions, which is sustainable economic growth. Sustainable economic growth does not come only from high-growth start-ups but also from other types of productive entrepreneurship (Baumol, 1990; Stam, 2015). Thus, from the macro-level perspective of regional policy, supporting the establishment of a start-up incubation ecosystem must be part of a more general policy of support for entrepreneurial ecosystems. Consequently, to discuss the logic of regional strategic support for establishing sustainable start-up incubation ecosystems, we will make use of the literature on regional innovation policy as well as the literature on entrepreneurial ecosystems.

ENTREPRENEURIAL ECOSYSTEMS

The concept of an *entrepreneurial ecosystem* is used to describe how the variety of individuals, organizations and institutions influence *entrepreneurial activity* in a particular context (Novotny et al., 2018). There are three main components in this definition: entrepreneurial, ecosystem, and entrepreneurial activity (Stam & Spigel, 2017). The first component, *entrepreneurial*, refers to the opportunity-exploiting characteristic. The second component, *ecosystems*, emphasizes the interdependency between actors, i.e. individuals, organizations, and institutions co-existing in a territorial area characterized by certain geographical features, or shared cultural, environmental or economic ties. The third component, *entrepreneurial activity*, is considered the process in which actors create opportunities for innovation.

Although the entrepreneurial ecosystem literature is derived predominantly from the strategy literature and the regional development literature, it is nevertheless considered distinct from both of these literature streams (Acs et al., 2017). From a regional development perspective, the entrepreneurial ecosystem is related to several approaches such as industrial clusters (Porter, 1998), industrial districts (Marshall, 1920), and regional innovation systems or "RIS" (Stam & Spigel, 2017; Terjesen et al., 2017). From the strategic management literature, entrepreneurial ecosystem research draws on concepts such as business ecosystems (Adner, 2017) and ecosystems surrounding a platform (Evans & Schmalensee, 2016; Parker & Van Alstyne, 2005). However, key features that distinguish entrepreneurial ecosystems from the other ecosystems considered in the literature include: (i) the focus on value creation by individual entrepreneurs; (ii) the existence of high-growth start-ups within a geographical boundary as a

Table 1.1   Comparison between cluster and regional innovation system (RIS) theory and entrepreneurial ecosystem theory

Theme	Cluster and RIS	Entrepreneurial Ecosystem
Role of the state	The state is the lead organizer and a significant investor (top-down)	Entrepreneurs are the primary leaders (bottom-up); the state only supports
Accessing regional resources and benefits	Little differentiation between large firms and small start-ups and new ventures	Focus on solving specific difficulties for start-ups and entrepreneurs
Role of knowledge	Focus on technical and market knowledge	Focus on entrepreneurial knowledge besides technical and market knowledge
Key actors	Large firms, public agencies, universities	Entrepreneurs
Industry	Strengthen knowledge flow and innovation in industries	More focus on underlying technology, less on industry or market

Source: Adapted from Spigel and Harrison, 2018.

key indicator; and (iii) a complex mix of public–private governance (Acs et al., 2017). The second feature is the reason we choose entrepreneurial ecosystems as the theoretical reference point for discussing start-up incubation ecosystems.

These three distinguishing features of entrepreneurial ecosystems have resulted in divergences between entrepreneurial ecosystems theory and regional development theory with respect to five themes: the role of the state; accessing regional resources and benefits; the role of knowledge; key actors; and the role of industry (Spigel & Harrison, 2018). A summary of these differences can be found in Table 1.1.

INNOVATION POLICIES

Innovation policy is "a broad concept that contains research and technology policy and overlaps with industrial, environmental, labor and social policies" (Kuhlmann & Edler, 2003, p. 620). Its goal is to strengthen the competitiveness of an economy and to increase societal welfare through economic success (Kuhlmann & Edler, 2003; Rinkinen, 2016). Innovation policy is a broad category that encompasses different objectives for innovation. Following Foray (2018, p. 7), we categorize innovation policies into three groups. The first group comprises innovation and industrial policies focusing on creating framework conditions for innovation, such as a favorable institutional environment for developing generic innovation capacities or increasing innovation diversity. The second group refers to innovation policies aimed at increasing the rate of innovation, that is, using public sector interventions to generate growth. The policies in the third group are designed to influence the *direction* of innovation – aiming for a trajectory towards sustainability – by combining relevant and complementary elements selected from various approaches.

Policies in the first two groups, though important, are not well equipped to tackle the unprecedented problems involved in designing and developing "new activities targeting the transformation of economic or technological structure" (Foray, 2018, p. 823), for example addressing a grand challenge such as climate change, or forming a new high-tech sector, or enabling a region to create a new specialty. This chapter places more emphasis on the third group, especially the smart specialization strategy and its role in providing strategic support for entrepreneurial ecosystems. As will be elaborated later, smart specialization, with its focus on regular renewal and adjustment of the particulars of the strategy, is a policy tool with the flexibility required to respond to continuous changes in the economic environment, and also takes regional differences fully into account whereas other policies remain largely undifferentiated regarding regional specificities (Foray, 2018). These characteristics of the policy facilitate the establishment and development of entrepreneurial ecosystems.

Smart Specialization

Background of the concept: The smart specialization approach was an attempt to overcome the weaknesses of an innovation policy focused on macro-level indicators, i.e. the national innovation system approach. Smart specialization takes a multi-level perspective. It connects macro-level analysis with support for micro-level entrepreneurial discoveries, facilitating the creation of start-up firms. The initial work on the smart specialization concept and methodology was carried out between 2008 and 2012 by the Knowledge for Growth group sponsored by the European Commission, which consisted of policymakers, academics, and innovation experts. One outcome was a broad framework, put together in 2009 by Dominique Foray and his colleagues (Foray, David, & Hall, 2009) and developed into a book in 2015 (Foray, 2015), which integrated different innovation theories and innovation policy principles under the smart specialization label. The approach was implemented in a large-scale

European innovation policy experiment in 2011 and officially entered European Union policy in 2015. So far, smart specialization principles and methodologies have been adopted by 18 national governments in the European Union and implemented in 170 regions across the EU and beyond, covering a combined area inhabited by hundreds of millions of people (Smart Specialization Platform, 2019). Even though a rich body of empirical evidence documenting the implementation of smart specialization policies in Europe is rapidly accumulating, Foray, one of the creators of the concept, has conceded that the theoretical base is in a nascent state of development (Foray, 2015, p. 16).

Working definitions: Smart specialization is a "dynamic of the development of new specialties that can emerge spontaneously in the economy" (Foray, 2015, p. 37). It can be considered a policy, strategy, approach, or a complex and involving process; any single definition will reduce the meaning of the smart specialization concept. We introduce several working definitions with the aim of providing different perspectives on the term. Smart specialization can refer to:

- An *innovation policy approach* "that aims to boost national and regional innovation, contributing to growth and prosperity by helping and enabling Member States and regions to focus on their strengths" (European Commission, 2016, p. 1).
- A *place-based approach* "characterized by the identification of strategic areas for intervention based both on the analysis of the strengths and potential of the economy and on an Entrepreneurial Discovery Process (EDP) with wide stakeholder involvement" (Gianelle, Kyriakou, Cohen, & Przeor, 2016, p. 10).
- A *process* aimed at "transforming the economic structures of a region or any other geographical unit through the formation and development of new transformative activities" (Foray, 2018, p. 818). Transformative activities are a collection of innovation capacities and actions that can contribute to a certain structural change towards economic and technological growth.

Therefore, smart specialization strategy means "the national or regional innovation strategies which set priorities in order to build competitive advantage by developing and matching research and innovation own strengths to business needs in order to address emerging opportunities and market developments in a coherent manner, while avoiding duplication and fragmentation of efforts; a smart specialization strategy may take the form of, or be included in, a national or regional research and innovation (R&I) strategic policy framework" (EU Regulation no. 1303, 2013, p. 338).

Basic mechanism: The basic mechanism for smart specialization is the entrepreneurial discovery process (EDP). The EDP is a collective learning process in which fragments of knowledge from various actors combine to enable a new understanding of the opportunities available to a region. Starting this journey of self-discovery requires a collective actor capable of pulling things together and making sense of the opportunities available to the regional economy in a new way (Virkkala, 2019).

Entrepreneurs continually search for, identify, and evaluate new business opportunities. This process is called entrepreneurial discovery in the business theory literature (Shane, 2003, pp. 4–6). The individual entrepreneur exploits an opportunity and organizes and recombines resources in a novel way. The opportunities an entrepreneur exploits may arise as a result of social, demographic, technological, political, or regulatory change, or in connection with grand challenges like climate change (Shane, 2003).

The EDP is a collaborative process involving a public sector agency, entrepreneurs, and scientists. The public sector actor uses a smart specialization strategy to support innovation activities that have a good fit with the economy. The strategy applies a principle of vertical intervention, "[favoring] some technologies, fields, population of firms" (Foray, 2013, p. 55), justified on the grounds that such intervention can help solve coordination and other collective action problems that would have prevented the private sector from achieving a similar transformation of regional capacities on its own (Foray, 2018; Foray & Rainoldi, 2013, pp. 2–3). The EDP provides a new conceptualization of the entrepreneur, broadening the scope of the term to include "innovative firms, research leaders in higher education institutions, independent inventors and innovators" (Foray, 2015, p. 40). EDP involves a collaborative set of entrepreneurial actors from the business world, science, and government. Through a collective process of self-discovery, the partners of these institutional spheres are supposed to open up an exploitation-biased economy to exploration. The systemic nature of this conceptualization of entrepreneurship contrasts with the traditional literature, which looks at entrepreneurship as opportunity discovery and exploitation by individuals (Shane & Venkataraman, 2000), not a collective effort by a set of actors.

Ecosystem Approach for Innovation Policy

Constant evolutionary change in the economic environment necessitates a policy approach that takes the ecosystem perspective into account (Rinkinen, 2016). While this perspective can draw on a relatively long tradition of theoretical work, its normative aspect – how policymakers can devise an ecosystem-friendly innovation policy in concrete terms – has

been comparatively neglected, especially compared to the smart specialization framework, which has been widely adopted in the real world.

The most prominent characteristic of innovation ecosystems is their
complex and self-organizing nature (Rinkinen, 2016), a characteristic that
imposes certain limitations on what an ecosystem-based innovation policy
can hope to achieve. In particular, it is futile for policymakers to aspire to
organize ecosystems according to a predefined blueprint since ecosystems
are self-organizing and too complex to be directed from above. Instead, an
ecosystem-based innovation policy must be flexible and leave room for the
unexpected. Table 1.2 describes the characteristics of such a policy.

Thus the core principles of ecosystem-based innovation policy are as
follows (Rinkenen, 2016):

*Table 1.2   Characteristics of innovation ecosystems and corresponding
elements of ecosystem-based innovation policies*

Innovation ecosystem characteristic	Matching elements of ecosystem-based innovation policy
1. Complex and self-organizing	• Innovation orchestration and facilitation; funding • Leaving room for serendipity; flexible projects to ensure dynamism • Prioritizing the fields from which innovative collisions are expected but without defining what collisions are and who collides
2. Niche development	The flexibility to directly support fields showing potential and growth
3. Find innovation potential from interfaces and unexpected combinations	• Intentional mixing • Looking for the unknown and unexpected
4. Ecosystem management; peer-to-peer management	Providing platforms for development; fostering ecosystem formation through public procurement
5. Global business ecosystems based on local/regional innovation ecosystems	Access to successful global ecosystems
6. Open innovation; co-creation; users	Quadruple helix cooperation
7. Trial-based; experimental; rapid prototyping in the real world	Experimentation culture; offering platforms; supporting pilots; trials and demo phases; constant feedback mechanisms

Source: Adapted from Rinkinen, 2016.

- Providing funding through public procurement, not through individual projects
- Orchestrating, enabling, and facilitating, rather than steering directly
- Network facilitation, not network management
- Promoting quadruple-helix cooperation rather than triple-helix cooperation
- Experimentation culture, not planning culture.

In fact, the elements in Table 1.2 and the core principles describe the smart specialization approach in a nutshell: a policy for ecosystems should prioritize the field for innovative collisions without predefining it, use public procurement to foster ecosystem formation, and provide platforms for development. Therefore, we argue that smart specialization is a policy tool that is consistent with an ecosystem-based view of the regional economy, specifically, an ecosystem-as-structure perspective, albeit with the highly specific entrepreneurial value propositions of Adner (2017) replaced by policymakers' more aggregated visions of what can be achieved by supporting particular domains at the regional level.

DISCUSSION OF THE SYNERGY BETWEEN ENTREPRENEURIAL ECOSYSTEMS AND SMART SPECIALIZATION

As mentioned in the section on "Entrepreneurial Ecosystems," entrepreneurial ecosystems have features that cause ecosystem-based innovation policy theory to diverge from regional development theory with respect to five themes: the role of the state; accessing regional resources and benefits; the role of knowledge; key actors; and industry (Table 1.1). Consequently, cluster strategies and regional innovation system (RIS) strategies are not ideally suited to supporting the establishment of entrepreneurial ecosystems. On the other hand, smart specialization, by virtue of bridging the aforementioned gaps, is arguably a more appropriate strategy for building entrepreneurial ecosystems in a territory. Table 1.3 compares the three approaches.

Role of the Public Sector (State-Region)

In the entrepreneurial ecosystem approach, the ecosystems are primarily led by entrepreneurs (Spigel & Harrison, 2018). By contrast, cluster and RIS policies typically focus on policy entrepreneurship, facilitating

Table 1.3   *How smart specialization bridges the gaps between*
entrepreneurial ecosystems and cluster/RIS strategies

Theme	Cluster and RIS	Entrepreneurial ecosystems	Smart specialization
Role of the state	The state is the lead organizer and a significant investor (top-down)	Entrepreneurs are the primary leaders (bottom-up); the state only supports	Entrepreneurs discover new domains of technological and market opportunities; the state decides which domain to prioritize (top-down and bottom-up)
Accessing regional resources and benefits	Little differentiation between large firms and small start-ups and new ventures	Focus on solving specific difficulties for start-ups and entrepreneurs	Focus on developing transformative activities that contribute to new domains of opportunities
Role of knowledge	Focus on technical and market knowledge	Focus on entrepreneurial knowledge (including but not limited to technical and market knowledge)	Focus on creating entrepreneurial knowledge with transformative potential
Key actors	Large firms, public agencies, universities	Entrepreneurs	State and innovation actors (including large firms, entrepreneurs, public agencies, universities)
Industry	Strengthen knowledge flow and innovation in industries	More focus on underlying technology, less on industry or market	More focus on transformative activities and new domains of opportunity, less focus on sector/industry

Source: Adapted from Spigel & Harrison, 2018; smart specialization column added by the authors.

institutional solutions which enable innovations (Isaksen, Kyllingstad, Rypestøl, & Schulze-Krogh, 2019) in which the state plays a dominant role. The smart specialization approach is a combination of top-down and bottom-up approaches, which may help to reduce the power distance between the state and entrepreneurs.

In the smart specialization policy framework adopted by the European Union, EU member states and regions are expected to provide analysis identifying competitive domains (areas of regional vertical specialization) as well as the need for horizontal policies such as supporting digitalization and the adoption of Key Enabling Technologies. The analysis, undertaken in collaboration with various quadruple helix stakeholders, is expected to lead to regional or national strategies including prioritization of public resources in development of these domains, and the establishment of institutional systems of governance for implementation and correction of the strategies.

However, these top-down initiatives only identify opportunities at a general level and are supplemented by a micro-level strategy of implementing EDP. EDP is an experimental search – continuously adjusted and corrected by feedback loops – for new growth opportunities. In this context the role of the public sector is to provide venture capital, evaluate outcomes, provide support for successful cases, terminate experiments that fail, and adjust the strategy (Foray, 2015).

Regional Resources

The entrepreneurial ecosystem approach requires sufficient resources from regional policy institutions to solve specific difficulties for start-up firms and entrepreneurs.

Whereas cluster policies and policies promoting regional systems of innovation tend to regard "all kinds of innovation" as desirable, the smart specialization approach focuses on entrepreneurial discoveries that open new areas of business, either based on existing domains (related variety) or through new path creation (unrelated variety). In the first phase of smart specialization, the focus was on place-based development, using resources available in the region. However, this approach proved to be insufficient to generate growth in lagging regions with weak institutions. Accordingly, the focus is now on combining place-based development with various forms of transnational thematic partnerships and strengthening the regional institutional capacity (Mariussen, Virkkala, Finne, & Aasen, 2018).

Knowledge

In the entrepreneurial ecosystem approach, the most important type of knowledge is entrepreneurial knowledge. The cluster/RIS approach, by contrast, focuses more narrowly on technology and market knowledge. Entrepreneurial knowledge includes these knowledge domains but is not limited to them; crucially, entrepreneurial knowledge also encompasses knowledge about the entrepreneurship process, i.e. issues such as opportunity identification, business planning, and venture capital financing (Spigel & Harrison, 2018).

The smart specialization approach focuses on generating entrepreneurial knowledge with a transformative potential. It achieves this through a process of combining, converting, and restructuring fragmented knowledge resources. More specifically, smart specialization aspires to combine three forms of knowledge: entrepreneurial insights into market opportunities; expertise on regional strategic orientations; and scientific insights. Such a process of knowledge integration is demanding as it relies heavily on connectivity between triple helix actors which are not always closely aligned (Blažek & Morgan, 2019). However, the involvement of the public sector facilitates knowledge diffusion and spillovers since public sector agencies, unlike private firms, do not have a strong incentive to keep entrepreneurial knowledge to themselves (Foray, 2018). The smart specialization approach, if conscientiously implemented, links directly into start-up formation and industrial upscaling and provides a supporting regional ecology for organizing start-up incubation.

Key Actors

In the entrepreneurial ecosystem approach, the key actors are entrepreneurs. In the cluster/RIS approach, they are public agencies, universities, and large firms. In the smart specialization approach, the key actors are all of the above – public agencies, universities, and all types of firms including start-ups.

EDP is an explorative search for new opportunities, potentially leading to diversification and climbing in value chains within existing domains but also to the identification of new paths based on existing strengths. EDP is not classic economic entrepreneurship. Instead, it is expected to be undertaken through a collaborative effort of public sector actors, entrepreneurs who know the market, and entrepreneurial scientists, each group complementing the strengths of the others (Foray, 2015).

Industry

While the entrepreneurial ecosystem approach focuses on an industry's underlying technologies and the cluster/RIS approach concentrates on strengthening knowledge flows and innovation within an industry, the focus of the smart specialization approach is on opening up new or related domains of technology and market opportunity – in other words, the same focus as entrepreneurs.

Based on a micro-macro approach that combines micro-level theories of learning through new knowledge creation with evolutionary economic theories of growth (Boschma, 2017; Nguyen & Mariussen, 2019), smart specialization connects the discussion of sustainable start-up incubation ecosystems to a modern theory of growth in the economy. The long-term ambition of smart specialization is to create sustainable macro-level growth in the economy, with EDP as a fundamental engine of growth.

To conclude: The smart specialization approach goes beyond theories of clusters and RIS – which tacitly assume that any kind of innovation creates growth – by emphasizing the importance of EDP.

The starting point of smart specialization is to leverage the current strengths of regions. Its ultimate aim is to transform regional econo-mies by discovering new potential growth domains and supporting the development of these through regional policy. New potential growth domains are found through a collaborative search process involving entrepreneurial actors in a broad sense, including firms, universities, public agents, and NGOs. In this sense, start-ups are important actors capable of embracing the opportunities that exist in a region as a result of the region's specific characteristics and developing new growth domains with the support of the regional smart specialization strategy. Entrepreneurial discoveries leading to growth may emerge through experiments that combine learning across value chains, sectors, and countries. Actors involved in defining or implementing a smart speciali-zation strategy should regularly reexamine and evaluate the priorities of the strategy and the assumptions on which it is based, learning from their own experience as well as from the experience of others, and adjust the policy accordingly.

The ambition of smart specialization is to create regional growth through better ways of using and combining place-based resources and macro-regional networks. A key element in achieving this is improving regional governance and facilitating cooperation among entrepreneurial actors in a broad sense including public sector agencies, universities, and businesses, with the aim of creating and refining the knowledge that can fuel entrepreneurial transformation activities. This is the synergy between smart specialization strategy and the entrepreneurial ecosystems approach, which likewise assumes that the co-existence and interaction of entrepreneurial actors is a driver of economic sustainability. Smart spe-cialization policies, with their experimental nature, enable the conditions for establishing domain priorities in the regions and initiating transforma-tive activities associated with those priorities, ultimately leading to the evolution of what could be called entrepreneurial ecosystems. The synergy will be discussed further in the next section.

IMPLICATIONS FOR POLICY AND CONTRIBUTION

It is important to understand that deploying smart specialization innovation policy does not mean dismissing other innovation policies such as cluster policy or national innovation system policy. These horizonal policies are essential to building a fundamental framework for strengthening regional innovation capacities and institutions. Policies offering support to a generalized category of activities or actors (e.g. R&D activities, or start-up firms) can be a crucial means of increasing innovation rates. Smart specialization is an additional option that regions may choose to embrace if they have a sufficiently high level of institutional sophistication and commitment to transforming their economic structure towards differentiation and specialization (Foray, 2018).

Implications for Policy

There are several implications for policy design if a smart specialization strategy is adopted to support the development of entrepreneurial ecosystems. As mentioned in the section on "Innovation Policies," the synergy between smart specialization and entrepreneurial ecosystems lies in the *experimental nature* of smart specialization, which will help enable the conditions for *establishing the domain priorities* in the regions and for *developing transformative activities* associated with those domain priorities (Foray, 2018).

Establishing the domain priorities in the regions refers to the process of exploring new ways of matching specific regional characteristics and innovation capacities with entrepreneurial opportunities in order to identify key domains that have the potential to transform the economic structure of the region. This process should involve intensive interactions between public and private sectors within a robust and transparent policy framework (Foray, 2018). *Developing transformative activities* refers to policies that help create the critical mass of involvement and activity within a prioritized domain that will enable it to produce sustainable economic growth. The priorities and transformative activities should be *experimental*, i.e. gradually and jointly discovered by a diverse set of actors in the regions through EDP. The policy must therefore be flexible and subject to regular evaluation using objective performance indicators and feedback from relevant stakeholders (Feldman, Hadjimichael, Lanahan, & Kemeny, 2016).

For illustration, consider the case of the Nordland region of Norway, which has adopted a smart specialization strategy. The regional government of Nordland has identified three domains to prioritize: seafood, tourism, and the process industry (OECD, 2016). Rather than provide financial support to these industries in an indiscriminate fashion, which would run counter to the ideas of smart specialization, the Nordland government has implemented three *transformative activities* (OECD, 2016, p. 198):

- "Supporting co-operative projects between business and R&D institutions"
- "Brokering education projects within clusters"
- "Supporting competence building in universities and R&D institutes that align with cluster development in the region."

Several policy implications are reflected in this example. First, a vision of regional transformation does not necessarily have to focus on high-tech areas of the economy, although it should facilitate the adoption of relevant advanced technological solutions by potential users in the prioritized domains. Second, the policy should aim to develop specialized human capital and capabilities before, or at least in parallel with, increasing demand for R&D within the priority domains. Third, the public sector agency should support knowledge diffusion in the domains in order to mitigate the problem of private sector actors tending to keep information private. Fourth, the policy should not be based on any preconceived notions of how the domains ought to evolve but should instead facilitate a process of collective learning aimed at enabling entrepreneurs to define the new economic structure of the region in a bottom-up fashion.

Contribution

In this chapter we have discussed the role of smart specialization in providing regional strategic support for the establishment of sustainable start-up incubation ecosystems. We did so in three steps. First we introduced the ecosystem concept in economics and management. We then turned to innovation policy, discussing two approaches to innovation policy in particular: smart specialization, which has been widely implemented in practice but is relatively loosely grounded in theory, and the ecosystem-based approach, which rests on a relatively strong theoretical base but has not been developed into a practitioner-friendly framework. Finally we compared these two approaches and argued that smart specialization essentially *is* an ecosystem-based approach – or at least consistent with ecosystem-based approaches in most respects – while retaining some elements of traditional innovation policy, and that it therefore "bridges the gap" between the traditional and ecosystem-based views of innovation. This finding has practical significance. Smart specialization is currently being implemented on a large scale in the European Union, imbuing the concept with empirical substance and facilitating its adoption by policymakers elsewhere. Although smart specialization is not the be-all and end-all of innovation policy, we argue that it is currently the most useful answer to the question of how ecosystem-based notions of innovation policy can be implemented.

In the context of supporting entrepreneurial ecosystems at the regional level through smart specialization, lending support to *start-up incubation* ecosystems is a small but vital component. It is small because, by definition, only firms at the earliest stage of their lifecycle can be in a state of incubation, and thus only a small minority of entrepreneurial actors (recall that smart specialization takes an expansive view of this term) will belong to a start-up incubation ecosystem at any given time. Yet it is also vital because smart specialization has a strong focus on new entrepreneurial opportunities, and start-ups are designed to seize those.

The contribution of the present chapter to the entrepreneurship literature is three-fold. First and foremost, to the best of our knowledge this chapter is the first attempt in the academic literature to examine explicitly how smart specialization is connected to entrepreneurship theories, offering in the process a new conceptualization of entrepreneurship as a collective (rather than individual) effort to discover opportunities.

Second, this chapter addresses the question of how the sustainability of entrepreneurial ecosystems can be ensured, raised by Cavallo et al. (2018), who draw special attention in this context to the distinction between "natural" and "artificial" governance mechanisms. To the extent that smart specialization can promote sustainable entrepreneurial ecosystems (an idea to which we are sympathetic), our conclusion is that a combination of top-down ("artificial") and bottom-up ("natural") mechanisms is called for. Indeed the notion that the two should be combined is absolutely essential to smart specialization.

Third, in extension of the above, we explain how policymakers can intervene in order to facilitate and enable (as opposed to regulate) the "natural" drivers of dynamism in entrepreneurial ecosystems. In a nutshell, our answer is that policymakers should implement a smart specialization strategy. That is to say, they should encourage an entrepreneurial discovery process involving the public sector and academia in addition to private entrepreneurs, identify domains to prioritize as an outcome of this process, support transformative activities within those domains, and so on, as described at length in this chapter and elsewhere.

Some aspects of smart specialization leave room for interpretation, and one might argue with some justification that the concept is more of an idealized vision loosely based on a miscellany of theories than a rigorous theoretical framework in its own right. Yet the undeniable political and economic reality of smart specialization makes it urgent and imperative for scholars to engage with the concept. We hope the present chapter will inspire more research on the theoretical underpinnings of smart specialization and the linkages between smart specialization and entrepreneurship theory in particular.

REFERENCES

Acs, Z. J., Stam, E., Audretsch, D. B., & O'Connor, A. (2017). The lineages of the entrepreneurial ecosystem approach. *Small Business Economics*, *49*(1), 1–10.

Adner, R. (2017). Ecosystem as structure: An actionable construct for strategy. *Journal of Management*, *43*(1), 39–58.

Baumol, W. J. (1990). Entrepreneurship: Productive, unproductive, and destructive. *Journal of Political Economy*, *98*(5, Part 1), 893–921. doi:10.1086/261712.

Blažek, J., & Morgan, K. (2019). The institutional worlds of entrepreneurial discovery: Finding a place for less developed regions. In Å. Mariussen, S. Virkkala, H. Finne, & T. M. Aasen (Eds.), *The entrepreneurial discovery process and regional development. New knowledge emergence, conversion and exploitation.* Abingdon: Routledge.

Boschma, R. (2017). Relatedness as driver of regional diversification: A research agenda. *Regional Studies*, *51*(3), 351–364.

Byrne, D., & Callaghan, G. (2014). *Complexity theory and the social sciences: The state of the art.* New York: Routledge.

Cavallo, A., Ghezzi, A., & Balocco, R. (2018). Entrepreneurial ecosystem research: Present debates and future directions. *International Entrepreneurship and Management Journal.* doi:10.1007/s11365-018-0526-3. https://ssrn.com/abstract=3192411.

European Commission (2016). Roadmap smart specialization: A fresh approach to the European growth and jobs through regional research and innovation strategies, in *Commission Communication on Smart Specialization*, December.

EU Regulation (2013). No. 1303/2013 of the European Parliament and of the Council, *Official Journal of the European Communities*, 20. https://eur-lex.europa.eu/legal-content/EN/TXT/PDF/?uri=CELEX:32013R1303&from=LV.

Evans, D. S., & Schmalensee, R. (2016). *Matchmakers: The new economics of multisided platforms.* Boston: Harvard Business Review Press.

Feldman, M., Hadjimichael, T., Lanahan, L., & Kemeny, T. (2016). The logic of economic development: A definition and model for investment. *Environment and Planning C: Government and Policy*, *34*(1), 5–21.

Foray, D. (2013). The economic fundamentals of smart specialization. *Ekonomiaz*, *83*(2), 55–78.

Foray, D. (2015). *Smart specialization: Opportunities and challenges for regional innovation policy* (Vol. 79). New York: Routledge.

Foray, D. (2018). Smart specialization strategies as a case of mission-oriented policy: A case study on the emergence of new policy practices. *Industrial and Corporate Change*, *27*(5), 817–832.

Foray, D., David, P. A., & Hall, B. (2009). Smart specialization: The concept. *Knowledge Economists Policy Brief*, *9*(85), 100.

Foray, D., & Rainoldi, A. (2013). Smart specialisation programmes and implementation report EUR 26002 EN (S3 Policy Brief Series. No. 02/2013). Seville: European Commission, JRC-IPTS.

Gianelle, C., D. Kyriakou, C. Cohen and M. Przeor (eds) (2016), Implementing smart specialization: A handbook, Brussels: European Commission, EUR 28053 EN, doi:10.2791/53569.

Isaksen, A., Kyllingstad, N., Rypestøl, J. O., & Schulze-Krogh, A. C. (2019). Entrepreneurial discovery processes in different regional contexts: A conceptual discussion. In Å. Mariussen, S. Virkkala, H. Finne, & T. M. Aasen (Eds.), *The entrepreneurial discovery process and regional development. New knowledge emergence, conversion and exploitation.* Abingdon: Routledge.

Kuhlmann, S., & Edler, J. (2003). Scenarios of technology and innovation policies in Europe: Investigating future governance. *Technological Forecasting and Social Change, 70*(7), 619–637.

Mariussen, Å., Virkkala, S., Finne, H., & Aasen, T. M. (2018). *The entrepreneurial discovery process and regional development: New knowledge emergence, conversion and exploitation.* Abingdon: Routledge.

Marshall, A. (1920). *Principles of economics.* London: Macmillan and Co.

Nguyen, N., & Mariussen, Å. (2019). Moving beyond related variety, creating firm-level ambidexterity for economic growth via the entrepreneurial discovery process. In Å. Mariussen, S. Virkkala, H. Finne, & T. M. Aasen (Eds.), *The entrepreneurial discovery process and regional development. New knowledge emergence, conversion and exploitation.* Abingdon: Routledge.

Novotny, A., Clausen, T., Rasmussen, E. & Wiklund, J. (2018). Call for chapters – *Research Handbook on Start-up Incubation Ecosystems.*

OECD. (2016). *OECD Regional Outlook 2016.*

Parker, G. G., & Van Alstyne, M. W. (2005). Two-sided network effects: A theory of information product design. *Management Science, 51*(10), 1494–1504.

Porter, M. E. (1998). *Clusters and the new economics of competition* (Vol. 76). *Harvard Business Review.* Boston.

Qian, H., Acs, Z. J., & Stough, R. R. (2013). Regional systems of entrepreneurship: The nexus of human capital, knowledge and new firm formation. *Journal of Economic Geography, 13*(4), 559–587. doi:10.1093/jeg/lbs009.

Rinkinen, S. (2016). Clusters, innovation systems and ecosystems: Studies on innovation policy's concept evolution and approaches for regional renewal. *Acta Universitatis Lappeenrantaensis.* Retrieved from http://lutpub.lut.fi/handle/10024/129972.

Rinkinen, S., & Harmaakorpi, V. (2018). The business ecosystem concept in innovation policy context: Building a conceptual framework. *Innovation: The European Journal of Social Science Research, 31*(3), 333–349.

Shane, S. A. (2003). *A general theory of entrepreneurship: The individual-opportunity nexus.* Cheltenham: Edward Elgar Publishing.

Shane, S., & Venkataraman, S. (2000). The promise of entrepreneurship as a field of research. *Academy of Management Review, 25*(1), 217–226.

Smart Specialization Platform (2019, April 1). Retrieved from http://s3platform.jrc.ec.europa. eu/. Accessed 23/4/2019.

Spigel, B. (2017). The relational organization of entrepreneurial ecosystems. *Entrepreneurship Theory and Practice, 41*(1), 49–72.

Spigel, B., & Harrison, R. (2018). Toward a process theory of entrepreneurial ecosystems. *Strategic Entrepreneurship Journal, 12*(1), 151–168. doi:10.1002/sej.1268.

Stam, E. (2015). Entrepreneurial ecosystems and regional policy: a sympathetic critique. *European Planning Studies, 23*(9), 1759–1769.

Stam, E., & Spigel, B. (2017). Entrepreneurial ecosystems. In R. Blackburn, D. De Clercq, J. Heinonen, & Z. Wang (Eds.), *Handbook for Entrepreneurship and Small Business.* London: Sage.

Terjesen, S., Acs, Z., Audretsch, D., Hechavarria, D., Stam, E., & White, R. (2017). Entrepreneurial ecosystems: The search for performance. *University of Tampa, unpublished.*

Virkkala, S. (2019). Entrepreneurial discovery processes, knowledge creation and knowledge space. In Å. Mariussen, S. Virkkala, H. Finne, & T. M. Aasen (Eds.), *The entrepreneurial discovery process and regional development. New knowledge emergence, conversion and exploitation*. Abingdon: Routledge.

Virkkala, S., & Mariussen, Å. (2019). Emergence of new business areas in regional economies through entrepreneurial discovery processes. In Å. Mariussen, S. Virkkala, H. Finne, & T. M. Aasen (Eds.), *The entrepreneurial discovery process and regional development. New knowledge emergence, conversion and exploitation*. Abingdon: Routledge.

2. Incubating start-ups in entrepreneurial ecosystems: A multilevel perspective on entrepreneurial resources

Shruti Sardeshmukh, Allan O'Connor, and Ronda Smith

Entrepreneurial ecosystems are emerging as an important area of research in the entrepreneurship literature (Spigel, 2017). At the regional level, entrepreneurship has been linked to economic growth, long-term productivity as well as job creation (Isenberg, 2010). Entrepreneurial ecosystems are the contexts within which start-up firms are incubated and nurtured, fuelling this economic activity. Policymakers are increasingly interested in understanding and exploring the best practices in building entrepreneurial ecosystems in cities, towns, and regions (Isenberg, 2010; Mason & Brown, 2013, 2014; O'Connor, Stam, Susan, & Audretsch, 2018). Incubating start-ups that can grow and create jobs can be an engine of economic growth for many regions. Yet, many policy initiatives devoting resources to boost the economy do not always succeed (Lerner, 2010). Given the multitude of components, actors, and interconnections involved in the ecosystem, not much is yet known about how effective local entrepreneurial ecosystems operate and may be developed, nor do we know about how such ecosystems evolve (Ács, Stam, Audretsch, & O'Connor, 2017; Autio, Nambisan, Thomas, & Wright, 2018). Van De Ven (1993: 211) astutely observed early on that while "infrastructure facilitates and constrains individual entrepreneurs, it is the latter who construct and change the industrial infrastructure". Therefore, a better understanding of resources in the ecosystem can help us understand the mechanisms of growth and development of the entrepreneurial ecosystem and can also contribute to policy initiatives to boost regional economies.

Traditional theories of resources, such as the resource-based view (RBV), argue that resources are a property of the firm, yet it is also very clear that start-ups operate in a resource-constrained environment, borrowing resources from others and leveraging them to create value through mechanisms such as bricolage (Baker & Nelson, 2005). Resources in the entrepreneurial ecosystem provide the necessary inputs for start-up activity, just as the start-up activity contributes to the resources in the ecosystem.

While extant research has found that the abundance of resources can help entrepreneurial action (Zott & Amit, 2007), or an injection of resources can contribute to the entrepreneurial ecosystem (Roundy, Bradshaw, & Brockman 2018), there is little research examining the dynamic bottom-up emergence processes. From a bottom-up perspective, the resources at the higher ecosystemic level emerge from and are affected by resources held by the lower levels of individuals and organizations.

Spigel (2017: 53) espouses that the advantages of a well-performing entrepreneurial ecosystem are to be found with the ready access to related resources specific to "the entrepreneurship process such as start-up culture and financing rather than other types of industrial benefits found in clusters that accrue to firms of all sizes and ages". For example, Spigel (2017) discusses the importance of regional resources such as shared cultural understanding, shared labour pool, and social networks that facilitate knowledge spill-overs. However, while these are regional resources, it is unclear how the "regional" resources emerge from resources and actions of individuals. Similarly, resources such as a start-up culture emerge from the attitudes and activities of individuals within the ecosystem. An ecosystem analysis traces and exposes these levels of interdependence and is particularly amenable to multilevel, complex systems thinking. Therefore, a multilevel perspective can add value as a tool for understanding the functioning of places with respect to their entrepreneurial performances and resource behaviour.

To better understand the role of resources in the entrepreneurial ecosystem, and how they emerge from the micro level to perform the function of incubating a new generation of start-ups, we apply a multilevel framework to the construct of entrepreneurial ecosystems. We then discuss both the top-down and bottom-up processes of ecosystem development to articulate the process of emergence at the level of the ecosystem. Thus, we contribute to the process of developing a deeper understanding of resources in entrepreneurial ecosystems and how they nurture and incubate start-ups.

RESOURCES IN AN ENTREPRENEURIAL ECOSYSTEM

In the strategy literature, the Resource-Based View (RBV) of a firm defines resources as those that are owned and/or controlled by the firm (Barney, 1991). However, the start-up context implies that firms themselves are in the process of being born. Starting a new venture, which by definition has not reached a fully developed organizational form, is a process of firm emergence. Resources, as commonly explained in the RBV theory, are a property of the firm that can deliver a sustainable competitive advantage (SCA) when they are owned and controlled by the firm. However, in the process of emergence of the firm, success is often contingent upon how well the entrepreneurs can muster and receive support from others in order to access a larger pool of resources (Hanlon & Saunders, 2007) which they do not own. In other words, resources, in the entrepreneurial context of new firm creation, are not necessarily all owned or controlled by the entrepreneur (Stevenson & Jarillo, 1990). Therefore, the entrepreneur's strategic links to the entrepreneurial ecosystem are extremely important in terms of gaining access to various forms of resources and constructing the foundations of the resources of the firm in the long run. Resources at the ecosystemic level, therefore, play a significant role in enabling and/or constraining start-up activity.

To illustrate, the specific types of resources to which we refer to and discuss are:

- *Financial resources* (e.g., money) potentially transferable to a start-up through business angels, venture capital funds, banks, and government grants, family and friends, etc.
- *Human resources* (e.g., as labour and/or knowledge and connections) that may be attracted from the ecosystem and accumulated within or committed to the start-up. Also embedded in human resources are the attitudes and behaviours of individuals in the ecosystem.
- *Informational resources* (e.g., technical, legal, financial advice as well as entrepreneurial process and/or procedural advice) that a start-up can readily access through such technical and professional service firms and organizations such as universities, lawyers, accountants, and mentors.

These resources are clearly valuable to the entrepreneur; however, many of these resources may be owned by others within the ecosystem. In some instances, it may be that resources are acquired by transactional processes (e.g., borrowing money based on collateral and a principal and interest repayment schedule or buying the services from lawyers or accountants). However, in some instances, it would be a characteristic of the ecosystem, such as the start-up culture or the pattern of institutional infrastructure that sustains and supports the start-up activity and resource flows.

Given the definitional limitation of RBV in the start-up entrepreneur's resource acquisition context, a more appropriate starting point is Penrose (1995) who viewed resources as those things put to use for service of the firm rather than for ownership as theorized by Barney (1991). A more aligned theoretical base, therefore, is the extended resource-based view

(ERBV) that adopts a perspective that firms are able to draw on a wide array of external resources, through market-mediated transactions, various approaches to resource exchange, and capabilities to leverage resource relations (Mathews, 2003). Not only do entrepreneurial resources need to exist in the ecosystem, but they need to be generated, distributed, and recombined in order to sustain the start-up incubation activity. Networks, both formal and informal, are important conduits for such a flow of resources.

To better understand the emergent and complex nature of resource exchange, we view them as a multilevel phenomenon. In the next section, we articulate the complex and multilevel nature of entrepreneurial ecosystems.

ENTREPRENEURIAL ECOSYSTEMS AS MULTILEVEL COMPLEX SYSTEMS

In spite of the increasing research interest in the entrepreneurial ecosystems, the concept continues to remain "fuzzy" (Stam, 2014). The research to date has demonstrated that systemic and institutional conditions that form the context of entrepreneurial ecosystems are important for the generation of start-up activity. However, it is clear that entrepreneurs are not only acting within the context of the social and institutional environment, but also act to shape the environment through emergent processes. The start-ups incubated within the entrepreneurial system, grow, and develop to become contributors of resources to the ecosystem. Entrepreneurial ecosystems are thus an emergent phenomenon, such that the actions of individuals impact the context, and the context shapes the actions and behaviours of entrepreneurs, in particular during the start-up activity.

Entrepreneurial ecosystems, self-organizing and emergent (Roundy et al., 2018), are often portrayed as analogous to biological ecosystems (Colombo, Dagnino, Lehmann, & Salmador, 2017). They are complex systems where all the elements including human, knowledge, financial and other resources, and their interaction influence entrepreneurship through the actions of individuals (Ács, Audretsch, Lehmann, & Licht, 2016), institutions (Stam, 2015) and/or other entrepreneurial actors (Isenberg, 2010; Spigel, 2017). Not surprisingly, a variety of definitions of an entrepreneurial ecosystem have been developed focusing on various social, political, cultural and economic (Spigel 2017) elements (Isenberg, 2010; Spigel, 2017), factors (Stam, 2015), or processes (Mason & Brown, 2014), often described as dynamic and institutionally embedded (Ács, Autio, & Szerb, 2014). The elements in the entrepreneurial ecosystem span contextual factors such as the institutional environment, established firms, and support institutions. Stam (2014) articulates that entrepreneurial ecosystems can be decomposed into two types of conditions (a) Framework conditions (institutions, physical conditions), and (b) Systemic conditions (e.g., networks, leadership, finance, talent). These conditions provide the context for individual entrepreneurs to operate within. Also broadly common amongst entrepreneurial ecosystem definitions is some form of performance outcome, be it innovative start-ups (Spigel 2017), venture creation and growth (Isenberg 2010), allocation of resources (Ács et al., 2014), productive entrepreneurship (Stam, 2015), or some type of unspecified performance (Mason & Brown 2014).

Ecosystems are also considered in more holistic terms that include institutional frameworks, leadership, existing entrepreneurs, and the complex interactions between the diverse elements (Isenberg, 2010), as well as the networks between different components (Motoyama & Watkins, 2014). While it is clear that multiple actors, including individuals, firms, and institutions play a role, it is also the interaction between their activities that constitutes a thriving ecosystem. An important role of such an ecosystem is to incubate and nurture start-ups whereby entrepreneurs start their firms in the context of the ecosystem and draw resources from the ecosystem. Audretsch and Keilbach (2005: 458) discuss the notion of entrepreneurship capital as "the capacity of a society to generate new firms" which is important for improving the region's productivity. To understand this phenomenon the ecosystem perspective becomes increasingly important when the value of multi-lateral relationships cannot be decomposed into an additive form of binary relationships (Adner, 2017). That is, an ecosystemic study is useful when the phenomenon is holistic, and the decomposed parts such as the framework and systemic conditions have interdependencies. For instance, to understand the systemic conditions of financing, there may be an interdependency on the institutional framework condition of taxation law, or an influence through institutional culture such as may be the case with Buddhist or Muslim religions (Audretsch, Bönte, & Keilbach, 2008). Roundy, Bradshaw and Brockman (2018, p. 5) state that "[a]n entrepreneurial ecosystem is a self-organized, adaptive, and geographically bounded community of complex agents operating at multiple, aggregated levels, whose non-linear interactions result in the patterns of activities through which new ventures form and dissolve over time". Similar to this definition, we offer a more concise definition that ecosystems consist of *institutionally embedded elements influencing actors who bring about entrepreneurial performance*. In other words, entrepreneurial ecosystems nurture (i.e., produce, incubate, and support the development of) start-ups.

Appreciating the self-organizing nature of entrepreneurial ecosystem interactions and the interdependence and interactions among elements and actors in the ecosystem, the concept of emergence becomes central. Emergence is defined as "the creation of new 'order' – structures, processes, and system-wide properties that come into being within and across system levels" (Lichtenstein, 2011: 486). Furthermore, emergence is observed as a characteristic of complex systems due to the interdependent interaction of processes between levels and with the system as a whole (Fuller & Moran, 2001; Lissack & Letiche, 2002).

There has been some qualitative research that investigated the complex nature of ecosystems. For example, a study of accelerators in the entrepreneurial ecosystem of Bangalore, India (Goswami, Mitchell, & Bhagavatula, 2018) or Polish migrants in Glasgow, Scotland (Lassalle & Johnston, 2018) both used a qualitative lens to understand ecosystems and the resources. On the other hand, studies of emergence can be represented by work done in Seattle, Washington involving social impact entrepreneurs and businesses (Thompson, Purdy, & Ventresca, 2018). However, generally, quantitative studies have been fewer and have also tended, although not exclusively, to focus on elemental contributions and econometrics to address issues of measurement (c.f., Bruns, Bosma, Sanders, & Schramm, 2017) or accounts of entrepreneurial ecosystems (Stam, 2018). Quantitative multilevel studies on emergence appear relatively rare with the exception of Sohns and Diez (2018) who used multilevel methods to explain micro-entrepreneurship in rural Vietnam.

Given the emergent nature of entrepreneurial ecosystems, we apply the multilevel lens to understand the phenomenon. A multilevel perspective defines the different levels and articulates how the micro phenomena are embedded in the macro contexts and how the macro context emerges as a result of the dynamics between the micro-level elements. We define three levels of analysis by drawing upon the field of organizational studies (Kozlowski & Klein, 2000). We specifically choose this view, as we are interested in the organizing process of nurturing start-ups and the distribution of resources. The levels are defined as:

- The macro (e.g., the normative and regular social behaviours of the community in focus).
- The micro (e.g., the population of individual actors undertaking and associated with the start-up behaviour).
- The meso (e.g., the interaction level where established organizations create opportunities for interaction among individual actors and facilitate aggregation and flow of resources).

Critically, *ecosystem* as portrayed in this chapter at the macro level is not to be taken as separable from the meso and micro levels. An ecosystem is a holistic concept that includes the meso and micro levels but manifests as a higher level of order. The meso level is of particular importance as it represents the *organization of exchange* between the actors that form the components of the ecosystem. It allows us, "both to understand the whole and keep an eye on the parts" (Kozlowski & Klein, 2000: 54). This is so for two reasons: (a) individual entrepreneurs take action, including undertaking an entrepreneurial activity, and (b) it is the interrelationships between individuals and other entities that are key to the existence of ecosystems.

Kozlowski, Chao, Grand, Braun, and Kuljanin (2013: 582) define two distinct processes that characterize multilevel phenomena. They define top-down processes as "contextual effects whereby higher-level phenomena constrain, shape, and influence different lower-level phenomena". On the other hand, they argue that bottom-up processes signify "emergence whereby dynamic interaction processes among lower level entities (i.e., individuals, teams, units) – over time – yield phenomena that manifest at higher, collective levels". We first articulate these top-down and bottom-up processes. To fully comprehend the multilevel nature of the resources in the entrepreneurial ecosystem, we need to understand both the contextual influences (i.e., how the resources of the ecosystem affect individuals' start-up activity) and the emergent processes (how the individuals' resources, behaviours, and attitudes lead to resources at the ecosystemic level). While previous research has tended to focus on the top-down effects, we focus on both top-down and bottom-up processes.

Top-down Processes – Contextual Influences

An individual's entrepreneurial activity is both constrained and enhanced by the surrounding context. Most of the entrepreneurial ecosystems research has focused on the top-down phenomenon perpetuated by a view that an ecosystem is independent and situational for entrepreneurship (Isenberg, 2010; Mack & Mayer, 2015). To illustrate, the argument that a lack of availability of financial resources in an ecosystem may constrain the activity and scale of individual ventures positions the entrepreneur as a passive recipient of funds distinct from the ecosystem. It follows, therefore, that a sudden injection of resources can contribute to increased start-up activity (Roundy et al. 2018). Similarly, the view that by being part of an ecosystem, an entrepreneur may be able to access resources such as informational and human resources that they might not otherwise have access to, assumes that the ecosystem provides for and drives entrepreneurial activity. Through knowledge spill-overs within an ecosystem, start-ups can get access to information, a key ingredient in the process of opportunity recognition. Further, involvement in the ecosystem can help the development of connections and relationships with other entrepreneurs and support institutions such that it can help foster innovation and further entrepreneurship. In this manner, entrepreneurship is viewed as dependent on the context for the provision of resources, and, from the top-down perspective, enriching the context will drive more entrepreneurship.

Bottom-up Process – The Emergence

The complement to top-down is described by Stam (2015) who argued that the entrepreneurial ecosystem emphasized a bottom-up, emergent nature as individual level resources and entrepreneurial behaviours aggregate to form entrepreneurial ecosystems. The bottom-up or emergent processes articulate how the constructs at the micro level can lead to an emergent phenomenon observed at the macro level such that it cannot then be reduced or discretely assigned to its lower-level individual elements. In a multilevel model, the phenomenon is said to be emergent "when it originates in the cognition, affect, behaviours or other characteristics of individuals are amplified by their interaction and manifests as a higher level collective phenomenon" (Kozlowski & Klein, 2000: 55). Emergent phenomena can be through either the process of composition or through the process of compilation (Kozlowski et al., 2013; Kozlowski & Klein, 2000). Composition assumes that phenomena at the lower can coalesce at a higher level, yielding a macro-level property. Phenomena that emerge through composition processes emerge as shared properties at the macro level. Compilation, on the other hand, does not require such a process of coalescing. In fact, the pattern of individual-level attributes generates configural properties at the macro level. Patterns of networks among the individual actors, for example, can lead to an emergent configural property of ecosystems.

To illustrate, the properties of an organization in an aggregated sense can reflect both coalesced and configured properties. For instance, an organization may hold a reputation for excellent customer service. This sensed or observed characteristic must also be *lived* by the members of the organization. Hence, the shared vision, culture, and way of operating to produce the service excellence reputation is both composed by and observed as a common attribute among employees. Although each and every employee may not exhibit the attribute in the exact same way, this commonality in approach comes together and coalesces as an organizational property, providing service excellence. Furthermore, service excellence is also experienced and is a sum of what employees actually do.

Delivering service excellence can be attributed to how the combination of difference among the skills, world-views, expertise and knowledge sets of individuals are compiled through a certain organizational configuration to deliver the observable organizational output; service excellence. In our case, the entrepreneurial ecosystem is equally dependent on the entrepreneurial activity to define it at the macro level by observed aggregation of the coalesced composition of common attributes and the compiled configuration of different actors and forms of actors to articulate the properties of an ecosystem that frequently nurture start-up firms.

Role of the Meso

While much of the action takes place at the individual level and becomes aggregated and manifested at the macro level (the observed properties of the ecosystem), mesostructures such as existing firms, infrastructure, and support institutions have an important role to play in this process. Traditionally, in organizational studies, the meso level is taken to be the integrating level of organizational science between the macro, generalized organization and the particulars of individuals at the micro level (Kozlowski & Klein, 2000). We apply and extend the multilevel framework such that the meso level is the interactive and integrative level between the macro (ecosystem) and the activities of individuals, which hosts a variety of organizational forms. Social interaction and the resource exchange between individuals and between organizations are crucial to emergence, and the structure and processes exhibited among these various organizations provide the opportunities for interaction at the meso level. Incubators, financial institutions, and other support organizations can play an important role in facilitating the emergence of macro-level phenomena.

It is also important to note that the start-up activity itself, over time, may augment the organizational infrastructure of the ecosystem. Individual entrepreneurs undertake entrepreneurial action and start new firms. As in most entrepreneurship literature, we consider the start-up ventures and entrepreneurs at the same level, the micro level. However, over time as the ventures grow and develop into established and potentially larger organizations, they may become a part of the meso organizational framework. For example, while Microsoft and Google began as start-ups, over time, they have become integral to the structure of the Silicon Valley ecosystem. As Kozlowski et al. (2013: 585) articulate: "The process of emergence begets structure in the form of an emerged phenomenon that then shapes subsequent processes." This also resonates with the view that entrepreneurial "successes" can shape and drive the growth of an entrepreneurial ecosystem.

Resources Conceptualized as Compositional Properties of an Ecosystem

From an emergent perspective, properties at the level of the ecosystem may originate from the micro level as the experiences, human capital, information and other resources of the individuals that are aggregated at the macro level. We argue that the financial, human, informational and cultural resources of individuals in an ecosystem can signal a compositional property aggregated at the macro level. Composition implies "isomorphism between manifestations of constructs at different levels; the constructs share the same content, meaning, and construct validity across levels" (Kozlowski & Klein, 2000: 30). When resources are conceptualized as a compositional property, it also implies coherence (Roundy et al., 2018) among entrepreneurial activity.

Financial resources conceptualized as compositional properties of the ecosystem. The availability of financial resources in terms of investment capital is quite critical for start-ups in the ecosystem. However, such financial resources are aggregated from the existing organizational framework of the ecosystem, including, venture capital funds, incubators, accelerators as well as individuals, informal angel investors and the entrepreneur's own personal wealth. The greater the amount of resources available to these actors, the greater is the potential for the aggregate availability of finance in the ecosystem. Furthermore, successful start-ups that grow and show strong financial performance also may contribute to the financial resources available in the ecosystem. From a compositional perspective, it is both the quantum of financial resources and the number of entrepreneurial firms that through an application of those financial resources reach sustained and perpetual success that affirms the presence of an entrepreneurial ecosystem and distinguishes a "wealth" attribute. However, while "wealth" may be a feature, it will not be a uniform attribute of all individual entrepreneurs even though they may share a common "wealthy" environment. Instead, the coalescence of the quantum, application, and prominence of profitable firms signals the shared property of "wealth" at the level of the entrepreneurial ecosystem.

Human resources conceptualized as compositional properties of the ecosystem. Human resources, such as a skilled labour force and professionals to help the needs of new ventures, are highly important for the ecosystem. Without access to human resources, start-ups would struggle to survive. Thriving ecosystems can create a self-sustaining cycle such that top human resources are attracted to the start-ups and businesses in the ecosystem, adding to the aggregate human resources available at the meso level. Similarly, working in a start-up may allow individuals to develop feasibility cognitions for creating their own venture, thus developing a start-up-friendly workforce, with a positive attitude towards entrepreneurial failure and acceptance of porous boundaries (Mason & Brown, 2014). The resulting start-up culture can emerge as a resource at the ecosystemic (macro) level. The composition of the workforce and behaviours at the meso level create social norms reflected at the regional ecosystem level. It suggests an ecosystem that frequently supports start-up formation. However, decomposing to the individual level and the discrete elements of human resources will not articulate the one entrepreneurial culture of the ecosystem. Instead, entrepreneurial culture is a collectively observed and shared attribute.

Informational resources conceptualized as shared properties of the ecosystem. Finally, informational resources, key knowledge and new opportunities generated by the individual can contribute to the development of the agglomerated shared resources at the ecosystem level. Opportunities are created by connecting dots from among diverse information (Baron, 2007). Such entrepreneurial activity also creates new information and new knowledge, adding to the aggregate knowledge and informational resources within the ecosystem. The composition of potential informational resources and knowledge into an opportunity-rich entrepreneurial landscape amounts to a third shared property defining the entrepreneurial ecosystem. Again, not all entrepreneurs at the individual level will be equally endowed with all available information and knowledge resources, but the scale and scope of innovative start-ups emerging from the interactional meso level will signal a shared attribute of an ecosystem able to frequently nurture firms operating at or near the innovation frontier.

Resources Conceptualized as Configural Properties of Entrepreneurial Ecosystems

Configural unit properties originate at the micro level but unlike shared properties, don't coalesce. Instead, it is their pattern of contributions and relationships that can be captured through configural unit properties. While convergence or coherence is essential for compositional properties, divergence and complex non-linear dynamics within the micro-level elements is important for configural properties, through a process of compilation (Kozlowski et al. 2013). Such compilation processes are marked by the generation of higher-level phenomena through complex combinations of lower-level contribution (Costa et al. 2013).

Spigel (2017: 56) clarified these relationships in his statement, "An ecosystem's attributes are sustained and reproduced through their relationships with other attributes" indicating that the pattern of individual contributions and relationship emerges as a configural unit property of the ecosystem. Some of the measures articulated by Stangler and Bell-Masterson (2015) articulate the configural nature of resources in an ecosystem, where rather than similarity or coherence, diversity or configuration of the resources contribute to the macro-level phenomena. The configurational perspective also allows us to articulate relationships that differ across different levels – what may be negative for any individual start-up, may indicate a positive for the ecosystem.

Financial resources conceptualized as configural properties of the ecosystem. While wealth and financial resources in a regional economy help the availability of resources, they do not guarantee a thriving start-up component of the regional economy. Thus, the quantum of resources may be a necessary, but not a sufficient, condition for entrepreneurial activity. Equally critical is how the resources are distributed and accessed throughout the ecosystem. For example, a diverse range of actors, informal investors, incubators, accelerators, angels as well as venture capitalists, offering financial resources at different stages of the entrepreneurial process, can tremendously help create a thriving entrepreneurial ecosystem. Further, entrepreneurial recycling (Mason & Brown, 2014) and the *flow* of resources across firms can lead to the fluidity of investment capital, fostering a greater number of start-ups. In fact, such recycling may even involve the demise of some start-ups that create fertile grounds for other start-ups as financial resources are recycled. From an emergence perspective, understanding an entrepreneurial ecosystem requires more than an observance of composed elements. Rather, comprehension of exactly how those elements are configured in such a way so as to encourage a flow of financial resources from a source through to start-up, then used by the firm before being recycled back to nourish the sources for further financing activity is also needed.

Human resources conceptualized as configural properties of the ecosystem. Beyond ethnic diversity of the population, the diversity of human capital (skills and talents in the labour force) can facilitate the combination and recombination of resources, thereby fostering innovation and new ventures. For example, ethnocultural diversity in the Silicon Valley ecosystem is argued to be important for the ecosystem (Saxenian, 2002). Similarly, flows of human capital across organizations can help start-ups access top human resource talent to thrive, and further contribute to the entrepreneurial ecosystem. Finally, as research has already pointed out, such flow of resources often takes place over social networks, emphasizing the importance of connectivity within the ecosystem. The configuration of types and characteristics of the human resources as well as the cultural influence and social norms will all influence the flow of human resources and hence be a defining attribute of an entrepreneurial ecosystem. Similar to financial resources, the churn of entrepreneurial start-ups can enhance the flow of human capital in the ecosystem.

Information resources conceptualized as configural properties of the ecosystem. The flow of human capital across the organization can also create knowledge spill-overs across the ecosystem. Such access to knowledge, ideas and information resources can help start-ups combine new ideas. Finding entrepreneurial opportunities (Baron & Ensley, 2006) requires entrepreneurs to make sense of diverse information. Through the social networks within an ecosystem, diverse information can flow, creating opportunities for new ideas to emerge. Such new informational resources can drive the start-up process, and the configurational structure of interactions, leading to deliberate or serendipitous collisions of ideas, becomes a third configurational aspect that has an influence on an entrepreneurial ecosystem. As Aldrich and Fiol (1994) pointed out, the flow of informational resources in the form of imitability can fuel growth at the macro level, yet, such imitability can even have a detrimental effect on survival of the individual ventures.

Thus, the experimentation and failure of early start-ups and imitability of resources can create additional informational resources for all stakeholders and legitimizes the new start-up activity at the eco-systemic level.

SYNTHESIS

A start-up ecosystem is not a monolithic structure but rather is made up of strata or levels. In this chapter, we have drawn from the field of organizational studies to more explicitly develop a multilevel view of a start-up ecosystem. At the base are the individuals who exhibit certain forms of behaviour. These individuals are not only entrepreneurs but other actors who make up the essential components of a start-up ecosystem. In our discussion, we have portrayed three resource types – financial, human, and informational – that are owned and/or controlled by the various entrepreneurial actors but to a large extent will not be the entrepreneur herself. At the meso level, we have portrayed the "organization of exchange" that hosts various organizational forms, from interactions between individuals to exchanges between individuals and organizations and transactions between organizations. We have argued that it is the transactional configurations between the micro and meso that give rise to coalesced attributes at the holistic macro, start-up ecosystem. Principally, a strong ecosystem will be wealthy and an opportunity-rich environment that regularly produces "successful" firms operating at the innovation frontier. Figure 2.1 illustrates this multilevel conceptualization.

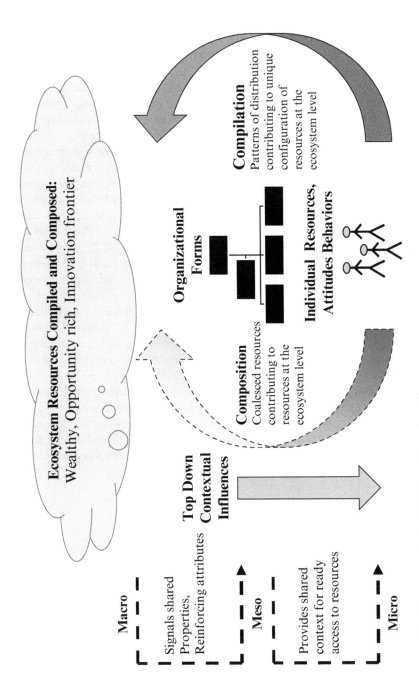

Figure 2.1   Resources in the Multilevel Framework

53

Previous studies of the ecosystem have tended to treat it as a phenomenon of top-down (left-hand side of Figure 2.1) construction whereby resources merely have to be proliferated within the ecosystem to create the context that drives entrepreneurship. In our work, we adopt the complementary perspective that the ecosystem is an emergent phenomenon (right-hand side of Figure 2.1) that is subject to resource compositions and compilations. We further propose that the patterns and configurations of interactions between the micro and meso level facilitate the start-up activity. Such patterns of start-up activity encompassing organizations and successful start-ups, accumulation and recycling of wealth, opportunities for individuals to recognize start-up potential, and persistent exposure to continually renewed information and knowledge contribute to resources at the ecosystemic level. The implication, therefore, is that the mere injections of resources within an ecosystem is insufficient without paying attention to the interactional processes that enable flows of financial resources, human capital diversity and movement, and information exchange among individuals through sharing and exchange-oriented regional organizational structures.

To be recognized as a strong start-up ecosystem, there is a secondary, processing layer that features coalescence of shared attributes. This will mean that the ecosystem appears wealthy, opportunity-rich, and a hotbed of innovative activity. These attributes are beyond just provisioning and enriching the ecosystem but require specific and persistent effort to both improve and strengthen the configurational processes upon which coalescence of shared resource attributes will be dependent. Importantly though, the coalescence and composition patterns of resources in the ecosystem is key to the self-reinforcing nature of the emergent phenomenon that generates financial, human, and information resources to sustain further innovative start-up activity.

LIMITATIONS AND FUTURE RESEARCH

While this research views ecosystems through a multilevel lens, it is important to articulate several limitations that can be addressed through future research. Both the processes of composition and compilation are two distinct anchors on the continuum of the emergence process. While we discuss the two contrasting ways to view resources as they emerge as ecosystemic resources, it is important to note that the patterns may be compositional, compilational, or a combination of both. Future research needs to theoretically specify and empirically test the model of emergence as it applies to the ecosystem.

While we focus on financial, human and informational resources, we acknowledge the importance of social network resources which facilitate the flow of all the resources in an ecosystem. We consider this a limitation that social network resources are omitted from our current chapter. While social network resources are interactional, we believe that future research should identify the multilevel nature of social network resources with greater detail.

Methodologically, traditional multilevel approaches assume that the lower level is neatly nested in one and only one higher level structure (Mathieu & Chen, 2011). In ecosystems, one may rarely observe such neat nesting. Entrepreneurs may belong to multiple support institutions (banks, entrepreneur support groups, incubators) and their membership may be fluid depending on the changing needs of the venture. Further, individuals belonging to multiple groups may actually enhance the network connections between the meso-level structures, improving the performance of the ecosystem. The meso level may furthermore contain individuals transacting in partnered relationships or teams, firms as organizations and institutional influences of both formal and informal nature. Such a complex structure requires a correspondingly complex meso-theory along with the appropriate methods.

CONTRIBUTIONS AND IMPLICATIONS FOR RESEARCH AND PRACTICE

Embracing a multilevel perspective of an entrepreneurial ecosystem brings into focus the emergent properties of resources that can support start-ups. This view has several implications for research and practice. While the aggregated quantum of resources matters, the resources of the ecosystems are more than just the aggregates of the micro-level resources – they are complex combinations argued by some to be characterized by diversity, fluidity, and connectivity (Stangler & Bell-Masterson, 2015). Therefore, static, merely additive accounts of elemental properties will not adequately explain the complexity of configural patterns that may be unique to a specific place. However, as Paruchuri, Perry-Smith, Chattopadhyay, & Shaw (2018) lament, extant research often assumes homologous behaviour across levels, without taking into account the complexity of interactional patterns. By articulating that the complex interplay of micro-level resources can lead to a unique compilation of financial, human, informational and knowledge resources, we contribute to deepening the theory of entrepreneurial ecosystems.

Resources in the entrepreneurial ecosystems are both a function of top-down and bottom-up processes. In general, although top-down strategies may manifest a resource influence more quickly, they may not account for the behavioural and configurational influences of bottom-up emergent effects that define the entrepreneurial ecosystem. Sustainable entrepreneurial ecosystems may evolve over a long period of time through an interplay of top-down and bottom-up dynamics. While changes at the micro level may take place more quickly, emergent ecosystemic changes may only become apparent over a longer period of time. Our contribution lies in bringing to fore the processes that may lead to the emergence of resources at the ecosystemic level.

Conceptualizing entrepreneurial ecosystems as a multilevel phenomenon also opens up research methods designed to understand the top-down and bottom-up processes. Qualitative research methods are more common in the field which includes retrospective case studies as well as prospective observance of emergence over time through action research and ethnographic methods. Similarly, quantitative research exploring existing ecosystems, in particular incubators, accelerators, and other meso start-up ecosystems structures can help us understand the top-down and bottom-up effects retrospectively as well as prospectively through longitudinal studies.

This study also has implications for policy. Emergent effects in entrepreneurial ecosystems may be misinterpreted as reliance on the "invisible hand", with no need for governance structures. In fact, without the framework of meso-level institutions, and legal structures, the emergent processes may not be able to coalesce at all; the configurations may be poor. Understanding the governance structures in the context of bottom-up and top-down multilevel phenomena can further add to our understanding of developing better ecosystems for start-up incubation.

Second, this study also provides a deeper conceptual rationale for the generation of unique resources for each ecosystem. Complex combinations of resources that make one ecosystem work do not necessarily do the same in other contexts. On the other hand, different combinations of resources, with a configurational architecture that responds to contextual conditions appropriately, may yield better results for the outcomes of the entrepreneurial ecosystem in general, and the start-up incubation in particular. This principle of equifinallity suggests that rather than emulating the established "Silicon Valley" entrepreneurial ecosystems models, it is important to nurture and cultivate regional ecosystems that provide the configuration of resources suitable to that region. In other words, just allocating more resources may not have the intended benefits. Finally, emergent processes may unfold over a longer time period as compared to top-down effects, and an understanding of these differing timeframes is important to design policy initiatives and assess their effect on the ecosystems.

CONCLUSION

The fields of both management and entrepreneurship are enhanced by borrowing multidisciplinary theories and methods from many fields, i.e., Anthropology, Sociology, Economics, Education, and Psychology, as well as Marketing and Finance. The multilevel framework allows us to integrate different theories of entrepreneurial behaviour to understand how the ecosystem may provide context for micro-level entrepreneurial action, and how micro perceptions, attitudes, and behaviours may aggregate to the ecosystem level. Answering the call for research to develop "theoretical frameworks to understand the processes through which ecosystems emerge, change, and influence the activities of entrepreneurial actors" (Spigel, 2017), this chapter argues for a multilevel framework to theorize how resources of the ecosystem may emerge and contribute to start-up incubation. A vibrant ecosystem can "help more ideas blossom, more job-creating start-ups launch, more companies find skilled labour and innovations, and more enterprises grow and compete in global markets" (Kanter, 2012: 141).

REFERENCES

Ács, Z. J., Audretsch, D. B., Lehmann, E. E., & Licht, G. (2016). National systems of entrepreneurship. *Small Business Economics*, *46*(4), 527–535. doi:10.1007/s11187-016-9705-1.

Ács, Z. J., Autio, E., & Szerb, L. (2014). National systems of entrepreneurship: Measurement issues and policy implications. *Research Policy*, *43*(3), 476–494.

Ács, Z. J., Stam, E., Audretsch, D. B., & O'Connor, A. (2017). The lineages of the entrepreneurial ecosystem approach. *Small Business Economics*, *49*(1), 1–10.

Adner, R. (2017). Ecosystem as structure: An actionable construct for strategy. *Journal of Management*, *43*(1), 39–58. doi:10.1177/0149206316678451.

Aldrich, H., & Fiol, C. M. (1994). Fools rush in? The institutional context of industry creation. *Academy of Management Review*, *19*, 645–670.

Audretsch, D. B., Bönte, W., & Keilbach, M. (2008). Entrepreneurship capital and its impact on knowledge diffusion and economic performance. *Journal of Business Venturing*, *23*(6), 687–698. doi:http://dx.doi.org/10.1016/j.jbusvent.2008.01.006.

Audretsch, D. B., & Keilbach, M. (2005). Entrepreneurship capital and regional growth. *The Annals of Regional Science*, *39*(3), 457–469.

Autio, E., Nambisan, S., Thomas, L. D., & Wright, M. (2018). Digital affordances, spatial affordances, and the genesis of entrepreneurial ecosystems. *Strategic Entrepreneurship Journal*, *12*(1), 72–95.

Baker, T., & Nelson, R. E. (2005). Creating something from nothing: Resource construction through entrepreneurial bricolage. *Administrative Science Quarterly*, *50*(3), 329–366.

Barney, J. (1991). Firm resources and sustained competitive advantage. *Journal of Management*, *17*(1), 99.

Baron, R. A. (2007). Behavioral and cognitive factors in entrepreneurship: Entrepreneurs as the active element in new venture creation. *Strategic Entrepreneurship Journal*, *1*(1–2), 167–182. doi:10.1002/sej.12.

Baron, R. A., & Ensley, M. D. (2006). Opportunity recognition as the detection of meaningful patterns: Evidence from comparisons of novice and experienced entrepreneurs. *Management Science, 52*(9), 1331–1344.

Bruns, K., Bosma, N., Sanders, M., & Schramm, M. (2017). Searching for the existence of entrepreneurial ecosystems: A regional cross-section growth regression approach. *Small Business Economics, 49*(1), 31–54. doi:10.1007/s11187-017-9866-6.

Colombo, M. G., Dagnino, G. B., Lehmann, E. E., & Salmador, M. (2017). The governance of entrepreneurial ecosystems. *Small Business Economics.* doi:https://doi.org/10.1007/s11187-0 17-9952-9.

Costa, P. L., Graça, A. M., Marques-Quinteiro, P., Santos, C. M., Caetano, A., & Passos, A. M. (2013). Multilevel research in the field of organizational behavior: An empirical look at 10 years of theory and research. *SAGE Open, 3*(3), doi:10.1177/2158244013498244.

Fuller, T., & Moran, P. (2001). Small enterprises as complex adaptive systems: A methodological question? *Entrepreneurship & Regional Development, 13*(1), 47–63.

Goswami, K., Mitchell, J. R., & Bhagavatula, S. (2018). Accelerator expertise: Understanding the intermediary role of accelerators in the development of the Bangalore entrepreneurial ecosystem. *Strategic Entrepreneurship Journal, 12*(1), 117–150. doi:10.1002/sej.1281.

Hanlon, D., & Saunders, C. (2007). Marshaling resources to form small new ventures: Toward a more holistic understanding of entrepreneurial support. *Entrepreneurship Theory and Practice, 31*(4), 619–641. doi:doi:10.1111/j.1540-6520.2007.00191.x.

Isenberg, D. (2010). How to start an entrepreneurial revolution. *Harvard Business Review,* June, 41–50.

Kanter, R. M. (2012). Enriching the ecosystem. *Harvard Business Review, 90*(3), 140–147.

Kozlowski, S. W. J., Chao, G. T., Grand, J. A., Braun, M. T., & Kuljanin, G. (2013). Advancing multilevel research design: Capturing the dynamics of emergence. *Organizational Research Methods, 16*(4), 581–615. doi:10.1177/1094428113493119.

Kozlowski, S. W. J., & Klein, K. J. (2000). A multilevel approach to theory and research in organizations: Contextual, temporal and emergent processes. In K. J. Klein & S. W. J. Kozlowski (Eds.), *Multi-level theory, research and methods in organizations.* San Francisco: Jossey-Bass.

Lassalle, P., & Johnston, A. (2018) Where are the spiders? Proximities and access to the entrepreneurial ecosystem: The case of Polish migrant entrepreneurs in Glasgow. In A. O'Connor, E. Stam, F. Sussan, & D. B. Audretsch (Eds.), *Entrepreneurial ecosystems: Place-based transformations and transitions* (pp. 131–152). Cham: Springer International Publishing.

Lerner, J. (2010). The future of public efforts to boost entrepreneurship and venture capital. *Small Business Economics, 35*(3), 255–264.

Lichtenstein, B. B. (2011). Complexity science contributions to the field of entrepreneurship. *The Sage handbook of complexity and management,* 471–493.

Lissack, M. R., & Letiche, H. (2002). Complexity, emergence, resilience, and coherence: Gaining perspective on organizations and their study. *Emergence, A Journal of Complexity Issues in Organizations and Management, 4*(3), 72–94.

Mack, E., & Mayer, H. (2015). The evolutionary dynamics of entrepreneurial ecosystems. *Urban Studies, 53*(10), 2118–2133. doi:10.1177/0042098015586547.

Mason, C., & Brown, R. (2013). Creating good public policy to support high-growth firms. *Small Business Economics, 40*(2), 211–225.

Mason, C., & Brown, R. (2014). Entrepreneurial ecosystems and growth oriented entrepreneurship. *Final Report to OECD, Paris.*

Mathews, J. A. (2003). Competitive dynamics and economic learning: An extended resource-based view. *Industrial and Corporate Change, 12*(1), 115–145.

Mathieu, J. E., & Chen, G. (2011). The etiology of the multilevel paradigm in management research. *Journal of Management, 37*(2), 610–641. doi:10.1177/0149206310364663.

Motoyama, Y., & Watkins, K. K. (2014). Examining the connections within the startup ecosystem: A case study of St. Louis. *Louis (September 1, 2014). Kauffman Foundation Research Series on City, Metro, and Regional Entrepreneurship.*

O'Connor, A., Stam, E., Sussan, F., & Audretsch, D. B. (2018). Entrepreneurial ecosystems: The foundations of place-based renewal. *Entrepreneurial Ecosystems* (pp. 1–21): Springer.

Paruchuri, S., Perry-Smith, J. E., Chattopadhyay, P., & Shaw, J. D. (2018). New ways of seeing: Pitfalls and opportunities in multilevel research. *Academy of Management Journal, 61*(3), 797–801.

Penrose, E. (1995). *The theory of the growth of the firm.* New York: Oxford University Press [1959].

Roundy, P. T., Bradshaw, M., & Brockman, B. K. (2018). The emergence of entrepreneurial ecosystems: A complex adaptive systems approach. *Journal of Business Research, 86*, 1–10. doi:10.1016/j.jbusres.2018.01.032.

Saxenian, A. (2002). Silicon Valley's new immigrant high-growth entrepreneurs. *Economic Development Quarterly, 16*(1), 20–31.

Sohns, F., & Diez, J. R. (2018). Explaining micro entrepreneurship in rural Vietnam – a multilevel analysis. *Small Business Economics, 50*(1), 219–237.

Spigel, B. (2017). The relational organization of entrepreneurial ecosystems. *Entrepreneurship Theory and Practice, 41*(1), 49–72. doi:10.1111/etap.12167.

Stam, E. (2014). The Dutch entrepreneurial ecosystem. Available at SSRN 2473475.

Stam, E. (2015). Entrepreneurial ecosystems and regional policy: A sympathetic critique. *European Planning Studies, 23*(9), 1759–1769. doi:10.1080/09654313.2015.1061484.

Stam, E. (2018). Measuring entrepreneurial ecosystems. In A. O'Connor, E. Stam, F. Sussan, & D. Audretsch (Eds.), *Entrepreneurial ecosystems* (pp. 173–197). Germany: Springer.

Stangler, D., & Bell-Masterson, J. (2015). Measuring an entrepreneurial ecosystem. *Kauffman Foundation. March.*

Stevenson, H. H., & Jarillo, J. C. (1990). A paradigm of entrepreneurship: Entrepreneurial management. *Strategic Management Journal, 11*(5), 17–27.

Thompson, T. A., Purdy, J. M., & Ventresca, M. J. (2018). How entrepreneurial ecosystems take form: Evidence from social impact initiatives in Seattle. *Strategic Entrepreneurship Journal, 12*(1), 96–116. doi:10.1002/sej.1285.

Van De Ven, H. (1993). The development of an infrastructure for entrepreneurship. *Journal of Business Venturing, 8*(3), 211–230. doi:https://doi.org/10.1016/0883-9026(93)90028-4.

Zott, C., & Amit, R. (2007). Business model design and the performance of entrepreneurial firms. *Organization Science, 18*(2), 181–199.

3. The domains of entrepreneurship support
Tiago Ratinho

INTRODUCTION

Entrepreneurial activity is the engine of economic prosperity. This realization motivated many private and public institutions to dedicate efforts to vigorously support entrepreneurship in the past decades. Notably, governments enacted policies benefitting new and small businesses, universities began to support efforts to transfer technology from faculty and students to markets, and new forms of organizations sprung into existence with the sole purpose of supporting entrepreneurs (for instance, business incubators or more recently, business accelerators). This Cambrian explosion of entrepreneurship support (ES) efforts caused a fragmented landscape in both practice and scholarly research for two main reasons. First, the rapid diversification and evolution of some ES efforts keeps research in this field at a perennial initial stage with many descriptive studies discussing typologies and few actually studying impact in entrepreneurial activity. Second, many of these studies often consider a single ES effort largely overlooking other sources of support that the entrepreneur may be enjoying or how this variety of ES may interfere with the long-term prospects of the new venture.

Two further observations motivate the current book chapter and justify its timing. First, as scholarly research in entrepreneurship is maturing, there seems to be a consensus around the fact that new businesses do not emerge in a void. The context is increasingly recognized as crucial to enable or prevent entrepreneurs to pursue their business ideas (Autio, Kenney, Mustar, Siegel, & Wright, 2014). Entrepreneurial ecosystems (EE) is emerging as a plausible candidate framework to differentiate regions along a range of characteristics that explain varying levels of startup activity (Isenberg, 2011; Stam, 2015). Second, research in ES has repeatedly shown that support initiatives often overlook the context as an input for design which may lead to ambiguous results of most studies investigating the impacts of ES. For instance, policies aimed at supporting high growth entrepreneurship have been found inappropriate due to a poor understanding of both the startups and the specific environments in which they operate (Mason & Brown, 2013). In fact, the empirical setting of many studies is a single region or country which makes it impossible to investigate the impact of variation of contextual factors and pose critical questions regarding the generalization of the results (Lindelof & Lofsten, 2005; Ratinho & Henriques, 2010).

In this chapter, I draw on EE literature to provide a uniform theoretical framework to understand ES. My working research proposition is to explore how a systemic perspective on the context in which support takes place impacts ES design and operation, and ultimately leads to the emergence of a startup incubation ecosystem. This chapter will appeal to scholars who are interested in ES by providing a modest contribution towards a general understanding of how support initiatives impact the whole EE. Practitioners – ES designers and managers – will find value in the discussion of how the multiple attributes of EE should be considered when designing and operating ES initiatives towards the desired outcome of increasing entrepreneurial activity.

This chapter is organized as follows. I begin by reviewing the literature on ES and EEs seeking common frameworks and base definitions. I then argue that ES manifests itself in three domains – institutional, organizational, and individual – and discuss their main characteristics, examples of current ES initiatives, and common expected outcomes. Finally, I outline future research opportunities for scholars interested in pursuing a better understanding of ES.

WHAT IS ES?[1]

ES infuses new ventures and entrepreneurs with resources intended to increase their long-term survival prospects and development. It is widely accepted that entrepreneurship drives economic prosperity; at the same, new ventures are fragile and the overwhelming majority fails within its first years. These two stylized facts have historically motivated ES as a way to promote entrepreneurship, either by helping aspiring entrepreneurs or sensitizing others to start businesses. ES is defined as:

> Provision of valuable resources to entrepreneurs by individuals or organizations through structured activities designed to facilitate the imminent establishment of a new independent firm, increase survival chances, or promote long-term growth. (Adapted from Hanlon & Saunders, 2007)

ES consists of sources of support and types of support (Hanlon & Saunders, 2007). Sources of support are organizations or individuals who provide a given resource to entrepreneurs while types of support are the resources being provided. One particular source of support can provide multiple types of support as well as one given type of support can be provided from several sources of support. For instance, known sources of support, such as business incubators, provide their tenants with mainly three types of support: infrastructure, business assistance, and access to networks (Bruneel, Ratinho, Clarysse, & Groen, 2012). Each of these types of support can however be provided by other sources of support such as science parks (provides infrastructure) (Amirahmadi & Saff, 1993), professional investors (provide business assistance) (Hellmann & Puri, 2002), or incidental entrepreneurship training programs (provide access to networks) (Gorman & McCarthy, 2006).

Common Sources of ES

Perhaps the most common source of ES is business incubation (BI). With an established industry and a history of a few decades (Adkins, 2002), BIs are seen today as a cornerstone of regional development policy and industrial revitalization strategies. BIs deliver support along three vectors: infrastructure, business assistance, and access to networks (Bruneel et al., 2012). A multitude of models has emerged with more or less emphasis in each of these vectors as well as different geographical and strategic orientations (Carayannis & Von Zedtwitz, 2005; Clarysse, Wright, Lockett, Van de Velde, & Vohora, 2005; Grimaldi & Grandi, 2005). More recently, business accelerators emerged as a cohort-based program geared towards growth of promising startups in what may be considered as an extension of prior incubation models (Cohen, 2013; Cohen & Hochberg, 2014; Pauwels, Clarysse, Wright, & Van Hove, 2016).

There is a vast body of research about BIs as an attempt to understand what precisely the impact of being incubators is for a new venture (Hackett & Dilts, 2004; Hausberg & Korreck, in press). Results are disappointingly inconclusive; the majority of studies are descriptive, phenomenological, and make use of small samples which renders findings non-generalizable or highly idiosyncratic. The exception is a comprehensive study by Amezcua and colleagues (2013) that shows that in the US university-based BIs contribute to startup longevity contingent to the fit of resources being provided and surrounding environmental factors such as density of existing businesses.

Second to BIs, entrepreneurship policy is among the most popular sources of ES and, as a result, has a considerable body of literature (Audretsch, Grilo, & Thurik, 2007). The link between entrepreneurship and economic prosperity has led national and regional governments to enact laws and regulations intended to increase the levels of entrepreneurial activity in the economy. Examples range from the establishment of business development centers locally to nation-wide tax breaks or credits to newly formed and/or innovative companies (Gilbert, Audretsch, & McDougall, 2004). While in some regions the emergence of entrepreneurship policy may be simultaneous to an increase of business ownership, academic research has yet to find undisputable evidence that there is a universal causal relationship.

Common Types of ES

The most common type of support is finance often available from many sources such as business angels, venture capitalists, or governmental programs (Berger & Udell, 1998; Rothwell, 1985). The notion that money is the quintessential resource for an entrepreneur to succeed was recently popularized by TV shows such as *Shark Tank*, in which an aspiring entrepreneur presents her idea to a panel of experts in order to access the capital needed to build a first prototype. Reality is however at odds with this picture.

Most entrepreneurs never access substantial amounts of money and, as a result, types of support such as business assistance or access to network become extremely important (Aldrich & Kim, 2007; Birley, 1985; Greve & Salaff, 2003). Several sources of support deliver programs based on networking and training – for instance business accelerators – before a final celebratory event in which some startups may finally come in contact with professional investors. Studies about impact yield mixed results as with other types of support although there is evidence that, in some contexts, this type of support can be effective. For instance, Autio and Rannikko (2016) show positive results in terms of growth using data from a governmental program consisting of access to networks with the aim to internationalize new companies and boost their growth. The program delivers essentially networking activities with domestic and international investors, sponsors expert consultations, and facilitates best practice exchange among participants who are periodically monitored and must meet milestones to remain in the program.

Impacts of ES

Despite some promising evidence that ES may be beneficial under certain conditions, research on the impacts of ES (sources and types of support) is far from being generalizable for several reasons. First, the ever-changing multitude of initiatives to support entrepreneurship involving a vast array of combinations of sources and types of support causes researchers to often change empirical settings to follow the most recent form of ES while, at the same time, rendering prior research results obsolete. Second, studies often focus on specific sources and/or types of ES and rarely include detailed data about the entrepreneurs receiving support. Entrepreneurs are often advised to get all the help they can and, as a result, ES can only be fully understood by focusing on the entrepreneur and investigating the impact of all the support she receives. This simple empirical improvement unleashes a range of new research avenues. For instance, a given source or type of ES may have different effects on the entrepreneur when combined with other sources of types of ES; the initial conditions (resource endowments) in which an entrepreneur begins to receive support are also worthy of attention to understand exactly how much she gained from a given source or type of ES. Finally, the lack of longitudinal studies hinders our understanding of the dynamics of ES sources and types. Some ES initiatives are also temporary (e.g. tax breaks, training programs) which represents an additional difficulty when trying to understand the long-term impacts of ES.

We now turn our attention to EE, a nascent framework to understand entrepreneurial activity in a given geographical region. I argue that this perspective is adequate to understand the phenomenon of ES, to develop improved future initiatives, and to better assess its impacts.

ENTREPRENEURIAL ECOSYSTEMS

Entrepreneurial ecosystems (EE) are emerging as a promising framework for studying entrepreneurial activity at a regional level. Inspired by the biological concept of ecosystem and earlier efforts to adapt the concept to business environments (Moore, 1993, 1999), EE are conceptualized as interconnected complex systems that enable entrepreneurial activity in a given location (Stam, 2015). At this nascent stage of research, EE is yet a fuzzy concept used by practitioners and researchers as an umbrella term to represent the complexity and interdependence of multiple actors that collectively create an environment more or less conducive to entrepreneurial activity. Practitioner-oriented literature has devoted much attention to the components of EEs, that is, observable attributes that make up a well-functioning EE and can be used to differentiate across EEs (see Table 3.1). More recently, Spigel (2017) surveyed the extant academic literature to find examples of studies investigating each of the attributes (Table 3.2). The list of attributes and its categorization in three broad categories – cultural, social, and material – is used to differentiate across different configurations of EE.

In both cases, the nature of EE attributes is unclear as well as their

Table 3.1   Attribute of an entrepreneurial ecosystem

Attribute	Description
Leadership	Strong group of entrepreneurs who are visible, accessible and committed to the region being a great place to start and grow a company.
Intermediaries	Many well-respected mentors and advisors giving back across all stages, sectors, demographics and geographies as well as a solid presence of effective, visible, well-integrated accelerators and incubators.
Network density	Deep, well-connected community of startups and entrepreneurs along with engaged and visible investors, advisors, mentors and supporters. Optimally, these people and organizations cut across sectors, demographics and culture engagement. Everyone must be willing to give back to his community.
Government	Strong government support for and understanding of startups to economic growth. Additionally, supportive policies should be in place covering economic development, tax and investment vehicles.
Talent	Broad, deep talent pool for all levels of employees in all sectors and areas of expertise. Universities are an excellent resource for startup talent and should be well connected to community.
Support services	Professional services (legal, accounting, real estate, insurance and consulting) are integrated, accessible, effective and appropriately priced.
Engagement	Large number of events for entrepreneurs and community to connect, with highly visible and authentic participants (e.g. meet-ups, pitch days, startup weekends, boot camps, hackathons and competitions).
Companies	Large companies that are the anchor of a city should create specific departments and programs to encourage cooperation with high-growth startups.
Capital	Strong, dense and supportive community of venture capitalists, angels, seed investors and other forms of financing should be available, visible and accessible across sectors, demographics and geography.

Source: Feld, 2012, pp.185–187.

relationship with entrepreneurial activity. For instance, government is seen as an active source of ES by intervening at many levels that include enacting new venture creation policies, devising specific regulation, creating tax incentives, and establishing investment vehicles that directly fund startups. The underlying assumption behind this particular attribute is

Table 3.2   Types of attributes of an entrepreneurial ecosystem (Spigel, 2017)

Type of Attribute	Attribute	Description
Cultural	Supportive culture	Cultural attitudes which support and normalize entrepreneurial activities, risk taking, and innovation.
	Histories of entrepreneurship	Prominent local example of successful entrepreneurial ventures.
Social	Worker talent	Presence of skilled workers who are willing to work at startups.
	Investment capital	Availability of investment capital from family and friends, angel investors, and venture capitalists.
	Networks	Presence of social networks that connect entrepreneurs, advisors, investors, and workers and that allow the free flow of knowledge and skills.
	Mentors and role models	Local successful entrepreneurs and business people who provide advice for younger entrepreneurs.
Material	Policy and governance	State-run programs or regulations that either support entrepreneurship through direct funding or remove barriers to new venture creation.
	Universities	Universities and other higher education institutions which both train new entrepreneurs and produce new knowledge spillovers.
	Support services	Firms and organizations that provide ancillary services to new ventures, for example, patent lawyers, incubators, or accountancies.
	Availability of sufficient office space	Availability of sufficient office space, telecommunication facilities, and transportation infrastructure to enable venture creation and growth.
	Open markets	Presence of sufficient local opportunities to enable venture creation and unimpeded access to global markets.

that government is multipurposed in that it supports startups through varied sources (policies and seed capital); government further intervenes at various levels such as institutional by adjusting the economic conditions in which new ventures operate, and organizational by investing directly in startups. In locations in which higher education is tendentially state-operated, government also indirectly supports individuals' training programs in entrepreneurship. Finally, this attribute's description includes a qualitative assessment about governmental activities such as barrier removal or strength of understanding of a startup's contribution to economic growth that cast ambiguity over what the government's role, scope, and impact is within EEs. Additionally, the categorization of attributes is convoluted in that it combines elements of the legal and economic background (e.g. presence of skilled workers, access to global markets, universities, market openness) with individual behaviors (willingness to work in startups, leadership roles, events, engagement). Further, some attributes presuppose initial conditions that can be seen as outputs; for instance, successful entrepreneurial ventures whose founders share their histories and could take leadership roles in promoting the region as a good place to start and grow a business are a result of a well-functioning EE.

These circular definitions of attributes are cause for concern particularly from an ES design and operation standpoint. In each EE attribute, a cacophony of sources and types of ES is found and are often ambiguous in their intended outcomes. For instance, removal of barriers to entrepreneurial activity and the creation of open international markets may be at odds with strong intervention to support startups. Further, the need for anchor companies in the region that can work with startups justifies public policy to support established companies as part of entrepreneurship support policies.

There are two dominant views currently emerging from the nascent body of literature on EEs: the *qualitative* view that regards EEs as different in kinds of ventures they nurture and harbor (Spigel, 2017; Spigel & Harrison, 2017); and the *quantitative* view arguing that EEs are more or less dynamic depending on the rate of new business creation (Mack & Mayer, 2016). According to the qualitative view, EEs are a bundle of interconnected resources and benefits that affect entrepreneurial activity in a given location. Different combinations of each of the attributes seen as their presence or intensity will originate different types of EEs. This view is not concerned with the rate of new business creation but rather with the kind of businesses that are nurtured in each EE. The quantitative view, embodied by Mack and Meyer (2016), argues that EE go through several stages: birth, growth, sustaining, and decline. These stages are characterized by different combinations of attributes that are, without exception, described in quantitative terms. For instance, finance and the availability of investors is "becoming available" in the birth stage and "decline[s]" in the decline stage. This view implies that a functioning EE necessitates a series of attributes to be present and well-articulated but also, and crucially, a certain level of each of the attributes above which the rate of new business creation rises.

THE DOMAINS OF ES

The bodies of literature of ES and EE share two important underlying theoretical assumptions: first, the view that entrepreneurial activity does not occur in a void; and second, the context can be acted upon to increase the rate of startup creation as well as the types of startups in a given region. The EE perspective views the context as an enabler that shapes entrepreneurial activity depending on the presence and intensity of a series of attributes and, importantly, how those are articulated to create a more or less active startup incubation ecosystem. Different combinations of attributes and linkages will lead to different EEs (Spigel, 2017) and varying rates of new business creation (Mack & Mayer, 2016). In a similar vein, ES literature sees the context as a crucial aspect of entrepreneurial activity and, consequentially, worthy of intervention. ES literature is, in a broad sense, concerned with active and purposeful interventions to enable and enhance entrepreneurial activity in the context as well as in the new ventures and entrepreneurs.

I propose that ES manifests itself in three domains: institutional, organizational, and individual. Table 3.3 summarizes the characteristics of

Table 3.3   Characteristics of domains of entrepreneurship support

Domain of ES	Affected EE's attributes	Scope	Duration	Delivery	Examples of sources
Institutional	Worker talent, Anchor companies, Open markets	May affect all companies and industries	Long	Passive	Government
Organizational	Support services, Office space, Investment capital	Judicious selection	Medium	Active and Passive	Business incubators, Science Parks, Universities, Venture Capitalists, Business angels
Individual	Universities	Judicious and self-selection	Short	Active	Entrepreneurship support programs, business development centers, Education programs

each domain, the EE attributes that are affected, and examples of existing ES sources.

Institutional ES refers to attempts to shape the environment in which entrepreneurship takes place. This kind of ES interferes mostly with attributes such as availability of skilled workforce (worker talent), presence of anchor companies, or openness of markets. Governmental policymaking affecting changes in regulations, fiscal or legal frameworks is an example of these types of ES sources. While there are clear examples of governmental policies dedicated to startups – for instance in the US (Gilbert et al., 2004) – there are other examples of policies that affect whole industries regardless of company age (Aoyama, 1999; Mowery, 2011). While the institutions shaping the context can be seen as actors (Autio et al., 2014) actively pursuing the goal of raising entrepreneurial activity in a given region, the delivery of this kind of ES is passive in that there is often no direct contact between the source of support (government) and the entrepreneurs. Further, institutional support affects all companies equally as it interferes with the common rules by which all entrepreneurs have to develop these companies. The duration of this source of ES tends to be long term and its effects observable after decades.

Organizational ES refers to support directed at companies. This kind of ES is intended to provide the new venture with tangible resources that mitigate the difficulties of its early stages. Organizational ES interferes mostly with EE attributes such as support services, availability and quality of office space for startup and investment capital (venture capitalists or business angels). Judicious selection is common in organizational ES. For instance, business incubators often have sophisticated selection criteria motivated by their missions and strategic objectives (Bergek & Norrman, 2008). Venture capitalists also carefully select which startups to invest in according to personal and professional characteristics of the entrepreneurial team (Chen, Yao, & Kotha, 2009). The duration of this source of support ranges from a few years in the case of business incubators to longer timeframes depending on investment conditions, in the case of business angels or other professional investors. Finally, the intervention of organizational ES sources in startups can be active like in the case of more recent models of business incubation (Bruneel et al., 2012) or rather passive like in the case of science parks which may not have structured support programs in place (Phan, Siegel, & Wright, 2005).

Individual ES refers to entrepreneurship skills training. This kind of ES intervenes at the entrepreneur level through specialized training in the form of mentorship/coaching. Intended to guide aspiring entrepreneurs to enter business ownership (Chrisman, McMullan, & Hall, 2005) by accelerating their learning curve, these sources of support have different selection practices. Some support programs are designed to help a specific population of aspiring entrepreneurs (Benson, Lies, Okunade, & Wunnava, 2011; Pernilla, 1997; Ram & Smallbone, 2003) while others rely on each entrepreneur's desire to seek advice (Cumming & Fischer, 2012; Lambrecht & Pirnay, 2005). The duration of individual sources of ES is short, in some cases, incidental and it is delivered actively, often through one-on-one consultation.

DISCUSSION

Using an EE lens to understand ES extends the literature in several directions. The introduction of institutional, organizational, and individual domains shows which attributes of the EE are likely to be actively and directly acted upon by ES sources and types. For instance, attributes such as leadership, role models, or supportive culture are likely to be outputs of a combination of ES interventions rather than direct results of a given ES source. Further, by emphasizing the area of intervention breaking with the prevalent ES source/type dualism allows practitioners to improve the design and operation of each ES effort. For instance, ES interventions to shape the institutional context do not need to be limited to entrepreneurship policy but should take into consideration other companies that can serve as anchor companies or drivers for skilled labor concentration. Additionally, this systemic view of entrepreneurship implies that each ES source should look at the EE and not just its intended area of intervention. For instance, supporting financial new ventures will not necessarily be effective if the entrepreneur herself lacks managerial capabilities.

The conceptualization of the three domains of support extends to prior literature on ES. For instance, organizational sponsorship (OS) refers to attempts to shape the environment by direct intervention in organizations (Flynn, 1993b) and is often linked to the existence of infrastructure (Amezcua et al., 2013; Flynn, 1993a). The conceptualization of ES along three domains allows for a more holistic perspective on support considering antecedents of entrepreneurial activity – for instance, entrepreneurial competence development – as well as public policy to shape the environment not necessarily targeted at startups. Further, I add to the literature on ES by suggesting that the direct link between individual entrepreneurial competence development and the act of starting a business (cf. Rotger, Gørtz, & Storey, 2012). Interventions in the EE can be supportive of entrepreneurial activity regardless in a longer time frame or act on indirect attributes such as increasing the availability of skilled labor or attracting anchor companies.

CONCLUSION

This manuscript is a modest attempt at exploring how a systemic perspective on the context in which support takes place impacts ES design and operation, and how it leads to the emergence of a startup incubation ecosystem. I use the main tenets of the nascent literature on EE to propose that ES manifests itself along three dimensions. Institutional, organizational, and individual ES intervene in the cultural, material, and social attributes of an EE to create an environment conducive to entrepreneurial activity in a given location. I hope that these insights will inspire practitioners involved in designing and managing ES initiatives to improve their offer and, as a result, the effectiveness of the support being provided. The scholarly community of ES and EE researchers also stands to gain with a more systemic view of ES that emphasizes how and why to act to shape the ecosystem.

NOTE

1. This section follows the systematic review of the Entrepreneurship Support work by Ratinho, Amezcua, Honig, and Zeng (Ratinho, Amezcua, Honig, & Zeng, 2016).

REFERENCES

Adkins, D. (2002). *A Brief History of Business Incubation in the United States*. Athens, Ohio: National Business Incubation Association.

Aldrich, H. E., & Kim, P. H. (2007). Small worlds, infinite possibilities? How social networks affect entrepreneurial team formation and search. *Strategic Entrepreneurship Journal*, *1*(1–2), 147–165. https://doi.org/10.1002/sej.8

Amezcua, A. S., Grimes, M. G., Bradley, S. W., & Wiklund, J. (2013). Organizational sponsorship and founding environments: A contingency view on the survival of business incubated firms, 1994–2007. *Academy of Management Journal*, *56*(6), 1628–1654.

Amirahmadi, H., & Saff, G. (1993). Science parks: A critical assessment. *Journal of Planning Literature*, *8*(2), 107–123.

Aoyama, Y. (1999). Policy interventions for industrial network formation: Contrasting historical underpinnings of the small business policy in Japan and the United States. *Small Business Economics*, *12*(3), 217–231. https://doi.org/10.1023/A:1008060108220

Audretsch, D. B., Grilo, I., & Thurik, A. R. (2007). *Handbook of Research on Entrepreneurship Policy*. Cheltenham: Edward Elgar.

Autio, E., Kenney, M., Mustar, P., Siegel, D., & Wright, M. (2014). Entrepreneurial innovation: The importance of context. *Research Policy*, *43*(7), 1097–1108. https://doi.org/10.1016/j.respol.2014.01.015

Autio, E., & Rannikko, H. (2016). Retaining winners: Can policy boost high-growth entrepreneurship? *Research Policy*, *45*(1), 42–55. https://doi.org/10.1016/j.respol.2015.06.002

Benson, D. A., Lies, A. K., Okunade, A. A., & Wunnava, P. V. (2011). Economic impact of a private sector micro-financing scheme in South Dakota. *Small Business Economics*, *36*(2), 157–168.

Bergek, A., & Norrman, C. (2008). Incubator best practice: A framework. *Technovation, 28*(1–2), 20–28. https://doi.org/10.1016/j.technovation.2007.07.008

Berger, A., & Udell, G. (1998). The economics of small business finance: The roles of private equity and debt markets in the financial growth cycle. *Journal of Banking & Finance, 22*(6), 613–673.

Birley, S. (1985). The role of networks in the entrepreneurial process. *Journal of Business Venturing, 1*(1), 107–117. https://doi.org/10.1016/0883-9026(85)90010-2

Bruneel, J., Ratinho, T., Clarysse, B., & Groen, A. (2012). The evolution of business incubators: Comparing demand and supply of business incubation services across different incubator generations. *Technovation, 32*(2), 110–121. https://doi.org/10.1016/j.technovation.2011.11.003

Carayannis, E. G., & Von Zedtwitz, M. (2005). Architecting gloCal (global-local), real-virtual incubator networks (G-RVINs) as catalysts and accelerators of entrepreneurship in transitioning and developing economies: Lessons learned and best practices from current development and business incubation practices. *Technovation, 25*(2), 95–110. https://doi.org/10.1016/S0166-4972(03)00072-5

Chen, X.-P., Yao, X., & Kotha, S. (2009). Entrepreneur passion and preparedness in business plan presentations: A persuasion analysis of venture capitalists' funding decisions. *Academy of Management Journal, 52*(1), 199–214. https://doi.org/10.5465/AMJ.2009.36462018

Chrisman, J. J., McMullan, W. E., & Hall, J. (2005). The influence of guided preparation on the long-term performance of new ventures. *Journal of Business Venturing, 20*(6), 769–791. https://doi.org/10.1016/j.jbusvent.2004.10.001

Clarysse, B., Wright, M., Lockett, A., Van de Velde, E., & Vohora, A. (2005). Spinning out new ventures: a typology of incubation strategies from European research institutions. *Journal of Business Venturing, 20*(2), 183–216. https://doi.org/10.1016/j.jbusvent.2003.12.004

Cohen, S. (2013). What do accelerators do? Insights from incubators and angels. *Innovations, 8*(3–4), 19–25.

Cohen, S., & Hochberg, Y. V. (2014). *Accelerating startups: The seed accelerator phenomenon* (SSRN Scholarly Paper No. ID 2418000). Rochester, NY: Social Science Research Network. Retrieved from http://papers.ssrn.com/abstract=2418000

Cumming, D. J., & Fischer, E. (2012). Publicly funded business advisory services and entrepreneurial outcomes. *Research Policy, 41*(2), 467–481.

Feld, B. (2012). *Startup Communities: Building an Entrepreneurial Ecosystem in Your City.* Hoboken, NJ: John Wiley & Sons.

Flynn, D. M. (1993a). A critical exploration of sponsorship, infrastructure, and new organizations. *Small Business Economics, 5*(2), 129–156.

Flynn, D. M. (1993b). Sponsorship and the survival of new organizations. *Journal of Small Business Management, 31*(1), 51–62.

Gilbert, B. A., Audretsch, D. B., & McDougall, P. P. (2004). The emergence of entrepreneurship policy. *Small Business Economics, 22*(3–4), 313–323. https://doi.org/10.1023/B:SBEJ.0000022235.10739.a8

Gorman, G. G., & McCarthy, S. (2006). Business development support and knowledge-based businesses. *The Journal of Technology Transfer, 31*(1), 131–143.

Greve, A., & Salaff, J. W. (2003). Social networks and entrepreneurship. *Entrepreneurship Theory and Practice, 28*(1), 1–22. https://doi.org/10.1111/1540-8520.00029

Grimaldi, R., & Grandi, A. (2005). Business incubators and new venture creation: An assessment of incubating models. *Technovation, 25*(2), 111–121. https://doi.org/10.1016/S0166-4972(03)00076-2

Hackett, S. M., & Dilts, D. M. (2004). A systematic review of business incubation research. *The Journal of Technology Transfer, 29*(1), 55–82.

Hanlon, D., & Saunders, C. (2007). Marshaling resources to form small new ventures: Toward a more holistic understanding of entrepreneurial support. *Entrepreneurship Theory and Practice, 31*(4), 619–641.

Hausberg, J. P., & Korreck, S. (in press). Business incubators and accelerators: A co-citation analysis-based, systematic literature review. *The Journal of Technology Transfer*, 1–26. https://doi.org/10.1007/s10961-018-9651-y

Hellmann, T., & Puri, M. (2002). Venture capital and the professionalization of start-up firms: Empirical evidence. *The Journal of Finance*, *57*(1), 169–197.

Isenberg, D. J. (2011). *The Entrepreneurship Ecosystem Strategy as a New Paradigm for Economic Growth: Principles for Cultivating Entrepreneurship*. Dublin, Ireland: Institute of International European Affairs.

Lambrecht, J., & Pirnay, F. (2005). An evaluation of public support measures for private external consultancies to SMEs in the Walloon Region of Belgium. *Entrepreneurship & Regional Development*, *17*(2), 89–108.

Lindelof, P., & Lofsten, H. (2005). Academic versus corporate new technology-based firms in Swedish science parks: an analysis of performance, business networks and financing. *International Journal of Technology Management*, *31*(3), 334–357.

Mack, E., & Mayer, H. (2016). The evolutionary dynamics of entrepreneurial ecosystems. *Urban Studies*, *53*(10), 2118–2133. https://doi.org/10.1177/0042098015586547

Mason, C., & Brown, R. (2013). Creating good public policy to support high-growth firms. *Small Business Economics*, *40*(2), 211–225. https://doi.org/10.1007/s11187-011-9369-9

Moore, J. F. (1993). Predators and prey: A new ecology of competition. *Harvard Business Review*, *71*(3), 75–86.

Moore, J. F. (1999). *The Death of Competition – Leadership & Strategy in the Age of Business Ecosystems*. Chichester, UK: Wiley.

Mowery, D. C. (2011). Nanotechnology and the US national innovation system: Continuity and change. *The Journal of Technology Transfer*, *36*(6), 697–711. https://doi.org/10.1007/s10961-011-9210-2

Pauwels, C., Clarysse, B., Wright, M., & Van Hove, J. (2016). Understanding a new generation incubation model: The accelerator. *Technovation*, *50–51*, 13–24. https://doi.org/10.1016/j.technovation.2015.09.003

Pernilla, N. (1997). Business counselling services directed towards female entrepreneurs – some legitimacy dilemmas. *Entrepreneurship & Regional Development*, *9*(3), 239–258. https://doi.org/10.1080/08985629700000014

Phan, P. H., Siegel, D. S., & Wright, M. (2005). Science parks and incubators: Observations, synthesis and future research. *Journal of Business Venturing*, *20*(2), 165–182. https://doi.org/10.1016/j.jbusvent.2003.12.001

Ram, M., & Smallbone, D. (2003). Policies to support ethnic minority enterprise: The English experience. *Entrepreneurship & Regional Development*, *15*(2), 151–166.

Ratinho, T., Amezcua, A., Honig, B., & Zeng, Z. (2016). Entrepreneurial support: Making sense of decades of practice and research. *Academy of Management Proceedings*, *2016*(1), 14044. https://doi.org/10.5465/AMBPP.2016.14044abstract

Ratinho, T., & Henriques, E. (2010). The role of science parks and business incubators in converging countries: Evidence from Portugal. *Technovation*, *30*(4), 278–290. https://doi.org/10.1016/j.technovation.2009.09.002

Rotger, G. P., Gørtz, M., & Storey, D. J. (2012). Assessing the effectiveness of guided preparation for new venture creation and performance: Theory and practice. *Journal of Business Venturing*, *27*(4), 506–521. https://doi.org/10.1016/j.jbusvent.2012.01.003

Rothwell, R. (1985). Venture finance, small firms and public policy in the UK. *Research Policy*, *14*(5), 253–265. https://doi.org/10.1016/0048-7333(85)90008-3

Spigel, B. (2017). The relational organization of entrepreneurial ecosystems. *Entrepreneurship Theory and Practice*, *41*(1), 49–72. https://doi.org/10.1111/etap.12167

Spigel, B., & Harrison, R. (2017). Toward a process theory of entrepreneurial ecosystems. *Strategic Entrepreneurship Journal*, *12*, 151–168. https://doi.org/10.1002/sej.1268

Stam, E. (2015). Entrepreneurial ecosystems and regional policy: A sympathetic critique. *European Planning Studies*, *23*(9), 1759–1769. https://doi.org/10.1080/09654313.2015.1061484

4. In support of university spinoffs – what drives the organizational design of technology transfer ecosystems?
Matthew Good and Mirjam Knockaert

1. INTRODUCTION

Over the past 30 years, universities have increasingly recognized the role they play in generating new knowledge and in facilitating the commercialization of that knowledge often referred to as either technology transfer (TT) or academic entrepreneurship (Grimaldi et al., 2011). Commercialization occurs in multiple ways including through the formation of highly innovative university spin-offs and student-led startups (Mosey et al., 2017; Wright et al., 2017). To facilitate commercialization, an ecosystem of organizations dedicated to supporting the TT process has emerged around universities that includes incubators, science parks, university investment funds, TT offices and others (Siegel and Wright, 2015). We refer to this set of organizations as the "TT ecosystem" – a form of startup incubation ecosystem focused on the university context.

Recent research has begun to recognize the importance of the TT ecosystem in supporting research commercialization (e.g. Good et al., 2019; Hayter et al., 2018). With the recognition of its importance, there is a need to understand how these complex systems can be shaped to better support commercialization. In this chapter, we aim at understanding how the characteristics of TT ecosystems differ between universities and what drivers can explain such variation. Specifically, we employ a comparative case study design to investigate TT ecosystems in eight different Scandinavian universities and use an organizational design perspective to compare the different ecosystems. By doing so, we identify leverage points for influencing the design of ecosystems, which is critical for improving its effectiveness (Nadler and Tushman, 1997; Adner, 2017).

Following Djokovic and Souitaris's (2006) approach to organizing the university spinout literature, we identify drivers of TT ecosystem design at the micro-, meso-, and macro-levels. At the micro-level, we identify initiatives taken by different types of individuals (i.e. entrepreneurs, managers, students, and academics) and collaborations between them that impact TT ecosystem design. At the meso-level, we identify major organizational change projects as drivers of design. At the macro-level, we identify governmental actions, public organization initiatives, private organization engagement, availability of human capital, macro trends, and mimetic forces affecting TT ecosystem design.

Understanding the drivers of TT ecosystem design has important implications for policy and practice. Particularly, our study shows that policy makers have a significant influence on the design of TT ecosystems through the creation of policies and regulations and need to be conscious of how those policies affect TT ecosystems. Further, university and ecosystem managers need to be aware of the challenges and opportunities that emerge from changes at the meso-level so that they can take advantage of them to optimize ecosystem design. Finally, the study identifies characteristics at the micro-level that are important for TT ecosystem design and may help managers in selection, recruitment and evaluation of TT ecosystem builders.

From a research perspective, we contribute to the ecosystem literature by taking a unique organizational design perspective. By elaborating on the antecedents of the design of ecosystems in the context of TT and the incubation of university-based startups, we build upon structural approaches to understanding ecosystems (Adner, 2017). Additionally, we contribute to the TT and academic entrepreneurship literature by taking a broader approach to studying TT (Siegel and Wright, 2015) and applying a novel theoretical perspective to elaborate on the TT ecosystem (Good et al., 2019).

The next section discusses the theoretical background guiding this study followed by an explanation of our methodology. We then present our results and finish with a concluding section highlighting the implications of this study.

2. THEORETICAL BACKGROUND

2.1. TT Ecosystems

TT is a complex, non-linear process whereby university research is translated into innovative products and services (Bradley et al., 2013). Recent research has called for a more holistic and theory-based approach to understanding TT support mechanisms at universities (Siegel and Wright, 2015; Hayter et al., 2018) as a complement to the rather case-based and descriptive work on TT. To fill this gap, we use an ecosystem perspective combined with an organizational design framework to understand TT ecosystems at different universities. We define TT ecosystems as the set of organizations affiliated with a university that directly support TT and startup incubation in a university context (Good et al., 2019).

The term "ecosystems" is typically used in the context of biological systems where multiple interdependent organisms interact in complex ways within a specific environment. The ecosystem concept has been applied in many different contexts including digital ecosystems (Sussan and Acs, 2017), tourism (Brandt et al., 2017), knowledge ecosystems (Jarvi et al. 2018), entrepreneurial ecosystems (Stam, 2015) and innovation ecosystems (Adner and Kapoor, 2010). Despite the use in several domains, there does not appear to be a clear definition of ecosystems. However, the common features appear to be the concepts of interdependent actors, interaction between actors, a specific context and a common purpose or outcome.

Criticism of the ecosystem perspective, particularly in the related contexts of entrepreneurship and innovation, focuses on its similarity to other bodies of work such as the systems of innovation and clusters literature, the lack of a clear conceptual and analytical framework that also identifies possible cause-and-effect relationships, the lack of comparative work, the lack of research using a strong theoretical foundation, unclear boundaries and the need for a more systems-based approach (Alvedalen and Boschma, 2017; Oh et al., 2016; Stam, 2015).

Using an organizational design framework, we address some of these criticisms by providing a theoretical base through which we analyze and compare different TT ecosystems and identify causal drivers of the organizational design of TT ecosystems.

2.2.   Organizational Design and TT Ecosystems

Organizations can be defined as a collection of actors that work together in achieving an overarching goal (Scott, 1998). In this respect, an organization can be conceptualized as either a collection of individuals or, as is the case with TT ecosystems, as a collection of organizations working toward a common goal (Fombrun, 1986; Gulati et al., 2012). The design of organizations can be studied by analyzing the four basic design elements of purpose, structure, activities and people (Scott, 1998). These elements are dependent on each other and maintaining alignment between these elements is necessary to successfully achieve an organization's goals (Nadler and Tushman, 1997; Scott, 1998).

Purpose refers to the main reason the organization exists. Organizations, and the actors within those organizations, will pursue a set of goals or outcomes that they identify as being important for fulfilling their purpose. Organizations can have multiple purposes and may even present different purposes to different audiences (Warriner, 1965).

Structure relates to the configuration of relationships and processes internal to each component of the ecosystem and between components. The structure of TT ecosystems varies in terms of ownership, governance, internal structure, size, and physical location (Scott, 1998). Ownership relates to who owns components in the ecosystem, whether it is primarily just the university or a combination of public and private organizations with the university. Governance is concerned with the degree to which components are integrated within the university organizational structure or set up as independent organizations. Internal structure relates to the degree of centralization, formalization and specialization within the ecosystem (Alter, 1990; Campbell et al., 1974). Size refers to the average size of components measured as number of employees. Location refers to the degree to which components are located on campus and co-located. Finally, structural relations refer to the degree to which the components of the ecosystem interact with one another, either formally or informally.

Activities are the tasks and routines that the organization performs in pursuit of its goals. Activities are highly diverse and can include anything from daily activities to complex and creative routines performed over a longer period. Howells (2006) developed a framework for classifying activities related to TT which we use to structure our analysis. He identified 10 different categories of intermediation activities: foresight and diagnostics; scanning and information processing; knowledge processing, generation and combination; gatekeeping and brokering; testing, validation and training; accreditation and standards; regulation and arbitration; intellectual property; commercialization; and assessment and evaluation.

People refers to the capabilities and experience of the individuals employed by the different components and the culture in which those people reside. In the context of TT ecosystems, we look at the extent to which actors within the ecosystem have academic, industry, or entrepreneurial experience. Experience is an important element of human capital which is likely to affect performance in executing tasks (Dimov and Shepherd, 2005) and reaching entrepreneurial performance (Unger et al., 2011).

3. METHODOLOGY

3.1. Research Design

To conduct this study, we employed a comparative case study with the unit of analysis being the TT ecosystem at eight different universities in Scandinavia (Yin, 2014). Using a theoretical sampling approach, we selected cases based on both a replicative (i.e. similar cases) and divergent logic (i.e. major differences in cases) (Eisenhardt, 1989). To minimize contextual factors and improve comparability, Scandinavia was chosen due to similarities in culture, innovation output, and many other factors (Eurostat, 2016). Furthermore, we focused on universities ranked in the top 200 of international rankings since these universities have higher research capacity and are more likely to be active in TT, which ensures the relevance of the selected cases.

Two universities were selected per country. The first case in each country was the highest ranked university (replication logic). The second case was chosen based on divergent characteristics such as a specialized research focus (divergent logic). The details of each case are presented in Table 4.1.

For reliability, a case study protocol was maintained and updated throughout the process. A pilot study was conducted at Case A to test and revise the initial version of the case protocol. An anonymized case database has also been maintained.

3.2.   Data Collection and Analysis

We conducted 38 unstructured interviews with managers at each component of each TT ecosystem between April 2016 and June 2017. Thirty-one of the interviews were recorded and transcribed while the remaining seven were unrecorded with summaries written up after the interview. Interview questions centred on gathering information about each organizational design element in our theoretical framework combined with how the interviewee's organization interacts with other organizations in the ecosystem. To enable triangulation and improve construct validity, we collected archival data which included websites, annual reports and strategic documents.

Analysis was completed in multiple stages using a case-oriented strategy concerned with identifying categories into which the various cases could be placed (Miles et al., 2014). The first author coded the transcriptions and summaries using a provisional coding approach which used codes derived from our theoretical framework. The results were then categorized and summarized in tables to allow for easier comparison. Diagrams were also created to visualize aspects of how each ecosystem is designed. The resulting tables and diagrams were used to conduct a cross-case analysis to compare the designs of each ecosystem. Interview transcripts were revisited a second time to identify statements that directly or indirectly elaborated on design choices. Throughout the process, the co-authors had repeated discussions using the previously mentioned materials as aids to further understand the data. The findings from this process are discussed in the next section.

Table 4.1 Case details

| | | | | | General university-level information | | | TT-related information | | | |
| | | | | | Size (5-year average) | | | | TT outcomes (5-year average) | | |
Case	Number of Interviews	Country	Location	Scientific specialization	Students	Academic Staff	General Income (mill. €)	TT Ecosystem Components	Spinouts	License	Disclosures
A	5	Norway	City	General	27,000	3,400	770	TTO, incubator, science park, student org	9	42	241
B	3	Norway	City	Specialized	39,000	3,700	750	TTO, proof of concept fund, incubator, student hub	16	15	149
C	5	Denmark	City	General	40,000	3,500	1,100	TTO, science park, incubator, student hubs	2	20	72
D	7	Denmark	City	General	37,000	4,400	850	TTO, science park, incubator, student hubs	3	18	60
E	6	Sweden	City	Specialized	6,000	2,400	650	Innovation office, incubator, science park	Not available	Not available	152
F	4	Sweden	Suburban	General	42,000	3,900	670	Innovation office, incubator, venture fund, other	Not available	Not available	97
G	3	Finland	City	General	33,000	4,200	720	TTO, student hub	2	2	75
H	5	Finland	Suburban	Specialized	19,000	2,800	390	TTO, incubator, accelerator, student hub, student orgs	7	26	159

4.   WHAT DRIVES THE DESIGN OF TT ECOSYSTEMS?

In the interest of brevity and to keep the focus of this chapter on the drivers of ecosystem design, we begin this section with a summary of the organizational design characteristics of each case in Table 4.2. We then present and discuss the drivers of ecosystem design we identified.

We identified drivers of design at three different levels: micro, meso and macro (Djokovic and Souitaris, 2006). The micro-level focuses on drivers emerging from the action of individuals within the ecosystem. The meso-level includes drivers caused by the actions of the university and TT ecosystem members. The macro-level includes drivers related to governmental, economic, or institutional mechanisms acting on the ecosystem. Table 4.3 summarizes the drivers we identified during our study and clearly illustrates how they impact ecosystem design. This table is useful for identifying overlaps between design impacts and shows that not all drivers impact every aspect of design.

4.1.   Micro-level

At the micro-level, we observed the importance of individuals possessing an entrepreneurial mindset, having access to resources and having been inspired to act. These influential individuals can affect every aspect of organizational design from shifting or expanding purposes (e.g. Case H), increasing the range of activities conducted (e.g. Case A), changing structure through the creation or renewal of components (e.g. Case F), or recruiting skilled individuals to the ecosystem (e.g. Case A).

Such individuals can include previously successful entrepreneurs (from inside and outside the university), academic scientists, or students. For example, the renewal of the science park in Case A is the result of hiring an ex-entrepreneur and investor who then engaged a second group of successful entrepreneurs to create the connected incubator. In this case, the motivation of these entrepreneurs appears to be a desire to give back to their community, the challenge of renewing and building these components and an interest in creating attractive investment opportunities. Case H has a thriving set of components created and driven by an inspired group of students with the support of other actors behind the scenes. In this case, the students were driven by the negative attitude of a business professor toward entrepreneurship in combination with their experiences visiting highly successful entrepreneurial environments in the U.S. Academic scientists have also been inspired by their experience at innovative universities or working with industry to develop supporting components such as an entrepreneurial internship program (Case A).

Table 4.2 Organizational design of TT ecosystems by case

	Case A	Case B	Case C	Case D	Case E	Case F	Case G	Case H
Purpose								
Encourage and support academic scientists to participate in commercialization	X	X	X	X	X	X	X	X
Encourage and support student participation in entrepreneurship		X	X	X			X	X
Facilitate the creation of valuable products and services based on university research	X	X	X	X	X	X	X	X
Support and facilitate the licensing of university research	X	X	X	X	X	X	X	X
Support establishment and growth of startups and university spinoffs	X	X	X	X	X	X	X	X
Support establishment and growth of established businesses	X	X	X	X	X	X		X
Regional economic development	X	X		X		X		X
Protect the rights of the university	X	X	X	X			X	X
Generate profit for owners			X	X	X	X		
Activities (adapted from Howells, 2006)								
Articulation of needs and requirements	X	X	X	X	X	X	X	X
Scanning and information processing	X	X	X	X	X	X	X	X
Gatekeeping and brokering	X	X	X	X	X	X	X	X
Prototyping and pilot facilities		X	X	X	X	X		X
Intellectual property rights	X	X	X	X	X	X	X	X
Marketing, support and planning	X	X	X	X	X	X	X	X
Sales network and selling	X	X	X	X	X	X	X	X
Finding potential capital funding and organizing funding or offerings	X	X	X	X	X	X	X	X
Venture capital	X		X	X	X	X		X
Initial public offering					X			
Assessment and evaluation	X	X	X	X	X	X	X	X
Structure								
Ownership								
University only components?			X	X	X	X	X	X
Component-owned components?	X	X	X					
Multiple owner components?	X	X	X	X	X	X	X	X
Governance								
Primarily internal to the university			X	X				X

Table 4.2   (continued)

	Case A	Case B	Case C	Case D	Case E	Case F	Case G	Case H
Primarily external organizations	X	X					X	
Mix of internal and external					X	X		
Internal Structure								
Centralization	Med.	Med.	High	High	Low	Low	High	High
Formalization	Med.	Med.	High	High	Low	Low	High	Low
Specialization	Med.	Low	Low	Low	High	Med.	Low	Low
Size								
Primarily small components	X	X			X	X	X	X
Primarily large components			X	X				
Location								
On campus	X	X	X	X	X	X	X	X
Off campus		X	X				X	X
Mostly co-located?	Yes	No	Yes	Yes	Yes	Yes	No	No
Structural Relations								
Primarily formal, contract based	X	X	X	X			X	X
Primarily informal	X	X			X	X		X
People								
Entrepreneurial experience	X	X	X	X	X	X	X	X
Industry experience	X	X	X	X	X	X	X	X
Research experience	X	X	X	X	X	X	X	X
Business experience	X	X	X	X	X	X	X	X
Legal experience	X	X	X	X	X	X		
Finance experience	X	X	X	X	X	X	X	
Clinical trials experience	X		X	X	X	X		

The collaborations between these individuals can also impact TT eco-system design. The clearest example of this is the interaction between managers in the ecosystem. For example, managers can develop a shared vision for the ecosystem which acts as a guiding design proposition for the ecosystem. This is true in Case F, where both university and component managers developed a shared vision that prioritized collaboration and minimization of duplication. This has a clear effect on the overall structure of the ecosystem in Case F, where components are co-located in the same office space and in which structural relations are characterized by significant knowledge sharing and communication.

In Case D, collaboration between an engaged student, a faculty researcher and faculty management led to the conversion of an empty space into an innovation and incubation hub. This initiative has since developed its own identity and branding and has grown to support

Table 4.3 Overview of drivers of organizational design of TT ecosystems

	Event(s)	Impact of events initiated by diverse drivers on TT ecosystem organizational design			
		Purpose	Activities	Structure	People
Micro-level drivers					
Individual initiatives					
Entrepreneurs	Successful entrepreneurs renewed a component (science park in Case A; TTO in Case H) or create new components (incubator in Case H)	Purposes were changed or expanded to include the support for startups and university spin-offs	Activities were expanded to include greater support for startups	The creation of a new component in Case A had the effect of reducing centralization Formalization reduced in both cases	Human capital of the ecosystem was developed through the inclusion of these entrepreneurs and through individuals they recruited from their network
Academics	Academic scientists were instrumental in developing components such as an entrepreneurial internship program (Case A) or initiated the formation of the ecosystem (Case F)	Introduction of new purposes including inspiring students to be entrepreneurs (Case A) or to support the commercialization of research generally (Case F)	Activities expanded to include student engagement (Case A)	Creation of centrally run, student focused component (Case A) increases centralization and formalization	Indirectly encourages students to participate in the ecosystem (Case A) Recruitment of leaders to start building the ecosystem (Case F)
Students	In Case H, an inspired group of students established a startup accelerator, student internship program and two annual events to support startups	Expansion of purpose to include inspiring students to be entrepreneurs and supporting startups	Introduced startup acceleration, network building, student engagement	Formation of student-led components reduces centralization and formalization	Engaging fellow students to participate in ecosystem (part- or full-time)

Table 4.3 (continued)

	Event(s)	Impact of events initiated by diverse drivers on TT ecosystem organizational design			
		Purpose	Activities	Structure	People
Collaborations between individuals					
Collaboration between individuals in the ecosystem	Collaboration between component managers led to the development of a shared vision for the ecosystem (Case F)	Creation of a coherent unifying purpose to which all components support (Case F)	Reduction of overlap or duplication of activities (Case F)	Shared vision in Case F encouraged decentralization and moderate specialization combined with co-location of components and significant formal and informal structural relations	-
Collaboration between students, academic scientists and administrators	Collaboration between students, academics and administrators led to the creation of new component focused on supporting student startups (Case D)	Expanded purpose to include support of student startups (Case D)	Addition of startup support and acceleration, provision of physical space for student startups (Case D)	Reduced centralization due to distance from other components, formalization reduced due to lack of formal management and specialization increased due to attachment to specific faculty or department	-
Meso-level drivers					
Large organizational change projects	The merger of universities (Case H) and an externally	Broadening overall purpose of ecosystem to include startup	Activities expanded to include startup support, acceleration,	Every aspect of an ecosystem's structure can be affected by	Required the recruitment of individuals to lead and develop the new components (Case D)

funded entrepreneurship project (Case D) enabled the creation of new components (i.e. incubator, accelerator and others) and reorganization of the ecosystem	support and increasing university–industry collaboration	industry engagement, student engagement	such projects and the impact is unique to each project	
Macro-level drivers				
Governmental			–	
Government –regulations — Government regulations affect or incentivize specific purposes (e.g. spin-off creation) and activities (e.g. patenting activities) and affect who owns the TT ecosystem (e.g. the university) and how it is governed (e.g. central to the university administration)	Prescribe or incentivize specific purposes such as supporting startups	Impacts which activities are conducted or prioritized such as startup creation or licensing	Regulations can determine ownership (such as mixed ownership) and governance structures (such as all external organizations)	
Government – funding — Reduction of government funding due to changes in government priorities or economic decline	Led to the narrowing of purpose to those that can be realistically be achieved or those considered "core"	Reduction of activities based on resources (e.g. elimination of proof of concept funding)	Elimination of components (e.g. closure of science park in Case E)	Inability to hire new individuals or potentially reducing the number of individuals in the ecosystem

Table 4.3 (continued)

| Event(s) | Impact of events initiated by diverse drivers on TT ecosystem organizational design | | | | |
| | Purpose | Activities | Structure | People | |

Event(s)	Purpose	Activities	Structure	People
Public organizations' initiatives	Public organizations provide funding for ecosystem components (e.g. proof of concept funds) or invest directly in new components (i.e. as owners of science parks or incubators)	Incentivizes or requires certain purposes (e.g. student support, creation of startups)	Enables a broader range of activities (e.g. proof of concept testing)	Supports the creation of new components (e.g. science parks or incubators)	Supports the recruitment of talent (e.g. to lead the new components)
Economic Private organizations' engagement	Private organizations' engagement in the ecosystem through collaboration or direct investment/ownership.	Influence the purpose of the ecosystem through collaboration requirements or ownership control (e.g. more profit oriented)	Increases types of activities conducted by the ecosystem (e.g. startup support, specialized commercialization support, investment)	The structure of the ecosystem will have a greater degree of mixed ownership and external organizations combined with a greater degree of specialization. Supports formation of new components, can act as owners, can increase specialization	Private organizations can also provide access to human capital within their organization or through their network
Availability of human capital	The failure or decline of a large local company such as in Case F provided	—	—	—	Provides a significant pool of human capital to recruit into the ecosystem

Institutional Trends and mimetic forces	The pressure to follow current trends and mimic successful ecosystems (i.e. all cases) has a significant impact on ecosystem design	Choice of purposes influenced by need for legitimacy, copying successful ecosystems, or specific trend characteristics (i.e. creation of startups, economic development)	Range of activities depends on purpose. Activities reflect best practices or learnings from other jurisdictions. (i.e. copying the "Stanford model" or attending community of practice conferences)	Structures are then adapted to reflect these other jurisdictions but are adapted for the differences in context (e.g. only external organizations or co-location)	The people recruited into the ecosystem reflect these choices (e.g. recruiting patent lawyers or entrepreneurs)

ecosystems with the ability to recruit highly talented individuals to participate in the ecosystem.

multiple student-led companies but lacks defined routines and business development expertise. Similar instances are now being developed in other faculties but in a more formal, top-down process led initially by faculty leadership. From an organizational design perspective, this dynamic collaboration between students, researchers and faculty management is an example of a driver that increases the range of activities conducted by the ecosystem and affects the structure of the ecosystem by adding components, which increases specialization and reduces centralization.

4.2.   Meso-level

At the meso-level, we found two cases (Case D and H) where a critical event, specifically a large, externally funded organizational change project at the university, had a significant impact on the types of components present and how those components were integrated into the ecosystem. In Case H, the education authorities in Finland decided to merge multiple universities into a single, multidisciplinary university, as part of renewing the higher education sector in Finland and with a goal of creating a university that fosters innovation. The merger enabled both academic scientists and student-related actors from the merging institutions to claim spaces that became available due to these changes. These spaces became the starting point of hubs for university–industry collaborations, entrepreneurship-related events and startup acceleration. In Case D, the university secured funding for a project attempting to enhance its entrepreneurial activity. Specifically, this project enabled the creation of an incubator and spin-off related program, which were subsequently merged and centralized into the internal TTO. As a result, the ecosystem's purpose in each case was broadened to include the support of startup companies (both student and external) and increasing university–industry collaboration. Furthermore, the activities of the ecosystem were expanded to include business acceleration, entrepreneurial internships, entrepreneurship related events, hackathons and industry sponsored design workshops. Every aspect of ecosystem structure was affected by these projects but in different ways. For example, while both became more centralized, in Case H, self-governed student-led components were created whereas Case D does not have student-led components. Finally, the addition of these elements increased the numbers of people involved in the ecosystem.

4.3.   Macro-level

Influential actors at the macro-level reside outside the TT ecosystem and include government, public organizations, private organizations, macro-trends and mimetic forces. Government has arguably the greatest impact on ecosystem design through the creation of policies and programs directed at regulating academic TT. In many cases, government policies define the boundaries of the TT process and the freedom universities and other actors have in organizing for academic entrepreneurship. For example, Swedish universities are not allowed to directly earn profit but have been allowed to create holding companies that can profit from TT activities. In addition, the Swedish government provides funding for innovation offices that support TT internally at a limited number of universities (Cases E and F). Government policies and programs can, therefore, affect the overall purpose, activities and structure of TT ecosystems. Specifically, governments can prescribe or heavily incentivize particular purposes such as setting a mandate for publicly owned components or tying financial support to specific performance measures, which influences the activities prioritized by the ecosystem. Finally, government policies can require specific structures such as the holding company structure in Sweden.

Another government-related driver was the reduction of university budgets due to economic decline (Case C, E, H and G). This had a major impact on resources available to some components. The lack of financial resources narrowed the purpose of the ecosystem to what could reasonably be accomplished, reduced the range of activities conducted and limited the ability to hire additional people.

Public organizations that support TT also impact the design of TT ecosystems. Public organizations are government-owned organizations that operate as independent companies and act to fulfil a mandate set by government. In a TT context, these organizations typically provide some form of funding that can be accessed for the purposes of research or the development of proofs of concept. In some countries such as Norway, public organizations also provide support and direct investment for the creation of incubators and science parks which can affect the prevalence and internal configuration of these organizations. Overall, public organizations can influence an ecosystem's activities, structure and people by providing dedicated funding for specific outcomes, creation of new components, and recruitment of skilled individuals.

Private organizations influence primarily the activities in the ecosystem. For instance, they can affect the types of technologies that are prioritized for commercialization by the ecosystem. In some cases, private organizations will even partly own different components allowing for influence over their operations. This can even lead to the ecosystem specializing or creating specialized components focused on that particular industry. An example of this is Case B where local companies invested in the university incubator and provide funding for one of the student entrepreneurship organizations. Another example is Case A where an industry cluster organization supported the creation of an incubator focused on medical technologies. Overall, private organizations can have an impact on the purpose, activities and structure of the ecosystem.

Another driver related to private organizations (Case F, G and H) was the failure or decline of large industrial actors in the region. Individuals who previously worked in these large companies stayed in the region and with their expertise either joined the ecosystem, started their own companies, or became investors. This is consistent with the concept of recycling within entrepreneurial ecosystems where individuals from failed or closed ventures re-enter the ecosystem in other capacities bringing with them their resources and experience (Spigel and Harrison, 2018). These recycled resources enabled the creation or expansion of components and enabled collaborations with industry. Such events have the greatest impact on the people aspect of organizational design since these individuals take up roles within the ecosystem, adding their human capital to the system. For example, in Case H, one of these individuals was an influential leader and became a micro-level driver of change within the ecosystem.

Macro-trends and mimetic forces impacted the design of ecosystems in all of the cases. The increasing focus on TT from universities combined with the digitalization of society are examples of trends that have put pressure on ecosystems to adapt their designs. For example, the incubator in Case A is primarily focused on supporting startups developing machine learning or artificial intelligence-based products. Mimetic forces have led ecosystem components to adopt "best practices" from other ecosystems to their context in a bid to increase legitimacy and solve operational challenges. For example, the TTOs or similar components at each of the universities implemented very similar approaches to their commercialization processes often referred to as the "Stanford model" or "Oxford model." It was also quite common for leaders from different universities to take "field trips" and visit other universities to better understand what other universities were doing related to TT. Both trends and mimetic forces have a pervasive effect on every aspect of organizational design with purposes being adapted to the requirements of the trend and copied from other jurisdictions with the hope of building legitimacy and potentially recreating success. Similarly, activities may be adapted to reflect what is considered "best practice" in the relevant communities of practice or to show that the ecosystem is adapting to emerging trends. Structure will then need to be changed to support these changes and this can take the form of changing ownership, creation or elimination of components, modifications in governance, reorganization of internal structures, or changing of structural relations.

5.   IMPLICATIONS AND CONCLUSIONS

In our study of the TT ecosystems of eight different universities in Scandinavia, we have identified a range of micro-, meso- and macro-level drivers that affect the overall organizational design of TT ecosystems (see Figure 4.1). At the micro-level, we identify influential entrepreneurs, academics and students whose actions and interactions affect TT ecosystem design. At the meso-level, we identify one major driver of design which stems from university or ecosystem level organizational development projects. Finally, at the macro-level, we identify government policy and programs, public organizations, private organizations, macro-trends, and mimetic forces as drivers of ecosystem design.

From a research perspective, we build on the structural perspective of ecosystems (Adner, 2017) by identifying dynamic mechanisms that impact ecosystem design. Future research can study these mechanisms in more detail to understand how these drivers impact alignment, how the different drivers

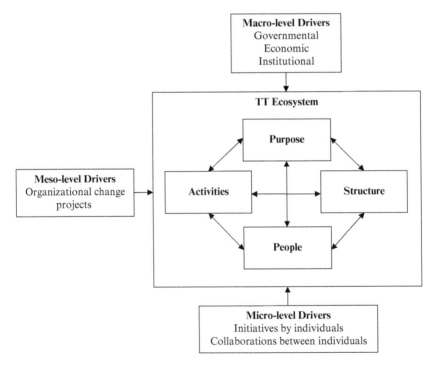

Source: Scott, 1998.

Figure 4.1   Drivers of the organizational design of TT ecosystems

interact, and how they influence TT outcomes. Furthermore, we contribute to the TT and academic entrepreneurship literatures by responding to calls for studying the broader context in which TT occurs (Siegel and Wright, 2015) by elaborating on the TT ecosystem concept (Good et al., 2019). We also contribute by applying a well-understood theoretical perspective in a novel way that adds to what has been a largely atheoretical body of work (e.g. Lamine et al., 2018; Spigel and Harrison, 2018).

From a practitioner's perspective, each of these drivers are potential leverage points that practitioners can use to influence the design of the ecosystem in order to achieve alignment between the different components and thereby improving effectiveness.

Our study provides a deeper understanding of how TT ecosystems are designed to help research scientists and students to turn their ideas and technologies into new businesses. By doing so, we contribute to the ecosystem, TT and academic entrepreneurship literatures.

REFERENCES

Adner, R. (2017). Ecosystem as structure: an actionable construct for strategy. *Journal of Management*, 43(1), 39–58.

Adner, R., & Kapoor, R. (2010). Value creation in innovation ecosystems: How the structure of technological interdependence affects firm performance in new technology generations. *Strategic Management Journal*, 31(3), 306–333.

Alter, C. (1990). An exploratory study of conflict and coordination in interorganizational service delivery systems. *The Academy of Management Journal*, 33(3), 478–502.

Alvedalen, J., & Boschma, R. (2017). A critical review of entrepreneurial ecosystems research: Towards a future research agenda. *European Planning Studies*, 25(6), 887–903.

Bradley, S. R., Hayter, C. S., & Link, A. N. (2013). *Models and methods of university technology transfer*. Delft, Netherlands: Now Publishers Incorporated.

Brandt, T., Bendler, J., & Neumann, D. (2017). Social media analytics and value creation in urban smart tourism ecosystems. *Information & Management*, 54(6), 703–713.

Campbell, J.P., Bownas, D.A., Peterson, N.G., & Dunnette, M.D. (1974) The measurement of organizational effectiveness: A review of relevant research and opinion. Retrieved from Personnel Decisions Research Inst, Minneapolis MN.

Dimov, D.P., & Shepherd, D.A. (2005). Human capital theory and venture capital firms: Exploring "home runs" and "strike outs". *Journal of Business Venturing*, 20(1), 1–21.

Djokovic, D., & Souitaris, V. (2006). Spinouts from academic institutions: A literature review with suggestions for further research. *The Journal of Technology Transfer*, 33(3), 225–247.

Eisenhardt, K. M. (1989). Building theories from case study research. *The Academy of Management Review*, 14(4), 532–550.

Eurostat. (2016) *Key European Statistics*. Available at: http://ec.europa.eu/eurostat. Accessed 12 October 2016.

Fombrun, C. J. (1986) Structural dynamics within and between organizations. *Administrative Science Quarterly*, 31(3), 403–421.

Good, M., Knockaert, M., Soppe, B., & Wright, M. (2019). The technology transfer ecosystem in academia. An organizational design perspective. *Technovation*, 82, 35–50.

Grimaldi, R., Kenney, M., Siegel, D. S., & Wright, M. (2011). 30 years after Bayh–Dole: Reassessing academic entrepreneurship. *Research Policy*, 40(8), 1045–1057.

Gulati, R., Puranam, P., & Tushman, M. (2012). Meta-organization design: Rethinking design in interorganizational and community contexts. *Strategic Management Journal,* 33(6), 571–586.

Hayter, C. S., Nelson, A. J., Zayed, S., & O'Connor, A. C. (2018). Conceptualizing academic entrepreneurship ecosystems: A review, analysis and extension of the literature. *The Journal of Technology Transfer,* 43(4), 1039–1082.

Howells, J. (2006). Intermediation and the role of intermediaries in innovation. *Research Policy,* 35(5), 715–728.

Jarvi, K., Almpanopoulou, A., & Ritala, P. (2018). Organization of knowledge ecosystems: Prefigurative and partial forms. *Research Policy,* 47(8), 1523–1537.

Lamine, W., Mian, S., Fayolle, A., Wright, M., Klofsten, M., & Etzkowitz, H. (2018). Technology business incubation mechanisms and sustainable regional development. *The Journal of Technology Transfer,* 43(5), 1121–1141.

Li, L. (2005). The effects of trust and shared vision on inward knowledge transfer in subsidiaries' intra- and inter-organizational relationships. *International Business Review,* 14(1), 77–95.

Mosey, S., Guerrero, M., & Greenman, A. (2017). Technology entrepreneurship research opportunities: Insights from across Europe. *The Journal of Technology Transfer,* 42(1), 1–9.

Miles, M. B., Huberman, A. M., & Saldana, J. (2014). Qualitative data analysis: A method sourcebook. *CA, US: Sage Publications.*

Mintzberg, H., & Westley, F. (1992). Cycles of organizational change. *Strategic Management Journal,* 13, 39–59.

Nadler, D., & Tushman, M. (1997). *Competing by design: The power of organizational architecture.* New York: Oxford University Press.

Oh, D.-S., Phillips, F., Park, S., & Lee, E. (2016). Innovation ecosystems: A critical examination. *Technovation,* 54, 1–6.

Pearce, C.L., & Ensley, M.D. (2004). A reciprocal and longitudinal investigation of the innovation process: The central role of shared vision in Product and Process Innovation Teams (PPITs). *Journal of Organizational Behavior,* 25(2), 259–278.

Rasmussen, E., Moen, O., & Gulbrandsen, M. (2006). Initiatives to promote commercialization of university knowledge. *Technovation,* 26, 518–533.

Scott, W. Richard. (1998) *Organizations: Rational, natural, and open systems.* 4th ed. Upper Saddle River, N.J: Prentice Hall.

Siegel, D. S., & Wright, M. (2015). Academic entrepreneurship: Time for a rethink? *British Journal of Management,* 26(4), 582–595.

Spigel, B., & Harrison, R. (2018). Toward a process theory of entrepreneurial ecosystems. *Strategic Entrepreneurship Journal,* 12(1), 151–168.

Stam, E. (2015). Entrepreneurial ecosystems and regional policy: A sympathetic critique. *European Planning Studies,* 23(9), 1759–1769.

Sussan, F., & Acs, Z. J. (2017). The digital entrepreneurial ecosystem. *Small Business Economics,* 49(1), 55–73.

Swamidass, P. M. (2013). University startups as a commercialization alternative: lessons from three contrasting case studies. *The Journal of Technology Transfer,* 38(6), 788–808.

Unger, J. M., Rauch, A., Frese, M., & Rosenbusch, N. (2011). Human capital and entrepreneurial success: A meta-analytical review. *Journal of Business Venturing,* 26(3), 341–358.

Warriner, C. K. (1965). The problem of organizational purpose. *The Sociological Quarterly,* 6(2), 139–146.

Wright, M., Siegel, D. S., & Mustar, P. (2017). An emerging ecosystem for student startups. *The Journal of Technology Transfer,* 42(4), 909–922.

Yin, Robert K. (2014). *Case study research: Design and methods* (Fifth). London, UK: Sage publications.

5. The support system's influence on nature-based business start-ups in a rural context

Jorunn Grande and Espen Carlsson

INTRODUCTION

Small businesses and sole proprietorship are important for employment and wealth both nationally and regionally, and as argued by Mayer and Baumgartner (2014, p. 16), "entrepreneurship and innovation processes are important dynamics that shape the development of peripheral regions". Rural policies in many European countries thus often have high aims for increasing entrepreneurship as a tool to boost regional economic development and livelihood.

In this chapter, we investigate the role of regional formalized supporters – understood as public actors backing and enhancing entrepreneurial efforts in nature-based firms in a non-core[1] Nordic region. Nature-based businesses build their value creation on resources from land, forest, garden or the rural environment (see e.g. Sörensson et al. 2018, p. 53).

The Norwegian support system consists of several public actors with local and regional presence that can help rural entrepreneurs in the start-up and development phases (Ministry of Agriculture and Food 2015). The municipality has a first-level service, which implies they are the first contact point where entrepreneurs might get assistance, for instance via the agricultural office, regular business advisors or other innovative milieus they might organize. The devoted resources depend on the size of the municipality, location and regional characteristics. At the regional level, there are resources to follow up the entrepreneurial initiatives by both Siva – that governs national business incubator and business gardens programs – and Innovation Norway, having the greatest variety of instruments, advice and applicable financial support and programs. The county governor and the county council focus more broadly on mobilizing activities and measures regarding regional business development. All the public actors have a responsibility to guide the entrepreneurs and business operators to the most appropriate assistance/helpers.

Several studies suggest that innovative nature-based start-ups may need other systemic attributes and policy instruments that go beyond their traditional industries. Rabinowicz et al. (2012) find that rural entrepreneurs in Sweden perceive it time consuming and confusing to find the appropriate support and network for developing ideas. Clark (2009) suggests that entrepreneurial farmers in England need more sophisticated assistance from advisory services than currently available. Furthermore, North and Smallbone (2006) ask for more coordinated and strategic policy approaches for rural enterprise development. Finally, Klerkx et al. (2017) explain that advisory arrangement must be adapted to the needs and contexts of the companies. However, few studies seem to look at entrepreneurship from a truly interdisciplinary and systemic perspective (Alvedalen and Boschma 2017), making it harder to adapt to entrepreneurs that cross industry boundaries like many rural businesses do.

In this context, the entrepreneurial ecosystem (EE) concept seems promising for investigating the interaction and benefits in entrepreneurial environments across industries. While acknowledging the complexity of the system in total, EE highlights the mechanisms, institutions, networks, and cultures supporting entrepreneurs. So far, however, the literature on EE seems mostly concerned with the system's ingredients (Malecki 2018; Spigel and Harrisson 2018), partly ignoring the processes for their combination into a "sustainable milieu with entrepreneurial vitality" (Malecki 2018, p. 5). Furthermore, Roundy and Fayard (2019) argue that the topic is under-theorized and that the specific ecosystem mechanisms influencing entrepreneurs are unclear. Other shortcomings stressed in the literature are related to which interactions matter the most, what is cause and effect in an EE, and which institutions have an impact on the components and performance of EE (Alvedalen and Boschma 2017). Finally, much of the work on EE has been conceptual or based on data from an urban high-growth-technological-Anglo-American angle and it is not yet clear whether EE is a useful concept for all regions and types of firms (Malecki 2018, p. 8). Empirical research focusing on the interaction between supporters and entrepreneurs in endogenous regional development is therefore much needed (Stam 2015; Spigel and Harrison 2018).

To increase knowledge on these issues we contribute to the EE and start-up incubation literature by exploring the roles and interactions influencing nature-based start-ups in a rural context in the Trøndelag region in Norway. We ask the following research questions:

1. What peculiar contextual challenges do nature-based start-ups face in non-core EEs?
2. How do the formalized supporters in the rural (non-core) EE strengthen start-up quality, entrepreneurial efforts and value creation?

Theoretically, we draw and build on EE, the resource-based view and absorptive capacity-literature. This allows for investigating the underlying mechanisms on how start-up entrepreneurs interact and extract benefits from a supportive EE.

EEs, FORMALIZED SUPPORT, ENTREPRENEURSHIP AND FIRM RESOURCES

Baumgartner et al. (2013) show that different types of entrepreneurship and mechanisms stimulating endogenous regional development are at work in European non-core regions. The pioneering work of Marshall (1890/1920) and Schumpeter (1934) focuses on the industrial milieu and entrepreneurs – respectively – as nodes in their analysis of economic change, inspiring a number of theoretical concepts and territorial entrepreneurial and innovation models in the last decades. There is now scholarly consensus that knowledge, learning, and different kinds of entrepreneurship and innovation are key factors for firm competitiveness and regional and national economic development. This also applies to non-core regions (Mayer and Baumgartner 2014). Social networks and interaction between stakeholders who are different enough to provide new knowledge, but still closely enough linked to understand each other, seem to be important (Granovetter 1985). Arrangements, actions and instruments must be context-oriented and take regional peculiarities and different assumptions and capacities for entrepreneurship and innovation into account (Tödtling and Trippl 2005). Supporting intermediary organizations may thus cover a diversity of functions (Nauwelaers 2011; Klerkx et al. 2017). Spilling (1996) uses, for instance, the concept entrepreneurial system and argues that the interaction between various elements, actors and institutions, roles played and environmental factors, make up such a regional system of a region.

Investigations of bibliometric evidence by Malecki (2018) show that the usage of the "EE" term has overtaken other concepts such as "environments for entrepreneurship" and "entrepreneurial system". The ecosystem's tradition draws on concepts like clusters and regional innovation systems (RIS) (Spigel and Harrison 2018). According to Alvedalen and Boschma (2017), the EE-literature does not make a sharp distinction between the terms ecosystem and system, often using these interchangeably and citing entrepreneurial system work. Malecki (2018) explains that the inclusion of (public/private) organizations supporting new and growing firms is similar to the innovation system literature, but entrepreneurs and spin-offs are more central in the EE tradition. Spigel (2017, p. 66) suggests further, "ecosystems are defined by the connections between the attributes that produce them and the benefits they provide to the entrepreneurs." EE are thus concerned with and influenced by system conditions constituted by the presence of and interaction between entrepreneurs, knowledge, leadership, finance and (other) supportive services that change over time (Stam 2015; Malecki 2018).

Spigel and Harrison (2018) explain that the EE concept addresses weaknesses in how RIS and cluster theories approach entrepreneurship. This especially relates to three aspects: 1) There is a need to consider the ability of entrepreneurs to access specific resources (e.g. knowledge) and involvement in the entrepreneurial process. 2) Entrepreneurs should lead ecosystems, since policymakers do not have sufficient knowledge about entrepreneurship and may be a major barrier to effective state support. As argued by Spigel and Harrison (2018, p. 156) "entrepreneurs are the best group to identify the issues that should be addressed through public intervention". 3) The EE research has largely been industry-agnostic such that there is less competition between the start-ups in an ecosystem compared to, for instance, a more or less specialized cluster. This means that entrepreneurs within the ecosystem might share experiences and learn from each other more openly.

Nature-Based Entrepreneurs, Resources and Capacities

Entrepreneurial skills (competence) and access to resources are likely to be especially important for start-ups in the initial phase of exploring and carrying out ideas. For instance, agricultural entrepreneurs may face significant challenges in implementing new knowledge and technology (Grande 2014). They have to deal with new business areas and markets in which they have little experience, and new organization of the business (Vesala et al. 2007). External conditions – such as politics and markets – can limit the scope of their action making it particularly important for such businesses to explore how firm internal resources contribute to value creation. To this, the resource-based view (RBV) literature argues that valuable and rare resources controlled by a business – and difficult for others to copy or substitute – may give a business long-lasting advantages over its competitors (Barney 1991; Priem and Butler 2001). The complexity of a resource may provide information about its potential to be transformed or combined into a unique advantage (Brush et al. 2001). Recent RBV studies also emphasize the importance of the versatility of resources (Nason and Wiklund 2018), the role of the entrepreneur in bringing resources together to create value, and the need of differentiating between organizing/using existing resources and developing new resources and capacities (Kraaijenbrink et al. 2010).

A strong EE should ideally help alleviate start-up resource needs which cannot easily be satisfied otherwise (Spigel 2017). Resources available to rural start-ups may vary substantially depending on the entrepreneurs' personal skills, property resources (farm resources) and other accessible assets (Alsos and Carter 2006). Many diversifying farmers seem to benefit from resources and capabilities tied to their traditional farm if these are abundant (Alsos and Carter 2006; Fitz-Koch et al. 2018). Building appropriate networks is also likely to be important to start-ups since external networks will give better access to information, resources and markets (Moreno and Casillas 2007; Gulati et al. 2000).

In order to benefit from resources available within the EE, the start-up must be able to access it and make use of it. The start-ups ability to do that will depend on their absorptive capacity, which is "the ability of a firm to recognise the value of new, external information, assimilate it, and apply it to commercial ends" (Cohen and Levinthaal 1990, p. 128). This capacity can be split into two phases; potential absorptive capacity (acquisition and assimilation capabilities) and realized absorptive capacity (transformation and exploitation capabilities) (Todorova and Durisin 2007). Zahra and George (2002) argue that acquiring is a prerequisite to the exploiting of knowledge, but it is still possible to acquire and assimilate knowledge without the capacity to transform and exploit it.

METHODOLOGICAL APPROACH

Based on the literature review, we investigated the interaction between selected entrepreneurs and formalized supporters in the start-ups' environment. In particular, we looked at the formalized supporter's role in helping start-ups to identify and explore resources, supplement resources and contribute to their internal resource development.

In order to analyze start-up resources and ecosystem interaction, we have conducted an analytical assessment based on the RBV with six different resource categories extracted from previous research: physical, financial, human, social, technological and organizational (Greene et al. 1997; Brush et al. 2001). We have also considered the degree of complexity of resources as suggested by Brush et al. (2001). Simple resources are explained as material, distinct or property-based, while complex resources are immaterial, intangible, and system or knowledge-based.

In total, we interviewed 13 nature-based firms in the northern part of Trøndelag, Norway, about developing their business and their experience with the formalized support system. Data was collected in the period 2015–2017. We categorized eight of these firms as nature-based start-ups

Table 5.1 The start-up sample

Firm	Industry segment	Est.*	Org.	Revenue**	Employees	Gender
N1	Micro-energy, alternative energy solutions	2016	Corporation	2.4	4	M
N2	Special/ancient grain flours	2015	Corporation	0.75	0.5*	2xF
N3	Bakery – bread and bakery goods	2011	Corporation	1.7	4	F
N5	Meetings, dining accommodation	2010/2013	Sole proprietorship (SP)/Corporation	3.2	3 + extra	F/M
N6	Milk, meeting facilities and dining	2008/2012	2xSP	0.6	5-6 +extra	F/M
N7	Farm, milk, cheese factory	2008/2014	2xSP	0.2 + farm	3	F/M
N8	Open farm, Green care/Welfare services	2005/2012	SP/Corporation	1.2	9 incl. part-time	F/M
N10	Glassblowing, dining, creative meeting place	2002/2008	2xSP	Test-phase	2	M/F

Notes:
* Year of establishment associated with the informants. Two years are due to that some are couples with two separate registered Sole proprietorships (SP) organizing a common new start-up initiative not yet registered.
** 2017 million NOK.

Source: Proff.no, interviews.

with reference to their age, industrial segment and/or phase in their entrepreneurial start up process. Merriam-Webster (2018) defines "start-up" as "a fledgling business enterprise," i.e. an immature, inexperienced or underdeveloped firm.

The findings and discussion are based on primary data from these eight firms, identified using a combination of strategic selection and the snowball method (Miles and Huberman 1994; Thagaard 2013). Some start-ups had two informants and/or consisted of couples. We also got help from support-actors to recommend suitable firms. This procedure ensured a good variety in type of businesses. The research team used a theory-based semi-structured interview guide covering topics such as the entrepreneurial process, growth, use of formalized support, work life and competition. The interviews lasted two–three hours; they were tape-recorded and then transcribed verbatim. We categorized the transcribed data in an interview protocol. Websites, policy documents, four workshops with support organizations – with further processing and discussion of the preliminary findings, services offered, formal and informal roles and types of inter-mediation – gave us additional data. Further, we analyzed the data in a thematic and interpretive approach and related the findings to previous research and theoretical background.

RESULTS, ANALYSIS AND DISCUSSION

Entrepreneur/Firm-Perspective on Resources and System-Interaction

Physical and financial resources

A basic premise for entrepreneurs in most rural and natural-based indus-tries are the physical primary resources, the "premises at the farm," as explained by firm-informant N3 and shown in Table 5.2. Such resources are not necessarily unique or inimitable, but are often an important basis for a resource mix that adds value, for example, through a farm hotel or meeting facilities in harmonic countryside surroundings. These may be considered versatile resources (Nason and Wiklund 2018) having a poten-tial for several purposes. The mix of resources may however be harder to copy, thus also indicating importance of the "synergistic combination or bundle of resources created by the firm" as suggested by Kraaijenbrink et al. (2010, p. 356). We find that formal support influence (SI) is often con-nected to helping explore latent combinations of resources and give ideas on how to implement them in start-ups. We define SI as the identified results from direct help from support organizations. As physical resources, we also include EE resources such as well-functioning infrastructure providing access and transport opportunities in the outskirts. This adds to the resource value in the start-ups by increasing access to markets and customers.

Investment capital is a critical component of an entrepreneurial econ-omy. In start-ups risk capital is usually channelled through social networks of investors, and as argued by Spigel (2017), local investors connected with the entrepreneurial community are necessary to facilitate growth of entre-preneurial firms. However, small rural businesses do not have the growth potential or scale-ability to make them interesting for investors, hence, the investigated rural start-ups seem to a larger degree dependent on gov-ernmental funding/loans. The lack of financial resources (capital/money) and "risk offload" (N5) remains critical for some of the entrepreneurs. Several informants refer to low profitability – especially in the starting and development phase of the firm – as one of the biggest inhibitory factors:

"It has been a long process; the start-up has taken many years" (N1) and "A critical point when you quit previous employment and bet 100 percent on your own business" (N2). Many of the investigated start-ups combine employment with running their own business. However, the start-ups that have been able to focus fully on their start-up business report that it has been critical to their success. As well as having money to invest, this point also relates to human resources and time. We find that these factors relate to the versatility criteria as suggested by Nason and Wiklund (2018) in that they increase internal fungibility and flexibility to the resource use.

Since investor financing to a great degree is absent in our cases, formalized mentors and dealmakers seem more important. This suggest that in rural EEs, formal support might partly substitute the role of investors and experienced entrepreneurs in high-growth urban EEs.

Human resources

Human resources center on the entrepreneur in person, his/her aspirations, knowledge and experience, as well as other employees/persons involved in the start-up. The entrepreneurs stress the need for being proactive and possess personal characteristics that are consistent with business establishment and development. This may be exemplified by arguments that highlight the importance of "guts and stamina over years" (N8), and "your own motivation and commitment" (N6), implying the importance of having faith in yourself and your business idea, as well as the ability to meet the internal and external requirements when needed. The fact that the entrepreneurs have a solid will and passion for being active in the green industry is a strong impetus for the development of new businesses, as also pointed out in earlier research (Cardon et al. 2009). However, several entrepreneurs argue that it is important to let go of some personal control and involve others in developing the start-up in order to grow and become financially sustainable: "you must dare to give up some responsibility and go ahead" (N3).

Here, *SI* seems to focus on helping start-ups access business and industry knowledge, explore further opportunities and so forth. This can be linked to the ability to build organizational resources internally, for instance via "an external chair of the board (. . .) ensures more conscious decisions" (N3), or formal (part-time) education; "the opportunities for adult education in agriculture (. . .) has been important" (N2). Several entrepreneurs also draw attention to the lack of knowledge about marketing and the ability to reach new customers as one cause of poor profitability, for instance related to limited access to sales channels. Formalized supporters in an EE may thus contribute to start-up competence and flexibility (versatility) of resources through courses and intermediary activities.

Network and social resources

As argued in the theoretical section, interaction between stakeholders who are different enough to have new knowledge, but closely enough linked to understand each other, is essential. Our data indicate that private networks and family are of great importance to the nature-based start-ups, both as knowledge and work resources, personal support and discussion partners. Furthermore, different sorts of formal and informal cooperation are pointed at as important: "Many contacts are required" (N1). Here *SI* may facilitate programs and courses, which start-ups can attend, in addition to giving supervision on potential allies and customer segments. Through social resources and external assistance from formal supporters in the EE, start-ups can acquire organizational resources from leveraged knowledge of what is available to them. Two of the informants explained: "Attended establishment course and met others with start-up ambitions" (N3) and "participating in training courses contributes to networking and new knowledge" (N6). Network also indirectly stimulates learning depending on the businesses' absorptive capacity as suggested by Zahra and George (2002), indicating an indirect benefit from participating in activities provided by the support system.

N10 emphasizes the importance of a supporting local community network: "The local (supporting actors) should have stronger belief in the 'green' ones with ideas" and explain that "community thinking in some local contexts and traditional agricultural industry segments is inhibitory," indicating path-dependency and lock-in tendencies both in regard to industry and location and a lack of complementarity. Here, EE reflects a mind-set where entrepreneurs are an important group for identifying issues and guiding formal support actors (Spigel and Harrison 2018). Hence, in our cases there seems to be a potential for more interaction creating mutual understanding for the entrepreneurial prospects in the rural community. Still the entrepreneurs ask for more community involvement as start-up informant N6 argues: "The municipality should have had a greater role in coordinating the tourism industry," hence reflecting the need for intermediaries as a public support function in the geographical context and industrial segment the start-ups are part of.

Technological and organizational resources

The interviewed businesses point at local banks, accounting agencies and business advisors as important support functions and success factors for helping out with technological and organizational resources. The majority of the start-ups indicates that public support through counselling and mentoring has been crucial for setting up the business. This support provides opportunities for competence development, information access

Table 5.2   *Critical resources identified by the rural start-ups and suggested*
support influence (SI)* on these resources

	Physical/financial	Human	Social	Technological/organisational
Material ↑↓ *Immaterial*	• The farm, animal, soil, grain and the mill • Equity • Bank financing (SI) • Other financial support in the start-up phase/capital (SI) • Good infrastructure • Location – relative physical proximity to e.g. airport and city centres/customers **Unique (im)material resource combinations:** • The farm/physical resources + family + business network • Location/place and rural community + customers	• Time • Formal qualifications (SI) • Informal competence • Market knowledge (SI) • Experience-based knowledge, e.g. on business management • Proactivity, creativity and own drive • Intuition – sensing • The ability to create experiences	• The family • Business collaboration (SI) • Personal network (SI) • Exchange of experience with experts, similar businesses (SI) • Network for sharing knowledge and experience (SI)	• Business consultants / support (SI) • Accounting Agencies (SI) • Digital tools (SI) • External chairman who can see the company from outside (SI) • Quotas/contracts/formalized agreements (SI) • Mentoring (SI) • Outreach Work • Business concept, design (SI)

Note: *SI markings indicates direct influence. Resources that are not marked may be affected indirectly by SI involvement. To simplify, we have in the table and presentation combined physical and financial, technological and organizational resources.

Source: partly based on Sörensson et al. 2018.

and guidance. However, some of the start-ups experience "high risk for small firms" and argue that "there is a need for better arrangements" (N6). We recognize that learning and developing routines is very dependent on the knowledge and capacity of the start-up team, often involving support assistance in parts of the start-up process.

In some areas, an adequate level of industry-specific knowledge seems to be lacking in order to provide needed help or to work well as a formal supporter. This indicates a lack of match between the start-ups' needs and offerings in the ecosystem. Examples of referred support system barriers are e.g. "individual treatment" (N2); "more room for people to experiment" (N10), and; "more targeted follow-up to start-ups" (N6). Finally, another entrepreneur stated: "It is important that the business actors are respected and appreciated for their knowledge and not taught how to do it" (N5). For this reason, some of the start-ups address wishes of more flexible support tailored to their needs.

Ecosystem Perspectives on Formalized Support, Resources and Start-up/Entrepreneur Interaction

The formalized start-up supporters in our non-core EE have in general several tools to aid entrepreneurs: For instance, regarding finance, business modelling knowledge, social and business network knowledge, peer advisory services, mentoring, motivation and general mobilizing and intermediary functions, all identified as important elements of successful EEs in the theoretical section.

The regional support actor informants explain that quite many entrepreneurs drop out of the process from idea to incubation; they say this is "natural" because they do not have the right product or market, not sufficient stamina or do not fit in the system. We might ask if there is a potential in working more or differently with the "dropouts"? To get more entrepreneurial ideas into start-ups and value creation – as asked for by regional developers and policy makers – either more ideas are needed or those who have ideas or resources categorized as "not good enough" must be further explored on extracting the potential. As previously suggested, to take advantage of external knowledge and learn the start-ups must possess a realized absorptive capacity enabling them to leverage and transfer this knowledge to value creating outcomes. As Spigel and Harrison (2018, pp. 158–159) explain, "it cannot be assumed that all entrepreneurs are equally able to access and use these resources. Their positions within social networks, their internal capabilities, perceived legitimacy as entrepreneurs, and their personal characteristics will affect their ability to draw on the resources available in an ecosystem." This suggests a risk for missed opportunities; those who are not typically high-growth entrepreneurs may fall outside the formalized support arrangements and resign further development of their nature-based start-up idea.

We also found a tendency of support-actor "competition" about the "best entrepreneurs" indicating a potential lock-in tendency regarding which type of ideas and start-ups that are preferred in the supporters' portfolio of entrepreneurs. As entrepreneur involvement, support and interventions through government and regulatory frameworks are important pillars of EEs (Stam 2015), the creation and recycling of entrepreneurial resources is a key factor to the success of EEs. It therefore seems important that governments at different geographical scales through regulations and support facilitate and encourage flow of such processes, contributing to the dynamics between the actors and elements in an EE, as suggested by Spigel (2017).

Our data indicate that start-ups in the green industries often need two different perspectives of advice, partly a business but also an industry-specific. Two of the regional supporters have an agreement of sharing types of counselling between them. One has expertise related to product development and production processes in the food sector, while the other follows up the business side such as budget, pricing and market development. This model has been developed and adopted regionally and seems to be working well according to several of the interviewed start-ups receiving help from both intermediaries.

Through the interviews, it emerged that the supporters' knowledge, commitment and personal chemistry often can be as important as the actual formal structure. The helper does not only work as a direct help to the entrepreneur, but also as a facilitating in-between of help and information about where other knowledge and resources exist.

CONCLUSIONS, VALUE AND IMPLICATIONS

Formal supporters contributing to the incubation of start-up initiatives in non-core-regions are diverse but represent, quite generally, an important sub-group in a regional entrepreneurial ecosystem. This applies especially to sparsely populated areas having fewer experienced entrepreneurs and investors than in urban areas.

This chapter has investigated the benefits of and challenges in how formalized regional supporters enhance resource development in rural nature-based start-ups. Our study contributes to the EE and business start-ups literature in several ways. First, we add knowledge on how context may influence the role of support system actors. Our study suggests that rural EEs display other dynamics than EEs in an urban/high growth context. Since investors and experienced entrepreneurs have a less dominant role and/or are missing, formalized supporters seem to take over some of their roles regarding funding, knowledge supply and mentoring. Thus, we suggest that the interaction and resource development between *supporters* and *start-ups* is likely to be more important in a rural/nature-based context than in urban/high growth industries. Second, we also contribute to literature on start-up incubations and EE by showing how the resource-based and absorptive capability perspectives may serve as analytical tools to assess the interaction between two specific actors of the EE, i.e. the start-ups and formal supporters. These frameworks help us explore mechanisms of resource development in EE, and may aid the exploration of possible causes and effects, as asked for by Alvedalen and Boschma (2017).

The study shows a complex picture of combinatory entrepreneur/firm, environmental and formal support factors that promote nature-based business start-ups and employment. We observe that some types of help/ support are more easily transferred into value creation streams, whereas other types may have indirect effects by inducing beneficial processes in the start-ups. To both the RBV and start-up literature our study suggests a need to focus more on the synergistic potential of the resource mix in the businesses rather than on individual resources as also suggested by Kraaijenbrink et al. (2010). The investigated start-ups combine available resources into unique service-products based on their knowledge and characteristics of their property. Their ability to combine the farm premises into new uses also increases versatility of the resource base and value creative potential thus supporting Nason and Wiklund (2018) concerning the importance of flexibility in resources.

The results evidence different abilities in start-ups for building and making use of resources available in the EE, providing empirical evidence for the suggestion by Spigel and Harrison (2018) that less experienced entrepreneurs may have lower absorptive capacity than established businesses. We also find support for splitting absorptive capacity into two phases as suggested by Zahra and George (2002): To make use of acquired knowledge from support system actors the start-ups need to leverage the knowledge that has been absorbed. This depends on their transformation and exploitation capabilities or "realized absorptive capability" as labelled by Zahra and George (2002).

Start-ups with the greatest need for help may not know how to ask for it, or have less capacity to internalize the knowledge and resources offered. A practical implication of this dilemma is that advisory services need to address the businesses' ability to internalize (make use of) acquired knowledge and resources from support services. When developing EEs for start-up incubation in the nature-based industries, it is thus important to keep in mind the heterogeneity of entrepreneurs.

The combination of inadequate financial resources and labor capacity (time) seems to be especially inhibiting regarding growth of start-ups. A second practical implication is that the formal support system in rural EEs needs to address time/economic constraints facing start-ups in critical phases for a larger share to succeed. Finally, nature-based businesses span many different types of industries, challenging formal supporters' ability to possess adequate knowledge of industry-specific conditions. As our findings indicate, there is a need for more flexible support and tailor-made solutions due to non-core contextual attributes. This may include the need for specific knowledge, but also flexibility in relation to financial support.

While this study shows some aspects of start-ups' use of formalized support and their interactional dynamics, we still lack knowledge of what contributes to development for those who need it the most but rarely seek help. For non-core EEs to prosper, we suggest more research on methods for identifying and involving this "quiet" group of nature-based entrepreneurial initiatives in non-core EEs.

A case study design limits the possibility of generalizing to the population as such and other peripheral regions. The results thus indicate areas for further studies and possible verification. There is a potential bias through the selection method in that some start-ups may have a higher level of interaction with the support system than rural start-ups in general.

NOTE

1. We use non-core as an umbrella-term featuring attributes of the rural, remote and/or peripheral (see Baumgartner et al. 2013). Or as considered by Leick and Lang (2018, p. 214), non-core are spaces outside of the major agglomerations with contexts often described with terms such as rurality and peripherality or as structurally weak with a need to mobilize resources for learning and "upgrading."

REFERENCES

Alvedalen, J., and Boschma, R. (2017), 'A critical review of entrepreneurial ecosystems research: Towards a future research agenda', *European Planning Studies*, 25, 887–903.

Alsos, G.A., and Carter, S. (2006), 'Multiple business ownership in the Norwegian farm sector: Resource transfer and performance consequences', *Journal of Rural Studies*, 22(3), 313–322.

Barney, J.B. (1991), 'Firm resources and competitive advantage', *Journal of Management*, 17, 97–120.

Baumgartner, D., Pütz, M., and Seidl, I. (2013), 'What kind of entrepreneurship drives regional development in European non-core regions? A literature review on empirical entrepreneurship research', *European Planning Studies*, 21(8), 1095–1127.

Brush, C.G., Greene, P.G., and Hart, M.M. (2001), 'From initial idea to unique advantage: The entrepreneurial challenge of constructing a resource base', *The Academy of Management Executive*, 15(1), 64–78.

Cardon, M.S., Wincent, J., Singh, J., and Drnovsek, M. (2009), 'The nature and experience of entrepreneurial passion', *Academy of Management Review*, 34(3), 511–532.

Clark, J. (2009), 'Entrepreneurship and diversification on English farms: Identifying business enterprise characteristics and change processes', *Entrepreneurship and Regional Development*, 21(2), 213–236.

Cohen, W.M., and Levinthal, D.A. (1990), 'Absorptive capacity: A new perspective on learning and innovation', *Administrative Science Quarterly*, 35(1), 128–152.

Fitz-Koch, S., Nordqvist, M., Carter, S., and Hunter, E. (2018), 'Entrepreneurship in the agricultural sector', *Entrepreneurship Theory and Practice*, 42(1), 129–166.

Grande, J. (2014), 'Entreprenørskap i landbruket. – hva bidrar til verdiskaping og verdika-
    pring? I Grande, J., Husby, M., og Moa, P.F. (Ed). *Natur og Næring i samspill*. Trondheim,
    Akademika forl, 133–157.
Granovetter, M. (1985), 'Economic action and social structure: The problem of embedded-
    ness', *The American Journal of Sociology*, 91(3), 481–510.
Greene, P.G., Brush, C.G., and Brown, T. (1997), 'Resources in small firms: An exploratory
    study', *Journal of Small Business Strategy*, 8(2), 25–40.
Gulati, R., Nohria, N., and Zaheer, A. (2000), 'Strategic networks', *Strategic Management
    Journal*, 2(3), 203–215.
Klerkx, L. Stræte, E.P., Kvam, G.T., Ystad, E., and Renate Butli, R. (2017), 'Achieving
    best-fit configurations through advisory subsystems in AKIS: Case studies of advisory
    service provisioning for diverse types of farmers in Norway', *The Journal of Agricultural
    Education and Extension*, 23(3), 213–229.
Kraaijenbrink, J., Spender, J.C., and Groen, A J. (2010), 'The resource-based view: A review
    and assessment of its critiques', *Journal of Management*, 36(1), 349–372.
Leick, B., and Lang, T. (2018), 'Re-thinking non-core regions: planning strategies and
    practices beyond growth', *European Planning Studies*, 26(2), 213–228.
Malecki, E.J. (2018), 'Entrepreneurship and entrepreneurial ecosystems', *Geography
    Compass*, 12(3), e12359.
Marshall, A. (1890/1920), 'Principles of Economics'. London: Macmillan and Co., Ltd.
    http://www.econlib.org/library/Marshall/marP.html. Accessed August 15, 2018.
Mayer, H., and Baumgartner, D. (2014), 'The role of entrepreneurship and innovation in
    peripheral regions', Guest Editorial, *The Planning Review*, 50(1), 16–23.
Merriam-Webster (2018), https://www.merriam-webster.com/dictionary/start-up. Accessed
    August 8, 2018.
Miles, M.B., and Huberman, A.M. (1994), *Qualitative Data Analysis: An Expanded
    Sourcebook*. Thousand Oaks, CA: Sage.
Ministry of Agriculture and Food (2015), 'Garden som ressurs – marknaden som mål. Vekst
    og gründerskap innan landbruksbaserte næringar', Meld.St.31 (2014–2015).
Moreno, A.M., and Casillas, J.C. (2007), 'High-growth SMEs versus non-high-growth
    SMEs: A discriminant analysis', *Entrepreneurship and Regional Development*, 19, 69 88.
Nason, R.S., and Wiklund, J. (2018), 'An assessment of resource-based theorizing on firm
    growth and suggestions for the future', *Journal of Management*, 44(1), 32–60.
Nauwelaers, C. (2011), 'Intermediaries in regional innovation systems: Role and chal-
    lenges for policy', In Cooke et al. (eds), *Handbook of Regional Innovation and Growth*.
    Cheltenham, UK, Edward Elgar, 467–481.
North, D., and Smallbone, D. (2006), 'Developing entrepreneurship and enterprise in
    Europe's peripheral rural areas: Some issues facing policy-makers', *European Planning
    Studies*, 14(1), 41–60.
Priem, R.L., and Butler, J.E. (2001), 'Is the resource-based "view" a useful perspective for
    strategic management research?' *Academy of Management Review*, 26, 22–40.
Rabinowicz, E., Ferguson, R., Kaspersson, E., and Lind, L. (2012), '*På spaning efter ett inno-
    vationssytem för landsbygdsföretag*', Rapport 2012:3. Lund: AgriFood economics Centre.
Roundy, P.T., and Fayard, D. (2019), 'Dynamic capabilities and entrepreneurial ecosystems:
    The micro-foundations of regional entrepreneurship', *The Journal of Entrepreneurship*,
    28(1), 94–120.
Schumpeter, J.A. (1934), *The Theory of Economic Development. An Inquiry into Profits
    Capital, Credit, Interest, and the Business Cycle*, London, Transaction publishers.
Sörensson, A., Dalborg, C., Grande, J., and Carlsson, E. (2018), 'Entreprenørskap i natur-
    baserte næringer – faktorer som fremmer og hemmer idéutvikling og sysselsetting', *Søkelys
    på arbeidslivet*, 35(3), 52–68.
Spigel, B. (2017), 'The relational organization of entrepreneurial ecosystems', *Entrepreneurship
    Theory and Practice*, 41(1), 49–72.
Spigel, B., and Harrison, R. (2018), 'Toward a process theory of entrepreneurial ecosystems',
    Strategic Entrepreneurship Journal, 12(1), 151–168.

Spilling, O.R. (1996), 'The entrepreneurial system: On entrepreneurship in the context of a mega-event', *Journal of Business Research*, 36(1), 91–103.

Stam, E. (2015), 'Entrepreneurial ecosystems and regional policy: A sympathetic critique', *European Planning Studies*, 23(9), 1759–1769.

Thagaard, T. (2013), 'Systematikk og innlevelse. En innføring i kvalitativ metode', 4. Utgave. Bergen, Fagbokforlaget, Vigmostad og Bjørke.

Todorova, G., and Durisin, B. (2007), 'Absorptive capacity: Valuing a reconceptualization', *The Academy of Management Review*, 32(3), 774–786.

Tödtling, F. and Trippl, M. (2005), 'One size fits all? Towards a differentiated regional innovation policy approach', *Research Policy*, 34, 1203–1219.

Vesala, K., Peura, J., and McElwee, G. (2007), 'The split entrepreneurial identity of the farmer', *Journal of Small Business and Enterprise Development*, 14, 48–63.

Zahra, S.A., and George, G. (2002), 'Absorptive capacity: A review, reconceptualization, and extension', Academy of Management. *The Academy of Management Review*, 27(2), 185–203.

6. Transnational entrepreneurial ecosystems: The perspectives of Finnish and Estonian born-global start-ups

Hannes Velt, Lasse Torkkeli, and Sami Saarenketo

INTRODUCTION

The entrepreneurial-ecosystem concept has gained much attention from scholars in diverse research disciplines during recent years (Maroufkhani, Wagner, & Wan Ismail, 2018); it is, however, still a young stream of research and lacks coherent insights required to expose how the ecosystem influences entrepreneurial activities and thus the consequent value creation. In previous decades, studies have focused on the established concepts of industrial districts, clusters and innovation systems to describe unique entrepreneurial environments (Autio, Nambisan, Thomas, & Wright, 2018). Yet, newer studies focusing on the co-creation of the setting and the aspirations of local entrepreneurs (Spigel & Harrison, 2018) have gained their place at the heart of international business and entrepreneurship studies. All the recent advancements in ecosystem contextualisation have been fruitful, however, Mack and Mayer (2016) argue that previous efforts to identify entrepreneurial ecosystems are still too narrow and are based on already well-performing communities, and that they should be updated to create the grounds for additional investigations focusing on the entrepreneurial entities.

Moreover, consensus on what constitutes a successful ecosystem has not yet been reached, thus there is a need to produce studies to better capture the phenomenon in full. For example, how are entrepreneurial environments constructed (Kshetri, 2014) and how do they promote entrepreneurially driven firms during rapid progress towards global markets (Acs, Audretsch, Lehmann, & Licht, 2016)? In addition, the advancement of new theoretical frameworks and views on the ecosystem construct would allow us to challenge the status quo and gain insights into the conditions supporting firm growth and international expansion across regional geographies (Zander, McDougall-Covin, & Rose, 2015). Hence, following venture creation in the regional entrepreneurial context (Acs,

Estrin, Mickiewicz, & Szerb, 2017; Alvedalen & Boschma, 2017; Cavusgil & Knight, 2015) would help us to elaborate the structural conditions (Stam, 2014) facilitating the risk-taking actions of entrepreneurs in finding opportunities to globally enhance societal value propositions.

Subsequently, to explore the entrepreneurial-ecosystem context, it is essential to understand the prerequisites affecting the entrepreneurial activities in developing enterprises whose business is globally scalable. Thus, exploring the ecosystem's structural elements through the views of the founders shaping the environment becomes the focal point. In other words, studying how rapidly internationalising firms develop in the entrepreneurial ecosystem and which elements are critical in supporting high-risk–high-reward activities (Cavallo, Ghezzi, & Balocco, 2018) would explain the uniqueness of the regional entrepreneurial ecosystems and how are they perceived by the entities operating in them. Therefore, the context becomes relevant and an appropriate setting should be chosen for further exploration.

Traditionally, international growth-oriented firms that have a strong capability towards creating an innovation-driven environment (Cannone & Ughetto, 2014) are common in countries with small domestic markets (Kuivalainen, Saarenketo, Torkkeli, & Puumalainen, 2015; Luostarinen & Gabrielsson, 2006). However, as smallness often refers to deficiencies, entrepreneurial ecosystems tend to share and compete for the same resources (e.g. human capital). Fortunately, unlike many regions in the world, in the European Union, the free movement of labour is part of the four economic freedoms (European Union, 2012). This is a strong enabler for small countries to compete over and acquire appropriate resources. In the light of this transformative process, there is potential for transnational entrepreneurship (Bailetti, 2018; Lundberg & Rehnfors, 2018). As small ecosystems are bound to share resources, they may perhaps converge certain goals and policies, and create a transnational entrepreneurial ecosystem on the regional level.

Considering the above, countries such as Finland and Estonia would be good case examples, as both are small economies while being start-up-intensive and familiar with nurturing "unicorn" (i.e. start-ups valued at over 1 billion dollars) born-global start-ups (BGs; e.g. Rovio, Supercell, Skype, TransferWise and Bolt). Finland and Estonia, both Finnic nations, could be considered a transnational region with a substantial human resource concentration in their capital regions (Sergeevich & Alekseevna, 2015), making these countries share and complement their sources of goods, services, labour and capital. This, in turn, enables them to collaborate and create economic synergies (Nauwelaers, Maguire, & Marsan, 2013) and form the antecedents for the integration of regional skills and capabilities. Hence, it is relevant to look at these entrepreneurial ecosystems from the transnational viewpoint (Velt, Torkkeli, & Saarenketo, 2018b) to determine what makes these converging environments unique from the vantage point of local entrepreneurs and how they support the internationalisation of high-growth firms.

Subsequently, there is a need for further exploration regarding how transnational entrepreneurial ecosystems and their structural elements influence BG start-up development. In addition, it is suitable to examine how specific characteristics of a firm impact the perceptions of the regional ecosystem by focusing on intra-group attributes, such as age, team size and allocation, revenue reach, product-service orientation, ownership origin, rapidity of internationalisation and market scope. Along these lines, the present study aims to address how an incubating ecosystem augments and encourages BG start-ups' development and internationalisation by seeking answers to two research questions (RQs) in particular:

RQ1. Which elements of the transnational ecosystem are critical for BG progress during the early stages?

RQ2. How do BG perceptions differ depending on the intra-group characteristics?

The remainder of the study is structured as follows: In the next section, we review key concepts and outline the research methodology, after which the results are presented. In the last section, we discuss our findings with respect to the RQs and conclude with the theoretical and managerial implications, limitations of the study and avenues for future research.

ENTREPRENEURIAL ECOSYSTEMS AND BORN-GLOBALS

The concept of an entrepreneurial ecosystem was proposed late in the last century (Bahrami & Evans, 1995; Moore, 1993; Spilling, 1996; Van De Ven, 1993) as more reputable concepts (e.g. clusters and networks) were found to have limitations for elaborating the role of the entrepreneur in the local economic context (O'Connor, Stam, Sussan, & Audretsch, 2017). Hence, in recent years, the entrepreneurial ecosystem has gained renewed attention (Acs, Szerb, Lafuente, & Lloyd, 2018; Autio et al., 2018; O'Connor et al., 2017; Spigel & Harrison, 2018) to comprehend how the local environment nurtures the entrepreneurial lifeforce. Thus, the entrepreneurial ecosystem has been defined as a "combination of social, political, economic and cultural elements within a region that support the development and growth of innovative start-ups and encourage nascent entrepreneurs and other actors to take the risks of starting, funding and otherwise assisting high-risk ventures" (Spigel, 2017, p. 50). Based on Stam's (2015) belief regarding the surrounding ecosystem, there are two sets of conditions relevant for nurturing entrepreneurial activities on the framework and systemic levels. Framework conditions (i.e. governmental institutions, culture of the local community, physical infrastructure and access to demand) guide the systemic level. Whereas, systemic conditions (i.e. leadership, finance, talent, knowledge, networks and support setting) are the key core of the ecosystem and the driving force behind BG firm development by directly regulating the interactions between individuals. Henceforth, we use Velt, Torkkeli, and Saarenketo's (2018a) view of the systemic elements and sub-elements to elaborate the local context. However, as we have proposed a two-country context where both systems are sharing resources across a border, we introduce a "transnational" dimension to the context and refer to it as a transnational entrepreneurial ecosystem.

Moreover, entrepreneurial activities, domestic or international, are processes that encompass "the discovery, evaluation and exploitation of opportunities for creating future goods and services" (Shane & Venkataraman, 2000, p. 218), however, these processes commence on home ground. Hence, local conditions are relevant for capturing the creation of value and nurturing the needs of new ventures under conditions of resource scarcity (Sasi & Arenius, 2012) and rapid progress (Nummela, Saarenketo, & Loane, 2016). In addition, constant attention is placed on growth-oriented ventures in the current literature on entrepreneurial ecosystems (Alvedalen & Boschma, 2017; Mason & Brown, 2014). Thus, focusing on BG firms (Knight & Cavusgil, 2005; Oviatt & McDougall, 1994) in the entrepreneurial-ecosystem context is a suitable approach to take as BG refers to the most prospective start-ups internationalising from the local ecosystem to create global value "through the identification and exploitation of opportunities that cross national borders" (Peiris, Akoorie, & Sinha, 2012, p. 296). However, to shed light on the dynamic relationships and aspects of the ecosystem influencing BGs, it is important to concentrate on the criticality of the elements and how they affect the processes in each of the firm's life-cycle stages. Thus, we chose the Marmer Stages (Marmer, Herrmann, Dogrultan, & Berman, 2011) that have been widely used by practitioners in start-up communities. Therefore, we focus on the first stages of discovery and validation, arguably because the regional ecosystem has its strongest influence on BGs as they are still homebound while being launched and supported with the aim of starting rapid internationalisation. Broadly put, the discovery stage includes entrepreneurial processes involved in forming and launching new BG start-ups, and the validation stage includes the authentication activities of the offer and visible expansion into foreign markets.

Subsequently, by incorporating all sides of the framework, we elaborate the ecosystem's systemic structure in the international entrepreneurship context to comprehend the relevance of such elements for the wider setting and mainly for BGs. All the systemic elements have received attention in the international entrepreneurship literature (e.g. leadership, see Mets, 2015; financial capital, see Gabrielsson, Kirpalani, Dimitratos, Solberg, & Zucchella, 2008; Gabrielsson, Sasi, & Darling, 2004; talent, see Jantunen, Nummela, Puumalainen, & Saarenketo, 2008; Luostarinen & Gabrielsson, 2004; networks, see Gabrielsson & Kirpalani, 2004; Laanti, Gabrielsson, & Gabrielsson, 2007; knowledge, see Gabrielsson et al., 2008; Loane, Bell, & McNaughton, 2007; Rialp, Galván-Sánchez, & García, 2012; support, see Harrington, 2017; Pauwels, Clarysse, Wright, & Van Hove, 2016). However, these studies have tended to examine only one or a couple of the systemic elements at a time, thus neglecting the role of the entrepreneurial ecosystem from a holistic point of view, which would thus enable considering the effects of all its respective elements. Hence, it is important to clarify how a transnational ecosystem powers entrepreneurial internationalisation (Andersson, Evers, & Griot, 2013; Coviello, 2006) and to elaborate the relations between the structure of the system and its influence on the development and subsequent value for BG firms (Alvedalen & Boschma, 2017; Stam, 2015).

There are six main domains of systemic elements (Stam, 2014) and it is necessary to subdivide some of them to elaborate their relevance for the life-cycle stages of the BGs (Velt et al., 2018a). These elements are entrepreneurial leadership, financial capital sub-elements, two types of talent, knowledge as a singular concept, networks and sub-elements of the support services. Therefore, we briefly explain all of them, starting with entrepreneurial leadership, which is defined as "influencing and directing the performance of group members toward the achievement of organisational goals that involve recognising and exploring entrepreneurial opportunities" (Renko, El Tarabishy, Carsrud, & Brännback, 2015, p. 55). In the context of this study, this leadership is visible in the ecosystem, as established entrepreneurs motivate others to follow in their footsteps. Also, it trickles down to the firm level as the founders reflect their leadership abilities on their team members. These entrepreneurial leaders are crucial for a healthy ecosystem to create strong firms (Feld, 2012; Mets, 2015; Vissak, 2007).

Furthermore, financial capital is one of the main topics affecting firm growth and progress (Gabrielsson et al., 2004). There are multiple ways to raise capital or to secure financial resources creatively without lending money or selling equity such as empowering bootstrapping or minimising funding need (Harrison, Mason, & Girling, 2004). Yet, in the context of rapidly evolving BG start-ups, the founders need to raise capital from lenders (e.g. credit institutions, family and friends) and from equity investors (e.g. business angels [BAs], venture capitalists). Lenders usually use official collateral requirements to allocate a credit line and run their due diligence to assess the risks (Winton & Yerramilli, 2008). However, family and friends behave similarly (Chua, Chrisman, Kellermanns, & Wu, 2011; Wu, Steven, & Wu, 2016) while using trust as a form of collateral. However, it is not only about lending capital, but also holding an equity stake to directly engage in the firm's activities. Thus, previous sources should not be considered as strategic partners, instead equity investors should, like BAs, who use a hands-on approach to improve the firm's survival (Kerr, Lerner, & Schoar, 2014) by providing "seed capital" (Wong, Bhatia, & Freeman, 2009). Similarly, venture capital (VC) firms and corporate VC (CVC) investors utilise their networks to back their investment and use their extensive knowledge and capabilities to enhance the success of the firms (Denis, 2004; Kaplan & Strömberg, 2000). The main difference with the latter two is that CVC investors have corporate agendas and often integrate the focal company into their business platform ecosystem (e.g. GAFA) (Miguel & Casado, 2016). In addition, the most recent concept of "crowdfunding" is a way to raise capital from many individuals over the internet at once (Mollick, 2014) and has become a valid substitute for other forms of capital sources.

Moreover, every city, region and country has its own talent pool that is considered a critical resource for firm development and consequent success in the ecosystem (Cohen, 2006; Stam, 2014). Hence, talent is fundamental for creating entrepreneurial activities and often becomes visible in diverse and open societies (Lee, Florida, & Acs, 2004), thus talented individuals attract others to join their efforts in creating a sustainable environment to thrive in (Bahrami & Evans, 1995; Cohen, 2006). In addition, welcoming societies have an agglomeration of such talent, which creates the right conditions for the launch and growth of new ventures (Thomas, Sharapov, & Autio, 2018). However, when the opposite deglomeration occurs, potential entrepreneurs tend to move out from such environments to establish their businesses in another location where there is an abundance of talented people to hire and collaborate with (Neck, Meyer, Cohen, & Corbett, 2004), thus making talent critical for new venture success (Drexler et al., 2014).

Correspondingly, with the movement of talent, specific and appropriate knowledge moves into the entrepreneurial ecosystem. The knowledge build-up under resource constraints (Oviatt & McDougall, 1994) helps in recognising opportunities, which entrepreneurs then exploit by creating new innovations and building firms around novel solutions. However, knowledge creation does not usually happen in isolation (Huggins & Thompson, 2015), rather the entities capture the knowledge spill-overs by externally screening for innovations (Katila, 2002). Thus, entrepreneurs recognise opportunities by exploiting these spill-overs and then create new ventures to convert this revealed knowledge into commercial knowledge (Acs, Audretsch, & Lehmann, 2013). In parallel, the needed knowledge, information, resources, activities and capabilities are shared and acquired from a complex set of relationships among the entrepreneurs and network participants. Thus, there is a need for established networks that are "defined by the enduring exchange relations established between organisations, individuals and groups" (Weber & Khademian, 2008, p. 334) inside and extending outside of the local entrepreneurial ecosystem.

Last of all, there is a set of support conditions that needs to be present to cater to the needs of entrepreneurial firms such as consulting services, intermediaries, networking providers and engagement events. Consultants are "a sophisticated service infrastructure [that] allows start-up firms to focus on their chosen steeple of expertise, rather than dissipate their energies across a broad range of peripheral or supporting activities" (Bahrami & Evans, 1995, p. 63), meaning that entrepreneurs should focus on their core activities and outsource the rest. Zhang and Li (2010) argued that firms' innovation capability is related to professionals who share new knowledge, information on inventions, and reduce costs (McEvily & Zaheer, 1999) and mitigate the risks of disrupting the innovation process (Saxenian, 1990).

Similarly, intermediaries provide "support to start-ups to improve the probability of survival of the portfolio companies and accelerate their development" (Pauwels et al., 2016, p. 14). Incubators target very early-stage firms with greenhorn founders with scalable business models (Isabelle, 2013; Stagars, 2014) and accelerators focus on already established fast-tracking knowledge-intensive ventures (Bosma & Stam, 2012; Pauwels et al., 2016) by validating their businesses. Likewise, there is a set of network mediators (e.g. industry associations, alumni) which provides networking support and smoothens out information exchange and other interactions (Howells, 2006; Suresh & R. Ramraj, 2012) to enable new firms to gather the required resources. In addition, engagement services play a crucial role in motivating firms to launch. These meeting events enable entrepreneurs and community members to collaborate, initiate, pursue and combine new innovations (e.g. via start-up weekends and hackathons) (Feld, 2012; Harrington, 2017).

In sum, all the above-mentioned elements reflect the ecosystem's moral and inspirational conditions and highlight the value of the resources essential for developing business proposals based on the newest technological advancements. These forces are accessed, enriched, upheld and enabled by relationships between stakeholders, who in turn are supported early on to reach sustainable growth and development in the transnational entrepreneurial-ecosystem setting.

RESEARCH METHODOLOGY

The list of BG start-ups for the empirical part of this study was extracted and combined from a set of secondary sources: Startup 100, Crunchbase, FunderBeam and ActicStartup. All the firms found in the databases have been certified by start-up community leaders and investors, affirming that these firms possess the potential to become next-generation BG ventures. We introduced the stratified sampling method (cf. Neyman, 1934) to only target firms that had reached the second life-cycle stage of validation to account for their timely knowledge regarding both of the preliminary stages. Further, we applied the online survey method and managed to gather responses from 51 founders from Finland and 33 from Estonia. As the sample collection only targeted BG start-ups, we then verified their speed of internationalisation, market scope and export extent (Kuivalainen, Saarenketo, & Puumalainen, 2012). However, we were less strict regarding the requirement for BG to be present in at least two continents (cf. Luostarinen & Gabrielsson, 2006; Nummela, Saarenketo, Jokela, & Loane, 2014) as this is arguably inessential in a small country context (Choquette, Rask, Sala, & Schröder, 2017). In addition, as we were looking at the first stages of the life-cycle, some of the firms had no revenue as they were still less than three years old and had become international via other value-chain activities (e.g. global team allocation, integration to platform ecosystem).

Additionally, we controlled for the common method bias (Podsakoff, MacKenzie, Lee, & Podsakoff, 2003). When composing the survey, it was important to elaborate the elements and split some of them into sub-elements (i.e. financial capital, talent and support systems) to make clear distinctions and comparisons. Hence, this distinction ensured that the respondents would assess the elements as objectively as possible based on their own experience, allowing for the mitigation of the common method bias risk. In addition, we conducted Harman's single factor test and did not detect any individual factor that was solely influencing the results. Hence, we argue that there were no obvious issues with the common method bias.

Furthermore, we developed a set of metrics (cf. Audretsch & Belitski, 2017; Corrente, Greco, Nicotra, Romano, & Schillaci, 2018; Liguori, Bendickson, Solomon, & McDowell, 2019) measuring the elements and sub-elements on a 100-point slider scale. We asked respondents to assess the criticality of the elements from 0 being non-critical and 100 very critical. Questions were in line with "How critical are engagement events for discovery stage?" and "How critical is venture capital for validation stage?". This allowed us to clearly demonstrate which elements were ranked as essential for the preliminary stages of the BG life-cycle. Then, to answer RQ1, all mean averages were calculated for each element in its discovery and validation stage for both countries combined. These arithmetic means were then used to calculate the aggregate equivalents as cut-off points to distinguish the critical elements from the non-critical ones associated with the firm's progress.

Thereafter, to answer RQ2, we collected data on multiple intra-group characteristics of the entrepreneurial firms regarding their organisational (i.e. age, team size, service-product orientation, revenue) and international features (i.e. team allocation, origin of the owners, speed of internationalisation, market scope) and divided the firms into binary groups. These characteristics elaborate how ecosystem elements have influenced BG development. We then applied an analysis of variance (ANOVA) to compare the statistical significance of the entrepreneurial perceptions to verify if there were any discrepancies in terms of how these firms interpreted their environment. Resulting from the above steps, we could then answer the RQs by identifying which elements were most critical for firm development and how BGs were influenced by the ecosystem during life-cycle stages, depending on their characteristics.

FINDINGS

The findings were divided into two sections corresponding to the RQs (see Table 6.1). In the first section, we arranged the elements in descending order based on their mean average values. This was essential to visualise the position of the elements and their rank in both stages. Then, after calculating the cut-off points, it became clear that there were six elements that were critical for both stages (i.e. entrepreneurial talent, knowledge, leadership, networks, worker talent and BAs), five were non-critical for advancement (i.e. intermediaries, networking services, crowdfunding, CVC, credit institution) and five were in a transition mode (i.e. informal debt, bootstrapping, engagement services, consultants, VC). In terms of the latter elements, their positions changed by around ten places with a deviation of up to 31.67 points (i.e. VC), indicating that the elements' configuration for BG development effectively changed when they moved from one stage to the other.

Table 6.1 Results

Results [Q1 & Q2] Elements	Criticality Rank [Q1] St.1.	St.2.	Δ	Mean Values [Scale 0-100] St.1.	St.2.	Δ	ANOVA [Q2] BG Characteristics	Stages [1&2] #	Stat.Sign [**;*;-] Coeff.	Mean Deviations [0;1] 0	1	Δ	Sd
Entrepreneurial Talent	1.	1.	0	85.83	84.75	-1.08	—	—	—	—	—	—	—
Knowledge	2.	2.	0	77.70	82.98	5.28	Age [0=4→6; 1=0→3]	St.1.	-0.207*	82.64	73.81	-8.83	21.27
							Team Size [0=1→9; 1=10→...]	St.1.	0.208*	73.98	82.91	8.93	21.27
							Revenue [0= pre-revenue; 1=revenue]	St.2.	-0.272*	88.84	80.49	-8.35	14.09
							Firm Offer [0=product; 1=service]	St.2.	0.170*	80.54	85.30	4.76	14.09
							# of Markets [0=5→9; 1=10→...]	St.2.	0.142*	81.17	85.16	3.99	14.09
Informal Debt	3.	13.	-10	77.07	47.21	-29.86	Age [0=4→6; 1=0→3]	St.1.	0.292*	69.68	82.89	13.21	22.60
							Ownership Origin [0=home; 1=foreign]	St.1.	0.166*	73.33	80.81	7.48	22.60
							Team Allocation [0= local; 1=global]	St.2.	-0.142*	71.33	64.87	-6.46	22.79
Leadership	4.	6.	-2	73.13	68.33	-4.80	—	—	—	—	—	—	—
Bootstrapping	5.	10.	-5	68.46	76.24	7.78	—	—	—	—	—	—	—
Networks	6.	4.	+2	68.46	76.24	7.78	—	—	—	—	—	—	—
Worker Talent	7.	3.	+4	64.70	81.67	16.97	—	—	—	—	—	—	—
Engagement Services	8.	12.	-5	64.31	52.89	-11.42	Revenue [0=pre-revenue; 1=revenue]	St.1.	0.230*	54.68	68.39	13.71	27.43
Business Angels	9.	7.	+2	61.37	62.57	1.20	Age [0=4→6; 1=0→3]	St.2.	0.154*	58.54	65.74	7.20	23.34
							Internationalization [0=1→3; 1=0→1]	St.2.	-0.222**	68.37	58.00	-10.37	23.34
Intermediaries	10.	11.	-1	52.76	55.01	2.25	—	—	—	—	—	—	—
Networking Services	11.	9.	+2	45.00	56.67	11.67	Ownership Origin [0=home; 1=foreign]	St.1.	0.228*	39.00	51.00	12.00	26.45
Consultants	12.	8.	+4	44.11	61.50	17.39	—	—	—	—	—	—	—
Venture Capital	13.	5.	+8	41.62	73.29	31.67	Ownership Origin [0=home; 1=foreign]	St.1.	0.220*	34.86	48.38	13.52	31.00
Crowdfunding	14.	15.	-1	35.87	42.02	6.15	—	—	—	—	—	—	—
Corp Venture Capital	15.	14.	+1	21.95	46.56	24.61	Revenue [0=pre-revenue; 1=revenue]	St.1.	-0.209*	29.52	18.75	-10.77	23.66
							Ownership Origin [0=home; 1=foreign]	St.1.	0.264*	15.74	28.17	12.43	23.66
Credit Institution	16.	16.	0	19.35	31.62	12.27	Internationalization [0=1→3; 1=0→1]	St.2.	-0.197*	37.78	26.77	-11.01	27.88
Cut-off points				56.57	61.17								

Note: (**) $p<0.01$;(*) $p<.05$; (−) no stat. sign. difference among BGs

119

Furthermore, in the second section, it was imperative to explore if there was any intra-group contrast in these perceived rankings. Ergo, we needed to analyse firms' intra-group variance to detect if there was any disparity among their characteristics. We applied the ANOVA method to analyse the 16 ecosystem elements in the context of eight BG attributes. Intra-group variance was detected for more than half of the elements, indicating that firms had assorted perceptions towards their entrepreneurial ecosystem. We found nine distinctions in the discovery stage and seven in the validations stage, of which two were statistically significant at the 1 per cent level and 14 were significant at the 5 per cent level. However, the ANOVA results explain the background of the relationship as none of the intra-group perceptions changed the ranking from critical to non-critical and vice versa. In addition, the correlation coefficients were not measurable because we compared continuous dependent variables with binary independent variables and thus utilised point-scale deviations to demonstrate their significance.

In summary, the above results revealed that some elements were more critical than others under transnational conditions, and intra-group variations explained the contextual differences in how these elements influenced BG launches and their consequent internationalisation. All these results will now be discussed in detail.

DISCUSSION

The RQs of this study examine the ecosystem elements by exploring their criticality levels for BG development and how BGs perceive these elements in various ways depending on their intra-group characteristics. Also, it is rational to discuss each element independently in the transnational entrepreneurial-ecosystem context to attain a sound outline of the results.

Leadership

Leadership (particularly entrepreneurial leaders in the ecosystem context) is considered as influential individuals who share their experience in discovering and exploiting opportunities for value creation with their community and indirectly with the rest of the world (Greenberg, McKone-Sweet, & Wilson, 2011). In this study framework, it became clear that the leadership element was critical for BG development in the preliminary stages. This stable influence is in line with the previous research indicating that entrepreneurial leaders should become role models for others and motivate them (McGrath & MacMillan, 2013) to embrace creativity

(Cardon, Wincent, Singh, & Drnovsek, 2009) and work towards entrepreneurial objectives and activities (Gupta, MacMillan, & Surie, 2004; Yukl, 2008). However, leadership in some sense is limited to the local context, thus this is why the ANOVA results indicated that BGs with local teams were more exposed to the leadership element during validation processes. From another perspective, BGs with team members allocated across borders have arguably commenced internationalisation activities and therefore perceive leadership as less critical for the validation stage. The above results are in line with Mets (2015), who argued that leadership is a main factor for early internationalisation, hence its high ranking in both stages and the visible discrepancy for already internationalised firms.

Finance

Entrepreneurial finance focuses on BGs' decision to raise financial capital. Entrepreneurs create innovations and transform these into viable products and services (Burgelman & Hitt, 2008). As this process is time-dependant (Suddaby, Bruton, & Si, 2015) and requires immense amounts of capital investment (Ebben & Johnson, 2006), this action of commercialisation (Luostarinen & Gabrielsson, 2006) makes financial capital a primary element for progress. Overall, our results are in line with the above reasoning as some elements are efficient in the first stage and others in the second. However, as there are multiple sources of capital, it is crucial to explore which of them matter for BGs.

Our results suggest that informal debt and bootstrapping are critical for the discovery stage, but as they cannot cope with the speed of commercialisation and the cash burn-rate, these elements become non-critical for the validation stage. The ANOVA suggests that younger BGs value informal debt as more critical than older BGs do. This clearly indicates that high-risk investments and raising capital from the inner circle have been accepted by the local community to support BG development. Confidence is determined as collateral and failures are accepted as part of the learning process. In addition, it is interesting to note that BGs with foreign equity investors perceive informal debt as more critical. Perhaps founders with solid business plans are confident in raising capital from their family and friends, as otherwise they would risk harming their relationships. Thus, this degree of legitimacy generates trust among and is attractive to professional investors.

Moreover, BAs and VC are more suited for commercialisation in the second stage, as they improve firm survival, integrate new talent and lead to higher online visibility and traction, while simultaneously consulting and extending founders' networks (Kerr et al., 2014; Luostarinen &

Gabrielsson, 2006). Our results indicate that BAs are critical in both stages as they are considered as the region's own private investors who invest "seed capital" (Chemmanur & Fulghieri, 2014; Wong et al., 2009) and support the development from there. This is visible in the validation stage, as the results demonstrate that younger start-ups perceive BAs as more critical, denoting that these consortiums of investors have become a suitable source of finance for BG growth. However, BGs that have internationalised during their first year after inception find BAs less critical than others do. This is an indication that BAs have tendencies to constrain aggressive scaling, which instead is in line with the strategies of VC (Gabrielsson et al., 2004). Thus, our results clearly support the previous statement that VC is one of the principal elements in the validation stage and a prerequisite for successful internationalisation. Nevertheless, intra-group perceptions reveal that VC is more critical for BGs with foreign equity shareholders in the first stage compared to BGs with only local owners. This suggests that BGs backed by foreign equity owners are more open, have already attracted VC funding (Gabrielsson et al., 2008), or local founders just might feel reluctant to share their business in the discovery stage, or the BG business model is not yet suited to VC strategies.

Other sources such as crowdfunding, CVC and credit institutions were not found to be critical in supporting BG development. Crowdfunding is one of the newest popular ways to raise funding (Mollick, 2014), however, as it is rather understudied (Maroufkhani et al., 2018), our results suggest that there might be a mismatch between "smart" and "capital" for founders, making such online platforms non-critical. We argue that the information potential investors receive is ambiguous, that they might easily lose their money due to high default rates, and for the founders, it does not include the required benefits of monitoring, advising, teaching, recruiting and connecting with the right people when compared to VC and BAs (Chemmanur & Fulghieri, 2014).

CVC is also seen as less critical, which might be due to its formal strategy of only targeting BGs suitable for longitudinal investment plans and aligned with corporate strategies. The ANOVA reveals that CVC is attractive for BGs with foreign equity owners, similarly to VC, except CVC's strategic position differs. However, an interesting find is that BGs with pre-revenue status perceive CVC as more critical for their discovery stage than those with revenue do. The simplest explanation could be that CVC firms only target BGs that can be integrated into their business ecosystems (e.g. Microsoft acquiring Skype, Facebook acquiring WhatsApp), making other BGs in the sample rank them less critically. As BG development incorporates high levels of uncertainty and risk (Gabrielsson et al., 2008), we argue that firms with complex product-services and longer R&D time horizons perceive CVC as a stable environment, where the focus is on building meaningful solutions for platform bundling and is less on making money straight away.

Lastly, the results show that credit institutions were ranked as the lowest form of capital source, arguably because first-time entrepreneurs lack the collateral instruments and proven track record, thus making them less attractive for the credit institutions (Zott & Huy, 2007). This is further verified by the intra-group perspectives, as highly rapid internationalising firms perceived these institutions as inhibitors of internationalisation compared to standard BGs, probably because any kind of a constraint on cash flow would hinder momentum and progress. Concluding the results on capital sources, it is apparent that informal types of funding are more critical in the first stage, formal ones for scaling and internationalisation, and traditional and online institutions were not seen as critical for BG development because they lack the hands-on approach, personal connection and cannot directly commit to the success of the new venture.

Talent

Talent is one of the main resources for firm development, as entrepreneurs are the ones initiating BGs and driving them, while worker talent is considered as a spectrum of specialists in their respective fields who join the venture when the tasks become too complex for the founders to handle alone. Hence, there is a direct connection between talent and well-performing start-ups (Rauch & Rijsdijk, 2013; Talaia, Pisoni, & Onetti, 2016).

The results indicate that entrepreneurial talent is the most critical element in BG development in both stages. The statement that founders with proactive mindsets search for opportunities and create innovations while taking a substantial risk (cf. Kuivalainen, Sundqvist, & Servais, 2007; Nummela, Saarenketo, & Puumalainen, 2010; Vissak, 2007) received support in the empirical analysis. Worker talent is slightly less critical in the discovery stage but becomes highly critical when validation begins. Hence, founders take charge in the first stage and as the processes become more complex, talented people will be integrated to create synergies and together confront the challenges.

Knowledge

Knowledge is the fundamental source and driving force of modern communities shaped by dynamic innovation processes (Acs et al., 2016). BGs leverage their inner capabilities to learn and create new knowledge to develop unique and specialised products and services (Gabrielsson &

Kirpalani, 2004). Our results confirm that knowledge accumulation is highly critical for both stages. However, there are some intra-group differences. In the discovery stage, for younger firms, specific knowledge is essential, but other abilities (e.g. raising less restrictive capital, composing a team and extending networks) also take on a principal role during firm establishment. In contrast, BGs with larger teams perceive knowledge as more critical than smaller ones do. Arguably, the more sophisticated the business model becomes, the more talent with appropriate knowledge is integrated, making the team's composition and volume essential to run the tasks. In the validation stage, BGs with revenue streams perceive knowledge as less critical compared to pre-revenue firms. The difference in perception could be based on the timeline, as pre-revenue firms can still conduct knowledge-intensive R&D activities. Hence, as the product-service is not yet marketable, revenue is absent. Similarly, service-oriented BGs stated that knowledge was more critical for product-oriented ventures. We suggest that service firms are vulnerable to demand fluctuations due to their shorter time-to-market periods, making them arbitrarily flexible so that they can respond promptly to constantly changing market requirements. In addition, firms with more than ten markets perceive knowledge as more critical. Resilient international aspirations require a certain mix of knowledge and capabilities to retain a strong market presence (Rialp et al., 2012). Thus, expansion via learning-by-doing is a distinctive factor for BGs with a stronger market presence.

Networks

Networks are relational structures that entrepreneurs and other community participants engage inside and outside the local ecosystem to link and share information, activities, resources and capabilities to fulfil the requirements for BG development (Mort & Weerawardena, 2006; Zhou, Wu, & Luo, 2007). The results from this study confirm that the network element in the ecosystem is also critical for the early development of BGs in both stages. This is in line with the results from previous research arguing that there is a direct connection between building and leveraging networks in the early stages to sustain successful growth (Gabrielsson & Kirpalani, 2004; Laanti et al., 2007) and facilitate rapid internationalisation (Gabrielsson et al., 2008).

Support Services

Support services play a crucial role in sustaining the development and speeding up internationalisation for BG-type start-ups (Zhang & Li,

2010). Our study concentrated on the elements of consultants, intermediaries, networking and engagement services. Consultants, a set of external specialists, deliver different kinds of support services to BGs, so the teams can concentrate on what matters the most and less on bureaucracy. According to the results, these services were non-critical during the first stage and critical in the second stage. Hence, this corresponds to the idea that BGs handle their issues themselves in the beginning, however, external help becomes more relevant when complexities increase and different support and professional services are looked for (Luostarinen & Gabrielsson, 2006).

Furthermore, intermediaries such as incubators and accelerators form micro-ecosystems to integrate BG start-ups. In both stages, these mediators were ranked just below the cut-off line, making them non-critical for supporting BG development. Previous research has found that these intermediaries play a critical role in firm development and in improving their survival rates and accelerating their development (Feld, 2012; Pauwels et al., 2016). Our argument is that as we focus on small economies, their relative insufficiencies are visible on the incubator and accelerator level. In other words, when the local environment functions under resource constraints and shorter external networks, these micro-entities encounter comparable issues. Hence, the quality and quantity of intermediaries reflects the quaintness of the local ecosystem.

Networking services support entrepreneurs to find needed resources from their own networks and mediate information and other exchanges to enable further development. From the results, these services were found to be non-critical, but they still influenced and benefited the ecosystem (Saxenian, 1990; Suresh & R. Ramraj, 2012). We suggest this is because these services do not satisfy the BG requirements as ecosystems in periphery regions have shorter network nodes. The intra-group difference shows that, during the discovery stage, firms with foreign equity investors view networking services as more critical than others do. Hence, we argue that foreign stakeholders themselves can behave as the network extension for the firm. These services (e.g. alumni organisations) might in fact have been the key for foreign capital entry in the first place.

Lastly, engagement events are held to build social relationships between entrepreneurs and other community contributors to uncover and pursue innovation frontiers. We realised that engagement services are critical in the discovery stage and non-critical during validation. Hence, these events are appropriate for creating new BGs by finding new team members and initial investors, but less relevant for validating business ideas and scaling. Previous studies have made clear that these events are significant to healthy ecosystems (Feld, 2012; Harrington, 2017). The ANOVA detected that BGs with revenue streams perceived these events as more critical in the discovery stage than the pre-revenue firms did. This difference explicitly shows that BG participation has a positive effect on achieving revenue streams. Hence, the appropriate team composition and generating captivating business propositions lead to successful sales activities. In sum, even though some of the elements were not depicted to be as critical as others were, they are all relevant in forming and sustaining a healthy entrepreneurial ecosystem in the transnational setting.

CONCLUSION

Reflecting on the decades of research on entrepreneurial environments, scholars have studied how to nurture entrepreneurial action in various ways. One of these focal points has been the entrepreneurial-ecosystem construct, which, unlike others, directly influences entrepreneurial activities in launching and growing rapidly internationalising firms. These systems consist of structural elements that each play their role in fostering the needs of a new venture. Therefore, our exploratory study aimed to shed more light on the arrangements in terms of how these ecosystems influence BG start-ups during the preliminary stages of a firm's life-cycle. We took the transnational viewpoint of two small economies sharing their regional resources, thus unintentionally converging their environments towards a more sustainable arrangement.

Theoretical Contribution

The entrepreneurial-ecosystem construct is a topic that has gained momentum in recent years, as researchers, practitioners and policy makers, among others, would like to figure out how to construct and sustain environments that are innovation-driven and focus on value creation for the global society. Therefore, we wanted to explore the topic by integrating the entrepreneurial ecosystem, BGs and life-cycle studies into one framework to comprehend how the ecosystem's structural elements influence the development of rapidly internationalising firms during their stages of life (Alvedalen & Boschma, 2017; Malecki, 2018). This framework is not new per se (cf. Velt et al., 2018b, 2018a), however, it takes an original perspective. Specifically, we integrate a new dimension of "transnational" into the entrepreneurial-ecosystem context. The relevance is that we focus on two countries that have a high concentration of BG start-ups, and as these economies are situated in close proximity, there is an allusion of convergence. This opens a new study avenue to explore transnational aspects of the ecosystems, but also the effects of regional agglomeration and successive deglomeration.

Furthermore, we assessed the ecosystem level in a balanced manner (Mack & Mayer, 2016) by analysing all the main elements in one study framework and concentrating on the combined perceptions of BG founders to elaborate how these entrepreneurs sense their transnational environment. In detail, we focused on the configurations of criticality (Cavallo et al., 2018) to see which systemic elements were necessary in the regional context to support rapidly internationalising firms. It was appropriate to elaborate these criticality levels based on the intra-group differences of the firms to gather new insights into which elements and their combinations in the various stages should be emphasised to improve the nurturing surroundings when launching new ventures with global aspirations. The division of the stages exposed an increasingly complex view of ecosystem interactions.

Practical Implications

For entrepreneurs, our results elaborate how the transnational ecosystem behaves in a regional setting. Defining the critical elements in the preliminary stages would familiarise ecosystem participants regarding where the emphasis should be directed when launching and growing new ventures. These results inaugurate a layout of the ecosystem so that novice entrepreneurs can clearly identify where to allocate their time and effort. For example, they should try to raise capital from established sources such as BAs and VC, rather than spending time with credit institutions and crowdfunding. Similarly, the firm's business model and strategy implementations play a crucial role in the success of a venture, thus, participating in the engagement events will raise the firm's potential to better secure revenue streams.

For governments and policy makers, they should try to create a supportive set of regulations that will counter the shortcomings of the local entrepreneurial environment. As the discussion is about the formulation of a transnational setting, all relevant institutions should start to align their goals and introduce common strategies to benefit the regional ecosystem. For example, the free movement of talent between the countries happens daily, however, it is not easy for start-ups to officially relocate as corporate regulations and laws are rather different. Hence, it is important to create a common framework and support the set-up for rapidly internationalising firms as they are on the frontline of creating new jobs and societal value. It would be a strong advantage for Finnish ICT start-ups to directly hire Estonian talent for their e-governance units without having to deal with tax-compliance issues, or for a new Estonian gene-tech firm to apply for funding from Finnish state grants as there is no considerable equivalent in Estonia. Thus, creating common policies would benefit both nations in the long-run by sharing the innovation capacity.

Limitations and Future Research

The current study is exploratory and stays relatively descriptive by focusing on the best-in-the-class firms such as BGs. Hence, there should be other studies introducing and comparing the perceptions of other types of firms which are rapidly internationalising but have not achieved BG status. Likewise, based on the firm type, a configuration study would be of great benefit to reveal the modifications of the ecosystem elements required. In addition, it is essential to dig deeper and prepare case studies to understand more about the founders' experience in terms of why some elements are more critical than others are and how intra-group differences have played out in real life.

Additionally, by introducing the transnational dimension into the framework, we open a new avenue for research. Yet, as this is the first study to propose this, we need to verify that transnationality fully applies to the entrepreneurial-ecosystem context. The main dispute could be that transnationality is suitable in a small-economy context where the ecosystem is more often defined on the country level. But, for example, if we address a large economy on a state level that is the size of a country, the local ecosystem does not extend beyond national borders. However, cross-border convergence still occurs, but not outside the country limits.

REFERENCES

Acs, Z. J., Audretsch, D. B., & Lehmann, E. E. (2013). The knowledge spillover theory of entrepreneurship. *Small Business Economics, 41*(4), 757–774. https://doi.org/10.1007/s11187-013-9505-9

Acs, Z. J., Audretsch, D. B., Lehmann, E. E., & Licht, G. (2016). National systems of entrepreneurship. *Small Business Economics, 46*(4), 527–535. https://doi.org/10.1007/s11187-016-9705-1

Acs, Z. J., Estrin, S., Mickiewicz, T., & Szerb, L. (2017). Institutions, Entrepreneurship and Growth: The Role of National Entrepreneurial Ecosystems. *SSRN.* https://doi.org/10.2139/ssrn.2912453

Acs, Z. J., Szerb, L., Lafuente, E., & Lloyd, A. (2018). The Entrepreneurial Ecosystem and Global Prosperity. In *Global entrepreneurship and development index 2018* (pp. 11–19). Cham: Springer International Publishing. https://doi.org/10.1007/978-3-030-03279-1_2

Alvedalen, J., & Boschma, R. (2017). A critical review of entrepreneurial ecosystems research: Towards a future research agenda. *European Planning Studies, 25*(6), 887–903. https://doi.org/10.1080/09654313.2017.1299694

Andersson, S., Evers, N., & Griot, C. (2013). Local and international networks in small firm internationalization: Cases from the Rhône-Alpes medical technology regional cluster. *Entrepreneurship and Regional Development*, *25*(9–10), 867–888. https://doi.org/10.1080/0 8985626.2013.847975

Audretsch, D. B., & Belitski, M. (2017). Entrepreneurial ecosystems in cities: Establishing the framework conditions. *Journal of Technology Transfer*, *42*(5), 1030–1051. https://doi. org/10.1007/s10961-016-9473-8

Autio, E., Nambisan, S., Thomas, L. D. W., & Wright, M. (2018). Digital affordances, spatial affordances, and the genesis of entrepreneurial ecosystems. *Strategic Entrepreneurship Journal*, *12*(1), 72–95. https://doi.org/10.1002/sej.1266

Bahrami, H., & Evans, S. (1995). Flexible re-cycling and high-technology entrepreneurship. *California Management Review*, *37*(3), 62–89. https://doi.org/10.2307/41165799

Bailetti, E. (2018). Transnational entrepreneurship: Distinctive features and a new definition. *Technology Innovation Management Review*, *8*(9), 28–38. https://doi.org/10.22215/tim review/1184

Bosma, N., & Stam, E. (2012). *Local policies for high-employment growth enterprises*. Copenhagen. Retrieved 6 August 2018 from https://www.oecd.org/cfe/leed/Bosma-Stam_ high-growth%20policies.pdf

Burgelman, R. A., & Hitt, M. A. (2008). Entrepreneurial actions, innovation, and appropriability. *Strategic Entrepreneurship Journal*, *1*(3–4), 349–352. https://doi.org/10.1002/sej.28

Cannone, G., & Ughetto, E. (2014). Born globals: A cross-country survey on high-tech start-ups. *International Business Review*, *23*(1), 272–283. https://doi.org/10.1016/j.ibusrev.2013.05.003

Cardon, M. S., Wincent, J., Singh, J., & Drnovsek, M. (2009). The nature and experience of entrepreneurial passion. *Academy of Management Review*, *34*(3), 511–532. https://doi. org/10.5465/AMR.2009.40633190

Cavallo, A., Ghezzi, A., & Balocco, R. (2018). Entrepreneurial ecosystem research: Present debates and future directions. *International Entrepreneurship and Management Journal*, 1–31. https://doi.org/10.1007/s11365-018-0526-3

Cavusgil, S. T., & Knight, G. (2015). The born global firm: An entrepreneurial and capabilities perspective on early and rapid internationalization. *Journal of International Business Studies*, *46*(1), 3–16. https://doi.org/10.1057/jibs.2014.62

Chemmanur, T. J., & Fulghieri, P. (2014). Entrepreneurial finance and innovation: An introduction and agenda for future research. *Review of Financial Studies*, *27*(1), 1–19. https://doi.org/10.1093/rfs/hht063

Choquette, E., Rask, M., Sala, D., & Schröder, P. (2017). Born Globals – Is there fire behind the smoke? *International Business Review*, *26*(3), 448–460. https://doi.org/10.1016/j. ibusrev.2016.10.005

Chua, J. H., Chrisman, J. J., Kellermanns, F., & Wu, Z. (2011). Family involvement and new venture debt financing. *Journal of Business Venturing*, *26*(4), 472–488. https://doi. org/10.1016/j.jbusvent.2009.11.002

Cohen, B. (2006). Sustainable valley entrepreneurial ecosystems. *Business Strategy and the Environment*, *15*(1), 1–14. https://doi.org/10.1002/bse.428

Corrente, S., Greco, S., Nicotra, M., Romano, M., & Schillaci, C. E. (2018). Evaluating and comparing entrepreneurial ecosystems using SMAA and SMAA-S. *Journal of Technology Transfer*, 44(2), 1–35. https://doi.org/10.1007/s10961-018-9684-2

Coviello, N. E. (2006). The network dynamics of international new ventures. *Journal of International Business Studies*, *37*(5), 713–731. https://doi.org/10.1057/palgrave.jibs.8400219

Denis, D. J. (2004). Entrepreneurial finance: An overview of the issues and evidence. *Journal of Corporate Finance*, *10*(2), 301–326. https://doi.org/10.1016/S0929-1199(03)00059-2

Drexler, M., Eltogby, M., Foster, G., Shimizu, C., Ciesinski, S., Davila, A., . . . Morris, R. (2014). *Entrepreneurial Ecosystems Around the Globe and Early-Stage Company Growth Dynamics*. Geneva, Switzerland: World Economic Forum. Retrieved 15 August 2018 from http:// reports.weforum.org/entrepreneurial-ecosystems-around-the-globe-and-early-stage-com pany-growth-dynamics/wp-content/blogs.dir/34/mp/files/pages/files/nme-entrepreneurship -report-jan-8-2014.pdf

Ebben, J., & Johnson, A. (2006). Bootstrapping in small firms: An empirical analysis of change over time. *Journal of Business Venturing, 21*(6), 851–865. https://doi.org/10.1016/j.jbusvent.2005.06.007

European Union. (2012). Treaty on the Functioning of the European Union. *Official Journal of the European Union,* 1–368. Retrieved 11 January 2019 from https://eur-lex.europa.eu/legal-content/EN/TXT/?uri=uriserv:OJ.C_.2012.326.01.0001.01.ENG&toc=OJ:C:2012:326:TOC

Feld, B. (2012). *Startup communities: Building an entrepreneurial ecosystem in your city.* Hoboken, New Jersey: John Wiley and Sons. https://doi.org/10.15713/ins.mmj.3

Gabrielsson, M., Kirpalani, V. H. H. M., Dimitratos, P., Solberg, C. A., & Zucchella, A. (2008). Born globals: Propositions to help advance the theory. *International Business Review, 17*(4), 385–401. https://doi.org/10.1016/j.ibusrev.2008.02.015

Gabrielsson, M., & Kirpalani, V. M. (2004). Born globals: how to reach new business space rapidly. *International Business Review, 13*(5), 555–571.

Gabrielsson, M., Sasi, V., & Darling, J. (2004). Finance strategies of rapidly-growing Finnish SMEs: Born Internationals and Born Globals. *European Business Review, 16*(6), 590–604. https://doi.org/10.1108/09555340410565413

Greenberg, D., McKone-Sweet, K., & Wilson, H. J. (2011). Entrepreneurial leadership: Shaping social and economic opportunity. In *The new entrepreneurial leader: Developing leaders who shape social and economic opportunity* (pp. 1–22). Berrett-Koehler Publishers.

Gupta, V., MacMillan, I. C., & Surie, G. (2004). Entrepreneurial leadership: Developing and measuring a cross-cultural construct. *Journal of Business Venturing, 19*(2), 241–260. https://doi.org/10.1016/S0883-9026(03)00040-5

Harrington, K. (2017). Entrepreneurial ecosystem momentum and maturity the important role of entrepreneur development organizations and their activities. *SSRN,* 1–30. https://doi.org/10.2139/ssrn.3030886

Harrison, R. T., Mason, C. M., & Girling, P. (2004). Financial bootstrapping and venture development in the software industry. *Entrepreneurship and Regional Development, 16*(4), 307–333. https://doi.org/10.1080/0898562042000263276

Howells, J. (2006). Intermediation and the role of intermediaries in innovation. *Research Policy, 35*(5), 715–728. https://doi.org/10.1016/J.RESPOL.2006.03.005

Huggins, R., & Thompson, P. (2015). Entrepreneurship, innovation and regional growth: A network theory. *Small Business Economics, 45*(1), 103–128. https://doi.org/10.1007/s11187-015-9643-3

Isabelle, D. A. (2013). Key factors affecting a technology entrepreneur's choice of incubator or accelerator. *Technology Innovation Management Review, 3*(2), 16.

Jantunen, A., Nummela, N., Puumalainen, K., & Saarenketo, S. (2008). Strategic orientations of born globals – Do they really matter? *Journal of World Business, 43*(2), 158–170. https://doi.org/10.1016/J.JWB.2007.11.015

Kaplan, S. N., & Strömberg, P. (2000). *How do venture capitalists choose investments?* Chicago, US. Retrieved 8 August 2018 from http://citeseerx.ist.psu.edu/viewdoc/download?doi=10.1.1.201.5607&rep=rep1&type=pdf

Katila, R. (2002). New product search over time: Past ideas in their prime? *Academy of Management Journal, 45*(5), 995–1010. https://doi.org/10.2307/3069326

Kerr, W. R., Lerner, J., & Schoar, A. (2014). The consequences of entrepreneurial finance: Evidence from angel financings. *The Review of Financial Studies, 27*(1), 20–55, https://doi.org/10.1093/rfs/hhr098

Knight, G. A., & Cavusgil, S. T. (2005). A taxonomy of born-global firms. *MIR: Management International Review, 45*(3), 15–35. https://doi.org/10.2307/40836141

Kshetri, N. (2014). Developing successful entrepreneurial ecosystems: Lessons from a comparison of an Asian tiger and a Baltic tiger. *Baltic Journal of Management, 9*(3), 330–356. https://doi.org/10.1108/bjm-09-2013-0146

Kuivalainen, O., Saarenketo, S., & Puumalainen, K. (2012). Start-up patterns of internationalization: A framework and its application in the context of knowledge-intensive SMEs. *European Management Journal, 30*(4), 372–385. https://doi.org/10.1016/j.emj.2012.01.001

Kuivalainen, O., Saarenketo, S., Torkkeli, L., & Puumalainen, K. (2015). International entrepreneurship among Finnish SMEs. In P. N. Ghauri & V. H. M. Kirpalani (Eds.), *Handbook of Research on International Entrepreneurship Strategy: Improving SME Performance Globally* (pp. 287–308). Cheltenham, UK: Edward Elgar Publishing Limited. https://doi.org/10.4337/9781783471584

Kuivalainen, O., Sundqvist, S., & Servais, P. (2007). Firms' degree of born-globalness, international entrepreneurial orientation and export performance. *Journal of World Business*, *42*(3), 253–267. https://doi.org/10.1016/j.jwb.2007.04.010

Laanti, R., Gabrielsson, M., & Gabrielsson, P. (2007). The globalization strategies of business-to-business born global firms in the wireless technology industry. *Industrial Marketing Management*, *36*(8), 1104–1117. https://doi.org/10.1016/j.indmarman.2006.10.003

Lee, S. Y., Florida, R., & Acs, Z. J. (2004). Creativity and entrepreneurship: A regional analysis of new firm formation. *Regional Studies*, *38*(8), 879–891. https://doi.org/10.1080/003434 0042000280910

Liguori, E., Bendickson, J., Solomon, S., & McDowell, W. C. (2019). Development of a multi-dimensional measure for assessing entrepreneurial ecosystems. *Entrepreneurship and Regional Development*, *31*(1–2), 7–21. https://doi.org/10.1080/08985626.2018.1537144

Loane, S., Bell, J. D., & McNaughton, R. (2007). A cross-national study on the impact of management teams on the rapid internationalization of small firms. *Journal of World Business*, *42*(4), 489–504. https://doi.org/10.1016/j.jwb.2007.06.009

Lundberg, H., & Rehnfors, A. (2018). Transnational entrepreneurship: Opportunity identification and venture creation. *Journal of International Entrepreneurship*, *16*(2), 150–175. https://doi.org/10.1007/s10843-018-0228-5

Luostarinen, R., & Gabrielsson, M. (2004). Finnish perspectives of international entrepreneurship. In L. P. Dana (Ed.), *Handbook of Research on International Entrepreneurship* (pp. 383–403). Cheltenham, UK: Edward Elgar Publishing.

Luostarinen, R., & Gabrielsson, M. (2006). Globalization and marketing strategies of Born Globals in SMOPECs. *Thunderbird International Business Review*, *48*(6), 773–801. https://doi.org/10.1002/tie.20122

Mack, E., & Mayer, H. (2016). The evolutionary dynamics of entrepreneurial ecosystems. *Urban Studies*, *53*(10), 2118–2133. https://doi.org/10.1177/0042098015586547

Malecki, E. J. (2018). Entrepreneurship and entrepreneurial ecosystems. *Geography Compass*, *12*(3), 1–21. https://doi.org/10.1111/gec3.12359

Marmer, M., Herrmann, B. L., Dogrultan, E., & Berman, R. (2011). Startup Genome Report: A new framework for understanding why startups succeed. Retrieved 9 August 2018 from https://s3.amazonaws.com/startupcompass-public/StartupGenomeReport1_Why_Startups _Succeed_v2.pdf.

Maroufkhani, P., Wagner, R., & Wan Ismail, W. K. (2018, 3 September). Entrepreneurial ecosystems: A systematic review. *Journal of Enterprising Communities*. *12*(4), pp. 545–564. https://doi.org/10.1108/JEC-03-2017-0025

Mason, C., & Brown, R. (2014). *Entrepreneurial ecosystems and growth oriented entrepreneurship*. Final Report to OECD, Paris.

McEvily, B., & Zaheer, A. (1999). Bridging ties: A source of firm heterogeneity in competitive capabilities. *Strategic Management Journal*, *20*(12), 1133–1156. https://doi.org/10.1002/ (SICI)1097-0266(199912)20:12<1133::AID-SMJ74>3.0.CO;2-7

McGrath, R. G., & MacMillan, I. (2013). *The Entrepreneurial Mindset: Strategies for Continuously Creating Opportunity in an Age of Uncertainty*. Harvard Business Press.

Mets, T. (2015). The role of leadership in hi-tech born-globals: Small emerging country cases. In C. Ingley & J. Lockhart (Eds.), *Proceedings of the 3rd International Conference on Management Leadership and Governance (ICMLG 2015)* (pp. 207–214). Reading,UK: Academic Conferences & Publishing International Limited. https://doi. org/10.1080/10826070701360277

Miguel, J. C., & Casado, M. Á. (2016). GAFAnomy (Google, Amazon, Facebook and Apple): The Big Four and the b-Ecosystem. In M. Gómez-Uranga, J. M. Zabala-Iturriagagoitia, & J. Barrutia (Eds.), *Dynamics of big internet industry groups and future trends: A view from epigenetic economics* (pp. 127–148). Cham: Springer International Publishing. https://doi.org/10.1007/978-3-319-31147-0_4

Mollick, E. (2014). The dynamics of crowdfunding: An exploratory study. *Journal of Business Venturing, 29*(1), 1–16. https://doi.org/10.1016/j.jbusvent.2013.06.005

Moore, J. F. (1993). Predators and prey: a new ecology of competition. *Harvard Business Review, 71*(3), 75.

Mort, G. S., & Weerawardena, J. (2006). Networking capability and international entrepreneurship. *International Marketing Review, 23*(5), 549–572. https://doi.org/10.1108/026513 30610703445

Nauwelaers, C., Maguire, K., & Marsan, G. A. (2013). *The Case of Helsinki-Tallinn (Finland-Estonia)-Regions and Innovation: Collaborating Across Borders* (OECD Regional Development Working Papers No. 2013/19). https://doi.org/10.1787/5k3xv0lrt1r6-en

Neck, H. M., Meyer, G. D., Cohen, B., & Corbett, A. C. (2004). An entrepreneurial system view of new venture creation. *Journal of Small Business Management, 42*(2), 190–208. https://doi.org/10.1111/j.1540-627x.2004.00105.x

Neyman, J. (1934). On the two different aspects of the representative method: The method of stratified sampling and the method of purposive selection. *Journal of the Royal Statistical Society, 97*(4), 558–625. https://doi.org/10.2307/2342192

Nummela, N., Saarenketo, S., Jokela, P., & Loane, S. (2014). Strategic decision-making of a born global: A comparative study from three small open economies. *Management International Review, 54*(4), 527–550. https://doi.org/10.1007/s11575-014-0211-x

Nummela, N., Saarenketo, S., & Loane, S. (2016). The dynamics of failure in international new ventures: A case study of Finnish and Irish software companies. *International Small Business Journal, 34*(1), 51–69. https://doi.org/10.1177/0266242614539363

Nummela, N., Saarenketo, S., & Puumalainen, K. (2010). A global mindset – A prerequisite for successful internationalization? *Canadian Journal of Administrative Sciences / Revue Canadienne Des Sciences de l'Administration, 21*(1), 51–64. https://doi.org/10.1111/j.1936-4490.2004.tb00322.x

O'Connor, A., Stam, E., Sussan, F., & Audretsch, D. B. (2017). Entrepreneurial ecosystems: The foundations of place-based renewal. In A. O'Connor, E. Stam, F. Sussan, & D. B. Audretsch (Eds.), *Entrepreneurial Ecosystems. International Studies in Entrepreneurship* (pp. 1–21). Adelaide, Australia: Springer, Cham. https://doi.org/10.1007/978-3-319-63531-6_1

Oviatt, B. M., & McDougall, P. P. (1994). Toward a theory of international new ventures. *Journal of International Business Studies, 25*(1), 45–64. https://doi.org/10.1057/palgrave. jibs.8490193

Pauwels, C., Clarysse, B., Wright, M., & Van Hove, J. (2016). Understanding a new generation incubation model: The accelerator. *Technovation, 50–51*, 13–24. https://doi. org/10.1016/j.technovation.2015.09.003

Peiris, I. K., Akoorie, M. E. M., & Sinha, P. (2012). International entrepreneurship: A critical analysis of studies in the past two decades and future directions for research. *Journal of International Entrepreneurship, 10*(4), 279–324. https://doi.org/10.1007/s10843-012-0096-3

Podsakoff, P. M., MacKenzie, S. B., Lee, J. Y., & Podsakoff, N. P. (2003). Common method biases in behavioral research: A critical review of the literature and recommended remedies. *Journal of Applied Psychology, 88*(5), 879–903. https://doi.org/10.1037/0021-9010.88.5.879

Rauch, A., & Rijsdijk, S. A. (2013). The effects of general and specific human capital on long-term growth and failure of newly founded businesses. *Entrepreneurship: Theory and Practice, 37*(4), 923–941. https://doi.org/10.1111/j.1540-6520.2011.00487.x

Renko, M., El Tarabishy, A., Carsrud, A. L., & Brännback, M. (2015). Understanding and measuring entrepreneurial leadership style. *Journal of Small Business Management, 53*(1), 54–74. https://doi.org/10.1111/jsbm.12086

Rialp, A., Galván-Sánchez, I., & García, M. (2012). An inquiry into born global firms' learning process: A case study of information technology-based SMEs. In M. Gabrielsson & V. H. M. Kirpalani (Eds.), *Handbook of research on born globals* (pp. 71–95). Cheltenham, UK: Edward Elgar Publishing.

Sasi, V., & Arenius, P. (2012). Strategies for circumventing born global firms' resource scarcity dilemma. In G. C. Aard Groen, Ray Oakey, Peter Van Der Sijde (Ed.), *New technology-based firms in the new millennium* (pp. 71–85). Emerald Group Publishing Limited. https://doi.org/10.1108/S1876-0228(2012)0000009008

Saxenian, A. (1990). Regional networks and the resurgence of Silicon Valley. *California Management Review, 33*(1), 89–112. https://doi.org/10.2307/41166640

Sergeevich, M. A., & Alekseevna, M. A. (2015). Geographies of cluster internationalization : Inter-organizational linkages on the Baltica. *International Journal of Econometrics and Financial Management, 3*(1), 32–37. https://doi.org/10.12691/ijefm-3-1-6

Shane, S., & Venkataraman, S. (2000). The promise of entrepreneurship as a field of research. *Academy of Management Review, 25*(1), 217–226. https://doi.org/10.5465/amr.2000.2791611

Spigel, B. (2017). The relational organization of entrepreneurial ecosystems. *Entrepreneurship: Theory and Practice, 41*(1), 49–72. https://doi.org/10.1111/etap.12167

Spigel, B., & Harrison, R. (2018). Toward a process theory of entrepreneurial ecosystems. *Strategic Entrepreneurship Journal, 12*(1), 151–168. https://doi.org/10.1002/sej.1268

Spilling, O. R. (1996). The entrepreneurial system: On entrepreneurship in the context of a mega-event. *Journal of Business Research, 36*(1), 91–103. https://doi.org/10.1016/0148-2963(95)00166-2

Stagars, M. (2014). Incubators and accelerators. In *University startups and spin-offs* (pp. 131–136). Berkeley, CA: Apress. https://doi.org/10.1007/978-1-4842-0623-2_13

Stam, E. (2014). The Dutch entrepreneurial ecosystem. *SSRN*, 1–41. https://doi.org/10.2139/ssrn.2473475

Stam, E. (2015). Entrepreneurial ecosystems and regional policy: A sympathetic critique. *European Planning Studies, 23*(9), 1759–1769. https://doi.org/10.1080/09654313.2015.1061484

Suddaby, R., Bruton, G. D., & Si, S. X. (2015). Entrepreneurship through a qualitative lens: Insights on the construction and/or discovery of entrepreneurial opportunity. *Journal of Business Venturing, 30*(1), 1–10. https://doi.org/10.1016/J.JBUSVENT.2014.09.003

Suresh, J., & Ramraj, R. (2012). Entrepreneurial ecosystem: Case study on the influence of environmental factors on entrepreneurial success. *European Journal of Business and Management, 4*(16), 95–102.

Talaia, M., Pisoni, A., & Onetti, A. (2016). Factors influencing the fund raising process for innovative new ventures: An empirical study. *Journal of Small Business and Enterprise Development, 23*(2), 363–378. https://doi.org/10.1108/JSBED-07-2014-0111

Thomas, L. D. W., Sharapov, D., & Autio, E. (2018). Linking entrepreneurial and innovation ecosystems: The case of AppCampus. In Elias G. Carayannis, Giovanni Battista Dagnino, Sharon Alvarez, & Rosario Faraci (Eds.), *Entrepreneurial ecosystems and the diffusion of startups* (pp. 35–64). Cheltenham, UK: Edward Elgar Publishing. https://doi.org/10.4337/9781784710064

Van De Ven, H. (1993). The development of an infrastructure for entrepreneurship. *Journal of Business Venturing, 8*(3), 211–230. https://doi.org/10.1016/0883-9026(93)90028-4

Velt, H., Torkkeli, L., & Saarenketo, S. (2018a). The entrepreneurial ecosystem and born globals: The Estonian context. *Journal of Enterprising Communities, 12*(2), 117–138. https://doi.org/10.1108/JEC-08-2017-0056

Velt, H., Torkkeli, L., & Saarenketo, S. (2018b). Uncovering new value frontiers: The role of the entrepreneurial ecosystem in nurturing born globals. *International Journal of Export Marketing, 2*(4), 1–27.

Vissak, T. (2007). The emergence and success factors of fast internationalizers: Four cases from Estonia. *Journal of East-West Business, 13*(1), 11–33.

Weber, E. P., & Khademian, A. M. (2008). Wicked problems, knowledge challenges, and collaborative capacity builders in network settings. *Public Administration Review, 68*(2), 334–349. https://doi.org/10.1111/j.1540-6210.2007.00866.x

Winton, A., & Yerramilli, V. (2008). Entrepreneurial finance: Banks versus venture capital. *Journal of Financial Economics, 88*(1), 51–79. https://doi.org/10.1016/j.jfineco.2007.05.004

Wong, A., Bhatia, M., & Freeman, Z. (2009). Angel finance: The other venture capital. *Strategic Change, 18*, 221–230. https://doi.org/10.1002/jsc.849

Wu, J., Steven, S., & Wu, X. (2016). Entrepreneurial finance and innovation: Informal debt as an empirical case. *Strategic Entrepreneurship Journal, 10*(3), 257–273. https://doi.org/10.1002/sej.1214

Yukl, G. (2008). How leaders influence organizational effectiveness. *Leadership Quarterly, 19*(6), 708–722. https://doi.org/10.1016/j.leaqua.2008.09.008

Zander, I., McDougall-Covin, P., & Rose, E. L. (2015, 9 January). Born globals and international business: Evolution of a field of research. *Journal of International Business Studies.* Palgrave Macmillan UK. https://doi.org/10.1057/jibs.2014.60

Zhang, Y., & Li, H. (2010). Innovation search of new ventures in a technology cluster: The role of ties with service intermediaries. *Strategic Management Journal, 31*(1), 88–109. https://doi.org/10.1002/smj.806

Zhou, L., Wu, W. P., & Luo, X. (2007). Internationalization and the performance of born-global SMEs: The mediating role of social networks. *Journal of International Business Studies, 38*(4), 673–690. https://doi.org/10.1057/palgrave.jibs.8400282

Zott, C., & Huy, Q. N. (2007). How entrepreneurs use symbolic management to acquire resources. *Administrative Science Quarterly, 52*(1), 70–105. https://doi.org/10.2189/asqu.52.1.70

7. A contingency approach to the incubation of new ventures in entrepreneurial ecosystems: Descriptive exploratory plots for continuous and survival outcomes
*Alan R. Johnson, Katherine E. Masyn, and Alexander McKelvie**

> *Wise researchers conduct descriptive exploratory analyses of their data before fitting statistical models.*
> Judith D. Singer and John B. Willett

INTRODUCTION TO PLOTS AND COLLATERAL ISSUES

The analysis of findings from data represents the core – original or value-added material – of most journal articles. Entrepreneurship researchers are becoming increasingly aware that their research can, and should, be both methodologically rigorous and relevant to theory and practice (Wiklund, Wright, & Zahra, 2018). To a considerable extent, the core material of journal articles determines their theoretical significance and practical relevance (Basbøll, 2018; Dunleavy, 2003). Applied researchers want to use recognized procedures that produce legitimate results for the effects of predictors on new venture development and growth. For most scholarly questions addressed with longitudinal data, researchers need to use two-sided statistical models – *model for means* and *model for variances* – using either multilevel or structural equation model procedures (Curran, Lee, Howard, Lane, & MacCallum, 2012; Hoffman, 2015; Little, 2013).[1] However, with large and unfamiliar databases, which are often drawn from one or more register data sources constructed for purposes other than academic research, it can be difficult to decide where to start. Most general data analysis textbooks recommend researchers examine descriptive statistics – means, standard deviations, and correlations – and a variety of scatter plots to check data cleaning procedures for coding errors, univariate plots for normality, and bivariate plots for non-linearity (e.g., Tabachnick & Fidell, 2013). Specialist longitudinal texts recommend similar descriptive preliminary analyses but rely less on cross-sectional descriptive statistics and more on connected subject-observations and group-means using descriptive exploratory plots for two or more variables (e.g., Singer & Willett, 2003). However, other methodologists argue that *looking* at data and results first constitutes HARKing – hypothesizing after results are known – and argue that to present *post-hoc* hypotheses informed by results and data, as if they were *a priori*, is inappropriate (Kerr, 1998). So, where to start?

There appears to be a disconnect in what methodologists recommend for how applied researchers approach multilevel and longitudinal data. On one hand, some methodologists argue that researchers need "to get . . . their feet wet and in touch with . . . data" to gain a more concrete and nuanced understanding of its clusters and dynamics using descriptive exploratory plots and to reduce misspecification of statistical models (Singer & Willett, 2003). On the other hand, methodologists argue that HARKing is a threat to cumulative knowledge (e.g., Kerr, 1998). So, must researchers deduce all hypotheses blind to data and results? And what about descriptive statistics and descriptive exploratory plots: do they count as 'snooping?' In this chapter, we take a pragmatic view to HARKing and argue that hypotheses *amended* using only descriptive exploratory plots of multilevel and longitudinal data have little potential to bias cumulative knowledge (c.f., Murphy & Aguinis, 2019). We argue that descriptive exploratory plots are not problematic for three reasons. First, misspecification of multilevel and longitudinal regression models is also a threat to cumulative knowledge. Second, amended hypotheses, informed only by plots, remain in considerable jeopardy pending multivariate regression analyses. Third, when restricted range of continuous variables is an issue, researchers should compare survival outcomes with continuous outcomes to check for consistency of relations to predictors.[2]

This chapter suggests that descriptive exploratory plots of continuous and survival outcomes can *both* suggest the effects of predictor variables on new venture development and growth *and,* despite some amendment to hypotheses, promote cumulative knowledge in the field. The study is based on 373 academic spin-off (ASO) firms that were active in Norway between 2000 and 2015. We use data from multiple archival sources to show how relations between incubation and new venture development and growth may be conditional on other attributes of entrepreneurial ecosystems, e.g., location and issued capital. We supply graphical and non-mathematical heuristics to guide researchers on where to start specifying fixed and random effects to manage dependency in multilevel and longitudinal statistical models. Our analysis of findings suggests that descriptive exploratory plots can offer researchers a concrete and nuanced first approximation of how shared variance in *censored* outcome variables – (semi-)continuous variables that do not vary across their full range but have a lower or upper limit – break down into between and within components, which are not discoverable using conventional descriptive statistics typically used with cross-sectional data. We offer both heuristic schemas and examples from our data to illustrate how to use plots to help decide whether to specify appropriate random intercepts or random slopes in multivariate regression models that are critical to draw valid statistical inferences when using clustered data (Hox, Moerbeek, & van de Schoot, 2018). Specifically, if researchers fail to specify the model for the variances to account for *dependency* – within-subject residual correlations – from repeated observations of firms in longitudinal data, then regression analyses assume more data than are actually there and type 1 errors are likely to be inflated (c.f., Bliese, Maltarich, & Hendricks, 2018), because standard errors are too small, test statistics too large, and *p*-values too small (Allison, 2009). More generally, dependency can produce standard errors for predictor fixed effects that are either too high or too low, according to the sampling dimension, i.e., subject, time, or predictor, and pose similar threats to statistical conclusion validity (c.f., Cook & Campbell, 1979).

The foregoing runs contrary to the research ethics literature because, if plots help to specify multivariate statistical models and fit them to data, then we suggest that some forms of 'snooping the data' may not be so problematic and, to the contrary, help progress cumulative knowledge. Figure 7.1 summarizes our conception of a 'wheel of science' where *three* interdependent spokes, labeled: 1) grounding of hypotheses, 2)

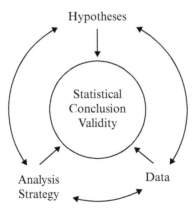

Figure 7.1   *Wheel of science; interdependencies between hypotheses, data, and analysis strategy to support statistical conclusion validity*

characteristics of the data, and 3) strategy for analyses, support statistical conclusion validity at the hub. In summary, each spoke needs to be sensitive to the other spokes but none of them determine the other. For example, researchers may adjust analysis strategy to characteristics of the data but should *not* impose their analysis strategy dogmatically to progress some polemical agenda. In addition, researchers may *amend* hypotheses in the light of characteristics in the data but should *not* introduce new *post hoc* hypotheses wholesale that are based solely on data and results.

USING DESCRIPTIVE EXPLORATORY PLOTS

New venture development and growth are defining constructs for entrepreneurship scholars. Development and growth for knowledge-intensive new ventures are especially important because they have high potential impact on social well-being, the local economy, firm profit, and individual employment (Fini, Rasmussen, Siegel, & Wiklund, 2018). While considerable public resources have been committed to support knowledge-intensive new venture creation, e.g., incubation, there is mixed evidence for whether and when that support is effective to help firms develop and grow (Amezcua, Grimes, Bradley, & Wiklund, 2013). We adopt the example of this mixed evidence about the effect of incubation on academic spin-off (ASO) development and growth conditional on other ecosystem attributes, to help outline the use of descriptive exploratory plots as a preliminary to multivariate modeling. About half of the ASOs in our sample, a sub-group of knowledge-intensive new ventures, were incubated (193 firms of 373) but there are no obvious positive main effects of incubation. We measure development and growth in four ways (McKelvie & Wiklund, 2010), i.e., sales, employees, traditional venture exit, and exit by merger and acquisition, with two potential moderating predictors, i.e., location, issued capital.

Operational definitions of performance, i.e., proxies for new venture development and growth, are a long-standing issue for the fields of management and entrepreneurship (Campbell, 1990; Delmar, 1997; Mathieu, Maynard, Rapp, & Gilson, 2008). However, we do not argue for any specific operational definition of performance here but merely voice some concerns about contamination and deficiency in outcome variables currently in use (Campbell, McCloy, Oppler, & Sager, 1992). Sales seems to be the preferred measure for new venture development and growth and most studies use it, e.g., 61 out of 82 (Shepherd & Wiklund, 2009). Absolute measures, e.g., sales value, are preferred over relative measures, i.e., percentage increases in sales value, because correlations between relative and absolute measures are typically weak, e.g., mean r = .095 for sales (Shepherd & Wiklund, 2009). However, sales is *deficient* as a measure of development because many knowledge-intensive new ventures in our data do not achieve sales in early years, if at all, e.g., 129 ASOs, 35 percent, have zero sales at any time (see Table 7.1). Further, sales is also deficient because it is not sensitive to developmental milestones that new ventures achieve 'on their way to' growth, i.e., sales is range restricted as an indicator of development. Employees seems to be the next most favored measure for development and growth perhaps because sales and employees are typically strongly and positively correlated, e.g., mean r =.34 (Shepherd & Wiklund, 2009). Employees is less deficient as a measure of development because it captures early hires to the venture, who presumably are working on its nascent offer, i.e., product, service, or technology, but in our data 93 ASOs, 25 percent, have zero employees at any time (see Table 7.1). In addition, employees is *contaminated* as a measure of growth because it is an input measure, or maybe an activity measure, as opposed to a measure of outcome. More generally, the methods literature discusses regression with *censored* dependent variables – a continuous outcome variable that does not vary across the full range of values but has a lower (floor) or upper (ceiling) limit (Muthén, Muthén, & Asparouhov, 2016). One response to a preponderance of zeros in continuous outcome variables, which entrepreneurship researchers have favored in earlier literature, is to operationalize new venture development and growth using survival outcome variables, e.g., time-to-traditional exit or time-to-merger and acquisition (Delmar, McKelvie, & Wennberg, 2013; Wennberg, Wiklund, DeTienne, & Cardon, 2010). Another response, used less frequently in the entrepreneurship literature, is to model the zeros by recoding (semi-)continuous variables as time-to-event outcomes, i.e., time-to-first sales, time-to-first employees, which addresses range restriction in continuous indicators of development and growth (e.g., Brush, Edelman, & Manolova, 2008; Schoonhoven, Eisenhardt, & Lyman, 1990). While we do not claim to solve the measurement problem for development and growth, we argue that continuous and survival outcome variable choices have consequences for statistical conclusion validity (Cook & Campbell, 1979). And thus, we recommend choosing two or more potentially analogous outcome measures to help increase statistical conclusion validity, especially if one outcome variable is (semi-)continuous then we recommend choosing another analogous outcome variable that is time-to-event.

In this chapter, we provide a heuristic framework and a set of applied examples for descriptive exploratory plots with two or more analogous outcome variables and the same predictors, emphasizing the situation where some outcomes are continuous, and others are survival. Although multilevel and longitudinal data are now used regularly in management and entrepreneurship research (Bliese et al., 2018), there is generally little discussion of the impact of different analytic approaches (see Alcácer, Chung, Hawk, & Pacheco-de-Almeida, 2018; Bliese et al., 2018 for important exceptions). More generally, different analytic approaches to multi-level and longitudinal modeling for social and behavioral science is well covered in several authoritative texts (e.g., Cleves, Gould, & Marchenko, 2016; Hoffman, 2015; Little, 2013; Rabe-Hesketh & Skrondal, 2012; Singer & Willett, 2003). However, even in these texts, procedures to accommodate both continuous and survival outcomes for complementary research questions are not well covered. In the context of the prevailing wisdom to specify a number of alternative models (Kline, 2016; Little, 2013), we argue that descriptive exploratory plots give a good idea about appropriate model specifications to start with. We review recommendations from the foregoing texts and pilot test them using our Norwegian ASO data to supply analogous plots for continuous and survival outcome variables, i.e., sales, employees, traditional exit, merger and acquisition, and predictors, incubation, location, and issued capital, for precisely the same sample of firms and precisely the same period. These procedures are not complicated but can be quite involved – more data management than statistical modeling (see Cleves et al., 2016; Mitchell, 2010).

Researchers need to understand why they are doing descriptive exploratory plots. The plots are less a substitute for multivariate regression analyses and more a step toward them. The plots and the tentative relations between constructs they reveal are part of a process of cleaning data and becoming familiar with it. Part of a process leading to a nuanced and relevant analysis of findings from data that are written in the authors voice, as opposed to some stylized template (Greve, 2017). As the quote at the beginning of the chapter suggest, methodologists recommend extensive descriptive exploratory plots before turning their attention to advanced multivariate statistical models. Singer and Willet (2003) argue that exploratory plots reveal general patterns in the data, supply insights into the functional form of relations between continuous outcomes and time at both the between- and within-subject levels and help find subjects who do not conform to the general pattern, i.e., outliers. They provide many examples of connected subject-observation plots for *continuous outcome variables*, often including both group-means and predictors (see Figures 7.4, 7.5 and 7.6, panels [a] and [b]). They argue that cross-sectional descriptive statistics are difficult to interpret with longitudinal data because correlations over time do not reveal between- and within-subject components of shared variance in the observations. Indeed, a principal reason for doing longitudinal research is that relations between constructs at the between-subjects level of analysis need not be, and often are not, the same as relations at the within-subjects level of analysis (Hoffman, 2015; Raudenbush & Bryk, 2002). Consequently, we recommend researchers bring data through a series of plots to compare connected subject-observations with group-means that may be conditional on one or more predictors. The plots help researchers to specify fixed and random effects to take care of residual correlations in the data and produce a coherent and accurate analysis of findings. Finally, while the relations observed in descriptive exploratory plots are important for subsequent modeling decisions they are also tentative; there is no guarantee they will remain, let alone be statistically significant, after controlling for other plausible explanations of the phenomena of interest (Murnane & Willett, 2011).

There is no direct analogue for connected subject-observations to plot for survival outcome variables. While plots of the hazard function look longitudinal (see Figures 7.4, 7.5 and 7.6, panels [c] and [d]), there is only one piece of event information per subject, as opposed to the many repeated subject-observations for continuous outcome variables. The underlying process, e.g., traditional exit (failure) or merger and acquisition (potential success), determines the height and shape of the hazard function (Singer & Willett, 2003). When the risk of failure (success) is zero, the hazard is zero. When the risk of failure is increasing (decreasing) over time, the hazard function is also increasing (decreasing) (see Figures 7.4, 7.5 and 7.6, panel [c]). Conversely, when the risk of success is increasing (decreasing) over time, the hazard function is also increasing (decreasing) (see Figures 7.4, 7.5 and 7.6, panel [d]). The whether and when of the event of interest (Singer & Willett, 2003) reflected in the hazard function is a group-level latent variable (Allison, 2014) with no subject-level analogue. Consequently, methodologists are less effusive about descriptive exploratory plots for survival outcome variables but, nevertheless, we believe there is a need for researchers to bring data through a series of plots to compare overall hazard rates with hazard rates conditional on predictors. Descriptive exploratory plots can assess the likely functional form of the hazard function and whether it remains proportional across the conditions of one or more predictors. Even though these plots cannot identify subject-level outliers, they can still help specify fixed and random effects to take care of residual correlations arising at the group-level, e.g., incubation, location, issued capital.

For survival outcomes, we recommend plotting hazard functions based on the Kaplan-Meier (KM) estimator because it places minimal restrictions on the functional form of relations and is thus analogous to the descriptive exploratory plots that we use with continuous outcome variables. Simply put, the hazard function (h0) plots are the inverse of the rate of change in the survival function (S0), explained in 'utter' detail in most survival and event history analysis texts (e.g., Cleves et al., 2016). On the positive side, the hazard function from the KM estimator can produce confidence intervals (CIs) to help assess sampling variability, which is not available after Cox regression. The CIs for the survival outcomes appear relatively wide, compared to the CIs for continuous outcomes, this is because of the relatively sparse information available to produce the hazard functions from single absorbing subject-events – events that happen once and are not repeated – compared to the abundant information to produce group-means for continuous outcomes from multiple subject-observations. On the negative side, there is some truncation of descriptive exploratory plots because some smoothing is required to produce the hazard function from the inverse of the rate of change in the survival function and therefore some events are lost from the beginning and the end of the function. However, using the Epanechnikov kernel in Stata (StataCorp, 2017) with a narrow width option reduces truncation to a minimum and keeps the function height and shape close to the original change dynamics in the data. We focus on hazard functions for single absorbing subject-events because they present as analogous to group-means with continuous outcome variables and they increase (decrease) over time, conditional on one or more predictors. Plots of the survival function are more difficult to interpret side-by-side with models for change using continuous outcome variables.

SPECIFYING MODELS FOR CHANGE

Researchers need to recognize that many combinations of fixed and random effects for subjects, time, and predictors can be used to model variation in outcome variables. Figures 7.2 and 7.3 guide researchers in a diagrammatic and non-mathematical way through how to specify fixed and random effects based on various patterns they may observe in descriptive exploratory plots. We offer these heuristic supports to help researchers *reduce* the number of 'garbage' parameters – theoretically uninterpretable terms specified *only* to improve model fit (Bentler & Bonett, 1981) – and the number of tests needed to specify multivariate statistical models. Figure 7.2 addresses both dependency and change in continuous outcome variables. Figure 7.3 addresses dependency and change in *single* event survival outcomes with predictor variables, as well as predictor conditions for continuous outcomes. As discussed above, connected subject-observations can be ignored for survival outcomes in Figure 7.3. In each panel of Figure 7.2 and 7.3, time is on the x-axis and

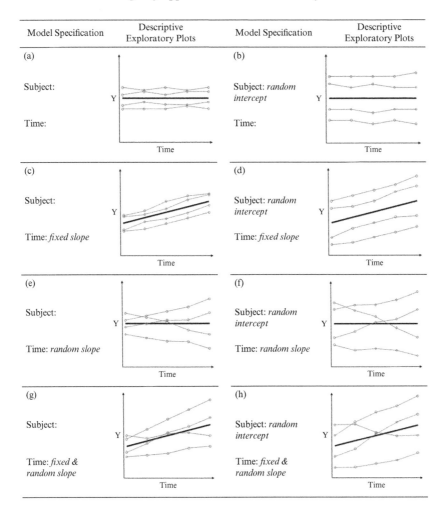

Source: adapted from Hoffman (2015).

Figure 7.2 *Fixed and random effects for subject and time*

the outcome variable is on the y-axis. The thick lines stand for *group-means* – reflecting fixed effects – and the thin lines stand for *connected subject-observations* – reflecting random effects – on outcome variables over time. Figure 7.3 extends the framework by introducing predictor conditions, e.g., incubation, location, or high (low) issued capital, where the short-dashed thick lines stand for group-means in one condition and the solid thick lines stand for group-means in another condition. Similarly,

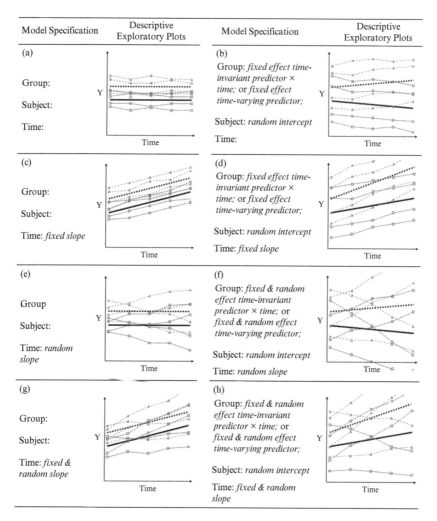

Source: adapted from Hoffman (2015).

Figure 7.3   Fixed and random effects for predictors over time

short-dashed thin lines stand for connected subject-observations in one condition and solid thin lines stand for connected subject-observations in another condition.

Descriptive exploratory plots support model specification decisions using two-sided multivariate statistical models: the model for means and the model for variances. Two-sided models allow researchers to manage dependency in multilevel and longitudinal data, which, if specified correctly, can offer more accurate parameter estimates and hypothesis tests (Hoffman, 2015). *Dependency* is the extent to which within-subject residual correlations exist, which arise from repeated observations of the same subject over time. Residual correlations violate the classical assumption that residual error terms are independent and identically distributed, i.e., drawn from a normal distribution with a mean of 0 and a standard deviation of 1 (Hox et al., 2018). For continuous outcome variables, researchers should always estimate residual correlations in a first step toward multivariate model specification because reliable variance is likely to be correlated with itself over time and, if residual correlations are not precisely zero, misfit can permeate to other parameter estimates in the model (Little, 2013). Thus, the two-sided modeling framework allows fixed and random effects to represent sources of dependency and, in so doing, produces more accurate hypothesis tests.

The model for means is the fixed effects side of the model, which researchers typically use for hypothesis testing, e.g., whether there are group-mean differences in outcome, Y, between conditions of predictors, X. In general, the model for means shows the extent to which the expected outcome, Y, varies with predictor conditions, X. The parameter estimates are labeled *fixed effects* because they are constant for all subjects (Singer & Willett, 2003). *The model for variances* is the random effects side of the model, which typically researchers are less familiar with but, if specified correctly, offers considerable benefit for cumulative knowledge. In general, the model for variances shows the pattern of within-subject variances and covariances for outcome residuals between observations over time. The parameter estimates in the model for variances are labeled *random effects* because they allow each subject to deviate from a corresponding fixed effect, to address dependency on one or more dimensions, i.e., subject, time, or predictors. Dependency in continuous outcome variables arises from *four* sources: 1) non-constant patterns of within-subject residual variances and covariances over time, 2) constant between-subject differences, 3) non-constant between-subject differences over time, and 4) non-constant between-subject differences in the effects of predictors over time.

The first source of dependency comes from the simple idea that residual correlations between observations that are closer together in time are likely to be larger than those that are further apart. Researchers can model unexplained *non-constant patterns of within-subject residual variances and covariances over time* for continuous outcome variables using one of several alternative residual correlation structures in *the model for variances*, e.g., n-order unstructured (least parsimonious but highest likelihood), compound symmetric (most parsimonious), auto-regressive, Toeplitz, n-1 order unstructured, which all describe patterns of variances and covariances over time to a lesser or greater extent of parsimony (see Hoffman, 2015 for more details). The model for variances in multilevel and longitudinal models gives access to alternative structures for residual correlations that go way beyond repeated measures ANOVA, which can only model constant variances and covariances over time, the equivalent of a *compound symmetric* residual correlation structure, with or without random intercepts (Hoffman, 2015). For example, Figure 7.2 panels (a)–(d) show connected subject-observations (thin lines) that run relatively parallel to group-means (thick lines) and a compound symmetric structure in the model for variances would likely adequately describe the constant pattern of residual variances and covariances over time. However, *constant* patterns of variances and covariances over time, i.e., *not* increasing or decreasing, are *rare* in applied data. Conversely, Figure 7.2 panels (e)–(h) show connected subject-observations (thin lines) that are dispersed at various angles around group-means (thick lines) and thus a more elaborate structure in the model for variances would be needed to adequately describe an *increasing* pattern of residual variances and covariances over time. In either case, researchers use the n-order unstructured (least parsimonious) latent means structure for residual variances and covariances as a baseline, which will always have the highest likelihood, to test more parsimonious models for residual variances and covariances. Having established a relatively parsimonious structure to describe the pattern in the model for variances, researchers add further fixed and random effects outlined in their research questions in an attempt to explain the residual variance. Thus, we next discuss models including random intercepts and then random slopes.

The second source of dependency comes from subjects showing consistently better (worse) outcomes. Researchers can model constant between-subject differences in outcomes using *random intercepts.* Random intercepts allow each subject to have their own constant deviation in outcome from the mean intercept (Hoffman, 2015). For example, Figure 7.2 panel (b) shows connected subject-observations (thin lines) dispersed relatively widely around the group-mean (thick lines) and a random intercept test of whether there are *constant between-subject differences in outcome* would likely reject the null hypothesis (be significant). Conversely, Figure 7.2 panel (a) shows connected subject-observations (thin lines) packed relatively tightly around the group-mean (thick lines) and a random intercept test would likely fail to reject the null hypothesis (not be significant). A similar pattern of results plays out down panels (d), (f), and (h) of Figure 7.2 that show connected subject-observations (thin lines) dispersed relatively widely around group-means (thick lines) and random intercept tests would likely reject the null hypothesis. Conversely, panels (c), (e), and (g) of Figure 7.2 show connected subject-observations (thin lines) packed relatively tightly around the group-means (thick lines), at least at some period, here time 1, and random intercept tests would likely fail to reject the null hypothesis.

The third source of dependency comes from subjects showing consistently faster (slower) rate of change in outcomes over time. Researchers can model between-subject differences in outcomes from the effects of time using *random slopes.* Random slopes allow each subject to have their own deviation in outcome from the group-mean slope (Hoffman, 2015). For example, Figure 7.2 panels (e)–(h) show connected subject-observations (thin lines) dispersed at various angles around the group-mean (thick lines) and random slope tests of whether there are *non-constant between-subject differences in outcomes over time* would likely reject the null hypothesis. Conversely, Figure 7.2 panels (a)–(d) show connected subject-observations (thin lines) that run almost parallel to the group-mean (thick lines) and random slope tests would likely fail to reject the null hypothesis. Figure 7.2 panel (h) shows, perhaps, the most common scenario with both fixed and random effects for subjects and time. A random intercept test of whether there are *constant between-subject differences* would likely reject the null hypothesis because the fixed intercept does not adequately describe the variation in starting positions shown in the connected subject-observations. And a random slope test of whether there are *non-constant between-subject differences in outcomes over time* would also likely reject the null hypothesis because the fixed slope does not adequately describe the variation in rates of change shown in the connected subject-observations.

The fourth source of dependency comes from subjects showing consistently stronger (weaker) effects of predictors over time. Researchers can model between-subject differences in outcomes from the effects of predictors over time by either of two alternative parameterizations: (a) using time-invariant predictors conditional on time or (b) using time-varying predictors whose effects increase (decrease) over time. Researchers can model these sources of dependency using *fixed* or *random effects.* As argued above, outcome variance is typically not homogenous over time (non-constant) and adding random slope variances to represent the different effects of predictors between-subjects is another way to model within-subject dependency (Hoffman, 2015).

For the *first parameterization,* researchers can model the fixed effects of time-invariant predictors conditional on time using a time-invariant predictor × time product term to test whether there are *non-constant between-subject differences in the effects of predictors on outcomes over time* (Hoffman, 2015). For example, Figure 7.3 shows group-means (thick lines) for a time-invariant predictor in two conditions, e.g., *location*, short dashed (Oslo) and long dashed (Trondheim), over time. Figure 7.3 panel (b) shows group-means for the time-invariant predictor conditions diverging over time where the fixed effect test of the product term would likely reject the null hypothesis. Conversely, Figure 7.3 panel (a) shows group-means for the time-invariant predictor conditions running parallel over time where the fixed effect product term test would likely fail to reject the null hypothesis. Figure 7.3, panels (d) and (c) show comparable results for the fixed effect of the product term but with the main effect of time significant. Note that neither of the main effects need to be significant for the product term to be significant, the time-invariant predictor is drawn to suggest a significant main effect only for pedagogical reasons, so that all the lines are not on top of each other. If further between-subject differences remain, researchers can add a random slope for the product term that allows each subject to have their own deviation from the group-mean slope. Figure 7.3, panels (f) and (h), show similar fixed effects to panels (b) and (d) but with connected subject-observations scattered at different angles around group-means that can be modeled using a random slope on the product term.

For the *second parameterization*, researchers can model the effect of time-varying predictors whose effects increase (decrease) over time using fixed or random effects of a time-varying predictor to test whether there are *non-constant between-subject differences in the effects of predictors on outcomes over time* (Hoffman, 2015). For example, Figure 7.3 can also illustrate group-means (thick lines) for time-varying predictors in two conditions, e.g., *issued capital*, short dashed (high) and solid (low), over time. Figure 7.3 panel (b) shows the group-means for time-invariant predictor conditions diverging over time where the fixed effect test of the main effect would likely reject the null hypothesis. Conversely, Figure 7.3 panel (a) shows group-means for the time-varying predictor conditions running parallel over time where the fixed effect test of the main effect would likely fail to reject the null hypothesis. If there are further between-subject differences, again researchers can add a random slope for the time-varying predictor that allows each subject to have their own deviation from the group-mean slope. More generally, random slopes allow connected subject-observations to get their own version of the effect of a predictor over time, so as not to constrain within-subject residual correlations to be constant and thus vary as a function of predictors and time. That completes our review of the four sources of dependency and how to anticipate them using descriptive exploratory plots and whether to try fixed or random effects to fit multilevel and longitudinal models to data. What about the research ethics problem with hypothesizing after looking at data and results?

COLLATERAL ISSUES WITH POST HOC HYPOTHESES

Most journal articles ostensibly follow the hypothetico-deductive (HD) model – theorize, predict, observe, test. The HD model for scientific method stipulates that researchers *first* articulate earlier theory, research, experience, or conjecture to deduce *a priori* hypotheses, and *later* test those hypotheses using data and recognized analytic procedures. However, the foregoing events often unfold in a different order 'in the lab', where researchers *first* look at their data and results, and *later* generate hypotheses to fit their results and work back to earlier 'theory', 'research', 'experience', or 'conjecture', which supposedly ground hypotheses, and *finally* use the same results to 'test' them *post hoc* (Kerr, 1998). The research ethics literature labels this practice 'HARKing' – hypothesizing after results are known – and argues that this is problematic because analyses of findings from data *capitalize on random chance* (Kline, 2016) and therefore have the potential to bias cumulative knowledge in the field. The potential for bias occurs because HARKing inflates the type 1 error rate – the probability of rejecting the null hypothesis given that it is true (false positives) – used in hypothesis testing (Simmons, Nelson, & Simonsohn, 2011). In practice, the type 1 error rate – is typically set at 5 percent, which is equivalent to admitting a 1/20 chance of incorrectly rejecting the null hypothesis is acceptable. The problem is that HARKing can potentially increase the false positive ratio to unacceptable levels, allowing 'results' that are unlikely to be replicated in other samples drawn for other subjects, times, and places, thus introducing potential bias to cumulative knowledge.

The difficulty for scientific ethics is that most methods used during 'researcher misconduct' can be legitimate under other circumstances. There are many forms of researcher misconduct ranging from ambiguously problematic, e.g., fishing for results with p < .05 using many tests, to potentially sackable offences, e.g., outright fabrication (Bettis, Ethiraj, Gambardella, Helfat, & Mitchell, 2016). However, even outright fabrication can be legitimate, e.g., simulation studies, provided researchers are transparent about what they have done and draw appropriate inferences from their analyses of findings. Nevertheless, ambiguously problematic forms of researcher misconduct such as HARKing are more relevant to the legitimate use of descriptive exploratory plots with multilevel and longitudinal data. Here, Murphy and Aguinis (2019) propose a taxonomy of HARKing behaviors from the *least* potential to bias for cumulative knowledge: 1) hypothesis proliferation, 2) THARKing, to *most* potential for bias 3) cherry-picking, and 4) question trolling. *Hypothesis proliferation* is when researchers amend hypotheses after they have looked at data and results. *THARKing* is when researchers HARK transparently, i.e., they disclose that they 'tested' *post hoc* hypotheses. *Cherry-picking* is when researchers choose the most favorable result from many tests that estimate *the same* population parameter. *Question trolling* is when researchers choose the most favorable results from many tests that estimate *different* population parameters. HARKing is not merely a hypothetical concern, over 90 percent of academic researcher respondents in management indicated that they had knowledge of faculty members who had developed hypotheses after results were known (Bedeian, Taylor, & Miller, 2010) and other studies suggest that at least 30 percent of researchers admit to similar practices themselves (e.g., John, Loewenstein, & Prelec, 2012).

In a simulation study, Murphy and Aguinis (2019) found hypothesis proliferation and THARKing are not likely to introduce bias to cumulative knowledge. However, more troublingly, they find that cherry-picking and question trolling have potential to introduce bias, especially question trolling. *For cherry-picking*, they found that population correlation coefficients of $r = .20$ were exaggerated by up to .10, i.e., *less than* 50 percent bias in most conditions. In some extreme conditions where, 1) 80 percent of estimates were cherry-picked, 2) the sample size was small, and 3) the number of estimates to choose from was large, i.e., 8–10, coefficients were exaggerated by a bit more than .10 (maximum .116). That translates to a *bit above* 50 percent bias in a small number of conditions. *For question trolling*, in 75 percent of conditions they found roughly the same .10 exaggeration in coefficients, i.e., *up to* 50 percent bias. However, more dramatically, in some extreme conditions, where 1) 60–80 percent of the estimates were question trolled, 2) the sample size was small, and 3) the number of estimates to choose from was large, i.e., 6–10, coefficients were exaggerated by .30 (maximum .40), equivalent to between 300 and 400 percent bias in 25 percent of conditions. The rationale offered for these results is as follows: for cherry-picking, there is a research question grounded in theory, before hypotheses are *amended* in response to patterns in the data. Therefore, the extent of bias is likely to be constrained to the extent of sampling error. For question trolling, in contrast, even the research question is 'up for grabs', so both the *post hoc* hypotheses and any theoretical rationale are reverse engineered to fit the data and results, without deference to an anchoring research question. That completes our review of the *four* types of HARKing and their potential to bias cumulative knowledge.

It appears that HARKing needs to be extreme before a sufficiently serious risk of bias to cumulative knowledge materializes that would outweigh the threats from model misspecification discussed above.

METHODS TO CREATE LONGITUDINAL DATA SETS

Approximately 10 people were involved in building the academic spin-off (ASO) data set over a period of about 10 years. The contributors have had different immediate goals but were guided by a dedicated principal investigator toward producing the data in its current form. While the data set is relatively small, it provides enough detail to be both a challenge and an instructive example for data management and descriptive exploratory plots for data sets that are several orders of magnitude larger. The exploratory procedures we recommend follow numerical and graphical strategies used routinely in cross-sectional work, but which tend to be a little more involved with longitudinal data. For example, there is the decision about whether to store data in the long-form, i.e., subject-period format where data for subjects at different times are coded on two or more rows, or the wide-form, i.e., subject-level format where all data are on just one row, but with many more columns (see Hoffman, 2015; Singer & Willett, 2003 for details). We recommend the long-form for data coding, cleaning and side-by-side checking reasons.

We merge each case history with data from other sources: establishment and exit data, accounting data, incubation data, grant funding data, and details about location. Most of these sources come with different date formats for time stamps, so there is considerable data cleaning and checking needed to ensure variables have been coded consistently before plotting. From our experience, keys to success when coding longitudinal data, especially when merging event dates with annual summary data, include the following:

1) Use *one* unique firm identification (id) code that specifies each firm unambiguously. These id codes are essential to merge tables of data from various sources correctly. The id also gives you the freedom to use more than one row to code things that happened to the firm on dates, e.g., date established, date of patent application, date of new CEO appointment, which leads into our next point.

2) Use a consistent format for time stamps, e.g., 10Aug1962, at the smallest interval that makes sense, and stick to it. We believe that the DD-MMM-YYYY date format is the most unambiguous and easy for people to use while coding date data from various sources.

This alpha-numeric format also circumvents inaccuracies based on different geographic traditions, such as how North Americans and Europeans write dates. If data are 'annual summaries,' then code start date and finish date, e.g., income statements and balance sheets can cover 6 to 18 months of operations in their first year. You can always collapse dates into calendar years, but it is *difficult* to get the dates back if you do not record them in the first place.

3)   Use as *many rows* as you want and as *few columns* as you can get away with to capture all the detail you need to record. Narrow tables sorted by firm and by date help when you want to cross-check what you have already coded side-by-side with another data source. Our experience is that it is easier to sort and search up-and-down, e.g., by id and date, than to scroll across-and-back, when looking for a specific field that you want to edit. Most statistical software now provides automated wide-to-long and long-to-wide data format transformations.

While we have implemented the physical coding from source data into structured tables in a series of spreadsheets in Excel (Microsoft Corporation, 2018) and merged these spreadsheets using Stata (StataCorp, 2017), we have drawn on the relational database thinking outlined above to assign combinations of unique identifiers for firms (id) and time stamps (date) to serve as primary and foreign keys in various tables. We use the keys in the excel sheets to merge data from the different sources in Stata (StataCorp, 2017). We recommend resisting the temptation to code data from all sources in one spreadsheet, our strategy was to use firm event data, especially establishment dates and exit dates, as an organizing template for including data from other sources. We added data to firms' time stamped envelopes from the other sources, usually one source at a time, and then started a new worksheet for the next source. Note that the -st- commands in Stata have a number of useful tools to check and repair consistency of event data with covariate data after merging, e.g., finding duplicates, filling empty cells (see Cleves et al., 2016 for details; Mitchell, 2010). For datasets less than one million rows, spreadsheets are still a practical alternative to relational database management systems (RDBMS). Our largest table only reached several thousand rows. For our purposes, primary and foreign keys are combinations of columns chosen to uniquely identify any and all rows in a spreadsheet that must contain a unique value for each row in the data set (i.e., id and date). As a rule, coding time at a lower level of aggregation (i.e., date), produces more precision in analyses of findings, including plots, which consequently are more likely to reveal relations of interest, if they are there (Hoffman, 2015; Little, 2013; Singer & Willett, 2003).

Specifically, in our data about half the firms were incubated through the Industrial Development Corporation's network of accelerators and science parks in Norway, SIVA.[3] We gathered establishment, exit, and location data from the company registration office in Norway, Brønnøysund.[4] In addition, we gathered data for each firm from Retriever – the largest media surveillance provider in the Nordic region – which we used to code firm acquisitions of significant value because trade sale transactions are not recorded by Brønnøysund.[5] Sales, employees, and issued capital data came from consolidated annual income statements and balance sheets provided by Proff Forvalt.[6] Grant funding data came from the Norwegian Research Council.[7] Here we adjusted sales using grant funding data because firms typically report moneys received via grants as sales in their income statements and, thus, overstate sales from actual paying customers.

ANALYSIS OF FIRM DEVELOPMENT AND GROWTH

We draw on detailed case histories for each firm to establish they were *bona fide* knowledge-intensive new ventures. Therefore, in Table 7.1, we must take seriously the quotient of firms with zero sales and zero employees (48 firms). Many studies using large firm databases might try to argue that firms with zeros on both metrics are inactive or just 'paper' firms. However, and importantly, we have evidence to the contrary and do *not* exclude these firms from further analyses. The company registration office in Norway provided establishment dates for all (373 firms), and traditional exit dates for about half (180 firms), i.e., liquidated, changed purpose, bankrupt, and legal proceedings, and using media data we coded merged and acquired dates for a further 14 percent (51 firms), with the remainder

Table 7.1   Number of firms with zero, low and high mean values for continuous outcome variables

Employees (dummy)	Sales (dummy)			
	Zero Sales	Low Sales	High Sales	Total
Zero Employees	48	38	7	93
Low Employees	53	60	28	141
High Employees	28	24	87	139
Total	129	122	122	373

Note: low is below the median (excluding zero) of the firm-mean over time; high is above the median (excluding zero).

Table 7.2   Number of firms and exit events

Exit Event (dummy)	Incubation (dummy)		
	Non-Incubated	Incubated	Total
Acquired	14	18	32
Merged	10	9	19
Liquidated	40	33	73
Change purpose	12	9	21
Bankrupt	12	17	29
Legal proceedings	2	4	6
Total	90	90	180

being right-censored. Table 7.2 presents the details of the number of firms and type of exit, with the split between non-incubated and incubated.

Exploring Between-Subject Differences in Outcomes

The simplest way of exploring *between-subject differences* in outcomes is to plot the entire set of firm observations, just simply connecting observations for each subject overtime, without any model fitting. Figure 7.4 panels (a) and (b) provide such plots for each subject (thin lines), showing the non-incubated firms on the left-hand side and the incubated firms on the right-hand side of each panel. Each panel also includes group-means (thick lines), using fractional polynomial functions with 95 percent confidence intervals, which help compare connected subject-observations with group-means over time. Both panels (a) and (b) suggest that the shape of group-means in sales and employees between firm age 1 and 14 is increasing modestly and seems approximately linear, especially up to age 10. Further, both panels suggest substantial between-subject heterogeneity in change; up to one-third of firms stay anchored to zero, c.f., Table 7.1, while some firms achieve more than double the group-mean, and there are plenty of firms in between. As suggested in Figures 7.2 and 7.3, it is possible to tell from these plots that a multilevel growth model with random intercepts and random slopes for time is likely to fit these data well. We can interpret the main effect of incubation by comparing the height and shape of the group-means over time (thick lines) in the left-hand and right-hand parts of each panel. These descriptive exploratory plots show only a small, if any, main effect of incubation on ASOs.

For survival outcomes, Figure 7.4 panels (c) and (d) show kernel smoothed hazard functions (h0) for traditional exit and merged and acquired (M&A), respectively. Again, the left-hand and right-hand parts of each panel represent non-incubated and incubated conditions. In panel (c), the first kernel-smoothed estimates appears at about 2.5 years in the left-hand panel and just over 3 years on the right-hand panel using the Epanechnikov kernel and a minimum bandwidth in Stata (StataCorp, 2017).[8] For these data, we suggest this as an acceptable compromise between describing the dynamics in the data, i.e., not smoothing too much, and not losing too much visibility of early and late parts of the hazard function (h0). Remember that panels (c) and (d) in Figure 7.4 show hazard functions (h0) for absorbing events, i.e., one-time, non-repeating, and thus cannot have subject-level random intercepts or random slopes for time. Although event occurrence was recorded by date, we divided each time by the length of an 'average' year, (i.e., 365.25 days), but retained fractional components so as not to lose precision in the measurement of time. Scaling time in years makes time more meaningful and easier to compare with plots for continuous outcomes because firm income statements summarize these data (i.e., sales and employees), into years. However, temporal precision is *not* lost because we have not rounded the time values. Again, we can interpret the main effect of incubation by comparing the height and shape of the hazard function in the left-hand and right-hand parts of the panel. The rate of traditional exit in panel (c) seems similar across the two groups, except for an early peak around age 5 in the left-hand part. This result could potentially be interpreted as higher 'liability of newness' among non-incubated firms. The rate of merger and acquisition in panel (d) seems higher in the right-hand part, especially in later years, which might be interpreted as a benefit from the 'incubation network' for appropriating value to the founders. Explanatory variables, in addition to incubation, can be added from here, to explore whether incubation is conditional on other attributes of the entrepreneurial ecosystem, which we come to next.

Exploring Between-Subject Differences in the Effects of Predictors on Outcomes

We now consider between-subject differences in the effects of two predictors, i.e., location and issued capital, on the relation between incubation and outcomes for knowledge-intensive new ventures. Asking whether new venture development and growth differ by geographical location allows us to explore where incubation is most effective, i.e., in the more agglomerated areas around Oslo, a regional innovation center around the technical university in Trondheim, or in other perhaps more peripheral areas around the country, by considering differences in the height and shape of group-means (thick lines) for each location (see Figure 7.5). Table 7.3

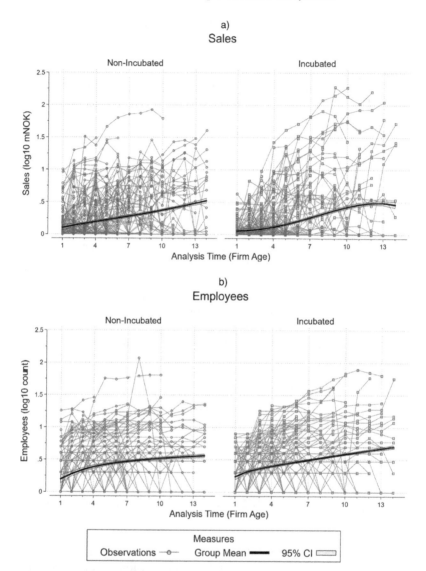

a)
Sales

b)
Employees

Source: adapted from Singer and Willett (2003).

Figure 7.4   *The effects of incubation on continuous and survival outcomes,*
(a) sales, (b) employees, (c) traditional exit, (d) merger and
acquisition

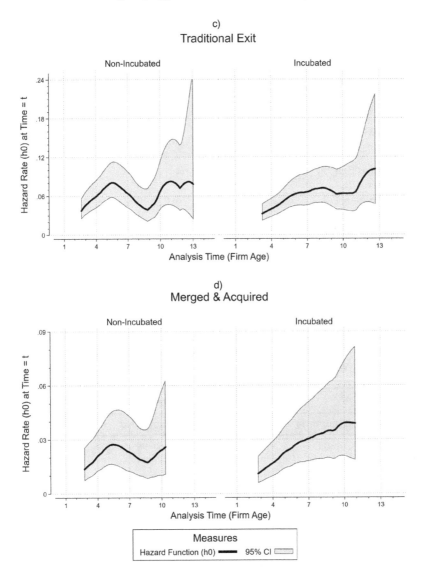

Figure 7.4   (continued)

shows the number of firms in each location and incubation predictors. At first glance, the three M&A events in the Oslo area for incubated firms and the six M&A events in Other areas for non-incubated events seem too low to yield reliable estimates. Thus, we need to consider the plots for those conditions with some caution.

Table 7.3   Number of firms and outcomes with categorical predictors

	Incubation (dummy)		
Location (dummy)	Non-Incubated	Incubated	Total
Oslo area	79	60	139
Trondheim area	46	64	110
Other areas	55	69	124
Total	180	193	373
Traditional Exit			
Oslo area	28	16	44
Trondheim area	19	20	39
Other areas	19	27	46
Total	66	63	129
Merger & Acquisition			
Oslo area	8	3	11
Trondheim area	10	13	23
Other areas	6	11	17
Total	24	27	51

Table 7.4   Number of firms and outcomes with continuous predictors

	Incubation (dummy)		
Issued Capital (dummy)	Non-Incubated	Incubated	Total
High Issued Capital	87	99	186
Low Issued Capital	93	94	187
Total	180	193	373
Traditional Exit			
High Issued Capital	19	25	44
Low Issued Capital	47	38	85
Total	66	63	129
Merger & Acquisition			
High Issued Capital	14	14	28
Low Issued Capital	10	13	23
Total	24	27	51

Note: low is below the median of the firm-mean over time; high is above the median.

Asking whether new venture development and growth differ by issued capital allows us to explore the resource conditions when incubation is more effective, i.e., with high (low) issued capital, by considering differences in the height and shape of group-means (thick lines) associated with the extent of issued capital (see Figure 7.6). Table 7.4 shows the number of firms in each issued capital and incubation condition. These cells seem better covered with observations because there are only four groups (as opposed to six in Table 7.3). Again, Figures 7.5 and 7.6 show separate panels for each outcome variable that distinguish between incubation conditions. If the predictor is categorical, e.g., location, constructing the display is straightforward. If the predictor is continuous, e.g., issued capital, we temporarily categorize values, e.g., above and below the median (kNOK 190), for the purposes of display. For later multivariate analyses, of course, we continue to use the original continuous values.

Figure 7.5 panels (a) and (b) show plots for the effects of location on continuous outcomes over time, with the non-incubated firms on the left-hand side and the incubated firms on the right-hand side of each panel. For the incubated condition, Trondheim (thick dashed lines) seems to have a slightly higher group-mean compared to other locations, especially before the age of 10. This suggests a three way-interaction, i.e., incubation × location × time. Alternatively, for both incubation conditions, Other geographic areas (thick solid lines) seem to have a lower group-mean compared to other locations, especially up to the age of 10, which suggests a two-way interaction, i.e., location × time. This pattern of results suggests the institutional frameworks and support networks available in Trondheim may complement incubation sponsorship to promote ASO development and growth better than alternative locations, and especially compared to other locations. Because there are only three location conditions, estimating random effects for the interaction term is unlikely to produce accurate results (Maas & Hox, 2005). However, between condition variability for the location variable can be assessed using a multiple group model containing a growth model within a structural equation modelling framework (Little & Rioux, 2019).

Figure 7.5 panels (c) and (d) show plots for the effects of location on survival outcomes over time, again with non-incubated firms on the left and incubated on the right. For the incubated group, Trondheim (thick dashed lines) has lower hazard rates for traditional exit and higher hazard rates for M&A than Other locations (thick solid lines). This result appears consistent with continuous outcomes in panels (a) and (b). Again, for the incubated group, the separation over time of hazard functions by location for Trondheim (thick dashed lines) and Other (thick solid lines) reinforces the importance of location predictors on both traditional exit

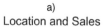

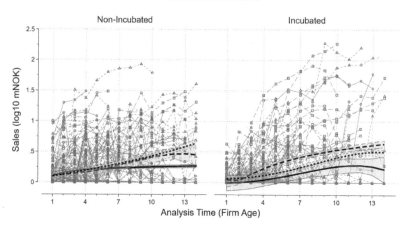

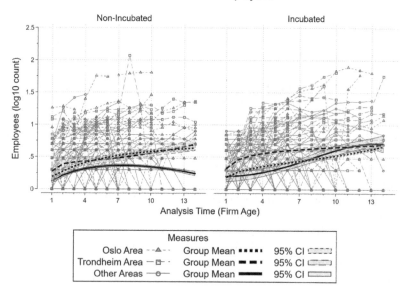

Source: adapted from Singer and Willett (2003).

Figure 7.5   *Moderation effects of location on relation between incubation and continuous and survival outcomes, (a) sales, (b) employees, (c) traditional exit, (d) merger and acquisition*

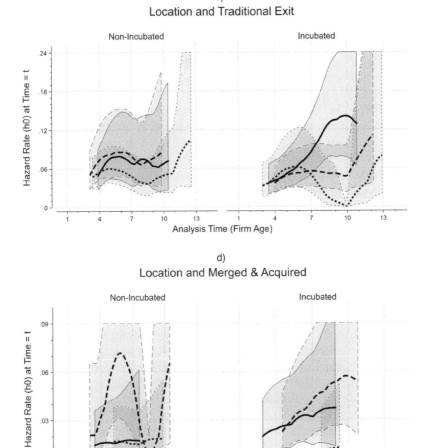

c)
Location and Traditional Exit

d)
Location and Merged & Acquired

Figure 7.5   (continued)

and M&A. However, for both incubation conditions, the Oslo area (thick short-dashed lines) has the lowest hazard rate for both traditional exit and M&A in incubated groups, which is not consistent with the continuous outcomes in panels (a) and (b). Nevertheless, the confidence intervals on all hazard functions are relatively wide because of sparse events across three of the location conditions, especially M&A in Oslo for the incubated condition, which has only three events (cf., Table 7.3). Finally, the high rate of M&A in the Trondheim area, especially during early years of venture development, again suggests strength in the institutional and support networks in that area. Curiously, the rate of M&A in the incubated group is almost the same for Other areas as it is for Trondheim, especially during early years. Taken together, there is some, but not perfect, consistency across relations between the predictors and the four outcome variables. While it remains possible to find a model that will fit all four outcomes in an analogous way, that model will clearly be more parsimonious, with fewer predictors and restrictions, than the best fitting model for any one outcome variable considered alone. This is a good result for cumulative science.

Figure 7.6 panels (a) and (b) show plots for the effects of issued capital on continuous outcomes, again with non-incubated firms on the left and incubated on the right. For both incubation conditions, high issued capital (thick short-dashed lines) seems to be higher, which suggests that new ventures with greater resource endowments develop and grow a little faster, even if their initial positions are not that different. However, because we know a large quotient of firms have zero continuous outcomes, there may be random as well as fixed effects of issued capital on the continuous outcome variables.

Figure 7.6 also plots the effects of issued capital on survival outcomes in panels (c) and (d), with non-incubated firms on the left and incubated on the right as before. For both incubation conditions, high issued capital (thick short dashed lines) seems to have a lower hazard rate for traditional exit. This is consistent with continuous outcomes. In addition, for the non-incubation condition, the 'liability of newness' appears again in the low issued capital condition (thick solid lines). This is consistent with Figure 7.4 panel (c) and suggests that 'liability of newness' is at least partly explained by lack of financial resources. Further, for the incubated condition, there seems to be a lower rate of traditional exit for low issued capital (thick solid lines) compared to the non-incubated group, at least under age 10. This suggests that incubation could act as a resource buffer for firms, at least in early years of firm development (Amezcua et al., 2013). For both incubation conditions, the M&A hazard function is about the same height for the high issued capital condition (thick short-dashed lines) but the shape for the incubation condition seems to start low and end high, while the non-incubation condition remains relatively constant. More curiously, the highest rate of M&A is for the low issued capital and incubated group. These trade sales could be accounted for by resource scarcity preventing the founders from bringing the new venture to the next development and growth stage.

DISCUSSION

In this chapter, we address several data management and analysis issues and challenges facing researchers who want to develop, code, and use multilevel and longitudinal data to study development and growth processes in knowledge-intensive new ventures. For example, specification of fixed and random effects in models fit to clustered data and forming hypotheses *post hoc* after looking at data and when results are known, all of which if done inappropriately can lead to bias in cumulative knowledge. In response to these issues and challenges, we provide several recommendations to help researchers find their way through what often appear to be conflicting demands put on them from both methodologists and advocates of rigor in research ethics. We offer our thoughts in all humility as we have developed them initially to reconcile the apparently conflicting demands for ourselves; to find a way through the rocks and row toward clear water. The size of the prize is large because multilevel and longitudinal data opens many new processual research questions that are not amenable to cross-sectional data. However, the price for these new discoveries is also high because we need to take care of more details in data and analyses. Many of these details are getting resolved by specialists in methodology and statistics and the philosophy of science but it takes time for these breakthroughs to 'trickle down' to applied researchers (see Little, 2013; Murnane & Willett, 2011; Pearl & MacKenzie, 2018 for important exceptions). We hope this chapter makes some contribution to researchers doing multilevel and longitudinal work and brings the opportunities and threats for cumulative science to a wider audience.

In doing so, we provide an illustration based on a sample of academic spin-offs in Norway over a period of 15 years to show an alternative approach to research questions about relations between incubation and knowledge-intensive new venture growth and development that may be conditional on other attributes of the entrepreneurial ecosystem. Specifically, we focus on ecosystem attributes that are likely to complement the effect of incubation on new venture outcomes, i.e., location, issued capital. We observe both constant between-subject differences and

a)

Issued Capital and Sales Value

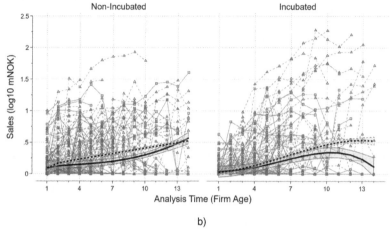

b)

Issued Capital and Employees

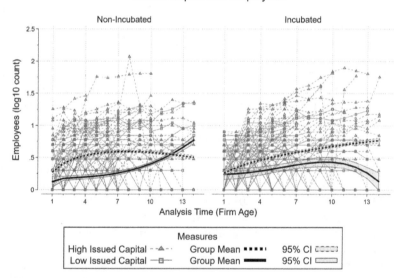

Source: adapted from Singer and Willett (2003).

Figure 7.6   *Moderation effects of issued capital on relation between incubation and continuous and survival outcomes, (a) sales, (b) employees, (c) traditional exit, (d) merger and acquisition*

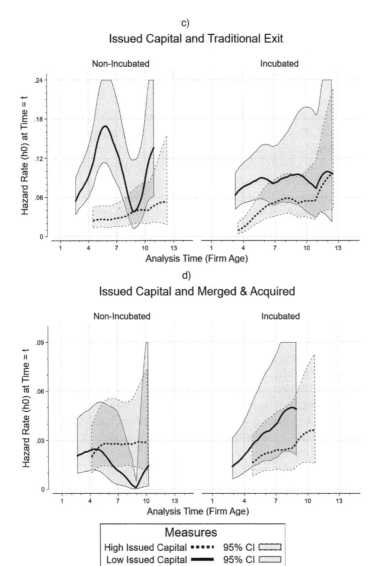

Figure 7.6 (continued)

non-constant between-subject differences over time that need to be modeled using random intercepts and fixed and random slopes, respectively
(see Figure 7.4 panels [a] and [b]). We also observe non-constant between-
subject differences in the effects of predictors over time (see Figures 7.5
and 7.6 panels [a] and [b]). Specifically, we find support for the notion that
some locations, i.e., Trondheim, provide a better institutional context for
incubation to promote new venture development and growth than other
locations, i.e., Oslo, other. In addition, we find support for the notion
that high issued capital conditions provide a better context for incubation
to promote new venture development and growth than low issued capital
(no surprises there). However, it is surprising that for the incubation
condition, that firms with low issued capital have a considerably higher
M&A hazard function than firms with high issued capital. This is a result
worthy of further exploration, perhaps, distinguishing between acquired
firms bought by other firms for relatively large amounts, which were
reported in the media, and merged firms that joined with other firms
for undisclosed amounts. We suggest four main implications of our
illustration.

First, descriptive exploratory plots provide insights that help to inform
subsequent detailed examination with more complex multivariate analyses. For instance, we have already discussed the benefits to cumulative
science from using both continuous and survival outcome variables
to triangulate results across analogous outcome variables for specific
combinations of predictors. The argument for using both continuous
and survival outcome variables is especially strong for censored dependent variables. Indeed, in the future, researchers studying new venture
development and growth research might consider further extending
their modeling repertoire from multilevel growth and survival models
to include two-part models that explicitly model both the zeros and the
growth for (semi-)continuous outcome variables (Muthén et al., 2016).
Two-part regression models have a binary part describing the probability
of being below or above the censoring threshold and a continuous part for
the rest of the distribution. Typically, a log transformation is made of the
positive part of the outcome variable distribution to allow the assumption
of normally distributed residual variances after the log transformation
(Muthén et al., 2016, p. 289). However, wide adoption of two-part models
may still be a way off because they are not widely available in statistical
software packages.[9]

Second, in the meantime, there are improvements to measurement and
analysis strategy using conventional tools for new venture development
and growth scholars to consider. To improve measures of new venture
development, as opposed to growth, entrepreneurship scholars could intro-

duce a broader range of (semi-)continuous outcome variables and model both their continuous and time-to-event realizations, e.g., number of patents and time-to-first patent, sales and time-to-first sales, venture capital funding and time-to-venture capital funding, etc. Indeed, maybe entrepreneurship scholars can cast the measurement net a bit wider and add new indicators to address contamination and deficiency issues on conventional measures of new venture development and growth. However, failing a dramatic breakthrough on new proxies for development and growth, a more eclectic range of multilevel growth and survival modelling approaches, including those we outlined above, will help move the field toward cumulative knowledge.

Third, we see that choices of dependent variables are important to understand the true impact of focal independent variables. In the case of our illustration, we elected to include two types of outcome variable, continuous and survival. We do so because there are no grounds, from previous entrepreneurship research or from statistical theory, to assume that both types of outcome variable will produce consistent results for a combination of predictors. Although earlier entrepreneurship research has suggested links among sales and employees (e.g., Chandler, McKelvie, & Davidsson, 2009; Shepherd & Wiklund, 2009), there have been limited grounds to illustrate systematic relations using longitudinal data. Indeed, before conducting the analysis of findings for these data, our assumption was that the results would differ in several striking and informative ways. Therefore, it is important for researchers to consider evaluating one or more outcome variables of each sort, i.e., continuous and time-to-event, to provide evidence that findings are consistent with effects in similar directions, even if one or more sets of results are not statistically significant.

Fourth, we show that time is important. In addition to taking care of the maturation effects over time, which can be thought of as a proxy for any and all unmeasured explanatory variables (Allison, 2009), time is essential for teasing out both constant and non-constant between-subject differences over time, which are essential to correct model specification. In addition, and more important for hypothesis testing with fixed effects in the model for means, time allows us to tease out non-constant between-subject differences in the effects of predictors over time, which are essential to the whether and when of management and policy implications arising from any analysis of findings from data. For example, the relation between location and outcomes being contingent on time, especially in the incubation condition shown in Figure 7.5. New venture development studies employing longitudinal data have also been able to examine these changing patterns of time, whether they affect changes in growth dynamics (e.g., Wennberg, Delmar, & McKelvie, 2016) or the relationship among key outcome variables (e.g., Delmar et al., 2013).

CONCLUSION

Descriptive exploratory plots of continuous and survival outcomes can *both* suggest the effects of incubation and other ecosystem variables on new venture development and growth *and* promote cumulative knowledge in the field. Using a sample of 373 ASO firms active in Norway between 2000 and 2015, we outline a preliminary analysis strategy using descriptive exploratory plots to show how the relation between incubation and new venture development and growth may be conditional on other attributes of entrepreneurial ecosystems, e.g., location, issued capital. In addition, we outline analogue heuristics with no equations to guide researchers on where to start with specifying fixed and random effects in multilevel and longitudinal models that manage dependency in clustered data. Our analysis of findings from archival data suggest that descriptive exploratory plots can give researchers a concrete and nuanced first approximation of how shared variance in censored outcomes breaks down into between- and within-subject components that are not discoverable using conventional approaches to descriptive statistics typically used with cross-sectional data. Our heuristic schemas and examples using archival data show researchers how to do preliminary analyses to help them specify appropriate fixed and random effects when fitting multivariate regression models to their data. Modeling dependency in multilevel and longitudinal data using appropriate fixed and random effects is critical for researchers to draw valid inferences from clustered data (Hox et al., 2018).

The foregoing qualifies concerns in the research ethics literature about amending hypotheses after looking at data and results. It could be argued that the preliminary analytic strategies we recommend inflate type 1 error (increase false positives) because encouraging researchers to look at descriptive exploratory plots might 'tempt' them to capitalize on chance relations occurring in the data. The concern is that hypotheses formulated after results are known produce findings data that are unlikely to generalize to other subjects, times, and places or replicate with data from other sources and thus do not contribute to cumulative knowledge. We think of ourselves as thoughtful researchers from a pragmatic empiricist tradition who are sympathetic to research ethics concerns and take these arguments seriously. We are also concerned about inadvertently providing a loop hole in the hypothetico-deductive scientific method for 'data snoopers' to use as a defense for question trolling (data mining) procedures with large quantities of data scraped from the internet (Hox, 2017). On the contrary, our intention is to facilitate thoughtful and comprehensive analyses using appropriate statistical models with modest amounts of relevant data from research designed to address specific questions with important theoretical and practical implications. Our concern is that some researchers are now so concerned about doing something illegitimate during analysis of findings that they do *not* look at the data at all. For all the reasons outlined above, if this is the case, then it is a problem. Our discussion of descriptive exploratory plots for continuous and survival outcomes to help researchers specify fixed and random effects in multilevel and longitudinal models is an attempt to push the pendulum back in the other direction, but without damaging the finely tuned mechanism of the clock.

NOTES

*   The first author thanks the Norwegian Research Council, Handelsbanken, Sweden and Soderberg Foundation, Sweden, for part funding this work. The authors thank Todd Little for thoughtful remarks on an earlier version of this chapter.
1.   We follow Hoffman (2015) and use the terms '*model for means*' and '*model for variances*' to help interpret results from fixed and random effects using multilevel and longitudinal models. The model for means and model for variances are heuristic to interpret results in **G** – model for means – and **R** – model for variances – matrices after specifying fixed and random effects in various combinations. The model for means and model for variances are not 'separate' models because all parameters in both parts of the heuristic are estimated simultaneously. The multilevel and longitudinal modeling literature typically distinguishes between- and within-subject variation, because classical analysis, e.g., ANOVA, OLS regression, reveals only between-subject variation. However, the between- and within-subject variance composition of shared variation is not directly analogous to model for means and model for variances. Labels for other between vs. within variation effects include; level 2 vs. level 1, macro vs. micro, inter-subject vs. intra-subject (e.g., Hox, Moerbeek, & van de Schoot, 2018; Nesselroade, 1991; Nesselroade & Ram, 2004; Snijders & Bosker, 2012).
2.   We use the term, 'survival outcomes' to refer to time-to-event outcomes, in our examples time-to-traditional exit, time-to-merger and acquisition, but also potentially to study new venture development and growth with time-to-first sales, time-to-first employees, time-to-intellectual property registration, which can be assessed on either a discrete or continuous time scale, e.g., date, month, year. We use 'survival' synonymously with 'time-to-event' throughout the chapter with a relatively continuous time scale, i.e., date. However, please note that we use the term 'continuous outcomes' to refer to outcome variables measured on a ratio scale, e.g., sales, employees, that have nothing to do with the time scale for the survival outcomes.
3.   SIVA, www.regjeringen.no
4.   Brønnøysund, www.brreg.no
5.   Retriever, www.retriever-info.com
6.   Proff Forvalt, www.forvalt.no
7.   Norwegian Research Council, www.forskningsradet.no
8.   Details of the Stata syntax used to manage the data and create the plots in these examples are available from the first author.
9.   At the time of writing we are only aware of two-part model procedures available in Mplus and a user contributed command in Stata, -twopm-.

REFERENCES

Alcácer, J., Chung, W., Hawk, A., & Pacheco-de-Almeida, G. (2018). Applying random coefficient models to strategy research: Identifying and exploring firm heterogeneous effects. *Strategy Science, 3*(3), 533–553. https://doi.org/10.1287/stsc.2018.0064

Allison, P. D. (2009). *Fixed Effects Regression Models.* Thousand Oakes, CA: Sage.

Allison, P. D. (2014). *Event History and Survival Analysis* (2nd ed.). Thousand Oaks: Sage.

Amezcua, A. S., Grimes, M. G., Bradley, S. W., & Wiklund, J. (2013). Organizational sponsorship and founding environments: A contingency view on the survival of business-incubated firms, 1994–2007. *Academy of Management Journal, 56*(6), 1628–1654. https://doi.org/10.5465/amj.2011.0652

Basbøll, T. (2018). Inframethodology: Introduction. Retrieved January 22, 2019, from http://blog.cbs.dk/inframethodology/?page_id=649

Bedeian, A. G., Taylor, S. G., & Miller, A. N. (2010). Management science on the credibility bubble: Cardinal sins and various misdemeanors. *Academy of Management Learning & Education, 9*(4), 715–725. https://doi.org/10.5465/amle.9.4.zqr715

Bentler, P. M., & Bonett, D. G. (1981). Significance tests and goodness of fit in the analysis of covariance structures. *Psychological Bulletin, 88*(3), 5SS – 606. https://doi.org/10.1037/0033-2909.88.3.588

Bettis, R. A., Ethiraj, S., Gambardella, A., Helfat, C., & Mitchell, W. (2016). Creating repeatable cumulative knowledge in strategic management. *Strategic Management Journal, 37*(2), 257–261. https://doi.org/10.1002/smj.2477

Bliese, P. D., Maltarich, M. A., & Hendricks, J. L. (2018). Back to basics with mixed-effects models: Nine take-away points. *Journal of Business and Psychology, 33*(1), 1–23. https://doi.org/10.1007/s10869-017-9491-z

Brush, C. G., Edelman, L. F., & Manolova, T. S. (2008). The effects of initial location, aspirations, and resources on likelihood of first sale in nascent firms. *Journal of Small Business Management, 46*(2), 159–182. https://doi.org/10.1111/j.1540-627X.2008.00238.x

Campbell, J. P. (1990). Modeling the performance prediction problem in industrial and organizational psychology. In *Handbook of Industrial and Organizational Psychology, Vol. 1, 2nd ed* (pp. 687–732). Palo Alto, CA, US: Consulting Psychologists Press.

Campbell, J. P., McCloy, R. A., Oppler, S. H., & Sager, C. E. (1992). A theory of performance. In N. Schmitt & W. C. Borman (Eds.), *Personnel Selection in Organizations* (pp. 35–70). San Francisco, CA: Wiley.

Chandler, G. N., McKelvie, A., & Davidsson, P. (2009). Asset specificity and behavioral uncertainty as moderators of the sales growth – Employment growth relationship in emerging ventures – ScienceDirect. *Journal of Business Venturing, 24*(4), 373–387.

Cleves, M., Gould, W. W., & Marchenko, Y. (2016). *An Introduction to Survival Analysis Using Stata* (Revised 3rd ed.). College Station, TX: Stata.

Cook, T. D., & Campbell, D. T. (1979). *Quasi-experimentation: Design & Analysis Issues for Field Settings* (Vol. 351). Boston, MA: Houghton Mifflin.

Curran, P. J., Lee, T., Howard, A. L., Lane, S., & MacCallum, R. (2012). Disaggregating Within-Person and Between-Person Effects in Multilevel and Structural Equation Growth Models. In J. R. Harring & G. R. Hancock (Eds.), *Advances in Longitudinal Methods in the Social and Behavioral Sciences* (pp. 217–253). Charlotte, NC: Information Age.

Delmar, F. (1997). Measuring growth: methodological considerations and empirical results. In R. Donckels & A. Miettinen (Eds.), *Entrepreneurship and SME Research: On its Way to the Next Millennium* (pp. 199–215). Oxford: Routledge.

Delmar, F., McKelvie, A., & Wennberg, K. (2013). Untangling the relationships among growth, profitability and survival in new firms. *Technovation, 33*(8), 276–291. https://doi.org/10.1016/j.technovation.2013.02.003

Dunleavy, P. (2003). *Authoring a PhD: How to Plan, Draft, Write and Finish a Doctoral Thesis or Dissertation.* Basingstoke, UK: Palgrave.

Fini, R., Rasmussen, E., Siegel, D., & Wiklund, J. (2018). Rethinking the commercialization of public science: From entrepreneurial outcomes to societal impacts. *The Academy of Management Perspectives*, *32*(1), 4–20. https://doi.org/10.5465/amp.2017.0206

Greve, H. R. (2017). From the Editor. *Administrative Science Quarterly*, *62*(2), v–vi. https://doi.org/10.1177/0001839217707199

Hoffman, L. (2015). *Longitudinal Analysis: Modeling Within-Person Fluctuation and Change.* New York, NY: Routledge.

Hox, J. J. (2017). Computational social science methodology, anyone? *Methodology*, *13*(Supplement 1), 3–12. https://doi.org/10.1027/1614-2241/a000127

Hox, J. J., Moerbeek, M., & van de Schoot, R. (2018). *Multilevel Analysis: Techniques and Applications* (3rd ed.). Oxford, UK: Routledge.

John, L. K., Loewenstein, G., & Prelec, D. (2012). Measuring the prevalence of questionable research practices with incentives for truth telling. *Psychological Science*, *23*(5), 524–532. https://doi.org/10.1177/0956797611430953

Kerr, N. L. (1998). HARKing: Hypothesizing after the results are known. *Personality & Social Psychology Review (Lawrence Erlbaum Associates)*, *2*(3), 196. https://doi.org/10.1207/s15327957pspr0203_4

Kline, R. B. (2016). *Principles and Practice of Structural Equation Modeling* (4th ed.). New York, NY: Guildford.

Little, T. D. (2013). *Longitudinal Structural Equation Modeling* (1st ed.). New York, NY: Guilford.

Little, T. D., & Rioux, C. (2019). On the Merits of Longitudinal Multiple-Group Fixed Effects Modeling: A Valid and Often Preferred Approach to Intervention Evaluations. *Working Paper Texas Tech.*

Maas, C. J. M., & Hox, J. J. (2005). Sufficient sample sizes for multilevel modeling. *Methodology: European Journal of Research Methods for the Behavioral and Social Sciences*, *1*(3), 86–92. https://doi.org/10.1027/1614-2241.1.3.86

Mathieu, J. E., Maynard, M. T., Rapp, T., & Gilson, L. (2008). Team effectiveness 1997-2007: A review of recent advancements and a glimpse into the future. *Journal of Management*, *34*(3), 410–476.

McKelvie, A., & Wiklund, J. (2010). Advancing firm growth research: A focus on growth mode instead of growth rate. *Entrepreneurship Theory and Practice*, *34*(2), 261–288. https://doi.org/10.1111/j.1540-6520.2010.00375.x

Microsoft Corporation. (2018). Excel (Version Office 365 (32-bit)) [Windows 10]. Seattle, WA: Microsoft Corporation.

Mitchell, M. N. (2010). *Data Management Using Stata: A Practical Handbook.* Stata press College Station, TX.

Murnane, R. J., & Willett, J. B. (2011). *Methods Matter: Improving Causal Inference in Educational and Social Science.* New York, NY: Oxford University Press.

Murphy, K. R., & Aguinis, H. (2019). HARKing: How badly can cherry-picking and question trolling produce bias in published results? *Journal of Business and Psychology*, *34*(1), 1–17. https://doi.org/10.1007/s10869-017-9524-7

Muthén, B. O., Muthén, L. K., & Asparouhov, T. (2016). *Regression and Mediation Analysis using Mplus.* Los Angeles, CA: Muthen & Muthen.

Nesselroade, J. R. (1991). The warp and woof of the developmental fabric. In R. M. Downs, L. S. Liben, & D. S. Palermo (Eds.), *Visions of Aesthetics, the Environment & Development: the Legacy of Joachim F. Wohlwill* (pp. 213–240). Hillsdale, NJ: Erlbaum.

Nesselroade, J. R., & Ram, N. (2004). Studying intraindividual variability: What we have learned that will help us understand lives in context. *Research in Human Development*, *1*(1–2), 9–29. https://doi.org/10.1080/15427609.2004.9683328

Pearl, J., & MacKenzie, D. (2018). *The Book of Why: The New Science of Cause and Effect.* Colchester, UK: Penguin.

Rabe-Hesketh, S., & Skrondal, A. (2012). *Multilevel and Longitudinal Modeling Using Stata* (3rd ed., Vol. 1–2). College Station, TX: Stata.

Raudenbush, S. W., & Bryk, A. S. (2002). *Hierarchical Linear Models: Applications and Data Analysis Methods* (2nd ed.). Thousand Oakes, CA: Sage.

Schoonhoven, C. B., Eisenhardt, K. M., & Lyman, K. (1990). Speeding products to market: Waiting time to first product introduction in new firms. *Administrative Science Quarterly*, *35*(1), 177–207. https://doi.org/10.2307/2393555

Shepherd, D. A., & Wiklund, J. (2009). Are we comparing apples with apples or apples with oranges? Appropriateness of knowledge accumulation across growth studies. *Entrepreneurship Theory and Practice*, *33*(1), 105–123.

Simmons, J. P., Nelson, L. D., & Simonsohn, U. (2011). False-positive psychology: Undisclosed flexibility in data collection and analysis allows presenting anything as significant. *Psychological Science*, *22*(11), 1359–1366.

Singer, J. D., & Willett, J. B. (2003). *Applied Longitudinal Data Analysis: Modeling Change and Event Occurrence*. New York, NY: Oxford.

Snijders, T. A. B., & Bosker, R. (2012). *Multilevel Analysis: An Introduction to Basic and Advanced Multilevel Modeling* (2nd ed.). London, UK: Sage.

StataCorp. (2017). Stata Release 15.1 Statistical Software (Version IC for Windows 64-bit x86-64). College Station, TX: StataCorp LLC.

Tabachnick, B. G., & Fidell, L. S. (2013). *Using Multivariate Statistics*. Essex, UK: Pearson.

Wennberg, K., Delmar, F., & McKelvie, A. (2016). Variable risk preferences in new firm growth and survival. *Journal of Business Venturing*, *31*(4), 408–427. https://doi.org/10.1016/j.jbusvent.2016.05.001

Wennberg, K., Wiklund, J., DeTienne, D. R., & Cardon, M. S. (2010). Reconceptualizing entrepreneurial exit: Divergent exit routes and their drivers. *Journal of Business Venturing*, *25*(4), 361–375. https://doi.org/10.1016/j.jbusvent.2009.01.001

Wiklund, J., Wright, M., & Zahra, S. A. (2018). Conquering relevance: Entrepreneurship research's grand challenge. *Entrepreneurship Theory and Practice*, *43*(3), 419–436. 1042258718807478. https://doi.org/10.1177/1042258718807478

PART II

START-UP SUPPORT ORGANIZATIONS

8. Organizational sponsorship: An overview of the state of knowledge and future research directions
Marit Breivik-Meyer

INTRODUCTION

New firms often face difficulties in accessing resources from the environment because they lack a track record and have low levels of legitimacy. Stinchcombe (1965) describes this as the *liability of newness*, since new firms' risk of failure is much higher than established firms' risk. Moreover, new firms are often small and face the *liability of smallness*, which refers to the vulnerability of small firms and the impact of size on available resources (Aldrich & Auster, 1986). Recognizing these constraints, start-up incubation ecosystems (SUPIEs) provide sponsorship to new firms in the form of public and private actors, such as business incubators, accelerators and other efforts that support new firms in their early development. This could be labelled *organizational sponsorship* (Amezcua, Grimes, Bradley, & Wiklund, 2013).

Organizational sponsorship is an emerging theory that bridges the conversation between scholars of different types of sponsorship in SUPIEs and entrepreneurial policy (Amezcua et al., 2013). Actors in SUPIEs use considerable amounts of public and private capital to support new firms (Bergek & Norrman, 2008), and there is therefore a tremendous value in understanding the mechanisms that make sponsorship more effective. Hence, this chapter addresses the following key questions:

(1) How good is our understanding of organizational sponsorship and its mechanisms?
(2) What do we need to know more about?

To answer these questions, the remainder of this chapter is divided into three sections. The first section is a presentation of how the systematic literature review was conducted. Second, the papers and their contributions to the development of organizational sponsorship theory are presented. The third section discusses the status and future research directions, and lastly a conclusion for the chapter is presented.

METHODOLOGY

A systematic literature review, which is characterized by a transparent and objective review process, was used to identify key contributions (Jesson, Matheson, & Lacey, 2011). First, I used the influential article by Amezcua et al. (2013) to identify relevant search terms by going through the article's reference list and doing a citation search on the article. The reference list yielded two articles by Flynn, and I also went through these two papers' reference lists and found three proceedings by Flynn that used the term *sponsorship* in their titles. I tried to obtain access to the conference papers, but I was unable to obtain copies. Therefore, the three proceedings were excluded from further analysis. In the citation and final searches, I chose Web of Science (WoS) and Scopus as databases because they are the most extensive databases and differ substantially in their coverage (Mongeon & Paul-Hus, 2016). The citation search yielded 31 articles from WoS and 40 articles from Scopus. I read the articles' abstracts and keywords, searching for articles using the term *sponsorship*, and this resulted in six articles from WoS and two additional articles from Scopus. These articles made the foundation for creating the search terms: 'organizational sponsorship', 'organizational sponsors', 'public sponsorship', 'government sponsorship', 'sponsorship of incubators' and 'incubator sponsors'.

The final searches were conducted in December 2018. In WoS, the Web of Science Core Collection was chosen, which covers the leading scholarly literature. The search was conducted between 1955 and 2018 with topic as the field search, which included title, abstract, keywords and keywords plus (additional keywords created by Thomson Reuters). This yielded a total of 18 articles when limiting to the English language and the 'business' and 'management' categories. In the Scopus database, the search yielded 102 articles when limiting to the English language and 'business, management and accounting' and 'social sciences' as the subject areas.

All the articles were exported into Endnote (N = 120), and duplicates were deleted. After the deletion of duplicates, 100 articles remained. Most of the duplicates existed because I completed the search in two databases. Scopus retrieved the highest number of articles, which is not surprising since Scopus is the larger database of the two (Mongeon & Paul-Hus, 2016). Scopus also covered most of the articles found in WoS.

I read through the titles and abstract of the 100 articles. The inclusion and exclusion criteria were as follows:

- Studies had to focus on the sponsorship of organizations.
- Papers that, for instance, focus on government sponsorship to increase innovation through collaboration between university and

industry were excluded, and papers addressing government sponsorship of research were excluded.

- Papers that focus on sponsorship in other contexts than entrepreneurship, such as banking, refugees, sport events, education or advertising, were excluded.
- Papers that are just sponsored by the government and do not study sponsorship were excluded.

When the titles of the papers clearly indicated that the papers were irrelevant, their abstracts were not read. These were mainly articles focusing on banking, refugees, sport events, education and advertising. This step reduced the sample to only 14 relevant papers, which were read in their entirety. A data-extraction sheet with author(s), research question(s)/purpose, definition of sponsorship, context of sponsorship, data, method and key findings was used to code the articles. Another criterion was implemented in the full-paper reading: Only publications that contribute to organizational sponsorship as a theoretical perspective were considered in the final sample. Articles that use incubator sponsors, public sponsorship and government sponsorship as a term but do not contribute to the theoretical perspective of organizational sponsorship were excluded. After this step, 10 articles remained. I did not get access to the full-paper version of one article, which was a conference proceeding. I included two papers that contribute to organizational sponsorship but did not appear in the final searches. The final sample consists of 11 articles.

THE EVOLUTION OF THE LITERATURE ON ORGANIZATIONAL SPONSORSHIP

Flynn and Falbe (1986) triggered the first wave of publications (1986–1993) on organizational sponsorship. Flynn himself has written all the publications in the first wave (five publications), and the first three publications are conference proceedings (Flynn, 1988, 1990; Flynn & Falbe, 1986). Amezcua et al. (2013) triggered the second wave of publications, and research using organizational sponsorship as a theoretical perspective is in an upward trend, with eight publications in the last three years. The next sections will present the papers and their contributions to the evolution of the literature on organizational sponsorship (see Appendix A for an overview of the papers).

The Pioneering Studies

The first published article by Flynn (1993b) was a conceptual paper using population ecology and resource dependence theory in the context of sponsorship. These two theoretical perspectives consider organizations' levels of control on their environments. The population ecology model explains the relationship between organizations and their environments and the specific environmental conditions that lead to the establishment, growth and death of organizations and populations of organizations (Aldrich, McKelvey, & Ulrich, 1984). For high-density markets, the founding effect is negative and the failure effect is positive (Flynn, 1993b). Therefore, organizational survival is seen as organizational success in the population ecology view. In comparison to the population ecology model, new organizations more actively attempt to adapt to the environment in the resource dependence approach (Flynn, 1993b). Resource dependence theory highlights the strategies new organizations undertake to obtain resources. New organizations are not self-reliant, and they must obtain resources from the external environment. To increase the level of resources available, new organizations develop inter-organizational relationships. This leads to dependencies between organizations. The degree of dependence is determined by resource availability and importance (Pfeffer & Salancik, 1978).

Flynn (1993b) discusses how sponsorship can affect organizational survival by (1) protecting the sponsored organization from competitors until it is ready to stand on its own and (2) providing links to external actors. Flynn (1993b) argues that the outcome of sponsorship depends on whether the sponsored organization uses its endowments to differentiate itself from competitors. Additionally, the type of sponsorship may affect the organization's learning opportunities, since the sponsor imprints the new organization with features that will affect its chances of survival. Flynn (1993b) also stresses that sponsorship should focus on creating organizations that are self-organizing. It is important that the sponsored organization is not too dependent on the sponsor, because over-dependency could make it difficult for the organization to adapt to an unsponsored environment. It is also important to consider the regional infrastructure, and Flynn states that the infrastructure is important for the long-term survival of organizations. Sponsorship should contribute to enriching an area's resource base in the long term.

The second article uses register data on 14 regions in the United States to study the effect of public sponsorship and regional infrastructure on new organizations' emergence and survival (Flynn, 1993a). Flynn (1993a) found that sponsorship enriches the local infrastructure.

The Second Wave of Studies

Amezcua et al. (2013) started the second wave of studies on organizational sponsorship by laying the groundwork for a new theory, the theory of organizational sponsorship. Since there is sparse literature on organizational sponsorship, Amezcua et al. (2013) draw several parallels to sociology's attention to patronage to describe organizational sponsorship. Both organizational sponsorship and patronage emphasize efforts to resolve structural imbalances of power and resources.

Organizational sponsorship includes different types of sponsorship (e.g. small business loans, venture capital, business incubation, franchising), and until now, research efforts on the different types of sponsorship have evolved in isolation from each other (Amezcua et al., 2013). Amezcua et al. (2013) argue that this framework bridges the conversation between scholars of different types of sponsorship by introducing mechanisms of sponsorship across contexts. They identify two mechanisms applied via sponsorship, *bridging* and *buffering*. Some cases of sponsorship can focus on one mechanism, while others use both to mediate the relationship between new organizations and their environments. Organizational sponsorship playing a buffering role refers to the development of internal resources in the new organization, simultaneously protecting the organization against the external environment (Flynn, 1993b). The buffering mechanism helps the new firm to develop an initial resource base by focusing on developing internal resources. The sponsor (the organization that supports the new organization) protects the new organization until it is able to attract resources from the environment. Governmental efforts, such as tax subsidization for new organizations, provide a buffer against particular environmental obligations, in this case taxes. Business incubators can also buffer a new organization by helping the organization accumulate resources and build operating procedures, thereby making the organization less dependent on the external environment (Amezcua et al., 2013). Flynn (1993a) realizes that new organizations can be overprotected in a stable environment and therefore face challenges adapting to an uncertain environment.

Mobilizing resources from the environment is a great challenge for new organizations. In the second view, organizational sponsorship plays a bridging role in which the sponsor connects the new firm to external resources. The bridging mechanism focuses on enhancing relationships between the new organization and the external environment. The new organization can struggle to attract resources because it lacks a reputation and a track record (Brush, Greene, & Hart, 2001). The sponsor serves as a connective intermediary between the social network of the sponsor and the new organization and encourages the new organization to actively engage in the external environment to attract resources from it (Amezcua et al., 2013). However, before the sponsor connects the new organization to potential external resource providers, the sponsor and the nascent organization have to find out which resources are needed and thereafter identify and target potential suppliers of that resource (Brush et al., 2001). For example, if the needed resource is capital, an incubator can connect the new organization to a venture capital fund. Thus, the organization has a chance to attract financial resources.

Through the bridging mechanism, organizational sponsorship increases social capital (Flynn, 1993b) and legitimacy (Amezcua et al., 2013). The sponsor can help the new organization to build and increase its social capital by improving the quantity and quality of the organization's external relationships. Social capital can be defined as 'the aggregate of resources embedded within, available through, and derived from the network of relationships possessed by an individual or organisation' (Inkpen & Tsang, 2005, pp. 150–151). Through building social capital, the likelihood of attracting resources and knowledge increases, and new organizations can improve competitiveness and chances of survival (Amezcua et al., 2013). Good relationships indicate that the organization has a leading edge in the market, which can increase legitimacy (Zimmerman & Zeitz, 2002). Legitimacy can be defined as 'a generalized perception or assumption that the actions of an entity are desirable, proper, or appropriate within some socially constructed system of norms, values, beliefs, and definitions' (Suchman, 1995, p. 574). Stinchcombe (1965) describes legitimacy as the cure for the liabilities facing new organizations. Zimmerman and Zeitz (2002) argue that legitimacy is an important intangible resource, because increased legitimacy enables new organizations to acquire resources from external actors. Therefore, acquiring and increasing social capital and legitimacy are important for new organizational survival, development and growth and are two central concepts in the organizational sponsorship perspective.

In addition to defining bridging and buffering, Amezcua et al. (2013) categorizes the actual activities associated with buffering and bridging into direct support, networking and field-building and find that sponsorship's effectiveness is dependent on how particular sponsorship activities fit with the founding density of an environment. Sponsorship of new firms in high-density markets should focus on networking and direct support, while sponsorship of new firms in markets characterized by lower market density should focus on field-building efforts. The study also shows that those same services in other environments have a negative effect on new organizational survival.

Autio and Rannikko (2016) state that organizational sponsorship theory has focused on survival and paid less attention to the growth of new firms. Their study proposes a third mechanism, the capacity-boosting mechanism (*boosting*), to better understand how sponsorship can increase the growth of new firms. In this mechanism, the focus is on the formation and achievement of milestones, and the amount of support provided to a firm will depend on the reaching of these milestones. The focus is also on serving as a connective intermediary between firms.

Pandey, Lall, Pandey, and Ahlawat (2017) extend the literature on organizational sponsorship by suggesting that sponsoring organizations, particularly social accelerator programmes, engage in another mechanism, *bolstering*. The authors describe bolstering mechanisms as sponsors providing mentoring, additional fundraising, and credibility and awareness to sponsored organizations. Further, the bolstering mechanism is described as supporting already-founded, early-stage social firms. The study found that social accelerators engage in buffering, bridging and bolstering mechanisms by offering seven services: (1) training, (2) mentoring, (3) networking with partners and customers, (4) networking with other entrepreneurs, (5) direct seed capital funding, (6) indirect funding through investors and (7) building awareness and credibility.

Cohen, Bingham, and Hallen (2018) focus on how entrepreneurs access, interpret and process external information and suggest that sponsors help entrepreneurs to react to external knowledge, learn from peers and focus on where to search and gather information.

Dutt et al. (2016) contribute to the development of organizational sponsorship as a theoretical perspective by examining how different types of sponsorship of incubators (private, government, academic and non-governmental organizations [NGOs]) influence the incubators' mix of services. This paper finds that private-, academic- and NGO-sponsored incubators tend to specialize (private on finance, academic on space and consulting, NGO on training), while government-sponsored incubators provide a mix of services. Mrkajic (2017) contributes to the organizational sponsorship perspective by supporting Dutt et al.'s (2016) findings that services offered by incubators depend on the type of sponsorship the incubators have.

Seidel, Packalen, and O'Mahony (2016) address how entrepreneurs sustain their autonomy while being affiliated with organizational sponsors. This paper identifies three types of threats to entrepreneurs' autonomy and solutions to address the threats: First, mentor role conflict is addressed by problem-focused advice and the notion that the entrepreneur has the decision rights. Second, gatekeeper control is reduced by entrepreneurs engaging in knowledge- and experience-sharing with other entrepreneurs and the incubator facilitating forums for this peer exchange. Third, affiliation dissonance is addressed by entrepreneurs engaging with incubators in the early stages while trying to distance themselves in later stages.

Motoyama and Knowlton (2016) examine the effect of government sponsorship in an ecosystem and the process of how start-ups access local resources and develop networks. This study characterizes the effects of sponsorship into different dimensions of the ecosystem. First, it is the interaction and learning between entrepreneurs that has facilitated firm development. Second, start-ups have received access to multiple local resources and used these for different purposes and during different stages of their development. Third, the public–private partnership has acted as a coordinator between the local support organizations.

Jourdan and Kivleniece (2017) state that the nascent literature on organizational sponsorship remains elusive and provides limited insights into the concept of sponsorship and its effects on organizations. Using the population of French film enterprises between 1998 and 2008, this study found an inverted U-shaped relationship between the quantity of public sponsorship obtained for a sponsored organization and its market performance. The breadth, depth and focus of the sponsored organization's resource accumulation and allocation moderated this relationship.

DISCUSSION AND FUTURE RESEARCH DIRECTIONS

The Mechanisms of Organizational Sponsorship

Table 8.1 summarize the assumptions of the mechanisms of organizational sponsorship. The table is adopted from the paper by Amezcua et al. (2013). The mechanisms differ in respect to focus, how they perceive the environment and sponsorship activities. The suggested boosting mechanism by Autio and Rannikko (2016) focuses on growth, but they also state that the bridging mechanism, through access to external resources, enhances survival and facilitates growth through knowledge and experience exchanges. In their study, Autio and Rannikko (2016) argue that the buffering mechanism promotes survival through insulation of resources and that survival will not automatically lead to growth. I agree that survival will not automatically lead to growth but that buffering, through consulting services, also could lead to enhanced knowledge and experience, which in turn would facilitate growth. The boosting mechanism is added to the table because it plays a different role than bridging and buffering. Organizational sponsorship plays a boosting role when the

Table 8.1   Distinguishing assumptions of the mechanisms of organizational sponsorship

Characteristics	Buffering	Bridging	Boosting
Entrepreneurial resources	Focus on the development of internal resources	Focus on the acquisition of external resources	Focus on the boosting of organizational capacities for growth
Founding environment	Environment is a source of competition and resource dependencies	Environment is a confluence of potential stakeholders that can provide the new firm with social capital and legitimacy	NA
The role of sponsorship	Focus on maintaining a protective environment that allows new firms to develop internal resources while minimizing resource dependencies	Focus on serving as a connective intermediary allowing new firms to acquire social capital and legitimacy for the purpose of building a sustainable competitive advantage	Focus on the formation and achievement of milestones. The amount of support will depend on the reaching of milestones. The focus is also on serving as a connective intermediary between firms.
Sample sponsorship activities	Tax shelters, subsidized office space, subsidized back office support, subsidized product development, consulting services, small business loans, labor force training	Networking services, structural incentives and programmes encouraging early-stage investments. Science park co-location, memberships and associations	Imposed milestones, networking between firms

sponsor imposes milestones and tries to boost organizational capacities for growth (Autio & Rannikko, 2016). Firm growth depends on having an organizational capacity for growth and actively pursuing it (Zahra, Sapienza, & Davidsson, 2006). This mechanism is especially designed for growth firms.

Pandey et al. (2017) introduce another mechanism, *bolstering*, in which sponsors provide mentoring, additional fundraising, and credibility and awareness. This mechanism is supposed to target already-founded, early-stage firms. However, I find it difficult to understand exactly what is unique with the bolstering mechanism. According to Amezcua et al. (2013), bridging consists of, for example, mentoring from persons outside of the incubator and access to potential funding sources. In the bridging mechanism, the sponsor helps new firms to acquire social capital and legitimacy through serving as a connective intermediary. Since the activities in the bolstering view already exist in the bridging view, the uniqueness of the bolstering mechanism is missing. Therefore, I have not included the bolstering mechanism in Table 8.1.

Sponsorship of Sponsors and Types of Sponsoring Organizations

Flynn and Falbe (1986) defined the process of sponsorship as attempts from state and local agencies to help new firm formation. Flynn (1988) refers to sponsorship as government, business and/or university efforts to create a nurturing environment that supports and contributes to the birth and survival of firms (Flynn, 1993b). Amezcua et al. (2013, p. 1628) define organizational sponsorship as 'attempts to mediate the relationship between new organizations and their environments by creating a resource-munificent context intended to increase survival rates among those organizations'. As we can see from the methodology chapter, there are also other terms used, such as *public sponsorship* and *government sponsorship*. The different terms relate to the sponsorship of sponsors. As I see it, organizational sponsorship is the overarching term, including private, government, academic, and non-governmental organizations. Public and government sponsorship are synonyms and sub-categories of organizational sponsorship. Therefore, I agree with Jourdan and Kivleniece (2017) that public sponsorship is one form of organizational sponsorship.

In addition to defining sponsorship by the 'sponsorship of sponsors', sponsorship could be categorized by the type of sponsoring organization. Organizational sponsorship includes many types of sponsorship, such as venture capital, business incubators and franchising (Amezcua et al., 2013). Jourdan and Kivleniece (2017) suggest the need to clarify the difference between sponsorship and contract-based or equity-based resource acquisition. Therefore, there is a need to classify all the types of organizational sponsorship and the similarities and differences between each type of sponsoring organization. Of the studies discussed in this chapter, four use business incubation as a context, two use acceleration and four use sponsorship directly from the government. As Amezcua et al. (2013)

mention, the mechanisms of bridging and buffering should be appropriate to all types of sponsorship, but the activities and services used likely differ. This indicates a need for research in different contexts, and future research should focus on three different aspects: First, research should investigate whether or not the mechanisms are applicable to new contexts, such as venture capital and franchising. Second, it should investigate if there are any new mechanisms that take place in these contexts. Third, organizational sponsorship has highlighted different mechanisms, but the actual content of those mechanisms is somewhat unclear, and may differ across sponsorship phenomena (types of sponsoring organizations and the sponsorship of sponsors). Dutt et al. (2016) and Mrkajic (2017) found that the sponsorship of sponsors affects the services provided to new firms. Future studies should examine the actual activities in the mechanisms in different contexts.

Firm Stage, Type of Firm and Environmental Conditions

There is also a need for process studies that investigate the interplay between the mechanisms and in which stage of firm development each mechanism should be introduced. Also, how much of each mechanism and which activities should be introduced in the different stages of firms' early development needs to be investigated. Mrkajic (2017) distinguishes between the nascent stage and seed stage of the entrepreneurial life cycle and suggests that sponsors supporting firms in nascent stages should emphasize business capability development and that sponsors supporting firms in the seed stage should emphasize market reach development. Future research should pursue longitudinal studies that follow new firms' development. A related area is to study how the mechanisms and activities are customized to firms' resource needs. High-growth firms have different needs than those who just want to survive. Therefore, it is expected that sponsors supporting different types of firms offer different types of services. There has to be a match between the sponsored organization's needs and the services provided by the sponsor. Autio and Rannikko (2016) propose boosting as a mechanism for supporting growth-oriented firms. Future research should address this further.

Some parts of the literature focus on the positives with organizational sponsorship, while others focus on the conditions under which sponsorship has positive and negative effects. Jourdan and Kivleniece (2017) look at the relationship between the amounts of public sponsorship received for a sponsored organization and the organization's market performance. In their study, they found an inverted, U-shaped relationship. This is another research area to pursue in order to develop the sponsorship theory further. The questions to be addressed concern how much of each mechanism is the right amount and whether the amount depends on the type of firm and/or firm stage. Another research area is to further study under which environmental conditions the mechanisms and activities have positive and negative effects. It is also important to address how the sponsors create organizations that are ready to adapt to an unsponsored environment.

Defining Organizational Sponsorship

Literature on organizational sponsorship is emerging. However, the literature is not clear on the definition of organizational sponsorship (see Appendix A). Organizational sponsorship is recognized by different names that reflect the sponsorship of sponsors. In addition, organizational sponsorship includes many types of sponsoring organizations who sponsor different types of firms and firms in different stages of development. Both Flynn and Amezcua emphasize the survival of new organizations in their definitions. However, Jourdan and Kivleniece (2017) have a broader definition that includes all organizations, not only new organizations. On the other hand, Autio and Rannikko (2016) criticise that organizational sponsorship has only considered survival rather than growth. The reason for the emphasis on survival is that the literature, as mentioned earlier, builds on population ecology, in which survival is the primary dependent variable. Jourdan and Kivleniece (2017) also suggest that there is a need to clarify how sponsorship differs from contract-based or equity-based resource acquisition. Future research should address these criticisms and discuss what should be included in the definition of organizational sponsorship.

CONCLUSION

SUPIEs use considerable amounts of capital to provide sponsorship to new firms, and there is a great value in understanding the mechanisms that make sponsorship more effective. The aim of this chapter has been to provide an overview of the literature on organizational sponsorship and its mechanisms and to suggest future research directions. Organizational sponsorship is an emerging theory, which is quite complex and multi-faceted. To develop the theory further, the literature needs to clarify which sponsoring organizations are included in organizational sponsorship and which types of firms the theory targets. It is also important for future research to further address under which conditions the mechanisms and activities in organizational sponsorship have positive and negative effects for firms' emergence, survival and growth.

REFERENCES

Aldrich, H., & Auster, E. R. (1986). Even dwarfs started small: Liabilities of age and size and their strategic implications. In B. M. Staw & L. L. Cummings (Eds.), *Research in organizational behavior* (Vol. 8, pp. 165–198). Greenwich: CT: JAI Press.

Aldrich, H., McKelvey, B., & Ulrich, D. (1984). Design strategy from the population perspective. *Journal of Management, 10*(1), 67–86.

Amezcua, A. S., Grimes, M. G., Bradley, S. W., & Wiklund, J. (2013). Organizational sponsorship and founding environments: A contingency view on the survival of business-incubated firms, 1994–2007. *Academy of Management Journal, 56*(6), 1628–1654.

Autio, E., & Rannikko, H. (2016). Retaining winners: Can policy boost high-growth entrepreneurship? *Research Policy, 45*(1), 42–55.

Bergek, A., & Norrman, C. (2008). Incubator best practice: A framework. *Technovation, 28*(1–2), 20–28.

Brush, C. G., Greene, P. G., & Hart, M. M. (2001). From initial idea to unique advantage: The entrepreneurial challenge of constructing a resource base. *The Academy of Management Executive, 15*(1), 64–78.

Cohen, S. L., Bingham, C. B., & Hallen, B. L. (2018). The role of accelerator designs in mitigating bounded rationality in new ventures. *Administrative Science Quarterly*, 1–45. doi:10.1177/0001839218782131

Dutt, N., Hawn, O., Vidal, E., Chatterji, A., McGahan, A., & Mitchell, W. (2016). How open system intermediaries address institutional failures: The case of business incubators in emerging-market countries. *Academy of Management Journal, 59*(3), 818–840.

Flynn, D, M. (1988). Sponsorship, Infrastructure and New Organizations: Exploration of an Ecological Model into Fourteen Regions. In B. A. Kirchhoff, W. A. Long, W. E. McMullen, K. H. Vesper, & W. E. Wetzel Jr. (Eds.), *Frontiers of Entrepreneurship* (pp. 238–253). Wellesley, Mass: Babson College.

Flynn, D. M. (1990). An Exploration of the Effects of Sponsorship and Infrastructure on High Technology Industries. *Proceedings, United States Association for Small Business and Entrepreneurship*, 30–36.

Flynn, D. M. (1993a). A critical exploration of sponsorship, infrastructure, and new organizations. *Small Business Economics, 5*(2), 129–156.

Flynn, D. M. (1993b). Sponsorship and the survival of new organizations. *Journal of Small Business Management, 31*(1), 51–62.

Flynn, D. M., & Falbe, C. M. (1986). Sponsorship, Infrastructure, and New Organizations: An Exploration of an Ecological Model into Six Regions. *Proceedings, Eastern Academy of Management*, 162–166.

Inkpen, A. C., & Tsang, E. W. (2005). Social capital, networks, and knowledge transfer. *Academy of Management Review, 30*(1), 146–165.

Jesson, J., Matheson, L., & Lacey, F. M. (2011). *Doing your literature review: Traditional and systematic techniques.* London: Sage.

Jourdan, J., & Kivleniece, I. (2017). Too much of a good thing? The dual effect of public sponsorship on organizational performance. *Academy of Management Journal, 60*(1), 55–77.

Mongeon, P., & Paul-Hus, A. J. S. (2016). The journal coverage of Web of Science and Scopus: a comparative analysis. *Scientometrics, 106*(1), 213–228.

Motoyama, Y., & Knowlton, K. (2016). From resource munificence to ecosystem integration: The case of government sponsorship in St. Louis. *Entrepreneurship & Regional Development, 28*(5-6), 448–470.

Mrkajic, B. (2017). Business incubation models and institutionally void environments. *Technovation*, *68*, 44–55.

Pandey, S., Lall, S., Pandey, S. K., & Ahlawat, S. (2017). The appeal of social accelerators: What do social entrepreneurs value? *Journal of Social Entrepreneurship*, *8*(1), 88–109.

Pfeffer, J., & Salancik, G. (1978). *The external control of organizations: A resource dependence perspective*. New York: Harper & Row.

Seidel, V. P., Packalen, K. A., & O'Mahony, S. (2016). Help me do it on my own: How entrepreneurs manage autonomy and constraint within incubator organizations. In L. E. Cohen, M. D. Burton, & M. Lounsbury (Eds.), *The Structuring of Work in Organizations (Research in the Sociology of Organizations, Volume 47)* (pp. 275–307). Emerald Group Publishing Limited.

Stinchcombe, A. L. (1965). Social structure and organizations. In J. G. March (Ed.), *Handbook of organizations* (pp. 142–193). Chicago: Rand McNally.

Suchman, M. C. (1995). Managing legitimacy: Strategic and institutional approaches. *Academy of Management Review*, *20*(3), 571–610.

Zahra, S. A., Sapienza, H. J., & Davidsson, P. (2006). Entrepreneurship and dynamic capabilities: A review, model and research agenda. *Journal of Management Studies*, *43*(4), 917–955.

Zimmerman, M. A., & Zeitz, G. J. (2002). Beyond survival: Achieving new venture growth by building legitimacy. *Academy of Management Review*, *27*(3), 414–431.

APPENDIX A: ARTICLES ANALYZED IN THE LITERATURE REVIEW

Author(s)	Research question(s)/ purpose	Definition of sponsorship	Context of sponsorship	Data	Method	Key findings (with emphasis on organizational sponsorship)
Flynn (1993b)	Understand the phenomenon of sponsorship through integrating population ecology and resource dependence.	'Sponsorship includes the intervention by government agencies, business firms, and/ or universities to create an environment conducive to the birth and survival of organizations' (Flynn, 1988, p. 51).	NA	NA	Conceptual	This paper argues that sponsorship programmes should consider the existing and expected environmental conditions, the opportunities in existing populations and the regional infrastructure. Sponsorship may be most effective when it improves the existing infrastructure for the long term.
Flynn (1993a)	Provide a preliminary empirical test of the joint effects of infrastructure and sponsorship initiatives on the existence and emergence of new organizations in 14 urban regions.	Uses Flynn's (1988) definition of sponsorship.	Public sponsorship: Sponsorship from the state	Register data on 14 regions in the United States.	Quantitative, factor analysis and correlation	The analysis suggests that (1) sponsorship supports industry development that fits with the local infrastructure, (2) direct and indirect support enriches the local infrastructure and (3) for a firm to overcome the over-dependency on sponsors, it needs to include mechanisms for organizational learning.

Amezcua et al. (2013)	Offer a nuanced theory that better accounts for sponsorship effects in different environments.	Organizational sponsorship 'attempts to mediate the relationship between new organizations and their environments by creating a resource-munificent context intended to increase survival rates among those organizations' (p. 1628).	Public sponsorship: Incubators	Register data on all university-based incubators in the United States.	Quantitative, regression	The results suggest that sponsorship's different services (direct support, networking and field-building) have both positive and negative effects on new organizational survival, depending on the environmental conditions.
Autio and Rannikko (2016)	Can policy boost high-growth entrepreneurship?	'Public sponsorship promotes new organizations' (p. 43).	Public sponsorship: A high-growth entrepreneurship policy initiative	Panel data on 160 growth-oriented firms in Finland.	Quantitative, descriptive analysis and propensity score matching	This study proposes a third mechanism, boosting, which facilitates new firm growth by developing the organisational capacity for growth. This study also demonstrates that policy initiatives can deliver a real impact on new firm growth.
Dutt et al. (2016)	Examine business incubators in emerging markets and their emphasis on developing markets versus developing specific businesses. The study further examines how	No definition of sponsorship.	Business incubators	Interviews with incubators and incubatees. Dataset of 133 incubators in 68 countries.	Mixed methods: Qualitative and quantitative, descriptive and Tobit regression	The study contributes to the literatures on organizational sponsorship and institutional entrepreneurship: The services incubators offer are dependent on the type of sponsorship incubators have.

Appendix A (continued)

Author(s)	Research question(s)/ purpose	Definition of sponsorship	Context of sponsorship	Data	Method	Key findings (with emphasis on organizational sponsorship)
	different types of sponsorship of incubators influence the mix of services that incubators provide.					
Seidel et al. (2016)	How do entrepreneurs sustain their autonomy while seeking resources and support from a sponsoring organization?	Uses Amezcua et al.'s (2013) definition but uses the term *organizational sponsors*.	Public sponsorship: High-technology business incubator	Five entrepreneurial firms in a business incubator. Silicon Valley, United States.	Qualitative, Grounded-theory approach: Field observations, interviews and archival data. Longitudinal.	The results suggest that there are three types of threats to entrepreneurs' autonomy (mentor role conflict, gatekeeper control and affiliation dissonance). This study also proposes how to address the threats.
Motoyama and Knowlton (2016)	What is the course of development for new firms that received government sponsorship in the context of accessing local resources and developing networks?	"Government sponsorship" is an attempt to mediate the relationship between new organizations and their environment, primarily by creating a resource-munificent	Public–private sponsorship: Arch Grants.	Case study: Interviews with 46 recipient firms and 15 support organizations. St. Louis, United States.	Qualitative	The results suggest that (1) interaction and learning between entrepreneurs are important for business development, (2) the Arch Grants opened up access to multiple local resources, which were used for

Author	Purpose	Definition	Concept	Sample	Method	Findings
		context intended to increase survival rates among supported firms' (p. 450). Uses Flynn (1993a) and Amezcua et al. (2013) to define government sponsorship.				different purposes and during different stages of start-up development and (3) the public–private partnership enhanced coordination between the local support organizations.
Jourdan and Kivleniece (2017)	Develop a nascent theory on sponsorship by examining the relationship between public sponsorship and market performance.	Public sponsorship is 'a provision of external resources to a focal organization by a public actor (e.g. state, political or governmental agency), whereby such provision takes place outside market exchange mechanisms with an aim to selectively alter the focal organization's emergence, survival or performance' (p. 56).	Public sponsorship	The entire population of film production enterprises in France between 1998 and 2008.	Quantitative, descriptive statistics and fixed-effect regression	This study suggests that the relationship between the amount of public sponsorship received and the organization's market performance is an inverted U-shaped relationship moderated by the breadth, depth and focus of the organization's resource accumulation and allocation patterns. While increased breadth (resources across the horizontal scope of the firm) and reduced depth (resources across the vertical chain of activities, i.e. resource profile) strengthen the relationship, increased focus (supplying to explicit market needs, i.e. market orientation) decreases it.

Appendix A (continued)

Author(s)	Research question(s)/ purpose	Definition of sponsorship	Context of sponsorship	Data	Method	Key findings (with emphasis on organizational sponsorship)
Pandey et al. (2017)	Are the most-publicized benefits of social accelerators also the ones most valued by social entrepreneurship? Does the social entrepreneur human capital – such as education, professional background and experience – shape the attractiveness of value propositions of different social accelerator benefits?	No definition of sponsorship.	Social Accelerators	4,125 self-identified social ventures that applied to social accelerator programmes. Multiple-country data.	Quantitative	The study suggests that sponsoring organizations, especially social accelerator programmes, also engage in bolstering mechanisms.
Mrkajic (2017)	Develop a conceptual framework of business incubation models in institutionally laggard environments.	No definition of sponsorship.	Public–private sponsorship: Business incubators	Five case studies of business incubators in Egypt. Survey and interviews with incubator managers,	Qualitative	This paper contributes to the literature on the development of incubation models. The findings add to the literature on organizational sponsorship and support Dutt et al.'s

	Research question	Theory/definition	Type	Data	Method	Findings
				observations, interviews with incubated and non-incubated entrepreneurs, etc.		(2016) findings that services offered by incubators are dependent on the sponsorship the incubator has. In addition, this study found that more severe institutional voids require two different incubation models to be able to react to the more heterogeneous needs of entrepreneurs, which are caused by different externalities.
Cohen et al. (2018)	How do accelerators' programme designs influence new ventures' ability to access, interpret, and process the external information needed to survive and grow?	Uses Flynn's (1993) definition of sponsorship.	Accelerators	Eight accelerator programmes in the United States. 37 ventures. Interviews with entrepreneurs, managers and mentors. Site visits. Archival data.	Qualitative	The study suggests that sponsors help entrepreneurs understand and address their own knowledge limitations and biases by (1) helping entrepreneurs to avoid under- or overreacting to external knowledge, (2) helping entrepreneurs learn from peers and (3) helping ventures to focus on where to search for and gather information.

9. Understanding startup development organizations in the context of startup incubation ecosystems

Cristiano Bellavitis, Michael Sargent, and Carlos M. DaSilva

INTRODUCTION

The first years of small to medium enterprises (SMEs) are often difficult. They face a hostile and turbulent environment with competition from larger companies who benefit economies of scale and support networks (Bøllingtoft, 2012; Buratti & Penco, 2001; Vanderstraeten & Matthyssens, 2012). Thus, SMEs suffer from a number of structural deficiencies that inhibit growth such as limited human resources, weak capitalization capacities and poor innovation management (Buratti & Penco, 2001). This phenomenon has become known as the liability of newness in which newer, smaller companies lack the networks and legitimacy held by older firms that allow them greater access to sought-after resources (Freeman & Reed, 1983; Hughes, Ireland, & Morgan, 2007; van Weele, van Rijnsoever, & Nauta, 2016). To bridge this period of high risk, fledgling companies will often seek out support via startup incubation ecosystems (SUPIEs), which are defined as a set of interdependent development organizations and actors aimed at supporting startup companies.

In recent years a wide variety of organizations have been launched by governments, private investors, corporates, universities, research institutes and others in order to foster the creation and growth of start-up companies. In this chapter, we define this set of organizations as "startup development organizations" or SDOs – a set of organizations that aim to support the growth and development of startups. Whilst past literature on support mechanisms for entrepreneurs do agree startup development organizations are useful and relevant, it also reveals a need for identifying their heterogeneity (Barbero, Casillas, Ramos, & Guitar, 2012) given their evolution over time (Bruneel, Ratinho, Clarysse, & Groen, 2012). In fact, examples of SDOs today include incubators (business support), co-working spaces (work stations), accelerators (structured programs) and other variants (Hallam & DeVora, 2009; Vanderstraeten & Matthyssens,

2012). Thus, it is relevant to understand the different models employed by different SDOs in order to address their specificities, contexts, procedures and possible impact on SUPIEs (Barbero et al., 2012; Pauwels, Clarysse, Wright, & Van Hove, 2016).

In this chapter, we will discuss in detail each type of SDO. While all have a common purpose to support startup organizations, we identify major differences in their practices and models. Specifically, we will cover three major types of SDOs: 1) incubators, 2) accelerators and 3) co-working spaces. Within the incubator category, we will distinguish between traditional and university incubators. Within the accelerator category, we will distinguish between traditional and corporate accelerators. We will not only review the existing literature to justify such typology, but also interview practitioners on their views concerning SDOs' typologies. Table 9.1 provides an overview of the chapter and a summary of the main differences across the SDOs covered. The next sections will analyze in detail each typology and will draw conclusions in the form of practical implications and further research avenues.

INCUBATOR

The incubator model dates back to the late 1950s with the foundation of incubators in the startup ecosystem. The model has a heavy focus on the provision of shared office space to startups with an additional mentorship and networking role providing sustained value to incubated firms. While incubators usually have a selection process, they are open ended in duration, meaning that they have no set length and will typically, as a result, have a rolling admission (Bone, Allen, & Haley, 2017). Consequently, incubation programs will often extend a number of years with great levels of variance between different companies. In the next section, we will distinguish between two types of incubators: traditional incubators (an incubator subtype paid for through discounted rent-based fees) and university incubators (an incubator subtype launched by universities and usually free of charge for students and other staff from the university).

Traditional Incubator

Some of the earliest attempts at mapping out what scholars defined as the incubator model were explored by Smilor (1987) who conceptualized two major models of incubation as a business. The first focused on the renovation of older vacant buildings and then leasing this space to entrepreneurs at inexpensive rates. The success of this model was measured by a tenant

Table 9.1   Summary of different startup development organizations classifications

	Incubator		Accelerator		Co-Working Space
	Incubator	University Incubator	Accelerator	Corporate Sponsored Accelerator	
Investment	Not common, but will offer access to capital	Typically will offer access to capital but no direct investment	Typically offers seed investment in exchange for equity	On a case-by-case basis	None
Equity	On a case-by-case basis	Typically does not take equity	Typically yes	On a case-by-case basis	None
Time	1–5 years	1–4 years	Typically 3–6 months	Typically 3–6 months	Indefinite
Co-location/ Office Space	On-site	On-site	Typically on-site	Typically on-site	On-Site
Selection	Local	Internal	Local and global	Internal, local and global	Local
University Affiliation	Varies, typically moderate	Very high	Typically low	Low	Low
Selection Type	Continuous	Continuous	Cohort	Cohort	Continuous
Stage	Seed to later stage	Idea to seed stage	Seed to early stage	Seed to early stage	Seed to later stage
Demo Day	No	No	Yes	Yes	No
Primary Services	Office space, mentoring, networking	Mentoring, technology and patent access/ expertise, student and faculty entrepreneurship education	Mentoring, cohort training, seed capital investment	Investment opportunities, mentoring, training, access to large corporate network	Office space and some networking

firm's ability to meet monthly expenses. The second model focused significantly more on company building through the leveraging of incubator resources.

While the exact line between what is and is not considered a business incubator is often ill defined, what is clear is the nature of business incubation to facilitate and support the formation and growth of new enterprises. There have been several attempts to classify incubators into different typologies. The work of Allen and McCluskey (1991), classifies incubators into four basic archetypes: For profit property development incubators, non-profit development corporation incubators, academic incubators and for profit seed capital incubators. Allen's model examines the incubator archetypes along a spectrum of value-added services from a basic real estate business of renting space to firms to a more business development approach where the incubator capitalizes on an equity investment opportunity. Building on Allen and McCluskey's work (1991), Bøllingtoft and Ulhøi (2005) add on the continuum of their value-added services, by bringing in the hybrid model that combines elements of the four basic archetypes.

While these different architypes have overlapping features, the literature still lacks an overall consensus. This has been attributed in large part to the heterogeneity of incubator services and resources offerings (Rubin, Aas, & Stead, 2015) and, as such, the concept of business incubation has been defined in innumerable ways across literature. The National Business Incubation Association (NBIA), defines business incubation as a catalyst tool for the economic development of SMEs providing entrepreneurs with a range of business resources and services. This definition, in line with both Allen and McCluskey (1991) as well as Bøllingtoft and Ulhøi (2005), then categorizes incubators into five types: for profit property development ventures, non-profit development corporations, academic institutions, venture capital firms, and hybrids of the aforementioned categories (Rubin et al., 2015).

Example
Launch 22. Launch 22 is a traditional fee-based incubator located in the United Kingdom. Launch 22 offers several different fee-based plans. The incubator purports its commitment to creating a foundation through which participants can build a startup. Their offerings include a fully equipped communal workplace as well as significant mentorship as a part of the program and access to company held events including workshops and networking opportunities. This highlights the primary goal of incubators which is to provide an environment that facilitates the growth of startups.

University Incubator

Primarily in line with their non-university counterparts, a university incubator is similar to other incubator type organizations, which themselves often have relations with a university. However, a university incubator can be distinguished by its foundation and typically operates out of one or more universities. As a result, they will often have goals and capabilities that are in line with the core capabilities of the university they come from.

In many cases, this may be access to university research, IP, lab equipment, university personnel, knowledge base or university contacts. These services may require a fee-based or some kind of arrangement between the startups and the university. For example, Cicada Innovations takes an equity stake in the startups incubated:

Example

Cicada Innovations. Cicada Innovations (formally ATP Innovations) is a prominent Australian university incubator, ranked highly in Australia and the eigth globally according to the university incubator global ranking (UBI Global, 2015). Cicada's incubation program lasts up to five years and has a competitive rolling entry. Stated offerings include aiding the startup with growing their business, accessing grants and research through the universities, capital raising, sale of the business and access to facilities and technology.

ACCELERATOR

While the accelerator model has begun to be explored in the literature with defining characteristics being largely compared against more traditional incubator models, its rapid expansion has led to it being conceptually linked with incubator models with some research even using accelerator nomenclature to describe an incubator (Bliemel et al., 2016; Malek, Maine, & McCarthy, 2014; Pauwels et al., 2016). However, accelerators have different characteristics and peculiarities. In this section, we will distinguish between traditional accelerators and corporate accelerators.

Traditional Accelerator

Accelerators are often defined as structured programs that help entrepreneurs bring their technologies, ideas or products into the market place (Dempwolf, Auer, & D'Ippolito, 2014). They aim at fostering the creation and scaling up of "high-impact" startups (Pauwels et al., 2016). The literature clearly acknowledges that accelerators add value to startups by speeding time-to-market and the acquisition of customers (Miller & Bound, 2011; Pauwels et al., 2016).

While parallels can be drawn with incubators, accelerators differ considerably (Cohen & Hochberg, 2014). First, incubators and accelerators differ in their duration. Startups are usually incubated for one–five years with no strict dates or timelines, while accelerator programs typically have strict entry and exit dates with a typical program lasting about three months. Second, accelerators run programs in cohorts. Accelerators will typically have a call for applications, a selection process and a cohort or batch of startups who enter the accelerator program at a certain point in time. Third, most accelerators seek an equity stake or interest in the start-ups being accelerated. Fourth, accelerator programs incorporate a demo day at the culmination of the program. This refers to a meeting in which the startup founders pitch their businesses to an audience of potential investors or corporates (Cohen & Hochberg, 2014).

Example
Y Combinator. The Y Combinator Accelerator (United States of America) has accelerated several successful companies such as Dropbox and Airbnb since its creation in 2005. The program recruits two batches of companies per year. Each selected startup receives seed capital, mentoring, training and networking opportunities in exchange for 7 percent equity. The program aims to accelerate startups into a high growth business.

Corporate Accelerator

Corporate accelerators usually match the traditional accelerator by having a time-based cohort structure, possible equity interest and a pitch day to conclude the program. However, all corporate accelerators are character-ized by the backing of a large corporate body for usage of financing, networks, facilities and/or other amenities that will be provided for the growth of new startups (Bauer, Obwegeser, & Avdagic, 2016; Freeman & Engel, 2007; Guttman, 2015; Kanbach & Stubner, 2016). This interac-tion between the corporate body and the utilization of their economies of scale and networks provides the foundation of value for this model (Guttman, 2015). Corporate accelerators typically look for startups work-ing with technology and innovations that have the potential to impact their industry in the future (Bauer et al., 2016). The emergence of corpo-rate accelerators is related to the speeds at which companies innovate. There is a common perception among the literature that larger corporate bodies move slowly, unable to mobilize their resources at the pace that innovative startups can (Bauer et al., 2016). Corporate accelerators then are an intermediary facilitating the merging of a large corporate resource base with the swift innovation and validation found in startups (Bauer et al., 2016). Corporate accelerator programs are typically structured in two ways: an external accelerator company run on behalf of the corporate partner; or an internal accelerator run internally. TechStars for example runs multiple corporate-sponsored accelerator programs internationally (Kanbach & Stubner, 2016).

Example

TechStars. Techstars for example runs multiple corporate sponsored programs internationally. Some examples of these include Barclays, Cedars-Sinai, SAP.IO, Ford, Amazon, Comcast, Target and an internet of things accelerator comprised supported by GE, Bosch, PwC, SAP, Verizon and next47 (Siemens). Each of the corporate accelerators offers the same formula as standard Techstars accelerators, with a $100,000 convertible note in addition to $20,000 in return for equity. However, the accelerators are more industry focused, for example, the target accelerator focuses on retail-based startups while the Barclays accelerator focuses financial services including machine learning, lending, digital banking solutions, trading, cyber security, data analytics, payments, cryptocurrency, insurance and wealth management.

Barclays outlines their role in the corporate accelerator in this way:

> We're committed to supporting entrepreneurs and startups. We'll provide tools, equipment and facilities – plus support for startups to get their products or services to market. In conjunction with Techstars, we'll also provide mentorship from carefully selected business leaders and entrepreneurs to help you develop your business model. These mentors will be able to give you unparalleled advice with networking, marketing, PR, pitching and more – helping you accelerate your company's development. (https://www.barclaysaccelerator.com/#/faqs/)

CO-WORKING SPACE

A co-working space is a physical workspace provided to companies in return for rent-based fees, which in many cases is reserved for younger companies (Bone et al., 2017; Bouncken & Reuschl, 2018). Some co-working spaces however offer additional support mechanisms that will help growing companies develop, such as light mentorship or networking activities, specialized spaces or access to stakeholder groups like investors (Gandini, 2015). These are referred to as a co-working space plus (Bone et al., 2017). As a result, co-working space plus will typically exist in a spectrum with other incubator and accelerator models. As a result, the literature has found difficulty in defining the lines between what is considered a standard co-working space, co-working plus and an incubator or accelerator (Moriset, 2013). The main distinction of these models from incubator types is a very limited focus on business support services as well as non-competitive entry criteria.

Furthermore, the primary focus of co-working space or co-working space plus models is the facilities which they provide to their client companies (Capdevila, 2015). These facilities will often include hotdesking, fixed desks, dedicated office space as well as meeting rooms and other desired amenities such as phone/desk services, storage, office supplies and meeting rooms (Schuermann, 2014). The co-working environment is expected to encourage sharing of knowledge and resources between residences thus offering enhanced value to those located in the space through unofficial networking channels (Bouncken, Laudien, Fredrich, & Görmar, 2018; Bouncken & Reuschl, 2018; Spinuzzi, Bodrozic, Scaratti, & Ivaldi, 2018; Sundsted, Jones, & Bacigalupo, 2009).

Example
Level 39. Level 39 from the U.K. provides a workspace tailored to small fast-growth companies in the finance, cybersecurity, retail and smart-city technology businesses and tailor any workshops and mentorship around these particular industries by providing access to experts from the financial sector. These practices are said to help the startups better identify their challenges and identify a route to market thus improving the speed at which the startup can gain traction. Additional services provided by the company include access to an investment community and additional networking.

A PRACTITIONER LENS: HYBRIDIZATION

The confusion in defining and classifying SDOs partly stems from the fact that, in practice, many SDOs offer services spanning across different categories. This has led to a growing overlap between models, increasing the difficulty in defining exactly where a company sits due to the hybrid nature of many SDO models. This often leads to labels that companies may or may not be happy to associate with due to them not being a true reflection of their business's activities. As a result, neatly categorizing any SDO company by a narrow set of criteria can often be difficult. In order to complement our understanding of this phenomenon, we have conducted interviews in New Zealand with managing directors of different SDOs to extend the literature with a practitioner lens:

> I'm not sure that there is a really good way to describe them (SDOs).

> We've always considered ourselves as an incubator + accelerator in that we've tended to work with very early stage business ideas right through to capital raising and being independent of the needs of an incubator.

> We do hate labels. We're trying and we've been trying to think of a better term for an accelerator forever.

> There is a lot of confusion. The first thing that we usually do when we speak publicly anywhere is to lay down our definitions of what we're talking about, how we define accelerators is that it is a three-month residential program that has a fixed intake. So, there's a date and there is a submission period, there's a selection period and then there is a set starting date.

> With incubation . . . it's essentially a fluid model and it doesn't have the same time frames as an accelerator, so our incubation cycles are typically somewhere between 12 and 15 months.

> We're constantly evolving. It's not actually a static business that sort of just stays the same, the models are constantly evolving.

These quotes from practitioners may represent an aversion to strict labelling of SDOs, as hybridization might not be the exception in the future, but the rule. A prominent example of a hybrid organization is WeWork. Although WeWork can be considered a co-working space where individual entrepreneurs rent a desk for themselves and their team, sometimes on a short-term basis, WeWork is much more than a simple co-working space. The company claims to offer "space, community, and programming to help [entrepreneurs] fulfil their destiny". Among the advantages of WeWork is the fact that they organize mentoring events, pitch nights and workshops, and introduce entrepreneurs to investors. In addition, it is not uncommon for WeWork to partner with typical incubators and accelerators in the local ecosystem they operate in.

Hybridization might bring added challenges when effectiveness measurement is concerned. The literature still lacks concrete criteria to measure how SDOs perform versus others. Universities leverage SDOs as means to promote student entrepreneurship, corporates as a means to foster innovation, co-working spaces as a real estate business and accelerators as a means for return on investment. Different objectives require different criteria.

IMPLICATIONS AND FUTURE RESEARCH DIRECTIONS

This chapter defined and explained the different types of startup development organizations that populate SUPIEs, providing an overview over the three major types of organizations that support startup development, namely incubators, accelerators and co-working spaces. In addition, we discussed the hybrid model that is emerging in practice. While we agree SDOs are unified via a common aim of promoting an environment supportive of startup organizations, we believe hybrid models will continue to evolve merging elements of the three major types. As a result, more empirical research is needed in order to understand where the trends are heading, and how SDOs will evolve in the future.

The SDO characterizing variables present in Table 9.1 can be used to position different SDOs within the overall ecosystem. We suggest that initial advisors to startups such as government support agencies, mentors, entrepreneurship educators, among others, should consider the different SDOs and their associated characteristics in order to advise and guide nascent entrepreneurs toward particular types that may best meet their needs and stage of development. On the same note, it allows entrepreneurs seeking support to better understand which particular SDO best meet their needs. Working as a potential selection criterion, the characterizing variables presented in Table 9.1 allow for a straight-forward contrast analysis between the different SDOs. The diversity of SDOs we have identified also has implications for policymakers in supporting different SDOs and assessing their role in the ecosystem. Rather than assessing SDOs based on a fixed set of criteria, there is a need to develop accountability that takes into account the different peculiarities and goals of different types of SDOs. Policymakers usually have a concrete agenda, from regional development to employment. As a result, policymakers must realize that certain types of SDOs may not necessarily be profitable in the short to medium horizon, if ever. The stage of development of the startups they support, the services offered and their strategic aims do not always allow for such. As SDOs become popular, entrepreneurs and organizations such as universities, government and corporates feel compelled to launch an SDO. Universities perceive it as a means to foster student entrepreneurship, corporates as a bridge towards innovation and re-invention, and governments as a means to encourage economic growth. However, the sustainability of their models over a long period of time is still a question, as it is still early days, especially for investment/equity-based models encountered in traditional accelerators.

While this chapter emphasizes the difference between SDOs, it does not address the dynamics embedded in the exchange relationship between SDOs and entrepreneurs. Future research should consider examining the process that unfolds when startups join a particular type of SDO. To date, most research that examines ventures that join SDOs are more focused either on the beginning or the end of the process, with little insights on the transformation that occurs in-between. Furthermore, future research should consider studying performance differences across and within SDOs. To date, limited empirical research has studied the performance implications and associated impact of the different types of SDOs within the SUPIE.

REFERENCES

Allen, D. N., & McCluskey, R. (1991). Structure, policy, services, and performance in the business incubator industry. *Entrepreneurship Theory and Practice, 15*(2), 61–77.
Barbero, J. L., Casillas, J. C., Ramos, A., & Guitar, S. (2012). Revisiting incubation performance: How incubator typology affects results. *Technological Forecasting and Social Change, 79*(5), 888–902.
Bauer, S., Obwegeser, N., & Avdagic, Z. (2016). Corporate Accelerators: Transferring Technology Innovation to Incumbent Companies. In MCIS 2016 Proceedings. Paper 57.
Bliemel, M. J., Flores, R. G., de Klerk, S., Miles, M. P., Costa, B., & Monteiro, P. (2016). The role and performance of accelerators in the Australian startup ecosystem. Department of Industry, Innovation & Science (Made public 25 May 2016).
Bøllingtoft, A. (2012). The bottom-up business incubator: Leverage to networking and cooperation practices in a self-generated, entrepreneurial-enabled environment. *Technovation, 32*(5), 304–315.
Bøllingtoft, A., & Ulhøi, J. P. (2005). The networked business incubator – leveraging entrepreneurial agency? *Journal of Business Venturing, 20*(2), 265–290.
Bone, J., Allen, O., & Haley, C. (2017). Business incubators and accelerators: The national picture. *BEIS Research Paper, 7.*
Bouncken, R. B., Laudien, S. M., Fredrich, V., & Görmar, L. (2018). Coopetition in coworking-spaces: Value creation and appropriation tensions in an entrepreneurial space. *Review of Managerial Science, 12*(2), 385–410.
Bouncken, R. B., & Reuschl, A. J. (2018). Coworking-spaces: How a phenomenon of the sharing economy builds a novel trend for the workplace and for entrepreneurship. *Review of Managerial Science, 12*(1), 317–334.
Bruneel, J., Ratinho, T., Clarysse, B., & Groen, A. (2012). The evolution of business incubators: Comparing demand and supply of business incubation services across different incubator generations. *Technovation, 32*(2), 110–121.
Buratti, N., & Penco, L. (2001). Assisted technology transfer to SMEs: Lessons from an exemplary case. *Technovation, 21*(1), 35–43.
Capdevila, I. (2015). Co-working spaces and the localised dynamics of innovation in Barcelona. *International Journal of Innovation Management, 19*(03), 1540004.
Cohen, S., & Hochberg, Y. V. (2014). Accelerating startups: The seed accelerator phenomenon. *Available at SSRN 2418000*. Retrieved July 23, 2018 from http://papers.ssrn.com/sol3/Papers.cfm?abstract_id=2418000
Dempwolf, C. S., Auer, J., & D'Ippolito, M. (2014). Innovation accelerators: Defining characteristics among startup assistance organizations. *Small Business Administration*, 1–44.
Freeman, J., & Engel, J. S. (2007). Models of innovation: Startups and mature corporations. *California Management Review, 50*(1), 94–119.
Freeman, R. E., & Reed, D. L. (1983). Stockholders and stakeholders: A new perspective on corporate governance. *California Management Review, 25*(3), 88–106.
Gandini, A. (2015). The rise of coworking spaces: A literature review. *Ephemera, 15*(1), 193.
Guttman, A. (2015). Why Corporate Accelerators Can Be Better For Startups Than Traditional Ones. Retrieved September 28, 2016, from http://www.forbes.com/sites/amyguttman/2015/11/13/why-corporate-accelerators-can-be-better-for-startups-than-traditional-ones/
Hallam, C. R., & DeVora, N. (2009). Technology-based business incubation: A study of the differences and similarities between private, university, and government incubation. In *Management of Engineering & Technology, 2009. PICMET 2009. Portland International Conference on* (pp. 1875–1887). IEEE.
Hughes, M., Ireland, R. D., & Morgan, R. E. (2007). Stimulating dynamic value: Social capital and business incubation as a pathway to competitive success. *Long Range Planning, 40*(2), 154–177.
Kanbach, D. K., & Stubner, S. (2016). Corporate accelerators as recent form of startup engagement: The what, the why, and the how. *Journal of Applied Business Research, 32*(6), 1761.

Malek, K., Maine, E., & McCarthy, I. P. (2014). A typology of clean technology commercialization accelerators. *Journal of Engineering and Technology Management*, *32*, 26–39.

Miller, P., & Bound, K. (2011). *The Startup Factories: The rise of accelerator programmes to support new technology ventures*. NESTA. http://www.nesta.org. uk/library/documents/ StartupFactories. pdf.

Moriset, B. (2013). Building new places of the creative economy. The rise of coworking spaces. *Territoire En Mouvement*. https://doi.org/10.4000/tem.3868. Accessed July 23, 2018.

Pauwels, C., Clarysse, B., Wright, M., & Van Hove, J. (2016). Understanding a new generation incubation model: The accelerator. *Technovation*, *50*, 13–24.

Peters, L., Rice, M., & Sundararajan, M. (2004). The role of incubators in the entrepreneurial process. *The Journal of Technology Transfer*, *29*(1), 83–91.

Rubin, T. H., Aas, T. H., & Stead, A. (2015). Knowledge flow in technological business incubators: Evidence from Australia and Israel. *Technovation*, *41*, 11–24.

Schuermann, M. (2014). *Coworking Space: A Potent Business Model for Plug 'n Play and Indie Workers*. epubli. https://eur01.safelinks.protection.outlook.com/?url=https%3A%2F% 2Fwww.amazon.co.uk%2FCoworking-Space-Potent-Business-Workers

Smilor, R. W. (1987). Managing the incubator system: Critical success factors to accelerate new company development. *IEEE Transactions on Engineering Management*, (3), 146–155.

Spinuzzi, C., Bodrozic, Z., Scaratti, G., & Ivaldi, S. (2018). "Coworking is about community" but what is "community" in coworking? *Journal of Business and Technical Communication*. *33*(2), 112–140.

Sundsted, T., Jones, D., & Bacigalupo, T. (2009). *I'm Outta Here: how co-working is making the office obsolete*. Lulu.com. Accessed July 23, 2018.

UBI Global. (2015). Global Benchmark 15/16 Report: Top University Business Incubators. UBI Global. (2015). Retrieved July 23, 2018, from Retrieved from http://ubi-global.com/ rankings/

van Weele, M., van Rijnsoever, F. J., & Nauta, F. (2016). You can't always get what you want: How entrepreneur's perceived resource needs affect the incubator's assertiveness. *Technovation*. *59*, 18–33.

Vanderstraeten, J., & Matthyssens, P. (2012). Service-based differentiation strategies for business incubators: Exploring external and internal alignment. *Technovation*, *32*(12), 656–670.

10. Distinguishing self-sufficient business incubators in start-up incubation ecosystems
Oliver Straub, Peter M. Bican, and Alexander Brem

1. INTRODUCTION

Ecosystems play a vital role in jumpstarting businesses and fostering entrepreneurial activity in general (Spigel 2017), since sustainable business success is difficult to achieve in isolation. Thereby, incubators are seen as "[...] the hot new way to nurture and grow start-ups in the Internet economy", indicating a key role within the start-up incubation ecosystem (Hansen et al. 2000, p. 75). Ironically, with the main objective to foster development and growth, many incubators cannot meet their goals to become self-sufficient themselves (Chandra & Chao 2011). Most incubators in Hansen et al.'s (2000) study have failed, only few survived. Especially public business and innovation centres (BICs) with government funding faced this issue (European Commission 2002; Knuth 2009; Etzkowitz 2002).

Literature on incubators analyses why incubators exist and how to differentiate the various incubator types from one another, e.g. depending on profit orientation, stakeholder structure, strategic objectives, service offerings, or competitive focus (Pauwels et al. 2016, Lukeš et al. 2018). Based on these definitions, research has mainly been conducted on success factors of incubators (e.g. Smilor 1987; Lee & Osteryoung 2004; Bøllingtoft & Ulhøi 2005; Gerlach & Brem 2015), analysing these business models more from the top (Alberti 2011). Few studies describe the incubation process in detail, predominantly on specific focus areas. Approaches to business incubators from a business model perspective are difficult to identify, leaving core questions, like the profit formula, unanswered, with single-sided views on value propositions. Recommendations for the implementation of viable long-term business models could not be drawn from prior research.

With this background, this chapter will focus on the comparison of self-sufficient and non-self-sufficient incubators in order to answer the following research question:

Which measures determine self-sufficient incubators' business models?

An online survey with 71 incubators was conducted to analyse differences in the value proposition, the profit formula, and the key activities and resources used. On the one hand, the findings support previous claims regarding the need for a profit-driven nature, regardless of a profit or non-profit business orientation, as well as generating diverse income streams to cover operational costs. On the other hand, new insights on key elements of incubators' business models are shown. Based on these findings, practitioners as well as researchers will gain a clearer understanding of the factors enabling the set-up of self-sufficient incubators in the future.

2.   THEORETICAL BACKGROUND

Since the first incubators were founded in the 1950s, many synonyms emerged (Mian et al. 2016), with no general definition for business incubators (BI). Grimaldi and Grandi (2005), for example, see business incubators as an economic development tool to accelerate the creation of entrepreneurial firms and the exploitation of technology.

The overarching objectives is to provide resources, services, and assistance to start-up-firms (e.g. Bøllingtoft & Ulhøi 2005; Diamantopoulou et al. 2018). As each incubator type has further objectives, scholars built clusters for differentiation. While some assign incubators based on their competitive scope, such as industry, location or segment (Carayannis & von Zedtwitz 2005), Grimaldi and Grandi (2005) adopted Allen and Rahman's (1985) incubator differentiation based on sponsor type.

On one end of the spectrum, there are public incubators whose services are oriented towards the provision of tangible assets and market commodities. Business Innovation Centres (BICs) provide office space and partially coaching services with a mid- to long-term orientation towards regional development, technology transfer and job creation (Chandra & Chao 2011). University Business Incubators (UBIs) are at the interface of public and private sponsorship and are initiated by universities, which aim to foster technology transfer (Markman et al. 2005).

On the other end of the model, there are privately owned incubators, whose services are oriented towards the provision of finance and intangible assets with a short-term orientation. Corporate Private Incubators (CPIs) are mainly operated by private firms or research institutes and aim to set up new business units (Hausberg & Korreck 2018). Independent Private Incubators (IPIs) are set up by private individuals or a group of investors, which have personally invested in a venture. These profit-oriented incubators are also called company-builders or accelerators (Kreusel et al. 2018).

2.1. Success Factors and Customer Value Proposition

Alberti (2011) and Gerlach and Brem (2015) highlight the importance of considering the incubator's objectives when analysing its success factors. Thereby, Carayannis and von Zedtwitz (2005) identified five crucial services that incubators should provide: Access to physical resource, office support, access to financial resources, as well as networks and support in entrepreneurial start-ups. Besides these main service elements, the provided service mix depends on the focus of the incubator as well as the needs and preferences of the entrepreneur (e.g. Chandra & Fealey 2009).

Amongst those, the access to physical resources, such as provision of office space is seen as the most beneficial aspect for tenants (Chan & Lau 2005). Further physical services range from administrative services or accessibility to meeting rooms (McAdam & McAdam 2006) to the provision of laboratories (von Zedtwitz & Grimaldi 2006). In addition to the physical services, incubators provide office support in forms of book-keeping, IT infrastructure, or secretarial services (Carayannis & von Zedtwitz 2005; Samaeemofrad & Van den Herik 2018).

Supporting start-ups with financial resources is another service provided by incubators. The access to venture capital is generally a mix of private funds provided by the incubator or capital provided by firms, venture capitalists or local institutions (Carayannis & von Zedtwitz 2005).

2.2. Profit Formula

Depending on the orientation of the incubator, operational costs vary significantly, especially regarding the initial set-up costs and investments (Lazarowich & Wojciechowski 2002). The average cost of setting up a business incubator is just under four million euros, with the majority of financing coming from public sources (European Commission 2002). While 20 per cent of initial investments are subsidised by the international agencies and 50 per cent by governmental institutions, only 13 per cent of set-up costs were covered directly from private sector sponsors (Lazarowich & Wojciechowski 2002). Furthermore, Scaramuzzi (2002) argues that rental and provision of space are not sufficient to cover all costs of an incubator and only 40 per cent of incubators set a breakeven point for the future development (Lazarowich & Wojciechowski 2002). In general, the revenue generation of incubators was not in the focus of prior research (Alberti 2011; Grimaldi & Grandi 2005). Sources of revenue may stem from selling equity in incubatees or through the payment of royalties for a limited time (Scaramuzzi 2002). All incubators with own revenue streams see self-sustaining or self-sufficient business models as a crucial mean to maintaining financial independency from long-term subsidies.

Despite the widely acknowledged effectiveness, the dependency on public funds shows considerable disadvantages (European Commission 2002). Incubators that are mostly financed from public funds, are often endowed for a limited time only and with a capital stock that is too small, and are therefore constantly striving for further financial support from the state (Duff 1999; Knuth 2009). This can also lead to a rather rigid structure that hinders successful development (Tötterman & Sten 2005). As a consequence, scholars (Duff 1999; Lalkaka 2000; Hackett & Dilts 2004), argued that the shift from a former publicly financed incubator to a self-sufficient business model has numerous advantages, like increased professionalism, flexibility in HR issues, or reinvestment of profits.

2.3. Definition of Incubator Self-Sufficiency

Why is it important to differentiate between self-sufficient and non-self-sufficient incubators? Because there are quite some differences in how such incubators are set up and run. Also, in terms of survival rates and success measures, a differentiation makes sense. While incubator self-sufficiency (also referred to as financial sustainability, as contrary to ecological sustainability) is posing one of the main challenges for the incubators' management (Scaramuzzi 2002), the terms are not generally defined yet. Lalkaka (2000, p. 87) described financial sustainability as "the state where operating revenues consistently exceed operating expenditures", even after external subsidies have declined (Lalkaka 2006, p. 46). Financial streams, like depreciation or reserve for bad debts are accrued to cover actual costs, resulting from replacing and repairing equipment and facilities. Initial start-up costs such as building acquisition and facility construction or renovation, and the resulting operating deficit, are not included in this definition of sustainability/self-sufficiency. Lalkaka (2006) formulated sustainability/self-sufficiency assessment criteria like: Generating revenue surplus, recovering the service costs, leveraging university-business and state policies, and aiming for stakeholder and tenant satisfaction.

Similarly, Duff (1999) defines financial sustainability as operational expenses being more than offset by income generated through incubation. "Core income" (Duff 1999, p. 38) streams should cover the recurring operating costs. A dependency on highly variable forms of income – such as revenue through royalties or the sale of equity held in incubatees – to cover operating expenses, is considered as a riskier approach. Bhasin and Gupta (2016, p. 3) argue that self-sufficiency is attained when institutions "are able to cover all administrative costs, loan losses, and financing costs from operating income, after adjusting for inflation and subsidies and treating all funding as if it had a commercial cost". Consequently, incubators that do not fall under this understanding of self-sufficiency are deemed non-self-sufficient in our understanding.

3.   METHODOLOGY

Descriptive survey methods are generally used to understand the relevance of a phenomenon (Cooper & Schindler 2014). Forza (2002) states that descriptive surveys are especially beneficial to analyse problems that are interesting to practitioners, academics and policymakers. In that matter especially online surveys are beneficial when the study is addressing individuals that are difficult to contact or at distant locations (Wright 2005). An assessment of the different survey instruments based on the factors from Miller and Salkind (1991) support an online survey method.

3.1.   Research Design

The survey was designed following Forza's survey research process (2002). It considers aspects such as linking the survey to its theoretical background, followed by establishing the research design and testing, to the collection and analysis of data. Hence, a systematic literature review, a collection of all relevant measures used in previous studies and a conceptual analysis was performed prior to the survey (Sekaran & Roger 2016).

Different scaling types were used in this chapter and were chosen based on Flynn's findings (1990) to further keep participants engaged in the completion of the survey (Cooper & Schindler 2014). Given the high sensibility of data, assurance of confidentiality increased the participants' motivation (Cooper & Schindler 2014). To increase the exploratory capability, open questions were stated at the end of the questionnaire (Appendix 10.A.1 provides a summary of the questionnaire).

3.2.   Research Context and Survey Partners

As many business incubators are struggling to operate their business in a self-sufficient way, it is necessary to see how different incubator types generate revenue and cover their costs. Therefore, this research was not limited to specific incubator types and thus also included science parks, corporate incubators and accelerators. The International Business Innovation Association (INBIA) website was assessed, as well as platforms like crunchbase and angel.co were used to generate a list of potential incubators. Thereof, survey partners were selected based on their position. In order to reduce random or even bias error, only knowledge-able respondents were identified, with CFOs as primary source followed by CEOs and business developers.

3.3. Data Collection

Data was collected through an online survey between August and September 2017. Prior to that, a pilot survey was conducted to test the clearness of the questions and necessities for further refinement (Cooper & Schindler 2014). After the pilot phase, the survey invitations were e-mailed to 977 INBIA members and other identified respondents via the Qualtrics web interface. Subsequently two reminders were sent out, one in the middle and one shortly before the end of the survey, leading to a total number of survey responses of 71 (response rate of around 7.3 per cent). As some surveys were incomplete, yet still contained valuable data, surveys were not discarded in general, but were assessed separately. Consequently, 53 incubators where used for the group analysis. Additionally, data and responses were validated through a desktop research.

We checked for nonresponse bias by comparing early with late respond-ents (e.g. Etter and Perneger 1997; Studer et al. 2013), based on the assumption that late respondents behave similar to non-respondents (Voigt et al. 2003). Nonresponse bias could not be observed. To analyse the data set in terms of significant differences in the mean values of the two independent populations, a non-parametric Mann-Whitney U test was performed (Mann & Whitney 1947). Given the characteristics of the data set, the Mann-Whitney U test is more suitable as it does not require the assumption of normal distributions, and has advantages when analys-ing different group sizes, scale types and smaller samples (Nachar 2008; Lozano 2006).

Based on the definition of self-sufficient business models in the sec-tion "Definition of Incubator Self-Sufficiency", we distinguished self-sufficiency and non-self-sufficiency based on annual revenues exceeding (or not exceeding) expenses, adjusted for donations and subsidies.

4.   FINDINGS

To get a better understanding of the survey's participants, the sample characteristics, central tendencies and frequency distributions will be explained and findings presented.

4.1. Respondent Characteristics

Organizational structure
Incubators from 19 different countries participated in the survey, with the highest percentage coming from France (17 per cent), Israel (14 per cent), United States (14 per cent), Germany (12 per cent) and Switzerland (9 per cent).

An analysis of the stockholder structure showed that five (7 per cent) distinct governmental, two (3 per cent) university, four (6 per cent) corporate and 11 (15 per cent) private incubators with respectively one stakeholder participated in the survey. With only few incubators having a distinct major stakeholder, the remaining 69 per cent could be classified as hybrid institutions with a diverse stakeholder structure. To facilitate the analysis, the participating incubators were clustered in the four incubator types, based on their major stakeholders. Thus, 27 per cent could be classified as BICs, 11 per cent as UBIs, 30 per cent as CPIs and as 32 per cent IPIs.

Fostering an entrepreneurial culture can be regarded as the overall main objective, being the highest ranked objective for governmental, corporate and private incubators (Table 10.1). University incubators strive to enhance university spin-offs from technological innovations and showed a significantly higher focus on technology transfer than corporations and private incubators. The corporate incubator's main goal is fostering

Table 10.1   *Overarching objectives of different incubator types based on a 6-star scale (t-test differences in mean values: a[i] significance level of 5%; b[i] significance level of 10%; example: value a4 varies significantly from IPI)*

Objectives	BIC		UBI		CPI		IPI	
	Mean	Std. Error	Mean	Std. Error	Mean	Std. Error	Mean	Std. Error
Technology Transfer	4.42	0.345	5.38[a3,4]	0.375	3.95[a2]	0.417	3.91[a2]	0.332
Profits	2.26 [a4,b3]	0.314	3.13	0.693	3.14[a3]	0.421	4.65[a1,2,3]	0.285
Corporate Innovation	3.95	0.422	4	0.535	4.29	0.379	4.43	0.294
Real Estate Appreciation	2.11	0.35	2.5	0.627	1.95	0.312	2	0.243
Foster Entrep. Culture	5.16	0.233	5.13	0.515	5.1	0.323	5.22	0.235
International Outreach	3.37[b3]	0.317	3.88	0.581	4.24[b1]	0.344	4.13	0.409

an entrepreneurial culture within the firm and to increase its innovation performance, while also increasing its international outreach. Private incubators were shown to be significantly more profit-driven.

Most incubators in this survey are focused on specific industries ranging from Life Science, Engineering, Energy and Health Tech to Fashion, Media and Communication, with the majority focused on digitalisation and engineering technologies.

Incubation structures

Most of the incubators provided a core bundle of services, such as business development, access to financing, and network access. Equipment and marketing services for incubatees or consulting for external firms are not common within the sample. From the incubators perspective the services that added the most value to their member firms are (in descending order): networking (1. corporate, 2. mentors, 3. financing), coaching (1. start-up methods, 2. business development, 3. consulting), and access to finance (1. funding, 2. investment ready, 3. convertible loans). Only 4 per cent of incubators had start-ups in a mature profitable growth stage with more than $2M in revenue. Also, the graduation times of incubatees varied from less than three months to more than four years.

Financial structures

As shown in previous studies there are many different sources of financing. The share of annual revenues and expenses for the incubators are presented in Table 10.2.

Corporate sponsorships, subsidies, or donations account for over half of the incubators' income. The main sources for generated revenue are rent or membership fees, followed by external consulting activities, return on equity sold, and event and educational fees (Table 10.2). Salaries for staff and covering building costs are the biggest single expenses. The reliance of incubators on government support and subsidies can also be seen in this sample with over 51 per cent indicating to reduce or cease operations, if government support drowns.

About 40 per cent of the respondents take equity (38 per cent cash) in exchange for services provided, with incubatees also asked to actively contribute to the entrepreneurial culture or provide revenue shares. About one-third (N=25) of the incubators maintained an affiliate seed fund to provide financial backing in exchange for equity in the incubatees, with an approximate average fund size of between $5M and $10M (only recently established, so no profit returns).

Table 10.2   Percentage of annual a) revenues and b) expenses, for the most recent fiscal year of business incubators

a) Percentage of annual revenues	N	Mean	Std. Deviation	b) Percentage of annual expenses	N	Mean	Std. Deviation
Membership/ Rent for office space	55	18,04	23,916	Building costs	57	19,6	16,886
Educational Program Participation fees	54	4,04	11,085	Utilities, Internet, Telephone	57	6,51	8,277
Event & Social Revenues	55	4,49	7,827	Staff Salaries	57	36,95	20,028
Corporate Sponsorship/ Subsidies	55	37,82	34,651	Legal and Accounting	57	4,14	7,102
Donations/ Grants	55	14,64	28,299	Consultants/ Outside	57	6,56	10,334
Returns from Client Stock	55	5,13	14,213	Contractors	57	3,95	8,457
External Consulting Activities	55	8,11	18,254	Marketing	57	5,72	5,882
Other revenues	55	4,18	7,543	Event Costs	57	6,46	5,603
				Other expenses	56	4,93	7,767

4.2.   Business Model Analysis: A Comparison of the Variables

The following section identifies factors influencing a self-sufficient business model for incubators; the sample was clustered in self-sufficient and non-self-sufficient institutions. Consequently, 14 incubators were identified as having self-sufficient businesses, while 39 incubators could not cover their expenses independently. In the following sections, the two clusters will be analysed based on the key elements derived from prior literature.

Customer value proposition

While the start-up stage did not have a significant impact on the incubator performance, the graduation time varied considerably. Self-sufficient incubators have a significant shorter incubation time, with about 57 per cent having an incubation time of no more than six months. Forty-seven per cent of non-self-sufficient incubators on the other hand had incubation times of more than two years, with 16 per cent having no time limit. Also,

Table 10.3   Comparison of value propositions of self-sufficient and non-self-sufficient incubators

Value Proposition	Cluster	N	Mean	Std. Deviation	Mann-Whitney U	Asymp. Sig. (2-tailed
Technology Transfer	Non-Self-Sufficient	39	4,23	1,477	271	0,967
	Self-Sufficient	14	4,14	1,748		
Profits	Non-Self-Sufficient	39	2,59	1,585	271	0
	Self-Sufficient	14	4,64	1,393		
Corporate Innovation	Non-Self-Sufficient	39	3,97	1,581	177,5	0,048
	Self-Sufficient	14	4,93	0,997		
Real Estate Appreciation	Non-Self-Sufficient	39	2,03	1,386	264,5	0,854
	Self-Sufficient	14	2,21	1,626		
Fostering Entrepreneurial Culture	Non-Self-Sufficient	39	5	1,277	211	0,16
	Self-Sufficient	14	5,57	0,756		
International Outreach	Non-Self-Sufficient	39	3,82	1,233	227	0,344
	Self-Sufficient	14	4,07	1,979		
Jobs created p.a.	Non-Self-Sufficient	33	25,55	27,192	42,5	0
	Self-Sufficient	10	98,2	78,953		
International Partners	Non-Self-Sufficient	21	9,71	12,993	72	0,305
	Self-Sufficient	9	11	8,093		
Fostering Entrepreneurial Culture (1 decreased, 5 sig. increased)	Non-Self-Sufficient	33	4,3	0,684	209	0,565
	Self-Sufficient	14	4,43	0,646		

goals and objectives in formulating a value proposition differ, as shown in Table 10.3.

As Table 10.3 suggests, self-sufficient incubators are significantly more profit-driven than non-self-sufficient ones. Self-sufficient incubators were shown to be more profit-driven with all incubators relying on financing themselves through their own revenues. As 20 per cent of self-sufficient incubators (compared to 30 per cent) were non-profit institutions, this fact is further supported.

Although self-sufficient incubators had a lower corporate stakeholder percentage, the focus on corporate innovation is significantly higher, suggesting that offering value to established firms is a key factor for a long-term viable business.

Although they are profit-driven, self-sufficient incubators tend to fulfil the main objective of governmental incubators of creating local jobs to a significantly higher extent. Policymakers who are interested in job creation would presumably be satisfied with identifying those incubators

Table 10.4   Reward for services provided to incubatees

Reward for services to incubatees	Cluster	N	Mean	Std. Deviation	Mann-Whitney U	Asymp. Sig. (2-tailed
Equity Stakes	Non-Self-Sufficient	39	0,23	0,427	121,5	0
	Self-Sufficient	14	0,79	0,426		
Money for services	Non-Self-Sufficient	39	0,33	0,478	169	0,015
	Self-Sufficient	14	0,71	0,469		
Neither	Non-Self-Sufficient	39	0,54	0,505	165	0,011
	Self-Sufficient	14	0,54	0,363		

that produce the largest number of jobs, regardless of whether this is the incubators' goal or not (Bergek & Norrman 2008).

Profit formula

Self-sufficient incubators financed their expenditures significantly higher through their own revenues (71 per cent of participants) or through private ownership with partner support (57 per cent). Significantly more non-self-sufficient incubators indicated a financing through governmental support. There was no significant difference in affiliation with universities, private persons, corporations and non-profit institutions, nor did cost differ substantially. To cover these, incubators received equity stakes or cash for services provided (Table 10.4).

As for the descriptive analyses, the variation between self-sufficient and non-self-sufficient incubators seems significant. While self-sufficient incubators ask for both, non-self-sufficient ones tend to have no monetary benefits (significant on 5 per cent). These differences also become visible in the revenue positions of incubators. The average standard deviation of the percentage of income sources of 19,063 and 9,054 differs significantly, i.e. a more diverse revenue stream returns a more self-sufficient incubator. Furthermore, self-sufficient incubators had a significantly higher percentage of returns from consulting external firms, membership, or rent for office space and from events. Although the results in Table 10.4 suggest that self-sufficient incubators earned more revenue through equity shares, the difference was not significant. Services provided to customers were almost identical, with self-sufficient incubators having a significantly higher percentage of services provided by volunteers. On the contrary, 50 per cent of non-self-sufficient incubators did not have any support.

5. CONCLUSION

This chapter provides insights on success factors of incubators and their role within start-up incubation ecosystems. Elements of incubator business models that bear relevance for a self-sufficient operation, as well as management mechanisms for incubators are presented. Furthermore, different aspects of business models within incubation ecosystems imply a distinct, yet interrelated, impact on businesses' self-sufficiency. This indicates that some revenue streams might interest incubators more in operating their business self-sufficiently, i.e. without being reliant on external subsidies, while meeting main stakeholder or incubatee demands. Furthermore, aiming to generate income streams through less variable factors such as rents and long-term consulting or project work might support covering the operational costs, while fluctuating revenues through equity sold or events might provide the basis for further investments.

Certain means positively influence the self-sufficiency of business incubators and contribute to success in incubation ecosystems: Consistent with Duff (1999), Lalkaka (2000) and Scaramuzzi (2002), the need for establishing a self-sufficient incubator business model, which can cover expenses with revenue generated on its own, is proposed. The value generated for incubatees is analysed, and also how incubators capture value themselves, and what resources and activities are needed. Prior research on this topic is scarce, with most other studies centring around the general definition of incubators, their success factors and impact on tenant firms (e.g. Hughes et al. 2007).

Incubators were divided in self-sufficient and non-self-sufficient institutions based on the *ability to cover the operational costs through revenue generation without the dependence on subsidies*. The analysis implied differences between the two groups in regard to their business models, with indications of significant differences in the customer value proposition, the profit formula, as well as the key resources and processes provided.

While it had been shown that incubators have to be profit-driven and have to aim at diversifying those profits through different income streams, activities like operating a seed fund or striving for revenues through sale of equity could not be supported by this study. Moreover, the stakeholder structure as well as the objectives of the incubators seem to significantly influence business viability and differentiation potential. Yet, inconsistencies in the results surfaced, like outcomes between revenue policy (equity stakes) and actual revenues (returns from client stocks). These might probably indicate another path between them, namely the performance enhancing role of equity stakes themselves. Considering the argument in Mowery and Ziedonis (2001), equity stakes potentially improve the performance of start-ups. This indirectly increases membership fees or office rental fees as long as they are coupled with the financial performance of incubatees.[1] No statistically significant differences between self-sufficient and non-self-sufficient incubators were observed in regard to an incubator's focus industry, its size (in terms of annual budget), or its founding year. Furthermore, the different start-up stages and the number of current start-ups incubated did not impact incubators' self-sufficiency.

While many papers argue that an incubator's performance is based on the provision of coaching and networking to tenant firms (e.g. Carayannis & von Zedtwitz 2005), this chapter indicates that these services are not influencing the incubator itself. Many scholars neglected the fact that incubators are often start-ups themselves, with identical problems, acting under the same constraints (Grimaldi & Grandi 2005). Viewing incubators as start-ups themselves is supported by their constant change in services provided or halting of unwanted offerings. Open questions on services that have already been discontinued or found highly valuable by customers furthermore support the notion that many incubators are on a constant search for monetisation opportunities. Hence, the appearance of company-builders or accelerators (Kreusel et al. 2018) may also lead to a more differentiated view on how to support start-ups in their development.

6.   LIMITATIONS AND FURTHER RESEARCH

A problem common to this study type is whether an individual response can represent the intended firm-level situations. Different skill sets and experiences of the participant population suggest that, despite good reliability statistics, responses may not reflect similar contexts. To mitigate this impact, the respondents addressed were at the board level, i.e. CFOs or CEOs, who best represent their firms and who are familiar with the topic analysed. Furthermore, the data reported could suffer from common method variance. Firm internal data is scarce in the literature, however, multiple sources were used to verify the dataset and to mitigate this risk.

Although non-response bias was accounted for, transferring the sample findings to the whole incubator population may be difficult due to its limited sample size and origin of the majority of participants, stemming from developed countries only. We therefore urge subsequent research on larger samples and econometric analyses to validate our findings. Lastly, the definition of self-sufficiency and the subsequent clustering may be susceptible to contrary classifications due to the scaling method of the questionnaire, striving between ensuring anonymity and gaining appropriate and accurate data. However, this serves as an interesting starting point for further research.

NOTE

1. An anonymous reviewer has pointed us towards this inconsistency and its impact, for which we are very grateful.

REFERENCES

Alberti, J. (2011): *Geschäftsmodelle für Inkubatoren. Strategien, Konzepte, Handlungsempfehlungen*. 1. Aufl. Wiesbaden: Gabler Verlag / Springer Fachmedien Wiesbaden GmbH, Wiesbaden (Gabler Research: Innovation und Technologie im modernen Management), pp. 83–187.

Allen, D. N.; Rahman, S. (1985): 'Small business incubators: a positive environment for entrepreneurship', *Journal of Small Business Management* (Vol. 23).

Bergek, A.; Norrman, C. (2008): 'Incubator best practice. A framework', *Technovation* 28 (1–2), pp. 20–28.

Bhasin, N.; Gupta, P. (2016): 'Drivers of sustainability of Indian microfinance institutions', *International Journal of Business Ethics in Developing Economies* 5(2), pp. 1–16.

Bøllingtoft, A.; Ulhøi, J. P. (2005): 'The networked business incubator – leveraging entrepreneurial agency?', *Journal of Business Venturing* 20 (2), pp. 265–290.

Carayannis, E. G.; von Zedtwitz, M. (2005): 'Architecting gloCal (global–local), real-virtual incubator networks (G-RVINs) as catalysts and accelerators of entrepreneurship in transitioning and developing economies. Lessons learned and best practices from current development and business incubation practices', *Technovation* 25 (2), pp. 95–110.

Chan, K. F.; Lau, T. (2005): 'Assessing technology incubator programs in the science park. The good, the bad and the ugly', *Technovation* 25 (10), pp. 1215–1228.

Chandra, A.; Chao, C.-A. (2011): 'Growth and evolution of high-technology business incubation in China', In *Human Systems Management* (Vol. 30, No. 1–2), pp. 55–69.

Chandra, A.; Fealey, T. (2009): 'Business incubation in the United States, China and Brazil. A comparison of role of government, incubator funding and financial services', *International Journal of Entrepreneurship* (Volume 13), pp. 67–86.

Cooper, D. R.; Schindler, P. S. (2014): *Business research methods*. 12th edition, Boston: McGraw-Hill/Irwin (The McGraw-Hill/Irwin series operations and decision sciences), p. 324.

Diamantopoulou, V.; Androutsopoulou, A.; Charalabidis, Y. (2018): 'Towards a taxonomy of services offered by start-up business incubators: insights from the Mediterranean Region', *International Journal of Entrepreneurship and Small Business* 33(4), pp. 494–513.

Duff, A. (1999): 'Best practice in business incubator management', *AUSTEP Strategic Partnering Pty Ltd*, p. 38.

Etter, J.-F.; Perneger, T. V. (1997): 'Analysis of non-response bias in a mailed health survey', *Journal of Clinical Epidemiology* 50 (10), pp. 1123–1128.

Etzkowitz, H. (2002): 'Incubation of incubators. Innovation as a triple helix of university-industry-government networks', *Sci. and Pub. Pol.* 29 (2), pp. 115–128.

European Commission (2002): *Benchmarking of Business Incubators*, Final Report (Ref. Ares(2014)77245 – 15/01/2014), pp. 20.

Flynn, B. (1990): 'Empirical research methods in operations management', *Journal of Operations Management* 9 (2), pp. 250–284.

Forza, C. (2002): 'Survey research in operations management. A process-based perspective', *International Journal of Operations and Production Management* 22 (2), pp. 95–194.

Gerlach, S.; Brem, A. (2015): 'What determines a successful business incubator? Introduction to an incubator guide', *International Journal of Entrepreneurial Venturing* 7 (3), pp. 286–307.

Grimaldi, R.; Grandi, A. (2005): 'Business incubators and new venture creation. An assessment of incubating models', *Technovation* 25 (2), pp. 111–121.

Hackett, S. M.; Dilts, D. M. (2004): 'A systematic review of business incubation research', *The Journal of Technology Transfer* 29 (1), pp. 55–82.

Hansen, M. T.; Chesbrough, H., Nohria, N.; Sull, D. N. (2000): 'Networked incubators. Hothouses of the new economy', *Harvard Business Review* (Sep-Oct), pp. 74–84.

Hausberg, J. P.; Korreck, S. (2018): 'Business incubators and accelerators: a co-citation analysis-based, systematic literature review', *The Journal of Technology Transfer*, pp. 1–26.

Hughes, M.; Ireland, R. D.; Morgan, R. E. (2007): 'Stimulating dynamic value. Social capital and business incubation as a pathway to competitive success', *Long Range Planning* 40 (2), pp. 154–177.

Johnson, M. E. (2010): *Seizing the White Space: Business Model Innovation for Growth and Renewal*. Boston, MA: Harvard Business Press.

Knuth, A. (2009): *Gründungsnetzwerke im Wissenschafts-und Hochschulbereich*. Wiesbaden: Springer Fachmedien (Gabler Edition Wissenschaft: Innovation und Technologie im modernen Management).

Kreusel, N.; Roth, N.; Brem, A. (2018): 'European business venturing in times of digitisation-an analysis of for-profit business incubators in a triple helix context', *International Journal of Technology Management* 76 (1–2), pp. 104–136.

Lalkaka, R. (2000): 'UNESCO – Manual on technology business incubators', *UNISPAR Series of Toolkits on Innovation*, pp. 46–87.

Lalkaka, R. (2006): 'Technology business incubation: A toolkit on innovation in engineering, science and technology', *UNESCO Pub* (v. 255).

Lazarowich, M.; Wojciechowski, M. John (2002): *Russian Business Incubator Program, Prospect Development & Strategic Plan*. University of Waterloo, pp. 19–29.

Lee, S. S.; Osteryoung, J. S. (2004): 'A comparison of critical success factors for effective operations of university business incubators in the United States and Korea', *Journal of Small Business Management* 42 (4), pp. 418–426.

Lozano, J. (2006): 'Nonparametric statistics. Graduate seminar in applied statistics.' University of Goettingen. Available online at http://www.statoek.wiso.uni-goettingen.de/veranstaltungen/graduateseminar/Nonpar2006.pdf. Accessed: October 30th, 2018.

Lukeš, M.; Longo, M. C.; Zouhar, J. (2018): 'Do business incubators really enhance entrepreneurial growth? Evidence from a large sample of innovative Italian start-ups', *Technovation* (in press).

Mann, H. B.; Whitney, D. R. (1947): 'On a test of whether one of two random variables is stochastically larger than the other', *The Annals of Mathematical Statistics* 18 (1), pp. 50–60.

Markman, G. D.; Phan, P. H.; Balkin, D. B.; Gianiodis, Peter T. (2005): 'Entrepreneurship and university-based technology transfer', *Journal of Business Venturing* 20 (2), pp. 241–263.

McAdam, M.; McAdam, R. (2006): 'The networked incubator', *The International Journal of Entrepreneurship and Innovation* 7 (2), pp. 87–97.

Mian, S.; Lamine, W.; Fayolle, A. (2016): 'Technology business incubation. An overview of the state of knowledge', *Technovation* 50–51, pp. 1–12.

Miller, D. C.; Salkind, N. J. (1991): *Handbook of research design & social measurement*, pp. 168. 5. ed. Thousand Oaks, Calif.: Sage.

Mowery, D. C.; Ziedonis, A. A. (2001): 'The commercialisation of national laboratory technology through the formation of "spin-off" firms: evidence from Lawrence Livermore National Laboratory', *International Journal of Manufacturing Technology and Management* 3 (1–2), pp. 106–119.

Nachar, N. (2008): 'The Mann-Whitney U. A test for assessing whether two independent samples come from the same distribution', *TQMP* 4 (1), pp. 13–20.

Pauwels, C.; Clarysse, B.; Wright, M.; van Hove, J. (2016): 'Understanding a new generation incubation model. The accelerator', *Technovation* 50–51, pp. 13–24.

Samaeemofrad, N.; Van den Herik, J. (2018): 'The Relation Between Support by Business Incubators and Performance of NTBFs', 2018 IEEE International Conference on Engineering, Technology and Innovation (ICE/ITMC), Stuttgart, Germany, pp. 1–7.

Scaramuzzi, E. (2002): 'Incubators in Developing Countries: Status and Development Perspectives', World Bank Working Paper. Available online at http://documents.worldbank. org/curated/en/186751468770425799/Incubators-in-developing-countries-status-and-develo pment-perspectives. Accessed: August 30th, 2019.

Sekaran, U.; Roger, B. (2016): *Research methods for business. A skill building approach*, 7th Edition. New York, NY: John Wiley & Sons.

Smilor, R. W. (1987): 'Managing the incubator system. Critical success factors to accelerate new company development', *IEEE Trans. Eng. Manage.* EM-34 (3), pp. 146–155.

Spigel, B. (2017): 'The relational organization of entrepreneurial ecosystems', *Entrepreneurship Theory and Practice* 41(1), pp. 49–72.

Studer, J.; Baggio, S.; Mohler-Kuo, M.; Dermota, P.; Gaume, J.; Bertholet, N. (2013): 'Examining non-response bias in substance use research-are late respondents proxies for non-respondents?', *Drug and Alcohol Dependence* 132 (1–2), pp. 316–323.

Tötterman, H.; Sten, J. (2005): 'Start-ups. Business incubation and social capital', *International Small Business Journal: Researching Entrepreneurship* 23 (5), pp. 487–511.

Voigt, L. F.; Koepsell, T. D.; Darling, J. R. (2003): 'Characteristics of telephone survey respondents according to willingness to participate', *American Journal of Epidemiology* 157 (1), pp. 66–73.

von Zedtwitz, M.; Grimaldi, R. (2006): 'Are service profiles incubator-specific? Results from an empirical investigation in Italy', *Journal of Technology Transfer* 31 (4), pp. 459–468.

Wright, K. B. (2005): 'Researching internet-based populations. Advantages and disadvantages of online survey research', Online Questionnaire Authoring Software Packages, and Web Survey Services, *Journal of Computer-Mediated Communication* 10 (3).

APPENDIX

Table 10A.1 Summary questionnaire

Question	Question
Preliminary questions	*Services and Operations*
Q1 In what country is your incubator based? *(Open question)*	Q11 Please indicate the services that you are providing: *(11 options, multiple choice)*
Q2 When did you start your incubator? *(Open question)*	Q12 What do you want in reward for your offered services? *(4 options, multiple choice)*
Q3 Rate the importance of the following overarching goals in your organization? *(7 goals, scale (1-6))*	Q13 Does your organization have an affiliate seed fund that provides cash in exchange for a percentage of equity in start-up companies in your programs? *(Binary (0/1))*
Q3a How many graduate jobs do your incubatees approximately create per year? *(Open question, numerical)*	Q13a In how many start-ups are you investing in average per year? *(3 ranges, single choice)*
Q3b How many international partners are you helping per year? *(Open question, numerical)*	Q13b What is your approximate fund size? *(5 ranges, single choice)*
Q3c Since your operation of the incubator, you could see that the innovation activities of your local environment or partners have... *(Scale (1–3)*	Q13c How high is your average Investment approximately? *(5 ranges, single choice)*
Q4 Please indicate the topics that your incubator specifically focuses on: *(10 topics, single choice)*	Q13d What is your average APR? *(5 ranges, single choice)*
Q5 Please indicate how many corporate strategic partners you have: *(Open question, numerical)*	Q14 Approximately, what are your organization's total annual expenses? *(5 ranges, single choice)*
Q6 How many tenants/incubatees do you currently have? *(6 ranges, single choice)*	Q15 For the most recent fiscal year, please indicate the approximate percentage of total expenses for each of the following: *(9 categories, open question)*
Q7 In what stage are most of your start-ups? *(5 stages, multiple choice)*	Q16 How many employees of your core team are involved in coaching incubatees? *(Open question, numerical)*
Q8 After what time do your tenants graduate? *(6 ranges, single choice)*	Q17 What percentage of your start-up services is carried out by volunteers? *(4 ranges, single choice)*

Table 10A.1   (continued)

Question	Question
Q9 Are you depended on a parental institution's/company's decisions? *(3 options, multiple choice)* Q10 Please indicate the approximate percentage of your Stakeholders: *(5 stakeholders, open question)*	*Income/Funding* Q18 What is your organization's total annual budget/revenue including subsidies? *(5 ranges, single choice)* Q19 How is your institution financed? *(8 options, multiple choice)* Q20 For the most recent fiscal year, please indicate approximately what percentage of your revenue totals came from the following: *(9 categories, open question)* Q21 If the government funding would be stopped: *(3 options, single choice)* Q22 Please share some of your experiences / insights. *(Open question)*

Note: The full questionnaire is available upon request from the authors.

11. Incubators' coopetition strategy in the start-up incubation ecosystem
Christina Theodoraki and Karim Messeghem

INTRODUCTION

Entrepreneurial ecosystem research has received high consideration from the academic society in the last years (Malecki, 2018). The entrepreneurial ecosystem is broadly defined as a set of interconnected and interdependent actors, entrepreneurial processes and factors coordinated in such a way that enable productive entrepreneurship while sustaining a local entrepreneurial environment (Mason & Brown, 2014; Stam, 2015; Brown & Mason, 2017). The entrepreneurial ecosystem is considered as a multifaceted, multi-layered, multi-nodal, multi-modal and multi-lateral phenomenon which further complicates its understanding (Carayannis, Grigoroudis, Campbell, Meissner, & Stamati, 2018). To reduce this complexity, it is necessary to clarify the importance of each actor for the effective function of the overall system (Morris, Neumeyer, & Kuratko, 2015). Likewise, business incubators play a key role in the entrepreneurial ecosystem as they act as intermediaries that connect tenants with the external entrepreneurial environment (Bergek & Norrman, 2008; Spigel, 2017). However, the entrepreneurial ecosystem is composed of several interconnected sub-ecosystems in different levels of analysis (Moore, 1996; Simatupang, Schwab, & Lantu, 2015; Theodoraki & Messeghem, 2017). Based on Theodoraki and Messeghem (2017), we consider that the incubation process evolves in the micro-level of analysis (or intra-incubator level); the relationships between incubators establish the meso-level of analysis (or inter-incubator level); and the incubators' relationships with other ecosystem actors such as policy makers or funding entities design the ecosystem-level of analysis.

The term of incubator is an 'umbrella word' used to describe organizations facilitating creation and successful development of start-ups by supplying offices, shared services and entrepreneurial support (Aernoudt, 2004; Hackett & Dilts, 2004b; Bøllingtoft, 2012). In the past 30 years, the number of incubators has strongly increased worldwide (Bruneel, Ratinho, Clarysse, & Groen, 2012; Vanderstraeten & Matthyssens, 2012). Incubators evolve in coopetitive environments characterized by cooperation and competition relationships (Adner, Oxley, & Silverman,

2013). The lack of entrance barriers in the ecosystem threatens incubators' survival because of new competitors, such as accelerators. The European debt crisis context reinforces the need for a broader research on this issue which has theoretical and practical interests (Grimaldi & Grandi, 2005; Schwartz & Hornych, 2008; Vanderstraeten & Matthyssens, 2012). Therefore, the term 'coopetition' appears useful to describe cooperation and competition relationships. Coopetition is described as the combination of two existing and conflicting concepts: cooperation and competition (Bengtsson & Kock, 1999, 2000; Bengtsson, Eriksson, & Wincent, 2010; Yami, Castaldo, Dagnino, & Le Roy, 2010; Akdoğan & Cingšz, 2012). Even though the concept of coopetition has been studied in various fields such as the spatial industry (Fernandez, Le Roy, & Gnyawali, 2014), information and communication technology (ICT) (Ritala, Hallikas, & Sissonen, 2008), biotechnology (Quintana-Garcia & Benavides-Velasco, 2004), it still remains little explored (Dagnino & Padula, 2002; Walley, 2007; Gnyawali & Park, 2011) and less studied during the entrepreneurial process (Galkina & Lundgren-Henriksson, 2017). Some articles underline the need for broader research on the concept of coopetition in different contexts, sectors (Dagnino & Padula, 2002; Ritala et al., 2008; Gnyawali & Song, 2016) or ecosystems (Minà, Dagnino, & Ben Letaifa, 2015).

Furthermore, previous studies invite researchers to develop frameworks for building 'sustainable entrepreneurial ecosystems' to promote innovation, stimulate long-term economic development, successful new firms, and sustainable employment growth within a specific geographical area (Simatupang et al., 2015; Theodoraki, Messeghem, & Rice, 2018). Despite the increasing interest in exploring incubators to understand the functioning of the entrepreneurial ecosystem, little research is done on the entrepreneurial process (Spigel & Harrison, 2018). In addition, few studies explore coopetition strategies between incubators (Chan & Harayama, 2011), while neglecting to examine these strategies during the incubation process. Therefore, more research is needed to understand the coopetition impact during the incubation process on building entrepreneurial ecosystems. To address this research gap, we focus on the Start-up Incubation Ecosystem (SUPIE), where incubators have a leading role with the goal to support new business creation and development through the incubation process. This type of ecosystem is characterized by an intensification in competitive dynamics and a need for cooperation due in part to the stakeholders' demands. This chapter explores the following research question: How do coopetition strategies evolve during the incubation process in the Start-up Incubation Ecosystem?

To answer this question, we use a qualitative explorative study of 39 semi-structured interviews, conducted in the South of France with key actors of the Start-up Incubation Ecosystem. Furthermore, this chapter is organized into three parts. First, we will present the theoretical framework of coopetition in the French Start-up Incubation Ecosystem. Second, we will describe the research design of the qualitative method used by detailing the data collection and analysis. Finally, we will show and discuss our findings on how coopetition is articulated with the incubation process. We will formulate three propositions based on coopetition strategies in the incubation process. To conclude, we consider that coopetition relationships should be encouraged by policy makers to improve incubators' efficiency and ecosystems' long-term sustainability. Setting up funding plans and evaluation tools may indeed affect these relationships.

THEORETICAL FRAMEWORK

Coopetition has been used in strategic management as a theoretical framework which forms a better understanding of relationships between firms. This framework also applies to SUPIEs.

Start-up Incubation Ecosystem: Functioning and Incubation Process Model

An entrepreneurial ecosystem and its sub-ecosystems are made up of economic communities in which firms share their business practices to benefit the entire economic community (Moore, 2006). Entrepreneurial support has merely been identified as an emerging ecosystem. It is designed to reinforce economic growth, promote innovation and support new high potential tech firms (Aernoudt, 2004; Bergek & Norrman, 2008; Schwartz & Hornych, 2008; Bøllingtoft, 2012; Bruneel et al., 2012). In this chapter, we focus on a specific type of the entrepreneurial ecosystem, i.e. the Start-up Incubation Ecosystem. The latter is composed of a multitude of actors collectively covering a large range of needs for the tenants. Thus, SUPIEs are widely diverse and complex due to the large number of stakeholders and incubators' models (Gstraunthaler, 2010). It involves a variety of industries in which organizations co-evolve by developing new competencies. More precisely, SUPIEs are composed of customers, suppliers, producers, communities and other actors who interact to produce goods and services (Moore, 1993). The ecosystem-view perspective also adds several groups of stakeholders such as professional organizations, governmental and institutional organisms (Isenberg, 2011, 2016).

The wide variety of incubators, services and incubation processes are the basis for a complex and dynamic environment (Bøllingtoft, 2012; Messeghem, Bakkali, Sammut, & Swalhi, 2018), which encourages coopetition strategies. Indeed, the concept of incubator is used to describe organizations set up to create a positive environment, secured and favourable to the development of new firms in the early stages of their lives (Chan & Lau, 2005; Bergek & Norrman, 2008; Chandra & Fealey, 2009). The main source of complexity derives from the diversity of incubation processes. The synthesis of previous literature review reveals three main mechanisms of the incubation process: 1) selection, 2) supply of resources and skills, 3) network access (Hackett & Dilts, 2004a, 2004b; Bergek & Norrman, 2008). The first mechanism relies on the selection process that involves decisions of accepting (or not) the entry of potential tenants. The second mechanism consists of the entrepreneurial support and facilities to tenants. This mechanism also contains human and financial resources and skills that contribute to support tenants. The last mechanism refers to the ability of the incubator as intermediator to connect tenants with other ecosystem actors.

Even though there are a large number of incubators with different ambitions defined by the investors' priorities, they all share the same goal of supporting the emergence, development and survival of new firms (Hannon, 2005; McAdam & Marlow, 2007). However, there is also competition between incubators and consulting firms, real estate agencies or firms that offer entrepreneurial support services (Carayannis & Von Zedtwitz, 2005). While ecosystem actors may compete among each other, they also should cooperate due to the lack of resources. Cooperation and competition dynamics compose the phenomenon of coopetition as it will be explained below.

Coopetition: A Trend to Explore

Since the 1990s, coopetition has become a point of interest in major areas (Dagnino & Padula, 2002; Yami et al., 2010). Coopetition is a neologism that cannot be found in any dictionary except Wikipedia (Yami et al., 2010). Practitioner Ray Noorda, CEO of Novell, first used the word 'coopetition' in 1993 as an attempt to describe the simultaneous relationships of competition and cooperation. Brandenburger and Nalebuff (1995) popularized the word through game theory, which states that players can simultaneously adopt two contrasting behaviours (Brandenburger & Nalebuff, 1995; Chiambaretto & Dumez, 2016; Dagnino & Padula, 2002; Luo, 2007; Yami et al., 2010). Coopetition is often described with other terms: 'competitive-alliance', 'opportunistic collaboration', 'cooperative competitiveness', 'collaboration with competitors', etc. (Ritala & Hurmelinna-Laukkanen, 2013). Meyer (1998) uses it to describe the 'strange-bedfellow arrangements' that firms form by cooperating with competitors or even with enemies. Coopetition is indeed described as a paradoxical and dyadic phenomenon since it simultaneously combines relationships based on competition and relationships based on cooperation with one (or several) partner(s)-competitor(s) (Brandenburger & Nalebuff, 1995; Bengtsson & Kock, 1999, 2000; Bengtsson et al., 2010; Bengtsson & Johansson, 2014; Fernandez et al., 2014; Raza-Ullah, Bengtsson, & Kock, 2014; Bengtsson, Raza-Ullah, & Vanyushyn, 2016)

Coopetition strategy is often found in industries with complex and dynamic environments as well as in the service industry (Bengtsson et al., 2010; Carayannis & Alexander, 1999). In these environments, being knowledgeable is essential to being more competitive. Moreover, the heterogeneity of unique resources initiates a coopetitive behaviour (Bengtsson & Kock, 2000; Carayannis & Alexander, 1999). SUPIEs, as dynamic and complex environments, need to master as much information as possible to ensure quality service to tenants (Carayannis & Alexander, 1999). To master and gain access to multiple information, most incubators create networks and collaborate by adopting collaborative behaviours that will lead to benefits and profits (Bengtsson & Kock, 2000). Incubators are also competing with each other since they have the same mission, the same funders and the same success factors: entrepreneurial support for fast-growing firms or *gazelles*,[1] that reinforce the added value of the incubator through job creation (Aernoudt, 2004; Chan & Harayama, 2011; Henrekson & Johansson, 2010). Combining cooperation and competition will lead to coopetitive behaviours among incubators. These behaviours are more beneficial than cooperation and competition strategies applied separately. Coopetition allows one to benefit from both strategies simultaneously (Bengtsson & Kock, 1999, 2000; Ritala et al., 2008; Yami et al., 2010).

Nonetheless, coopetition is neither the outcome of research on competition nor cooperation (Dagnino & Padula, 2002). Therefore, it deserves to be studied as a singular phenomenon with its own set of research, investigation, questioning and studies. Even though coopetition is considered as a singular phenomenon, it is often studied through competition and cooperation concepts (Bengtsson et al., 2010). More precisely, Bengtsson and Kock (2000) describe coopetitive relationships as a continuum made up of two extremes: cooperation and competition. The authors distinguish three types of coopetitive relationships:

1. Cooperation-dominated relationship (cooperation prevails in the coopetitive relationship).
2. Equal relationship (the coopetitive relationship is equally balanced between cooperation and competition).

3. Competition-dominated relationship (competition prevails in the coopetitive relationship).

In the first case, individuals share common goals to protect collective interests. In the second case, the relationship is equally balanced between cooperation and competition interactions. In the third case, individuals aim at maximizing their own interests through egocentric and opportunistic behaviours. This study uses the same approach to understand coopetition strategy in SUPIEs. Moreover, Chan and Harayama (2011) point out that cooperation and competition exist between incubators but they fail to study the reasons for this co-existence. This leads us to ask the following question: How do these relationships affect the incubation process?

METHOD

To identify coopetition relationships in the incubation process, we used an explorative qualitative research protocol which is convenient for studying novel and underexplored phenomena such as SUPIEs (Miles & Huberman, 2003; Creswell, 2013). To do so, we collected data from 39 semi-structured interviews in the South of France between May 2013 and November 2014, corresponding to approximately a hundred hours of audio recording. The South of France is a dynamic regional entrepreneurial ecosystem and it is suitable for this study as we may find all ecosystem components and benefits of geographical proximity. More specifically, this location is suitable for our study as it includes all necessary elements, such as research entities, entrepreneurial culture and favourable atmosphere to business creation, support entities, success stories, large firms, funding sources and skilled labour (Isenberg, 2011).

The semi-structured interviews were conducted in person by following a twofold guide questioning: 1) the role of the actor in the SUPIE and 2) the relations with other actors during the incubation process. Semi-structured interviews allowed us to obtain all necessary information on the topic while giving participants the opportunity to highlight their ideas and raise emerging concepts. To strengthen the ecosystem view of the study, we carried out interviews by proceeding in a purposive sampling with several ecosystem actors: policy makers (2), network coordinators (4), incubator managers (13) and staff (7), tenants (5), funding entities (3), research entities (2), independent consultants (3). All interviews were recorded, transcribed while respecting informant anonymity and data confidentiality. Other sources were also added to increase validity and reliability of results using data triangulation: websites, documentary analysis, audit reports, observation of quality and certification meetings, etc. (Mathison, 1988).

Data analysis was performed through a thematic coding with Nvivo software which allowed us to create the code tree, consistent with the structure of the interview guide (Bazeley & Jackson, 2013). The thematic coding proceeded in three steps by combining emerging and predetermined codes (Creswell, 2013). In the first step, some codes were created based on the interview guide, while others were created based on our intuition of the data and settings (general themes). All data were coded to the general themes, while we created new codes when necessary. The second step merged in a re-contextualization process where codes were grouped together by creating higher-level categories and aggregated dimensions based on the incubation process (code tree). Once we had the hierarchical structure of data, we used Nvivo Assistant Matrix and Queries to identify similarities and differences on coopetition dynamics through the incubation process (Bazeley & Jackson, 2013). To ensure the encoding process quality, the data was coded twice with an interval of several months.

FINDINGS AND DISCUSSION

Combining the above theoretical framework, we linked the types of coopetition relationships, proposed by Bengtsson and Kock (2000), with each of the three incubation process mechanisms: selection, resources and skills, network access (Figure 11.1). A synthesis of connections between the incubation process and the types of coopetition are shown in Table 11.1.

Coopetition in the Selection Phase

Cooperation relationships in SUPIEs are necessary during the selection phase. Indeed, incubators are driven to gather selection committees to evaluate submitted projects, especially their potential value and the risks associated with them. These committees are composed of economic actors: bankers, institutional representatives, business angels, other incubators' advisors, etc. Thus, we can assume that cooperation relationships between

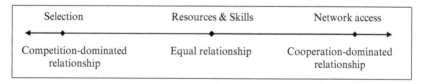

Selection	Resources & Skills	Network access
Competition-dominated relationship	Equal relationship	Cooperation-dominated relationship

Figure 11.1   Coopetition relationships during the incubation process

Table 11.1   *Intensity of the coopetition relationships during the incubation process*

Incubation Process	Cooperation intensity	Competition intensity	Coopetition Type
Selection	Low	High	Competition-dominated relationship
Resources & Skills	High	High	Equal relationship
Network Access	High	Low	Cooperation-dominated relationship

actors of SUPIEs reinforce the selection phase, which is crucial to the beginning of the incubation process. An incubator staff says:

> We are always aware that someone of the Regional Economic Development Agency is part of our selection committees because one day or another they will see this project when it will be created, so we involve them in our committees. Also, we invite independent consultants who are charged to conduct a 'flash expertise' on the project and they present their conclusions and recommendations on the project.

However, this selection phase is characterized even more by a strong competition between incubators. This competition results from the efforts made to attract the best projects with a high potential, which will in turn add value to the incubator for other clients or investors. For some actors, competition is limited to a regional level (where it is more intense). For others it takes place at a national, or even an international level. For instance, in spin-out[2] cases, Clarysse, Wright, Lockett, Van de Velde, and Vohora (2005) show three incubation models: low selective model, supportive model and incubator model. It is in this last model that the selection phase is the most competitive. Only the best projects are selected and supported by the incubator. Incubators are going to confront each other to attract the most promising projects. An incubator staff stated that:

> There are incubators that compete with each other to attract the best projects. . .Sometimes, there are some projects that haven't decided yet their incubator, and so, some incubators try to attract them at any cost.

Furthermore, an incubator manager testifies that:

> My role is to select the best projects and the talents that will settle in the territory and attract firms that are going to stay in the territory and make it shine. . .We hunted a lot of talents. For a while, we needed to look for talents to shine.

Moreover, incubators can be more aggressive for not losing their market shares and maintain a good image vis-à-vis policy makers who contribute in large parts to their funding and therefore to their long-term sustainability. The funding source affects the incubator's strategy as well as the selection criteria for tenants (Chandra & Fealey, 2009; Gstraunthaler, 2010). In some cases, strict selection criteria allow one to mainly choose shiny projects to improve incubator's image. An independent consultant said that:

> I also used this argument, because I was a platform president. It's very easy to have good records when you reject all the bad ones. If you take out all the bad records, you have a rate that is higher than the national average, it's not complicated.

The selection mechanism is therefore characterized by a coopetitive relationship dominated by competition with a highly competitive intensity and a low cooperative intensity. We can therefore assume the following proposition.

Proposition 1: During the selection stage, coopetition strategy is dominated by competition (mainly because of high-potential projects selection and market-share logics).

Coopetition vis-à-vis Resources and Skills

The variety of provided services strengthens the ecosystem's complexity even more. Even though these services are essential to ensure an efficient incubation, it may be difficult for an incubator to offer all of them simultaneously. Therefore, incubators will develop cooperative behaviours that would in turn complement each other. However, the variety of actors and the market evolution drive incubators to develop strategies which will allow them to survive and earn competitive advantages. An incubator staff said that:

> For us, as we co-support projects, it is essential that we have good relations and that we are in collaboration, in partnership with all the actors. . .You cannot do everything alone. There are lots of services that are provided, that are subcontracted. For example, the accommodation, we do not have offices to host tenants, in fact they are hosted in research organizations or universities that have set up offices, because they are members of our association.

Previous studies confirm this finding as coopetition enables an access to rare and complementary resources to improve methods, techniques or processes and to create new competencies by transforming existing skills (Yami et al., 2010). Cooperation helps obtain rare competencies, knowledge of the market and customers' needs, a solid reputation, access to other products, services and necessary resources (Bengtsson & Kock, 1999). Firms, and especially small and medium-size businesses, encounter the same challenges and difficulties in their relative markets. Collaborating and using similar and complementary resources enable them to reinforce their expertise and to create opportunities (Gnyawali & Park, 2009; Bengtsson & Johansson, 2014). Indeed, Chan and Harayama (2011) explain that cooperation between incubators permits them to share information, good practices, knowledge, experience, ideas and reciprocal support. This win-win coopetitive relationship allows an access to necessary resources for offering a complete and better-quality service to tenants and to decrease support costs for being more competent and efficient. On one hand, cooperation strengthens competitiveness, and on the other hand, competition is necessary to take advantage of the expertise generated by this collaboration (Lado, Boyd, & Hanlon, 1997).

Even though European incubators are most often publicly funded, they still need to ensure their survival. To do so, they compete with other ecosystem actors. Brandenburger and Nalebuff (1995) use the cake metaphor to describe the market. According to this metaphor, coopetitors first collaborate to make the best cake possible and then they compete to take the biggest part of that cake. Competition intensifies when incubators look for an access to financial resources to obtain more public funding. Incubators also compete to host and organize events initiated by policy makers. Regarding logistics, incubators compete on the amount of space offered or rent costs as means to attract high potential firms (Chan & Harayama, 2011). An independent consultant said:

> Everyone tries to fund his activity and justify the provided support. So, from the moment you have several actors, we have to push others to take their place.

On the coopetition relationship continuum, cooperation and competition are balanced in the incubators' search for resources and skills with a high intensity for both. Competition and cooperation are necessary since competition contributes to a company's awareness and continuous will to improve itself, and second, this happens thanks to the sharing of information, knowledge and experience brought through cooperation (Bengtsson et al., 2010). Based on this analysis, we formulate the following proposition:

Proposition 2: In the search for resources and skills, the coopetition strategy is equal between cooperation (mainly thanks to information sharing) and competition (mainly because of logistics).

Coopetition in Network Access

According to Peters, Rice, and Sundararajan (2004), the incubator's role is to offer office facilities, training, knowledge, guidance but also an access to networks. Incubators are intermediators between tenants and funding entities as well as potential partners: customers, suppliers, etc. (Bergek & Norrman, 2008; Bøllingtoft & Ulhøi, 2005). Competition may exist between incubators in terms of visibility, image and reputation vis-à-vis networks since these factors contribute to attract new projects (Schwartz & Hornych, 2008). However, the need to belong to a network reinforces even more the need for cooperation between incubators.

The incubator's role is to connect tenants with useful actors and resources (universities, venture capitalists, investors...) necessary to the project's development. Incubators establish actions that encourage inter-actions with internal and external actors of the incubator. To reinforce the reputation of tenants and generate opportunities, they must organize meetings with investors, banks and external actors of the incubator, including recruitment offices, commerce agencies, sales and marketing departments, etc. Through the mechanism of network access, the incubator offers advantages to its stakeholders and tenants. Moreover, the incubator adds value to the human and social capital of tenants by offering them the possibility to gain credibility and social acceptance (Bergek & Norrman, 2008; Bøllingtoft & Ulhøi, 2005). An incubator staff adds that:

> The interactions we have with other actors are based on a logic of advancement and continuity. Let's admit that a tenant wants to benefit from a regionally funded zero-rate loan or a state-funded zero-rate loan; you have actors who are empowered to study the request, we will play a relay or intermediary role.

Thus, the mechanism of network access is a coopetition relationship in which cooperation prevails. It is characterized by a high intensity in cooperation and a low intensity of competition. This analysis leads us to a third proposal:

Proposition 3: In network access, coopetition strategy is dominated by cooperation (mainly thanks to the key role of incubators as intermediators in the SUPIE).

CONCLUSION

Entrepreneurial support and coopetition concepts are often studied in the literature but rarely used simultaneously. To better understand the convergence of these two concepts, this chapter focused on exploring coopetition in SUPIEs. We also focused on the key factors facilitating this phenomenon and on the coopetition relationships during the incubation process. We used the continuum approach developed by Bengtsson and Kock (2000), composed of two extremes: cooperation and competition by applying it to SUPIEs. Three forms of coopetition are found in the incubation process: competition-dominated relationships in the selection phase, equal coopetition in resources and skills contribution and cooperation-dominated relationship in network access. Competitive dynamics in the SUPIEs are related to public funding. This chapter contributes to introducing and demonstrating the relevance of coopetition strategies in SUPIEs and highlights the important role of public policies in the development of new measures to reinforce territorial economic growth. More precisely, public policies facilitate coopetition strategies by simultaneously using tools that promote cooperation and assessment measures designed to increase competition and incubators' efficiency. This chapter is restricted to a qualitative exploration of this reflection and future research should measure the impact of coopetition strategy on incubators' and SUPIEs' performances. From a managerial point of view, this study is fruitful to policy makers who are looking to promote incubators' coopetition relationships to increase regional competitiveness. Policy makers act as keystone players and have a leading role in the governance of SUPIEs as they create and fund business incubators, and they establish the rules of the game. Thus, it is necessary to understand the coopetition dynamics in SUPIEs to optimize its functioning through upgraded rules. It is also useful for incubators' managers who are confronted with an intensification of the competitive game. As highlighted by Chan and Harayama (2011), incubator managers should improve incubator practices and outcomes to attract collaborations with other incubators and at the same time they compete for public funding which is essential for the survival of the incubator. They are drawn to rethink their strategy and even their business model. To that extent, coopetition may be a framework well adapted to this new context. We hope that this explorative study will inspire future research and the academic society for providing further knowledge of these phenomena.

NOTES

1. Innovative firms with a high potential for growth and which are not necessarily new or small (Henrekson and Johansson 2010).
2. A spin-out (or spin-off) is known as a new activity that emerges through intrapreneurship and is outsourced through the creation of a new firm.

REFERENCES

Adner, R., Oxley, J.E., & Silverman, B.S. (2013). *Collaboration and Competition in Business Ecosystems.* Bingley, UK: Emerald Group Publishing Limited, 429 p.
Aernoudt, R. (2004). Incubators: tool for entrepreneurship? *Small Business Economics,* 23 (2), 127–135.
Akdoğan, A.A., & Cingšz, A. (2012). An empirical study on determining the attitudes of small and medium sized businesses (SMEs) related to coopetition. *Procedia – Social and Behavioral Sciences,* 58, 252–258.
Bazeley, P., & Jackson, K. (2013). *Qualitative Data Analysis with NVivo.* Sage Publications Limited.
Bengtsson, M., Eriksson, J., & Wincent, J. (2010). Co-opetition dynamics–an outline for further inquiry. *Competitiveness Review: An International Business Journal Incorporating Journal of Global Competitiveness,* 20 (2), 194–214.
Bengtsson, M., & Johansson, M. (2014). Managing coopetition to create opportunities for small firms. *International Small Business Journal,* 32 (4), 401–427.
Bengtsson, M., & Kock, S. (1999). Cooperation and competition in relationships between competitors in business networks. *Journal of Business & Industrial Marketing,* 14 (3), 178–194.
Bengtsson, M., & Kock, S. (2000). "Coopetition" in business networks – to cooperate and compete simultaneously. *Industrial Marketing Management,* 29 (5), 411–426.
Bengtsson, M., Raza-Ullah, T., & Vanyushyn, V. (2016). The coopetition paradox and tension: The moderating role of coopetition capability. *Industrial Marketing Management,* 53, 19–30.
Bergek, A., & Norrman C. (2008). Incubator best practice: A framework. *Technovation,* 28 (1–2), 20–28.
Bøllingtoft, A. (2012). The bottom-up business incubator: Leverage to networking and cooperation practices in a self-generated, entrepreneurial-enabled environment. *Technovation,* 32 (5), 304–315.
Bøllingtoft, A., & Ulhøi, J.P. (2005). The networked business incubator – leveraging entrepreneurial agency? *Journal of Business Venturing,* 20 (2), 265–290.
Brandenburger, A.M., & Nalebuff, B.J. (1995). The right game: Use game theory to shape strategy. *Harvard Business Review,* 73 (4), 57–71.
Brown, R., & Mason, C. (2017). Looking inside the spiky bits: A critical review and conceptualisation of entrepreneurial ecosystems. *Small Business Economics,* 49 (1), 11–30.
Bruneel, J., Ratinho, T., Clarysse, B., & Groen, A. (2012). The evolution of business incubators: Comparing demand and supply of business incubation services across different incubator generations. *Technovation,* 32 (2), 110–121.
Carayannis, E.G., & Alexander, J. (1999). Winning by co-opeting in strategic government-university-industry R&D partnerships: The power of complex, dynamic knowledge networks. *The Journal of Technology Transfer,* 24 (2–3), 197–210.
Carayannis, E.G., Grigoroudis, E., Campbell, D.F., Meissner, D., & Stamati, D. (2018). 'Mode 3' universities and academic firms: Thinking beyond the box trans-disciplinarity and nonlinear innovation dynamics within coopetitive entrepreneurial ecosystems. *International Journal of Technology Management,* 77 (1–3), 145–185.
Carayannis, E.G., & von Zedtwitz, M. (2005). Architecting gloCal (global–local), real-virtual incubator networks (G-RVINs) as catalysts and accelerators of entrepreneurship in transitioning and developing economies: Lessons learned and best practices from current development and business incubation practices. *Technovation,* 25 (2), 95–110.
Chan, W., & Harayama, Y. (2011). *Exploring the Interactions among Incubators: A Case Study on Incubators in the Hsinchu Region,* in Technology Management in the Energy Smart World – Proceedings of PICMET, pp. 1–6.
Chan, K., & Lau, T. (2005). Assessing technology incubator programs in the science park: The good, the bad and the ugly. *Technovation,* 25 (10), 1215–1228.
Chandra, A., & Fealey, T. (2009). Business incubation in the United States, China and

Brazil: A comparison of role of government, incubator funding and financial services. *International Journal of Entrepreneurship*, 13 (13), 67–86.

Chiambaretto, P., & Dumez, H. (2016). Towards a typology of coopetition: A multilevel approach. *International Studies of Management and Organization*, 46 (2–3), 110–129.

Clarysse, B., Wright, M., Lockett, A., Van de Velde, E., & Vohora, A. (2005). Spinning out new ventures: A typology of incubation strategies from European research institutions. *Journal of Business Venturing*, 20 (2), 183–216.

Creswell, J.W. (2013). *Research Design: Qualitative, Quantitative, and Mixed Methods Approaches*. London: Sage.

Dagnino, G.B., & Padula, G. (2002). Coopetition strategy: A new kind of interfirm dynamics for value creation. EURAM Conference, Stockholm, available at https://www.researchgate.net/publication/228605296_Coopetition_Strategy_A_New_Kind_of_Interfirm_Dynamics_for_Value_Creation

Fernandez, A.-S., Le Roy, F., & Gnyawali, D.R. (2014). Sources and management of tension in co-opetition case evidence from telecommunications satellites manufacturing in Europe. *Industrial Marketing Management*, 43 (2), 222–235.

Galkina, T., & Lundgren-Henriksson, E.-L. (2017). Coopetition as an entrepreneurial process: Interplay of causation and effectuation. *Industrial Marketing Management*, 67, 158–173.

Gnyawali, D.R., & Park, B.R. (2009). Co-opetition and technological innovation in small and medium-sized enterprises: A multilevel conceptual model. *Journal of Small Business Management*, 47 (3), 308–330.

Gnyawali, D.R., & Park, B.-J.R. (2011). Co-opetition between giants: Collaboration with competitors for technological innovation. *Research Policy*, 40 (5), 650–663.

Gnyawali, D.R., & Song, Y. (2016). Pursuit of rigor in research: Illustration from coopetition literature. *Industrial Marketing Management*, 57, 12–22.

Grimaldi, R., & Grandi, A. (2005). Business incubators and new venture creation: An assessment of incubating models. *Technovation*, 25 (2), 111–121.

Gstraunthaler, T. (2010). The business of business incubators: An institutional analysis–evidence from Lithuania. *Baltic Journal of Management*, 5 (3), 397–421.

Hackett, S.M., & Dilts, D.M. (2004a). A real options-driven theory of business incubation. *The Journal of Technology Transfer*, 29 (1), 41–54.

Hackett, S.M., & Dilts, D.M. (2004b). A systematic review of business incubation research. *The Journal of Technology Transfer*, 29 (1), 55–82.

Hannon, P.D. (2005). Incubation policy and practice: Building practitioner and professional capability. *Journal of Small Business and Enterprise Development*, 12 (1), 57–75.

Henrekson, M., & Johansson, D. (2010). Gazelles as job creators: A survey and interpretation of the evidence. *Small Business Economics*, 35 (2), 227–244.

Isenberg, D. (2011). The entrepreneurship ecosystem strategy as a new paradigm for economic policy: Principles for cultivating entrepreneurship. *Institute of International European Affairs,* Dublin, Ireland.

Isenberg, D. (2016). Applying the ecosystem metaphor to entrepreneurship: Uses and abuses. *The Antitrust Bulletin*, 61 (4), 564–573.

Lado, A.A., Boyd, N.G., & Hanlon, S.C. (1997). Competition, cooperation, and the search for economic rents: A syncretic model. *Academy of Management Review*, 22 (1), 110–141.

Luo, Y. (2007). A coopetition perspective of global competition. *Journal of World Business*, 42 (2), 129–144.

Malecki, E.J. (2018). Entrepreneurship and entrepreneurial ecosystems. *Geography Compass*, 12 (3), 1–21.

Mason, C., & Brown, R. (2014). *Entrepreneurial Ecosystems and Growth-Oriented Entrepreneurship*. Paris, Final Report to OECD.

Mathison, S. (1988). Why triangulate? *Educational Researcher*, 17 (2), 13–17.

McAdam, M., & Marlow S. (2007). Building futures or stealing secrets? Entrepreneurial cooperation and conflict within business incubators. *International Small Business Journal*, 25 (4), 361–382.

Messeghem, K., Bakkali, C., Sammut, S., & Swalhi, A. (2018). Measuring nonprofit incubator performance: Toward an adapted balanced scorecard approach. *Journal of Small Business Management*, 56 (4), 658–680.

Meyer, H. (1998). My enemy, my friend. *Journal of Business Strategy*, 19 (5), 42–46.

Miles, M. B., & Huberman, A. M. (2003). *Analyse des données qualitatives*. Paris, de Boeck, 632 p.

Minà, A., Dagnino, G.B., & Ben Letaifa, S. (2015). Competition and cooperation in entrepreneurial ecosystems: A life-cycle analysis of a Canadian ICT ecosystem. In *Innovation, Alliances, and Networks in High-Tech Environments*. London and New York: Routledge, pp. 65–81.

Moore, J.F. (1993). Predators and prey – a new ecology of competition. *Harvard Business Review*, 71 (3), 75–86.

Moore, J.F. (1996). *The Death of Competition: Leadership and Strategy in the Age of Business Ecosystems*. Harper Business, New York.

Moore, J.F. (2006). Business ecosystems and the view from the firm. *The Antitrust Bulletin*, 51 (1), 31–75.

Morris, M.H., Neumeyer, X., & Kuratko, D.F. (2015). A portfolio perspective on entrepreneurship and economic development. *Small Business Economics*, 45 (4), 713–728.

Peters, L., Rice, M., & Sundararajan, M. (2004). The role of incubators in the entrepreneurial process. *The Journal of Technology Transfer*, 29 (1), 83–91.

Quintana-Garcia, C., & Benavides-Velasco, C.A. (2004). Cooperation, competition, and innovative capability: A panel data of European dedicated biotechnology firms. *Technovation*, 24 (12), 927–938.

Raza-Ullah, T., Bengtsson, M., & Kock, S. (2014). The coopetition paradox and tension in coopetition at multiple levels. *Special Issue on Co-Opetition Cooperation and Competition*, 43 (2), 189–198.

Ritala, P., Hallikas, J., & Sissonen, H. (2008). Coopetitive networks in the ICT sector. *International Journal of Business Environment*, 2 (1), 1–16.

Ritala, P., & Hurmelinna-Laukkanen, P. (2013). Incremental and radical innovation in coopetition – The role of absorptive capacity and appropriability. *Journal of Product Innovation Management*, 30 (1), 154–169.

Schwartz, M., & Hornych, C. (2008). Specialization as strategy for business incubators: An assessment of the Central German Multimedia Center. *Technovation*, 28 (7), 436–449.

Simatupang, T.M., Schwab, A., & Lantu, D.C. (2015). Introduction: Building sustainable entrepreneurship ecosystems. *International Journal of Entrepreneurship and Small Business*, 26 (4), 389–398.

Spigel, B. (2017). The relational organization of entrepreneurial ecosystems. *Entrepreneurship Theory and Practice*, 41 (1), 49–72.

Spigel, B., & Harrison, R. (2018). Toward a process theory of entrepreneurial ecosystems. *Strategic Entrepreneurship Journal*, 12 (1), 151–168.

Stam, E. (2015). Entrepreneurial ecosystems and regional policy: A sympathetic critique. *European Planning Studies*, 23 (9), 1759–1769.

Theodoraki, C., & Messeghem, K. (2017). Exploring the entrepreneurial ecosystem in the field of entrepreneurial support: A multi-level approach. *International Journal of Entrepreneurship and Small Business*, 31 (1), 47–66.

Theodoraki, C., Messeghem, K., & Rice, M.P. (2018). A social capital approach to the development of sustainable entrepreneurial ecosystems: An explorative study. *Small Business Economics*, 51 (1), 153–170.

Vanderstraeten, J., & Matthyssens, P. (2012). Service-based differentiation strategies for business incubators: Exploring external and internal alignment. *Technovation,* 32 (12), 656–670.

Walley, K. (2007). Coopetition: An introduction to the subject and an agenda for research. *International Studies of Management and Organization*, 37 (2), 11–31.

Yami, S., Castaldo, S., Dagnino, B., & Le Roy, F. (2010). *Coopetition: Winning Strategies for the 21st Century*. Cheltenham, UK: Edward Elgar Publishing.

12. A comparative analysis of USA enterprise support organizations for conscious capitalism and conventional capitalism

Kerul Kassel, Shelley F. Mitchell, and Guénola Abord-Hugon Nonet

INTRODUCTION

In order to gain a better understanding of Start-Up Incubation Ecosystems (SUPIEs) and contribute to this field, our research examines different types of enterprise support organizations (ESOs) involving principles for conscious capitalism. The shared value contributed by ESOs is part of a larger endeavour by this handbook to better understand the phenomenon of SUPIEs and to target the intersections between start-up firms, incubation and ecosystems. Bringing these topics together will provide a better understanding about the relationships between innovative start-ups and their supportive environment. We sought to study start-up enterprise support organizations in the context of conscious capitalism. Our findings indicate that support for start-up enterprises embracing conscious capitalism is growing, as support organizations for this type of enterprise are popping up, both in the United States and across the globe.

Over the past decade we have seen the growth of a new breed of ESOs: those aimed at supporting a more conscious capitalism also described as sustainable, responsible and social. To embrace the different aspects of conscious capitalism represented in the United Nations Sustainable Development Goals (UN General Assembly, 2015), we choose to focus on a gold standard of ESOs that have the potential to more fully embody the triple bottom line (Elkington, 1997); thus, we call these entities ESOs for conscious capitalism.

Our review of the existing literature to date identified a gap in that very little theoretical and empirical research has been dedicated to identifying and studying these new types of ESOs (Levinsohn, 2015). The researchers studied two specific types of ESOs: those that strive to support conscious capitalism and those supporting conventional capitalism, all located in the United States market. Our goal is to contribute to this field by understanding the institutional support from ESOs to assist start-up entrepreneurs considering issues of social and environmental innovation, triple bottom line and sustainability-related aspects in their business models. This research provides a rich contribution to the handbook's broader encompassing overview that targets the intersections between start-up firm, incubation and ecosystems.

According to the *Financial Times* lexicon (http://www.lexicon.ft.com), Corporate Social Responsibility (CSR) is a business approach that commits to sustainable development by providing social, environmental and economic benefits to all stakeholders. This is in alignment with our conceptualization of ESOs for conscious capitalism related to stakeholder theory (Freeman, 1984) and essentially a key strategy for achieving sustainability within the enterprise arena.

Based on the growth of new types of entities aimed at supporting sustainability and social/environmental enterprises, we began our research using terms such as sustainable enterprise and social entrepreneurship. We then incorporated related terms such as impact enterprise and conscious capitalism. As our theoretical review reveals, conscious capitalism is most in sync with our intention of understanding organizations that support enterprises designed to address social and environmental concerns in addition to economic profit. These are issues, that conventional capitalism ("business as usual") mostly treats as illegitimate or unnecessary at worst, and window dressing at best, due to the largely exclusive focus on short-term financial returns.

This chapter investigates a sampling of ESOs for conventional capitalism and for conscious capitalism to better describe their identity, their main characteristics and how they operate. This formed the following research questions:

1. What substantial differences exist between ESOs for conventional capitalism and ESOs for conscious capitalism?
2. How do the different types of ESOs identify themselves, measure their own success, and measure the success of the start-up enterprises they support?
3. How do the two different types of ESOs' offerings compare with one another and with the literature?

In the next section, we will start with a review of the relevant theoretical background to address the gaps we identified.

THEORETICAL BACKGROUND

To understand how ESOs are defined, we look at the literature related to incubators and accelerators for business-as-usual organizations. For clarity, we use the term *enterprise support organizations for conventional capitalism* when talking about incubators, accelerators, co-working spaces and related organizations focusing most primarily on economic/financial return on investment. More particularly, these ESOs do not mention social and/or environmental concerns in their strategy, apart from that jobs are created by the supported enterprises (although this metric is certainly important in the social and economic bottom lines).

In addition, we looked for literature on ESOs founded on sustainability-related principles, those which seek to create support for enterprises desiring to integrate social and environmental concerns into their business models and practices, which we label *ESOs for conscious capitalism*. In the next section we delve deeper into the literature in regard to definitions and conceptualizations used in our study.

Definition of Enterprise Support Organizations (ESOs)

Lewis, Harper-Anderson and Molnar (2011), note that some industry professionals use the term "accelerator" and "incubator" interchange-ably. In the overview of the 2013 annual general meeting of the Academy of Management, accelerators were defined as including components of time limitation, education, cohorts, mentorship, funding and networking (AOM, 2013). Miller and Bound (2011) describe accelerators as character-ized by five features: an open and highly competitive application process, the provision of funding, smaller teams (as opposed to individual found-ers) and a relatively short period of planned events. Business incubators are defined as "facility established to nurture young (startup) firms during their early months or years. It usually provides affordable space, shared offices and services hand-on management training, marketing support and, often access to some form of financing" (*Business Dictionary*, online).

In addition to the above characteristics, Cohen (2013) and Borella (2012) added a sixth characteristic: organizing demo events to introduce entrepreneurs to investors. Lall, Baird and Bowles (2013) comment that accelerators have a tendency to target companies with already existing customers and revenue, while incubators would focus more on early stage ventures. Cohen (2013), however, claims that accelerators often focus on early stage ventures.

Levinsohn (2015, pp. 35–36) offers a detailed definition of accelerators "as a non-formal program of entrepreneurship education." Due to the varied use of the terms, we choose to use the generic term enterprise support organizations (ESOs).

ESOs for Conscious Capitalism

Our conceptualization of ESOs for conscious capitalism encompasses Freeman's (1984) stakeholder theory of creating as much value as possible for stakeholders without resorting to trade-offs, including the practice of sustainable value creation (Phillips, 2003; Bidhan et al., 2010) by including the environment and society at large (Bansal, 2005; Kolk & Pinkse, 2007; Sharma & Henriques, 2005). The concept of *social entrepreneurship* also reveals how ESOs can broaden their commitments to their stakeholders by taking a broader look than sole financial consideration and encompassing a larger social agenda and, increasingly, an environmental agenda too (Austin, Stevenson, & Wei-Skillern, 2006); "social entrepreneurs pursue sustainable solutions to neglected problems with positive externalities that increase value or utility for society's members" (Waddock & Steckler, 2016, p. 720). *Sustainability enterprise*, yet another twist on the nomenclature, is described as a transformative force in "creating a better world" (Wiklund, Davidsson, Autresch, & Karlsson, 2011, p. 1). Social enterprise, a conceptual form for business organizations that offers a financially viable return while solving mostly social but also environmental problems by providing solutions in the form of services or goods, itself is a nascent research topic (Boyd, Henning, Reyna, Wang, & Welch, 2009; Hamschmidt & Pirson, 2011). A call for new business models that simultaneously address the economic, ecological and social challenges facing society has been made by governments, the civil society, for-profit organizations and supported by the United Nations Sustainable Development Goals Agenda (Shrivastava, Ivanaj, & Persson, 2013).

ESOs for Conventional Capitalism

Our conceptualization of ESOs for conventional capitalism is based on Milton Friedman's approach to the role of corporation, namely maximizing profits for the purpose of returning a portion of these profits to shareholders (Friedman, 1962).

The National Business Incubation Association (NBIA), headquartered within the United States, defines ESOs as:

> A business support process that accelerates the successful development of a start-up and fledgling companies by providing entrepreneurs with an array of targeted resources and services. These services are usually developed or

orchestrated by incubator management and offered both in the business incubator and through its network of contacts. A business incubator's main goal is to produce successful firms that will leave the program financially viable and freestanding [. . .] critical to the definition. (NBIA, 2009)

Enterprise support organizations have emerged within universities, local governments, private industry, and through public/private collaboration, often in hi-tech (Grimaldi & Grandi, 2005). Correspondingly, and more recently, ESOs for conscious capitalism have similarly begun to operate. While the generation of research on social entrepreneurship and conscious capitalism itself is a recent development (Weerawardena & Mort, 2006), studies attempting to understand and assess ESOs for conscious capitalism constitute a gap in ESO research.

Differences Between ESOs for Conscious Capitalism and ESOs for Conventional Capitalism

Casasnovas and Bruno's (2013) research indicates that ESOs for conscious capitalism embrace a great diversity of educational approaches compared to those for conventional capitalism, both with regards to the content of education and in relation to the length of time entrepreneurs spend at the ESO. ESOs for conscious capitalism have a tendency to reach far beyond their regional borders to recruit new start-ups, in contrast to ESOs for conventional capitalism: Lall, Bowles and Baird's research (2013) studied 52 "impact-oriented" accelerators and incubators and shows the diversity of recruitment, as only 43 per cent of the start-ups are recruited from a single country.

Research confirms that beyond these few studies, little theoretical and empirical research has been dedicated to understanding ESOs for conscious capitalism and even less so to compare these entities with ESOs for conventional capitalism. Review of the literature also reveals a diversity of approaches and understandings of the various concepts related to ESOs. Our research seeks to determine the differences between ESOs for conscious capitalism and conventional capitalism, how they identify themselves, and how their offerings compare with one another and the literature.

RESEARCH QUESTIONS AND FINDINGS

With these questions in mind, we conducted a qualitative research study, interviewing enterprise support organizations, both those aiming at developing more of a conscious capitalism approach encompassing social and/or environmental criteria in their strategy, and other enterprise support organizations supporting conventional capitalism, driven primarily by a financial return on investment. We aimed for a sample of director level leaders within both types of ESOs. Secondary data was obtained from the websites, social media, and media reports of the ESOs in the study, to round out any data that was not expressly provided in the interviews.

Our study includes a total of 21 ESOs, 12 characterized as conscious capitalism ESOs and nine ESOs for conventional capitalism, all within the United States, spread broadly across the nation. See Table 12.1 for a summary of information regarding how these ESOs identified their organization, when they began operations, their primary affiliations, and geographical locations.

DISCUSSION

Defining Differences Between ESOs for Conscious Capitalism and ESOs for Conventional Capitalism

Labelling
Our results confirm the literature (Lewis et al., 2011), in that ESOs tend to use various defining terms interchangeably. Most of the ESOs for conventional capitalism identified by a single label, two as "accelerator" and five as "incubator". In contrast, only three ESOs for conscious capitalism identified as an "accelerator", two as "co-working spaces", and the rest as some combination of incubator, accelerator, and/or co-working space. However, two ESOs for conscious capitalism and one for conventional capitalism didn't use any of these terms, although they are enterprise support organizations. They used terms such as, "thought leadership and research hub", "local economy leadership network", and "education programs for entrepreneurs".

ESOs' connection with the not-for profit sector
A higher percentage of these ESOs for conscious capitalism characterized themselves as being most closely associated with a non-profit organization than the ESOs for conventional capitalism: six versus two. Only one ESO for conscious capitalism characterizes as a stand-alone organization versus three ESOs for conventional capitalism. While all of the ESOs for conventional capitalism used the terms incubator or accelerator except for one, none of them use the term co-working space, in contrast with ESOs for conscious capitalism, five of which used the term.

Table 12.1   Summary of ESO participants

	Conscious Capitalism ESOs	Conventional Capitalism ESOs
Identity		
Accelerator	3	2
Incubator	0	5
Co-working Space	2	0
Incubator/Accelerator	2	1
Incubator/Accelerator/Co-working space	2	0
Incubator/Co-working Space	1	0
Other terms	2	1
Start Year		
Pre-2000	1	4
Earliest	1997	1985
Most recent	2014	2013
Between 2008–2013	8	5
Affiliation		
University	4	4
Non-profit	6	2
Stand-alone	1	3
Hybrid (University/Non-profit/ Standalone)	0	1
Not stated	1	0
Location		
Arizona	0	1
California	1	0
Colorado	0	1
Florida	1	3
Georgia	0	1
Louisiana	1	0
Maine	1	0
Michigan	0	1
New Hampshire	2	1
New Jersey	1	0
New York	0	1
Oregon	1	0
Pennsylvania	1	0
Rhode Island	1	0
Washington	2	0

ESOs for conscious capitalism have a clear triple bottom line approach

This study's results show that ESOs for conscious capitalism pay great attention to environmental health and social equity. In contrast, all ESOs for conventional capitalism except for two mentioned these concerns, instead envisioning sustainable enterprise from a financial or longevity perspective.

In regard to use of terms, our findings align with Lewis, Harper-Anderson and Molnar (2011): as a group, the organizations we interviewed and surveyed use the terms incubator and accelerator somewhat interchangeably or loosely, or they offer hybrid services or use multiple labels. For example, some ESOs self-identifying as accelerators offer programmes for very early-stage start-ups versus an existing enterprise that is scaling up. Some ESOs self-identifying as accelerators work with the entrepreneurs individually versus as a cohort, or act primarily as co-working spaces with business services and classes, but more limited mentoring and access to investment capital opportunities.

More than one self-identified co-working space ESO offered workshops, mentoring, and assistance with finding funding. Overall, however, and particularly for conventional capitalism ESOs, accelerators offer services aligned with Levinsohn's (2015, pp. 35–36) findings: a selective selection process, some seed funding, a short intensive period of mentoring and networking, and presentation to funders. The terms "impact enterprise" and "conscious capitalism" (Mackey & Sisodia, 2014) and "shared value" (Porter & Kramer, 2011) came out of our interviews, although some of these are also evident in enterprise literature.

Sustainable enterprise

Our results showed that the word "sustainable", as part of the term "sustainable enterprise" is used loosely, leading to confusion. Table 12.2 offers the different interpretations in the answers to the question, "How do you define being a sustainable enterprise?". For ESOs for conventional capitalism, *sustainable enterprise* is primarily about the financial longevity of the company and does not relate to the concept of sustainable development (World Commission on Environment and Development, 1987) or the triple bottom line (Elkington, 1997).

In contrast, six of the 12 ESOs for conscious capitalism cited the triple bottom line and/or people/planet/profit as integrated into the business model as the definition for sustainable enterprise. More interestingly, however, five of these ESOs avoided making this particular distinction, even though they appeared to understand the terms as we conceptualized them for the purpose of the study. The reasons for this were because these ESOs did not want to limit the potential businesses they supported

Table 12.2   *Definitions of sustainable enterprise offered by directors at Conscious Capitalism ESOs compared to definitions offered by directors at Conventional Capitalism ESOs*

"How do you define sustainable Enterprise?"	
Conscious ESOs	Conventional ESOs
"Ideally the businesses created are all socially, environmentally and economically integrated through a holistic approach." ConcESO1	"I'm not sure." ConvESO1
"Strives to integrate the economic, people, and ecological factors into [. . .] strategic decisions and operating decisions." ConcESO2	"Companies that are profitable, that want to stay here in our area and grow and create jobs." ConvESO2
"We don't really use that term, but [. . .] where ownership is broadly distributed and where product or service has integrated benefit for society and where profits are used for the wellbeing of most." ConcESO3	"Can grow and eventually run a profit where the cash flow feeds the growth of the business as opposed to ongoing investment." ConvESO3
"Social ventures, both for profit and non-profit; you need to approach it from both sides." ConcESO4	"A long-term viable market and organization that continues on into the future." ConvESO4
"Sustainable business practices with respect to environment, [. . .] how they treat their employees, [. . .] corporate social responsibility." ConcESO5	"Partnerships with various other organizations to support the community and state to build sustainable businesses. "ConvESO5
"I try not to define sustainable enterprise [. . .] I also try not to define impact. But [. . .] 2 billion people have moved up to not being poor and hungry through for profit enterprise and so we need to do the same for the rest of the world." ConcESO6	"Structurally stable financial and business model." ConvESO6
"Thinking about people, planet, as well as profit so with a triple bottom line principle." ConcESO7	"Program revenues cover 70% or more of expenses." ConvESO8
"People planet profit [. . .] balance among those three things [. . .] actually maximize profits because of it." ConcESO9	"Strives to reduce energy consumption, waste generation, consume resources at a rate compatible with renewal or generation." ConvESO9
"Technologies that have the potential for a positive impact along at least two of the TBL areas." ConcESO11	
"Having the ability to change and seek new opportunities." ConcESO12	

by effectively pre-screening applicants. Rather, most of the ESOs for conscious capitalism preferred to work with the entrepreneurs they served, to help integrate these concerns into their business models if they were not already taken in account. Additionally, the pace with which terms are evolving in the enterprise and ESOs' space was a consideration; ESOs wanted to avoid creating confusion or using an outdated term. Our findings illustrate how terms can be controversial and nuanced, even among ESOs for conscious capitalism.

ESO success metrics
Both ESOs for conscious and for conventional capitalism emphasized the ongoing success and longevity of the enterprises they supported, the ability to attract deal flow, job creation through the supported enterprises, and their own profitability as key metrics of their organization's success. ESOs for conscious capitalism, however, emphasized additional social and environmental impacts of their supported enterprises, "We utilize several criteria such as financial success, relevance, ability to build community, efficient and effective, responsible with resources, positive workplace culture". In Table 12.3, research participants speak to enterprise success metrics.

When asked about familiarity with the triple bottom line concept, all ESOs for conscious capitalism responded affirmatively. Of ESOs for conventional capitalism, however, four were not familiar with the concept, and the rest were familiar but said their organizations were not working with the model but instead focused on financial sustainability; one said,

> *I could mark that, yes, we fit that, we have activities that fit that model, but I think most of those things where they are trying to fit the environmental piece and they're meeting economic as well as real social need (social in terms of creating sustainable jobs) the environmental piece is usually marketing [nonsense].* (ConvESO3)

Enterprise success metrics
Of the ESOs for conscious capitalism, seven of the ESOs self-evaluated the success of the enterprises they supported. Many of these ESO supported enterprises had already self-reported their success and impact. In terms of the ESOs' knowledge about enterprise success or impact, three did not have a process for evaluating the success or impact of the enterprises they supported, and three mentioned that each enterprise had differing success and impact metrics, based on the industry and business model of the individual enterprise.

Overall, however, a number of these ESOs for conscious capitalism used the word "impact" in answering how they evaluate the success of

Table 12.3   Comparison of ESO success metrics

"As an organization, how do you measure your success?"	
Conscious	Conventional
"The number of students we work with, variety of disciplines represented and level of engagement with the community mentors and the ability to attract resources and capital." ConcESO1	"Outcomes of the enterprises" ConvESO1
"How many corporations support us through membership? [. . .] How much evidence is there of impact on their practices of understanding?" ConcESO2	"The number one parameter is job creation. The second benchmark is how many companies [. . .] are in business five years later and have sustained their job and job growth." ConvESO2
"Connecting leadership, spreading solutions, attracting investment for healthy local economies." ConcESO3	"Return on investment, invested funds." ConvESO3
"The metrics are tied to Global Impact Investing Rating System (GIIRS) [. . .] throughout the program and after." ConcESO4	"How many hi-tech companies have we started? How many jobs have been created [. . .] what is the wealth creation? Start seven companies a year [. . .] to create 63 jobs." ConvESO4
"How many of our [enterprises] are still running [. . .] companies must keep profit." ConcESO6	"The number of businesses we launch; the number of business that leave because of growth; our own ability to be self-sustaining." ConvESO5
"The success of our members [. . .] whether or not we as a business, are profitable [. . .] reputation and continued growth and an increasingly saturated market." ConcESO7	"Performance metrics (jobs, investment, sales) and customer satisfaction measures." ConvESO6
"Our ventures' growth, job creation [. . .] different community impacts." ConcESO8	"Number of student businesses started, student businesses still in business after five years, number of businesses served, number of employees gained vs started, new business starts, sponsor dollars." ConvESO7
"How many start-ups [. . .] how many clients we assist every year [. . .] how many businesses actually are acting more [socially or environmentally] sustainably." ConcESO9	

Table 12.3   (continued)

"As an organization, how do you measure your success?"	
Conscious	Conventional
"Jobs created, revenue earned, and follow-on funding awarded to the companies we've served. We are in the midst of developing environmental and social impact metrics as well." ConcESO11 "Financial success, relevance, ability to build community, efficient and effective, responsible with resources, positive workplace culture." ConcESO12	

their enterprises, as compared with the ESOs for conventional capitalism. For example, one sends out a survey asking their enterprises about their impact, another stated, "impact metrics are self-reported." Some are quite thorough in their tracking; one such organization reported that "we do modular and metrics and we work one on one with the ventures and try to get them to adopt a pretty sophisticated and robust metrics dashboard" as well as revenue growth. Sustainability reporting and the growth of impact were mentioned by one ESO for conscious capitalism. One reported that they "conduct surveys on connections they have made, collaborations through the centre or other members (strategic partnerships, finding employees, funding, value received through events)."

In comparison, ESOs for conventional capitalism collected information on the enterprises they supported. They focused mostly on enterprise revenue growth and funding with outside investment and grants, although three of these ESOs incorporated jobs or employment in their evaluations. Somewhat surprisingly, only one mentioned return on investment as a part of their assessment metrics.

CONCLUSION

As we had identified a gap in literature with very little theoretical and empirical research dedicated to defining ESOs for conscious capitalism, our research sought to understand what ESOs for conscious capitalism are, how they are defined and also how they potentially differ from ESOs for conventional capitalism. We distinguished between these two types of organizations by conducting a comparative survey to compare how they identify themselves, their offerings, and their understanding of the notion of sustainable enterprise/social entrepreneurship. In comparing incubators, accelerators and other types of enterprise support organizations, we found that the gap is not so pronounced in terms of services provided to start-up enterprises or techniques utilized between those supporting enterprises for conscious capitalism as opposed to more conventional ones. The core goal of all start-up ESOs is financial viability of the enterprise, but the conscious capitalism ESOs helped focus their enterprises in terms of the social and environmental impact, as well as the economic, by providing a context that draws attention to the triple bottom line.

The pronounced differences between the ESO groups occurred in how they articulated purposes and degree of stakeholder inclusion and values. Other distinguishing differences were the level of emphasis placed on the triple bottom line, certain success criteria and the time length ESOs supported their clients. Our analysis highlights key similarities between ESOs for conscious capitalism and those for conventional capitalism which included a success measure of financial soundness, ROI, funding options, number of jobs created, mentoring programmes, and shared work space available to start-ups or existing enterprises.

Use of terminology within ESO types shared commonality up to a point. For example: the word sustainable had different interpretations between ESOs for conscious capitalism and for conventional capitalism, as well as within each category. This reflected a difference in the use of terminology or language describing activities within the ESOs. ESOs for conscious capitalism described sustainability on a spectrum from encompassing the triple bottom line to being a multidimensional construct involving all key stakeholders including society and the environment. This is aligned with our conceptualization of conscious capitalism with enterprises designed as a means to reduce poverty and/or environmental damages and create overall stakeholders' welfare (Freeman, 1984; Bansal, 2005; Austin et al., 2006; Waddock & Steckler, 2016). This may serve more of an indicator of an evolving "state of sustainability" within these ESOs.

Levinsohn (2015) eloquently discussed the economic "systems" of business as social processes, which dovetails with the purposes of conscious capitalism ESOs, while others define sustainability on their own terms; such was the case with the ESOs for conventional capitalism. These latter ESOs tended to define sustainability in financial terms to ensure the longevity of an enterprise.

In general, our findings are novel and render insights, but are not generalizable due to the relatively small number of interviews and online responses to our survey. This was a limitation of the research study. Through our work on this study, we have been introduced to several outlets and organizations for continuing our research. Being able to increase the response rate with a future online survey by working more closely with these organizations would address this limitation along with incentivizing participation. Also, extending our study on an international basis would increase the sample size and add a dimension not previously addressed.

Future research opportunities could lead us to examine the affect university ESOs have in developing social entrepreneurs, how ESOs for conscious capitalism have evolved over time, the success rate of enterprises in each type of ESO, or how the support of other entities influences the success of each type of ESO. Lastly, an intriguing finding which may be anecdotal yet warrants additional research has to do with why ESOs are at different stages of organizational sustainability as addressed in the Discussion section. This aspect intrigued us as researchers and could potentially give rise to developing a framework for use in analysing a range of business models from ESOs for conscious capitalism to conventional capitalism. As our world faces inevitable social and environmental challenges more entrepreneurs will be called upon to meet those challenges with innovation, an entrepreneurial spirit and sustainability mindset.

REFERENCES

Academy of Management (AOM). (2013) Professional Development Workshop: Accelerating Research on Accelerators. 2013 Annual Meeting Program. Academy of Management.
Austin, J., Stevenson, H., & Wei-Skillern, J. (2006). Social and commercial entrepreneurship: Same, different, or both? *Entrepreneurship Theory & Practice*, 30(1): 1–22.
Bansal, P. (2005). Evolving sustainability: A longitudinal study of corporate sustainable development. *Strategic Management Journal*, 26: 197–218.
Bidhan, L. Parmar, Freeman, R. Edward, Harrison, S. Jeffrey, Wicks, C. Andrew, Purnell, Lauren, & de Colle, Simone. (2010). Stakeholder theory: The state of the art. *Academy of Management Annals*, 4(1): 403–445.
Borella, P. (2012). Startup Sauna: Accelerating Startups from Northern Europe & Russia. Espoo: Aalto University Center for Entrepreneurship / TEKES.
Boyd, B., Henning, N., Reyna, E., Wang, D. E., & Welch, M. D. (2009). *Hybrid organizations: New business models for environmental leadership*. Sheffield, UK: Greenleaf.
Business Dictionnary, retrieved from http://www.businessdictionary.com/definition/business-incubator.html. Accessed on September 16, 2019.
Casasnovas, G., & Bruno, A. (2013). Scaling social ventures: An exploratory study of social incubators and accelerators, *The Journal of Management for Global Sustainability* 1(2): 173–197.
Cohen, S. (2013). What do accelerators do? Insights from incubators and angels. *Innovations* 8(3/4): 19–25.
Elkington, J. (1997). *Cannibals with forks: the triple bottom line of twenty first century business*. Mankato, MN; Capstone.

Freeman, R.E. (1984). *Strategic management: A stakeholder approach.* Boston: Pitman.

Friedman, M. (1962). *Capitalism and freedom.* Chicago: University of Chicago Press.

Grimaldi, R., & Grandi, A. (2005). Business incubators and new venture creation: An assessment of incubating models. *Technovation* 25(2): 111–121. doi: http://dx.doi.org/10.1016/S0166-4972(03)00076-2

Hamschmidt, J., & Pirson, M. (Eds.). (2011). *Case studies in social entrepreneurship and sustainability.* (Vol. 2). Sheffield: Greenleaf.

Kolk, A., & Pinkse, J. (2007). Towards strategic stakeholder management? Integrating perspectives on sustainability challenges such as corporate responses to climate change. *Corporate Governance: The International Journal of Effective Board Performance* 7: 370–378.

Lall, S., Bowles, L., Baird, R. (2013). Bridging the "pioneer gap": The role of accelerators in launching high-impact enterprises. *Innovations* 8(3–4): 105–137.

Levinsohn, D. (2015). *No entrepreneur is an island, an exploration of social entrepreneurial learning in accelerators.* Jönköping International Business School Dissertation Series No. 105.

Lewis, D., Harper-Anderson, E. Molnar, L. (2011). *Incubating Success. Incubation Best Practices That Lead to Succesful New Ventures.* Michigan: U.S. Department of Commerce Economic Development Administration / Institute for Research on Labor, Employment, and the Economy, University of Michigan.

Mackey, J., & Sisodia, R. (2014). *Conscious capitalism: Liberating the heroic spirit of business.* Boston, Mass: Harvard Business Review Press.

Miller, P. & Bound, K. (2011). The startup factories – The rise of accelerators programmes to support new technology ventures. NESTA Discussion paper: June 2011.

National Business Incubation Association (NBIA) (2009). *What is Business Incubation?* http://www.nbia.org/resource_library/what_is/index.php. Accessed June 9, 2009.

Phillips, R. (2003). *Stakeholder theory and organizational ethics.* San Francisco: Berrett-Koehler.

Porter, M.E., & Kramer, M.R. (2011). Creating shared value. *Harvard Business Review* 89(1/2): 62–77.

Sharma, S., & Henriques, I. (2005). Stakeholder influence on sustainability practices in the Canadian forest products industry. *Strategic Management Journal* 26: 159–180.

Shrivastava, P., Ivanaj, S., & Persson, S. (2013). Transdiciplinary study of sustainable enterprise. *Business Strategy and the Environment* (22): 230–244.

UN General Assembly. (2015). *Resolution adopted by the General Assembly on 25 September 2015,* Seventieth session, 21 October 2015.

Waddock, S., & Steckler, E. (2016). Visionaries and wayfinders: Deliberate and emergent pathways to vision in social entrepreneurship. *Journal of Business Ethics* (133): 719–734.

Weerawardena, J., & Mort, G. S. (2006). Investigating social entrepreneurship: A multidimensional model. *Journal of World Business* 41(1): 21–35. doi: http://dx.doi.org/10.1016/j.jwb.2005.09.001

Wiklund, J., Davidsson, P., Audretsch, D. B. & Karlsson, C. (2011), The future of entrepreneurship research. *Entrepreneurship Theory and Practice* 35: 1–9. doi:10.1111/j.1540-6520.2010.00420.x

World Commission on Environment and Development. (1987). *Our common future.* Oxford: Oxford University Press.

13. Incubation and founders' champion behaviour

Are Jensen, Nhien Nguyen, and Jens Ø. Hansen

INTRODUCTION

We view incubators through the theoretical lens of entrepreneurial eco-systems. An entrepreneurial ecosystem has been defined as "a set of interdependent actors and factors coordinated in such a way that they enable productive entrepreneurship within a particular territory" (Stam & Spigel, 2017, p. 1). More loosely, the concept is often used to refer to geographic regions with a high concentration of entrepreneurs which are also characterized by significant degrees of self-sustainability and self-regulation (Isenberg, 2016). A self-sustainable system is one in which entrepreneurs within the system rely predominantly on each other for critical resource inputs, whereas a self-regulating system is one that adapts and evolves without centralized control.

An incubator is a purpose-built economic environment designed to provide resident NTBFs with access to critical physical and intangible resources by connecting them to relevant service providers and other entrepreneurs within the environment (Hackett & Dilts, 2004; Mian, Lamine, & Fayolle, 2016). Since an incubator connects economic actors for the purpose of exchanging resources for mutual benefit, and since the ultimate goal of an incubator is to facilitate entrepreneurship, one could argue that an incubator – at least a *successful* one – must possess the interdependency and entrepreneurship-enabling characteristics of an entrepreneurial ecosystem as described above. Some scholars view NTBFs as nested within larger ecosystems rather than being ecosystems in their own right (Mian et al., 2016).

To succeed in commercializing new technologies, the founders of NTBFs may have to confront established industry practices and shape an entirely new market while convincing the surroundings of the merit of their ideas – an undertaking that requires considerable persistence and enthusiasm (Cardon & Kirk, 2015; Gompers, Kovner, Lerner, & Scharfstein, 2010; Schumpeter, 1934; Walter, Parboteeah, Riesenhuber, & Hoegl, 2011). To succeed, NTBFs typically depend critically on the personal efforts and resourcefulness of their founders (Mian et al., 2016).

Arguably the founder's behaviour is one of an NTBF's most important properties (McKenzie, Ugbah, & Smothers, 2007), if not *the* most important property (Gartner, 1988). Therefore, to the extent that incubation can influence founders' behaviours, this is potentially an important way for incubators to create value. A recent line of research has started to examine value-creating processes in the interplay among founder-managers of incubated firms (Ahmad & Ingle, 2011; Branstad, Saetre, & Matlay, 2016; Rice, 2002), but few studies focus on the effects of incubation on individuals and how the incubation process contributes to outcomes at the founder-manager level.

The particular behaviour we examine is *champion behaviour*. Classical entrepreneurship research shows that successful entrepreneurs "get things done" (Schumpeter, 1934), and more recent theorizing shows that they have "entrepreneurial drive" (Chandler & Jansen, 1992), including willpower and courage to tackle challenges and obstacles head on (Schumpeter, 1934). Champion behaviour recently emerged as a theoretical meta concept (Howell, Shea, & Higgins, 2005; Walter et al., 2011) that encompasses many of these behaviours. In the NTBF setting, we know that champion behaviour is beneficial for both the evolution of innovations (Howell et al., 2005; Taylor, Cocklin, Brown, & Wilson-Evered, 2011) and the success of NTBFs (Walter et al., 2011). For example, the "getting the right people involved" dimension of champion behaviour invigorates innovation activities in university-based spin-offs – a type of NTBF (Walter et al., 2011). Walter et al. (2011) found that the "persistence" and "enthusiasm" dimensions also invigorate innovation activities, albeit only to a certain extent. Still, they deemed champion behaviour to be closely tied to successful innovation activities. The dimensions mentioned above are abstract, so a concrete example from Reid, Keogh, Mitchell, and McAdam (2007) is helpful: In their case study, the champion invigorates innovation activities as she sets goals and encourages those around her to persistently and enthusiastically strive towards those goals regardless of the cost. Through such encouragement, she overcomes hindrances that would force the non-champion into capitulation. Such behaviours are the essence of champions and is what makes them useful for NTBF founders. How this behaviour is created within founders remains unknown. Reflecting this lack of knowledge, we address the following research question:

How can incubators promote champion behaviour in incubated founders?

Our research question is developed into a set of hypotheses which are tested against empirical survey data collected among 210 firms in Norwegian R&D incubators. Through our examination we find that champion behaviour is affected by the incubation process, in several interacting ways.

CHAMPIONS AND THEIR BEHAVIOUR

As demonstrated in the introduction, NTBFs must overcome barriers and challenges impeding the development and commercialization of their innovation. NTBFs are typically resource-constrained, so their founder-managers' behaviour becomes crucially important (Gartner, 1988; McKenzie et al., 2007). Founder-managers unwilling or unable to "do what it takes" in order to overcome barriers and obstacles have slim prospects of success.

Acting as charismatic leaders, founder-managers project enthusiasm (Shamir, House, & Arthur, 1993), motivate and involve the right people, and thus build a power base through which they grow their firms (Chandler & Jansen, 1992; Pavett & Lau, 1983). In short, NTBFs' founder-managers benefit from a type of behaviour scholars refer to as "champion behaviour". Such behaviour allows founders to compensate for lacking resources by increasing their resilience to setbacks and hardship. When Howell, Shea, and Higgins (2005) reviewed the literature on champions while creating and validating a measure of their behaviour, they found champion behaviour to be characterized by three features: *enthusiasm, persistence,* and *getting the right people involved.* These behaviours coincide with the entrepreneur and manager role of Chandler and Jansen (1992), providing a means to study founder behaviours associated with new venture success. Following Howell, Shea, and Higgins' (2005) study, further theorizing on (Pinto & Patanakul, 2015), and evidence of (Pinto & Patanakul, 2015; Liozu, Hinterhuber, & Somers, 2014; Walter et al., 2011), the importance of champion behaviour have emerged. Yet, our understanding of how champion behaviour develops remains sketchy – particularly in new firms.

Since NTBFs are an important source of innovation, policymakers have created incubators whose purpose is to help the development of NTBFs, hopefully imprinting both the firms and their founders with beneficial patterns of behaviour. The reason as to why incubators ought to imprint founders relates to incubators' role as a resource munificent learning environment. Additionally, incubators can be conceptualized as a sheltered environment (Amezcua, Grimes, Bradley, & Wiklund, 2013) where the mechanisms involved in nurturing champion behaviour are particularly visible. For example, as further discussed below, business incubator managers (henceforth IMs) typically aim to develop founders' managerial skills (Pena, 2004), help founders establish communication and interaction with others (such as other incubated founders, henceforth IFs) (McAdam & McAdam, 2008) or external stakeholders (Scillitoe & Chakrabarti, 2010; Soetanto & Jack, 2013), and offer rich personal interaction through business monitoring and assistance (Hackett & Dilts, 2004). Below we discuss the incubation context and its relation to champion behaviour in more detail.

BUSINESS INCUBATION AND ITS VALUE-ADDING MECHANISMS

A business incubator (henceforth BI) can be defined as "a shared-office space facility that seeks to provide its [incubated founders] [. . .] with a strategic, value-adding intervention system [. . .] of monitoring and business assistance. This system controls and links resources with the objective of facilitating the successful new venture development of the [incubated firms]" (Hackett & Dilts, 2004, p. 57). The same authors also add that the totality of the BIs are important: inside the incubator ecosystem there are networks of incubated founders, incubator staff, cooperation partners, etc., who play complementary roles during the incubation process (Hackett & Dilts, 2004, 2008).

Scholars of co-production theory provide further insights into these ecosystems in their studies of how interactions between IMs and IFs create value. In co-production theory added value from incubation does not emerge spontaneously. Rather, value is created in relationships characterized by frequent interdependent actions (Ahmad & Ingle, 2011; Rice, 2002) in addition to resource exchange. As summarized by Rice (2002, p. 165): "co-production involves joint efforts between two parties, who jointly determine the output of their collaboration". Recent theorizing has extended these arguments, claiming that dyadic interactions among the incubatees themselves are another value-creating mechanism of the incubation process (Ahmad & Ingle, 2011). Under the assumption that co-production theorizing is valid, sharing of resources and knowledge within the incubator among incubated firms and their founder-managers is an important aspect of the way the incubation process generates value. Moreover, Hughes, Ireland, and Morgan (2007) argue that incubator managers may facilitate and improve the dyadic interaction between incubated firms and founders, acting as an intermediary agent between incubated firms, thus forming a triad. In such cases intervention by the incubator manager would affect the incubatee–incubatee dyad's value creation and reduce information asymmetries among incubatees (Ahmad & Ingle, 2011).

In terms of co-production theory, interactions within these dyads and triads are points of origin for learning. Incubators seek to help "weak-but-promising" young ventures, implying that their founders are also in a vulnerable position. According to imprinting theory, it is during such vulnerable moments that impressions are most likely to take hold and become entrenched (Marquis & Tilcsik, 2013; Simsek, Fox, & Heavey, 2015). Imprinting theory shows us that human learning interactions have a profound effect on individuals' behaviours. Within the incubator setting, the interactions within dyads and triads of incubator managers and incubated founders are likely a rich source of such behaviour-learning interactions. Therefore, interactions within the incubator will likely generate outcomes within founders, and particularly on their behaviours.

GENERATION OF CHAMPION BEHAVIOUR THROUGH THE INCUBATION PROCESS

Enthusiasm: As Howell, Shea, and Higgins (2005, p. 642) point out, enthusiasm in the champion literature relates to the "expression of enthusiasm and confidence about the success of the innovation". Hence, enthusiasm as a champion behaviour describes what others perceive the champion to be or do enthusiastically. This differs from enthusiasm as a mood or state of mind. In the champion behaviour literature the mood of enthusiasm is certainly part of the underlying behaviour pattern, but as a behaviour, enthusiasm can be instilled in other ways.

In our context the IM can encourage the IF to appear enthusiastic in the company of others regardless of the IF's mood, and thereby instill in them a behaviour pattern of appearing enthusiastic. Similarly, IFs might observe other IFs' champion enthusiasm, conclude that it is beneficial, and subsequently adopt the behaviour and thereby be imprinted by vicarious learning from other incubated founders. Enthusiasm is strengthened upon recurring task success, as one acquires mastery over them (Lazarus & Folkman, 1984; Tuckey, Searle, Boyd, Winefield, & Winefield, 2015). It follows that increased likelihood of task success increases enthusiasm, and *vice versa*, further strengthening founders' behaviours of enthusiasm.

Failure reduces enthusiasm (Lazarus & Folkman, 1984; Tuckey et al., 2015). Thus, incubators' reduction of task failure severity through resource provision and linking keeps the newly created enthusiasm behaviours intact. Resource munificence also lets IFs focus on their areas of expertise, allowing them to stick to topics they are familiar with, further reducing task failures. The combination of letting the IF focus on their existing talents, while giving them resources and an environment to learn new ones at low costs, should generate and maintain enthusiasm.

Personal interactions between the IM and IF serve other purposes in addition to the ones mentioned above. For example, *a*) IMs' experience-whetted advice provides IFs with clarity and direction during difficulties (Patton, Warren, & Bream, 2009); *b*) IF firms suffer growth pains – mediation and adaptation by the IM ease this process (McAdam & Marlow, 2007); and, *c*) knowing the IF's ambitions, the IM can ease IFs' exit from the incubator. This should further the imprinting process by generating enthusiasm behaviours while reducing the likelihood of failure, an antithetical factor to enthusiasm. In sum, facilitation of task success, buffering from task failure, clarity-giving advice, easing of growth pains, and easing exits from the incubator should help build and maintain enthusiasm. These observations lead to our first hypothesis:

Hypothesis 1a: The incubator manager's support is positively related to the incubated founders' enthusiasm.

Communication within the BI also provides a place for IFs to learn from the success and failures of their peers, generating further enthusiasm. Access to communities of similar others allows IFs to receive support, resources and advice, and possibly partake in collaborations. Such communication and information-sharing should have the same enthusiasm-generating effect as support from incubator managers, as described above.

IFs are, however, often wary of sharing ideas and information among each other (McAdam & Marlow, 2007). In such cases IMs may act as mediators of communication among IFs. Being part of a larger group of similar others may also give IFs a sense of community and belonging (Cooper, Hamel, & Connaughton, 2012), possibly leading to changes in behaviour. There is evidence to suggest that entrepreneurs prefer face-to-face interaction as opposed to formal communication (Cooper et al., 2012; McAdam & McAdam, 2006). Incubator managers are in an ideal situation to facilitate such communication, maintaining the enthusiasm-building quality of interactions between IFs. These arguments in concert lead to the following hypothesis:

Hypothesis 1b: Incubatee–incubatee interaction is positively related to the incubated founders' enthusiasm.

Persistence: In the champion literature, persistence is usually related to the task of making sure a technology is brought to the market (see Howell et al., 2005; Markham & Griffin, 1998; Schon, 1963; Walter et al., 2011, for example). More specifically, and in line with champion literature, we will use the term "task persistence" to denote the extent of time an individual devotes towards achieving a goal (Sandelands, Brockner, & Glynn, 1988). An individual of high task persistence will, relative to others, spend more time on solving a problem before they give up. As with enthusiasm, being successful at tasks leads to task persistence (Aspinwall & Richter, 1999; Gompers et al., 2010). We have already discussed how the incubation process increases the chance of task success both in the short and long term. Below we focus on the particularities of task persistence and its relation to the incubation process.

Repeated task failure leads to "learned helplessness" – a situation where individuals consider their actions unrelated to task success or failure. Once learned helplessness is instilled in individuals, they begin to consider their behaviours to be unrelated to task outcomes (Eisenberger, 1992). In turn this decreases task persistence (*ibid.*). Through counseling the IM can brief the IF about likely difficulties when undertaking unfamiliar actions (Scillitoe & Chakrabarti, 2010; Starnes & Zinser, 1983). The IM can also give feedback after such actions have taken place (debriefing) (Medway & Venino, 1982; Scillitoe & Chakrabarti, 2010; Starnes & Zinser, 1983). As a consequence, the IFs' belief that their actions matter is strengthened, leading to increased task persistence. In other words, persistence is the opposite of the learned helplessness described above.

IFs' needs are idiosyncratic (Ahmad & Ingle, 2011) and these idiosyncrasies in turn decide the most effective use of the BI's offerings (Ahmad & Ingle, 2011; Amezcua et al., 2013; Hughes et al., 2007; Patton et al., 2009; Schwartz & Hornych, 2008). The idiosyncrasies of IFs and their needs are communicated through personal interaction between the IM and IF (Ahmad & Ingle, 2011; Amezcua et al., 2013). As a consequence, personal interactions characterize many parts of the incubation process. It follows that IMs which have frequent interactions with IFs are more in-tune with the needs, demands, and abilities of IFs. Thus, they are better able to buffer IFs from situations where IFs would learn to be helpless. This should further build IFs' persistence. In sum, through frequent interactions, incubator managers help prevent founders from spiralling into states of learned helplessness, help them manage their expectations regarding task success and outcomes, and strengthen their understanding of how their task persistence relates to successful outcomes. This leads us to our third hypothesis:

Hypothesis 2a: The incubator manager's support is positively related to the incubated founders' persistence.

As with enthusiasm, persistence can be built through belonging to a community of similar individuals. Within these communities individuals can overcome their feelings of helplessness, thus strengthening their persistence. For the sake of brevity, we refer to our arguments related to hypothesis 1b above. Additionally, psychology scholars have produced evidence that individuals, especially when in unfamiliar and unwelcoming environments, persist for longer periods of time when they have received social support by those around them both in the present and in the past (see Cross & Vick, 2001 for an applied example). This serves as an example of persistence generated through group interactions. This leads us to the following hypothesis:

Hypothesis 2b: Incubatee–incubatee interaction is positively related to the incubated founders' persistence.

Getting the right people involved: Incubator managers ought to be able to imprint on founders the behaviours of getting the right people involved. In the champion literature getting the right people involved relates to the ability to involve – and manage the relationships with – important stakeholders that have a say in the survival of the innovation (Burgelman, 1983; Howell et al., 2005; Markham & Griffin, 1998; Shane, 1994). A prerequisite of getting the right people involved is access to networks of the right people. The IM is likely to have larger networks than the IF, and they are likely more suited for developing new ventures (Hackett & Dilts, 2004; Hughes et al., 2007; Soetanto & Jack, 2013). Also, the IM has a relationship with both IFs and network members (Scillitoe & Chakrabarti, 2010; Soetanto & Jack, 2013). This leads to information asymmetry and puts IMs in a role as a bridge between IFs and the IM's network members (Scillitoe & Chakrabarti, 2010). Also, in many European countries, including the one where this study takes place, IMs are part of a greater public innovation system (Aerts, Matthyssens, & Vandenbempt, 2007). As an insider, the IM is likely to have considerable experience in how to approach other public institutions on behalf of its IFs. In our context that would include TTOs, tax deduction programmes for R&D projects, and similar. IFs may also benefit from interacting with institutions or individuals outside the BI. In such cases IMs may act as mediators between scientists, practitioners, and IFs (Schwartz & Hornych, 2010; von Zedtwitz, 2005).

As illustrated above, IMs can act as powerful bridges for IFs. There is evidence to suggest that IFs by themselves are unable to reliably communicate their intentions and ideas to potential stakeholders, and vice versa (Scillitoe & Chakrabarti, 2010), despite the importance of engaging with them. By actively promoting the importance of IFs' interactions with other actors, and through encouraging them to make use of them as network bridges, IMs should imprint on IFs' behaviours of getting the right people involved. This leads to our fifth hypothesis:

Hypothesis 3a: The incubator manager's support is positively related to the incubated founders' behaviours characterized by getting the right people involved.

In our literature review, we found no evidence of IF–IF interactions replacing the functions of the IM in the type of incubator we are concerned with in this study. We did, however, find literature supporting this replacement within "bottom-up" incubators (see the work of Bøllingtoft and colleagues, e.g., Bøllingtoft, 2012; Bøllingtoft & Ulhøi, 2005) – incubators where founders build their own incubator environment. Other scholars have also pointed out the valuable, but difficult, nature of IF–IF interactions when developing business ideas and strategies, and as an arena for discussing IFs' technologies (see e.g., McAdam & Marlow, 2007). Therefore, interactions between IFs ought to instill in them that getting the right people involved is an important endeavour.

IFs' networks may be useful to other founders besides themselves. By acting as bridges between other IFs and their own networks, IFs can act as bridges much in the same way as IMs. For example, IFs originating from a university environment may become an important network bridge for IFs who are dependent on knowledge only available at the university. By becoming such a bridge, IFs can replace or complement some "getting the right people involved" behaviours generated through interactions with the IM. In sum, interactions between IFs ought to instill behaviours in IFs of getting the right people involved. So should access to other IFs' networks. These observations lead to our sixth hypothesis:

Hypothesis 3b: Incubatee–incubatee interaction is positively related to IFs' behaviours characterized by getting the right people involved.

METHOD

Sample and data collection: A public agency overseeing all Norwegian R&D incubators provided us with names and e-mail addresses of the founder-managers of all the incubators' tenant firms. We distributed an email survey to the entire population during December 2008. The programme consisted of 22 R&D incubators, all Norwegian R&D incubators at the time. The incubator managers helped motivate incubated founders to respond. After two reminders, we had 207 responses out of a population of 390 incubated firms – a response rate of 53 per cent. Excluding cases with missing values left us with 210 cases. Descriptive statistics of the variables below can be found in the appendix (Table 13.1) together with a correlation table of the variables used in the regressions (Table 13.2).

Dependent variables: champion behaviour: We split the dependent variable, champion behaviour, into three dimensions (Howell et al., 2005). For the sake of brevity, we refer to these dimensions as "enthusiasm", "persistence", and "getting the right people involved". The constructs' items were translated into Norwegian but are otherwise identical to the original items. The items used were of 7-point Likert-type scales, as per the original paper (Howell et al., 2005). Items can be found in the appendix (Table 13.3).

Independent variables: the incubation process: The development of Hackett and Dilts' measures of the incubation process is based on their previous work, especially their literature review (Hackett & Dilts, 2004, 2008). As a result, the items we use from their measure can be classified within the "resource provision and linking" and "business monitoring and assistance" dimensions of the incubation process. It was necessary to adapt the measures as we study the incubation process from the view of incubated founders. For our measure representing the support given by the IM to the IF, we were left with six items. As for our measure of IF–IF interaction, we were left with three items. Items can be found in the appendix (Table 13.3).

Control variables: We use several control variables: the size of the founding team, the age, years of work experience, and education level of the primary founder. We also control for whether the primary founder has taken formal entrepreneurship classes, has founded but had to close a business in the past (sale of firm is not included here) and how many firms the founder currently manages and owns besides the incubated firm, if any. Finally, we employ a set of binary variables to control for the effect of which incubator the IFs are located in. These are not visible in the regression table (Table 13.4), due to space limitations.

Techniques: We use Principal Component Analysis (PCA) in order to establish the three dimensions of champion behaviour (Cronbach alphas: enthusiasm 0.95, persistence 0.94, getting the right people involved 0.83) and the two dimensions of the incubation process (Cronbach alphas: IM support 0.88, Incubatee–incubatee interaction 0.87). We employed an oblique rotation (oblimin) while predicting these five variables for the regression analysis. OLS regression was chosen as the regression technique.

ANALYSES AND RESULTS

The incubation process' latent constructs are regressed on the measures of champion behaviour using OLS regression with the R statistical software. As we can see from Table 13.4, we find that there is a significant effect from IM support on all three dimensions of champion behaviour. As for incubatee–incubatee interaction however, we note that it only has a significant, positive, relationship with the dimension of getting the right people involved. Hypotheses *1a, 2a, 3a,* and *3b* remain fully supported while hypotheses *1b* and *2b* are rejected. No Variance Inflation Factors were greater than 2 and residuals were approximately normal.

DISCUSSION AND IMPLICATIONS

According to Hackett and Dilts (2004) and more recently Mian, Lamine, and Fayolle (2016), most incubation studies focus on firm-related mechanisms and outcomes, for example, resource provision, growth, and survival. Conversely, few studies have focused on how such ecosystems affect individual-level outcomes.

Empirical testing of our model highlighted the role of the incubation process in affecting champion behaviour development. More specifically, the model shows that *a*) there is a direct effect on founders' champion behaviour from the support received from the incubator and its management, and that *b*) there is a direct effect from interactions with other incubated founders on behaviours characterized by getting the right people involved. In summary, the model provides evidence that the incubation process has individual-level outcomes. For this particular study the outcome is a behaviour pattern related to success in innovation efforts, namely champion behaviour. This serves as an example of how individual-level outcomes can be instilled in entrepreneurs through the incubation process.

The model analysed in this chapter relies on co-production theory to understand how individual-level behavioural outcomes are generated through the incubation process. The model serves as a test of the generalizability of the theory in the context of R&D incubators. In short, we find support for the model, while illustrating the importance of IMs' role in the process. Similar to Ahmad and Ingle (2011) we extend Rice's (2002) model through our inclusion of incubatee–incubatee interactions. While co-production theory is mainly concerned with the production process on the firm level, scholars working with co-production theory should be aware that their research can have even greater implications since the co-production process also has effects on individual-level outcomes.

Further, Rice's and Ahmad and Ingle's studies have provided us with great insight into the complexities of the incubation process; since they are case studies, however, no generalizations can be made based on their findings. Our study provides evidence of the generalizability of their study while also extending the boundaries of the model's outcomes.

Other case studies besides Rice (2002) and Ahmad and Ingle (2011) have attempted to unpack the relative importance of the co-production actors. Bøllingtoft and Ulhøi (2005) and Bøllingtoft (2012), for example, argue that incubators' management may play a secondary role and can in some cases be replaced by "bottom-up" efforts by founder-communities. Our study illustrates that such interactions are inadequate for generating the whole spectrum of champion behaviours. At face value, only considering incubatee–incubatee interactions, one could be led to believe that champion behaviour development is unrelated to the IM. Our analysis, however, revealed that the IM plays a focal role in this relationship. Thus, one should be careful not to ignore the importance of the incubator's management – they seem to be acting as an important part of the co-production triad (Ahmad & Ingle, 2011) and without them fruitful incubatee–incubatee interactions may fall apart.

Since the positive impact of champion behaviour on innovation and entrepreneurship is well established in the literature, discovering ways to promote champion behaviour has valuable practical implications. We have found evidence that business incubator environments provide fertile ground for the cultivation of champion behavior. Exploring whether the findings can be extended to other types of entrepreneurial ecosystems is an interesting opportunity for further research.

REFERENCES

Aerts, K., Matthyssens, P., & Vandenbempt, K. (2007). Critical role and screening practices of European business incubators. *Technovation, 27*(5), 254–267. https://doi.org/10.1016/j.technovation.2006.12.002

Ahmad, A. J., & Ingle, S. (2011). Relationships matter: Case study of a university campus incubator. *International Journal of Entrepreneurial Behavior & Research, 17*(6), 626–644. https://doi.org/10.1108/13552551111174701

Amezcua, A. S., Grimes, M. G., Bradley, S. W., & Wiklund, J. (2013). Organizational sponsorship and founding environments: A contingency view on the survival of business-incubated firms, 1994–2007. *Academy of Management Journal, 56*(6), 1628–1654. https://doi.org/10.5465/amj.2011.0652

Aspinwall, L. G., & Richter, L. (1999). Optimism and self-mastery predict more rapid disengagement from unsolvable tasks in the presence of alternatives. *Motivation and Emotion, 23*(3), 221–245. https://doi.org/10.1023/A:1021367331817

Bøllingtoft, A. (2012). The bottom-up business incubator: Leverage to networking and coop-eration practices in a self-generated, entrepreneurial-enabled environment. *Technovation, 32*(5), 304–315. https://doi.org/10.1016/j.technovation.2011.11.005

Bøllingtoft, A., & Ulhøi, J. P. (2005). The networked business incubator – Leveraging entrepreneurial agency? *Journal of Business Venturing, 20*(2), 265–290.

Branstad, A., Saetre, A. S., & Matlay, H. (2016). Venture creation and award-winning technology through co-produced incubation. *Journal of Small Business and Enterprise Development, 23*(1). Retrieved from http://www.emeraldinsight.com/doi/abs/10.1108/JSBED -09-2014-0156, 23 January 2019.

Burgelman, R. A. (1983). A process model of internal corporate venturing in the diversified major firm. *Administrative Science Quarterly, 28*(2), 223–244.

Cardon, M. S., & Kirk, C. P. (2015). Entrepreneurial passion as mediator of the self-efficacy to persistence relationship. *Entrepreneurship Theory and Practice, 39*(5), 1027–1050. https://doi.org/10.1111/etap.12089

Chandler, G. N., & Jansen, E. (1992). The founder's self-assessed competence and venture performance. *Journal of Business Venturing, 7*(3), 223–236. https://doi.org/10.1016/0883-9 026(92)90028-P

Cooper, C. E., Hamel, S. A., & Connaughton, S. L. (2012). Motivations and obstacles to networking in a university business incubator. *Journal of Technology Transfer, 37*(4), 433–453. https://doi.org/10.1007/s10961-010-9189-0

Cross, S. E., & Vick, N. V. (2001). The interdependent self-construal and social support: The case of persistence in engineering. *Personality and Social Psychology Bulletin, 27*(7), 820–832. https://doi.org/10.1177/0146167201277005

Eisenberger, R. (1992). Learned industriousness. *Psychological Review, 99*(2), 248–267. https://doi.org/10.1037/0033-295X.99.2.248

Gartner, W. B. (1988). Who is an entrepreneur? Is the wrong question. *American Journal of Small Business, 12*(4), 11–32.

Gompers, P., Kovner, A., Lerner, J., & Scharfstein, D. (2010). Performance persistence in entrepreneurship. *Journal of Financial Economics, 96*(1), 18–32. https://doi.org/10.1016/j. jfineco.2009.11.001

Hackett, S. M., & Dilts, D. M. (2004). A systematic review of business incubation research. *Journal of Technology Transfer, 29*, 55–82. https://doi.org/10.1023/B:JOTT.0000011181.11 952.0f

Hackett, S. M., & Dilts, D. M. (2008). Inside the black box of business incubation: Study B-scale assessment, model refinement, and incubation outcomes. *Journal of Technology Transfer, 33*(5), 439–471. https://doi.org/10.1007/s10961-007-9056-9

Howell, J. M., Shea, C. M., & Higgins, C. A. (2005). Champions of product innovations: Defining, developing, and validating a measure of champion behavior. *Journal of Business Venturing, 20*(5), 641–661. https://doi.org/10.1016/j.jbusvent.2004.06.001

Hughes, M., Ireland, R. D., & Morgan, R. E. (2007). Stimulating dynamic value: Social capital and business incubation as a pathway to competitive success. *Long Range Planning, 40*(2), 154–177. https://doi.org/10.1016/j.lrp.2007.03.008

Isenberg, D. J. (2016). Applying the ecosystem metaphor to entrepreneurship: Uses and abuses. *The Antitrust Bulletin, 61*(4), 564–573. https://doi.org/10.1177/0003603X16676162

Lazarus, R. S., & Folkman, S. (1984). Stress. *Appraisal, and Coping, 725*. Retrieved from https://ccme.osu.edu/WebCastsFiles/562The%20Management%20of%20Stress%20-%202. pdf, 23 January 2019.

Liozu, S., Hinterhuber, A., & Somers, T. (2014). Organizational design and pricing capa-bilities for superior firm performance. *Management Decision, 52*(1), 54–78. https://doi. org/10.1108/MD-05-2013-0279

Markham, S. K., & Griffin, A. (1998). The breakfast of champions: Associations between cham-pions and product development environments, practices and performance. *Journal of Product Innovation Management, 15*(5), 436–454. https://doi.org/10.1016/S0737-6782(98)00010-1

Marquis, C., & Tilcsik, A. (2013). Imprinting: Toward a multilevel theory. *The Academy of Management Annals, 7*(1), 195–245. https://doi.org/10.1080/19416520.2013.766076

McAdam, M., & Marlow, S. (2007). Building futures or stealing secrets? Entrepreneurial cooperation and conflict within business incubators. *International Small Business Journal*, *25*(4), 361–382. https://doi.org/10.1177/0266242607078563

McAdam, M., & McAdam, R. (2006). The networked incubator: The role and operation of entrepreneurial networking with the university science park incubator (USI). *The International Journal of Entrepreneurship and Innovation*, *7*(2), 87–97. https://doi.org/10.536 7/000000006776928663

McAdam, M., & McAdam, R. (2008). High tech start-ups in University Science Park incubators: The relationship between the start-up's lifecycle progression and use of the incubator's resources. *Technovation*, *28*(5), 277–290. https://doi.org/10.1016/j.technova tion.2007.07.012

McKenzie, B., Ugbah, S. D., & Smothers, N. (2007). "Who is an entrepreneur?" Is it still the wrong question? *Academy of Entrepreneurship Journal*, *13*(1), 23–43.

Medway, F. J., & Venino, G. R. (1982). The effects of effort feedback and performance patterns on children's attributions and task persistence. *Contemporary Educational Psychology*, *7*(1), 26–34. https://doi.org/10.1016/0361-476X(82)90004-2

Mian, S., Lamine, W., & Fayolle, A. (2016). Technology business incubation: An overview of the state of knowledge. *Technovation*, *50-51*, 1–12. https://doi.org/10.1016/j. technovation.2016.02.005

Patton, D., Warren, L., & Bream, D. (2009). Elements that underpin high-tech business incubation processes. *Journal of Technology Transfer*, *34*(6), 621–636. https://doi.org/10.1007/ s10961-009-9105-7

Pavett, C. M., & Lau, A. W. (1983). Managerial work: The influence of hierarchical level and functional specialty. *Academy of Management Journal*, *26*(1), 170–177. https://doi. org/10.2307/256144

Pena, I. (2004). Business incubation centers and new firm growth in the Basque country. *Small Business Economics*, *22*(3–4), 223–236. https://doi.org/10.1023/B:SBEJ.0000 022221.03667.82

Pinto, J. K., & Patanakul, P. (2015). When narcissism drives project champions: A review and research agenda. *International Journal of Project Management*, *33*(5), 1180–1190. https://doi.org/10.1016/j.ijproman.2015.01.013

Reid, R. S., Keogh, W., Mitchell, N., & McAdam, R. (2007). Implementing innovation management in manufacturing SMEs: A longitudinal study. *Journal of Small Business and Enterprise Development*, *14*(3), 385–403. https://doi.org/10.1108/14626000710773501

Rice, M. P. (2002). Co-production of business assistance in business incubators: An exploratory study. *Journal of Business Venturing*, *17*(2), 163–187.

Sandelands, L. E., Brockner, J., & Glynn, M. A. (1988). If at first you don't succeed, try, try again: Effects of persistence-performance contingencies, ego involvement, and self-esteem on task persistence. *Journal of Applied Psychology*, *73*(2), 208–216. https://doi. org/10.1037/0021-9010.73.2.208

Schon, D. A. (1963). Champions for radical new inventions. *Harvard Business Review*, *41*, 77–86.

Schumpeter, J. A. (1934). *The Theory of Economic Development: An Inquiry Into Profits, Capital, Credit, Interest, and the Business Cycle*. New Brunswick: Transaction Publishers.

Schwartz, M., & Hornych, C. (2008). Specialization as strategy for business incubators: An assessment of the Central German Multimedia Center. *Technovation*, *28*(7), 436–449. https://doi.org/10.1016/j.technovation.2008.02.003

Schwartz, M., & Hornych, C. (2010). Cooperation patterns of incubator firms and the impact of incubator specialization: Empirical evidence from Germany. *Technovation*, *30*(9–10), 485–495. https://doi.org/10.1016/j.technovation.2010.05.001

Scillitoe, J. L., & Chakrabarti, A. K. (2010). The role of incubator interactions in assisting new ventures. *Technovation*, *30*(3), 155–167. https://doi.org/10.1016/j.technovation.2009.12.002

Shamir, B., House, R. J., & Arthur, M. B. (1993). The motivational effects of charismatic leadership: A Self-Concept Based Theory. *Organization Science*, *4*(4), 577–594. https://doi. org/10.1287/orsc.4.4.577

Shane, S. A. (1994). Are champions different from non-champions? *Journal of Business Venturing, 9*(5), 397–421. https://doi.org/10.1016/0883-9026(94)90014-0

Simsek, Z., Fox, B. C., & Heavey, C. (2015). "What's past is prologue": A framework, review, and future directions for organizational research on imprinting. *Journal of Management, 41*(1), 288–317. https://doi.org/10.1177/0149206314553276

Soetanto, D. P., & Jack, S. L. (2013). Business incubators and the networks of technology-based firms. *Journal of Technology Transfer, 38*(4), 432–453. https://doi.org/10.1007/s10961-011-9237-4

Stam, E., & Spigel, B. (2017). Entrepreneurial Ecosystems. In R. Blackburn, D. D. Clercq, & J. Heinonen (Eds.), *The SAGE Handbook of Small Business and Entrepreneurship*. London: SAGE.

Starnes, D. M., & Zinser, O. (1983). The effect of problem difficulty, locus of control, and sex on task persistence. *The Journal of General Psychology, 108*(2), 249–255. https://doi.org/10.1080/00221309.1983.9711498

Taylor, A., Cocklin, C., Brown, R., & Wilson-Evered, E. (2011). An investigation of champion-driven leadership processes. *The Leadership Quarterly, 22*(2), 412–433. https://doi.org/10.1016/j.leaqua.2011.02.014

Tuckey, M. R., Searle, B. J., Boyd, C. M., Winefield, A. H., & Winefield, H. R. (2015). Hindrances are not threats: Advancing the multidimensionality of work stress. *Journal of Occupational Health Psychology, 20*(2), 131–147. https://doi.org/10.1037/a0038280

von Zedtwitz, M. (2005). Outsourcing R&D in the pharmaceutical industry: From conceptuatisation to implementation of the strategic sourcing process. *R & D Management, 35*(3), 355–356.

Walter, A., Parboteeah, K. P., Riesenhuber, F., & Hoegl, M. (2011). Championship behaviors and innovations success: An empirical investigation of university spin-offs. *Journal of Product Innovation Management, 28*, 586–598. https://doi.org/10.1111/j.1540-5885.2011.00826.x

APPENDIX

Table 13.1   *Descriptive statistics for variables used in regression analysis (see Table 13.4)*

Variables	N	Mean	SD	Min	Max	Range	Skew	Kurtosis	SE
Enthusiasm	210	0.00	1.00	−3.92	1.22	5.15	−1.21	1.32	0.07
Persistence	210	0.00	1.00	−4.38	1.28	5.66	−1.50	2.48	0.07
Getting right people involved	210	0.00	1.00	−3.02	1.31	4.33	−0.75	−0.14	0.07
IM support	210	0.00	1.00	−2.45	1.75	4.20	−0.30	−0.69	0.07
IF–IF interaction	210	0.00	1.00	−1.80	2.22	4.03	0.19	−0.83	0.07
No. founders	210	2.67	2.08	1.00	12.00	11.00	2.45	7.95	0.14
Founder age	210	42.57	10.04	23.00	70.00	47.00	0.37	−0.50	0.69
No. years work exp.	210	20.11	10.30	2.00	49.00	47.00	0.27	−0.58	0.71
Education level	210	3.54	0.78	1.00	5.00	4.00	−0.52	0.93	0.05
Formal entr. edu.	210	0.63	0.48	0.00	1.00	1.00	−0.53	−1.73	0.03
Closed firm	210	0.23	0.42	0.00	1.00	1.00	1.25	−0.43	0.03
No. prev. startups	210	1.35	1.87	0.00	10.00	10.00	2.56	7.75	0.13
No. prev. startups still active	210	1.20	1.36	0.00	11.00	11.00	4.14	26.00	0.09

Table 13.2 Correlation table for variables used in regression analysis (see Table 13.4)

Variables / No.	1	2	3	4	5	6	7	8	9	10	11	12
Enthusiasm												
Persistence	0.65***											
Get. people inv.	0.52***	0.57***										
IM support	0.26***	0.20**	0.26***									
IF–IF inter.	0.24***	0.15*	0.22**	0.40***								
No. founders	-0.05	-0.01	0.13	0.03	-0.09							
Founder age	-0.07	-0.07	0.00	0.02	-0.15*	0.03						
No. years w/exp.	-0.10	-0.06	-0.01	0.02	-0.11	0.01	0.92***					
Education level	0.15*	-0.09	-0.07	-0.05	-0.14*	0.06	0.04	-0.09				
Formal entr.edu.	-0.01	0.03	0.00	-0.11	0.03	0.04	-0.10	-0.11	-0.04			
Closed firm	0.05	0.12	0.12	0.03	-0.09	0.08	0.36***	0.37***	-0.15*	0.10		
No.prev.startups	0.00	-0.02	0.01	-0.12	-0.06	0.00	0.13	0.15*	0.06	-0.09	0.14*	
" still active	-0.22**	-0.15*	-0.06	-0.07	-0.02	0.01	0.02	0.05	0.05	-0.06	-0.05	0.55***

Table 13.3   Items used in Principal Component Analysis

Domain	Name	Item description
Enthusiasm	ent1	Enthusiastically promotes the innovation's advantages
	ent2	Expresses strong conviction about the innovation
	ent3	Expresses confidence in what the innovation can do
	ent4	Shows optimism about the success of the innovation
	ent5	Points out reasons why the innovation will succeed
	ent6	Keeps pushing enthusiastically
Persistence	per1	Sticks with it
	per2	Shows tenacity in overcoming obstacles
	per3	Continues to be involved with the innovation until it is implemented
	per4	Knocks down barriers to the innovation
	per5	Does not give up when others say it cannot be done
	per6	Persists in the face of adversity
Getting the right people involved	gtr1	Gets problems into the hands of those who can solve them
	gtr2	Gets the right people involved
	gtr3	Gets key decision makers involved
IM-support	i1_1	The incubator manager spends enough time assisting you
	i1_2	Interactions between the incubator manager and you have reduced the likelihood of you making expensive business-related mistakes
	i1_3	The incubator has provided operations-related advice of high quality
	i1_4	The incubator has provided you with access to investors or other capital providers
	i1_5	By being inside the incubator, you and your firm's credibility among stakeholders has increased
	i1_6	You follow the advice of the incubator manager
I–I int.	i2_1	Your firm has learned strategies for how success can be achieved through other incubated firms
	i2_2	You have acquired a great deal of knowledge from other incubated founders
	i2_3	You and your firm follow advice from other incubated founders

Table 13.4   *Regression analysis, IM support and IF-IF interactions on the three dimensions of champion behaviour*

	Enthusiasm		Persistence		Getting the right people involved	
	(1)	*(2)*	*(3)*	*(4)*	*(5)*	*(6)*
No. founders	−0.015	−0.013	0.011	0.011	0.074**	0.077**
	(0.035)	(0.033)	(0.035)	(0.035)	(0.036)	(0.034)
Founder age	−0.008	−0.003	−0.012	−0.010	0.012	0.019
	(0.019)	(0.018)	(0.019)	(0.019)	(0.020)	(0.019)
Work exp.	−0.004	−0.007	0.003	0.002	−0.020	−0.024
	(0.019)	(0.018)	(0.019)	(0.019)	(0.020)	(0.019)
Edu. lvl.	0.180**	0.229**	−0.070	−0.043	−0.113	−0.054
	(0.105)	(0.100)	(0.107)	(0.105)	(0.109)	(0.103)
Entr. edu.	−0.068	0.012	−0.030	0.038	−0.025	0.059
	(0.151)	(0.145)	(0.153)	(0.152)	(0.157)	(0.149)
Prev. closure	0.159	0.152	0.338*	0.316*	0.201	0.205
	(0.189)	(0.181)	(0.192)	(0.190)	(0.196)	(0.185)
Prev. founding	0.091*	0.116**	0.060	0.079*	0.033	0.060
	(0.047)	(0.045)	(0.048)	(0.047)	(0.049)	(0.046)
Founder owner	−0.233***	−0.242***	−0.155**	−0.160**	−0.076	−0.088
	(0.064)	(0.061)	(0.065)	(0.064)	(0.066)	(0.062)
IM support		0.232***		0.206**		0.234***
		(0.076)		(0.079)		(0.077)
IF-IF interact.		0.154*		0.036		0.216***
		(0.076)		(0.083)		(0.081)
Constant	0.192	−0.072	0.846	0.711	0.355	0.028
	(0.634)	(0.606)	(0.645)	(0.637)	(0.659)	(0.621)
Observations	210	210	210	210	210	210
R^2	0.187	0.275	0.158	0.200	0.122	0.240
Residual Std. Error	0.972	0.923	0.989	0.969	1.009	0.945
	(df=180)	(df=178)	(df=180)	(df=178)	(df=180)	(df=178)

Notes: Binary variables for associated incubator omitted; all models with IVs satisfy the Overall F-test of Significance, $p<.1$).

14. Multinational companies' roles in start-up incubation ecosystems: The case of Microsoft Innovation Centers in Brazil

Nadja Nordling, Elisa Thomas, Rhiannon Pugh, and Roberto Rivas Hermann

1. INTRODUCTION

Start-up incubators are recognized as public policy tools to enhance regional entrepreneurship and innovation. Policy makers view science parks, incubators and accelerators as a tool for promoting economic development, innovation and the emergence of new technology-based growth firms (Bergek & Norrman, 2008; Mian, Lamine and Fayolle, 2016).

The term "incubator" has been used to describe supportive environments for breeding and developing new firms (Lindholm-Dahlstrand and Klofsten, 2002). Whereas more "traditional" incubation approaches emphasize physical infrastructure and high technology. Kautonen, Pugh and Raunio (2017, 620) suggest that "incubation approaches are moving (. . .) to a more interactive, participatory and social mode of innovation, in line with broader developments in innovation policy and theory". This includes involving more actors, with the aim of stimulating new forms of collaboration between groups such as public, private, university, and third sectors (Etzkowitz, 2008).

Business management literature has examined the utilization of platform business models by large companies in order to gain outside knowledge and build an ecosystem to incubate creativity, innovation and entrepreneurship (Gawer & Cusumano, 2014). These discussions concentrate on large firms as the platform leaders or keystone companies within the ecosystem (Zahra & Nambisan, 2012; Gawer & Cusumano, 2014). These companies offer their own product or technology for others to complement and thus strengthen their market position (Gawer & Cusumano, 2014).

Within these discussions, we find little focus on large multinational companies (MNCs) delivering start-up incubation services and driving the development of entrepreneurial ecosystems (EE). Models usually focus on government, development agencies or higher education institutions delivering start-up incubation services (Etzkowitz, 2008). Where MNCs have been considered (Isenberg, 2010; Loganathan, 2018), there is evidence that they can have a positive effect on the wider entrepreneurial ecosystem provided they are truly locally embedded. However, in emerging economies such as Brazil, public supports for incubation, innovation and entrepreneurship activities are squeezed due to governance challenges and economic issues.[1] This chapter will fill this lacuna by studying the role of MNCs in such activities, presenting an exploratory case study of a large incubation programme in Brazil initiated and delivered by Microsoft. Specifically, we explore the different roles performed by MNCs, and seek to understand the organization of incubation activities within and between the various regional actors.

To guide our exploration, we devised the following research question:

What is the role of MNCs in delivering start-up incubation services and driving the creation of EEs?

We chose the case of the Microsoft Innovation Centers (MIC) programme in Brazil because of its scale and rapid expansion across several regions, and indeed countries. Briefly, the first MIC was established in Brazil in 2001. At its peak in Brazil, 15 centres were opened. Currently, there are three MICs in action in Brazil and more than 100 MICs worldwide (Microsoft, 2018). We found this to be an interesting case of an incubation mechanism driven by the private rather than public sector using novel approaches around community engagement.

2.   START-UP INCUBATION AND ENTREPRENEURIAL ECOSYSTEMS

Incubation policy and programmes are well established and researched over the past 30 years (Mian et al., 2016). Literature has widely explored the role of government, development agencies or universities and higher education institutions in business incubation (Etzkowitz, 2008; McAdam, Miller & McAdam, 2016; Soetanto & Jack, 2016). We can see research exploring incubation within large companies (Ford, Garnsey & Probert, 2010), open innovation (Mortara & Minshall, 2011) and "intrapreneurship" (Braunerhjelm, Ding & Thulin, 2018). A recent study from Loganathan (2018) studies the role of MNCs in EEs and their symbiotic relationship with start-ups in India. However, this work focuses merely on foreign direct investments and benefits for the MNC and start-ups, leaving the wider regional ecosystem and its collaboration with the MNCs aside. We find that discussions of large firms' involvements in incubation efforts in partnership with actors at the regional level are lacking.

Past incubation efforts focused on a narrow elite of innovators, with a science- and technology-based perspective on innovation (Kautonen et al., 2017). These were not always successful and sometimes led to "cathedrals in the desert" in less-favoured regions (Benneworth & Charles, 2005). Recently, trends have emerged towards platform-based approaches to incubation, less high-tech premised and more focused on local needs, involving the wider "community" in innovation and entrepreneurship activities (Kautonen et al., 2017). Conceptually, we can envisage incubation activities in relation to the development of EEs, encompassing a wide range of different actors and institutions.

EE refers to the relations among actors, policies and resources with the aim to support innovation and entrepreneurial activity (Stam, 2015). "Actors" in the ecosystem involve a heterogeneous group of customers, suppliers, institutions, venture capitalists, government agencies and educational institutions (Acs, Stam, Audretsch & O'Connor, 2017). Through continuous exchange with their environment (other actors, policies and resources), entrepreneurs identify new opportunities, develop commercial opportunities and translate them into new ventures (Alvedalen and Boschma, 2017).

Literature on EE has focused on publicly funded programmes to drive start-ups, and incubators are often included as a component of the system (see Spigel 2017 for a full presentation of components). As with the incubation literature, we find little discussion of MNCs within this body of work, which is partly understandable due to the focus on entrepreneurial start-ups, but potentially misses the roles and activities of a large and economically important group of actors. Indeed, it has been found that MNCs increasingly seek to coordinate their value chains and relations within their local ecosystems (Pitelis and Teece, 2018). The literature also indicates that MNCs have positive spillover effects, enhancing the innovation potential of smaller firms (Almeida and Phene, 2004) and that they tap into local resources and link them to R&D activities while benefiting the local ecosystem (Nordling, 2014). However, the integration of MNCs into regional ecosystems has proved problematic, leading to what are known as "branch-plant economies" in some of the struggling post-industrial regions of the UK (Phelps, 2009). Research shows that gains from MNCs' inclusion in an ecosystem depends much on the heterogeneity of the ecosystem and the absorptive capacity of firms (Bhawe and Zahra, 2019).

The case study presented here explores the integration of an MNC into regional ecosystems via incubation activities, and discusses the different roles and interdependency of the MNC and regional stakeholders. The design of the MIC programme, with explicit aims to incubate start-ups and enrich EEs addressing gaps of local needs for innovation support, fits into emerging platform- and community-based trends in incubation.

3.   DATA AND METHOD

We conducted an exploratory case study of the Microsoft Innovation Center (MIC) programme in Brazil, which was the first partner-country to build centres towards fostering EEs and creating start-ups. The intrinsic case study approach (Stake, 2005) helped us understand the process of incubating start-ups developed by an MNC in partnerships with local actors, rather than viewing it as a phenomenon isolated from the local context.

We used interviews, documents and observations as data sources. The lead author visited three MICs in Brazil, in the cities of Belo Horizonte, São Paulo and Fortaleza, in November and December 2013. Additional data was gathered via email questionnaires in March 2014. The second author made follow-up calls in 2018 to confirm and update information with the three MICs currently operating in Brazil, in the cities of Campinas, Curitiba and Fortaleza. The three locations from the original study vary from each other in terms of socio-economic situation and cultural aspects.[2]

We conducted 11 interviews with key actors in each MIC. The semi-structured interviews for MIC managers and hosts had four themes: establishment of the centres, practical activities and actors involved; connections to the region and other MICs; different actors' roles and modes of interaction; and motivation and incentives of different stakeholders' engagement. Interviews with the participants of MIC programmes dealt with involvement and experiences from the activities; interaction in the community and what networks participation had enabled; tasks and responsibilities in the centre; motivation and incentives for participation and; future plans with lessons taken from the programme.

Observation generated understanding of everyday life in each MIC; relationships and interactions in the MIC community; collaboration and knowledge sharing between the actors; support for participants in entrepreneurship and innovation and; the overall atmosphere in the centre. The MIC website and programme documents were analysed to understand the general MIC model and the "toolkit" Microsoft offers. Additional material was gathered at an international workshop in Belo Horizonte in 2013. Different local and international actors gathered to enhance innovation and development in that region. Data was analysed inductively using the following categories: interaction between actors in the ecosystems; the role of the MNC in the EE; benefits and pitfalls of the approach; the model of fostering and incubating start-ups; and incubation platform policies. A bottom up approach to the data was implemented, allowing topics and issues to emerge as we went through the data, and triangulated across the research team's individual and group analysis.

4. MICROSOFT INNOVATION CENTRES IN BRAZIL

4.1 MIC Organization and Actors' Roles

MICs are Microsoft's initiative in which the company works together with local partners to help build competence, foster entrepreneurship and incubate start-ups. Local partners are typically private or public higher education institutions, technical schools or local development agencies. Hosts collaborate with local industries thus expanding the network of MICs. Each centre has a manager whose role is central in the interaction between the MNC, the host, other regional institutions as well as the participants of the MIC programmes, who are developers, entrepreneurs, start-ups, IT professionals, students and academic researchers.

The various actors take different roles within the centre. Microsoft brings in a toolkit with the latest technologies, programmes and concepts designed to advance innovation and entrepreneurship (Table 14.1). These may be recurrent or non-recurrent programmes including training, lectures and events, developed for different groups. Each local host decides which tools to utilize and implement in practice. The length of activities vary, from days to several months or years. Even though most of the programmes are run by the local hosts some global ones are the responsibility of Microsoft (e.g. annual Imagine Cup innovation competition).

Table 14.1 Examples of programmes and concepts from the Microsoft toolkit

Microsoft toolkit programme	Description
Partnership accelerator programme for networking	A tool for community building, an example event being breakfast meetings that bring together companies, MIC participants and Microsoft IT professionals to discuss technology and opportunities.
Global BizSpark programme for start-up development	Designed to support start-ups for a three-year-period through which Microsoft provides a monthly allowance of USD 200. The programme also includes free software, training, mentoring, visibility, etc.
Local Innovation accelerator programme	Enhancing local capacity for innovation through hands-on engagements. The centres provide labs for innovation and development work for participants.
Skills development	Developing intellectual capital with courses in software, business management and marketing, and employment programmes for students.

Even though most centres are focused on technology and software development, some emphasize vocational training and diversified fields such as business and marketing. Besides training, MICs provide valuable contacts and networks for the entrepreneurs or start-ups participating in the programmes.

> MIC has also some ties to the government. I made a call and some start-ups got the fund and contacts from the sponsors of the Imagine Cup. MIC manager 2

Besides the MIC toolkit programmes, the centres are also a home to the "core MIC" teams, with a varying structure by centre: some emphasize start-up teams, some are more based on IT-professionals or student teams. In these centres the participants may enter the programme either as trainees or they may get paid for their participation. These teams work in open, hierarchy-free environments: the participants and teams are self-organized, working to meet deadlines. The manager provides support when needed. Atmosphere in the visited centres was enthusiastic and focused. In one of the centres, three student teams were working towards the Imagine Cup innovation competition and were eager to show the case they were working on.

> Sometimes we spend more time on things than professional teams. . .but on the other hand we can do something that anyone can't do because we are not afraid to fail, they are students they are not afraid to fail – yet. This is good because we can do different things. MIC manager 3

4.2   Business Model and Collaboration

For Microsoft, the business model offers a channel to root technology to new locations, expand its market share, and test products with local users. As local hosts organize the physical facilities and activities, and are also responsible for the costs, the model is fairly risk-free for Microsoft in terms of investments. In addition, local hosts pay a fee to Microsoft when setting up the centre. In return the host gains access to the MIC toolkit. In some cases Microsoft has approached the local host with a suggestion to launch a centre but most often it has been the local host approaching Microsoft with an interest to establish an MIC. There is no standard business or financial model, though. In some cases the activities may be funded solely by the hosts, or by revenues from the activities and services the centre provides either to local industry or to Microsoft (e.g. software development or concept-building). In some cases the projects or start-ups are sold, along with the intellectual property rights. In others, entrepreneurs or student teams use the facility to work on their own ideas.

Thus, there is a multi-dimensional nature of the business model, where collaboration and ecosystem building may be found at the institutional or individual levels.

Centres may also offer business opportunities to participants, connecting national and international networks, allowing the start-ups to build their ecosystems by utilizing the network structure. Online tools can establish connections that go beyond the regional ecosystem and tap into knowledge and resources across the country.

> The MIC has established relations with the universities in the area and provided them with the opportunity to have students in the MIC volunteer programme. Especially the private universities have responded well to this because they are always looking for new opportunities for their students to get involved in business. MIC manager 1

> For the students of PUC University, MIC is a window to the world, to work with Microsoft professionals and a door to great careers. University Professor

Single centres may be closed in case they do not meet or serve regional needs and competence building. For example, one centre in Brazil was established around agricultural studies but the added value of the centre was not clear therefore it was closed. In another example, the local host of MIC Sao Paulo reported in 2013 that the support of Microsoft was no longer necessary as it was when launching the centre. The activities, concepts and brand of the facility had grown so strong that they were thinking of becoming independent. In the follow-up in 2018 MIC Sao Paulo had exited the programme, confirming this.

5.   DISCUSSION

Having outlined the structure of MICs, we now discuss their role within regional start-up incubation ecosystems. Our aim is neither to make any pronouncement on whether the involvement of MNCs in incubation activities is a "good" or "bad" thing, nor to provide a full evaluation of the MIC programme, but to open up the discussion of MNCs' roles in start-up incubation ecosystems.

Our research reported positive experiences of those involved in the MIC programme in Brazil. However, it is worth pointing out that our research methodology was in some ways "self-selecting" as we interviewed those involved with the centres – we did not have access to those who had for instance been denied access to a centre, or who had been involved and left. Such actors may have reported different experiences, of course, and for a full evaluation of the programme we would attempt such counterfactual research that is less self-selecting than our methodology here. From our exploratory research, experiences from MICs in their aim to incubate start-ups and foster entrepreneurial ecosystems are reported positively among respondents. In MIC Fortaleza there are some start-ups established by the people who were part of the MIC core team (these participants started as volunteers in the centre to learn technical skills). MIC Fortaleza has also conducted a teacher-training project for the governments of seven cities reaching 5000–6000 students. In MIC Sao Paulo some start-ups were founded every year, usually after an innovation competition. MICs are part of these activities and even though it may not always be possible to straight-forwardly report these as "MIC start-ups", the centre is an enabler and has played an active role in incubating and training start-up entrepreneurs. During five years of operation, MIC Belo Horizonte supported 132 start-ups with training and lectures and partnered up with 20 start-ups. At the time of the research, all start-ups involved with the three MICs were working nationally, however Microsoft offers channels for internationalization.

Regarding the perceived benefits of the MIC approach, local ecosystems and businesses evolve through these activities, which is beneficial to wider regional economies. Through the platform- and community-based initiative, Microsoft benefits by gaining outside knowledge of the company's R&D activities, by spreading its technology and by getting complementary components to the company's products (as the start-ups use Microsoft technology and build their business around the MNC). Thus the programme strengthens the MNC's market position. If the city or the regional government was running an incubator, they would be unlikely to have that technology to offer, or would have to buy it. Another potential benefit of MNC involvement in start-up incubation is the ability to link with international platforms and connect the local ecosystem on a global level. Also, the MNC has a global view of ecosystem development and may be able to share best practices from around the world in a way that a regional government focused only on one set of experiences and contexts may not be able to.

However, there is also a potential darker side of having greater involvement of MNCs in start-up incubation activities. It is the case that an MNC such as Microsoft has huge technological resources and international networks to offer, but the question arises over motivation and goals, and whether an MNC is mostly concerned with local ecosystem development and economic outcomes (as a public actor would be assumed to be in a well-functioning society), or with its own growth and development. In the best case scenario these two objectives are balanced well and both parties are gaining from the programmes and collaborations. In another scenario, the model would be biased towards supporting the MNC. Local partners would pay for technology, spreading or selling the MNC's technology and products, and providing free or cheap work force for the MNC in the name of training (via student teams and interns), rather than utilizing the talents in the local companies and for local development. In the case we researched, we see the more positive scenario. However, we should not assume benevolence; MNCs are indeed targeting emerging economies in order to embed their technologies and increase market share. Our respondents had a pragmatic approach to MNC involvement in incubation: although there might be some negative flip-sides to MNC involvement, it would be better to have the programmes and facilities than not, and it is worth some compromise in order to enjoy the benefits of the centres.

An important discussion point is the recent closure of so many MICs in Brazil. It raises the question of whether Microsoft, once it had embedded its technology and derived maximum value from its involvement in the local ecosystem, no longer saw a benefit of supporting start-ups and running the centres and so moved on. We cannot say this was necessarily the case, and from a more optimistic perspective perhaps the centres had embedded new activities and strengthened the local ecosystem to the point that support was no longer needed and that's why they moved on (as we described earlier in the case of MIC Sao Paulo). But a question mark has been raised as the programme progressed. This should be investigated in future research: exactly why were so many centres in an emerging economy closed? Another important issue to follow up is, in the case of closure, what traces from the MNC involvement remain: does the MNC simply leave without a trace and the collaborations end, or does the ecosystem retain its imprint and continue to benefit from its presence? As is the case with exploratory research, our case study findings throw up further interesting questions on the topic of MNCs' involvement in incubation, all of which we cannot answer at the exploratory stage.

6.   CONCLUSIONS

This chapter presents an exploratory research on the role of MNCs in start-up incubation and in fostering ecosystem development while previous literature has focused on activities stemming from the public and education sectors (McAdam et al., 2016; Soetanto & Jack, 2016). The MIC programme emerged as a salutary case with which to "fill in the blanks" on this topic due to its size and rapid emergence. The MIC model offers the experience of an MNC providing start-up incubation in partnership with the local actors and may offer value-added for the local start-up ecosystem.

We link this programme to trends in the incubation literature and public policy towards interaction and community building (cf. Kautonen et al., 2017; Etzkowitz, 2008), and towards platform business models where companies can engage outside knowledge to their R&D activities (cf. Gawer & Cusumano, 2014). Our case illustrates how an MNC utilizes a business platform model encompassing both physical infrastructures and digital spaces to engage in local ecosystem development.

Within this programme, we were especially interested to find out whether such an incubation initiative stemming from an MNC can create mutual benefits both for the company and the local region. We do not aim to make a definitive judgement whether or not MNC involvement in delivering incubation services is a "good" or "bad" thing, and we found both benefits and potential issues or compromises. The partnership and community-building between the MNC and local actors is key. The grounding of digital platforms enables both parties (the company and the region) to benefit: the former through integration of outside knowledge and ideas into the company's R&D activities, access to networks within the region and nation, and capture of market-share; and the latter benefiting from well-designed tools and initiatives stemming from the MNC that they would not otherwise have had access to, and channels for internationalization for local partners.

Our case study illuminates discussions about what happens when different actors from the public, private, and university spheres take on each other's roles, as the proponents suggest they should do in a well functioning innovation ecosystem (Etzkowitz, 2008). However, a large MNC is not a public agency nor an education institution, and we cannot assume that the whole process is philanthropic. Public actors should pay attention to which companies they are inviting for collaboration to ensure that this is done in the spirit of mutual benefit. However, who or what type of actor is delivering the incubation support may not be the most important consideration, and instead we should consider whether the incubation models are well designed, clear and accessible for a range of local stakeholders to participate in, and based on a participatory or platform design to spread benefits into the local ecosystem widely.

In short, the match to the needs and strengths of the local ecosystem is the crucial factor. It is important that the MNC is placing regional needs at the core of their activities, and that the programme is working harmoniously to deliver benefits to both the supporting MNC and the local economies. Research indicates that well-designed ecosystem business models offer value for the MNC as well as positive spill-over effects on the local start-up scene (cf. Almeida and Phene, 2004) as well as on the competence building of local partner institutions.

We find that in our cases in Brazil, the MNC has filled an empty space and stimulated incubation supports to develop the local start-up ecosystem, considering the context of countries in the Global South where the public sector may be less stable and resourced as is usually assumed in the literature on incubation support, which is focused on Europe and North America. More work is needed in the emerging economy context to understand the similarities and differences to the extant cases presented in the literature stemming from the Global North (such as: Almeida, 2008; Rapini, et al., 2009). Whilst we report quite a positive experience of MNC involvement in incubation from our research with participants in the MIC programme, we do issue a caution in that support for local ecosystems should not become merely a sales pitch or market capture by MNCs, which is an inherent danger of this approach. The needs and priorities of the MNC should not override the local ecosystems'.

NOTES

1. The OECD (2018) estimates that growth in Brazil will slow and that "public spending has crowded out private investment in the past" (p.10). Recommendations to help return investments to the country range from simplifying taxes and allowing stronger competition so that high-performing enterprises can thrive and enhance further investment triple helix opportunities (OECD, 2018).
2. The State of São Paulo is the leading economic State in Brazil, representing 33 per cent of the national GDP. The State of Minas Gerais, from which Belo Horizonte is the capital, is in third place (9 per cent of GDP). The State of Ceara, from which Fortaleza is the capital, is 12th. Comparing the cities, São Paulo has the highest GDP, Belo Horizonte is fourth and Fortaleza is the 10th. Although it may seem that the two first cities are close in economic situation, São Paulo's GDP is almost 7.5 times bigger than of Belo Horizonte (IBGE, 2018).

REFERENCES

Acs, Z. J., Stam, E., Audretsch, D. B., & O'Connor, A. (2017), The lineages of the entrepreneurial ecosystem approach, *Small Business Economics*, *49*, 1–10.

Almeida, M. (2008), Innovation and entrepreneurship in Brazilian universities, *International Journal of Technology Management & Sustainable Development*, *7*(1), 39–58.

Almeida, P., & Phene, A. (2004), Subsidiaries and knowledge creation: the influence of the MNC and host country on innovation, *Strategic Management Journal*, *25*(89), 847–864.

Alvedalen, J., & Boschma, R. (2017), A critical review of entrepreneurial ecosystems research: towards a future research agenda, *European Planning Studies*, *25*(6), 887–903.

Benneworth, P., & Charles, D. (2005), University spin-off policies and economic development in less successful regions: Learning from two decades of policy practice, *European Planning Studies*, *13*(4), 537–557.

Bergek, A., & Norrman, C. (2008), Incubator best practice: A framework, *Technovation*, *28*(1–2), 20–28.

Bhawe, N., Zahra, S.A. (2019), Inducing heterogeneity in local entrepreneurial ecosystems:

the role of MNEs, *Small Business Economics*, *52*(2), pp 437–454. https://doi.org/10.1007/s11187-017-9954-7

Braunerhjelm, P., Ding, D. & Thulin, P. (2018), The knowledge spillover theory of intrapreneurship, *Small Business Economics*, *51*(1), 1–30.

Etzkowitz, H. (2008), *The triple helix: university-industry-government innovation in action*, New York: Routledge.

Ford, S., Garnsey, E. & Probert, D. (2010), Evolving corporate entrepreneurship strategy: technology incubation at Philips, *R&D Management*, 40(1), 81–90.

Gawer, A., & Cusumano, M. A. (2014), Industry platforms and ecosystem innovation, *Journal of Product Innovation Management*, *31*(3), 417–433.

IBGE – Instituto Brasileiro de Geografia e Estatística – Coordenação de Contas Nacionais (2018). *Produto interno bruto dos municípios: 2010-2015*. Rio de Janeiro.

Isenberg, D. (2010) Multinationals' Unique Role in the Entrepreneurial Ecosystem, *Forbes*, Nov 22, 2010.

Kautonen, M., Pugh, R. & Raunio, M. (2017), Transformation of regional innovation policies: from 'traditional' to 'next generation' models of incubation, *European Planning Studies*, *25*(4), 620–637.

Lindholm-Dahlstrand, A., & Klofsten, M. (2002), 'Growth and innovation support in Swedish science parks and incubators', in Ray Oakey, Wim During, Saleema Kauser (eds), *Vol 2 / New technology-based firms in the new millennium*, Oxford: Elsevier Science Ltd, pp. 31–46.

Loganathan, M. (2018), 'Exploring MNC-startup symbiotic relationship in an entrepreneurial ecosystem, *Asian Journal of Innovation and Policy*, *7*(1), 131–149.

McAdam, M., Miller, K., & McAdam, R. (2016), Situated regional university incubation: A multi-level stakeholder perspective, *Technovation*, *50*, 69–78.

Mian, S., Lamine, W., & Fayolle, A. (2016), Technology Business Incubation: An overview of the state of knowledge, *Technovation*, *50*, 1–12.

Microsoft (2018), Microsoft Innovation Centers, accessed 6 August 2018 at https://www.microsoftinnovationcenters.com/.

Mortara, L. & Minshall, T. (2011), How do large multinational companies implement open innovation? *Technovation*, *31*(10–11), 586–597.

Nordling, N. (2014), *Innovation Platforms Integrating Global Human Capital into Knowledge Economy*, University of Tampere, Tampere, Finland.

OECD (2018), OECD Economic Surveys: Brazil 2018, OECD Publishing, Paris.

Phelps, N. (2009), From branch plant economies to knowledge economies? Manufacturing industry, government policy, and economic development in Britain's old industrial regions. *Environment and Planning C: Government and Policy*, *27*(4), 574–592.

Pitelis, C.N., Teece, D.J. (2018), The new MNE: 'Orchestration' Theory as envelope of 'Internalisation' Theory, *Management International Review*, *58*, 523–539.

Rapini, M. S., Albuquerque, E. d. M., Chave, C. V., Silva, L. A., De Souza, S. G. A., Righi, H. M., & Da Cruz, W. M. S. (2009), University–industry interactions in an immature system of innovation: evidence from Minas Gerais, Brazil, *Science & Public Policy*, *36*(5), 373–386.

Soetanto, D., & Jack, S. (2016), The impact of university-based incubation support on the innovation strategy of academic spin-offs, *Technovation*, *50*, 25–40.

Spigel, B. (2017), The relational organization of entrepreneurial ecosystems, *Entrepreneurship Theory and Practice*, *41*(1), 49–72.

Stake, R. (2005), 'Qualitative case studies', in Denzin, N., and Lincoln, Y. (eds) *The Sage Handbook of Qualitative Research*, London: Sage, pp. 443–466.

Stam, E. (2015), Entrepreneurial ecosystems and regional policy: A sympathetic critique, *European Planning Studies*, *23*(9), 1759–1769.

Zahra, S. A., & Nambisan, S. (2012), Entrepreneurship and strategic thinking in business ecosystems, *Business Horizons*, *55*(3), 219–229.

15. Outsider support, firm births and outcomes
Lars Kolvereid and Espen J. Isaksen

INTRODUCTION

This study concerns outsider support to Norwegian nascent entrepreneurs and the relationship between such support and subsequent firm outcomes. We investigate two types of support to nascent entrepreneurs: (1) capital in the form of loans and grants and (2) good advice. We further compare the impact of government support to nascent entrepreneurs with the impact of equivalent support from banks. Nascent entrepreneurs are individuals who try to start a business; in this survey defined as individuals who own a newly registered firm. These individuals become actual entrepreneurs when the firm is born. The year of business birth is here defined as the year in which the firm carries out an initial economic transaction and reports earnings or losses.

Isenberg (2011) argues that there are six domains of entrepreneurship ecosystems: conductive policy, markets, financial capital, human skills, culture and supports. In the present study, we focus on two of these domains, financing and advice, which both constitute key parts of an entrepreneurial ecosystem (Mason & Brown, 2014). The goal of the present study is to answer the following two research questions:

RQ1: Among nascent entrepreneurs, is receiving support from government or banks associated with increased probability of business birth?

RQ2: What is the association between government and bank support to nascent entrepreneurs and subsequent business outcomes in terms of firm earnings, employment, sales and endurance?

In this study, we focus on support to individual nascent entrepreneurs and the extent to which support from government and banks contribute to the creation of viable new ventures. The first step in this process is business birth, here defined as a business that has economic transactions. Since new firms in Norway have to register and obtain a legal status before they are allowed to start selling or hiring, many business that are registered will never have any economic transactions, such as sales income or labour costs, and never report any earnings or losses. The second step is associated with business outcomes among firms that are born and have carried out economic transactions, such as earnings, employment, sales, and endurance. This research concerns two of the most central actors in the national entrepreneurial ecosystem in Norway: the government and the banking industry. It contributes to the literature on ecosystems of new firms by investigating the effects of government support on new firms and comparing this type of support with support from banks.

The starting point of this study is a representative sample of 1048 new business registrations during four successive weeks in Norway in May/June 2002. Using tax records, we monitor the annual transactions of these businesses from 2003 to 2015.

LITERATURE REVIEW

Governments in many countries actively support new firm formation. There is, however, a debate regarding which types of firms should be supported and which are the most appropriate and effective policy initiatives (Shane, 2009; Mason & Brown, 2014). Shane (2009) argues that policy makers should stop subsidizing the formation of typical start-up firms and instead focus on a small subset of firms with substantial growth potential. A way to facilitate high growth entrepreneurship using a more holistic and system-based approach is to focus on entrepreneurial ecosystems (Mason & Brown, 2014). According to Alvedalen and Boschma (2017), the entrepreneurial ecosystem literature mainly aims to explain high quality or ambitious entrepreneurship. According to them, the performance of ecosystems depends on three elements: individuals, organizations and institutions. A national entrepreneurial ecosystem is a national system of entrepreneurship with "a dynamic, institutionally embedded interaction between entrepreneurial attitudes, abilities and aspirations, by individuals which drives the allocation of resources through the creation and operation of new ventures" (Acs, Autio, & Szerb, 2014, p. 479). Key players in this system are the individual entrepreneurs, but also agents that provide capital and advice to nascent entrepreneurs, such as government agencies and banks.

Theoretical Perspectives

The resource-based view of the firm is appropriate to explain and predict the effect of government support programmes to small and new businesses. According to this view, competitive advantage can stem from resources that are valuable, rare, imperfectly imitable and non-substitutable (Barney, 1991).

Both financial and human capital resources are key prerequisites for founders of new businesses (Chandler & Hanks, 1998). External advice may compensate for the nascent entrepreneurs' lack of relevant entrepreneurial human capital. According to Robson and Bennett (2000), analyses have shown that external advice has been used by SMEs in order to fill gaps in internal staff and management expertise. Chrisman and McMullan (2000) argue that an increase in knowledge acquired from counselling can become an intangible firm-specific resource that increases competitive advantage.

Pergelova and Angulo-Ruiz (2014) claim that financial resources through government support can boost competitive advantage by converting such support into firm-specific in-imitable assets and capabilities. Seeking financial capital in the initial phase is related to the strategy the business might pursue (Cooper, Gimeno-Gascon, & Woo, 1994). Nascent entrepreneurs seeking and getting external financial capital are likely to have higher growth ambitions for the new business compared with nascent entrepreneurs not involved in such activities. Further, initial financial capital buys time (Cooper et al., 1994) giving the nascent entrepreneur possibility to learn and overcome initial challenges in the business start-up process.

Empirical Evidence

Scholars have carried out empirical investigations of the effect of government financial support to small businesses in several countries. For example, researchers have investigated the effect on credit guarantees to small firms in the UK (Cowling, 2010; Cowling & Mitchell, 2003), in Spain (Garcia-Tabuenca & Crespo-Espert, 2010), and Korea (Oh, Lee, Heshmati & Choi, 2009). Others have investigated the effect of government equity (Hart & Lenihan, 2006) and grant support to small businesses in Ireland (Roper & Hewitt-Dundas, 2001). Roper and Hewitt-Dundas (2001) investigated the effect of government grant support to small businesses in Ireland. They found that such support had a positive effect on employment growth, but no effect on turnover growth or profitability. Many previous studies concern the effect of various forms of government financial support to small firms, but very few have investigated the effect of government loans and grants on new business birth, performance, growth or survival. Pergelova and Angulo-Ruiz (2014) conducted one of the few studies that have focused on the effect of government financial support to new firms. Using data from the USA, they investigated the effect of government loans, guarantees, and equity on new firm competitiveness and performance. Their results suggested that government financial support had an indirect effect on new firm performance because it increased firms' competitive advantage.

Chrisman and associates have published several articles on the effect of outsider government sponsored assistance for new and small businesses in USA. They have found that such advice and guidance is positively associated with new firm creation (Chrisman, 1999), long-term performance (Chrisman & McMullan, 2000; Chrisman, McMullan, & Hall, 2005), and firm survival (Chrisman & McMullan, 2004). They often report an inverted U-shaped relationship between the amount of outsider assistance and firm outcomes, indicating that there are diminishing returns to outsider assistance over a certain number of hours of such assistance.

Studies from the UK have reported more mixed results of the effects of government supported business advice. Wren and Storey (2002) did not find any positive effects of consultancy advice on firm survival among small firms, but reported positive effects among mid-range SMEs with regard to survival and growth. Robson and Bennett (2000) investigated the relationship of SME growth in Britain with the acquisition of external business advice. They detected no effect on growth of government or bank advice. Mole, Hart, Roper, and Saal (2009) found no effect of business advice on sales growth, but that such advice was positively associated with employment growth. Rotger, Gørtz, and Storey (2012) found that a programme that involved guided preparation of new firms had a positive effect on the size and survival of new firms, but that the effect on growth was less clear.

This brief review of the literature and empirical findings suggests that both government and bank financial support and advisory services may influence firm births and their subsequent performance, growth and survival. However, governments and banks in different countries have different policies towards new businesses and use different methods to support nascent entrepreneurs. The effect of support to new businesses may therefore vary between countries.

METHODOLOGY

Sample

In Norway, all new businesses are required to register before they can start trading or hire personnel legally. This makes it possible to identify new businesses at a very early stage. The data collection for this study started in May 2002. We acquired contact information to all new businesses registered during four sequential weeks in May/June 2002 and mailed out 3121

Table 15.1   Industry distribution in the sample

Industry	N	%
Agriculture and fishing	77	7.3%
Manufacturing	48	4.6%
Construction	106	10.1%
Trade	182	17.4%
Transport	63	6.0%
Finance	62	6.9%
Information Technology	76	7.3%
Business services	233	22.2%
Personal services	124	11.8%
Leisure	77	7.3%
Total	1048	100%

questionnaires to the lead entrepreneur in all new business registered. After one reminder, we received 1048 questionnaires, a response rate of 35 per cent. We received most of the completed questionnaires during only a few weeks after businesses' registration.

In November 2016, we acquired annual tax accounts from all the businesses from 2003 to 2015 from the Norwegian tax authority. This data contained information about annual sales, labour costs and earnings (or losses) for all businesses that had transactions during each year from 2003 to 2015 (we did not include data from 2002 in the analysis since accounting figures from non-incorporated businesses that year were unavailable). As Table 15.1 illustrates, the sample is very heterogeneous with regard to industry.

Measures

Government support to nascent entrepreneurs in Norway can come from the central government and national actors, but also from counties and municipalities. Further, the support can be grants, loans and guarantees or non-financial support such as advice and guidance to entrepreneurs. Some government actors offer financial support only, some advice only, and yet others both capital and advice.

Independent variables
We measure financial support from government with a binary variable indicating whether the business had received capital in the form of loans or grants from government sources. Similarly, we measure financial support from banks using a binary variable indicating that the business

had received loans from banks. Among the respondents, 27 per cent had received capital from banks and 8 per cent had received government financial support.

In another question we asked respondents to indicate along a 7-point scale (from 1=not at all to 7=to a very large extent) to what degree they had received valuable advice from banks and four different government actors (Innovation Norway, SIVA, NFR and the municipality). We recoded the responses into binary variables so that a score of five or higher indicates that the entrepreneur had received good advice from banks or from any of the four government actors. This recoding was necessary because most respondents had only been in contact with one or two of the four government actors. Among respondents, 14 per cent had received good advice from banks and 7 per cent from government actors.

Dependent variables

Firm births can be operationalized in many different ways, including founder's interpretations, new business registrations, initial transactions, initial profits, and initial employees (Reynolds, 2017). Since many new firms never hire employees and never become profitable, we define a business being born the year the firm carries out its initial transaction. This definition of business birth leads to an image of a fast start-up requiring little effort, with a high potential for successful birth, but with limited survival and low level of job creation (Reynolds, 2017).

Using data from the Norwegian tax authority, we coded annual transactions for each of the firms as earnings (or losses) different from zero. We calculated the proportion of businesses born between 2003 and 2015 as the accumulated percentage of firms that each year had carried out at least one transaction since registration in 2002. This variable indicates whether or not the firm is born (0=not born) and the number of years with transactions among firms that are born (endurance).

The outcome variables include accumulated figures for firm earnings, employment, sales (from 2003 to 2015) and endurance. The figures from the tax authorities contained annual earnings (or losses) before interests and taxes (EBIT), total labour costs (salaries and the firm's contribution to pension and social security), and sales revenues in each business (excluding VAT). We assigned a value of zero to businesses with missing values because they had no sales, labour costs or profits (losses) in a specific year. We adjusted all figures for inflation, and measure earnings, labour costs and sales in 2015 Norwegian Kroner. Our last measure of firm outcomes is endurance, measured by the number of years between 2003 and 2015 the firms had transactions, that is, earnings (or losses) different from zero. We measure endurance rather than firm survival because the year of firm birth in our data varies from 2003 to 2015 and since a firm that is born can have successive years as dormant with no economic transactions.

RESULTS

Support and Firm Births

Research question 1 concerns the relationship between receiving support from government and banks and business birth. Figures 15.1 and 15.2 illustrate how capital from banks and government is related to business birth. Here we compare firms with and without bank loans and government financing. In 2003, about 40 per cent of the firms with capital from banks were born (see Figure 15.1). Note that this means that 40 per cent of firms receiving bank loans were born and not that 40 per cent of born firms had received bank loans. This proportion gradually increases to close to 80 per cent in 2015. In other words, about 20 per cent of firms that did receive bank loans were never born. In comparison, less than 30 per cent of firms without bank loans were born in 2003, and only about 60 per cent of the firms were born by 2015. Loans from banks appears to have a strong and lasting positive effect on the probability of business birth.

Figure 15.2 illustrates the effect of government capital support. Firms that have received government capital are only slightly more likely to be born than firms that have not received such support. About 35 per cent of firms that did receive government funding were never born. The two lines concerning government financing in Figure 15.2 appear to be approximately parallel all years from 2003 to 2015, indicating that government capital support has a very small, but lasting effect on the probability of firm birth.

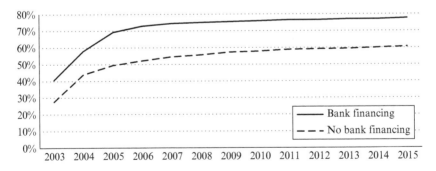

Figure 15.1   Accumulated percentage of born firms, bank financing

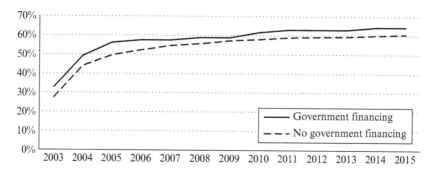

Figure 15.2   Accumulated percentage of born firms, government financing

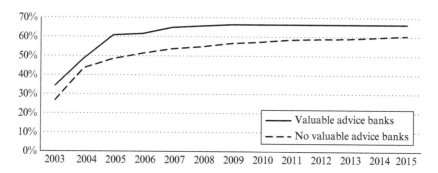

Figure 15.3   Accumulated percentage of born firms, valuable advice from banks

Figure 15.3 illustrates the effect of receiving good advice from banks. Good advice from banks appears to have a relatively strong and lasting effect on the probability of firm birth. In comparison, good advice from government (Figure 15.4) appears to have a relatively strong effect on the probability of firm birth the first years after registration, but this effect seems to decline over the years. The figures also suggest that good advice from government has a stronger effect on firm births the first years after registration (Figure 15.4) than capital from government (Figure 15.2).

Support and Firm Outcomes

Research question 2 concerns the relationship between government and bank support and subsequent business outcomes. The study of firm outcomes is only meaningful for firms that are born. Therefore, in this analysis we excluded the 411 firms (39.2 per cent) that never did carry

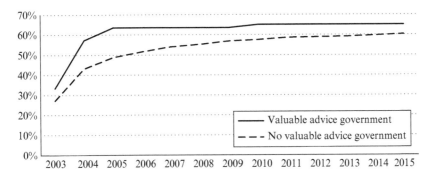

Figure 15.4   Accumulated percentage of born firms, valuable advice from government

Table 15.2   Spearman correlations between sources of finance, advice, and firm outcomes (n=603)

	Bank finance	Government finance	Bank advice	Government advice
Finance				
Bank finance	1			
Government finance	0.15*	1		
Advice				
Bank advice	0.42*	0.13*	1	
Government advice	0.06*	0.35*	0.17*	1
Firm outcomes				
Earnings	0.16*	−0.02	0.05	−0.04
Employment	0.17*	0.08	0.08	0.03
Sales	0.22*	0.04	0.12*	−0.02
Endurance	0.15*	0.02	0.10*	0.02

Note: Levels of statistical significance. * indicates p<.05 (two-tailed).

out any annual transactions. We also removed 34 respondents with incomplete datasets, leaving 603 respondents for the analysis. Since the dependent variables have a difficult non-normal distribution, we did not carry out any multivariate analysis, and only report non-parametric Spearman correlations. Table 15.2 shows the results.

Table 15.2 shows that bank loans to new businesses are significantly positively associated with all the dependent variables. In comparison, government capital to new businesses is not significantly associated with any of the four dependent variables. Good advice from banks is significantly positively associated with accumulated sales and endurance, that is, number of years with transactions. With respect to all the dependent variables, the effect of good advice from banks appears to be less positive than the effect of loans from banks. None of the correlations between good advice from government and firm outcomes are statistically significant.

To test the sensitivity of the findings, we examined the effect of recoding the advice items in different ways. The results remained robust and almost identical to those reported here. We also tested whether advice from different government agents influenced the results differently, but did not find that the effect of advice from the four government agents differed in any significant way.

DISCUSSION AND CONCLUSION

This study has focused on two key domains of entrepreneurial ecosystems – outsider support in terms of financing and good advice. The findings do not indicate any strong effect of government financial or non-financial support on business birth rates or subsequent firm performance. However, government advice to nascent entrepreneurs appears to be associated with slightly higher firm birth rates the first three years after registration. This finding is in line with Chrisman (1999) concerning the positive effect of government guidance on new firm creation. However, in contrast to Chrisman and McMullan (2000) and Chrisman et al. (2005), we failed to find any relationships between government advice and long-term performance. Loans from banks are associated with increased probability of business births. Further, such support is significantly associated with subsequent firm performance and endurance. Good advice from banks also relates significantly positively to sales revenues and firm endurance.

This study is a starting point for further research on the effects of government support on business birth and subsequent business outcomes. According to the entrepreneurship ecosystem literature there are several key players in the system such as, incubators and other policy initiatives. In this study we were not able to investigate how financing and advice interact with other domains of entrepreneurial ecosystems. Further research, using, for example, a case study methodology, could investigate how government support in terms of advice and financial capital can effectively contribute to new viable firms creating wealth and jobs. One issue to consider is the effect of government support through incubators.

Several factors determine the extent to which the government is willing to support the start-up of a new business in Norway. In an attempt to "pick winners", some new businesses receive government support because they have substantial potential for growth. However, growth prospects are usually not sufficient conditions for support. The government also emphasizes the extent to which the business is novel and represents something new to the marketplace. Innovative new businesses appear to be systematically favoured over businesses with high growth potential, possibly because the government fears that the growth in traditional new businesses comes at the expense of existing businesses.

To the extent the government in Norway is attempting to follow a strategy of "picking winners" among nascent entrepreneurs, they are not very successful. There are several political issues that make "picking winners" uncommon in Norway. For example, the government has a regional policy that favours the support to new businesses in rural areas threatened by depopulation. Many support measures are therefore aimed at agriculture and small businesses in sparsely populated areas. The government is also interested in increasing the rate of female entrepreneurs and is involved with promoting and supporting entrepreneurship among the unemployed and minorities, such as the Sami population and immigrants. Given this variety of political considerations, the effect of government support on business birth, growth, performance and survival is not likely to be particularly strong.

Limitations

It is possible that government support to new businesses stimulates new business among groups of entrepreneurs, such as entrepreneurs in areas with depopulation, women and minorities. The failure to investigate such possible effects is one of the shortcomings of the present study. Another possible limitation of this study is that we did not include a measure of the amount of capital and non-financial support provided by government agencies and banks. A further limitation is the representativeness of the sample. We are confident that the sample is representative of new businesses started during the four weeks of data collection, but cannot be certain that the sample is representative for all businesses registered in 2002 or successive years. Norway has had three different prime ministers since 2002, and changes in government sometimes means changes in politics. Therefore, the characteristics of nascent entrepreneurs and new businesses receiving government support in 2002 may be different from those eligible in later years. The current government support services may be more tuned towards high potential nascent entrepreneurs rather than charitable contributions to marginal new ventures, which appear to have been the case in 2002.

Implications

Despite the limitations, this study has several implications. The results presented here suggest that resources in terms of capital and advice obtained from banks are more important for firm birth and successive firm outcomes than resources obtained from government actors. According to the resource based view of the firm (Barney, 1991), this means that capital and advice from banks is either more valuable, more rare, more imitable or more non-substitutable than capital and advice from government actors.

Since support from banks is positively associated with business births and subsequent firm performance, government agencies should consider various strategic options to make their support more valuable to entrepreneurs. One possible strategy is a closer cooperation with banks. For example, the government should consider using more capital to top up funding of new ventures supported by banks, rather than base funding. Government funding agents should also consider evaluating new venture projects more similar to banks. This includes asking for collateral and checking the applicants' and the new ventures' ability to manage interests and loan repayments.

Nascent entrepreneurs who cannot get loans from banks or other commercial actors should consider this a serious warning about the prospects of the new venture. Managing a business without a serious bank to support you appears to be a very challenging task.

REFERENCES

Acs, Z. J., Autio, E., & Szerb, L. (2014). National systems of entrepreneurship: Measurement issues and policy implications. *Research Policy*, 43(3), 476–494.

Alvedalen, J., & Boschma R. (2017). A critical review of entrepreneurial ecosystems research: Towards a future research agenda. *European Planning Studies*, 25(6), 887–903.

Barney, J. (1991). Firm resources and sustained competitive advantage. *Journal of Management*, 17(1), 99–120.

Chandler, G. N., & Hanks, S. H. (1998). An examination of the substitutability of founders' human and financial capital in emerging business ventures. *Journal of Business Venturing*, 13(5), 353–369.

Chrisman, J. J. (1999). The influence of outsider-generated knowledge resources on venture creation. *Journal of Small Business Management*, 37(4), 42.

Chrisman, J. J., & McMullan, W. E. (2004). Outsider assistance as a knowledge resource for new venture survival. *Journal of Small Business Management*, 42(3), 229–244.

Chrisman, J. J., & McMullan, W. E. (2000). A preliminary assessment of outsider assistance as a knowledge resource: The longer-term impact of new venture counseling. *Entrepreneurship Theory and Practice*, 24(3), 37–53.

Chrisman, J. J., McMullan, E., & Hall, J. (2005). The influence of guided preparation on the long-term performance of new ventures. *Journal of Business Venturing*, 20(6), 769–791.

Cooper, A. C., Gimeno-Gascon, F. J., & Woo, C. Y. (1994). Initial human and financial capital as predictors of new venture performance. *Journal of Business Venturing*, 9(5), 371–395.

Cowling, M. (2010). The role of loan guarantee schemes in alleviating credit rationing in the UK. *Journal of Financial Stability*, 6(1), 36–44.

Cowling, M., & Mitchell, P. (2003). Is the small firms loan guarantee scheme hazardous for banks or helpful to small business? *Small Business Economics*, 21(1), 63–71.

Garcia-Tabuenca, A., & Crespo-Espert, J. L. (2010). Credit guarantees and SME efficiency. *Small Business Economics*, 35(1), 113–128.

Hart, M., & Lenihan, H. (2006). Estimating additionality and leverage: The interplay between public and private sector equity finance in Ireland (2000–2002). *Venture Capital*, 8(4), 331–351.

Isenberg, D. (2011). The entrepreneurship strategy as a new paradigm for economic policy: Principles for cultivating entrepreneurship, Babson Entrepreneurship Ecosystem Project, Babson College, Babson Park: MA.

Mason, C., & Brown, R. (2014). Entrepreneurial ecosystems and growth oriented entrepreneurship. Background paper prepared for the workshop organised by the OECD LEED Programme and the Dutch Ministry of Economic Affairs on Entrepreneurial Ecosystems and Growth Oriented Entrepreneurship, The Hague, the Netherlands.

Mole, K. F., Hart, M., Roper, S., & Saal, D. S. (2009). Assessing the effectiveness of business support services in England: Evidence from a theory-based evaluation. *International Small Business Journal*, 27(5), 557–582.

Oh, I., Lee, J.D., Heshmati, A., & Choi, G.G. (2009). Evaluation of credit guarantee policy using propensity score matching. *Small Business Economics*, 33(3), 335–351.

Pergelova, A., & Angulo-Ruiz, F. (2014). The impact of government financial support on the performance of new firms: The role of competitive advantage as an intermediate outcome. *Entrepreneurship and Regional Development*, 26(9–10), 663–705.

Reynolds, P.D. 2017. When is a firm born? Alternative criteria and consequences. *Business Economics*, 52(1), 41–56.

Robson, J. A., & Bennett, R. J. (2000). SME growth: The relationship with business advice and external collaboration. *Small Business Economics*, 15(3), 193–208.

Roper, S., & Hewitt-Dundas, N. (2001). Grant assistance and small firm development in Northern Ireland and the Republic of Ireland. *Scottish Journal of Political Economy*, 48(1), 99–117.

Rotger, G. P., Gørtz, M., & Storey D.J. (2012). Assessing the effectiveness of guided preparation for new venture creation and performance: Theory and practice. *Journal of Business Venturing*, 27(4), 506–521.

Shane, S. (2009). Why encouraging more people to become entrepreneurs is bad public policy. *Small Business Economics*, 33(2), 141–149.

Wren, C., & Storey, D.J. (2002). Evaluating the effect of soft business support upon small firm performance, *Oxford Economic Papers*, 54(2), 334–365.

PART III

UNIVERSITY-BASED SUPIEs

16. Bridging or isolating? The role of the university Technology Transfer Office in the start-up incubation ecosystem
Adam Novotny

1. INTRODUCTION

There is ambiguity regarding the idea of Technology Transfer Offices (TTO) in the current literature. Are they about maximizing the university's benefits from research activities, creating companies, or optimizing the business ecosystem? The TTO emerged in the literature as an actor with great potential for facilitating university–industry linkages owing to the Bayh-Dole Act (1980), which permitted higher education institutions to commercialize employees' inventions born from government-funded research (Agrawal, 2001). However, the number of TTOs, TTO staff and university patents started to grow in the U.S. well before the Bayh-Dole Act, already in the 1960s and 1970s (Mowery & Sampat, 2005). Initially, TTOs were created to protect and manage the intellectual property (IP) of higher education institutions and to provide additional research funding by selling the rights to use university-owned IP to firms (Feldman, Feller, Bercovitz, & Burton, 2002). Since then, establishing TTOs has become a worldwide trend at universities, and their interpretation has also broadened. Nowadays the TTO is seen as a significant promoter of research commercialization, a bridge between academia and industry (O'Gorman, Byrne, & Pandya, 2008), a key element in the creation and development of university spin-off firms (USOs) (Algieri, Aquino, & Succurro, 2013). This view of the TTO is in line with the entrepreneurial or "third mission" of universities, that is, the aspiration of becoming the engine for regional economic development and technological innovation (Etzkowitz, 1983; Florida, 1999; Wright, Clarysse, Mustar, & Lockett, 2007).

While some earlier findings show that the TTO has a positive impact on USO activity, more recent studies do not find such a clear relationship (Clarysse, Tartari, & Salter, 2011). The TTO's reputation has also been damaged by the fact that a significant proportion of university technologies reach industry application without any contribution or notice from the TTO (Huyghe, Knockaert, Piva, & Wright, 2016; Thursby & Kemp, 2002). Furthermore, it is unclear whether TTOs really aim at creating

USOs with strong potential for financial gain, that is, focus on quality, or rather regard a high spinout rate, that is, quantity, more important to show their relevance, improve their reputation, and attract more government funding (Djokovic & Souitaris, 2008). Critics highlight that formal changes in the university structure such as the creation of a TTO is not likely to cause "substantive" effects (e.g. high-growth firms) but remains a "symbolic" act that creates many lifestyle firms (Fini, Fu, Mathisen, Rasmussen, & Wright, 2016). While there is some evidence of the positive effect of the TTO on USO activity, it may be due to better data collection methods introduced as part of Bayh-Dole-type technology transfer systems rather than a real increase in the number of USOs created (Wright et al., 2007). Establishing TTOs and USOs is a simple way of complying with government initiatives but developing high-growth firms would need the entrepreneurial transformation of the whole university and the development of a new ecosystem, which is a complex and resource demanding process.

Nascent USOs need various resources to engage in entrepreneurial activities, but we regard participation in different ecosystem networks as a key resource that creates access to other vital resources. TTOs are often seen as critical actors in building and coordinating networks and partnerships within science-based entrepreneurial ecosystems by connecting nascent academic entrepreneurs with external actors to the firm and thus reshaping the "relational dynamics" in the region (Clayton, Feldman, & Lowe, 2018). While academic entrepreneurs regard the TTO as the primary source of connections, it often lacks the expertise to bridge the cultural gap between academia and industry (Muscio, 2010). We have scant knowledge on whether the TTO is capable of transforming "knowledge ecosystems" (hotspots of innovative start-ups centred around universities) into "business ecosystems" (complex networks of firms that combine skills and resources to create value), or it supports firms that follow an academic rather than commercial logic (Clarysse, Wright, Bruneel, & Mahajan, 2014). Bridging different social networks (academic and non-academic) is crucial for USO success, thus using a systems perspective is more suitable for understanding the role of external actors in USO development (Hayter, 2016).

This chapter investigates USOs' integration into the start-up incubation ecosystem (SUPIE) and the role of the TTO in building ecosystem networks for firms. It proposes a taxonomy of ecosystem networks in which USOs access support to survive and grow. We aim to contribute to the literature of technology transfer, academic entrepreneurship and entrepreneurial ecosystems by arguing that the TTO influences start-up success indirectly, by bridging firms with (or isolating them from) other ecosystem actors/networks that have the resources firms need to overcome their liabilities. We also contribute to network content research in the context of USOs by analysing the structure of spin-offs' ecosystem partners, and the types of stakeholder networks university start-ups are embedded in and which influence their resource profile and future growth potential. Exploring the main categories of USOs' ecosystem partners helps to better understand how entrepreneurial resources are generated, distributed and reconfigured within SUPIEs.

After reviewing the literature on the importance of the TTO in academic entrepreneurship and SUPIEs, this chapter empirically explores the role of the TTO in USOs' ecosystem networks. A key finding is that the TTO does not isolate USOs, but it seems to be less capable of integrating firms into non-academic/private ecosystem networks than academic/public ones. The findings are based on survey data collected from a representative sample of Norwegian USOs established between 1998 and 2012.

2. LITERATURE REVIEW

TTOs and Academic Entrepreneurship

The significance of TTOs in academic entrepreneurship is difficult to assess, as their organization, objectives and operations differ and evolve continuously, which process is influenced by their formal and informal activities and the different strategies and goals TTOs and their mother institution follow about the third mission (Cesaroni & Piccaluga, 2016; Muscio, 2010).

TTOs in the U.S., in particular, prefer licensing and IP protection to entrepreneurship and new venture creation (Jensen & Thursby, 2001; Markman, Phan, Balkin, & Gianiodis, 2005). Despite state-level economic policies, they incline toward maximizing cash flows and minimizing legal and financial risks associated with firm creation. TTOs are often seen as self-supporting, which expectation also reduces their willingness to take risks in equity (Feldman et al., 2002).

In Europe, competitiveness and innovation designated as a pan-European policy goal (European Council, 2000) have led to a stronger focus on USOs, considered as a driving force of modernizing industry (Algieri et al., 2013). The "European paradox" (i.e., the low impact of scientific research on industry development) also highlights the need for TTOs that can reduce information asymmetries between industry and universities (Debackere & Veugelers, 2005). A stronger emphasis on regional economic development in Europe is shown by the use of quality-related measures to evaluate USOs (e.g. income generated from ownership in firms, number of employees, turnover, equity value and time to exit) and a smaller lag behind the U.S. in USO activity compared to disclosures, patent applications and licenses (Balderi et al., 2007).

Technology transfer is more often associated with patenting and licensing than academic entrepreneurship (Agrawal, 2001; Geuna & Muscio, 2009) though USOs have high commercialization value as well (Rogers, Takegami, & Yin, 2001). The study of USOs as key technology transfer outcomes became more popular during the early 2000s (Siegel, Veugelers, & Wright, 2007). While creating USOs seems to be a better choice for the university than licensing, in reality very few disclosures (circa 3 per cent) are appropriate for commercialization via spin-off firms (Bray & Lee, 2000).

USOs need support to overcome their liabilities of newness and smallness (Freeman, Carroll, & Hannan, 1983; Stinchcombe, 1965), but the role of the TTO in academic entrepreneurship and especially after firm formation is debated (Rasmussen & Wright, 2015). Satisfaction with the TTO differs from country to country and even from one study to another. For example, TTOs appear to be more successful in the U.S. than in the U.K. (Chapple, Lockett, Siegel, & Wright, 2005) because American TTOs tend to employ staff with more industry experience (Gubitta, Tognazzo, & Destro, 2016). Another study found that American academic faculty is generally not satisfied with the capabilities of the TTO, which they regard as bureaucratic, inflexible (lacking "business-like" mentality) and in need of practical and marketing skills (Siegel, Waldman, & Link, 2003). The role of the TTO is regarded as "marginal" and "indirect" in commercialization and USO creation in Italy and the U.K. (Clarysse et al., 2011; Muscio, 2010). Algieri and colleagues (2013) find a "very high" probability for Italian TTOs to contribute to spin-off creation in the future. In Germany, the TTO is a must-have unit, a part of university bureaucracy, often without clear strategic orientation, which can hinder its additional effect (Hülsbeck, Lehmann, & Starnecker, 2013). Based on cases from Columbia University and Stanford University, Colyvas and colleagues (2002) suggest that the TTOs' competencies, in general, are not suitable for finding industry partners for ready-to-market technologies, but they can be crucial in managing embryonic innovations, when existing links with industry are weak, and participants of the transfer are not rooted in networks.

The TTO's performance can be related to organizational (internal) and environmental (external) factors (Chapple et al., 2005). Internal aspects include the TTO's size/number of staff (Caldera & Debande, 2010; Di Gregorio & Shane, 2003; O'Shea, Allen, Chevalier, & Roche, 2005), experience (Feldman et al., 2002; Powers & McDougall, 2005), skills and capabilities (Gómez Gras, Galiana Lapera, Mira Solves, Verdú Jover, & Sancho Azuar, 2008; Lockett & Wright, 2005), organizational structure (Battaglia, Landoni, & Rizzitelli, 2017; Brescia, Colombo, & Landoni, 2016; Chapple et al., 2005; Hülsbeck et al., 2013), internal reputation and legitimacy (Geuna & Muscio, 2009; O'Kane et al., 2015), business model and strategy (Markman et al., 2005), staffing, compensation and incentives practices (Markman et al., 2005), as well as its visibility within the university (Huyghe et al., 2016).

External aspects are independent of the TTO and include issues related to the university, as well as regional and national innovation policies (Chapple et al., 2005; Hülsbeck et al., 2013). University-level factors are, for instance, faculty quality, financial resources/research funding (Algieri et al., 2013; O'Shea et al., 2005), IP management policies, USO creation processes and faculty reward systems (Link & Siegel, 2005; Lockett & Wright, 2005).

TTO capabilities are often associated with regional characteristics and industrial clusters. A higher concentration of firms produces knowledge "spillovers" and more efficient supply of resources, including access to lawyers, venture capital (VC), consultants, entrepreneurs and industry-based researchers (Friedman & Silberman, 2003; Krugman, 1991). The growing number of USOs as we move from the south of Italy towards the north well illustrates the importance of the local ecosystem (Algieri et al., 2013). Focusing on profit-oriented firms with significant growth potential is a more common TTO strategy in innovative regions, suggesting a definite link between USO performance and regional innovation capabilities (Beraza-Garmendia & Rodríguez-Castellanos, 2015). Since entrepreneurship and USO incubation happen in the broader environment, we need to analyse the contribution of the TTO to firm development from an ecosystems perspective.

TTOs within SUPIEs

Academic entrepreneurship is often seen as the responsibility of the TTO, yet extant literature implies that the TTO staff alone is unlikely to commercialize university-born technologies. It is more plausible that instead of providing business and technology development services itself, the TTO contributes to USO development indirectly, i.e., by supporting academic entrepreneurs in building successful networks and obtaining critical resources from external ecosystem actors. Hence, in what follows, we focus on what we consider a vital role of the TTO in academic entrepreneurship, i.e., fitting spin-off firms into SUPIE networks.

Not a single actor but the whole system, comprising the university, TTO and other regional conditions and organizations, is needed to improve the innovative capacity of start-ups and the economic development of regions (González-Pernía, Kuechle, & Peña-Legazkue, 2013). Fini and colleagues (2011) highlight the importance of the collective impact of different forms of academic entrepreneurship and the interaction of determinants at the national, regional and organization level. Instead of isolated individuals and organizations, the social networks of academic and industry scientists, university administrators, TTO directors, company managers and entrepreneurs make a difference in technology transfer processes (Siegel, Waldman, Atwater, & Link, 2003). Universities should devote resources to create a "networking environment" that is capable of strengthening the social capital of researchers vital for increasing USO intention and activity (Moutinho, Au-Yong-Oliveira, Coelho, & Manso, 2016).

The TTO is often seen as the central organization in academic entrepreneurship ecosystems (Fini et al., 2011). Hayter and colleagues (2018) find entrepreneurs, TTOs and entrepreneur support programmes as the most common independent variables of academic ecosystem papers (the most usual dependent variables are related to spinoff outcomes). The assumed importance of TTOs can be explained by their relatively easy availability for university researchers who intend to commercialize technologies. TTOs, like science parks, business incubators and accelerators, provide knowledge-intensive services to innovative small firms and help their networking with industry stakeholders (Comacchio, Bonesso, & Pizzi, 2012). They are "bridges" between technological and business expertise (Muller & Zenker, 2001) and "boundary spanners" within universities (Aldrich & Herker, 1977). They facilitate the transfer of knowledge and technologies between isolated ecosystem actors who would otherwise not be in contact with each other. These activities go far beyond typical brokerage, as boundary spanners are supposed to increase the network density among key ecosystem actors, stimulate interpersonal relations between universities and industry (Comacchio et al., 2012). TTOs are "anchors" that promote relationships between different types of ecosystem actors (Clarysse et al., 2014), they are "signalling" organizations as they influence VC funding and firm growth when they evaluate USOs by providing them with public funds (Gubitta et al., 2016).

Academic entrepreneurs tend to rely on similar actors, such as the TTO, university incubator and experienced colleagues when they create and consolidate their firms; however, building relationships with non-academic actors will sooner or later be inevitable for the further development of the firm (Fernández-Alles, Camelo-Ordaz, & Franco-Leal, 2015). USOs, to survive and grow, must gradually strengthen their ties with actors external to the university and distance themselves from the academic environment (Vohora, Wright, & Lockett, 2004). Their long-term success will depend on whether they can get critical resources from different ecosystem partners at the right development stage (Bjørnåli & Gulbrandsen, 2010; Vohora et al., 2004). These vital resources include business (i.e., managerial and commercial) competencies as well as experience, financing (venture and seed capital), technological resources and market credibility (Fernández-Alles et al., 2015; Mosey & Wright, 2007; Vohora et al., 2004). Different public and private organizations own resources important at different start-up development stages (Fernández-Alles et al., 2015), thus joining local and international networks is vital for the healthy development of these firms.

Figure 16.1 outlines the proposed relationship among ecosystem actors within a SUPIE. Using an analogy of natural ecosystems, the TTO acts like parent birds who work hard to provide vital resources for the healthy growth of their nestlings (i.e., firms). USOs, like altricial young chicks, must gradually increase their independence from their nest and parents (i.e., the university and TTO) and leave their protected environment in time to develop survival skills themselves. Staying too long under the TTO's "wings" would prevent nascent firms from learning the ecosystem and practising how to acquire resources themselves.

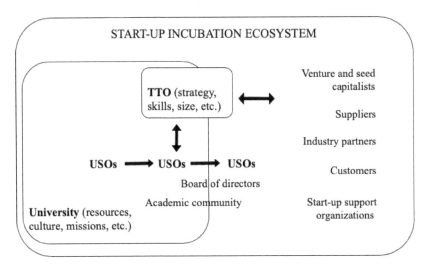

Figure 16.1   *The role of the TTO in the start-up incubation ecosystem. The TTO is a boundary spanner that helps USOs to develop and at the same time work themselves away from the academic environment*

Facilitating USOs' resource acquisition from external SUPIE actors, on the other hand, can be a challenging task. There is an "inherent tension" between academic and industry culture, and universities expect the TTO, a "resource constraint boundary spanner", to bridge the two distinct worlds (Huyghe & Knockaert, 2015, 2016). The success of USOs is much dependent on the quality and diversity of the university's stakeholder networks, but the network of the TTO is often limited (Hayter et al., 2018). While building collaborative networks is the most important driver of research commercialization, the role of the TTO in networks is generally perceived negatively by technology transfer stakeholders in Germany and Ireland (Boehm & Hogan, 2014). TTOs are supposed to become anchor tenants within knowledge ecosystems; however, they fail to achieve a "cross-realm transposition", that is, a transfer of logic among different organizations (Powell, Packalen, & Whittington, 2010). TTOs meet obstacles to gain legitimacy even within the university because of being a single agent of various principals (e.g., the university management and scientists) with different expectations (O'Kane et al., 2015).

Instead of centralizing the bridging role and controlling every interaction between academic faculty and industry partners ("hub model"), a dispersed technology transfer organization model could decrease the dependency on the limited capabilities of the TTO (Gümüsay & Bohné, 2018). Hiring professional, non-academic TTO managers can also help reduce cultural barriers, bridge the gap between scientists and industry, and make the creation of innovative start-ups and other forms of technology transfer less daunting (Friedman & Silberman, 2003; Muscio, 2010). TTOs who hire "hybrid employees" having both academic and industry experience can improve the "cognitive proximity" between academia and industry, which is especially useful for evaluating the feasibility of technology transfer projects (Villani, Rasmussen, & Grimaldi, 2015).

3.   CONTEXT

This chapter considers USO creation and development as the primary goal of TTOs, which is very relevant in the Norwegian context. A key policy tool for stimulating academic entrepreneurship in Norway is the FORNY programme, which was established during the 1990s to support the commercialization of publicly funded research in the country. The FORNY programme, operated by the Research Council of Norway, is implemented by allocating resources to TTOs that select and follow up technology transfer projects. The main direct output of the programme are start-up firms and licence agreements. In line with international trends,

Norway adopted the Bayh-Dole model of technology transfer in 2003, leading to an expansion in the number of TTOs between 2003 and 2005. While the number and organizational characteristics of TTOs are changing, at the time of the survey there were 14 TTOs (see Table 16.1): six in the Oslo region, four in southern and western Norway, two in mid-Norway and two in northern Norway. According to TTO websites, most of them emphasize commercializing technologies by creating and incubating start-up/spin-off ventures.

TTOs in Norway are heterogeneous regarding their size, strategy and location. Most are owned by a university or research institute, but large national and local companies can also have an ownership stake in them. Universities have a high level of autonomy in managing TTO operations, including staffing, specialization and strategies for commercialization. The largest TTOs with the most significant budget either operate at the largest universities (Trondheim, Oslo, Bergen) or serve a group of research institutes or university hospitals. They can obtain funds from the Research Council of Norway for various purposes including idea/project development, verification of technology, or competency building among their staff. TTO staff and managers can also receive incentive funding for top-notch technology transfer such as creating USOs with high potential for growth and external financing.

From a nationwide survey, Borlaug and colleagues (2009) found that establishing USOs and contributing to (regional) economic development is a major goal of TTOs, while they regard licensing and income generation less critical. TTOs' financial performance is skewed; Medinnova (Oslo), Sinvent (later SINTEF TTO), NTNU (Trondheim) and Bergen Technology Transfer together generated about 95 per cent of total TTO revenues when our survey was conducted. TTOs had seven employees on average in 2008 (NTNU was by far the largest in TTO staff) and relied on consultants occasionally, mainly in the field of business law. Among the average TTO staff, graduates of engineering, natural sciences, economics and business were overrepresented, and qualifications in medicine and law were underrepresented. Their boards had representatives from various areas including research, business, finance and the public sector.

TTOs apply different idea generation strategies; some are selective and focus on high-quality research groups, while others prefer a high number of disclosures. The majority of them have developed a formal procedure to evaluate projects; they typically assess ideas based on their market potential, available funding, business concept and stage of technology development. A key objective of Norwegian TTOs is selecting and taking equity positions in the highest growing USOs and choosing the right exit strategies. However, time to exit can take several years, and prospects

Table 16.1   The distribution of the sampled USOs by TTO

TTO	Location	Weight in the sample		Main ambition*
		Number of firms	Percentage of firms	
Oslo region		**57**	**36.79**	
1 Kjeller Innovation	Lillestrøm	29	18.7	Establishing successful companies providing solutions that society needs (in fields of energy, environment, community safety and bio-economics).
2 Inven2	Oslo	11	7.1	Building new businesses based on cutting-edge technology originating from its owners, University of Oslo and Oslo University Hospital.
3 Bioparken	Ås	8	5.2	Incubating and investing in technology companies (Bioparken AS has been discontinued).
4 Oslo Science Park	Oslo	5	3.2	Starting and growing businesses, contributing to economic growth and the commercialization of science, and being a catalyst for new companies (in ICT, biotech, medical technology, energy and environment).
5 Biomedical Innovation (BMI)	Oslo	3	1.9	Offering research and development of pharmaceutical products (later it started to focus on projects in later stages of commercialization).
6 Simula Innovation	Fornebu	1	0.7	Creating knowledge about fundamental scientific challenges that are of genuine value for society (in ICT).
Southern and Western Norway		**39**	**25.2**	
7 Prekubator	Stavanger	14	9.0	Commercializing innovations, identifying commercial potential, securing IP rights, licensing, business development and innovation management.

				Engaging as an active co-owner in innovative business ideas to create more scalable and innovative growth companies.
8 Coventure	Grimstad	12	7.7	
9 Bergen Technology Transfer (BTO)	Bergen	9	5.8	Helping owners and partners to bring their research results out to the market, ensuring that knowledge and inventions benefit individuals, the industry and society as a whole.
10 ForInnova	Bergen	4	2.6	Commercializing projects originating in research at the University of Bergen (predecessor to BTO).
Middle-Norway		**25**	**16.13**	
11 NTNU TTO	Trondheim	20	12.9	Securing, managing, developing, marketing and selling rights of use and property rights to knowledge, ideas, inventions and other intangible values created by NTNU and Helse Midt-Norge.
12 Sinvent (SINTEF TTO)	Trondheim	5	3.2	Developing commercial concepts from relevant research results (at SINTEF) and commercializing these either through selling technology, licensing or through establishing new spin-off companies.
Northern Norway		**38**	**24.52**	
13 Leiv Eiriksson Innovation (LEN)	Trondheim	17	11.0	Assisting start-up companies and budding entrepreneurs through consulting, courses and investor networks.
14 Norinnova	Tromsø	17	11.0	Developing research (developed at The Arctic University of Norway, The University Hospital of Northern Norway and Northern Research Institute) into new products and services with commercial value either by licensing or creating new start-ups.
Total		155	100	

Note: * Main goals are based on information gathered from TTO websites in 2018.

for successful exits are rather modest, which may be partly attributed to Norwegian USOs' modest market potential or TTO's ineffective technology selection strategies. Several TTOs, especially ones operating at multi-faculty universities, are likely to deal with embryonic technologies that are immature for VC funding. These technologies can expect finance from public support organizations such as Innovation Norway, which together with industry partners provide the majority of external capital for start-ups, and only a small proportion of USOs develop until the seed funding and VC phases.

4.   METHOD

The empirical part of the chapter is based on a questionnaire survey sent to USO founders in Norway between 2009 and 2013. The final sample consists of 155 firms who responded to the survey (response rate: 57.1 per cent) and were registered and observed in the FORNY programme. The responding firms were established between 2000 and 2012 and were about five years old on average (SD= 2.1). Response bias was not detected: chi-square tests revealed no significant difference at the 0.05 level between the respondents and non-respondents concerning technology type, industry partner, completed sales contract and VC acquisition. Hence, we can generalize from the sample to the population of Norwegian USOs.

A group of questions asked USO founders how important various ecosystem actors had been for the development of their firm. Likert-type scales were used to measure the perceived contributions received from different actors (0= not involved, 7= very important): the TTO, industry partners, the academic community (where the technology originated from), venture and seed capital firms, customers, suppliers, the board of directors, and public support organizations (e.g., government agencies, incubation programs). Contributions were measured to three development dimensions, that is, technology, firm and business/market credibility.

Table 16.2 presents the variables (contributions from different ecosystem actors) in decreasing order of their importance in USO development. USOs primarily rely on university researchers in developing technologies and establishing market credibility, but they mostly build on their board of directors in firm development. The TTO contributes more to the firm and its credibility than to technology development. After testing the unidimensionality and internal consistency of the three items (technology, firm, credibility) by principal component analysis and Cronbach's alpha respectively, we calculated composite scores for each ecosystem actor based on their means.

Table 16.2   *Descriptive statistics of SUPIE actor variables (n=155; 0=*
                not involved, 7= very important)

	Contribution to the development of. . .			Composite variables		
	Technology	Firm	Credibility	% of "not involved"	Mean	Std. Dev.
Academic community	4.30	3.13	4.47	8.40	3.97	2.15
Board of directors	2.82	3.92	3.77	11.0	3.51	2.05
TTO	2.33	3.38	3.28	16.1	3.00	2.13
Public support organizations	3.13	3.13	2.63	20.6	2.96	2.13
Customers	2.79	2.15	3.15	21.3	2.70	2.05
Industry partners	2.81	2.11	3.04	23.9	2.65	2.19
Venture and seed capitalists	1.24	1.87	1.62	48.4	1.58	2.04
Suppliers	1.72	1.19	1.55	43.2	1.49	1.75

Descriptive statistics revealed that during their early growth stages, USOs typically use the resources of academic/public ecosystem actors (university researchers, TTO, public support organizations) and those of their board of directors. Non-academic/private actors (customers, industry partners, venture and seed capitalists, suppliers) contribute less to early USO development.

We used correlational analyses and exploratory factor analysis (EFA) to investigate further the main categories of SUPIE actors used by USOs to develop. Correlations allow for testing whether reliance on TTO couples with more (or less) support from other actors. An inverse association between the contribution of the TTO and those of other actors indicated that the TTO isolates USOs within the ecosystem; while a positive relationship showed that the TTO acts as a bridge between actors. Furthermore, we used EFA to explore the taxonomy of ecosystem actors, i.e., groups of actors whose resources are likely to be combined by USOs during their early development.

5. RESULTS

Table 16.3 depicts the direction, strength and significance of the relationships between the studied variables. The first column relates to our central

Table 16.3   Correlation coefficients (in decreasing order of association with the TTO)

	(1)	(2)	(3)	(4)	(5)	(6)	(7)	(8)
(1) TTO	1							
(2) Academic community	0.331***	1						
(3) Public support organizations	0.247**	0.195*	1					
(4) Suppliers	0.199*	0.123	0.236**	1				
(5) Industry partners	0.184*	0.111	0.175*	0.438***	1			
(6) Venture and seed capitalists	0.173*	−0.010	0.209**	0.102	0.147	1		
(7) Board of directors	0.162*	0.279***	0.423***	0.238**	0.146	0.236**	1	
(8) Customers	0.043	0.089	0.172*	0.515***	0.381***	0.157	0.082	1

Notes: n=155; * p< 0.05; ** p< 0.01; *** p< 0.001.

question of interest, the association between the contributions of the TTO and those of other ecosystem actors. Pearson correlation coefficients show that firms who cooperate more with the TTO also rely more on other SUPIE actors, except for customers, in which case the association is not significant at the 0.05 level. More importantly, the TTO's contribution is more likely to be combined with support from the academic community and public support organizations than that of non-academic and private actors.

To propose a taxonomy of ecosystem networks, that is, groups of actors whose resources are used in combination by spin-off firms, we conducted EFA with oblique (promax) rotation warranted by the relatively strong correlations among factors. Four factors have been extracted, as shown by Table 16.4, identifying four types of ecosystem actors: "market partners" (industry partners, customers and suppliers), "support providers" (board of directors and public support organizations), "the university nest" (the TTO and university colleagues) and "financial mentors" (venture and seed capital firms). The contribution firms receive in the university nest is more likely to be accompanied by the resources of support providers than those of market partners and financial mentors (Table 16.5).

Table 16.4   Categories of ecosystem networks (oblique-rotated pattern matrix for the four-factor model)

Ecosystem actors	Factor 1 Market partners	Factor 2 Support providers	Factor 3 University nest	Factor 4 Financial mentors
Industry partners	**0.516**	−0.054	0.098	0.069
Customers	**0.680**	−0.008	−0.094	0.000
Suppliers	**0.680**	0.065	0.032	−0.045
Board of directors	0.002	**0.574**	0.033	0.019
Public support organizations	0.055	**0.467**	0.059	0.080
TTO	−0.025	−0.019	**0.508**	0.114
Academic community	0.014	0.135	**0.456**	−0.148
Venture and seed capitalists	−0.017	0.185	−0.047	**0.337**

Table 16.5   Bivariate correlations among factors

Factors	Market partners	Support providers	University nest	Financial mentors
Market partners	1			
Support providers	0.380	1		
University nest	0.372	0.631	1	
Financial mentors	0.501	0.503	0.279	1

6.   CONCLUSION

This chapter aimed to explore the role of the TTO in SUPIEs by examining its importance in bridging firms with other ecosystem actors that help USOs overcome their liabilities of smallness and newness. Literature suggests that university scientists are disposed to use the networks of the TTO to reach outside the academic sector and establish profitable partnerships with external SUPIE actors. However, previous results have questioned the role and capability of the TTO in bringing isolated ecosystem actors together to create an optimal combination of resources, embedded in various ecosystem networks, for USO development.

The university TTO is typically expected to provide IP management, technology development, and business development services for scientist and nascent USOs, as well as acting as a bridge builder, boundary spanner, or anchor organization within the broader ecosystem. In this chapter we focused on the latter roles of the TTO, that is, integrating USOs into

SUPIEs by connecting different types of ecosystem networks such as academic and non-academic, public and private. A key question for USOs is whether they can absorb resources, grow and gradually move away from the university and find their own places as standalone businesses. While TTOs try to provide several technology transfer services, it is more important that they help nascent spin-offs to fit into the ecosystem and maximize the inflow of resources to their balance sheets. However, accessing resources is a non-trivial issue owing to the clash of cultures between university spin-offs and those actors that might provide resources.

Based on correlations and exploratory factor analyses of the perceived importance of contributions received from various SUPIE actors, we found that (a) USOs rely more on the resources of academic/public ecosystem actors than on the resources of non-academic/private actors; (b) USO founders who depend more on the TTO also rely more on other ecosystem actors, including non-academic/private ones; however, (c) USOs' use of the TTO is more likely to be coupled with support from academic/public actors than non-academic/private ones. We also proposed a taxonomy of ecosystem networks, that is, groups of actors whose resources are typically used in combination by USOs. These are: *market partners* (industry partners, customers, and suppliers), *support providers* (board of directors and public support organizations), *the university nest* (TTO and the university) and *financial mentors* (venture and seed capitalists).

Findings imply that the role of the TTO is not black-and-white in start-up development. The TTO seems to have the capabilities to bridge USOs with other ecosystem actors external to the university, but it is more successful in connecting firms with academic and public actors that have a similar (not so much business-like) logic to the TTO. The TTO does not seem to inhibit the growth of diverse entrepreneurship networks vital for USO success, but it is liable to reinforce the academic nature of firms. In other words, USOs relying too heavily on the TTO's services will probably find it more difficult to distance themselves from the academic environment, which would be necessary for their survival and future development.

Findings also nuance our knowledge on how USOs gain access to resources embedded in SUPIEs, i.e., the role of the TTO in transferring key resources to USOs by bridging them with different types of ecosystem networks. An important implication for TTOs and universities is that they should put more effort into connecting USOs with non-academic and private SUPIE actors, such as venture capitalists, industry partners, customers and suppliers if they want to provide firms with a healthy combination of resources. The TTO should not encourage spin-off firms to "stick around" the university nest but rather help them move away from the academic culture and integrate into local, national, and international business ecosystems. Enjoying the safety of the university nest for long prevents firms from learning how to survive and develop on their own and can lead to more lifestyle firms, the unproductive use of resources, and eventually cause a social loss.

This study has some limitations deriving from its exploratory and cross-sectional nature. Thus, future research would benefit from paying closer attention to the effects of the TTO's involvement in firm development, for example, to the question of how different SUPIE networks and USO resource acquisition strategies influence the subsequent performance of firms and the outcomes of technology transfer processes. Since network resources facilitate the flow of all ecosystem resources, different types of networks or more diverse ecosystem relations are likely to have different performance outcomes for USOs and their stakeholders.

REFERENCES

Agrawal, A. K. (2001). University-to-industry knowledge transfer: Literature review and unanswered questions. *International Journal of Management Reviews, 3*, 285–302.

Aldrich, H., & Herker, D. (1977). Boundary spanning roles and organization structure. *Academy of Management Review, 2*(2), 217–230.

Algieri, B., Aquino, A., & Succurro, M. (2013). Technology transfer offices and academic spin-off creation: The case of Italy. *The Journal of Technology Transfer, 38*, 382–400. https://doi.org/10.1007/s10961-011-9241-8

Balderi, C., Butelli, P., Conti, G., Di Minin, A., Piccaluga, A., della Liberta, P. M., . . . per Monteroni, V. (2007). Towards an Italian way of public research valorisation. The importance of time and commitment. *R&D Management* (June 2016).

Battaglia, D., Landoni, P., & Rizzitelli, F. (2017). Organizational structures for external growth of University Technology Transfer Offices: An explorative analysis. *Technological Forecasting and Social Change*. https://doi.org/10.1016/j.techfore.2017.06.017

Beraza-Garmendia, J. M., & Rodríguez-Castellanos, A. (2015). Characteristics and effectiveness of university spin-off support programmes. *Academia Revista Latinoamericana de Administración, 28*(1), 14–44.

Bjørnåli, E. S., & Gulbrandsen, M. (2010). Exploring board formation and evolution of board composition in academic spin-offs. *The Journal of Technology Transfer, 35*(1), 92–112.

Boehm, D. N., & Hogan, T. (2014). 'A jack of all trades': The role of PIs in the establishment and management of collaborative networks in scientific knowledge commercialisation. *The Journal of Technology Transfer, 39*(1), 134–149.

Borlaug, S. B., Grünfeld, L., Gulbrandsen, M., Rasmussen, E., Rønning, L., Spilling, O. R., & Vinogradov, E. (2009). Between entrepreneurship and technology transfer: Evaluation of the FORNY programme. In *Report 19* (p. 160). Oslo: NIFU STEP.

Bray, M. J., & Lee, J. N. L. (2000). University revenues from technology transfer: Licensing fees vs. equity positions. *Journal of Business Venturing, 15*(5–6), 385–392. https://doi.org/10.1016/S0883-9026(98)00034-2

Brescia, F., Colombo, G., & Landoni, P. (2016). Organizational structures of Knowledge Transfer Offices: An analysis of the world's top-ranked universities. *Journal of Technology Transfer, 41*(1), 132–151. https://doi.org/10.1007/s10961-014-9384-5

Caldera, A., & Debande, O. (2010). Performance of Spanish universities in technology transfer: An empirical analysis. *Research Policy*, *39*(9), 1160–1173.

Cesaroni, F., & Piccaluga, A. (2016). The activities of university knowledge transfer offices: towards the third mission in Italy. *The Journal of Technology Transfer*, *41*(4), 753–777. https://doi.org/10.1007/s10961-015-9401-3

Chapple, W., Lockett, A., Siegel, D., & Wright, M. (2005). Assessing the relative performance of UK university technology transfer offices: Parametric and non-parametric evidence. *Research Policy*, *34*, 369–384.

Clarysse, B., Tartari, V., & Salter, A. (2011). The impact of entrepreneurial capacity, experience and organizational support on academic entrepreneurship. *Research Policy*, *40*, 1084–1093. https://doi.org/http://dx.doi.org/10.1016/j.respol.2011.05.010

Clarysse, B., Wright, M., Bruneel, J., & Mahajan, A. (2014). Creating value in ecosystems: Crossing the chasm between knowledge and business ecosystems. *Research Policy*, *43*(7), 1164–1176. https://doi.org/10.1016/j.respol.2014.04.014

Clayton, P., Feldman, M., & Lowe, N. (2018). Behind the scenes: Intermediary organizations that facilitate science commercialization through entrepreneurship. *Academy of Management Perspectives*, *32*(1), 104–124.

Colyvas, J., Crow, M., Gelijns, A., Mazzoleni, R., Nelson, R. R., Rosenberg, N., & Sampat, B. N. L. B. (2002). How do university inventions get into practice? *Management Science*, *48*, 61–72.

Comacchio, A., Bonesso, S., & Pizzi, C. (2012). Boundary spanning between industry and university: the role of Technology Transfer Centres. *The Journal of Technology Transfer*, *37*(6), 943–966.

Debackere, K., & Veugelers, R. (2005). The role of academic technology transfer organizations in improving industry science links. *Research Policy*, *34*(3), 321–342.

Di Gregorio, D., & Shane, S. (2003). Why do some universities generate more start-ups than others? *Research Policy*, *32*, 209–227. Retrieved from internal-pdf://0996535662/scholar. enw LB – 5.14

Djokovic, D., & Souitaris, V. L. B. (2008). Spinouts from academic institutions: a literature review with suggestions for further research. *Journal of Technology Transfer*, *33*, 225–247.

Etzkowitz, H. (1983). Entrepreneurial scientists and entrepreneurial universities in American academic science. *Minerva*, *21*(2–3), 198–233.

European Council. (2000). Presidency Conclusions. Lisbon Summit. *23-24 March. Nr: 100/1/00.*

Feldman, M., Feller, I., Bercovitz, J., & Burton, R. (2002). Equity and the technology transfer strategies of American research universities. *Management Science*, *48*(1), 105–121. https://doi.org/10.1287/mnsc.48.1.105.14276

Fernández-Alles, M., Camelo-Ordaz, C., & Franco-Leal, N. (2015). Key resources and actors for the evolution of academic spin-offs. *The Journal of Technology Transfer*, *40*(6), 976–1002.

Fini, R., Fu, K., Mathisen, M. T., Rasmussen, E., & Wright, M. (2016). Institutional determinants of university spin-off quantity and quality: a longitudinal, multilevel, cross-country study. *Small Business Economics*, 1–31. https://doi.org/10.1007/s11187-016-9779-9 LB – Fini2016

Fini, R., Grimaldi, R., Santoni, S., & Sobrero, M. (2011). Complements or substitutes? The role of universities and local context in supporting the creation of academic spin-offs. *Research Policy*, *40*(8), 1113–1127.

Florida, R. (1999). The role of the university: Leveraging talent, not technology. *Issues in Science and Technology*, *15*(4), 67–73.

Freeman, J., Carroll, G. R., & Hannan, M. T. (1983). The liability of newness: Age dependence in organizational death rates. *American Sociological Review*, 692–710.

Friedman, J., & Silberman, J. (2003). University technology transfer: Do incentives, management, and location matter? *The Journal of Technology Transfer*, *28*, 17–30.

Geuna, A., & Muscio, A. (2009). The governance of university knowledge transfer: A critical review of the literature. *Minerva*, *47*, 93–114.

Gómez Gras, J. M., Galiana Lapera, D. R., Mira Solves, I., Verdú Jover, A. J., & Sancho Azuar, J. L. B. (2008). An empirical approach to the organisational determinants of spin-off creation in European universities. *The International Entrepreneurship and Management Journal*, *4*(2), 187–198. https://doi.org/10.1007/s11365-007-0061-0

González-Pernía, J. L., Kuechle, G., & Peña-Legazkue, I. (2013). An assessment of the determinants of university technology transfer. *Economic Development Quarterly*, *27*(1), 6–17.

Gubitta, P., Tognazzo, A., & Destro, F. (2016). Signaling in academic ventures: the role of technology transfer offices and university funds. *Journal of Technology Transfer*, *41*(2), 368–393. https://doi.org/10.1007/s10961-015-9398-7

Gümüsay, A. A., & Bohné, T. M. (2018). Individual and organizational inhibitors to the development of entrepreneurial competencies in universities. *Research Policy*, *47*(2), 363–378.

Hayter, C. S. (2016). A trajectory of early-stage spinoff success: The role of knowledge intermediaries within an entrepreneurial university ecosystem. *Small Business Economics*, *47*(3), 633–656.

Hayter, C. S., Nelson, A. J., Zayed, S., & O'Connor, A. C. (2018). Conceptualizing academic entrepreneurship ecosystems: a review, analysis and extension of the literature. *The Journal of Technology Transfer*, 1–44.

Hülsbeck, M., Lehmann, E. E., & Starnecker, A. (2013). Performance of technology transfer offices in Germany. *The Journal of Technology Transfer*, *38*(3), 199–215. https://doi.org/10.1007/s10961-011-9243-6

Huyghe, A., & Knockaert, M. (2015). The influence of organizational culture and climate on entrepreneurial intentions among research scientists. *The Journal of Technology Transfer*, *40*(1), 138–160.

Huyghe, A., & Knockaert, M. (2016). The Relationship Between University Culture and Climate and Research Scientists' Spin-off Intentions. In *University Evolution, Entrepreneurial Activity and Regional Competitiveness* (pp. 3–26). Springer.

Huyghe, A., Knockaert, M., Piva, E., & Wright, M. (2016). Are researchers deliberately bypassing the technology transfer office? An analysis of TTO awareness. *Small Business Economics*, *47*(3), 589–607. https://doi.org/10.1007/s11187-016-9757-2

Jensen, R., & Thursby, M. (2001). Proofs and prototypes for sale: The licensing of university inventions. In *American Economic Review* (Vol. 91).

Krugman, P. (1991). Increasing returns and economic geography. *Journal of Political Economy*, *99*(3), 483–499.

Link, A. N., & Siegel, D. S. (2005). Generating science-based growth: An econometric analysis of the impact of organizational incentives on university–industry technology transfer. *European Journal of Finance*, *11*(3), 169–181.

Lockett, A., & Wright, M. (2005). Resources, capabilities, risk capital and the creation of university spin-out companies. *Research Policy*, *34*, 1043–1057.

Markman, G. D., Phan, P. H., Balkin, D. B., & Gianiodis, P. T. (2005). Entrepreneurship and university-based technology transfer. *Journal of Business Venturing*, *20*, 241–263.

Mosey, S., & Wright, M. (2007). From human capital to social capital : A longitudinal study of technology-based academic entrepreneurs. *Entrepreneurship Theory and Practice*, *31*(6), 909–935. https://doi.org/10.1111/j.1540-6520.2007.00203.x

Moutinho, R., Au-Yong-Oliveira, M., Coelho, A., & Manso, J. P. (2016). Determinants of knowledge-based entrepreneurship: An exploratory approach. *International Entrepreneurship and Management Journal*, *12*(1), 171–197.

Mowery, D., & Sampat, B. (2005). The Bayh-Dole act of 1980 and university-industry technology transfer: A model for other OECD governments? *Essays in Honor of Edwin Mansfield*, 233–245.

Muller, E., & Zenker, A. (2001). Business services as actors of knowledge transformation: The role of KIBS in regional and national innovation systems. *Research Policy*, *30*(9), 1501–1516.

Muscio, A. (2010). What drives the university use of technology transfer offices? Evidence from Italy. *The Journal of Technology Transfer*, *35*, 181–202.

O'Gorman, C., Byrne, O., & Pandya, D. (2008). How scientists commercialise new knowledge via entrepreneurship. *Journal of Technology Transfer, 33*(1), 23–43. https://doi.org/10.1007/s10961-006-9010-2

O'Kane, C., Mangematin, V., Geoghegan, W., Fitzgerald, C., O'Kane, C., Mangematin, V., . . . Fitzgerald, C. (2015). University technology transfer offices: The search for identity to build legitimacy. *Research Policy, 44*(2), 421–437. https://doi.org/http://dx.doi.org/10.1016/j.respol.2014.08.003

O'Shea, R. P., Allen, T. J., Chevalier, A., & Roche, F. (2005). Entrepreneurial orientation, technology transfer and spinoff performance of US universities. *Research Policy, 34*, 994–1009.

O'Shea, Rory P., Allen, T. J., Chevalier, A., & Roche, F. (2005). Entrepreneurial orientation, technology transfer and spinoff performance of US universities. *Research Policy, 34*(7), 994–1009. https://doi.org/10.1016/j.respol.2005.05.011

Powell, W. W., Packalen, K., & Whittington, K. (2010). Organizational and Institutional Genesis: The Emergence of High Tech Clusters in the Life Sciences. *The Emergence of Organizations and Markets*, 434–465.

Powers, J. B., & McDougall, P. (2005). Policy orientation effects on performance with licensing to start-ups and small companies. *Research Policy, 34*, 1028–1042.

Rasmussen, E., & Wright, M. (2015). How can universities facilitate academic spin-offs? An entrepreneurial competency perspective. *The Journal of Technology Transfer, 40*(5), 782–799.

Rogers, E. M., Takegami, S., & Yin, J. (2001). Lessons learned about technology transfer. *Technovation, 21*, 253–261.

Siegel, D. S., Veugelers, R., & Wright, M. (2007). Technology transfer offices and commercialization of university intellectual property: Performance and policy implications. *Oxford Review of Economic Policy, 23*(4), 640–660.

Siegel, D. S., Waldman, D. A., Atwater, L. E., & Link, A. N. (2003). Commercial knowledge transfers from universities to firms: Improving the effectiveness of university-industry collaboration. *Journal of High Technology Management Research, 14*(1), 111–133. https://doi.org/10.1016/S1047-8310(03)00007-5

Siegel, D. S., Waldman, D., & Link, A. (2003). Assessing the impact of organizational practices on the relative productivity of university technology transfer offices: An exploratory study. *Research Policy, 32*, 27–48.

Stinchcombe, A. L. (1965). Social structure and organizations. In J. P. March (Ed.), *Handbook of organizations* (pp. 142–193). Chicago: Rand McNally.

Thursby, J. G., & Kemp, S. (2002). Growth and productive efficiency of university intellectual property licensing. *Research Policy, 31*, 109–124.

Villani, E., Rasmussen, E., & Grimaldi, R. (2015). How intermediary organizations facilitate technology transfer: A proximity approach. *Academy of Management Proceedings, 2015*(1), 13440. Academy of Management Briarcliff Manor, NY 10510.

Vohora, A., Wright, M., & Lockett, A. (2004). Critical junctures in the development of university high-tech spinout companies. *Research Policy, 33*(1), 147–175.

Wright, M., Clarysse, B., Mustar, P., & Lockett, A. (2007). Academic entrepreneurship in Europe. In *Academy of Management Learning Education* (Vol. 8). https://doi.org/10.4337/9781847205575

17. The key drivers for emergence of an entrepreneurial ecosystem – the role of brokerage, role models and inspiration
Karolina Lesniak and Roger Sørheim

INTRODUCTION

In the last decades of the twentieth century, a little known environment surrounding a technical university in Norway generated a number of highly successful technological companies and gave rise to what became a high-tech entrepreneurial ecosystem (EE). Among these companies was Silicon Valley's first Scandinavian investment, the main competitor to Google's search engine, and future leading semiconductor design centers. However, new ventures are not created in a void; they need favorable conditions to emerge and grow. Fueled by the success of places such as Silicon Valley and Boulder Colorado, the concept of EE emerged as an approach to defining and understanding the structure and functioning of environments that positively stimulate the development of new innovation-based companies.

Previously, research has focused on EEs from a geographical perspective (Stam, 2015), university EEs (Miller & Acs, 2017), and the role of social capital within EEs (Theodoraki et al., 2018). Interestingly, past studies omitted a closer investigation into the origins of EEs (Mason & Brown, 2014). The purpose of this chapter is therefore to investigate the process of an organic emergence of an EE. It does so by looking into two research questions: *what are the key drivers for the emergence of an EE* and *how do the key drivers for the emergence of an EE operate?*

The empirical context of this study is a historical EE that grew out of a technical university. The university nurtured young talented students, who became tech entrepreneurs and key players in the developing new industries in Norway. This particular case was chosen for several reasons. First, at that point in time, neither entrepreneurship nor innovation were encouraged or stimulated in any way at the university. Second, both companies and individuals came from the same university environment. Third, the case shows a highly specialized ecosystem that hosted high-tech companies that either commercialized innovative research or developed new technologically advanced products. Furthermore, since it is a historical case, both the key drivers of the EE's emergence and its operation are possible to discern.[1]

Consequently, the study offers insights into the organic process by which a specialized ecosystem emerged. The key drivers of the process were engaged individuals, who operated through brokerage, role modeling, and inspiration to involuntarily create a high-performing and specialized ecosystem. Furthermore, the study presents the importance of interactions between committed professors and talented students in developing a university based EE. The subsequent section presents a short review of the relevant theoretical perspectives, which was developed through an iterative process with collected data. This is followed by a presentation of the methods applied and the results. The results section is in a narrative form to give background details to both the historical ecosystem and the empirical findings discussed in the subsequent section. The study is concluded with a summary of findings and the implications of the case for research and practice.

FRAME OF REFERENCE

EE is understood as a "set of interdependent actors and factors coordinated in such a way that enables productive entrepreneurship within a particular territory" (Stam & Spiegel, 2017). The most important element of the EE approach is the interdependency of both actors and institutions, which leads to new venture creation (Acs, Stam, Audretsch & O'Connor, 2017). Entrepreneurial ecosystems come to life "in response to specific circumstances, usually operating in combination" (Mason & Brown, 2014, p. 27). Companies that originate in EEs can create spillover effects that create further entrepreneurial opportunities (Audretsch & Belitski, 2017). In other words, an EE is fueled by new ventures that are established within it and operates on the assumption that such ventures will constantly spin off new ventures, thus contributing to the growth and evolution of the ecosystem (Mason & Brown, 2014). The character of an ecosystem may also influence the type of companies growing in it (Autio, Kenney, Mustar, Siegel & Wright, 2014).

Universities, as knowledge producing organizations (Stam, 2015), are crucial for entrepreneurial innovation (Autio et al., 2014). Recently, they gained the status of "hubs of entrepreneurship" (Miller & Acs, 2017) that have internal EEs (Mason & Brown, 2014). The greatest attention in the literature on university entrepreneurship has been placed on the institutionalized support system for commercialization, i.e., university policy, while there has been little focus on students' place in the process of technology transfer (Siegel & Wright, 2015). There is very little evidence regarding how EEs influence students and the actual role that students play in the further development of EEs (Siegel and Wright, 2015).

Following Feld (2012), Stam (2015) presents the attributes of a successful ecosystem as: leadership, intermediaries, network density, government, talent, support services, engagement, companies, and capital (p. 1762). Leadership is understood as a group of key entrepreneurs who are "visible" within the community and take an active role in its development. Stam (2015) continues to claim that the key factors for successful ecosystems are entrepreneurs, who act as "feeders" of the ecosystem – both entrepreneurs and specialized support organizations. Similarly, Hayter (2016) recognizes the role of "knowledge intermediaries" as connectors between academic and business knowledge in the case of university entrepreneurship. People also play an important role in the process of information brokerage that contributes to new ventures gaining legitimacy within and outside of the EE (Kuratko, Fisher, Bloodgood & Hornsby, 2017). Brokers are individuals who, through their access to various groups with various proficiencies and knowledge sets, can "connect" ideas and information by gapping the "holes" between them (Burt, 2005).

People within an EE can stimulate its development by serving as role models and inspiration (Isenberg, 2010). Role models, understood as individuals who are seen as worth acting like because they have desired features or achievements (Nauta & Kokaly, 2001), can influence others regarding the decision to start an entrepreneurial career (Stam, 2009). Role models also have a place in the learning process, as people can learn by observing and imitating the behavior of others in their environment (Bandura, 1986). Entrepreneurial role models can positively influence the tolerance toward risk and the understanding of entrepreneurial activity (Stam, 2009). In addition, role models can become a "trigger" for starting a new venture (Nabi, Linan, Fayolle, Krueger & Walmsley, 2017).

Role models can also serve as inspiration (Jung, 1986). Inspiration, in turn, combines motivation, willingness, and action toward a certain goal and can be triggered by a person or an event (Thrash & Elliot, 2003). It has two levels: theoretical (i.e., from external origins such as colleagues or literature), and practical (i.e., through active participation) (Nabi et al., 2017). In the context of entrepreneurship, inspiration is often seen in relation to the outcomes of entrepreneurship education (Nabi et al., 2017; Souitaris, Zerbinati & Al-Laham, 2007). As established by Souitaris et al. (2007), teachers in the university context can have a broader role than simply being disseminators of knowledge – they can trigger positive change in students' entrepreneurial attitudes and behaviors through the "change of hearts and change of minds."

Moreover, it has been shown that successful graduates can be both role models and inspiration for high school students (Tjas, Nelson & Taylor, 1997). When considering entrepreneurship in the university context, these important roles are played by both professors (Van Auken, Fry & Stephens 2006; Souitaris et al., 2007) and university peers (Kacperczyk, 2013). Van Auken et al. (2006) claims that direct interaction with role models such as professors will increase entrepreneurial awareness among students. Simultaneously, entrepreneurial peers can have a direct impact on the decision to start one's own company, as seeing peers who successfully established new ventures validates one's skills and abilities (Kacperczyk, 2013).

METHODOLOGICAL APPROACH

The study was initially motivated by an interest in the history of tech entrepreneurs coming from a specific class at a university and the connections between them and the environment. A case study design (Yin, 2014; Eisenhardt, 1989) is employed, with an abductive approach to the use of theory (Baxter, 2010). A case study approach was deemed suitable, as it is a relevant method for the in-depth exploration of a complex phenomenon that is not clearly divided from its context (Yin, 2014). Moreover, a single case study can be a compelling illustration of an unusual phenomenon (Siggelkow, 2007). The historical case explored in this study is an unusual example of how EEs emerge through people's interactions and engagements without outside stimulation due to the level of success of the ecosystem in question.

The primary data collection was proceeded by a desktop research phase to establish the timeline of events, a list of informants, and potential emerging themes for the interviews. In this phase, the secondary data was gathered (this comprised business databases, the LinkedIn profiles of entrepreneurs, and newspaper articles about the history of the companies involved). This phase was followed by informal interviews with people with knowledge of the ecosystem to establish factual details. The primary data collection took place between November 2016 and March 2017 and consisted of semi-structured interviews (Dunn, 2010) with 16 informants and a total of 24 hours of interviews. These interviews were with tech entrepreneurs who belonged to the class of 1991–1992 (8 informants, 12 hours), other students from the class (4 informants, 6 hours), professors who taught them (2 informants, 3 hours), and other professors (2 hours, 3 informants). Interview guides were prepared separately for each informant category, with the use of interview techniques suggested by Cook and Crang (2007) – that is, starting with factual information, going through informants' descriptions of the historical events, and then going on to more advanced questions about events and opinions. Interview data was supported by historical books about the Norwegian University of Science and Technology (NTNU, previously NTH) and its environment, business databases, officially accessible articles, and videos of and about individuals and companies involved in the case.

The data was analyzed according to an explorative matrix building approach, as suggested by Miles, Huberman, and Saldana (2014). First, the categories related to the EE in question were devised (including topics such as "university environment," "industry cooperation," or "social relations"). Then, more detailed matrices were created that focused on the key drivers of the emergence of the EE. Through an iterative approach, the categories were confronted with existing theoretical insights, as proposed by Baxter (2010), and this led to the development of the final categories: "key individuals," "brokers," "role models," and "inspiration."

From a methodological perspective, the study presents certain limitations. First, since the events in question took place 25 years ago, some key informants have passed away. Information about those people was gained through other interviews and secondary data. Second, one of the tech entrepreneurs in question was unavailable for interview despite many attempts to contact him. Information about him was gathered from other people in the case, particularly his co-founder, LinkedIn profile, newspaper articles, interviews, and podcasts he participated in. Third, as interviews concerned past events, the interviewer must be aware of the fact that people "tend to remember what they want to remember" (Denzin, 1989). Taking that into consideration, all factual information was triangulated with secondary data and other informants.

FINDINGS

Background – The Emergence of a High-tech Ecosystem

Origins of an entrepreneurial ecosystem – a research ecosystem
The EE evolved around what was initially a research ecosystem in Norway, with the Department of Physical Electronics at Norwegian University of Science and Technology (NTNU) as a central actor. In the second part of the twentieth century, NTNU was a leading teaching and research college in Norway. Beginning in the 1970s, and culminating in the 1980s, the university cooperated closely with other research organizations (among others Sintef, organization for industrial research, and FFI, organization for military research). The environment was characterized

324   *Research handbook on start-up incubation ecosystems*

by friendliness and openness toward both industry and industry research: "There were sort of invisible divisions between Sintef and NTNU at that time. People were going back and forth, and there was a very homogenous atmosphere, which really caused the culture to be very industry friendly" (Karl Klingsheim, leader of the research group at that time).

Great attention was also put on cooperation with existing industry, with two main goals – creating interest around university research and encouraging existing companies to apply it in their work – as well as learning about industry needs and specificities. The collaboration was governed by the engagement of individual professors, who developed extensive networks of contacts with the business world and encouraged them to be present at the campus. One notable example was an exchange forum for the university and industry regarding integrated circuit design, which was initiated by Professor Einar Aas. Importantly, both university professors and researchers from the industrial research organization were involved in teaching and student supervision.

First commercial activity
In the 1980s, the environment of physical electronics spun off two highly successful academic spin-offs: Nordic Semiconductor and Vingmed Ultrasound. Vingmed Ultrasound (later part of the GE Group) pioneered the use of ultrasound technology in the medical care sector. Importantly, one of the researchers behind the success of the venture, Professor Kjell Arne Ingebritsen, was actively engaged as both a university professor and a co-founder. In turn, Nordic Semiconductor (previously Nordic VLSI), was the direct fruit of the close cooperation between the university and the industrial research organization (Sintef), and it later became one of the leading Norwegian and international companies in integrated circuit design. Of crucial importance for the emergence of the ecosystem was the fact that Nordic Semiconductor remained in close cooperation with NTNU and the Department of Physical Electronics. The culmination of the collaboration came in 1989, when Oddvar Aaserud, the Nordic co-founder, came back to the university for a professor position. The remaining Nordic co-founders were actively engaged as lecturers or supervisors for project works and master's theses.

Graduates of 1991/1992 and their entrepreneurial impact
Highly talented individuals came into that environment: Haakon Bryhni, Egil Eide, Geir Førre, Sverre Dale Moen, John Markus Lervik, John Raaum, Svein Anders Tunheim, and Vegard Wollan; all graduated from the Department of Physical Electronics in either 1991 or 1992. Universities today are seen as "hotbeds" for entrepreneurship that are rich in support

structures and encourage both students and researchers to invent and commercialize. However, this was not the case in the 1980s and 1990s, when there was no direct encouragement toward innovation and entrepreneurship, and a focused support system was non-existent. As remembered by one of the students, Per Gunnar Kjeldsberg, who is now an NTNU professor: "We were encouraged to make new things, improve technology, but without it being spelled out like – make patent."

The focus at NTNU at that time was on research and teaching, neither of which was directly involved in the promotion of innovation and entrepreneurship. Nevertheless, students were encouraged to gain a strong theoretical knowledge base, develop new things, and enhance existing solutions, without it being named as "innovation" or "entrepreneurship." For future entrepreneurs, that was the value of the environment – as remembered by Sverre Dale Moen, co-founder of Chipcon: "Start-ups from 1991–92 classes, it's not because NTNU supported entrepreneurship, but because they supported high-tech education." Importantly, during their study time, students had the opportunity to apply their highly theoretical and advanced knowledge to real-life industry projects. Moreover, professors devoted time to supervision and education without compromising their research. They were also able to spot talent and direct it to the most promising technology areas.

Although Norway struggled with the aftermath of the financial crisis of 1989, those smart and highly ambitious students found jobs immediately after graduation in sought after places – in industrial research organizations (Sintef) or highly innovative companies (Nordic Semiconductor) – or they started their PhDs. Importantly, students who gained experience in industry and the industrial research sector prized this for being their "business school." Between 1995 and 2008, they established six highly successful companies within semiconductor design, digital signal processing, telecommunication, and radar technologies.

First in the case study was Atmel Norway. Established in 1995 by Wollan and another student of class of 1992 with the purpose of commercializing an innovative integrated circuit (IC) design, Atmel Norway was the first Silicon Valley investment in Scandinavia; this simultaneously created a positive precedent for their peers in the class of 1991–1992. A year later, Førre, Dale Moen, and Tunheim started Chipcon, a semiconductor design company that was later sold to a major player in the international market, Texas Instruments. Both Atmel Norway and Chipcon can be regarded as corporate spin-offs. In 1996, Haakon Bryhni started Advanced Communication Technologies with the aim of commercializing the knowledge he acquired during his PhD from the University of Oslo. In subsequent years, John M. Lervik, together with other PhD students from the groups of Professor Arne Halaas and Tor Ramstad at NTNU, established Fast Search & Transfer, which became the main competitor to Google's search engine. In 2001, Egil Eide commercialized radar technology that he had developed during his PhD at NTNU through a company named 3d-Radar. Finally, in 2008, John Raaum left Nordic Semiconductor and established Arctic Silicon Devices to commercialize industry specific IC design.

Some of the companies created by students of the class of 1991–1992 contributed with further spin-off activity (Chipcon spun off Energy Micro, which later spun off Disruptive Technologies, which is currently one of the most promising microchip companies in Norway). Other entrepreneurs of the class of 1991–1992 contributed to the growing entrepreneurial community through their mentor and board member roles (e.g., Wollan is a main investor, mentor, and board member of Mode Sensor, which is a sensor technology company established by NTNU students) and as venture capitalists, investors, and business developers. Some are also actively engaged in building entrepreneurial communities and interest toward innovation and commercialization.

Engaged Individuals as Key Drivers of the Emergence of an Entrepreneurial Ecosystem

All of the events presented above are strongly characterized by the actions of engaged individuals as key drivers of the EE emergence process. Both professors and students had important roles, which were visible in three distinctive ways: as brokers, role models, and inspiration.

Brokers

Professors had a significant place in the history of the EE. Their presence was not limited to being university teachers – they were also connectors between academia and the outside world. Some of them were actively engaged in developing relationships with industry – for example, Einar Aas through the exchange forum mentioned above. Others, such as Oddvar Aaserud, were connecting the scholarly world with practical applications of research through entrepreneurship. What is common among the key professors in the case study is their high engagement in connecting academia with the "external world" by sharing information about research and technology and its latest developments.

This sharing activity had very tangible fruits. For example, for Fast Search & Transfer, an NTNU spin-off, the initial business contacts and investors were found through professors' networks; Lervik, Fast's co-founder, recalled:

Neither prof. Ramstad nor prof. Halaas had business skills, nor particular business interests in terms of commercialization; this wasn't something they were really passionate about. But again, they both had great networks with many people and companies, and created excitement of what we were doing, and hence they were also connected with people in the commercial area. So through those relations, that's really how I got into business and what later became Fast.

In a similar manner, the information was shared by peers who established companies with those who were on the way toward entrepreneurship. For example, Atmel Norway co-founder shared his "tips and tricks" of entrepreneurial trade with Førre (co-founder of Chipcon), and Bryhni (founder of Advanced Communication Technologies) contributed business support and investment to Eide (founder of 3d-Radar).

Role models
Another theme that comes out strongly from the data is the importance of role models in the emergence of EE. Both professors, academic entrepreneurs, and peers were recognized as role models. The significance of role models can be seen as early as the first commercial activity at NTNU – the co-founder of Vingmed Ultrasound, Kjell Arne Ingeritsen was a definite role model for Oddvar Aaserud, co-founder of Nordic, in reaching new heights in technology application. "University didn't know what to do with people like us. Kjell Arne (Ingebritsen) and GE Ultrasound was a role model for us. When we started Nordic, we had people to talk to, exchange experience," as remembered by Oddvar Aaserud, one of the Nordic Semiconductor co-founders.

Students also saw clear role models in their professors and saw Oddvar Aaserud in particular as an academic entrepreneur: "Trond Sæther [. . .] and Oddvar (Aaserud), as founders of Nordic, they were, if you think of it, a seed for everything in the bigger picture, a seed for a lot of things. That was by itself important and interesting and encouraging having them as lecturers and in the corridors because we were looking at them as front figures" (Vegard Wollan). In this way, academic entrepreneurs were early entrepreneurial role models for students. But, importantly, professors were also seen as role models through their extensive expertise and attitude of constant technological development. Significantly, role models were professors from the same scientific specialty as students. Similarly, students served as entrepreneurial role models for their peers.

Inspiration
The third key driver of the emergence of EE was inspiring individuals. Professors were inspiration sources to their students; interestingly, this

was through being academic entrepreneurs, as Aaserud, and through their scientific expertise and ability to encourage people to develop new technological solutions, and choice of specializations in demanding but up-and-coming areas. All in all, professors were remembered for being inspirational, open. They were supportive and devoted to teaching and "doing much beyond their duty."

Clearly, the biggest source of inspiration was peers and their entrepreneurial successes: "Both Atmel and Chipcon were big influences for me. They've been some people to really look up to" (John Raaum, co-founder of Arctic Silicon Devices). As put in a more detailed way by Geir Førre, Chipcon co-founder during a conference presentation (Technoport 2015, Transistor Podcast):

> I think that if it wasn't for the fact that Nordic Semiconductor had started, and the fact that Atmel Norway had started, I don't think that Chipcon would have started, and if Chipcon didn't start, there wouldn't have been Energy Micro. So, there is a chain of reaction happening; so, to some extent it's coincidence, to some extent it's the inspiration, to some extent it's mutual realization, and some people go forward and saw the possibilities and open people's minds on what can be done.

ANALYSIS AND DISCUSSION

Entrepreneurial Ecosystem Emergence

According to Mason and Brown (2014), EE comes to life and develops when there are certain conditions, "usually operating in combination" (p. 27). The empirical findings presented above described this "combination" as strong technology related research in an environment of advanced university–industry collaboration, high technological expertise, extensive contact networks of key individuals, and a high degree of engagement with key individuals. The study found that the key drivers in turning the combination of supportive factors into an EE were engaged individuals who acted as brokers, role models, and inspiration.

Brokers

Brokers are individuals who possess information and through their position at the crossing points of various groups and networks share relevant information across those networks (Burt, 2005). The key element of brokerage is the ability to bridge the gaps between remote groups in terms of specialization (Burt, 2005). In terms of EEs, the role of brokers is somewhat similar to the "feeders" of the ecosystem (Stam, 2009) or "knowledge intermediaries" (Hayter, 2016), where the first is related to an entrepreneur who takes a "leadership role" or to specialized support system entities, and the second is an individual or an organization that is specialized (works professionally) in sharing information among various actors, particularly between research and business worlds in the context of university-based EEs. Both contribute to the growth of an ecosystem by sharing their specialized knowledge with the ecosystem members. However, those two terms refer to people and groups of specific specializations and whose purposeful/professional role is to connect entrepreneurs with relevant actors.

The empirical findings from the case study show, however, that in the organic process through which an ecosystem emerges, a crucial driving role belongs to individuals who share their knowledge in informal and voluntary ways (i.e., who are not specialized in sharing information or whose presence in the ecosystem is not designed as "connector" or "person sharing information"). Hence, the term "broker" appears to describe their activity in a more appropriate manner. During the organic emergence of an ecosystem from a research ecosystem, both professors and students can become brokers. The key to the brokerage process is the sharing information across groups of different specializations. As such, the case shows that the key brokers are those professors who actively engage in cooperation with the industry and business worlds with the aim of spreading research outside the "ivory tower." Through this, they create strong networks of contacts among various professional specialties, which enables the brokerage of many lines between "opposite worlds" – organizations with different logics and resource bases, such as academia and industry, basic and commercial research, and research and entrepreneurship. Being a broker involves the "distribution" of insights regarding the specificities of business/industry needs regarding the application of technology and the legitimization of new technologies within an ecosystem (Kuratko et al., 2017); thus, university professors contribute to new ventures within an ecosystem by lending them legitimacy and, through this, access to resources.

The case reveals that students are another group that operates as brokers. When starting their own companies, they gain insight into the "world of entrepreneurship" through their significant access to specialized information regarding entrepreneurial process, financing, and market entry strategies, etc. In the case of an organically emerging EE, where there is no specialized support system, all sources of information regarding the entrepreneurial process are significant. Access to this information is facilitated by individuals who are willing to share it. The willingness to share information in the brokerage process is conditioned by the prospect of an incentive or gain from the brokerage activity (Burt, 2005). The case revealed that the willingness of professors to share their knowledge and understanding of technology among various actors is a potent incentive for others to do so. Such professors help to create a supportive and collaborative atmosphere for research and develop timely and up-to-data educational programs. In doing so, they prioritize collaboration over purely financial gains.

Role models

Role models are defined as people "worth emulating" due to their possession of desirable traits or achievements (Nauta & Kokaly, 2001). The importance of role models within EEs was previously argued for by Isenberg (2010) and Stam (2009). However, little has been said about how role models influence other members of an ecosystem. The case demonstrates that university professors can be entrepreneurial role models for students and that entrepreneurial students can be role models for their immediate peers. Undeniably, being able to observe and learn from academics who have commercialized technology within one's environment is directly linked to the entrepreneurial role models impact suggested by Isenberg (2010). The case revealed that role models create a positive precedent and encouragement for entrepreneurial activity by being individuals worth emulating.

Professors can be entrepreneurial role models for their students through the type, quality, and innovativeness of the research they carry out; their attitude of openness and cooperation toward business/industry; the active creation of common projects with external partners; and by encouraging the constant development of existing technologies and further experimentation and creation. Those qualities can contribute to the development of both innovative and entrepreneurial attitudes among students, which acts as a promising base for future entrepreneurial activity. Importantly, both academic entrepreneurs[2] and entrepreneurial professors[3] can constitute role models for students – role models that contribute to the development of entrepreneurial attitudes. They are figures of high-end expertise – this is important when building a company based on technological innovation, as technological development is the first step toward commercialization. An important element revealed by the case is that role models are "most effective" when they relate to people who have the same professional and, in this case, scientific background.

Inspiration

The final and probably the most important driver of the emergence of the ecosystem in this study is inspiration. Similarly to Stam (2009), the case shows that people can benefit from the presence of entrepreneurial examples in their environment by learning entrepreneurial know-how from them. However, the case reveals that an important element in inspiration is how close the inspirational person or company is to the people in the ecosystem. Students can be inspired by their immediate peers to start new ventures (Kacperczyk, 2001); nevertheless, the case reveals that, even within one large class of students, it is more important for inspiration that students and professors have disciplinary proximity. Entrepreneurial examples that are loosely connected with a specific environment do, of course, have an impact on entrepreneurial attitudes; nevertheless, the fact that people have exactly the same background, and thus the same prerequisites to succeed, creates a positive precedent for others.

It has been found that professors may possibly be a good source of inspiration (Souitaris et al., 2007; Nabi et al., 2017). The case adds to those findings by establishing the inspirational role of an academic entrepreneur who teaches students. Such academics provide a positive example to students of the value of their knowledge and skills. Moreover, the inspiration from both professors and academic entrepreneurs can go beyond education and direct encouragement toward new venture creation – this involves stimulating constant technological development and applying technological knowledge to practical tests, which is of great importance to high technology ecosystems.

CONCLUSIONS AND IMPLICATIONS OF THE STUDY

The case presented above provides an empirical example of the process of emergence of an EE. It shows how a specialized research oriented environment can be turned into a high-tech EE through bottom-up movement. The key drivers of this organic emergence are found in engaged individuals, who influence the process by acting as brokers, role models, and inspiration. The case study contributes to the existing literature on EEs by showing the importance of engaged professors, academic entrepreneurs, and entrepreneurial students in the formation of environments conducive to entrepreneurship. In this process, professors have an important place as brokers of information between the university and outside world, particularly industry and business. Moreover, academic entrepreneurs and entrepreneurial professors can be role models and sources of inspiration for their students, not only regarding commercial activity but also in terms of constant technological development and innovation. Similarly, students who create successful companies also create an important precedent that serves as a source of inspiration for their peers. An important aspect revealed by the study is the importance of specialization proximity for role models to have an impact on future technology entrepreneurs.

As a single case, this study presents interesting aspects of EE emergence that should be investigated through a larger sample of EEs. It could be highly informative to investigate the role of brokers, role models, and inspiration in other organically grown EEs to specify their place and impact. However, it could also be interesting to further investigate the key drivers in engineered ecosystems. The case only touched upon the role of brokers in gaining legitimacy for new ventures (as theorized by Kuratko et al., 2017); hence, broader empirical studies on how new technology ventures, particularly student-led technology ventures, achieve legitimacy within an ecosystem could be purposeful. From the practitioner perspective, the study calls for greater attention to not only what organizations and resources are involved but *who* is part of an EE. For those working with engineering of EEs at universities, the study provides empirical examples of the value of "self-organization, individual autonomy, and flexibility" (as in Saxenian, 1994) among people residing in academia – both professors and students are indispensable actors in the environment, and they need to be activated wisely.

NOTES

1. In comparison to contemporary events, where effects are not visible; hence, it is challenging to determine which drivers of ecosystem emergence are the key drivers.
2. Academic entrepreneur defined as a researcher who successfully commercialized one's research outcomes and remained in academia to teach and do research (Rahim, Mohamed, & Amrin, 2015).
3. An entrepreneurial professor is understood as one who may not have commercialized their research but applies entrepreneurial methods to acquire new projects and contacts, as in Etzkovitz, 2003.

REFERENCES

Acs, Z. J., Stam, E., Audretsch, D. B., & O'Connor, A. (2017). The lineages of the entrepreneurial ecosystem approach. *Small Business Economics, 49*(1), 1–10.
Audretsch, D. B., & Belitski, M. (2017). Entrepreneurial ecosystems in cities: Establishing the framework conditions. *Journal of Technology Transfer, 42*(5), 1030–1051.
Auken, H. L., Fry, F., & Stephens, P. (2006). The influence of role models on entrepreneurial intentions. *Journal of Developmental Entrepreneurship (JDE), 11.*
Autio, E., Kenney, M., Mustar, P., Siegel, D., & Wright, M. (2014). Entrepreneurial innovation: The importance of context. *Research Policy, 43*(7), 1097–1108.
Bandura, A. (1986). *Social foundations of thought and action: A social cognitive theory.* Prentice-Hall series on social learning theory. Prentice-Hall, Inc.

Baxter, J. (2010). Case studies in qualitative research. In I. Hay, I. (Ed.), *Qualitative research in human geography*. Oxford University Press.

Bishop, K., D'Este, P., & Neely, A. (2011). Gaining from interactions with universities: Multiple methods for nurturing absorptive capacity. *Research Policy*, *40*(1), 30–40.

Burt, R. (2005). *Brokerage and closure*. Oxford University Press.

Cook, I., & Crang, M. (2007). *Doing ethnographies*. London: SAGE Publications.

Denzin, N. K. (1989). *Interpretive biography*. SAGE Publications.

Dunn, K. (2010). Interviewing. In I. Hay (Ed.), *Qualitative research in human geography*. Oxford University Press.

Eisenhardt, K. M. (1989). Building theories from case study research. *Academy of Management Review*, *14*(4), 532–550.

Etzkowitz, H. (2003). Research groups as quasi-firms: The invention of the entrepreneurial university. *Research Policy*, *32*(1), 109–121.

Feld, B. (2012). *Startup communities: Building an entrepreneurial ecosystem in your city*. New York: Wiley.

Guba, E. (1981). Criteria for assessing the trustworthiness of naturalistic inquiries. *ERIC/ECTJ Annual Review Paper*.

Hayter, C. S. (2016). A trajectory of early-stage spinoff success: The role of knowledge intermediaries within an entrepreneurial university ecosystem. *Small Business Economics*, *47*(3), 633–656.

Isenberg, D. J. (2010). How to start an entrepreneurial revolution. *Harvard Business Review*, June.

Jung, J. (1986). How useful is the concept of role model? A critical analysis. *Journal of Social Behavior and Personality*, *1*, 525–536.

Kacperczyk, A. J. (2013). Social influence and entrepreneurship: The effect of university peers on entrepreneurial entry. *Organization Science*, *24*(3), 664–683.

Kuratko, D. F., Fisher, G., Bloodgood, J. M., & Hornsby, J. S. (2017). The paradox of new venture legitimation within an entrepreneurial ecosystem. *Small Business Economics, 49 (1), 119–140*.

Mason, C., & Brown, R. (2014). Entrepreneurial Ecosystems and Growth Oriented Entrepreneurship. *OECD special report*.

Miles, M.B., Huberman, A. B., & Saldana, J. (2014). *Qualitative data analysis. A methods sourcebook* (3rd ed.). SAGE Publications.

Miller, D. J., & Acs, Z. J. (2017). The campus as entrepreneurial ecosystem: The University of Chicago. *Small Business Economics*, *49*(1), 75–95. https://doi.org/10.1007/s11187-017-9868-4

Nabi, G., Liñán, F., Fayolle, A., Krueger, N., & Walmsley, A. (2017). The impact of entrepreneurship education in higher education: A systematic review and research agenda. *Academy of Management Learning & Education*, *16*(2), 277–299.

Nauta, M. M., & Kokaly, M. L. (2001). Assessing role model influences on students' academic and vocational decisions. *Journal of Career Assessment*, *9*(1), 81–99.

Rahim, N. A., Mohamed, Z. B., & Amrin, A. (2015). Commercialization of emerging technology: The role of academic entrepreneur. *Procedia – Social and Behavioral Sciences*, *169*, 53–60.

Rasmussen, E., Moen, Ø., & Gulbrandsen, M. (2006). Initiatives to promote commercialization of university knowledge. *Technovation*, *26*(4), 518–533.

Rothaermel, F. T., Agung, S. D., & Jiang, L. (2007). University entrepreneurship: A taxonomy of the literature, *Industrial and Corporate Change*, *16*(4), 691–791.

Saxenian, A. (1994). *Regional advantage. Culture and competition in Silicon Valley and Route 128*. Harvard University Press.

Siegel, D. S., & Wright, M. (2015). Academic entrepreneurship: Time for a rethink? *British Journal of Management*, *26*(4), 582–595.

Siggelkow, N. (2007). Persuasion with case studies. *The Academy of Management Journal*, *50*(1), 20–24.

Souitaris, V., Zerbinati, S., & Al-Laham, A. (2007). Do entrepreneurship programmes raise entrepreneurial intention of science and engineering students? The effect of learning, inspiration and resources. *Journal of Business Venturing, 22*(4), 566–591.

Stam, L., & Spigel, B. (2017). Entrepreneurial ecosystems. In Z. Blackburn, D. Heinonen, & J. Wang (Eds.), *The SAGE handbook of small business and entrepreneurship*. London: SAGE.

Stam, E. (2009). Entrepreneurship, evolution and geography. *Papers in Evolutionary Economic Geography*.

Stam, E. (2015). Entrepreneurial ecosystems and regional policy: A sympathetic critique. *European Planning Studies, 23*(9), 1759–1769.

Theodoraki, C., Messeghem, K., & Rice, M. P. (2018). A social capital approach to the development of sustainable entrepreneurial ecosystems: An explorative study. *Small Business Economics, 51*(1), 153–170.

Thrash, T. M, and Elliot, A. J. (2003). Inspiration as a psychological construct. *Journal of Personality and Social Psychology, 84*(4), 871–889.

Tjas, K., Nelsen, E. A., & Taylor, M. (1997). Successful alumni as role models for high school youth authors. *The High School Journal, 80*(2), 103–110.

Van Auken, H., Fry, F. L., and Stephens, P. (2006). The influence of role models on entrepreneurial intentions. *Journal of Developmental Entrepreneurship, 1*(2), 157–167.

Yin, R. (2014). *Case study research. Design and methods.* SAGE Publications.

18. Toward a model for universities as incubation ecosystems: Facilitating students for an entrepreneurial career
B.W. Åmo, I.B. Pettersen, E. van der Lingen, K. Voldsund, and J.J. Bragelien

INTRODUCTION

Students tend to start firms close to their graduating university (Larson, Wennberg, Wiklund, & Carsrud, 2016). Hence, universities and their regions would benefit from well functional support systems facilitating students successfully starting and running their businesses (Wrigth, Siegel, & Mustar, 2017). Universities hold many roles, among these are facilitating entrepreneurship among their students. Entrepreneurship education aims for nurturing students' entrepreneurial abilities and mindsets. Exposing the students to entrepreneurship elements is supposed to enhance both their entrepreneurial abilities as well as to raise their awareness of their own entrepreneurial potential. In this way, universities act as incubators developing students' entrepreneurial capabilities and motivation. An incubator is a device that carefully provides support and assistance in a safe environment (Smith, & Zhang, 2012). This chapter contributes by developing a model for universities as incubation ecosystems.

Business incubators are often classified by their purpose; economic development, technology development, or basic research (Allen & McCluskey, 1990; Aernoudt, 2004) or by the actor installing them; government, non-government, independent, or corporate (Grimaldi, & Grandi, 2005; Becker, & Gassmann, 2006; Von Zedtwitz, & Grimaldi, 2006). Business incubators have evolved from facilities nurturing general-purpose business start-ups, through focusing on assisting young and emerging firms in selected technologies to focusing on single industry sectors. Hence, incubators have evolved over time, and now incubators usually facilitate diverse support for their clients; access to physical resources, office support services, access to capital, business counselling, and networking services in order to facilitate newly founded firms through growth and lift-off (Wright et al., 2017). Incubators are the seedbeds for new firms, and governments support such entrepreneurship enhancing processes worldwide (NBIA, 2018; OECD, 2018).

Pauwels, Clarysse, Wright, and Van Hove (2016) state that incubation managers need a clear vision and strategy guiding their effort. They further claim that insights into how different incubators support new firm formation and the impact different accelerator types have on their clients is necessary for generating new improved incubation models. The business incubation process has been treated uniformly by many research studies (Barbero, Casillas, Wright, & Garcia, 2014). Investigating the incubation process in isolation neglects the influence from the context and the dynamic interaction among the actors/stakeholders. To remedy this drawback, researchers position incubators as parts of an entrepreneurial ecosystem. An ecosystem is a result of various mechanisms and actors in different contexts that evolves over time where different parts of the ecosystem might have different and conflicting goals (Wright et al., 2017). Acs, Autio, and Szerb (2014, p. 479) have defined an entrepreneurial ecosystem as: "dynamic, institutionally embedded interaction between entrepreneurial attitudes, ability, and aspirations, by individuals, which drives the allocation of resources through the creation and operation of new ventures". In such a system, individual actors independently act under a set of more or less expressed rules or conditions constantly renegotiated by the actors and stakeholders that make up the system (Autio, & Levie, 2017). Business incubators are a part of such an entrepreneurial ecosystem developing and nurturing start-ups into growing viable businesses.

The role of universities differs from the role of incubators. The role of universities in an entrepreneurial ecosystem is to nurture and grow talents (Isenberg, 2011; World Economic Forum, 2013; Stam, 2015). Universities then contribute to the entrepreneurial ecosystem by providing students business related knowledge, developing entrepreneurial mind-sets as well as offering a network of equal minded entrepreneurs-to-be. Through training in performing entrepreneurship related activities, education on the pros and cons of entrepreneurship, universities enable students to cope with entrepreneurship challenges. These didactics engaging students in entrepreneurship activities also have a formative element, motivating the students to see themselves as entrepreneurs. Through these activities universities prepare students for an entrepreneurial career.

A new emerging incubation model is the incubation ecosystem model. Universities often engage external actors in fulfilling the university's mission to nurture students' entrepreneurial mind-sets. There is a need to explore the relationship between the actors within an entrepreneurial ecosystem and its key stakeholders (Mian, Lamin, & Fayolle, 2016). This chapter investigates the role universities have in fostering and nurturing students' entrepreneurial mind-sets by considering universities as incubation ecosystems. Studying the incubation process as an incubation ecosystem allows for a holistic view on the support structure universities, together with stakeholders, install to support and assist students in their own entrepreneurial expedition. Kepenek and Eser (2018) further ask for comparative analysis of university-based business incubation processes in different countries, as they see major inconsistencies in how student entrepreneurship is organized and nurtured. This study addresses universities in Norway and South Africa as part of an entrepreneurship incubation ecosystem, exploring how entrepreneurship education influences students' entrepreneurial intentions.

First, we offer a discussion in the theoretical framework section deriving hypotheses that explain how exposure to entrepreneurship during previous schooling, important others and previous real-life entrepreneurship experience links to students' intention to start a firm. The method section discloses how we measured entrepreneurship themes related to students and how the data is analysed through regressions in order to reach our conclusions. The results section concludes on our hypotheses while the implications for researchers and practitioners are offered at the end of the chapter.

THEORETICAL FRAMEWORK

The wanted output from a business incubation system is successful firms that produce value creation for the society through improved goods or services, employment and taxes, while offering profit and self-realization for its founders. A business incubation process facilitating these results usually includes supporting entrepreneurial processes such as the acquisition of business networks, business experiences, skills and access to financial resources. A business incubation system consists of some persons wanting aid in establishing and growing their business, and some organizational instalments providing this aid (Peters, Rice, & Sundararajan, 2004). The input to business incubation processes is then entrepreneurs-to-be or other persons with a business idea they would like to pursue (Voisey, Jones, & Thomas, 2013).

Universities aid this input as it enables students for an entrepreneurial career by providing training in entrepreneurial activities, delivering knowledge on entrepreneurship, as well as enhancing the student's motivation and entrepreneurial identity. Universities may engage key stakeholders in this process. An incubation ecosystem requires structured support involving key shareholders to nurture students' entrepreneurial mind-sets

(Fetters, Greene, & Rice, 2010). There is a strong need to understand the factors that characterize such an incubation ecosystem, exploring how to facilitate and support students' entrepreneurial capabilities (Van de Ven, Polley, Garud, & Venkataraman, 1999; Wright et al., 2017).

Exposure to Entrepreneurship Educational Elements During Previous Schooling

Research on entrepreneurship education has primarily focused on investigating to what extent students eventually end up establishing new firms. The formal education system makes an important contribution by developing entrepreneurial competencies. In many OECD countries, schools, vocational education and training institutions along with higher education institutions are focusing on delivering such entrepreneurial competencies and capacities among their learners (OECD, 2018). The conventional wisdom is that entrepreneurship education programmes induce students to become entrepreneurs (Zhao, Seibert, & Hills, 2005; Rasmussen, & Sørheim, 2006; Pittaway, & Cope, 2007; Bae, Qian, Miao, & Fiet, 2014; Wright et al., 2017). Supported by recent empirical findings (Pihie, & Sani, 2009; Beliaeva, Laskovaia, & Shirokova, 2017; Nabi, Walmsley, Liñán, Akhtar, & Neame, 2018), we state the following hypothesis:

Hypothesis 1: Exposure to entrepreneurship through entrepreneurship education increases the likelihood of establishing a new firm.

Entrepreneurship Influence from Important Others

Behaviour is predicted by intentions, and intentions are predicted by certain specific attitudes, situational and personal characteristics (Ajzen, 1991). Both personal and situational characteristics have an indirect influence on entrepreneurship through influencing key attitudes and motivation to act, among these variables are role models, entrepreneurial exposure, entrepreneurial experience and entrepreneurial training (Kreuger, Reilly, & Carsrud, 2010; Wilson, Kickul, & Marlino, 2007; OECD, 2018). Role models are linked to future entrepreneurial activity (Carsrud, Olm, & Eddy, 1987; Scott, & Twomey, 1988; Hoffmann, Junge, & Malchow-Møller, 2015; Zozimo, Jack, & Hamilton, 2017) and we need to identify the most important social influencers (Shapero, 1982) and among these are parents, family and friends (Kreuger et al., 2010).

Hypothesis 2: Exposure to entrepreneurship by influence from important others increases the likelihood of establishing a new firm.

Previous Real-life Entrepreneurship Experience

Previous entrepreneurial experience is also linked to entrepreneurial intentions (Zhao et al., 2005). The vast majority of research studying entrepreneurial learning is based upon the assumption that entrepreneurs do better as they grow entrepreneurial experience (i.e. Cope, 2003). Students are also more able to learn entrepreneurship when they can activate their own entrepreneurial experiences and relate these to the classroom didactics, according to Mueller and Anderson (2014). Empirical studies also find a link between entrepreneurial experience and opportunity recognition (Shane, & Khurana, 2003; Politis, & Gabrielsson 2005; Huovinen, & Tihula, 2008).

Hypothesis 3: Exposure to entrepreneurship by own real-life entrepreneurial experience increases the likelihood of establishing a new firm.

METHOD

In order to understand how universities prepare students for an entrepreneurial career, we addressed students studying business and engineering. These students will soon look for a job, either as employees or as self-employed. The students were 540 Norwegian engineering students participating in a compulsory course in entrepreneurship during their second year of their bachelors degree, as well as 259 South African business students participating in an entrepreneurship course during their second year of their bachelors degree. Our web-survey contained a measure on entrepreneurial intention; "how likely it is that you will start a new firm" on a Likert scale ranging from 1 (unlikely) to 7 (likely). In addition to control variables as gender, age and country, we also included items measuring exposure to entrepreneurship elements experienced during previous university and high-school education, items measuring if important others acting as role models own or run a firm, as well as items measuring aspects of previous own real-life entrepreneurial experiences. Our response rate was 31 per cent in the Norwegian sample and 34 per cent in the South African sample. T-tests show no significant differences on age and gender between responders and non-responders.

Gender is often included as a control variable when studying students' intention to start a new firm (Kolvereid, Shane, & Westhead, 1993), and females are often reported to engage less in entrepreneurship than do males (Wilson et al., 2007). This is further supported by GEM (GEM, 2018) who evidence that the level of entrepreneurship differs between countries, between genders, age groups and cohorts with different educational backgrounds.

We proposed five yes/no questions regarding exposure to entrepreneurship during previous schooling including participation in internships, developing business ideas, working with business cases, teamwork in product development and participating in entrepreneurship programmes or courses. These five items were then summed and averaged to derive a measure of the students' exposure to entrepreneurship didactical elements during previous schooling; Entrepreneurship Education Exposure. The influence from important others' (Denzin, 1966) entrepreneurial engagement included four yes/no items; regarding if their father, mother, close friends or spouse now or previously run a business. We then derived summed averaged scores for this Entrepreneurial Important Others influence measures. Our measure of previous own real-life entrepreneurship experience included four yes/no items on general job experience, job experience from a family business, involvement in projects trying to commercialize own ideas and if they had ever been part of a start-up firm as a founder or team member. We also derived summed averaged scores for this Own Real-Life Entrepreneurial Experience measures. See Table 18.1 displaying some descriptive statistics regarding the population and how the respondents relate to our measures.

RESULTS AND ANALYSIS

The correlation matrix in Table 18.2 reveals that students' intention to establish a firm is positively related to our measures of exposure to entrepreneurship elements during previous schooling, entrepreneurial influence from important others and own real-life entrepreneurship experience. The table also shows that South African students are more likely to establish a firm than are Norwegians, and that males are more likely to start a new firm. The correlation table also reveals that the students were 24 years of age on average; the female proportion was 51 per cent in South Africa and 28 per cent in Norway. The correlation table furthermore shows that multicollinearity is not a problem in our dataset (Hair, Anderson, Tatham, & Black, 1998).

The first column in the hierarchical regressions displayed in Table 18.3 includes the control variables age, gender and country. The regression in model 1 shows that on average, male students and older students are more in favour of establishing a new firm than are females and younger students. Likewise, students from South Africa are more in favour of establishing a new firm.

Table 18.1   Descriptive statistics, total responses n=799

	Norway	South Africa
Males	388	128
Females	152	131
Total respondents per country	540	259
Entrepreneurship Education Exposure		
– Have you participated in internships – in start-up firms or in innovative firms (e.g. product development/improvement, problem solving) – Yes	50	70
– Have you participated in extra-curricular entrepreneurship programmes where students/pupils can develop business ideas, or new products? – Yes	91	73
– Have you worked with real business cases (student consulting as a course ingredient)? – Yes	95	73
– Experience with working in teams to develop a business idea, new products, lean-processes, or organizational change? – Yes	236	167
– Participation in entrepreneurship programmes? – Yes	94	108
Entrepreneurial Important Others		
– Did/does your father own and run a business? – Yes	131	132
– Did/does your mother own and run a business? – Yes	51	93
– Did/do closest friends own and run a business? – Yes	120	115
– Did/does your spouse own and run a business? – Yes	16	19
Own Real-Life Entrepreneurial Experience		
– Job experience (part time/during summer holiday)? – Yes	451	190
– Do you currently work in a business owned by yourself, your spouse or your parents? – Yes	39	39
– Have you previously participated in projects in the past to commercialize your ideas? – Yes	62	64
– Are you currently or have been involved in a start-up firm (founder or team member)? – Yes	56	63

The second column adds the student's entrepreneurship educational exposure to the model, model 2. It shows that exposing students to educational elements engaging them in entrepreneur-like activities raises their interest for establishing their own firm later. As evidenced in model 3, adding the entrepreneurial influence from important others as well as previous real-life entrepreneurial experience, further adds to the explanatory power of the model.

As model 1 shows, the demographical variables alone explain 19 per

Table 18.2 Pearson Correlation table with country means, n=797

Pearson Correlation matrix		1	2	3	4	5	6	7
How likely is it that you will establish a new firm? (1-unlikely, 7-likely)	1	1						
Age	2	-.07*	1					
Gender: (female=0, male=1)	3	.00	.11**	1				
Country (South Africa = 0, Norway = 1)	4	.42***	.03	-.22***	1			
H1 Entrepreneurship Education Exposure (Summed score, 0 to 1)	5	.27***	-.06	-.09**	.32***	1		
H2 Entrepreneurial Important Others influence (Summed score, 0 to 1)	6	.36***	.08*	-.12***	.41***	.24***	1	
H3 Own Real-life Entrepreneurial Experience (Summed score, 0 to 1)	7	.31***	.10**	.01	.14***	.26***	.24***	1
Mean South Africa n=259		5.53	24		.49	.38	.35	.34
Mean Norway n=540		3.79	24		.72	.21	.15	.28

Note: * indicate $p \leq .05$, ** indicate $p \leq .01$, *** indicate $p \leq .001$.

Table 18.3   Hierarchical regressions predicting the likelihood of establishing a new firm

The likelihood of establishing a new firm (Std beta)	Model 1 Control variable only	Model 2 Influence from entrepreneurship education	Model 3 Full model
Age	0.05	0.06	0.03
Gender (female=0, male=1)	0.09**	0.09**	0.09**
Country (SA=0, NO=1)	0.45***	0.40***	0.33***
H1 Exposure to entrepreneurship during previous schooling		0.16***	0.09**
H2 Influence from important others			0.17***
H3 Previous real entrepreneurship experience			0.19***
Adjusted R square	0.193***	0.215***	0.279**
Adjusted R square change		0.02***	0.06***
F-value	61.98***	53.28***	50.10***

Note: ** indicate $p \geq .01$, *** indicate $p \geq .001$.

cent of the variance in students' intentions to establish their own firm. Model 2 explains 22 per cent of the variance. Model 2 includes elements of experienced entrepreneurship education. The full model, model 3, then explains 28 per cent of the variance. Model 3 adds measures of the respondents' previous own real-life entrepreneurial activity as well as of important others who act as the respondents' role models owning or running a firm.

The results from Table 18.3, utilizing demographical data, indicate that older students are more likely to start a firm than are younger students. Male students are also more likely to start a firm than are females. Likewise, students from South Africa are more likely to see themselves as starting a firm than are Norwegian students.

In line with the results from the correlation matrix in Table 18.2, Table 18.3 moreover displays that exposure to entrepreneurship didactics during previous schooling does link to their intention to start a new firm. Hence, hypothesis 1 is confirmed. Exposure to entrepreneurship through entrepreneurship education increases the likelihood of establishing a new firm. Adding measures of entrepreneurship influence from important others and own real-life entrepreneurship experience also increases the model's predictability as shown in Table 18.3. Hence, hypothesis 2 is confirmed, exposure to entrepreneurship by influence from important others increases the likelihood of establishing a new firm. Similarly, hypothesis 3 is confirmed. Exposure to entrepreneurship by own entrepreneurial real-life experience increases the likelihood of establishing a new firm. The students own real-life entrepreneurship experience does positively influence the students' intention to start a firm.

Introducing the entrepreneurial influence from important others as well as previous real entrepreneurial experience, as in model 3, replaces some of the explanatory effects of entrepreneurship education. Furthermore, Table 18.2 shows a positive correlation between entrepreneurial influence from important others (.24***) and previous real entrepreneurial experience (.26***) and entrepreneurship education. Including interaction effects in the regression shows that those already exposed to entrepreneurship by influential others or through their own actions are more affected by entrepreneurship educational elements.

Our study bears some limitations. The respondents in our study are soon facing a career choice, starting their own firm could be a realistic option. Even if Trice (1991) finds that intention is a good predictor of action, our respondents are still students and their potential intent have not yet been challenged. Besides, as we did not measure the students' intent to start a new firm before entering the educational system to compare it with their intent at the time we gauged it, we do not know what comes first; the propensity to ever start a firm, the entrepreneurial education exercises or the real-life entrepreneurship experience. Despite these drawbacks, this study evidences the benefits in combining single item measures into multiple items, that is, combining the effect from several influencing important others or combining different expressions of previous real-life entrepreneurship experience into one measure. We urge future studies to explore further how to construct multiple items to increase the validity of the findings.

CONCLUSIONS AND IMPLICATIONS OF UNIVERSITIES' ROLES IN INCUBATOR ECOSYSTEMS

The purpose of this study is to improve the understanding of the theoretical, empirical, managerial, and policy implications of an emerging model of entrepreneurial universities; the university as an incubator ecosystem. We do so by exploring how entrepreneurship education influences students' entrepreneurial intentions and thereby increases our understanding on how universities contribute to entrepreneurial ecosystems enhancing the student's entrepreneurial capacity. Universities are a key agent in any entrepreneurial ecosystem as their main responsibility is education, research and dissemination of knowledge (Guerrero, Urbano, Fayolle, Klofsten, & Mian, 2016).

This study answers the call of Mian, Fayolle, and Lamine (2012) asking how universities can be more responsive to the challenge of developing solid programmes providing quality services adding value to the student's entrepreneurial development. The influence from previous exposure to entrepreneurship didactics during schooling was significant. This influence fell when the effect from own real-life entrepreneurial experience and their entrepreneurial important others were accounted for. This finding indicates that entrepreneurship education breathes oxygen into an already existing entrepreneurial fire but misses out igniting such a fire for those not already alert to an entrepreneurial career path. This raises questions for entrepreneurship education scholars wanting to nurture the entrepreneurial spark among all their students. It still seems important to pursue the issue of how we as educators could unleash more of the entrepreneurial mind-sets that rest in our students given the relatively lower influence from previous entrepreneurship educational exposure. As entrepreneurship education is a developmental process informing the student on the pros and cons of entrepreneurship, they might realize the complexity and challenges involved in business start-up (Oosterbeek, van Praag, & Ijsselstein, 2010), preventing them from committing to entrepreneurship.

Isenberg (2011) identified pillars comprising a successful entrepreneurial ecosystem. An entrepreneurial ecosystem consists of knowledge-generation and exploiting sub-system linked to global, national and regional systems (Cooke, Heidenraich, & Braczyk 2004; Mian et al., 2012). Our study hints at the students' important others as well as the industry as key stakeholders to a university incubating and nurturing students' entrepreneurial mind-sets. Hence, interaction with these key stakeholders is an important pillar in a university incubation ecosystem. Our findings indicate that university incubation ecosystems would profit from engaging more strongly with these key stakeholders. This investigation shows that actors as entrepreneurial businesses and students' entrepreneurial important others are key to enhance students' entrepreneurial intentions. Universities could gain from engaging with these key stakeholders more profoundly.

Furthermore, our research also provides some new input to the ongoing debate about how to teach entrepreneurship at schools and universities. This study indicates a strong link between student's real-life entrepreneurial experience and their self-reported intention to start a firm. This insight triggers a need to know how to make the classroom didactics more realistic, as well as a need to know specifically what aspects of the real-life entrepreneurship experience actually trigger students' start-up intentions. Insights into these didactics will inform universities on how to engage industries and entrepreneurial important others as key players in a university incubation ecosystem, with the purpose of emulating real-life entrepreneurial challenges and experiences in students. Short- and long-term internships in entrepreneurial firms could, for example, offer students real-life entrepreneurship experiences. Universities should therefore strive to develop real-life entrepreneurship courses with the research-based didactics as an educational offering.

Even if this study indicates that important others, such as family and friends have an effect on students' intention to start a firm, it is hard to exploit this knowledge directly. These important others have made an effect on the students from earlier on, and often during their upbringing, externally and independently of the university. Yet, we may use this insight for education purposes. We as teachers could ask students to invite parents or friends who represent important others to discuss issues related to their firm in class, evidencing the success of proxy role models and so inspiring other fellow students. We could also connect students to other potential role models in the wider entrepreneurial ecosystem and local industries, by organizing student field visits and internships, observing and interacting with entrepreneurial-like role models. There are truly many opportunities to exploit our research insights to improve and strengthen the university as an incubation ecosystem.

REFERENCES

Acs, Z.J., Autio, E., & Szerb, L. (2014). National systems of entrepreneurship: Measurement issues and policy implications. *Research Policy*, 43:476–494.
Aernoudt, R. (2004). Incubators: Tool for entrepreneurship? *Small Business Economics*, 23(2):127–135.
Ajzen, I. (1991). The theory of planned behavior. *Organizational Behavior and Human Decision Processes*, 50(2):179–211.
Allen, D., & McCluskey, R. (1990). Structure, policy, services and performance in the business incubator industry. *Entrepreneurship Theory and Practice*, 15(2):61–77.
Autio, E., & Levie, J. (2017). Management of entrepreneurial ecosystems. In (Eds.) G. Ahmetoglu, T. Chamorro-Premuzic, B. Klinger & T. Karcisky, *The Wiley Handbook of Entrepreneurship*, John Wiley & Sons, N.Y., 423–449.
Bae, T.J., Qian, S., Miao, C., & Fiet, J.O. (2014). The relationship between entrepreneurship education and entrepreneurial intentions: A meta-analytic review. *Entrepreneurship Theory and Practice*, 38(2):217–254.
Barbero, J.L., Casillas, J.C., Wright, M., & Garcia, A.R. (2014). Do different types of incubators produce different types of innovations? *The Journal of Technology Transfer*, 39(2):151–168.
Becker, B., & Gassmann, O. (2006). Gaining leverage effects from knowledge modes within corporate incubators. *Regional and Development Management*, 36(1):1–16.

Beliaeva, T., Laskovaia, A., & Shirokova, G. (2017). Entrepreneurial learning and entrepreneurial intentions: a cross-cultural study of university students. *European Journal of International Management*, 11(5):606–632.

Carsrud, A., Olm, K., & Eddy, G. (1987). Entrepreneurs – mentors, networks, and successful new venture development: An exploratory study. *American Journal of Small Business*, 12(2):13–18.

Cooke, P., Heidenreich, M., & Braczyk, H.J., eds (2004), *Regional Innovation Systems*, 2 ed, Routledge, London.

Cope, J. (2003). Entrepreneurial learning and critical reflection: Discontinuous events as triggers for 'higher-level' learning. *Management Learning*, 34(4):429–450.

Denzin, N.K. (1966). The significant others of a college population. *The Sociological Quarterly*, 7(summer):298–310.

GEM (2018). *Global Entrepreneurship Monitor, World Report 2017/2018*. GERA, Babson College, MA, USA.

Grimaldi, R., & Grandi, A. (2005). Business incubators and new venture creation: An assessment of incubating models. *Technovation*, 25(2):111–121.

Guerrero, M., Urbano, D., Fayolle, A., Klofsten, M., & Mian, S. (2016). Entrepreneurial universities: Emerging models in the new social and economic landscape. *Small Business Economics*, 47(3):551–563.

Fetters, M.L., Greene, P.G., & Rice, M.P (2010). Babson college. In (Eds.) M.L. Fetters, P.G. Greene, M.P. Rice & J.S. Butler, *The development of university-based entrepreneurship ecosystems: Global practices*, Edward Elgar, Cheltenham, UK, 15–44.

Hair, J.F., Anderson, R.E., Tatham, R.L., & Black, W.C. (1998). *Multivariate data analysis*, 5th edition. Prentice Hall, Upper Saddle River, NJ.

Hoffmann, A., Junge, M, & Malchow-Møller, N. (2015). Running in the family: Parental role models in entrepreneurship. *Small Business Economics*, 44 (1):79–104.

Huovinen, J., & Tihula, S. (2008). Entrepreneurial learning in the context of portfolio entrepreneurship. *International Journal of Entrepreneurial Behavior & Research*, 14(3):152–171.

Isenberg, D. (2011). Introducing the entrepreneurship ecosystem: Four defining characteristics. *Forbes*, May, 25.

Kepenek, E.B., & Eser, Z. (2018). Impact of Pre-incubators on Entrepreneurial Activities in Turkey: Problems, Successes, and Policy Recommendations. In (Eds.) D. Meissner, E. Erdil & J. Chataway, *Innovation and the Entrepreneurial University. Sciences, Technology and Innovation Studies*. Springer, Cambridge:57–82.

Kolvereid, L., Shane, S., & Westhead P. (1993). Is it equally difficult for female entrepreneurs to start businesses in all countries? *Journal of Small Business Management*, 31(4):42–51.

Kreuger, N.F., Reilly, M.D., & Carsrud, A.L. (2010). Competing models of entrepreneurial intentions. *Journal of Business Venturing*, 15(5–6):411–432.

Larson, J., Wennberg, K., Wiklund, J., & Wright, M. (2016). Location choices of graduate entrepreneurs. *Research Policy*, 46:1490–1504.

Mian, S., Fayolle, A., & Lamine, W. (2012). Building sustainable regional platforms for incubating science and technology businesses: Evidence from US and French science and technology parks. *The International Journal of Entrepreneurship and Innovation*, 13(4):235–247.

Mian, S., Lamine, W., & Fayolle, A. (2016). Technology business incubation: An overview of the state of knowledge. *Technovation*, 50:1–12.

Mueller, S., & Anderson, A.R. (2014). Understanding the entrepreneurial learning process and its impact on students' personal development: A European perspective. *The International Journal of Management Education*, 12(3):500–511.

Nabi, G., Walmsley, A., Liñán, F., Akhtar, I., & Neame, C. (2018). Does entrepreneurship education in the first year of higher education develop entrepreneurial intentions? The role of learning and inspiration. *Studies in Higher Education*, 43(3):452–467.

NBIA (2018). National Business Incubation Association see: http://www.nbia.org/resource_library/bibliography/index.php, last accessed 12 December 2018.

OECD (2018). Developing entrepreneurship competencies. Parallel session 3. 22–23 February

2018. Mexico City. SME Ministerial Conference. Downloaded: 27.11.2018: https://www.
oecd.org/cfe/smes/ministerial/documents/2018-SME-Ministerial-Conference-Parallel-Sess
ion-3.pdf
Oosterbeek, H., van Praag, M., & Ijsselstein, A. (2010). The impact of entrepreneurship education on entrepreneurship skills and motivation. *European Economic Review*,
54(3):442–54.
Pauwels, C., Clarysse, B. Wright, M., & Van Hove, J. (2016). Understanding a new genera-
tion incubation model: The accelerator. *Technovation*, 50:13–24.
Peters, L., Rice, M., & Sundararajan, M. (2004). The role of incubators in the entrepreneurial
process. *Journal of Technology Transfer*, 29(1):83–91.
Pihie, Z.A.L., & Sani, A.S.A. (2009). Exploring the entrepreneurial mindset of students:
Implication for improvement of entrepreneurial learning at university. *The Journal of
International Social Research*, 2(8):340–345.
Pittaway, L., & Cope, J. (2007). Entrepreneurship education: A systematic review of the
evidence. *International Small Business Journal*, 25(5):479–510.
Politis, D., & Gabrielsson, J. (2005). Exploring the role of experience in the process of
entrepreneurial learning. *Lund institute of economic research working paper series*, 1:1–25.
Rasmussen, E.A., & Sørheim, R. (2006). Action-based entrepreneurship education.
Technovation, 26(2):185–194.
Scott, M., & Twomey, D. (1988). The long-term supply of entrepreneurs: Students' career
aspirations in relation to entrepreneurship. *Journal of Small Business Management*,
26(4):5–13.
Shane, S., & Khurana, R. (2003). Bringing individuals back in: The effects of career experi-
ence on new firm founding. *Industrial and Corporate Change*, 12 (3):519–543.
Shapero, A. (1982). Social Dimensions of Entrepreneurship. In (Eds.) C. Kent, D. Sexton &
K. Vesper, *The Encyclopedia of Entrepreneurship*. Englewood Cliffs: Prentice-Hall:72–90.
Smith, D.J., & Zhang, M. (2012). Introduction: The evolution of the incubator concept. *The
International Journal of Entrepreneurship and Innovation*, 13(4):227–234.
Stam, E. (2015). Entrepreneurial ecosystems and regional policy: A sympathetic critique.
European Planning Studies, 23(9):1759–1769.
Trice, A. (1991). Relationship between first aspirations, parental occupation, and current
occupation. *Psychological Reports*, 68(1):287–290.
Van de Ven, A.H., Polley, D.E., Garud, R., & Venkataraman, S. (1999). *The innovation
journey*. Oxford: Oxford University Press.
Voisey, P., Jones, P., & Thomas, B. (2013). The pre-incubator: A longitudinal study of 10
years of university pre-incubation in Wales. *Industry and Higher Education*, 27(5):349–363.
Von Zedtwitz, M., & Grimaldi, R. (2006). Are service profiles incubator-specific? Results
from an empirical investigation in Italy. *Journal of Technology Transfer*, 31(4):459–468.
Wilson, F., Kickul, J., & Marlino, D. (2007). Gender, entrepreneurial self-efficacy, and entre-
preneurial career intentions: Implications for entrepreneurship education. *Entrepreneurship
Theory and Practice*, 31(3):387–406.
World Economic Forum (2013). *Entrepreneurial ecosystems around the globe and company
growth dynamics*, Davos: World Economic Forum.
Wright, M., Siegel, D., & Mustar, P. (2017). An emerging ecosystem for student start-up.
Journal of Technology Transfer, 42(4):909–922.
Zhao, H., Seibert, S.E., & Hills, G.E. (2005). The mediating role of self-efficacy in the
development of entrepreneurial intentions. *Journal of Applied Psychology*, 90(6):1265–1272.
Zozimo, R., Jack, S., & Hamilton, E. (2017). Entrepreneurial learning from observing role
models. *Entrepreneurship & Regional Development*, 29(9–10):889–911.

19. Individual-level determinants of academic patent licensing to start-ups: impacts of principal investigators' embeddedness in the industry

*Dolores Modic and Tohru Yoshioka-Kobayashi**

INDIVIDUAL ACTORS INSIDE INCUBATION SYSTEMS

Entrepreneurial ecosystems are usually defined as systems of co-located elements with diverse actors, functions and institutions interacting to support the creation and growth of new ventures (Thompson et al., 2018; O'Connor & Reed, 2018; Isenberg, 2010). O'Connor et al. (2018 p. 2) assume that every 'place' has an entrepreneurial ecosystem, but 'the performance, practices, strengths, weaknesses, opportunities, threats, objectives and actors each vary'.

Focusing on individual actors is neither new in entrepreneurial eco-system research (e.g. Thompson et al., 2018) nor in university–industry collaboration literature (e.g. Ooms et al., 2018). If we understand start-up incubation ecosystems as a set of actors (and factors) that interact to provide a nurturing environment for the creation of start-ups, then, when speaking of university start-ups, we need to acknowledge the role the principal investigators (PIs) in technology transfer.[1]

From the ecosystem point of view, two ontologies are at our disposal (O'Connor et al., 2018); a balanced system, where the pushes come from external sources, and a transforming ecosystem, where one of the pushes is the actor-level cooperation (see also O'Connor & Reed, 2018). The pushes in the actor-level cooperation come both from actors directly connected to start-ups (e.g. CEOs and funders) and from influential actors in their environment, for example PIs creating the technology used by a certain start-up.

But why focus on PIs, defined as researchers, primarily responsible for the research and who (usually) assemble a scientific team to carry out the project under their scientific supervision (Melkers & Xiao, 2012; Kastrin et al., 2018)? PIs are an important part of the university technology transfer and incubation ecosystems. Their role is multiple; from being the source of invention and connecting multiple researchers together (indeed, most university inventions are co-invented in groups), having a role in the patenting process (often requesting the solution to be patented), to providing ties to potential licensees and improving the quality of technology transfer by follow-up research (Jensen et al., 2003). Some of them also successfully contribute to start-up creations by transferring cutting-edge scientific knowledge or establishing their own start-ups (Zucker et al., 1998).

We try to discern the PI's influence on the flourishing of start-ups within, what we believe to be, transforming incubation systems. We do so by looking at various factors connected to PIs' involvement in technology transfer. In particular we investigate if their prior technology transfer experiences, that is, acquired licensing capabilities, connections with large firms, strong regional cooperation or strong ties with existing firms, have moderating effects on licensing to start-ups, and thus on stimulating the start-up ecosystem. We empirically test these questions in the Japanese university licensing milieu.

THE INTERPLAY OF PI LICENSING AND START-UP INCUBATION SYSTEM

We extend the conceptual framework of academic technology licensing provided by Wu et al. (2015), who considered the PI's influence in technology transfer. They argue that applicability of research and marketability of invention are key determinants of licensing, and these two determinants are influenced by individual factors such as the PI's orientation towards commercialisation, follow-up research and industry collaboration (hereinafter: industry collaboration orientation). Their framework is static and does not say anything about the dynamism of industry collaboration orientation. A remaining question is: with whom are PIs likely to collaborate before or after a certain collaboration? Obviously, large firms and start-ups are fundamentally different. Their differences affect both barriers to collaboration and returns from them. They also affect the industry collaboration orientation of PIs. This chapter attempts to answer this question. We examine the question using patenting and licensing activity data, focusing specifically on the industry collaboration orientation.

Licensing to start-ups is not an easy choice for academic researchers, but is mitigated by their prior experience. There is a high level of uncertainty related to start-ups, including the fact PIs are often not confident about individual start-up's capabilities. However, the entrepreneurship literature has revealed that academic researchers are more likely to establish start-ups when they already have certain knowledge about the market and their potential customers (Shane, 2004) or experiences with translating their technologies to the market (Shane & Khurana, 2003). This prior knowledge (here a typical learning-by-doing activity) and prior experiences mitigate start-ups' insufficiencies. We believe the same to be true for licensing activities. Thus, especially in the absence of prior experience, licensing to known business entities like large firms seems to be a safer option. Furthermore, in systems like the Japanese one, where the general licensing culture is one of licensing to large companies (see also UNITT, 2018), the decision to engage in commercialisation activity with a start-up needs PIs that are able to recognise the benefits of licensing to start-ups and the limitations of licensing to existing firms. PIs will select the best licensees and business models to reduce uncertainty or increase returns based on their prior licensing experiences, that had increased licensing capabilities.

Hypothesis 1: Principle investigators' (PIs') licensing experiences, i.e. licensing capabilities, stimulate licensing to start-ups.

The moderating (complementarity) effects of different transfer channels on start-ups (including home university spin-offs as well as other start-ups) has not yet been fully examined. Crespi et al. (2011) present a comprehensive overview of research regarding the potential moderating effects of patenting (a more limited one is presented by Azagra-Caro et al., 2017), both on publishing and on technology transfer. They conclude first, that although there is some statistical evidence of a moderating effect (or complementarity effect) between publishing and patenting, there is also qualitative and quantitative evidence of crowding out; and second, they point out the inconclusive results regarding the moderating effect of patenting on other forms of knowledge transfer. In light of this, Crespi et al. (2011) present evidence, pertaining to the UK, showing that patent stock is positively correlated with a number of other technology transfer channels. However, it has an inverted U-shape for most of them, with the exception of establishing a university spin-off. *Inter alia*, bigger companies can affect the technology transfer landscape through various mechanisms such as donations and sponsorships, locking-in the licensing efforts through these mechanisms. Hence, our review of the literature dictates it is reasonable to assume prior technology transfer ties with larger firms will affect start-up licensing.

Hypothesis 2: There are moderating effects of license (and re-assignment) activities to existing large firms on start-up licensing.

The regional innovation systems literature makes a distinction between individual actors and regional innovation structures and emphasises that we need to understand the impact of individual actors on these structures (Toedtling & Trippl, 2013; Suvinen, 2014). When looking at the role of universities and the university–industry cooperation, PIs and their personal and professional ties can sometimes be seen as the glue (Ooms et al., 2018). PIs can nurture either regional ties or ties beyond the region. Simultaneously, home university spin-offs are usually based in the same region as the university. This dictates the conclusion that a wide regional business network can result in licensing especially to home spin-offs, thus invigorating the home incubation ecosystem.

Hypothesis 3: Larger regional business networks by principle investigators (PIs) have a positive effect on licensing to spin-offs.

University–industry collaboration is conducive to joint patenting (Hicks, 2000; Veuglers & Cassiman, 2005; Belderbos et al., 2014; Natalicchio et al., 2017). Funk (2012) points out several reasons why university–industry patents come into existence: a) joint patents born out of joint collaboration; b) joint patents due to external funding; and c) those arising from the fact that the researchers are principals in a firm, such as those associated with university incubators. Joint patents are hence quite common by-products of university–industry collaborations (Hagedoorn, 2003; Kwon, 2011; Petruzzelli, 2011; Funk, 2012; Wang et al., 2013; Agostini & Caviggioli, 2015). An important role of the PI can also be deduced from the above options; as joint collaboration is most often based on PI-firm interaction, donations are often specific (to a certain lab) or arise from personal ties the PI has with the industrial co-owner. The important takeaway is that joined patents indicate a relatively strong tie in the university–industry nexus and that PIs play a strong role therein (e.g. Bercovitz & Feldman, 2011).

PIs have a strong commitment to firms they have collaborated with previously. This is reflected in the fact that it is not easy to conduct follow-up research with firms other than former collaboration partners. PIs are sometimes obliged not to join a new partnership with a former partner's competitors. Even if they do not have any non-competition obligation, they can often be emotionally or personally committed to licensees or have incentives to increase running royalties. In other words, PIs are socially locked-in with their existing licensee network.

Hypothesis 4: Strong ties with existing firms (i.e. the joint application tradition) is negatively associated with licensing to start-ups.

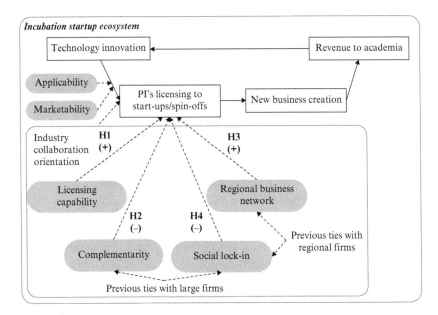

Figure 19.1   Hypotheses: the interplay of PI licensing and start-ups incubation system

We investigate these four hypotheses regarding PI licensing behaviour to start-ups and scrutinise this part of the entrepreneurial ecosystem more in-depth, whereby we position the PI as the facilitating factor for nurturing outputs inside the incubation systems (from new business creation to revenue and new innovation).

As shown in Figure 19.1, our hypotheses address elements of industry collaboration orientation; a behaviour of a PI in regard to a commercialisation engagement. We upgrade the framework provided by Wu et al. (2015) to identify in-depth the factors of industry engagement. Wu et al. (2015) took into consideration solely whether industry took part in the research leading to a patent (which is often mirrored in a joint patent application).

DATA AND METHODOLOGY

Research Design and Context

We empirically examined our hypotheses using licensing data in two Japanese universities. The regime shift toward academic entrepreneurship in Japan began in the mid-1990s, partly in response to the changing policy environment in the US (Walsh & Huang, 2014; Woolgar, 2007). When comparing the results of the AUTM licensing survey for the US with that of University Network for Innovation and Technology Transfer's (UNITT) survey for Japan, we can see several positive trends in licensing for the period 2008–2014. Whilst Japan doubled the amount of licensing agreements, the US increased its results only by about 30 per cent. This rise would indicate that the growth reached in this period was consistent with the catching up period of the Japanese system.

Focusing on where the university inventions end up when licensed to different organisations, we find a distinct lack of, otherwise potentially very valuable, licensing to start-ups. The data shows the predominant position of the licensing to large companies, with licensing to start-ups in the period of 2008–2014 at 1.5 per cent average according to the re-calculation of the UNITT data. UNITT reports show the establishment of university start-ups also seemed a rather fruitless effort up to 2014, both in absolute numbers as when compared to the US (with only 3.4 per cent of that observed in the US). Furthermore, Nagaoka et al. (2014) discovered that only about 16 per cent of the most important patents stemming from university–industry cooperation in Japan have ended up commercialised. However, 45 per cent of patents stemming from university–industry cooperation with smaller companies (i.e. those with fewer than twenty employees) were commercialised, compared to 10 per cent for large companies (Nagaoka et al., 2014). This indicates that stimulating technology transfer to smaller entities, foremost also start-ups, can prove very valuable.

The biggest advantage of using Japanese data is its specific environment. Nakayama et al. (2017) show the so-called hidden technology transfer via patenting is very low (16 per cent). Furthermore, the incidence of joined university patents, is much larger in Japan than elsewhere (Kneller, 2010). Nagaoka et al. (2014) list 47.7 per cent of patents with an industry co-owner during 2004–2007, and Ijichi and Nagaoka (2007), list at least 57 per cent. This activity brings Japan to the forefront of countries with (formal) joint university patents. Furthermore, the majority of joint applicants in our sample are large or medium entities at University A (79 per cent), with only 3 per cent of them being start-ups. Similarly, at University B, 86.5 per cent are large- and medium-sized companies and only 2.3 per cent are start-ups. We believe this can have important implications also for the creation of university start-ups, which is similar to sponsorship that can create lock-in situations (Bercovitz et al., 2019). This lock-in effect can be stronger when collaboration takes place with large firms.

Data

We constructed our databases based on administrative patenting and licensing records of two well-respected Japanese research universities. Due to confidentiality requirements they are referred to as University A and B. Data was enriched with information on joint patent applicants and with information on licensees. Both University A and University B exhibit strong patenting and licensing results according to the UNITT survey; ranking them among the top ten most successful Japanese universities in terms of technology transfer. Both are also members of the elite eleven research universities (RU11).

Our original dataset covered 809 unique licensing and re-assignment agreements (501 for A and 308 for B) and 8,357 patent filings between 2004 and 2014. As is in common in Japan, 59.9 per cent of the patent filings were joint patents with industry; 495 PIs in A and 724 in B were involved in academic patenting.

Even though licensing and re-assignments are not major technology transfer channels, each of the universities has 185 PIs who licensed their inventions in our observation period. However, few university researchers were committed to the start-up ecosystem. Among them, only 29 PIs in each university transferred (licensed or re-assigned) their inventions to start-ups, defined as firms that are within ten years from the date of their foundation that have a connection with their respective parent organisation. When we limit the data solely to focal universities' spin-offs, twenty PIs in A and 12 PIs in B contributed to academic entrepreneurial activities through patent transfers.

As seen in Figure 19.2, we first examined the characteristics of PIs who licensed or re-assigned their patent applications to start-ups and university spin-offs using PI-level performance data covering our whole observation period (hereinafter, whole period/static analysis, results reported in Table 19.2). We used data from both University A and University B. Due to differences in some variables between A and B, we tested them individually to ensure the robustness of our results. We adopted a logit regression analysis to estimate the probability to license to start-ups and spin-offs. In this estimation, we limited ourselves to PIs who had at least one licensed or re-assigned invention, in order to control the fundamental differences between PIs who never licensed their inventions and those who succeeded in technology transfer. Dependent variables are dummy variables that take a value of 1 if the focal PI licensed or re-assigned their patents to start-ups or university spin-offs. Independent variables correspond to Hypotheses 1, 3 and 4.

However, the first analysis cannot identify any causality. Hence, in

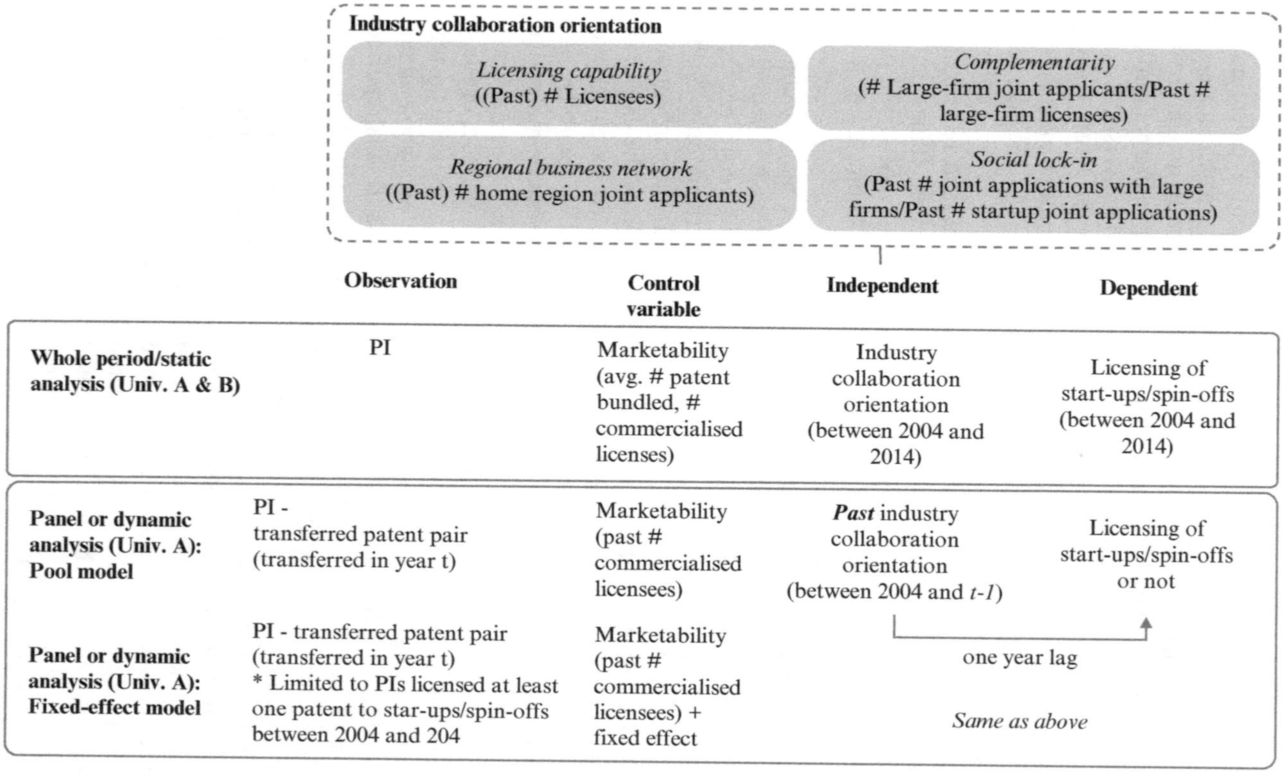

Industry collaboration orientation

- *Licensing capability* ((Past) # Licensees)
- *Complementarity* (# Large-firm joint applicants/Past # large-firm licensees)
- *Regional business network* ((Past) # home region joint applicants)
- *Social lock-in* (Past # joint applications with large firms/Past # startup joint applications)

	Observation	Control variable	Independent	Dependent
Whole period/static analysis (Univ. A & B)	PI	Marketability (avg. # patent bundled, # commercialised licenses)	Industry collaboration orientation (between 2004 and 2014)	Licensing of start-ups/spin-offs (between 2004 and 2014)
Panel or dynamic analysis (Univ. A): Pool model	PI - transferred patent pair (transferred in year t)	Marketability (past # commercialised licensees)	*Past* industry collaboration orientation (between 2004 and $t-1$)	Licensing of start-ups/spin-offs or not
Panel or dynamic analysis (Univ. A): Fixed-effect model	PI - transferred patent pair (transferred in year t) * Limited to PIs licensed at least one patent to star-ups/spin-offs between 2004 and 204	Marketability (past # commercialised licensees) + fixed effect	*Same as above*	*Same as above*

one year lag

Figure 19.2 Research design

the second fixed-effect logit regressions, using panel data of individual patent transfer contracts and corresponding PIs, we estimated the probability of a patent license or re-assignment to start-ups or spin-offs in year t (hereinafter, panel/dynamic analysis, results reported in Table 19.3). In cases when transfer agreements encompassed more than one patent, we split them into individual separate observations (thus, our total observations exceeded 809 licensing agreements). All independent variables are time-dependent on the contract date and we take into account solely the events before the focal contract date. In this analysis, we only used data from University A, due to limited availability of detailed contract information from University B. Dependent variables for our second analysis were dummy variables that took a value of 1 if the focal license or re-assignment contracts are with start-ups or university spin-offs, same as in our first analysis. The unit of analysis is a PI and the corresponding transferred patent (PI-patent) pair. Here we examined also Hypothesis 2. We used both a pool model and PI fixed-effect model. The fixed-effect model controls unobserved PI's characteristics. In this model, we excluded PIs who never licensed or re-assigned their patents to start-ups.

Table 19.1 shows the details of variables used, including their basic statistics.

RESULTS

Table 19.2 shows the logit regression estimation of PI-whole period performance. In University A, the number of licensees and re-assignees (# *Licensees*) is positively correlated with the probability to transfer their inventions to start-ups and spin-offs. By contrast, we did not find such a significant relationship for University B, even though its coefficients are close to University A's. The number of home region joint applicants (# *home region joint applicants*), is positively associated with the probability to license to spin-offs in both institutions. This result is consistent with our Hypothesis 3. Finally, the number of large firms that filed joint patents has only a significant negative correlation with licensing to spin-offs at University B. Our estimations are robust as almost all coefficients are similar in the estimation of the probability to licence or engage in joint applications with start-ups or spin-offs.[2]

These results imply a positive influence of the regional network on academic spin-off incubations. Other two factors – moderating effects between existing firms and start-ups, and constraints with large firms – seem to be reliant on institutional settings or geographical settings.

Table 19.1 Variables, basic statistics

Variables	Description	Whole period/static (Univ. A & B: PI = 370)		Panel/dynamic (Univ. A: PI = 21)		In dynamic analysis used as
		Mean	S.D.	Mean	S.D.	
License to start-ups (dummy)	Dummy variable takes the value of 1 if the focal PI has licensed his/her patent to a start-up (firm established within 10 years).	0.15	0.36	0.24	0.43	Past # start-up licensees
License to university spin-offs (dummy)	Dummy variable takes the value of 1 if the focal PI has licensed his/her patent to a university spin-off.	0.08	0.28	0.20	0.40	
# Licensees	Number of firms to which the PI licensed.	2.61	4.31	8.29	12.12	Past # licensees
# Large firm licensees	Number of large firms in licensees or assignees.	n/a	n/a	0.15	0.50	Past # large firm licensees
# Large firm joint applicants	Number of large firms (having 300+ employees) with which the PI jointly filed patents. We used the number of joint applications with large firms instead of the number of firms, since the total number of joint applications in essence mirrors the linkage with large firms.	1.25	2.54	5.13	8.60	Past # joint applications with large firms
# Home region joint applicants	Number of regional firms (headquartered in a same economic area as the university) with which the PI jointly filed patents. Dependent variables for our second analysis are dummy variables which take a value of 1 if the focal license or re-assignment contracts are with start-ups or university spin-offs, same as in our first examination.	0.52	1.20	1.05	1.60	Past # home region joint applicants

Variable	Description					
# Start-up joint applications	Number of start-ups with which the PI jointly filed patents.	n/a	n/a	0.15	0.50	Past # start-up joint applicants
# Commercialised licenses	Number of license or re-assignment cases that generated more than 20,000 JPY (approx. 200 USD.) For University A this means cases that generated more than 20,000 JPY as licensing revenues and, for University B, as estimated running royalties (in B). Both are indicators of the economic value of the PIs' patents.	0.35	1.39	5.35	10.86	Past # commercialised licences
Avr. # patent bundled	The average number of patents in a bundle reflects the average number of countries in INPADOC families of patents invented by the focal PI. This is the PI-level average number of international patent families bundled in contracts in university A or average number of countries in INPADOC family of PIs' patents from university B.	2.08	2.26	n/a	n/a	

Note: In our whole period or static analysis, these variables are computed in the whole observation period. In the panel/dynamic analysis, variables with prefix 'Past' are computed between 2004 and year $t-1$. The rest of variables are in year t.

Table 19.2   Estimation of probability to license or re-assign inventions to start-ups (whole period or static analysis: Logit model)

	Univ. A		Univ. B	
	License to start-ups	License to univ. spin-offs	License to start-ups	License to univ. spin-offs
# Licensees	1.400**	1.156†	1.139	1.156
	(0.121)	(0.0859)	(0.0906)	(0.110)
# Large-firm joint applicants	0.846	0.829	0.615	0.0898**
	(0.122)	(0.110)	(0.408)	(0.0773)
# Home region joint applicants	0.963	1.272†	1.468	4.014**
	(0.136)	(0.184)	(0.626)	(1.677)
Avr. # patent bundled	1.119	1.186*	1.544**	1.367*
	(0.0774)	(0.0830)	(0.198)	(0.189)
# Commercialised licenses	0.851	0.298†	1.142	1.848**
	(0.368)	(0.218)	(0.175)	(0.421)
Constant	0.0509**	0.0566**	0.0572**	0.0304**
	(0.0213)	(0.0217)	(0.0249)	(0.0152)
Observations	185	185	185	185
Pseudo R2	.230	.179	.091	.173
Log Likelihood	−60.58	−50.26	−69.93	−36.76

Notes: Odds ratio. Cluster robust standard errors are in parentheses. ** $p<0.01$, * $p<0.05$, † $p<0.1$.

Perhaps, since University B is located in a more globalised economic region, constraints with large firms are stronger than for University A.

Our fixed-effect logit regression estimations of PI-patent pairs panel data are shown in Table 19.3. Consistent with our first examination, the number of past licensees has a significantly positive effect on the incubation of start-ups and spin-offs. Also, the number of commercialised licenses increased the license to start-ups and spin-offs. The results are congruent with Hypothesis 1. The number of joint applications with large-firms and large-firm licensees are only significant in the probability of licensing to university spin-offs. Hypothesis 2 is partially supported. The number of joint applicants in the home region, however, is not consistently significant. This means Hypothesis 3 is not supported. Uniquely, both past licenses and joint applications to large

Table 19.3   Estimation of probability to license or re-assign inventions to start-ups in University A (panel or dynamic analysis: Logit model)

	License to start-up		License to univ. spin-off	
	Pool	FE	Pool	FE
Past # Licensees	1.227**	1.174*	1.595**	1.707**
	(0.0967)	(0.0960)	(0.193)	(0.277)
Past # home region	1.228	1.264	1.912*	2.048
joint applicants	(0.348)	(0.517)	(0.591)	(1.139)
Past # joint	0.842†	0.852	0.644**	0.600**
applications with	(0.0765)	(0.0841)	(0.0887)	(0.104)
large firms				
Past # start-up	0.0587**	0.00488**	0.0527**	0.00656**
joint applicants	(0.0409)	(0.00558)	(0.0390)	(0.00780)
Past # large-firm	0.847	0.956	0.528**	0.517**
licensees	(0.114)	(0.140)	(0.105)	(0.130)
Past # start-up	0.823	0.846	0.657*	0.588*
licensees	(0.124)	(0.131)	(0.122)	(0.137)
Past #	1.072**	1.121**	1.086**	1.130**
commercialised	(0.0228)	(0.0381)	(0.0253)	(0.0397)
licenses				
Constant	0.000752**		0.000205**	
	(0.000415)		(0.000147)	
Observations	848	375	854	280
# PIs	181	22	181	14
Log Likelihood	−250.7	−121.2	−179.4	−82.91

Notes: Odds ratio. Standard errors are in parentheses. ** $p<0.01$, * $p<0.05$, † $p<0.1$.

firms or start-ups have a negative influence on the licensing behaviour to university spin-offs. Our Hypothesis 4 is only supported in regard to university spin-offs.

DISCUSSION AND CONCLUSION

Our empirical analyses show that principal investigators (PIs) learn how to license the technologies to start-ups based on their past licensing activities. In addition, our panel analysis implies that PIs with more commercially successful licenses have a higher probability to license to start-ups. From past licensing activities, particularly those connected to fruitful licensing, PIs can get an overview of the market, potential licensees and increase their capability to license.

Nonetheless, previous license experiences are not always positive with regard to transferring to start-ups. Our panel analysis of PIs' licensing behaviour revealed that there is a negative moderating effect between licensing and joint applications with existing firms and licensing to spin-offs. Surprisingly, this effect was found not only in technology transfers to large firms, but also in transfers to start-ups. Having a joint application with a start-up dramatically reduces the probability to license or re-assign a PI's invention to start-ups and spin-offs. Joint applications with individual start-ups can be interpreted as mutual strong ties. Some PIs are shareholders or scientific advisers in these focal start-ups. Therefore, PIs might strive to prevent conflicts of interest between existing licensees and potential new licensees. When our analysis focused on PI-patent pairs, the results indicate that PIs having a link with start-ups are more likely to license inventions to firms other than start-ups. Licensing to start-ups denotes diminished social value returns as smaller firms show higher propensity in successful commercialisation (Nagaoka et al., 2014).

We also found that joint applications with home region firms do not contribute to licensing to spin-offs, although the total number of licensees is positively correlated with the probability to licensing to spin-offs in our whole period analysis. If we combine this with our previous finding, we conclude that regional network is not an antecedent, but rather a consequence. In other words, licensing to spin-offs works as a signal for regional firms and attracts local collaborators and licensees, thus it builds up the local ecosystem. *Mutantis mutandi* to ideas of spin-offs serving as 'ecosystem entrepreneurs' (Spigel, 2017) and contributing to the creation or improvement of the ecosystem, we find that PIs engaging in licensing to spin-offs might play a similar catalytic role.

These findings provide us three insights. First, even though some evidence indicates academic researchers prefer establishing spin-offs over the licensing to existing large firms in order to commercialise their technologies (Samson & Gurdon, 1993), and even though in Japan patents licensed to large firms are less likely to be implemented in the market (Nagaoka et al., 2014), PIs seem to realise complemental benefits of licensing to large firms, such as research collaboration, stable research funding and job opportunities for students. Thus, there are negative effects connected with licensing to large firms from the perspective of licensing to spin-offs.

Second, the regional ecosystem actors gather around the entrepreneurial challenge, signalled by licensing to start-ups. Regional entrepreneurial resources are often seen as accelerating start-up incubation, but our analysis illustrates that regional resources follow entrepreneurial activities at least in the early stages of regional entrepreneurial (i.e. of regional start-up incubation) ecosystem creation.

Finally, social constraints are negative determinants for licensing to start-ups. In short, we found a negative evidence of serial academic entrepreneurs engaged in nurturing multiple spin-offs. Academic researchers often place a high priority on existing ties with the industry or are locked-in by past collaboration partners. This fact implies challenges for start-up incubation ecosystems creation, as well as the importance of innovation policy to overcome these constraints.

From a theoretical perspective, this chapter expanded the PI-oriented framework provided by Wu et al. (2015). It allowed us to find interesting contradicting elements in PIs' industrial collaboration orientation, and to unveil that not only spin-offs as such, but also PIs can be 'ecosystem entrepreneurs' (Spigel, 2017), catalysing opportunities inside the transforming (O'Connor & Reed, 2018) start-up incubation ecosystems. However, their role in regard to supporting start-ups via licensing is contingent on the moderating effects of their overall licensing activities and prior technology transfer activities. Thus, in discussions about regional entrepreneurial and start-up incubation ecosystems and when pondering new exciting research opportunities, we should neither neglect individual actors nor interactions among technology transfer channels. Discovering and analysing lock-ins that effect new start-up opportunities (from the effects of sponsorship to effects of PIs' embeddedness in the industry, e.g. via prior licensing) will bring us a step closer to understanding the evolutionary paths of entrepreneurial ecosystems.

NOTES

*   Both authors are joint first authors. Modic would like to acknowledge Kakenhi Grant-in-Aid for JSPS Fellows grant 16F16774. Yoshioka-Kobayashi would like to acknowledge Ministry of Education, Culture, Sports, Science and Technology for the funding KAKENHI Grant Number 16K03907.
1.   Technology transfer employs many channels, with joint patents, licensing (including re-assignments) and start-ups representing well-established channels.
2.   We added the possibility to engage in joint applications in our main analysis. The mentioned robustness check results are not reported. Exceptionally in this unreported robustness check, for University B, # Licensees is statistically significant. However, we conclude that the volume of licensees is not an essential factor.

REFERENCES

Agostini, L., & Caviggioli, F. (2015). R & D collaboration in the automotive innovation environment: An analysis of co-patenting activities. *Management Decision*, 53(6), 1224–1246.

Azagra-Caro, J. M., Barberá-Tomás, D., Edwards-Schachter, M., & Tur, E. M. (2017).

Dynamic interactions between university-industry knowledge transfer channels: A case study of the most highly cited academic patent. *Research Policy*, 46(2), 463–474.

Belderbos, R., Cassiman, B., Faems, D., Leten, B., & Van Looy, B. (2014). Co-ownership of intellectual property: Exploring the value-appropriation and value-creation implications of co-patenting with different partners. *Research Policy*, 43(5), 841–852.

Bercovitz, J., Changoluisa, J., Feldman, M., & Modic, D. (2019). Pay to Play: Connecting university research funding to licensing outcomes. In F. J. Contractor & J. J. Reuer (Ed.). *Frontiers of Strategic Alliance Research: Negotiating, Structuring and Governing Partnerships*. Cambridge: Cambridge University Press.

Bercovitz, J., & Feldman, M. (2011). The mechanisms of collaboration in inventive teams: Composition, social networks, and geography. *Research Policy*, 40(1), 81–93.

Crespi, G., D'Este, P., Fontana, R., & Geuna, A. (2011). The impact of academic patenting on university research and its transfer. *Research Policy*, 40(1), 55–68.

Funk, M. (2012). Patenting partnerships by U.S. universities. *Journal of Business Administration Online*, Fall, 1–22.

Hagedoorn, J. (2003). Sharing intellectual property rights – an exploratory study of joint patenting amongst companies. *Industrial and Corporate Change*, 12(5), 1035–1050.

Hicks, D. (2000). 360 Degree linkage analysis. *Research Evaluation*, 9(2), 133–143.

Ijichi, H. & Nagaoka, S. (2007). *Nihon no daigaku tou to kenkyu kaihatu dokuritsu gyousei houjin ni okeru jyouryu kenkyu karano hatsumei no genjyou to titeki zaisanken no toriatsukai ni kansuru kenkyu houkoku [Management of IPRs for Upstream Research Inventions in Universities and National R&D Institutes in Japan: Results from the IIR IP Survey 2006]*. Kunitachi: Institute of Innovation Research, Hitotsubashi University.

Isenberg, D. J. (2010). How to start an entrepreneurial revolution. *Harvard Business Review*, 88(6), 40–50.

Jensen, R. A., Thursby, J. G., & Thursby, M. C. (2003). Disclosure and licensing of university inventions: 'The best we can do with the s** t we get to work with'. *International Journal of Industrial Organization*, 21(9), 1271–1300.

Kastrin, A., Klisara, J., Lužar, B., & Povh, J. (2018). Is science driven by principal investigators?. *arXiv preprint*. arXiv:1804.01062.

Kneller, R. (2010). The changing governance of Japanese public science. In R. Whitley, J. Glaser & L. Engval (Eds.). *Reconfiguring Knowledge Production: Changing Authority Relations in the Sciences and their Consequences for Intellectual Innovation* (pp. 110–145). Oxford: Oxford University Press.

Kwon, K. S. (2011). The co-evolution of universities' academic research and knowledge-transfer activities: The case of South Korea. *Science and Public Policy*, 38(6), 493–503.

Nagaoka, S., Nishimura, J., & Akaike, S. (2014). *Making university and industry collaboration: sources of seeds, needs and their matching process (preliminary version)*. Retrieved from http://www.iir.hit-u.ac.jp/doc/pdf-workshop/20140317Making%20university%20and%20industry%20collaboration_NagaokaNishimuraAkaikeHosono.pdf, accessed 10 March 2019.

Nakayama, Y., Hosono, H., & Tomizawa, H. (2017). *Kokuritsu daigaku no kenkyusha no hatsumei ni motozuita tokkyo syutsugan no mourateki chosa [Comprehensive Survey on Patent Applications Based on Inventions by National University Researchers]*. Tokyo: National Institute of Science and Technology Policy.

Natalicchio, A., Petruzzelli, A. M., & Garavelli, A. C. (2017). The impact of partners' technological diversification in joint patenting: A study on firm-PRO collaborations. *Management Decision*, 55(6), 1248–1264.

Melkers, J., & Xiao, F. (2012). Boundary-spanning in emerging technology research: Determinants of funding success for academic scientists. *The Journal of Technology Transfer*, 37(3), 251–270.

O'Connor, A., & Reed, G. (2018). Theorizing the University Governance Role in an Entrepreneurial Ecosystem. In A. O'Connor, E. Stam, F. Sussan, D. B. Audretsch (Eds.). *Entrepreneurial Ecosystems* (pp. 81–100). Cham: Springer.

O'Connor, A., Stam, E., Sussan, F., & Audretsch, D. B. (2018). Entrepreneurial ecosystems:

The foundations of place-based renewal. In A. O'Connor, E. Stam, F. Sussan, D. B. Audretsch (Eds.). *Entrepreneurial Ecosystems* (pp. 1–23). Cham: Springer.

Ooms, W., Werker, C., & Caniëls, M. (2018). Personal and social proximity empowering collaborations: The glue of knowledge networks. *Industry and Innovation*, 25(9), 833–840.

Petruzzelli, A. M. (2011). The impact of technological relatedness, prior ties, and geographical distance on university–industry collaborations: A joint-patent analysis. *Technovation*, 31(7), 309–319.

Samson, K. J. & Gurdon, M. A. (1993). University scientists as entrepreneurs: A special case of technology transfer and high-tech venturing. *Technovation*, 13(2), 63–71.

Shane, S. A. (2004). *Academic entrepreneurship: University spinoffs and wealth creation.* Cheltenham, UK and Northampton, MA: Edward Elgar.

Shane, S., & Khurana, R. (2003). Bringing individuals back in: The effects of career experience on new firm founding. *Industrial and Corporate Change*, 12(3), 519–543.

Spigel, B. (2017). The relational organization of entrepreneurial ecosystems. *Entrepreneurship Theory and Practice*, 41(1), 49–72.

Suvinen, N. (2014). Individual actors building an innovation network. In R. Rutten, P. Benneworth, D. Irawati, & F. Boekema (Eds.). *The Social Dynamics of Innovation Networks* (pp. 140–156). Oxon: Routledge.

Thompson, T. A., Purdy, J. M., & Ventresca, M. J. (2018). How entrepreneurial ecosystems take form: Evidence from social impact initiatives in Seattle. *Strategic Entrepreneurship Journal*, 12(1), 96–116.

Toedtling, F., & Trippl, M. (2013). Transformation of regional innovation systems: From old legacies towards new development paths. In P. Cooke (Ed.). *Re-Framing Regional Development: Evolution, Innovation and Transition* (pp. 297–317). Oxon: Routledge.

UNITT. (2018). *UNITT University Technology Transfer Survey FY2017.* Tokyo: University Network for Innovation and Technology Transfer (UNITT).

Veugelers, R., & Cassiman, B. (2005). R&D cooperation between firms and universities. Some empirical evidence from Belgian manufacturing. *International Journal of Industrial Organization*, 23(5–6), 355–379.

Walsh, J. P., & Huang, H. (2014). Local context, academic entrepreneurship and open science: Publication secrecy and commercial activity among Japanese and US scientists. *Research Policy*, 43(2), 245–260.

Wang, Y., Huang, J., Chen, Y., Pan, X., & Chen, J. (2013). Have Chinese universities embraced their third mission? New insight from a business perspective. *Scientometrics*, 97(2), 207–222.

Woolgar, L. (2007). New institutional policies for university–industry links in Japan. *Research Policy*, 36(8), 1261–1274.

Wu, Y., Welch, E. W., & Huang, W. L. (2015). Commercialization of university inventions: Individual and institutional factors affecting licensing of university patents. *Technovation*, 36–37, 12–25.

Zucker, L. G., Darby, M. R., & Brewer, M. B. (1998). Intellectual human capital and the Birth of U.S. biotechnology enterprises. *American Economic Review*, 88, 290–306.

20. The university ecosystem and the internationalization of spin-off firms
Eva Jenny B. Jørgensen and Adam Novotny

INTRODUCTION

In the last decade, several authors have pointed to the need for a better understanding of the context in entrepreneurship research (Hjorth, Jones, & Gartner, 2008; Welter, 2011; Zahra & Wright, 2011). The extant literature refers to the context as the circumstances, conditions, situations, or environment that are essential to the respective phenomenon and that enable or constrain it (Welter, 2011). It is claimed that although entrepreneurship always emerges in a particular context, research has been remarkably unable to integrate this context. Integrating context is essential in the advancement of entrepreneurship research (Zahra, Wright, & Abdelgawad, 2014) and is important for understanding more about when, how, and why entrepreneurship happens and who becomes involved (Welter, 2011). Specifically, the potential of viewing the context as an entrepreneurial ecosystem is emphasized (Autio, Kenney, Mustar, Siegel, & Wright, 2014). In this chapter, we aim to nuance our understanding of how a context, in terms of a start-up incubation ecosystem, can facilitate international entrepreneurship and the internationalization of university spin-offs (USOs).

We see the internationalization of USOs as the firms' exploitation of one or several international market opportunities (Di Gregorio, Musteen, & Thomas, 2008; Oviatt & McDougall, 2005), and thereby the likelihood to achieve international sales. Although USOs are founded on research results from universities and started by academic or student entrepreneurs, perspectives on internationalization have not received much attention in the academic entrepreneurship literature. The lack of knowledge on USO internationalization is a serious limitation of our understanding of these firms. This is because internationalization can provide USOs with important access to new markets, as well as new sources of supply, knowledge, or other valuable resources. Hence, internationalization represents an important but rather unexplored perspective for understanding the growth and development of USOs.

The internationalization of USOs does not emerge in a vacuum. These activities are embedded in a context, that is, a start-up incubation ecosystem that helps or hinders their development. A start-up incubation ecosystem can be defined as a set of interdependent actors and factors that interact as a system, providing a nurturing environment for the creation and successful development of start-ups. The academic entrepreneurship ecosystem is found to be essential for the creation and development of the firms that they spin out (Hayter, Nelson, Zayed, & O'Connor, 2018), and a particular feature of USOs is that they maintain a strong relationship with their parent university (Mathisen & Rasmussen, 2019). In addition, recent research in the international entrepreneurship literature has pointed to specific features of universities as important contexts for international entrepreneurship (Evers, Cunningham, & Hoholm, 2016).

Many small and new firms lack the motivation and resources to internationalize (Westhead, Wright, & Ucbasaran, 2001), but USOs are born in a university context which provides them with relatively freely available resources (e.g. human capital, research infrastructure, international networks and programmes) they can use to develop their international activities. In this chapter, we focus on supporting contexts in terms of university ecosystems for the development of internationalization of USOs. We regard the university as a start-up incubation ecosystem by its very nature. The university is a collection of different departments and other organizational units, scientists, students, managers, and administrative staff that interact as a system to achieve various individual and organizational goals including the creation, development and internationalization of spin-off firms. Based on these arguments, our research question is as follows: Whether and to what extent do the characteristics of a university ecosystem facilitate the internationalization of USOs?

The theoretical contribution of this chapter is twofold. First, by focusing on the internationalization of USOs we tighten the gap between academic and international entrepreneurship. Second, we contribute to a better understanding of whether and how the university context can function as a start-up incubation ecosystem that can facilitate USO internationalization.

THEORETICAL BACKGROUND

The Internationalization of USOs

USOs have traditionally been defined as new firms created by university faculty to commercially exploit some knowledge, technology, or research developed within a university; see for example Pirnay, Surlemont, and Nlemvo (2003). However, this definition has later been broadened to include firms that do not have a formal licensing agreement with a university, as well as firms established by individuals other than faculty, including postdocs and students (Hayter et al., 2018). USOs are knowledge- and technology-intensive and are found to be more innovative than companies that have been established via different methods (Lejpras, 2014). Generally, they are attracting massive venture capital and are internationalizing rapidly to the far corners of the world (Etemad, 2016).

The internationalization of USOs can be seen as an entrepreneurial process defined as "the discovery, enactment, evaluation and exploitation of opportunities – across national borders – to create future goods and services" (Oviatt & McDougall, 2005, p. 540). Based on this definition, we interpret USOs' internationalization as the likelihood to exploit international market opportunities. The opportunity-based view of internationalization has been a popular topic in the literature in recent years (see for example Mainela, Puhakka, & Servais, 2014). There is a broad agreement that an opportunity-based view involves two main processes (Muzychenko & Liesch, 2015; Vinogradov & Jørgensen, 2017). The first is international opportunity scouting (Hilmersson & Papaioannou, 2015) or opportunity recognition (Andersson & Evers, 2015), which is connected to the discovery of market opportunities. This process involves searches for possibilities that can create future goods and services. The second, often referred to as enactment (Laperrière & Spence, 2015) or opportunity realization (Åkerman, 2015), involves mobilizing, committing, and orchestrating resources to exploit international market opportunities. The focus of our study is on the likelihood of firms to reach the second stage, that is, exploiting one or several international market opportunities and achieving international sales.

The Influence of the University Ecosystem on USO Internationalization

In this chapter, we want to understand more about whether and to what extent characteristics of a university ecosystem may facilitate USO internationalization. USOs are born in a university context that can be viewed as an academic entrepreneurial ecosystem (Hayter et al., 2018). The emerging view of the university as an entrepreneurial system mirrors a growing focus on the wider social-economic role of universities (Foss & Gibson, 2015), including the establishment and development of USOs which are internationally oriented. The main idea behind the ecosystem thinking is the interconnectivity between constituent elements and their collective ability to provide knowledge and resources for firm success (Hayter, 2016). Reviewing the literature on academic entrepreneurial ecosystems, Hayter et al. (2018) identify several factors that are found to influence the establishment and development of USOs. These are the characteristics of the individual entrepreneur; the entrepreneurs' human capital and social networks; the entrepreneurial environment; financial resources; scientific, technical, and product characteristics; academic entrepreneurship programmes; and university management and policy. Below we argue that both the size and international orientation of the university ecosystem are important factors that can facilitate the internationalization of USOs.

The size of the university ecosystem
We aim to explore what impact the size of the university ecosystem has on the internationalization of USOs. Earlier research has demonstrated that the size of the university ecosystem has a significant impact on the creation of USOs (Horta, Meoli, & Vismara, 2016) and on the entrepreneurial effectiveness of the university (Van Looy et al., 2011). Based on the ecosystem perspective, it is likely that a larger university ecosystem, compared to a smaller one, will contain more elements that collectively can support the internationalization of USOs. At the individual level, a large university ecosystem will include more scientists and students who create firms that will internationalize. At the organizational level, it is more likely that a larger university system will have elements, as for example TTOs, incubators, venture funds, offices for academic mobility, international networks, exchange programmes, and educational programmes that directly or indirectly may benefit USOs' international opportunity exploitation. In addition, a large university ecosystem, compared to a smaller one, often has more resources to interconnect these elements to support USO internationalization. With this background, we suggest the following hypothesis:

H1: The size of the university ecosystem positively influences USO internationalization.

The international orientation of the university ecosystem
The two main activities at universities, teaching and research, are both increasingly international in nature. In this study, we will also explore how the internationalization of the university ecosystem may facilitate the internationalization of USOs. Global higher education rankings place large emphasis on the level of internationalization of universities, typically measured by the proportion of international mobility among students and scientists (Marginson & van der Wende, 2007). Academics and students who are internationally mobile serve as important carriers of knowledge across national borders. In order to internationalize, one of the

most important resources for USOs is "internationalization knowledge". Internationalization knowledge is typically related to a specific host country in terms of institutional knowledge (knowledge about language, laws, and rules) and business culture knowledge, as well as to knowledge about internationalization in general (Johanson & Vahlne, 2009). Mobility can provide potential scientist/student entrepreneurs with valuable international knowledge, in addition to international experience and networks. Hence, we suggest the following hypotheses:

H2a: International student mobility positively influences USO internationalization.

H2b: International scientist mobility positively influences USO internationalization.

METHOD

Sample

To analyse the relationship between USO internationalization and the university ecosystem, data was collected at both the firm and university level. Firm-level data was gathered from databases built within the framework of the Research Council of Norway's FORNY programme, which had been designed to support the commercialization of university research results in Norway. The start-up portfolio accumulated by the programme since 1996 consists of a significant number of USOs (374 in 2015) but is dominated by a few high-performing ventures. From the 374 registered USOs, 109 have spun out of research institutes and 26 do not have a confirmed academic affiliation, so we omitted them from the sample. Fifteen firms were excluded because of missing data on international sales, hence the final sample consists of 224 USOs. The sampled firms were established at 16 Norwegian universities and university colleges in the period between 1998 and 2012. USO activities were observed from firm foundation until 2015. The average firm was established in 2004 and was 11 years old at the end of the observation period. The oldest firm in the sample is 17 years of age.

Information on universities, shown in Table 20.1, was obtained from the Norwegian Centre for Research Data (http://www.nsd.uib.no/). The difficulty of assessing university ecosystems in Norway is that its higher education system has been continuously undergoing reforms since the end of the 1980s (Kyvik & Stensaker, 2016). As firms in the sample were

Table 20.1 University ecosystems (in order of their weight in the sample)

Name of university	Number of USOs in the sample	Distribution of USOs	Top university	University size[a]	Student mobility[b]	Scientist mobility[c]
1. Norwegian University of Science and Technology (NTNU)	68	30.36	Yes	20,262.8	801.1/663.7	162.4/166.1
2. University of Oslo (UiO)	45	20.09	Yes	29,708.0	826.3/748.3	188.6/195.4
3. University of Bergen (UiB)	21	9.38	Yes	15,740.8	654.6/495.2	151.5/197.6
4. Norwegian University of Life Sciences (NMBU)	20	8.93	Yes	3,041.4	120/105.7	39.1/45.6
5. University of Tromsø (UiT)	18	8.04	Yes	6,777.6	83.2/101.9	27.8/89.5
6. University of Agder (UiA)	17	7.59	No	8,143.1	153/229.3	18.6/42.4
7. University of Stavanger (UiS)	11	4.91	No	7,685.7	115.6/101.8	24.6/66.1
8. Sør-Trøndelag University College (HiST)	8	3.57	No	7,401.6	52.9/98.1	6.8/22.3
9. Narvik University College (HiN)	6	2.68	No	1,096.1	68.8/4.6	13/26.3
10. Akershus University College (HiAk)	2	0.89	No	4,347.9	13.9/42.5	10.5/20.4
11. Bergen University College (HiB)	2	0.89	No	6,274.4	51.6/147.8	12.6/25.9
12. Oslo University College (HiO)	2	0.89	No	11,118.2	166/243.8	36/84.9
13. Stord/Haugesund University College (HSH)	1	0.45	No	2,554.9	31.5/38.6	4.5/8.4
14. Nord-Trøndelag University College (HiNT)	1	0.45	No	4,306.8	15.6/10.8	6.2/16.6
15. Telemark University College (HiT)	1	0.45	No	5,421.4	83.2/33.4	10.9/27.5
16. Norwegian School of Veterinary Science (NVH)	1	0.45	No	436.9	9.1/7.8	10.4/20
Total	224	100		8,394.8	211/192.1	45.2/65.9

Notes:
a Mean of the number of students during the observation period.
b Mean of the number of incoming/outgoing students (exchange stays) during the observation period.
c Mean of the number of incoming/outgoing scientists (exchange stays) during the observation period.

established between 1998 and 2012, their ecosystems were influenced by the second wave of these reforms, when several university colleges merged to apply for university status. As a result, the development of some firms could have been influenced by more than one ecosystem, for example, if parent institutions merged around the time when the firm was created. Other measurement biases may derive from the inconsistent and incomplete data reporting of some universities, especially regarding scientist mobility.

Variables

The dependent variable is international sales that shows whether the firm has sold products and/or services abroad during the observation period or not, through direct or indirect exporting. About one-fifth of the sampled USOs have realized international sales during the observation period, that is, the first eight years of firm development on average. Firm-level control variables include technology type (software and biotech/pharmaceutical), firm location (core, i.e., located in Oslo and Akershus, or periphery), the attainment of venture capital during the observation period (yes/no), and establishment year (measuring the effect of time and macroeconomic conditions).

The main university ecosystem variables are ecosystem size (total number of students) as well as four international mobility variables measuring the international orientation of the university ecosystem: the total number of incoming and outgoing students and scientists. As a control for university quality, which may influence the international potential of USOs, we created a variable measuring whether the university is a top Norwegian higher education institution or not, according to THE (https://www.timeshighereducation.com). Table 20.2 contains the descriptive statistics of the measured variables.

The international orientation of the university ecosystem was measured by the volume of foreign and Norwegian students and scientists who completed an exchange stay (in any exchange programme) in Norway or abroad respectively, of a certain duration, in a given year. To mitigate the biases caused by the fluctuations in annual mobility figures, we averaged out the number of exchange stays using a five-year running window, that is, from two years before to two years after the year of firm establishment. The same procedure was applied to calculate ecosystem size but based on the average number of students. In what follows, we examine the effect of the university ecosystem on USOs' international opportunity exploitation by means of bivariate correlations and logistic regressions.

Table 20.2   Descriptive statistics (n = 224)

Variable	Mean/ Distribution	SD	Min.	Max.
Firm level variables:				
International sales (DV)	21.9%	–	0	1
Software firm	37.1%	–	0	1
Bio-pharma firm	25.9%	–	0	1
Core region	29.0%	–	0	1
Venture capital	33.5%	–	0	1
Establishment year	2004.8	3.69	1999	2012
University level variables:				
University size	15,935.6	9,536.9	433.8	33,349.4
Incoming students	498.3	349.1	6.4	1,390
Outgoing students	428.4	293.4	1.5	964.6
Incoming scientists	109.7	90.2	0	376.8
Outgoing scientists	129.9	92.1	0	341.4
University quality	top: 31.25%	–	0	1

ANALYSIS AND RESULTS

First, we explored the bivariate relationships between firm and university ecosystem characteristics by correlational analyses. Spearman's rho was used, as we supposed that variables change together in a monotonic fashion, but not necessarily at a constant rate or linear way (data transformations were not applied). Correlation coefficients in Table 20.3 show that the likelihood of entering international markets has a statistically significant relation with the acquisition of venture capital and the international mobility of scientists (Table 20.3). Regarding the hypotheses, scientists' international mobility has a stronger association with USOs' international activity than student mobility or university size.

The correlation table also reveals that there is a relatively strong association among international mobility variables and between university size and mobility figures. To make more accurate assessments of individual predictors, we ran a separate regression model for each key university ecosystem variable. Hence, we managed to keep the variance inflation factor value for each variable under 3, which is considered to be safe in general.

In the second step, we used logistic regression analysis for testing the impact of the university ecosystem on the international performance of

Table 20.3 Correlation coefficients (n = 224)

	(1)	(2)	(3)	(4)	(5)	(6)	(7)	(8)	(9)	(10)	(11)	(12)
(1) International sales	1											
(2) Software firm	0.13	1										
(3) Bio-pharma firm	−0.04	−0.37*	1									
(4) Core region firm	0.02	−0.12	0.18*	1								
(5) Firm est. year	−0.13	−0.17*	0.08	−0.14*	1							
(6) Venture capital	0.20*	−0.02	0.14*	0.00	−0.17*	1						
(7) University quality	0.11	−0.06	0.20*	0.26*	−0.15*	0.28*	1					
(8) University size	0.12	−0.01	0.11	0.32*	0.21*	0.15*	0.49*	1				
(9) Students – incoming	0.10	−0.04	0.17*	0.19*	0.38*	0.13	0.59*	0.88*	1			
(10) Students – outgoing	0.08	−0.02	0.11	0.13	0.38*	0.17*	0.50*	0.83*	0.86*	1		
(11) Scientists – incoming	0.18*	0.05	0.12	0.05	0.19*	0.22*	0.57*	0.77*	0.76*	0.73*	1	
(12) Scientists – outgoing	0.17*	0.07	0.14*	0.06	0.30*	0.17*	0.52*	0.69*	0.78*	0.71*	0.85*	1

Note: * $p < 0.05$.

374

firms. We anticipated that larger and internationally oriented university ecosystems are more likely to spin out firms that exploit international opportunities.

According to regression coefficients, shown in Table 20.4, university size does not influence firm internationalization; thus H1 is not supported. On the other hand, a stronger international orientation of the university ecosystem, and especially measured by scientist mobility, significantly (p < .01) increases the future probability of USOs' internationalization. Accordingly, for a one-unit increase in the number of outgoing or incoming scientists we can expect a 0.6–0.7 per cent increase in the odds of a firm to go international. Student exchange measures are weaker predictors of firm internationalization, with incoming students having a somewhat stronger effect of the two. Regarding the control variables, USOs are more likely (p < .05) to realize international sales if they have obtained venture capital or were established earlier (i.e., observed longer).

We also tested the hypotheses by applying logarithmic transformation to the original mobility variables as well as to university size, that is, the number of students. The high significance of the transformed values of outgoing scientists (p < .001) and incoming scientists (p < .01) indicates that there is almost certainly a true effect of scientist mobility on the internationalization of USOs. The transformed number of incoming students also has a statistically significant (p < .05) influence, but the transformed variable of ecosystem size remains insignificant.

To sum up, the positive effect of student mobility (H2a) is weakly supported, while the positive effect of scientist mobility (H2b) is clearly supported by the data. The models containing scientist mobility have better predictive ability than the ones containing student mobility. While ecosystem size does not tell much about the global impact of spin-off firms, the international orientation of the university ecosystem proved to be an important predictor of the internationalization of USOs.

In the models presented in Table 20.4, we measured the international orientation of university ecosystems with the total number of students and scientists registered in various international exchange programmes. We also tested the effects of relative international mobility variables (i.e., ones proportional to the number of students); however, these proportions are influenced by university size. Not surprisingly, relative mobility variables had little or no influence on USO internationalization, with the relative number of incoming scientists showing the strongest effect, but still not significant at the 0.05 level.

Table 20.4 Results from multiple logistic regression predicting international sales of USOs (log-odds, standard errors and odds ratios)

	Ecosystem size			Incoming students			Outgoing students			Incoming scientists			Outgoing scientists		
	B	SE	Exp(B)	B	SE	Exp(B)	B	SE	Exp(B)	B	SE	Exp(B)	B	SE	Exp(B)
Software firm	0.521	0.388	1.683	0.515	0.391	1.674	0.529	0.387	1.697	0.465	0.386	1.592	0.355	0.388	1.426
Bio-pharma firm	-0.181	0.432	0.834	-0.175	0.431	0.840	-0.173	0.434	0.841	-0.195	0.433	0.823	-0.316	0.427	0.729
Core region firm	-0.144	0.423	0.866	0.011	0.387	1.011	0.013	0.382	1.013	-0.020	0.386	0.980	-0.046	0.390	0.955
Firm est. year	-0.075	0.049	0.928	-0.119*	0.058	0.888*	-0.094	0.057	0.910	-0.111*	0.054	0.895*	-0.147*	0.062	0.863*
Venture capital	0.813*	0.361	2.254*	0.851*	0.360	2.341*	0.795*	0.366	2.214*	0.821*	0.361	2.273*	0.831*	0.361	2.296*
University quality	0.083	0.549	1.086	-0.272	0.632	0.762	0.079	0.565	1.082	-0.296	0.580	0.744	-0.350	0.605	0.705
University size	0.000	0.000	1.000												
Students – incoming				0.001	0.001	1.001†									
Students – outgoing							0.001	0.001	1.001						
Scientists – incoming										0.006**	0.002	1.006**			
Scientists – outgoing													0.007**	0.003	1.007**
Constant	146.987	99.286		235.303*	116.193		186.461	114.849		220.412*	109.061		291.842*	124.1	
McFadden's R²	0.074			0.078			0.071			0.091			0.097		
Chi-square	χ²=18.85, df=7, p<.01			χ²=19.84, df=7, p<.01			χ²=17.77, df=7, p<.05			χ²=20.59, df=7, p<.01			χ²=18.89, df=7, p<.01		

Note: † = p < .1; * = p < .05; ** = p < .01.

DISCUSSION

In this chapter, we examined whether and to what extent the characteristics of the university ecosystem facilitate the internationalization of the firms that they spin out. We expected to find that both the size and the international orientation of the university ecosystem would have a positive influence. Our results demonstrate that the international orientation of the university ecosystem positively influences the international opportunity exploitation of USOs. The mobility of scientists proved to be a better indicator of USO internationalization than student mobility. The results seem reasonable because there are more scientists than students creating USOs, but also because scientists probably gain more international knowledge (both country-specific and general), international networks, and experiences through international mobility compared to students. Moreover, these results seem to be in line with what Andersson and Berggren (2016) found in a case study of 10 USOs from Halmstad University, where scientists created USOs that were born global, and students created firms that were less internationally oriented.

We found no significant support for a positive impact of the size of the university ecosystem on USO internationalization. This contrasts with earlier findings which propose that larger ecosystems facilitate the creation of USOs (Horta et al., 2016) and the entrepreneurial effectiveness of the university (Van Looy et al., 2011). Our argument was that a larger ecosystem contains more elements that can support USO internationalization (TTOs, venture funds, international exchange programmes, and educational courses/programmes) and has more resources to connect these individual elements. We believe that our results indicate that even if a large university ecosystem contains many individual actors and factors, it does not necessarily mean that these factors also interact as a system providing a supporting environment for internationalization. This could be due, for example, to sharp borders between different departments and a rather closed university organizational culture. The lack of significant support for this hypothesis could also be due to the fact that we measured the size of the university ecosystem by the number of students. While enrolment is often used to measure university size, other proxies are also possible such as university budget and the number of departments or organizational units.

Earlier research has demonstrated that certain characteristics of an academic entrepreneurial ecosystem can facilitate both the creation and the development of USOs (see Hayter et al., 2018 for an overview). In our chapter, we explored a typical development strategy, that is, internationalization. Overall, our study demonstrates that the university context can be viewed as a start-up incubation ecosystem where individuals, certain organizational elements, and their interactions can support the development of the start-ups and their internationalization strategies. We thereby provide some novel insights into how an organization as an incubation ecosystem can facilitate spin-off firms' development through internationalization. From a theoretical point of view, we integrate academic entrepreneurship ecosystem influences into the international entrepreneurship literature. As such, this study tightens the gap between academic entrepreneurship, which has been occupied with the university context but not the internationalization of USOs, and international entrepreneurship, which has been occupied with the internationalization of SMEs but not the context.

Limitations and Possibilities for Further Research

An important limitation of this study is that we used only a single measure of internationalization (whether the firm has had international sales or not). Further research could use more elaborated measures of internationalization and hence increase our understanding of how university ecosystems can promote more rapid, extensive, and globalized forms of firm internationalization. Such research could use for example, the suggestions from Kuivalainen, Sundqvist, Saarenketo, and McNaughton (2012) on how to measure internationalization patterns. They suggest that three categories can be used to measure internationalization: speed (the time elapsed from the creation of the firm until the first international activity), scale (the extent, degree, or intensity of internationalization), and scope (the geographical scope of the international activities). Further research should also apply alternative ways to measure size of the university ecosystem. Alternative measures of size could be the number of academic staff, the number of departments and other organizational units, or university budget. Research on academic entrepreneurial ecosystems is criticized for being focused on individual ecosystem elements (Hayter, 2016). Hence, promising future research lies in more strategic and systemic conceptualizations of the university ecosystem, for instance, by taking some more characteristics of the university and the regional context into account. In this study, we simplified and treated data as if it was cross-sectional in nature. However, applying a more complex, panel data design and incorporating the effect of time and the changes of firm characteristics more efficiently in the models would provide a more nuanced picture of how, when, and why USOs internationalize.

REFERENCES

Åkerman, N. (2015). International opportunity realization in firm internationalization: Non-linear effects of market-specific knowledge and internationalization knowledge. *Journal of International Entrepreneurship, 13*(3), 242–259. doi:10.1007/s10843-015-0152-x

Andersson, S., & Berggren, E. (2016). Born global or local? Factors influencing the internationalization of university spin-offs – the case of Halmstad University. *Journal of International Entrepreneurship, 14*(3), 296–322. doi:10.1007/s10843-016-0182-z

Andersson, S., & Evers, N. (2015). International opportunity recognition in international new ventures – a dynamic managerial capabilities perspective. *Journal of International Entrepreneurship, 13*(3), 260–276. doi:10.1007/s10843-015-0149-5

Autio, E., Kenney, M., Mustar, P., Siegel, D., & Wright, M. (2014). Entrepreneurial innovation: The importance of context. *Research Policy, 43*(7), 1097–1108. doi:10.1016/j.respol.2014.01.015

Di Gregorio, D., Musteen, M., & Thomas, D. E. (2008). International new ventures: The cross-border nexus of individuals and opportunities. *Journal of World Business, 43*(2), 186–196. doi:10.1016/j.jwb.2007.11.013

Etemad, H. (2016). Special thematic issue on: International interactions and activities of university-based technology entrepreneurship. *Journal of International Entrepreneurship, 14*(3), 277–284. doi:10.1007/s10843-016-0189-5

Evers, N., Cunningham, J. A., & Hoholm, T. (2016). International entrepreneurship in universities: Context, emergence and actors. *Journal of International Entrepreneurship, 14*(3), 285–295. doi:10.1007/s10843-016-0188-6

Foss, L., & Gibson, D. V. (2015). *The Entrepreneurial University: Context and Institutional Change* (Vol. 37). London: Routledge.

Hayter, C. S. (2016). A trajectory of early-stage spinoff success: The role of knowledge intermediaries within an entrepreneurial university ecosystem. *Small Business Economics, 47*(3), 633–656. doi:10.1007/s11187-016-9756-3

Hayter, C. S., Nelson, A. J., Zayed, S., & O'Connor, A. C. (2018). Conceptualizing academic entrepreneurship ecosystems: A review, analysis and extension of the literature. *Journal of Technology Transfer, 43*(4), 1039–1082. doi:10.1007/s10961-018-9657-5

Hilmersson, M., & Papaioannou, S. (2015). SME international opportunity scouting – empirical insights on its determinants and outcomes. *Journal of International Entrepreneurship, 13*(3), 186–211. doi:10.1007/s10843-015-0155-7

Hjorth, D., Jones, C., & Gartner, W. B. (2008). Introduction for 'Recreating/Recontextualising Entrepreneurship'. *Scandinavian Journal of Management, 24*(2), 81–84.

Horta, H., Meoli, M., & Vismara, S. (2016). Skilled unemployment and the creation of academic spin-offs: A recession-push hypothesis. *The Journal of Technology Transfer, 41*(4), 798–817. doi:10.1007/s10961-015-9405-z

Johanson, J., & Vahlne, J.-E. (2009). The Uppsala internationalization process model revisited: From liability of foreignness to liability of outsidership. *Journal of International Business Studies, 40*(9), 1411–1431.

Kuivalainen, O., Sundqvist, S., Saarenketo, S., & McNaughton, R. (2012). Internationalization patterns of small and medium-sized enterprises. *International Marketing Review, 29*(5), 448–465.

Kyvik, S., & Stensaker, B. (2016). Mergers in Norwegian higher education. In R. Pinheiro, L. Geschwind, & T. Aarrevaara (Eds.), *Mergers in Higher Education: The Experience from Northern Europe* (pp. 29–42). Cham: Springer International Publishing.

Laperrière, A., & Spence, M. (2015). Enacting international opportunities: The role of organizational learning in knowledge-intensive business services. *Journal of International Entrepreneurship, 13*(3), 212–241. doi:10.1007/s10843-015-0151-y

Lejpras, A. (2014). How innovative are spin-offs at later stages of development? Comparing innovativeness of established research spin-offs and otherwise created firms. *Small Business Economics, 43*(2), 327–351. doi:10.1007/s11187-013-9534-4

Mainela, T., Puhakka, V., & Servais, P. (2014). The concept of international opportunity in international entrepreneurship: A review and a research agenda. *International Journal of Management Reviews*, *16*(1), 105–129. doi:10.1111/ijmr.12011

Marginson, S., & van der Wende, M. (2007). To rank or to be ranked: The impact of global rankings in higher education. *Journal of Studies in International Education*, *11*(3–4), 306–329. doi:10.1177/1028315307303544

Mathisen, M. T., & Rasmussen, E. (2019). The development, growth, and performance of university spin-offs: A critical review. *The Journal of Technology Transfer, https://doi. org/10.1007/s10961-018-09714-9* doi:10.1007/s10961-018-09714-9

Muzychenko, O., & Liesch, P. W. (2015). International opportunity identification in the internationalisation of the firm. *Journal of World Business*, *50*(4), 704–717. doi:https://doi.org/10.1016/j.jwb.2014.12.001

Oviatt, B. M., & McDougall, P. P. (2005). Defining international entrepreneurship and modeling the speed of internationalization. *Entrepreneurship Theory and Practice*, *29*(5), 537–553.

Pirnay, F., Surlemont, B., & Nlemvo, F. (2003). Toward a typology of university spin-offs. *Small Business Economics*, *21*(4), 355–369. doi:10.1023/a:1026167105153

Van Looy, B., Landoni, P., Callaert, J., van Pottelsberghe, B., Sapsalis, E., & Debackere, K. (2011). Entrepreneurial effectiveness of European universities: An empirical assessment of antecedents and trade-offs. *Research Policy*, *40*(4), 553–564. doi:https://doi.org/10.1016/j.respol.2011.02.001

Vinogradov, E., & Jørgensen, E. J. B. (2017). Differences in international opportunity identification between native and immigrant entrepreneurs. *Journal of International Entrepreneurship*, *15*(2), 207–228. doi:10.1007/s10843-016-0197-5

Welter, F. (2011). Contextualizing entrepreneurship – conceptual challenges and ways forward. *Entrepreneurship Theory and Practice*, *35*(1), 165–184. doi:10.1111/j.1540-6520.2010.00427.x

Westhead, P., Wright, M., & Ucbasaran, D. (2001). The internationalization of new and small firms: A resource-based view. *Journal of Business Venturing*, *16*(4), 333–358.

Zahra, S. A., & Wright, M. (2011). Entrepreneurship's next act. *Academy of Management Perspectives*, *25*(4), 67–83. doi:10.5465/amp.2010.0149

Zahra, S. A., Wright, M., & Abdelgawad, S. G. (2014). Contextualization and the advancement of entrepreneurship research. *International Small Business Journal*, *32*(5), 479–500. doi:10.1177/0266242613519807

21. The academic entrepreneurship ecosystem: The role of the university for societal impact of academic spin-offs*
Anders Billström

INTRODUCTION

Business ecosystems have grown in popularity among researchers and practitioners in the last decades. Ecosystems are important for the development and performance of firms. The business ecosystem literature emerged from the organizational ecology literature and concerns the interactions among organizations to achieve common goals (Moore, 1993). The concept has also been applied to the entrepreneurship context (e.g. Alvedalen and Boschma, 2017) and recently also to the academic entrepreneurship context (e.g. Hayter, Nelson, Zayed and O'Connor, 2018). Hence, entrepreneurship ecosystem research is yet a very young and immature stream of research.

The academic entrepreneurship ecosystem is a start-up incubation ecosystem promoting the development and performance of academic spin-offs. Academic spin-offs are firms commercializing knowledge, research and technology developed within a university (Pirnay, Surlemont and Nlemvo, 2003). This study uses the concept academic entrepreneurship ecosystem instead of the concept start-up incubation ecosystem because it is adapted to this specific context.

Academic entrepreneurship research has so far investigated single actors and organizations in the ecosystem while eschewing a system perspective, which provides a narrow view of new firm development (Hayter et al., 2018). Studies have frequently investigated university incubators, industry partners, science parks, Technology Transfer Officers – TTOs, and venture capitalists. Only a few studies have concerned accelerators, proof of concept centres, university seed funds and surprisingly, the university. The university is a very influential actor in the ecosystem (Civera, Meoli and Vismara, 2019) for several reasons.

First, the university takes by law (in U.S. and many European countries) an ownership share in these firms (Wright, Clarysse, Mustar and Lockett, 2007). Second, the university has by definition a natural connection to these firms because the technology and/or the inventor come from the university (Pirnay et al., 2003). Third, many universities have created a system of support actors including the incubator, science park, TTO and seed fund to support the development of academic spin-offs (Hayter et al., 2018). Finally, the university imprints the new firm with technical expertise, technology characteristics (Ferriani, Garnsey and Lorenzoni, 2012) and international behaviour (Civera et al., 2019). Hence, this study investigates the role of the ecosystem and particularly the university, in the performance of academic spin-offs.

There is a debate about the financial and economic performance of academic spin-offs. Studies of U.S. academic spin-offs show that these firms grow, create new jobs, generate tax income and contribute to regional development (Shane, 2004). In contrast, studies of European academic spin-offs indicate that most of these firms remain small, grow slowly (Mustar, Wright and Clarysse, 2008; Fini, Rasmussen, Siegel and Wiklund, 2018) and do not perform in the same way as corporate spin-offs (Wennberg, Wiklund and Wright, 2011). As a result, a few studies have recently changed focus from narrow financial and economic measures, to the societal impact of science commercialization (D'Este, Ramos-Vielba, Woolley and Amara, 2018; Fini et al., 2018). This is important because academic research aims to develop knowledge and address the grand challenges and sustainability goals (www.un.org), rather than creating financial and economic growth.

Research and literature is so far limited to empirical illustrations of social benefits. Examples of such benefits, also called societal impact, are firms creating new vaccines to treat diseases (Li and Garnsey, 2014), cleaner technologies to protect the environment (Kivimaa, Boon, Antikainen, 2017). However, theoretical knowledge regarding the societal impact of academic spin-offs from an ecosystem perspective is underdeveloped. This study addresses this gap by investigating the academic entrepreneurship ecosystem, and in particular the role of the university in the creation of academic spin-offs with societal impact.

The research questions are: how and why do the academic entrepreneurship ecosystem and in particular the university contribute to the creation of societal impact of academic spin-offs? The purpose is to develop a framework of the academic entrepreneurship ecosystem and in particular the role of the university in creating societal impact. To achieve this purpose, the study uses literature on academic entrepreneurship ecosystem and societal impact. The study employs a case study design and investigates academic spin-offs and for contrasting reasons, firms originating from research institutes.

THEORETICAL FRAME OF REFERENCE

This chapter combines literature on academic entrepreneurship ecosystem and societal impact of science commercialization.

The Academic Entrepreneurship Ecosystem

Entrepreneurship research has not yet clearly defined the concept entrepreneurship ecosystem, which provides a challenge to set its boundaries and scientifically investigate the phenomenon (Audretsch, Cunningham, Kuratko, Lehmann and Mente, 2019). This challenge also applies to the academic entrepreneurship ecosystem concept.

Several attempts have been made to describe the academic entrepreneurship ecosystem. Nelsen (2010) describes the ecosystem of the Massachusetts Institute of Technology (MIT) as businesses, investment communities and the university in a synergistic relationship that have emerged over several decades in a spontaneous way. Thus, the ecosystem contains entrepreneurs, industry scientists, university researchers and venture capitalists who interact continuously to transform the regional industry. Similarly, Hayter et al. (2018, p.1069) explain that *"Ecosystems, by definition, include a variety of different elements working in harmony"*. These and other descriptions lack the idea that an ecosystem generates value for the ecosystem itself (Audretsch et al., 2019). The ecosystem has a common goal and the firm contributes back to the ecosystem. This study defines the academic entrepreneurship ecosystem as the interactions between actors and organizations to commercialize academic knowledge or technology.

A review of academic entrepreneurship research reveals only a handful of papers published on academic entrepreneurship ecosystem. These are limited to the influence of the ecosystem before the creation of new firms, the firm development and firm performance. A policy study, an introduction to a special issue and literature reviews were also found.

Ecosystem research and *the intentions to start academic spin-offs*, show that the university has several functions. The university department promotes the social interactions among researchers and the TTO hosts informational events, which together encourage academic spin-off creation (Backs, Günther, and Stummer, 2019). Students' involvement in entrepreneurship programmes has a positive effect on the number of start-up activities while university financial support has a negative effect (Morris, Shriokovas and Tsukovas, 2017). Hence, the ecosystem contributes to start-up intensions and activities taken to initiate new firms.

The ecosystem is also essential for *academic spin-off development*. Academic intermediaries are important for the early commitment phase to promote the interactions between faculty members (Hayter, 2016). However, non-academic intermediaries are also important but for the interactions between academic entrepreneurs and industry. The university also encourages entrepreneurs to formulate a business plan (Slavtchev and Göktempe-Hulten, 2016), while networking with actors outside the university contributes to proof of concept funding and entrepreneurship education for researchers (Maia and Claro, 2013). Different university organizations such as the department, the research group and the TTO contribute directly to competence development in academic spin-offs, while the university management contributes indirectly to competence development in these firms (Rasmussen and Wright, 2015). As a result, the ecosystem provides education, start-up support and networks (van Stijn, Rijnsoever and van Veelen, 2018).

The ecosystem, and in particular the university, also influences *academic spin-off performance*. Firms with support from the university, a business idea related to patents, a business plan and venture capital, generate first sales earlier than firms without these characteristics (Slavtchev and Göktempe-Hulten, 2016). Academic spin-offs also internationalize more often than non-academic spin-offs (Civera et al., 2019). Taken together, the academic entrepreneurship ecosystem contributes to academic spin-off performance that enables the new firm to contribute back to the ecosystem.

In addition, universities promoting academic spin-off creation have different strategies that influence the new firm. The 'low selective model' maximizes the number of new firms (Clarysse, Wright, Lockett, Van de Velde, 2005), the 'supportive model' focus on growth orientated firms and the 'incubator model' relies on VC backed firms. Universities with an international strategy influence the firm to become more international (Civera et al., 2019). The university strategy influences academic spin-offs and the need for support from the other ecosystem organizations.

Finally, studies have also conceptualized student entrepreneurship in the university ecosystem (Wright, Siegel and Mustar, 2017) and academic entrepreneurship research as part of the academic entrepreneurship ecosystem (Hayter et al., 2018). Policy makers are also advised to promote TTOs, university employees and business communities to collaborate to create more new firms in the university ecosystem (Swamidass, 2013). In conclusion, academic entrepreneurship ecosystem research is a recent and vibrant stream of studies that has eschewed the societal impact.

Societal Impact of Academic spin-offs

The social value of firms has been framed in different terms such as business ethics, corporate social responsibility, social entrepreneurship, social innovation and societal impact. Historically, research has focused on business ethics in large firms and some decades ago also in new firms (Hannafey, 2003). Corporate social responsibility research emerged in the debate about the responsibility for social issues that started in municipalities and later involved also corporations, that is, large firms (Caroll and Shabana, 2010). Social entrepreneurship literature deals with value creating processes by combining resources to explore and exploit opportunities with the aim to create social value (Mair and Marti, 2000). Social innovation research concerns the creation of new ideas displaying a positive impact on the quality and/or quantity of life (Pol and Ville, 2009). Regardless of conceptual descriptions, none of the above-mentioned concepts include the type of impact values, corporations, opportunities or innovations have in society. Hence, this study uses the concept societal impact.

Societal impact concerns contributions to society usually, but not always, beyond financial and economic values. Several other concepts appear in the literature with similar meaning and there is no complete list of concepts or definitions. One concept is societal quality that means the relevance and impact of research in society (van der Meulen and Rip, 2000). Relevance means that research should address different issues such as health issues, environmental issues, social issues, learning or culture. The impact research means that the research needs to be in direct use to be relevant. Another concept, societal benefits means that research is beneficial if it informs policy, is useful for industry and/or leads to a solution to a real world problem (Roberts, 2009). Many research projects claim they will have a societal benefit in future but not all of the projects provide the promised solution. This implies that impact can be either intended or realized. The concept public value means consensus about the obligations of citizens to society, the state and one another (Bozeman and Sarewitz, 2011). This means that citizens have a mutual commitment to society and each other. Finally, the concept societal impact refers to the assessment of social, cultural, environmental and economic returns from publicly funded research (Bornmann, 2013). These concepts are developed in research evaluation literature but societal impact has recently been applied to science commercialization (see Fini et al., 2018). In this context, societal impact is:

> the effect on or change or benefit to the economy, society, culture, public policy or services, health, the environment, or quality of life from new or improved products or services based on scientific knowledge. (Fini et al., 2018, p. 5)

This study uses this definition as a starting point in the exploration of the contributions from the university to academic spin-offs in the creation of possible impact.

Academic entrepreneurship studies suggest that academic spin-offs have societal impact but it has not been expressed in these terms. Early studies indicate that these firms contribute to regional development by employing university graduates and act as role models for other entrepreneurs (Steffensen, Rogers and Speakman, 2000). Recent studies also found that academic spin-offs cooperate with the local university and regional firms by performing R&D tasks, consultancy work and joint R&D projects (Gabrielsson, Politis and Billström, 2019). These firms also contribute to the building of financial networks, sales networks and R&D networks (Iacobucci and Micozzi, 2015). As a result, empirical studies indicate that academic spin-offs directly and indirectly contribute to socioeconomic development (Urbano and Guerrero, 2013).

A few empirical studies provide illustrative examples of societal impact that contributes to human beings and the environment. A case study of biomedical firms from UK and China suggests that the vaccines are not only critical to cure tuberculosis but also to create a healthy population worldwide, especially in Asian and African countries (Li and Garnsey, 2014). Another case study of Cleantech firms started in Finland suggests that the accelerator is an important vehicle for supporting the firms to develop cleaner technologies that reduce the negative environmental impact (Kivimaa et al., 2017). A study of academic spin-offs of Norway suggests that the technologies these firms commercialize have four types of societal impact; environmental impact, health impact, pedagogical impact and safety impact (Billström, Høyvarde Clausen and Rasmussen, 2018). Research provides almost anecdotal case descriptions and fragmented empirical evidence that academic spin-offs create societal impact. Hence, there is still a void of theoretical knowledge regarding the academic entrepreneurship ecosystem and the contributions from the university to academic spin-offs in the creation of societal impact.

Taken together, this study uses literature on academic entrepreneurship ecosystem to conceptualize the creation of societal impact of academic spin-offs. This is important because "assessing the impacts of science commercialization should be considered within a broader context, accounting for all actors engaging with research organizations" (Fini et al., 2018, p. 4). By doing this, this study addresses the calls for more research on academic entrepreneurship ecosystems (e.g. Hayter et al., 2018) and societal impact of academic spin-offs (e.g. Fini et al., 2018).

METHOD

This study employs a case study design to address the exploratory status of academic entrepreneurship ecosystem and societal impact research. It builds on a selection of firms from a longitudinal dataset of 374 academic spin-offs registered between 1999 and 2012. The firms were registered by the 'FORNY programme' funded by the Research Council of Norway, with the aim to support research commercialization.

Selection of Firms

Several selection criteria were set up to identify relevant firms to investigate. *The first selection criteria* included firms that originate in universities and research institutes, and excluded corporate spin-offs. To make sure the results were not unique to academic spin-offs the study selected firms originating at research institutes because universities often are publicly owned while research institutes are privately owned in Norway, and private and public organizations have different purposes and goals (Moray and Clarysse, 2005). The study excluded 25 firms and 349 firms remained at this stage. *The second selection criteria* included firms that commercialize technology and excluded firms that were set up for service-based purposes such as a consultancy firms offering general business advice. Another 16 firms were excluded and 333 firms remained. *The third selection criteria* included the oldest firms, registered to the FORNY programme in the year 1999, because several firms were not part of the FORNY programme at firm start and it often takes at least seven to 10 years or longer before these firms create significant sales (Wennberg et al., 2011) and impact (van der Meulen and Rip, 2000). Another 311 firms were excluded and 22 firms remained. *The fourth selection criteria* included firms with sales because they can have a real societal impact when the product is in use (van der Meulen and Rip, 2000). Nine firms had no sales and 13 firms remained, whereof eight firms were spin-offs from universities and five firms were spin-offs from research institutes. For illustrative purposes typical cases were selected for the analysis (Yin, 2009), one from a university and one from a research institute. This study did not limit the sample of firms in other respects such as by industry or firm development, so as to be as open as possible at this explorative stage of theoretical development.

Data Collection

Since no data on economic and societal impact is readily available, electronic documents including firm official documents (e.g. presentations), news and media articles that were published online from firm registration to the end of 2016 and websites were collected to code societal impact. News articles often report significant firm events such as investments, product sales and firms' (positive and negative) influence on society and the environment. News and media articles are also a relevant source of information about potential and realized societal impact because journalists act in the interest of society when they write news articles for public interest. At this explorative stage of societal impact research at firm level (Fini et al., 2018), data sources such as documents and media articles were used to capture the phenomenon. Documents can provide different information than interviews (Yin, 2009) and societal impact is not easily captured in interviews.

Other publicly available documents including annual reports, firm announcements, firm documents, websites, YouTube movies, LinkedIn profiles and online databases were used to describe the firms, the founders and the parent organizations (research institutes and universities). The use of several data sources including traditional media and social media found support in Miller and Acs's (2017) single case study design of the University of Chicago. They collected data from traditional media and social media including publications, videos, Facebook, blogs, Twitter, and LinkedIn, and public databases, to explore the university ecosystem. However, not all firms and events are reported extensively on the Internet or in the media, which implies that the societal impact is likely to be underreported.

To retrieve information about societal impact of academic spin-offs, well-trained research assistants used two online search engines, the Atekst/Retriever media archive and Google internet. Senior entrepreneurship faculty supported and supervised the research assistants in regular meetings during the entire data collection and coding process. The assistants identified more than 4,100 news articles of the 374 sample of firms. They downloaded and registered the firm documents, news and media articles that contained information about societal impact. The assistants built a comprehensive database with the documents.

Analysis Method

This study is based on an inductive coding done by the author. More than 300 news and media articles and firm documents were read and coded using the software NVivo 12. The author followed the three steps in the coding process including 1st order concepts, 2nd order themes and aggregated dimensions (Gioia, Corley and Hamilton, 2012). The 1st order concepts are sentences and statements that indicate any type of societal impact. An example of a 1st order code is the statement "*It is stressful to travel with [potentially] sick children*". The 2nd order themes are the common denominators for 1st order concepts. An example is 1st order concept "*It is stressful to travel with [potentially] sick children*", that was coded in the 2nd order theme '*health impact*' because the technology for example reduces the parents' and the children's stress level. The aggregated dimension was the common denominator of the 2nd order themes, which was '*societal impact*'. To capture the role of the ecosystem and in particular the university, the author used the narrative strategy because it fits well to capture time in one or few cases (Langley, 1999). The narrative stories are structured over time to capture when, who and what role the ecosystem and in particular the university have in the creation of societal impact. The grounded theory method and the narrative method are high in accuracy but low in simplicity and generality (Langley, 1999).

To validate the author's coding, it was crosschecked with the coding done by the research assistants who collected the data. They coded a 641 news articles of 255 firms. The author's coding fitted the assistants' coding with one exception. The assistants used the 2nd order theme '*other impact*' for codes representing negative impact and codes they did not label. In this theme examples of codes associated with peoples' learning was found. In the author's coding these codes were coded in a new 2nd order theme labelled '*pedagogical impact*'. Hence, 1st order codes related to pedagogy and learning were not coded in the 2nd order theme '*other impact*'. In other words, the two independent coders corresponded. The author also compared the coding with an earlier coding, also done by the author, but 18 months earlier. The first coding was done in 2017 for a conference paper (Billström et al., 2018) and the second coding was done for this study. The coding of about 100 news and media articles corresponded without exceptions.

EMPIRICAL FINDINGS

The characteristics of the investigated firms are summarized in Appendix 21A.1. All firm names are fictious. The empirical findings show no clear differences between the spin-off firms from university and research institutes because they both create societal impact, and the ecosystem as well as the parent organization seem to play similar roles. Hence, two typical cases InfTec and LogOpt, the first from a university and the latter from a research institute, were selected to illustrate the ecosystem and the role of the university in the creation of societal impact.

The University and InfTec

Documents from the year 2007 were used because the firm was acquired at that point in time. The university is publicly owned with a traditional structure that contained six faculties in the year 2007. The university is now one of eight universities of Norway and has merged with several university colleges during the years. The main focus areas were biotechnology, fishery science, telemedicine among other areas. The university has grown from about 1,600 employees in the year 1999 to about 2,300 in the year 2007. The university budget was about 1,400,000 TNOK, whereof 260,000 TNOK was allocated for research.

Official documents of the university from the year 2008 clearly state the commercialization strategies. The university has taken several actions to organize, control and manage early commercialization projects. The organization has also clarified the roles of the students, teachers, researchers, industry partners, TTO and other actors involved in research commercialization. The university provides an entrepreneurship programme at Masters level to educate students about innovation and science commercialization. The university actively works with human resource management, waste management, energy consumption, transportation, social security, crisis management and cultural diversity. The university is the main owner of the TTO that has about five full-time equivalents. The TTO connects the university hospital, innovation organizations, public agencies, municipality, ministry of trade, investors, innovators and entrepreneurs. It has contributed to the creation of 32 new firms.

InfTec was founded in 1999 and launched a new information and communication technology for verbal and non-verbal online communication. InfTec targeted several potential customers nationally and internationally including the oil industry, the shipping industry and the health care industry. The CEO explained in a media interview:

> It is a coincidence that we have customers at these places [in Russia and United States of America]. Internationalization is not yet large numbers.

The idea was to improve security and thus enhance privacy of existing online communication technologies. The entrepreneurs added new product features that could transfer text, pictures and audio because existing technologies could only transfer text and pictures in a secure way. Security was paramount to convince customers. The CEO explained in a news article:

> Norway has come far, regarding communication in the health sector and we work in a culture with a strict focus on security [and privacy].

After an intensive period of product testing and real-life evaluations InfTec sold the first products to the health care industry. Sales revenue almost reached 400,000 Norwegian kronor (NOK) in the year 2004. The firm did not make any profit due to high costs for salary, research and development (R&D), material and equipment. At the end of the first year, the firm had seven employees. Product sales peaked at 11.9 MNOK and the number of FTEs was 14 in the year 2007.

Several actors with a relationship to the university got interested in the firm. The first venture capitalist entered the firm and became one of the main owners in the year 2001. The local science park and the TTO also became owners and funds were granted for R&D. InfTec was dependent on several providers of infrastructure such as health care actors. The project leader explained:

> This programme requires that the medical doctors [or other partners] are connected with the receivers, the hospitals, and that they want to join. Another important requirement is that the health network in the region follows all security standards set by The Norwegian Data Protection Authority.

The technology has several positive benefits for society. Several hundred children are screened every year for potential heart failure and only a few of them have heart problems. The technology transfer heart sounds fast and safely online, from doctors at primary care units to cardiologists at university hospitals. This technology is cheaper and more flexible compared to video conference because there is no need for the patient, the doctor and the specialist to meet at the same time, and the information can be evaluated asynchronously. A project leader from InfTec explained that 50 health care providers in Norway started to use the technology in the year 2002. The project leader answered the question whether the technology has any value for the society.

> Yes, are you crazy!? In Northern-Norway there are long distances. It is stressful to travel with [potentially] sick children. The parents need to travel with the child. This is a lost income. Usually, you also need to stay overnight at a hotel to catch the next flight back home.

A medical doctor explained that the reliability is more than 90 per cent, which is not worse than face-to-face evaluations. The medical doctor also explained the technology benefits from the health care perspective in the year 2002. "*On average I need two minutes to analyze the sound of the heart.*" InfTec was acquired in the year 2007 for about 25–30 MNOK and the CEO of the new the firm said:

> With the acquisition we establish a centre for coordinating health organizations in Norway, which is unique nationally.

The Research Institute and LogOpt

The Research Institute was founded by a Norwegian university but was reconstructed in the 1980s to an independent business organization. In the year 1999, the institute had a traditional industry structure that contained the four sub-institutes for marine research, electricity research, geography research and fishery and aquaculture research. In the year 2019, the institute contains six sub-institutes including construction, ICT, energy, industry, ocean and manufacturing. Currently, the institute says it has about 2,000 employees and 3,200 MNOK in sales.

The official website clearly states that the purpose is to develop society by conducting research in science, technology, health and social sciences. The institute is the main owner of the TTO, which has about eight employees, and collaborates with authorities, companies, industry clusters, institutes, new firms and universities. The TTO's main activity is to develop and commercialize research by selling, licensing, patenting or creating new firms. A strategy is to cover areas related to societal challenges such as clean energy, ICT and life sciences. The TTO has spun-off 26 research-based firms.

LogOpt was founded in 1999 and launched an optimization technology for logistics planning. LogOpt targeted the transportation industry and added the health care industry in the year 2015. In the beginning, the firm had relationships with national and international firms and universities, in, for example, France, Italy and Scotland. The idea was to provide environmentally friendly transportation options by automatically optimizing and scheduling freight transportation routes. The idea was also to reduce manpower, time and money at logistic companies. Around the time of founding the logistic planning was done by people, which required more time and money with fewer transportation alternatives. As a result, logistic firms did not use the available vehicles. The new technology was an option to improve the efficiency in the industry.

The second year in operation, LogOpt sold the first products to the transportation industry. According to the annual reports, the sales revenue was about 100,000 Norwegian kronor (NOK) the first year and about 1.1 MNOK the second year. The firm did not make any profit the first years, due to high costs for salary and research and development (R&D). At the end of the first year, the firm had one employee and at the end of year two it had two employees. Product sales peaked at 4.3 MNOK and the number of employees was three in the year 2014. At firm start, the TTO and the science park became owners. In the year 2008, a new owner and CEO entered the firm. The firm has not acquired any venture capital. The European Union and the Norwegian Research Council have granted funds for R&D and commercialization projects. An industry partner explained their role in the firm.

> We have primarily been selected as a partner because we are known for having developed our own, high quality logistic system for computer application. As the other project partners, we have financially supported this project [firm].

The automatic calculation of optimized transportation has several positive benefits for society. Logistic companies typically have several customers, different geographical locations, deadlines, rest schedule and a mix of freight and available vehicles. The road network is large with many options and limitations such as road conditions, speed limits and traffic intensity. In a news article, the CEO explained the customer benefits:

> The use of route optimization in combination with maps in logistics planning, provides an opportunity for considerable cost reduction, customer service, overview and organization of everyday activities for the traffic control.

The technology can also reduce the number of vehicles and make every day work easier for customers. A national organization for transportation and logistics has identified several benefits for the environment. The representative explains in a news article:

> A softer driving style reduces fuel consumption and the CO_2 omissions. The same effect will appear, when tires are removed and the cars are washed, less frequently.

A municipality identified an optimization problem after a financial loss and soon they became a customer. The firm is still in operation and a municipality manager explained the technology value:

> If we tell a user that we will be there at 14.00 [2.00 pm], we can keep the promise. Today, employees start the route at 08.00 am, and it is unclear when they will meet each user. /. . ./ We can set all the times [in the system,] for each user, for example when they are going to the day-care centre, take the medicine or visit the doctor.

DISCUSSION

This study develops a framework of the academic entrepreneurship ecosystem and the relationships between the actors and organizations in the creation of societal impact. This discussion focuses primarily on the academic spin-offs because almost all firms investigated create environmental and health impact. Half of the firms also create safety impact and few firms create pedagogical impact.

Most firms create health impact that is a treatment of a disease of a human being when the product is in use. The firm 'InfTec' developed a technology that made it possible to screen and diagnose more people and thus identify serious heart issues and treat the patients faster than before. This reduced the waiting time and the stress of patients and their families. This example corroborates with a study of biomedical firms in the UK showing that these firms create vaccines to cure tuberculosis and improve peoples' wellbeing nationally and worldwide (Li and Garnsey, 2014). Hence, academic spin-offs create direct health impact for people worldwide.

Almost all academic spin-offs also have environmental impact that is reduction in pollution or harm to the environment. Naturally, clean-tech firms have an environmental impact (e.g. Kivimaa et al., 2017). Interestingly, the firm 'InfTec' also shows that other types of firms can have an environmental impact because the patients, their parents and the doctors do not need to meet in person to diagnose the patients. The local doctor and the cardiologist, often at large university hospitals, can communicate at a distance by using the technology. In this way, the technology reduced the amount of travel by airplanes, which has an environmental impact. Hence, academic spin-offs have direct and indirect environmental impact.

The results also suggest that academic spin-offs have safety impact, which means that the technology prevents an accident from occurring. The high priority on secure transmission of digital information (text, picture and audio) online reduced the risk of hacking and intrude peoples' privacy, compared to previous technologies. Studies have also found other types of safety impact such as navigation systems to prevent accidents at sea (Billström et al., 2018). Hence, academic spin-offs are an important vehicle to create technologies with safety impact in different industries.

The firms also have pedagogical impact that is an increase in peoples' learning and economic impact. The firm 'CliMea' develops a wind measurement system that makes it possible to forecast and learn about storms and other weather conditions. Several firms also create what has been called 'socioeconomic impact' in research (e.g. Urbano and Guerrero, 2013). An example is the 'InfTecs' heart screening technology that saves money for the local government and the hospital. Hence, these firms contribute to regional development, which is in line with previous research (e.g. Shane, 2004; Urbano and Guerrero, 2013; Gabrielsson et al., 2019).

As a result, academic spin-offs create several types of societal impact including health impact, environmental impact, safety impact and pedagogical impact that is beyond the traditional financial and economic measures frequently found in current entrepreneurship research. As a result, it is interesting to discuss how and why the societal impact is created in the ecosystem.

Academic entrepreneurship ecosystem research has identified several actors who contribute to the development and performance of academic spin-offs (Hayter et al., 2018). The study shows that the academic entrepreneurship ecosystem and in particular the university contribute to the creation of societal impact (see Figure 21.1). The ecosystem and the university contribute before (1) and after (2) firm establishment. The new firms also contribute back to the ecosystem, the university and the society at large when they create societal impact (3).

Before the firms have been established, the university (and the research institute) formulate strategies that demonstrate the importance of science commercialization, which corresponds to previous studies (Clarysse et al., 2005). They also build relationships with authorities, governments, investors to establish and develop a support infrastructure that contains accelerators, incubators, science parks and TTOs, who can support the development of the new firms. Although universities have been criticized for establishing incubators that reduce the innovation quality (Kolympiris and Klein, 2017), support organizations seem to play a role in the composition and dynamics of the ecosystem. Hayter (2016) showed that non-academic intermediaries play an important role in connecting academic and non-academic (i.e. industry) actors. It is clear that the university is

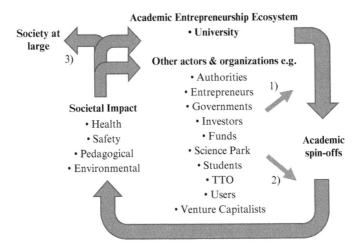

Figure 21.1   *The ecosystem and the creation of societal impact of academic spin-offs*

important in establishing and coordinating the support organizations in the ecosystem.

After the academic spin-offs have been established the ecosystem is more diverse. For example, the Science Park, TTO and venture capitalists often invest and thus take an ownership share in the new firms, while potential customers, users and industry partners take an active role in technology development and testing. This supports empirical studies showing that ecosystem members contribute in different ways and at different times during firm development (Hayter, 2016). The role of the university also decreases over time when firms connect to other actors outside the support system. Other organizations become more important such as authorities who both enable and hinder technology development. The Norwegian Data Protection Authority were crucial for one of the firms both legally and financially because the founders turned it into a customer value. Several hospitals also had to join to make the product possible to use. Hence, the leadership in the ecosystem changes from the university in early firm formation to business actors and institutional actors in subsequent phases of firm development and technology commercialization.

Taken together, the ecosystem provides various types of resources over time such as start-up support and networks (van Stijn et al., 2018). The university contributes with the strategy (Clarysse et al., 2005) and direct and indirect support that develops firm competences (Rasmussen and Wright, 2015). The ecosystem and in particular the university both push and pull the firm towards societal impact, which is a contribution back to the ecosystem and the society at large.

CONCLUSIONS

This study addresses the research questions, how and why do the academic entrepreneurship ecosystem and in particular the university contribute to the creation of societal impact of academic spin-offs? The study concludes that the university is the main organizer and the manager of several support actors and organizations in the academic entrepreneurship ecosystem. Other actors and organizations in the ecosystem provide different types of resources before and after the official establishment of the firms, which make it possible for the firms to develop and sell their own technology or be acquired by another firm. The ecosystem and in particular the university contributes to the creation of academic spin-offs for several reasons. A first reason is the strategy of the parent organization that is to develop and commercialize technologies that can contribute to societal development and address global challenges and sustainability goals. A second reason is to develop high growth firms that can contribute to the owners in financial terms and thus contribute to economic development. A third reason is to develop more functional technologies that in turn can have societal impact. Hence, these are only some indications of how and why the academic ecosystem, and in particular the university, contribute to the creation of societal impact of academic spin-offs. As a result, there is a need for more theoretical knowledge of each type of actor and organization within the ecosystem.

This study contributes to research on academic entrepreneurship ecosystem and societal impact in three ways. First, the study extends current research on academic entrepreneurship ecosystem that mainly has investigated the relationships between single actors and organizations and the firm (e.g. Morris et al., 2017; van Stijn et al., 2018). The study extends this focus by providing empirical indications of the relationships between several actors and organizations in the ecosystem and the academic spin-off. By showing that the ecosystem has a common goal, to develop society by science commercialization, and that the ecosystem contributes back to itself, the study also confirms previous business ecosystem research (Moore, 1993). Second, this study also extends and nuances societal impact research, by providing empirical illustrations and examples of different types of societal impact of the same firm. While there are few studies with case illustrations of one type of societal impact such as environmental impact (Kivimaa et al., 2017) and health impact (Li and Garnsey, 2014), this study shows that academic spin-offs can create several types of impacts that seem to be intertwined. Third, this study also extends current academic entrepreneurship research that has investigated academic spin-offs at one or few points in time (e.g. Gabrielsson et al., 2019). By employing a longitudinal case study design including firms registered in the year 1999 and following them over time (some firms are alive in the year 2019), this study could capture the ecosystem dynamics and change. The leadership changed from the university in early firm formation to business actors in the subsequent commercialization phases.

This study is not without limitations. It relies on a combination of fragmented and atheoretical studies taking the academic entrepreneurship ecosystem perspective and the societal impact perspective. Thus, there is a need to utilize existing theories such as the organizational imprinting theory, resource dependency theory and social networking literature to theorize the relationships between the ecosystem organizations and the academic spin-offs to explain the development of societal impact theoretically. Institutional theory can be utilized to further the explanations regarding the influence of rules and regulations as enablers or hinderers in the commercialization process. This study also relies on a case study design, with some empirical illustrations, which opens up new avenues to theory testing and longitudinal econometric analysis. Entrepreneurs and incubators are encouraged to consider not only financial performance but also societal impact in the new venture creation process. In this vein, policy makers should consider the importance of academic spin-offs as vehicles for the creation of societal impact. Hence, ecosystem and societal impact research need to develop from theoretical building to theoretical testing beyond the Norwegian context to inform researchers, entrepreneurs and policy makers.

NOTE

*   I would like to thank the editors of this book and the anonymous reviewer for constructive and very helpful feedback on previous manuscripts. However, the author is responsible for all remaining errors and mistakes. I would also like to thank "Regionale Forskningsfond Nord Norge" for financing.

REFERENCES

Alvedalen, J., & Boschma, R. (2017). A critical review of entrepreneurial ecosystems research: Towards a future research agenda, *European Planning Studies, 25*(6), 887–903.

Audretsch, D.B., Cunningham, J.A., Kuratko, D.F., Lehmann, E.E., & Mente, M. (2019). Entrepreneurial ecosystems: Economic, technological and societal impacts. *Journal of Technology Transfer, 44*(2), 313–325.

Backs, S., Günther, M., & Stummer, C. (2019). Stimulating academic patenting in a university ecosystem: An agent-based simulation approach. *Journal of Technology Transfer, 44*(2), 434–461.

Billström, A., Høyvarde Clausen, T., & Rasmussen, E. (2018). The economic and societal impact of academic spin-offs: A taxonomy and emerging empirical evidence. *Babson College Entrepreneurship Research Conference (BCERC)*, The Waterford Institute of Technology (WIT), Ireland, June 6–10.

Bornmann, L. (2013). What is societal impact of research and how can it be assessed? A literature survey. *Journal of the American Society for Information Science and Technology, 64*(2), 217–233.

Bozeman, B., & Sarewitz, D. (2011). Public value mapping and science policy evaluation. *Minerva, 49*(1), 1–23.

Caroll, A.B., & Shabana, K.M. (2010). The business case for corporate social responsibility: A review of concepts, research and practice. *International Journal of Management Reviews, 12*(1), 85–105.

Civera, A., Meoli, M., & Vismara, S. (2019). Do academic spin-offs internationalize? *The Journal of Technology Transfer, 44*(2), 381–403.

Clarysse, B., Wright, M., Locett, A., Van de Velde, E., & Vohora, A. (2005). Spinning out new ventures: A typology of incubation strategies from European research institutions. *Journal of Business Venturing, 20*(2), 183–216.

D'Este, P., Ramos-Vielba, I., Woolley, R., & Amara, N. (2018). How do researchers generate scientific and societal impacts? Toward an analytical and operational framework. *Science and Public Policy, 45*(6), 752–763.

Ferriani, S., Garnsey, E., & Lorenzoni G. (2012). Continuity and change in a spin-off venture: The process of reimprinting. *Industrial and Corporate Change*, *21*(4), 1011–1048.

Fini, R., Rasmussen, E., Siegel, D., & Wiklund, J. (2018). Rethinking the commercialization of public science: From entrepreneurial outcomes to societal impacts. *Academy of Management Perspectives*, *32*(1), 4–20.

Gabrielsson, J., Politis, D., & Billström, A. (2019). University spin-offs and triple helix dynamics in regional innovation ecosystems: A comparison of technology intensive start-ups in Sweden. *Global Business and Economics Review*, *21*(3/4), 362–381.

Gioia, D.A., Corley, K.G., & Hamilton, A.L. (2012). Seeking qualitative rigor in inductive research: Notes on the Gioia methodology. *Organizational Research Methods*, *16*(1), 15–31.

Hannafey, F.T. (2003). Entrepreneurship and ethics: A literature review. *Journal of Business Ethics*, *46*(2), 99–110.

Hayter, C.S. (2016). A trajectory of early-stage spin-off success: The role of knowledge intermediaries within an entrepreneurial university ecosystem. *Journal of Technology Transfer*, *47*(3), 633–656.

Hayter, C.S., Nelson, A.J., Zayed, S., & O'Connor, A.C. (2018). Conceptualizing academic entrepreneurship ecosystems: A review, analysis and extension of the literature. *Journal of Technology Transfer*, *43*(4), 1039–1082.

Iacobucci, D., & Micozzi, A. (2015). How to evaluate impact of academic spin-offs on local development: An empirical analysis of the Italian case. *Journal of Technology Transfer*, *40*(3), 434–452.

Kivimaa, P., Boon, W., & Antikainen, R. (2017). Commercialising university inventions for sustainability – A case study of (non-) intermediating 'cleantech' at Aalto university. *Science and Public Policy*, *44*(5), 631–644.

Kolympiris, C., & Klein, P.G. (2017). The effects of academic incubators on university innovation. *Strategic Entrepreneurship Journal*, *11*(2), 145–170.

Langley, A. (1999). Strategies for theorizing from process data. *Academy of Management Review*, *24*(4), 691–710.

Li, J.F., & Garnsey, E. (2014). Policy-driven ecosystems for new vaccine development. *Technovation*, 34(12), 762–772.

Maia, C., & Claro, J. (2013). The role of a proof of concept center in a university ecosystem: An exploratory study. *Journal of Technology Transfer*, *39*(5), 641–650.

Mair, J., & Marti, I. (2000). Social entrepreneurship research: A source of explanation, prediction and delight. *Journal of World Business*, *41*(1), 36–44.

Miller, D.J., & Acs, Z.J. (2017). The campus as entrepreneurial ecosystem: The university of Chicago. *Small Business Economics*, *49*(1), 75–95.

Moore, J.F. (1993). Predators and prey. A new ecology of competition. *Harvard Business Review*, *71*(3), 75–96.

Morris, M.H., Shirokova, G., & Tsukanova, T. (2017). Student entrepreneurship and the university ecosystem: A multi-country empirical exploration. *European Journal of International Management*, *11*(1), 65–85.

Moray, N., & Clarysse, B. (2005). Institutional change and resource endowments to science-based entrepreneurial firms. *Research Policy*, *34*(7), 1010–1027.

Mustar, P., Wright, M., & Clarysse, B. (2008). University spin-off firms: Lessons from ten years of experience in Europe. *Science and Public Policy*, *35*(2), 67–80.

Nelsen, L.L. (2010). Formation of an entrepreneurial ecosystem: The interaction of a research university and its city. *International Journal of Healthcare Technology and Management*, *11*(4), 296–303.

Pirnay, F., Surlemont, B., & Nlemvo, F. (2003). Toward a typology of university spin-offs. *Small Business Economics*, *21*(4), 355–369.

Pol, E., & Ville, S. (2009). Social innovation: Buzz word or enduring term? *The Journal of Socio-Economics*, *38*(6), 878–885.

Rasmussen, E., & Wright, M. (2015). How can universities facilitate academic spin-offs? An entrepreneurial competency perspective. *Journal of Technology Transfer*, *40*(5), 782–799.

Roberts, M.R. (2009). Realizing societal benefit from academic research: Analysis of National Science Foundation's broader impacts criterion. *Social Epistemology, 23*(3–4), 199–219.

Shane, S. (2004). *Academic entrepreneurship – university spinoffs and wealth creation.* Cheltenham, Edward Elgar Publishing.

Slavtchev, V., & Göktepe-Hultén, D. (2016). Support for public research spin-offs by the parent organizations and the speed of commercialization. *Journal of Technology Transfer, 41*(6), 1507–1525.

Steffensen, M., Rogers, E.M., & Speakman, K. (2000). Spin-offs from research centers at a research university. *Journal of Business Venturing, 15*(1), 93–111.

Svensson, G., & Wood, G. (2007). *Business ethics: Through time and across contexts.* Lund, Studentlitteratur.

Swamidass, P.M. (2013). University start-ups as commercialization alternative: Lessons from three contrasting case studies. *Journal of Technology Transfer, 38*(6), 788–808.

Urbano, D., & Guerrero, M. (2013). Entrepreneurial universities: Socioeconomic impacts of academic entrepreneurship in a European Region. *Economic Development Quarterly, 27*(1), 40–55.

van der Meulen, B., & Rip, A. (2000). Evaluation of societal quality of public sector research in the Netherlands. *Research Evaluation, 8*(1), 11–25.

van Stijn, N., Rijnsoever, F.J., & van Veelen, M. (2018). Exploring the motives and practices of university – start-up interaction: Evidence from Route 128. *Journal of Technology Transfer, 43*(3), 674–713.

Wennberg, K., Wiklund, J., & Wright, M. (2011). The effectiveness of university knowledge spillovers: Performance differences between university spin-offs and corporate spin-offs. *Research Policy, 40*(8), 1128–1143.

Wright, M., Clarysse, B., Mustar, P., & Lockett, A. (2007). *Academic entrepreneurship in Europe.* Cheltenham, Edward Elgar Publishing.

Wright, M., Siegel, D., & Mustar, P. (2017). An emerging ecosystem for student start-ups. *Journal of Technology Transfer, 42*(3), 909–922.

Yin, R.K. (2009), *Case study research: Design and methods.* Thousand Oaks, Sage.

APPENDIX 21A.1 CHARACTERISTICS OF THE SPIN-OFF FIRMS

Name[a]	Origin	Industry	Founders	Technology	VC year[a]	Sales year	Sales NOK[b]	Impact[c]	Status
CliMea	Institute	Scientific consultancy	Researcher, engineer	Climate measurement	–	1998	3.070.000	E, H, P, S	In operation
CovSys	Institute	Farming & forestry	Business person, engineer	Cover system	–	2000	870.000	E, H	In operation
DryMas	University[d]	Technical consultancy	Researchers	Drying machine	2001	2001	1.900.000	E, H	Failed 2014
EnvSys	Institute	Technical consultancy	Business persons, researcher	Environmental system	–	1999	800.000	E, H	Failed 2003
InfTec	University	ICT	Business person, unknown	Medical technology	2001	2000	390.000	E, H, S	Acquired 2007
IntPla	University	ICT	Students	Internet platform	2001	2001	150.000	–	In operation
LeaEqu	University[d]	ICT	Professors, researcher	Learning equipment	2002	1999	330.000	E, H, P, S	Failed 2012
LogOpt	Institute	ICT	Researchers	Logistic optimization	–	2000	100.000	E, H, S	In operation
NavSys	Institute	ICT	Business person, engineer	Navigation system	2001	1999	470.000	E, H, S	Acquired 2010
OilMea	University	Oil, gas, offshore	Professor	Oil measurement	–	2000	20.000	E, H, P, S	Acquired 2003
SofPro	University	Oil, gas, offshore	Researchers	Software, programmes	–	2000	1.700.000	E, H, S	In operation
VehCle	University	Technical consultancy	Professor	Vehicle	–	2006	20.000	E, H, S	In operation
WooPro	University	Forestry	Students	Wood protection	2001	2000	60.000	E, H	Acquired 2014

Notes:
a   VC year shows if and when the firm acquired venture capital.
b   Sales NOK is the first sales of the firm expressed in Norwegian kronor.
c   Impact shows the type(s) of societal impact the firm has created (E = Environmental impact, H = Health impact, P = Pedagogy impact, S = Safety impact)
d   The firm originated from a university and industry collaboration.

22. Urban universities as a start-up ecosystem: The case of academic spin-offs in Milan
Matteo Landoni

INTRODUCTION

The mission of universities in the age of the entrepreneurial society (Audretsch, 2014) is evolving from the primary scope of education and research, the two original missions, to a triple action that includes a return to the society in the form of economic and social development. From the university perspective, the third mission offers also the opportunity for new revenue streams in times of budget constraints (Etzkowitz and Leydesdorff, 1997, 2000; Gulbrandsen and Slipersaeter, 2007; Vorley and Nelles, 2010; Etzkowitz, 2014).

A core subject of the third mission is the transfer of knowledge to communities for social purpose. In the case of the commercial exploitation of research results, it is associated with the transfer of technology. It requires universities to research and develop technologies with valuable impact on society. For what concerns universities, technology transfer means the generation of value from research. The most entrepreneurial source of value generation from technology transfer is in the form of academic spin-offs, equal to say, new ventures founded to exploit a discovery made in an academic institution. Academic spin-offs have entered the policy agenda of many countries on the basis of their importance for the creation of wealth and jobs from academic research (Lackéus, 2015) and their role in the diffusion of new technologies and innovation (Wright et al., 2007; Rasmussen and Wright, 2015).

This chapter explores academic spin-offs in a two-level ecosystem, namely the university and the city. Universities and cities are entrepreneurial ecosystems, the two rely and thrive on mutual interaction. Universities are increasingly adopting measures to stimulate entrepreneurship as part of the third mission. The result is a return to society in the form of new business ventures, jobs, and innovation. Nevertheless, this is hardly a one-way, bottom-up process that lets the universities free and alone in serving their local communities with start-ups; instead, universities interact with the local government, businesses, and societies for the sake of entrepreneurship. How universities interact with the local environment – either adapt or react to it – is not clear and this creates a research gap. The aim of this chapter is to enhance our understanding of how universities arrange their internal entrepreneurial ecosystem with the external urban ecosystem. This means how the entrepreneurial behaviour of members and their outcome is shaped by the internal ecosystem and how it copes with the external ecosystem at the city level. The academic spin-off may provide a technological gatekeeper and nurture a cluster of spin-offs around a core technology. However, universities in an innovative city cannot act in isolation to sustain entrepreneurship (Wright and Stigliani, 2012); rather, they must take into account the local content (Audretsch and Belitski, 2017). For example, different university and local level strategies and organizational specializations may create either conflict or reinforcing mechanisms that hinder or facilitate spin-offs' activity.

The present chapter explores a case of multiple university spin-offs in a stable urban environment. It distinguishes supporting strategies (i.e. diversification, clustering) and then discusses the possible impact on cities. The chapter presents a theoretical framework, case selection and the analysis of four universities generating spin-offs in the city of Milan, and concludes with insights about universities' support for entrepreneurship, entrepreneurial strategies, and opportunities for the urban entrepreneurial ecosystem.

THEORETICAL FRAMEWORK

Academic Spin-offs and University Support

The literature on academic spin-offs is abundant and fragmented (see: Rothaermel, Agung, and Jiang, 2007; Schmitz et al., 2017; Miranda, Chamorro, and Rubio, 2018). The academic spin-off founding team involves at least one founder affiliated in some way with the parent university where the knowledge was originally generated (Nicolaou and Birley, 2003; Fryges and Wright, 2014), either a faculty member or a student or a technician. The debate concerning a shared definition of university and academic spin-offs is vast and, not surprisingly, fragmented (Pattnaik and Pandey, 2014, Belitski and Aginskaya, 2018). For the purpose of this chapter, the present study considers academic spin-offs the ventures that include a founder with a clear link with the universities (e.g. a current member), and are in every case officially attested as such on the university websites.

The number of academic spin-offs varies significantly among universities (Di Gregorio and Shane, 2003), as it reflects differences in the institutional settings at the university level; for example, different support mechanisms and organizational practices (Fini et al., 2011; Baroncelli and Landoni, 2017). Universities support a variety of policies and practices for institutions that enable academic entrepreneurship (Siegel, Waldman, and Link, 2003; Clarysse et al., 2005; Wright et al., 2007). Universities affect spin-offs in two ways. On one hand, the process of internal knowledge accumulation influences the university's ability to generate spin-offs; for example, the interaction between the founding team and external agents has a positive effect on spin-offs (Grandi and Grimaldi, 2003), meaning that often the internal knowledge is not enough. On the other hand, universities set up internal processes to support the creation of spin-offs (Lockett, Wright, and Franklin, 2003; O'Shea et al., 2005; Benassi, Landoni, and Rentocchini, 2017); for example, universities introduce entrepreneurship courses to stimulate an entrepreneurial attitude (Åstebro, Bazzazian, and Braguinsky, 2012). How universities support spin-offs is fundamental for their evolution at every stage, from the business idea's generation to the new venture creation, from the launch of the firm to the extraction of value (Ndonzuau, Pirnay, and Surlemont, 2002), and university departments may have a great impact (Rasmussen, Mosey, and Wright, 2014). Eventually, an iterative process emerges when a successful academic spin-off offers an example to others in the same university for starting a venture. This way, successful spin-offs orient the evolution of universities' support to favour their special needs (Rasmussen and Wright, 2015).

The institutional setting is fundamental for academic spin-offs. Despite it being not clear whether local governments and universities' policies are reinforcing or constraining each other (Rasmussen et al. 2014), institutions are particularly relevant in the start-up stages (Jong, 2006; Kenney and Goe, 2004; Moray and Clarysse, 2005; Rasmussen and Borch, 2010). Yet, the university of origin seems to have great influence on spin-off creation (Baldini, 2011; Colombo, D'Adda, and Piva, 2010; Fini, Grimaldi, and Sobrero, 2009; Lockett and Wright, 2005; Moray and Clarysse, 2005; Nosella and Grimaldi, 2009), with differences in universities' and departments' supporting practices greatly explaining spin-offs' determinants (Rasmussen et al., 2014; Baroncelli and Landoni, 2017).

Universities set up several initiatives to support the formation and growth of academic spin-offs. While some are dedicated to nurturing spin-offs, others are ill-equipped, non-interested, or simply adopt a mimetic approach to the issue, replicating what others are doing but without a strategy, or not corresponding to the resources needed. For example, universities may set up technology transfer offices but may miss the competences and experience to make them work effectively. Commitment to the third mission is only a necessary, not sufficient condition for having influence over spinoffs. Anyhow, the universities' internal processes are crucial to spin-offs' formation and development (Benassi et al., 2017).

Cities and Universities as Entrepreneurial Ecosystems

Cities are the fittest environment for innovative ventures (Florida, 2002, 2005). The reason is in complex emerging technologies that depend on resources and conditions found in the industrial diversity and density of local settings, which benefit from the concentration of services in metropolitan areas (Glaeser, Ponzetto, and Tobio, 2014; Henderson, Kuncoro, and Turner, 1995; Keeble and Nachum, 2002). In this respect, innovation is a branching process of clustered firms that generates growth for both cities and industries (Boschma and Frenken, 2006; Frenken and Boschma, 2007).

In an innovative city, clusters and spin-offs belong to the same environment. Clusters evolve when a leading firm takes the role of technological gatekeeper that paves the way to the spreading of spin-offs (Hervas-Oliver and Albors-Garrigos, 2014; Boschma and Fornahl, 2011; Menzel and Fornahl, 2010; Morrison, 2008). Social and physical conditions of the innovative city give rise to an entrepreneurial ecosystem, which includes a network of knowledge, talents, finance, and entrepreneurial opportunities (Stam and Spiegel, 2017).

Multiple clusters may co-exist in an innovative city; among them, universities are generative environments that provide gatekeepers and nurture spin-offs (Baroncelli and Landoni, 2018). Thus, academic spin-offs are important to the development of both the technological density and diversity of industries based in the city (Henderson et al., 1995; Quatraro, 2010).

Within the city as an entrepreneurial ecosystem, the university is an entrepreneurial ecosystem in itself. As widely acknowledged, universities greatly vary in their ability to generate spin-offs, in quantity, that is, the number of spin-offs per year, and in quality, that is, the potential for growth and longevity of spin-offs. The reason lies is in the spin-offs' dependence upon the institutional setting and policies of the universities, as depicted above. Norms, culture, and behavioural codes influence entrepreneurship. The last is particularly true in universities, where the approval of faculty fellows and peers may affect the entrepreneurial attitude of individuals (Grünhagen and Volkmann, 2014; Shane, 2004). The working environment – in this case the academic setting – is a relevant antecedent of entrepreneurial intentions, which offers not only approval, but examples too.

Heuristics is a recognized pattern of entrepreneurial discovery and exploitation of opportunities. Entrepreneurs get ideas and learn how to turn them into entrepreneurial ventures by observing other entrepreneurs. They imitate the behaviour of an extract information from predecessors (Baumol, 1986; Lieberman and Asaba, 2006). The demonstration of entrepreneurs encourages others, especially colleagues, to pursue a venturing opportunity (Nanda and Sørensen, 2010).

In the university as an entrepreneurial ecosystem spreading spin-offs, entrepreneurship is a socially accepted behaviour and faculty and departments effectively sustain new venture formation. In this ecosystem, entrepreneurs rely on the support mechanisms available in the university and learn from the experience of others by assuming an imitative strategy to reduce the uncertainty connected with entrepreneurship. That means, for example, to choose the same industry of other fellow entrepreneurs from the same university, and in doing so following a common path of venture development (Golman and Klepper, 2013; Baroncelli and Landoni, 2019).

At the city level, academic spin-offs interact with the industrial urban environment and may choose to enter the entrepreneurial landscape either in competition or diversification with the dominant industries at the city level. Of course, strategic implications underline the selection of a competitive sector or a non-contested industry, including the access to a flourishing environment for jobs and competencies already in place, or conversely, entering an open field arena with no competition as well as no resources available. The purpose of this chapter is to discuss how academic spin-offs position themselves in the university and urban entrepreneurial ecosystems.

EXPLORATION OF AN URBAN ECOSYSTEM

Case Selection and Data

The present study aims at offering to the readers an exploration of an urban setting comprehending multiple universities that have generated spin-offs. This way, the analysis embraces a two-level ecosystem. The first is the urban level, common to all the spin-offs; the second is the university, which differs for support, policies, resources, etc. For this purpose, the study selected the city of Milan in Northern Italy, a hub of innovation at country level thanks to the presence of a network of innovation that includes firms, research centres, and incubators. Essential to the present research, Milan is home to multiple universities, different in scope (research or teaching intensive university), size (large, medium, or small), focus (technical or generalist studies), and type (private or public).

The sample includes four universities. Although Milan counts at least seven universities in its urban area, without accounting for the larger metropolitan area, only four of them have generated at least five spin-offs over the last ten years. This selection strategy returned a population of 74 academic spin-offs generated between 2004 and 2013. This period is functional to the research because it keeps out the spin-offs that have existed less than five years in order to include only those spin-offs that survived the start-up phase, and it is centred around the starting year of the international financial crisis, 2008, which allows offsetting the overall economic downturn and its possible negative effect on entrepreneurial opportunities.

The final sample consists of 15 spin-offs from Bicocca University, six from the Università Cattolica, 27 from Politecnico, and 26 from the University of Milan (see Table 22.1). Besides financial and economic data available on public and proprietary databases (i.e. Chamber of Commerce of Milan; Bureau Van Dijk; Netval-*Italian Network of Technology Transfer Offices of Universities and Public Research Organizations*), two distinct surveys gathered information from the main informants about academic spin-off activity, and precisely 1) all the four universities' technology transfer offices (TTO), and 2) from 34 of the 74 spin-offs founders (response rate: 45.9 per cent). In both cases, the data collection process employed a semi-structured questionnaire; first, for the matter of the universities, interviews with the head of the TTO or a more similar position (e.g. vice-chancellor or delegates) were added; second, for the matter of the spin-offs, a questionnaire was sent to all the academic entrepreneurs, followed by a reminder email. The survey has been useful to grasp insights and triangulate data about the practices of support and the disposal of resources for the task in the case of the

Table 22.1   Sample

University	Scope	Dimension	N. of students	Focus	Type	Foundation	Spin-offs
Bicocca	Teaching/ Research	Large	>30K	Generalist	Public	1998	15
Cattolica	Teaching/ Research	Large	>30K	Generalist	Private	1922	6
Politenico	Research	Large	>30K	Technical	Public	1863	27
University of Milan	Teaching/ Research	Very large	>60K	Generalist	Public	1924	26

Source: author's elaboration.

universities; about the entrepreneurial attitude, the network interaction, opportunities recognition, motivation, and business development in the case of the spin-offs.

All this data presents a complex, multilayer ecosystem comprehending two levels, universities and the city, and at least two actors, academic spin-offs and the universities' supporting structure, i.e. the technology transfer offices. The academic spin-offs' industry selection is the unit of analysis, yet the observations include the multifaceted issues related to the phenomenon. The triangulation of data from multiple levels and actors aims at the illustration of a complex phenomenon more than in a robust empirical analysis, with the scope of providing useful insights for practitioners, policy-makers, and further research.

Universities Supporting Practices in Milan

The four universities in the sample are different in many ways – from status to strategy, from age to reputation – so are their supporting practices applied to spin-offs. Table 22.2 depicts the evidence gathered through the interviews with the universities responsible for technology transfer, which included support to spin-offs (see Table 22.2). Roughly, three main typologies are visible.

1) At Politecnico, the only technical university in the sample, the TTO sets up a strategy, defines industry preferences, trains entrepreneurs, and gives importance to the scientific content of spin-offs.
2) In generalist, public universities (i.e. Bicocca and University of Milan), there is no clear strategy; however, they provide some services and the staff has some experience in business development.
3) At the generalist, private Università Cattolica, the TTO is absent and there is no provision of services.

The questionnaire inquired about the perceptions of academic entrepreneurs concerning the support and assistance at the university. The survey returned the point of view of 34 founders of academic spin-offs. Two categories of answers distinguish for the university's assistance and the support provided. Assistance is regarded as concrete (implying direct involvement), positive (without involvement), indifferent, negative (hostile), or none. Support implies the provision of a set of services, namely financial support, laboratory and other infrastructure use, scientific, commercial, and administrative consultancy (see Table 22.3).

Entrepreneurs report a general positive attitude at the university towards spin-offs. Universities usually support spin-offs by granting the

Table 22.2   University supports

Support/service	Response[§]	Bicocca	Cattolica	Polimi	Unimi
Entrepreneurship class	Y/N	Yes	Yes	Yes	Yes
Class from year	"	2014	2012	2008	2014
Are there awards for entrepreneurs?	"	No	No	Yes	No
Are there training programmes for entrepreneurs?	"	No	No	Yes	No
Mentoring	"	Yes	No	Yes	Yes
Coaching	"	No	No	Yes	Yes
Proof of concepts	"	No	No	No	Yes
Patent assistance	"	Yes	No	Yes	Yes
Fund-raising support	"	No	No	Yes	No
Monitoring activity	"	Yes	No	Yes	Yes
When does monitoring happen?	"	On budget	n.a.	On budget	On request
Does the TTO have objectives:	"	Yes	No	Yes	Yes
Growth	*	2	0	1	3
Value	*	3	0	3	2
Employment	*	4	0	2	2
Scientific	*	1	0	4	3
None	*	0	4	0	0
Reward system for TTO staff	Y/N	No	No	No	No
Is the TTO strategy industry specific?	"	No	No	Yes	No
Help in start-up phase	*	4	0	3	4
Help in intermediate phase	*	0	0	2	2
Help in advanced phase	*	0	0	1	1
No help	*	0	4	0	0
Staff number	n.	2	0	2	3
Staff has no experience	%	75	n.a.	100	34
Staff experience low	%	0	n.a.	0	66
Staff experience high	%	25	n.a.	0	0

Notes:
§ = response: Y/N = Yes or No; * = order of importance (4= Higher: 1= Lower); % = in percentage; n. = number; n.a. = not applicable.
Polimi=Politecnico of Milan; Unimi=University of Milan. *Source*: author's elaboration.

Table 22.3   Academic entrepreneurs' perception of support and assistance

		Bicocca		Cattolica		Polimi		Unimi		Total	
		3	%	5	%	13	%	13	%	34	%
Assistance:	Concrete	0	*0*	1	*20*	2	*15.4*	4	*30.8*	**7**	***20.6***
	Positive	2	*66.7*	3	*60*	10	*76.9*	8	*61.5*	**23**	***67.6***
	Indifferent	1	*33.3*	0	*0*	0	*0*	0	*0*	**1**	***2.9***
	Negative	0	*0*	1	*20*	0	*0*	0	*0*	**1**	***2.9***
	None	0	*0*	0	*0*	1	*7.7*	1	*7.7*	**2**	***5.9***
Support:	Finance	2	*66.7*	0	*0*	5	*38.5*	4	*30.8*	**11**	***32.4***
	Laboratories	1	*33.3*	5	*100*	8	*61.5*	7	*53.8*	**21**	***61.8***
	Scientific	1	*33.3*	1	*20*	8	*61.5*	2	*15.4*	**12**	***35.3***
	Commercial	0	*0*	0	*0*	1	*7.7*	2	*15.4*	**3**	***8.8***
	Administrative	0	*0*	0	*0*	4	*30.8*	5	*38.5*	**9**	***26.5***

Note: Polimi=Politecnico of Milan; Unimi=University of Milan.

Source: author's elaboration.

use of laboratories; financial support is not reported as relevant, still, it is unneglectable. Entrepreneurs benefited from scientific consultancy from faculty members, particularly at Politecnico, much less elsewhere. Significantly, commercial support is widely provided. Indeed, academic entrepreneurs often require actual support in dealing with commercial issues, being the traditional mission of universities non-commercial in nature and scope.

Academic Spin-offs' Behaviour

The spin-offs from the four universities in Milan are the result of the influence of individuals, internal organizations, and institutional settings over entrepreneurial activity. Being the urban setting common to the whole sample, universities' influence has the greatest role in explaining the different attitude of members in choosing an entrepreneurial career. The first evidence is the number of spin-offs. All universities are large, having more than 30,000 students each, with the University of Milan accounting for around 60,000 students, the others between 30,000 and 40,000. However, the number of spin-offs is not astonishing, with differences that are only slightly explained by the size. The highest number of spin-offs is at Politenico (27), closely followed by the University of Milan (26), despite the fact that the University of Milan is almost double in size than Politecnico and Bicocca (15). Cattolica, which is almost the

Table 22.4   Academic spin-offs per industry and percentage of the city

Industry	Bicocca	%	Cattolica	%	Polimi	%	Unimi	%	Milan
ICT	8	66.7	–	–	2	16.7	2	16.7	12
Innovation Services	–	–	1	7.7	10	76.9	2	15.4	13
Energy and Environment	3	25	3	25	5	41.7	1	8.3	12
Life Sciences	2	18.2	1	9.1	1	9.1	7	63.6	11
Biotechnologies	2	10.5	1	5.3	3	15.8	13	68.4	19
Industrial automation	–	–	–	–	4	100	–	–	4
Nanotechnologies	–	–	–	–	1	50.0	1	50	2
Aerospace	–	–	–	–	1	100	–	–	1
Total	15	20.3	6	8.1	27	36.5	26	35.1	74

Note: Polimi=Politecnico of Milan; Unimi=University of Milan.

Source: author's elaboration.

same size of Politecnico and Bicocca, has generated only six spin-offs. Relevantly, these spin-offs started in the absence of any formal supporting measures.

The second evidence is the industrial choice of spin-offs. Table 22.4 shows the industry sector of the academic spin-offs with reference to the university of origin; it also shows the quota of spin-offs in a specific industry related to the city. Spin-offs tend to cluster around an industry according to the university of origin. Namely, eight of the 15 spin-offs from Bicocca are in *ICT technologies*; three out of the six spin-offs from Cattolica are in *energy technologies*; 10 of 27 spin-offs from Politecnico are in *innovation services*; lastly, 13 of the 26 spin-offs from University of Milan are in *biotechnologies* (see Table 22.4).

DISCUSSION

Apparently, there is an implicit industry selection around certain technologies. In fact, all universities but Politecnico do not have a strategy that targets any specific industry. At Politecnico, the strategy of industry choice favours *innovation services*, *energy technologies*, and *industrial automation*; however, Politecnico spin-offs choose different industries, more than in other universities that do not apply any sectorial strategy. Industry selection happens implicitly whether the university's strategy designed a target industry or not. This is an independent choice of the academic entrepreneurs that is probably favoured by a proximity effect with other academic entrepreneurs in the same technological or research area; this is in line with previous research that highlighted the importance of contexts on the outcomes of entrepreneurship learning (De Clercq et al., 2013; Walter and Dohse, 2012) and motivation and attitude towards entrepreneurship (Krueger et al., 2000; McMullen and Shepherd, 2006; Bae et al., 2014). In the case of entrepreneurial learning through imitation (Baroncelli and Landoni, 2019), missing a top-down strategy to orient entrepreneurship towards target technologies, it might be the example of others that provides members with imitation opportunities that led the entrepreneurial action (Neck and Greene, 2011). Scholars have pointed out how informal learning (Rasmussen, Mosey, and Wright, 2015; Lockett et al., 2017) and the influence of peers and fellow scientists (Kacperczyk, 2013; Tartari, Perkmann, and Salter, 2014) are relevant for the development of opportunity recognition and entrepreneurial competencies.

On one hand, the past experience of other entrepreneurs in the university forms a legacy of academic entrepreneurship that orients the behaviour of academic entrepreneurs towards specific industrial domains. On the other, universities tend to differentiate among themselves by the positioning of their spread of spin-offs in distinct industries. Each university specializes in a preferential area for entrepreneurial venturing for its members at the city level. The result is twofold; at the university level, the preferred industries are a non-overlapped area of development for academic spin-offs reinforced by shared experience based on the entrepreneurial legacy (Baroncelli and Landoni, 2019); at the city level, a variety of entrepreneurial sources combine multiple industrial domains' specialization at the university level with industry diversity at the city level. This way, the ecosystem of urban universities is able to provide both variety and specialization of entrepreneurial ventures.

CONCLUSION

More than supporting measures, something else must explain the entrepreneurial behaviour of academics. Universities are in this sense an ecosystem of a reinforcing pattern of behaviour. The example of fellow entrepreneurs sustains the effort of other faculty members to cope with the uncertainty of starting a new venture. Universities must take this into account when they orient their own internal processes towards an entrepreneurial model. Entrepreneurs are examples to others and stimulate their environment with a positive attitude that could influence more than universities' support.

Entrepreneurs are more diffused in cities. At a higher level, cities are ecosystems that combine different entrepreneurial sources. Universities interact with the city and among them, provide a focus on multiple industries that combine with others to enrich the variety within the entrepreneurial ecosystem.

The present exploration presents some insights worthy of consideration for possible further research. First, academic entrepreneurs tend to adopt an imitation strategy within the university, clustering predominantly around the same industry, presumably due to a reduction of risk and an increase in legitimation that leads to a preferred industry at the university level. Second, the universities form entrepreneurial clusters in separate, unrelated industries, a strategy that chooses diversification at the city level, enriching, in fact, the industrial environment of the urban landscape and flourishing the entrepreneurial ecosystem. This strategy is overall reinforced by the heritage of academic spin-offs that initially formed the cluster, posing a path-dependence effect on further ventures to come.

The university entrepreneurial ecosystem is a powerful network of knowledge and talents with a strong research orientation; yet, it is either reinforced or hindered by the business culture and attitude towards entrepreneurship, making incumbent entrepreneurs pioneers of innovation in disseminating examples of practices and processes. As in the case of the entrepreneurial ecosystem of innovative cities, social conditions create entrepreneurial opportunities (Stam and Spiegel, 2017). The universities being an entrepreneurial ecosystem often within a larger urban ecosystem, the two do not simply replicate each other but integrate strategies and specializations for a greater innovative network. That is expected to be even more complex and efficient in the case of a multiple universities ecosystem within the same urban ecosystem.

On the basis of this preliminary observation, the present chapter depicts a two-level ecosystem where different universities coexist in a common location. Whatever the support, academic entrepreneurs tend to cluster, possibly due to an imitative strategy, and to appear in different industries according to the university of origin. The city benefits from the variety of entrepreneurial sources. Interaction among these sources is of great importance to the entrepreneurial ecosystem.

REFERENCES

Åstebro, T., N. Bazzazian, and S. Braguinsky (2012), 'Startups by recent university graduates and their faculty: Implications for university entrepreneurship policy', *Research Policy*, 41 (4), 663–677.

414 Research handbook on start-up incubation ecosystems

414 Research handbook

Audretsch, D. B. (2014), 'From the entrepreneurial university to the university for the entrepreneurial society', *Journal of Technology Transfer*, 39 (3), 313–321.

Audretsch, D. B., and M. Belitski (2017), 'Entrepreneurial ecosystems in cities: Establishing the framework conditions', *Journal of Technology Transfer*, 42 (5), 1030–1051.

Bae, T. J., S. Qian, C. Miao, and J. O. Fiet (2014), 'The relationship between entrepreneurship education and entrepreneurial intentions: A meta-analytic review', *Entrepreneurship Theory and Practice*, 38 (2), 217–254.

Baldini, N. (2011), 'University spin-offs and their environment', *Technology Analysis & Strategic Management*, 22 (8), 859–876.

Baroncelli, A., and M. Landoni (2017), 'Exploring differences in university support practices and the effects on spin-off companies in Boston', *International Journal of Entrepreneurship and Innovation Management*, 21 (4–5), 366–394.

Baroncelli, A., and M. Landoni (2018), 'Academic Spin-offs and the Innovative City: Universities' Role in the Entrepreneurial Ecosystem of Boston', in Dallago, B. and E. Tortia, (eds) *Entrepreneurship and Local Economic Development. A Comparative Perspective on Entrepreneurs, Universities and Governments*, Abingdon & New York: Routledge, pp. 281–305.

Baroncelli, A., and M. Landoni (2019), 'Imitation and entrepreneurial learning. Insights from academic spin-offs', *Industry & Higher Education*, 33 (4), 233–245. doi.org/10.1177/0950422219832461.

Baumol, J. (1986), 'Entrepreneurship and a century of growth', *Journal of Business Venturing*, 1 (2), 141–145.

Belitski, M., and H. Aginskaya (2018), 'Defining Academic Spinoffs and Entrepreneurial University', in Presse, A., and O. Terzidis (eds) *Technology Entrepreneurship. Insights in New Technology-Based Firms, Research Spin-Offs and Corporate Environments*. FGF Studies in Small Business and Entrepreneurship, Cham: Springer, pp. 211–223.

Benassi, M., M. Landoni, and F. Rentocchini (2017), *University Management Practices and Academic Spin-offs*, Departmental Working Papers from Department of Economics, Management and Quantitative Methods at Università degli Studi di Milano, No. 2017–11.

Boschma, R., and D. Fornahl (2011), 'Cluster evolution and a roadmap for future research', *Regional Studies*, 45 (10), 1295–1298.

Boschma, R., and K. Frenken (2006), 'Why is economic geography not an evolutionary science? Towards an evolutionary economic geography', *Journal of Economic Geography*, 6, 273–302.

Clarysse, B., M. Wright, M. A., Lockett, E. V. A., de Velde, and A. Vohora (2005), 'Spinning out new ventures: A typology of incubation strategies from European research institutions', *Journal of Business Venturing*, 20, 183–216.

Colombo, M. G., D. D'Adda, and E. Piva (2010), 'The contribution of university research to the growth of academic start-ups: An empirical analysis', *The Journal of Technology Transfer*, 35 (1), 113–140.

De Clercq, D., D. S. K.Lim, and C. H. Oh (2013), 'Individual-level resources and new business activity: The contingent role of institutional context', *Entrepreneurship Theory and Practice*, 37 (2), 303–330.

Di Gregorio, D., and S. Shane (2003), 'Why do some universities generate more start-ups than others?', *Research Policy*, 32, 209–227.

Etzkowitz, H. (2014), 'The entrepreneurial university wave: From ivory tower to global economic engine', *Industry and Higher Education*, 28 (4), 223–232.

Etzkowitz, H., and L. Leydesdorff (1997), 'Introduction to special issue on science policy dimensions of the Triple Helix of university-industry-government relations', *Science and Public Policy*, 24 (1), 2–5.

Etzkowitz, H., and L. Leydesdorff (2000), 'The dynamics of innovation: From National Systems and 'Mode 2' to a Triple Helix of university–industry–government relations' *Research Policy*, 29 (2), 109–123.

Fini, R., R. Grimaldi, and M. Sobrero (2009), 'Factors fostering academics to start up new ventures: An assessment of Italian founders' incentives', *Journal of Technology Transfer*, 34, 380–402.

Fini, R., R. Grimaldi, S. Santoni, and S. Sobrero (2011), 'Complements or substitutes? The role of universities and local context in supporting the creation of academic spin-offs', *Research Policy*, 40 (8), 1113–1127.

Florida, R. (2002), 'The economic geography of talent', *Annals of the Association of American Geographers*, 92 (4), 743–755.

Florida, R. (2005), *Cities and the creative class*. New York: Routledge.

Frenken, K., F. Van Oort, and T. Verburg (2007), 'Related variety, unrelated variety and regional economic growth', *Regional Studies*, 41 (5), 685–697.

Fryges, H., and M. Wright (2014), 'The origin of spin-offs: A typology of corporate and academic spin-offs'. *Small Business Economics*, 43 (2), 245–259.

Glaeser, E. L., G. A. Ponzetto, and K. Tobio (2014), 'Cities, skills and regional change'. *Regional Studies*, 48 (1), 7–43.

Golman, R. and S. Klepper (2013), 'Spinoffs and Clustering.' *Papers in Evolutionary Economic Geography* (PEEG) 1309, Utrecht University.

Grandi, A., and R. Grimaldi (2003), 'Exploring the networking characteristics of new venture founding teams: A study of Italian academic spin-offs', *Small Business Economics*, 21 (4), 329–341.

Grünhagen, M. and C. K. Volkmann (2014), 'Antecedents of academics' entrepreneurial intentions–developing a people-oriented model for university entrepreneurship', *International Journal of Entrepreneurial Venturing*, 6 (2), 179–200.

Gulbrandsen, M. and S. Slipersaeter (2007), 'The Third Mission and the Entrepreneurial University Model', in Bonaccorsi, A., and C. Daraio (eds), *Universities and strategic knowledge creation*, Cheltenham, UK: Edward Elgar, pp. 112–143.

Henderson, V., A. Kuncoro, and M. Turner (1995), 'Industrial development in cities', *Journal of Political Economy*, 103 (5), 1067–1090.

Hervas-Oliver, J. L., and J. Albors-Garrigos (2014), 'Are technology gatekeepers renewing clusters? Understanding gatekeepers and their dynamics across cluster life cycles', *Entrepreneurship & Regional Development*, 26 (5–6), 431–452.

Jong, S. (2006), 'How organizational structures in science shape spin-off firms: The biochemistry departments of Berkeley, Stanford, and UCSF and the birth of the biotech industry', *Industrial and Corporate Change*, 15, 251–283.

Kacperczyk, A. J. (2013), 'Social influence and entrepreneurship: The effect of university peers on entrepreneurial entry', *Organization Science*, 24 (3), 664–683.

Keeble, D., and L. Nachum (2002), 'Why do business service firms cluster? Small consultancies, clustering and decentralization in London and Southern England', *Transactions of the Institute of British Geographers*, 27 (1), 67–90.

Kenney, M., and W. R. Goe (2004), 'The role of social embeddedness in professorial entrepreneurship: A comparison of electrical engineering and computer science at UC Berkeley and Stanford', *Research Policy*, 33 (5), 691–707.

Krueger, N. F., M. D. Reilly, and A. L. Carsrud (2000), 'Competing models of entrepreneurial intentions', *Journal of Business Venturing*, 15 (5), 411–432.

Lackéus, M. (2015), 'Entrepreneurship in Education. What, Why, When, How'. *OECD*, Paris.

Lieberman, M. B., and S. Asaba (2006), 'Why do firms imitate each other?' *The Academy of Management Review*, 31 (2), 366–385.

Lockett, A., and M. Wright (2005), 'Resources, capabilities, risk capital and the creation of university spin-out companies', *Research Policy*, 34 (7), 1043–1057.

Lockett, A., M. Wright, and S. Franklin (2003), 'Technology transfer and universities' spin-out strategies', *Small Business Economics*, 20, 185–200.

Lockett, N., C. Quesada-Pallarès, K. Williams-Middleton, A. Padilla-Meléndez, and S. Jack (2017), '"Lost in space": The role of social networking in university-based entrepreneurial learning', *Industry and Higher Education*, 31 (2), 67–80.

McMullen, J. S., and D. A. Shepherd (2006), 'Entrepreneurial action and the role of uncertainty in the theory of the entrepreneur', *The Academy of Management Review*, 31 (1), 132–152.

Menzel, M., and D. Fornahl (2010), 'Cluster life cycles – dimensions and rationales of cluster evolution', *Industrial and Corporate Change*, 19 (1), 205–238.

Miranda, F. J., A. Chamorro, and S. Rubio (2018), 'Re-thinking university spin-off: A critical literature review and a research agenda', *The Journal of Technology Transfer*, 43 (4), 1007–1038.

Moray, N., and B. Clarysse (2005), 'Institutional change and resource endowments to science-based entrepreneurial firms', *Research Policy*, 34, 1010–1027.

Morrison, A. (2008), 'Gatekeepers of knowledge within industrial districts: Who they are, how they interact', *Regional Studies*, 42 (6), 817–835.

Nanda, R., and J. B. Sørensen (2010), 'Workplace peers and entrepreneurship', *Management Science*, 56 (7), 1116–1126.

Ndonzuau, F. N., F. Pirnay, and B. Surlemont (2002), 'A stage model of academic spin-off creation', *Technovation*, 22 (5), 281–289.

Neck, H. M., and P. G. Greene (2011), 'Entrepreneurship education: Known worlds and new frontiers', *Journal of Small Business Management*, 49 (1), 55–70.

Nicolaou, N. and S. Birley (2003), 'Academic networks in a trichotomous categorisation of university spinouts', *Journal of Business Venturing*, 18 (3), 333–359.

Nosella, A., and R. Grimaldi (2009), 'University level mechanisms supporting the creation of new companies: An analysis of Italian academic spin-offs', *Technology Analysis and Strategic Management*, 21, 679–698.

O'Shea, R. P., T. J. Allen, A. Chevalier, and F. Roche (2005), 'Entrepreneurial orientation, technology transfer and spinoff performance of US universities', *Research Policy*, 34 (7), 994–1009.

Pattnaik, P. N., and S. C. Pandey (2014), 'University spinoffs: What, why, and how?', *Technology Innovation Management Review*, 4 (12), 44–50.

Quatraro, F. (2010), 'Knowledge coherence, variety and economic growth: Manufacturing evidence from Italian regions', *Research Policy*, 39, 1289–1302.

Rasmussen, E., and M. Wright (2015), 'How can universities facilitate academic spin-offs? An entrepreneurial competency perspective', *The Journal of Technology Transfer*, 40 (5), 782–799.

Rasmussen, E., and O. J. Borch (2010), 'University capabilities in facilitating entrepreneurship: A longitudinal study of spin-off ventures at mid-range universities', *Research Policy*, 39, 602–612.

Rasmussen, E., S. Mosey, and M. Wright (2014), 'The influence of university departments on the evolution of entrepreneurial competencies in spin-off ventures', *Research Policy*, 43, 92–106.

Rasmussen, E., S. Mosey, and M. Wright. (2015), 'The transformation of network ties to develop entrepreneurial competencies for university spin-offs', *Entrepreneurship & Regional Development*, 27 (7–8), 430–457.

Rothaermel, F. T., S. D. Agung, and L. Jiang (2007), 'University entrepreneurship: A taxonomy of the literature', *Industrial and Corporate Change*, 16 (4), 691–791.

Schmitz, A., D. Urbano, G. A. Dandolini, J. A. de Souza, and M. Guerrero (2017), 'Innovation and entrepreneurship in the academic setting: A systematic literature review', *International Entrepreneurship and Management Journal*, 13 (2), 369–395.

Shane, S. (2004), 'Encouraging university entrepreneurship. The effect of the Bayh–Dole Act on university patenting in the United States', *Journal of Business Venturing*, 19 (1), 127–151.

Siegel, D. S., D. A. Waldman, and A. N. Link (2003), 'Assessing the impact of organizational practices on the productivity of university technology transfer offices: An exploratory study' *Research Policy*, 32 (1), 27–48.

Stam, E., and B. Spiegel (2017), 'Entrepreneurial Ecosystem', in R. Blackburn, D. De Clercq, J. Heinonen, and Z. Wang (eds), *Handbook for Entrepreneurship and Small Business*. London: SAGE, pp. 407–422.

Tartari, V., M. Perkmann, and A. Salter (2014), 'In good company: The influence of peers on industry engagement by academic scientists', *Research Policy*, 43 (7), 1189–1203.

Vorley, T., and J. Nelles (2010), 'Gone corporate? The changing face of entrepreneurship in contemporary universities', *International Journal of Entrepreneurial Venturing*, 2 (2), 201–216.

Walter, S. G., and D. Dohse (2012), 'Why mode and regional context matter for entrepreneurship education', *Entrepreneurship & Regional Development*, 24 (9/10), 807–835.

Wright, M., and I. Stigliani (2012), 'Entrepreneurship and growth', *International Small Business Journal*, 31 (1), 3–22.

Wright, M., B. Clarysse, P. Mustar, and A. Lockett (2007), *Academic Entrepreneurship in Europe*. Cheltenham, UK: Edward Elgar.

23. Motivating universities to support spin-off firms: Stakeholders and start-up incubation ecosystems

Einar Rasmussen, Paul Benneworth, and Magnus Gulbrandsen

INTRODUCTION

Universities are important producers of new knowledge, with many examples of universities also contributing to the creation, development, and growth of technology businesses (Ghio et al. 2016). Entrepreneurial universities are often seen as a catalyst for economic and social development at regional level, and the creation of entrepreneurial university spin-off firms (USOs) can be an important aspect of regional development, at least for some universities (Guerrero et al. 2015). We define USOs as new ventures initiated within a university setting, based on knowledge derived from university research (Rasmussen and Borch 2010). Strengthening universities' entrepreneurial capacity has been a key area of most countries' innovation policy with legislative changes, altered university funding and incentives, and specific support arrangements for research commercialization and establishing USOs (Munari et al. 2015; Slaughter and Leslie 1997).

The creation of USOs is a rather marginal activity at most universities, compared to other pathways of knowledge transfer (Hayter, Rasmussen, and Rooksy 2018). Still, USOs are often seen as important for high-tech job creation and science commercialization (Fini et al. 2018). Garnsey and Heffernan (2005) showed that USOs played an important role in transforming the local economic activity in the Cambridge area into a high tech cluster, and studies have explicitly discussed the role of USOs in developing the regional innovation system (Benneworth 2007; Berggren and Dahlstrand 2009). Universities and their spin-offs can contribute to the development of an entrepreneurial ecosystem (Schaeffer and Matt 2016), taking the role of 'ecosystem entrepreneurs' enhancing the social, political, economic, and cultural elements of the ecosystem and the interplay between these elements (Spigel, 2017).

There is a tendency to view universities as being capable of promoting entrepreneurship, considering how fundamental research and training involve scientific and technological opportunities for high technology ventures (Hayter, Nelson, Zayed, and O'Connor 2018). This view downplays that universities are complex organizations that have internal structures whose function is pursuing missions that do not relate to promoting new ventures (Benneworth et al. 2015). While the characteristics of successful universities have been extensively studied (Di Gregorio and Shane 2003; Foss and Gibson 2015), a good understanding of the universities' motivation to develop their entrepreneurial capabilities is currently lacking. Policy initiatives are mainly top-down or linked to more or less external stakeholders such as regional actors and technology transfer offices (TTOs) (Breznitz et al. 2018; Rasmussen et al. 2008), while the key resources to develop new ventures are linked to the individual academics and their surroundings (Clarysse et al. 2011). Hence, designing effective policy measures is difficult without a clearer understanding of how the entrepreneurship process is aligned with the core tasks of the university and those of surrounding stakeholders. This chapter outlines some perspectives for how to better align the interests of universities and their USOs.

We contend that current approaches focus primarily on entrepreneurial transactions rather than considering the wider start-up incubation ecosystem (SUPIE) that emerges around universities in which USOs may be important participants, even if the USOs are not deemed to be important to the universities themselves. In this context we define the SUPIE as a set of interdependent actors and factors that interact as a system providing a nurturing environment for the creation and successful development of USOs. At the same time, we foreground that institutionalizing academic entrepreneurship is potentially problematic for universities (Benneworth et al., 2017). A number of authors have highlighted a clash of values between academic research and entrepreneurship, the 'dark side' of academic engagement (Bozeman et al. 2013; Slaughter and Leslie 1997). Barriers may exist in any university–company interaction: differences in outlook and values between universities and firms and problems in transactions may undermine universities' support for USO (Bruneel et al. 2010; Villani et al. 2017).

There is an interdependence between the extent to which universities and their wider communities can promote SUPIEs and the extent to which they can resolve the tensions that entrepreneurial activity may bring, particularly when the relative unimportance of USOs may lead universities not to favour USOs in their decision-making. We contend that understanding barriers to universities supporting USOs is not enough to explain either how these barriers can be addressed nor how universities might support the regional SUPIEs. This chapter argues that better policy interventions require a better understanding of both why universities support USOs, and what type of support the USOs themselves need from universities. This chapter claims that universities may respond to a variety of stakeholders when deciding to support USOs, but relatively little is known about this issue. We therefore proceed by discussing the following question: *How can external stakeholders associated with USOs influence the university to make better contributions to SUPIEs?*

THE POLICY CHALLENGE OF MAKING UNIVERSITIES SUPPORT USOs

Entrepreneurship is important for policy-makers, and universities are reactive to these policy-makers, but this does not mean that entrepreneurship is important to universities nor that they will take decisions to best promote university entrepreneurship (Benneworth et al. 2017). Although universities may seek to create high-impact spin-offs, the levels of uncertainty and resources demanded for USO creation create very strong disincentives to universities to invest resources in such ventures, and certainly not to prioritize directing scarce investments towards the SUPIEs necessary to make USOs become successful. This issue of potentially divergent actor interests in university entrepreneurship activities is seldom considered in existing research, policies or practice, despite it being a potentially interesting explanation of why policy to date has been less successful than might have been expected (Fini et al. 2017; Harrison and Leitch 2010).

Early policy efforts towards promoting university regional innovative entrepreneurship involved establishing science parks adjacent to universities (Link and Scott 2003), but their major shortcoming was failing to incentivize universities and academics to increase commercialization activities (Henrekson and Rosenberg 2001). Other policies have aimed to facilitate university engagement through legislative changes and funding universities' internal innovation activities. An important example is the US Bayh-Dole Act, which gave universities options to manage the intellectual property rights and spurred similar legislative changes in many European countries (Mowery and Sampat 2005). These changes have led to a rapid diffusion of infrastructure instruments for science-based entrepreneurship, such as TTOs, proof of concept programmes, and incubators. However, the associated initiatives have had mixed effects: the degree to which universities and departments create and develop high-growth businesses remains extremely uneven (Bercovitz and Feldman 2008; O'Shea et al. 2005).

Some argue that the relatively extensive policy measures to promote USOs seem to produce disappointing results (Fini et al. 2017; Harrison and Leitch 2010), and the ability of universities to create successful spin-offs remains a highly path dependent activity (O'Shea et al. 2005), associated with unique SUPIEs. The many initiatives aimed at stimulating universities to support USOs have tended to fail because they evoke a symbolic rather than a substantive change within the universities (Fini et al. 2017), again indicating that it is less important for universities.

Most of the literature concerning universities and USOs has looked at institutional factors related to the raw number of USOs created, without considering the potential impact of these firms or the extent to which these firms themselves form a coherent innovation community around the university (Harrison and Leitch 2010). Because of the disproportionate effect of a small subset of high-growth firms (Mason and Brown 2013), our objective is to understand how universities can stimulate high impact USOs rather than create more firms (Fini et al. 2017; Rasmussen et al. 2014). USOs typically emerging from an academic context lacking business experience and commercial skills need to assemble a range of resources to become new high-growth firms (Vohora et al. 2004). By bringing these resources together, these USOs may help to create the kinds of knowledge resources that other regional innovators can draw upon, thereby contributing to regional SUPIEs.

USOs have a low intrinsic value for universities, in that they are loosely aligned with universities' main strategic missions of excellence in teaching and research (Benneworth et al. 2017). We contend that USOs are only likely to be important to universities when they have an extrinsic (instrumental) value, in particular one that meets university stakeholders' key needs (McAdam et al. 2016; McAdam et al. 2012). If universities then respond to these USO needs, they may create services that are accessible to and valuable for other high-technology ventures, thereby potentially contributing to improving the SUPIE (Mason and Brown 2014). We therefore consider the ways that universities might choose to respond to USOs, the ways in which stakeholders might encourage those responses, and the consequences this may have for improving the overall SUPIE quality.

WHAT SUPPORT CAN UNIVERSITIES PROVIDE TO USOs?

The USO venture creation process is highly complex involving a range of different actors. Recent conceptualizations show that universities may support their USOs in gaining three kinds of entrepreneurial competencies that are important for their development (Rasmussen et al. 2014; Rasmussen and Wright 2015):

1) developing a viable business opportunity (opportunity development)
2) involving and supporting individuals that provide meaning and energy to the entrepreneurial process (championing)
3) accessing resources necessary to develop the new venture (resource leveraging).

First, USO founders' and managers' networks and experiences are usually more technologically oriented than market oriented. When exploring possible technology applications, USOs may limit their search to familiar knowledge areas or a few alternative uses (Zahra et al. 2007). Conversely, considering alternative applications more broadly and synoptically increases the chances of developing a high performing business (Gruber et al. 2013). This ability to improve and alter the opportunity according to new insights can be regarded as an opportunity development competency. This competency is dependent on high technology expertise combined with industry or market knowledge. Universities may support USO's opportunity development actively or passively. Active support may come through TTOs' activities aiming to actively place resources at USOs' disposal (Bozeman and Landsbergen 1989; Di Gregorio and Shane 2003; O'Shea et al. 2005). Passive support involves making resources (more) freely available for firms to access including research, knowledge, demand for services, complementary firms and human capital (Clark 1998; Moray and Clarysse 2005). For some USOs the university itself becomes a central first customer because the relevant product may be a research instrument or teaching technology.

Second, the role of the local work environment is particularly important for USOs because these firms are usually developed by teams where several persons play an active championing role (Vanaelst et al. 2006). Few USOs start without significant involvement from the inventors or the scientists behind the technology: the university environment can create incentives or barriers to active science participation. Potential university-based entrepreneurs may be discouraged where current local work environments are not actively entrepreneurial (Bercovitz and Feldman 2008). Hence, support from scientific colleagues, university managers, TTO staff, and people in the external network of the university is often critical, particular in early venturing stages. Moreover, it is crucial for emerging USOs that individuals with industry and business experience become involved. Universities as institutions may encourage their own stakeholders to support USOs. In early stages, the university's own business contacts may actively provide pathways allowing USOs to more easily attract champions with relevant expertise to join or support the venture, in advisory or management roles. Academics may champion ventures in which they hold a share, or seek to create future placement activities for their students, employers for their graduates, partners for research projects or customers for consultancy (D'Este and Perkmann 2011; Zomer et al. 2010).

Third, creating a new business activity based on research is typically extremely resource demanding because of parallel needs for technological, market and organizational development along lengthy paths (Colombo et al. 2014). A key resource for early stage USOs is involvement by the university scientists behind the commercialized technology (Agrawal 2006). Several studies have emphasized the role of academics' social capital and networks (Breznitz et al. 2018). Where new venture founders have relationships with venture investors they are most likely to receive venture funding and are less likely to fail (Shane and Stuart 2002). In addition to academic scientists' roles, the resource acquisition process is highly iterative involving many different actors with appropriate competencies (Rasmussen and Clausen 2012). Universities can also contribute by providing access to physical infrastructure and tangible resources such as laboratories, specific equipment, specific material (cell lines, etc.) and even venture financing (Etzkowitz and Klofsten 2005). Universities may also provide intangible resources: directly recommending USOs to investors, formally acknowledging their USOs, or offering locations, all of which may function as quality marks for potential stakeholders (Smith and Bagchi-Sen 2012). Universities' may use their wider networks to help USOs to access resources, for example building linkages between its own strategic partners and USOs.

HOW STAKEHOLDERS INFLUENCE UNIVERSITY MOTIVATION TO SUPPORT USOs

Much research on universities' entrepreneurial capability focuses on 'what' universities can do to support USOs (Berbegal-Mirabent et al. 2015; Bruneel et al. 2010) deftly avoiding the more complex question of 'why' universities might use their scarce resources on supporting USOs (Jongbloed et al. 2008; Benneworth et al. 2017). The university management literature (Clark 1998; Powell and Dayson 2013) has been rather normative, dodging this 'why' question by evoking 'heroic' university leaders who develop strategies that spread entrepreneurial enthusiasm and competence throughout their institutions. What is missing here is a more objective understanding of why these heroic university leaders would choose to support those activities, which are often at the institutional periphery, and how they fit within a university's core missions.

We contend that USOs are only likely to be important to universities when they have an extrinsic (instrumental) value, in particular one that meets university stakeholders' key needs (McAdam et al. 2016; McAdam et al. 2012). When USOs use their position within networks to access critical venturing competencies, and where universities perceive USOs as legitimate stakeholders, they may respond by providing relevant resources. Their support may then go beyond purely bilateral linkages between academics and firms towards creating more supportive environments for firms more generally (Mason and Brown 2014). The clear resonance here with emerging ideas about entrepreneurial ecosystems (Clarysse et al. 2014) leads us to suggest a future research and policy agenda where USOs are understood as one of many university stakeholders, but an important stakeholder that can trigger the universities to develop services that better contribute to SUPIEs.

There are plausible reasons that might explain why universities support their USOs; opportunity development could potentially lead to discussions with businesses leading to applied or joint research projects and USOs may improve graduate employability prospects. Likewise, there are also plausible reasons why universities might avoid supporting USOs; recommending USOs to industrial partners could, if those USOs failed to perform, potentially undermine industrial partners' trust in the academics (Guerrero and Urbano 2012). At its most extreme, universities may find themselves held financially liable for problems caused by their spin-offs (Benneworth, 2007).

Universities can be understood as highly complex, loosely coupled organizations undertaking many kinds of activities and with a range of different missions (Weick 1976). Universities' decision-making choices can be understood in terms of balancing competing interests and demands between different stakeholders (McAdam et al. 2015; McAdam et al. 2012). By stakeholders we here refer to Freeman's (1984) definition regarding an organization's stakeholders as those with a stake in the outcome of an organization's activity.

Mitchell et al. (1997) define a stakeholder's importance to an actor, or its 'salience', as the consequence of three variables, power (coercive, utilitarian, and normative), legitimacy (individual, organizational, societal) and urgency (time sensitivity, mission criticality). Given the range of pressures contemporary universities face, our diagnosis of the problem is that universities may not regard USOs as salient stakeholders and despite good intentions may choose not to take concrete steps to make resources available to support USOs (Auerswald and Branscomb 2003). Indeed, we see Bruneel et al.'s (2010) barriers between USOs and universities as symptomatic of USOs' lack of salience to universities: when universities must choose between working towards USO goals or those of other stakeholders, there is a tendency to prioritize the latter. Bjørkquist (2009) argues that networks of relationships between stakeholders can institutionalize what she calls 'stakeholder regimes'. These have definite effect on institutions' overall choices: if powerful stakeholders pressure a university to be more supportive of a third party (e.g. USOs), then that university may privilege that third party despite its low direct salience to the university. Conversely, if those stakeholders are uninterested in or antipathetic towards USO interests, then universities may be less willing to respond to USO needs.

A variety of stakeholders for the university (both internal and external) influence the extent to which USOs are seen as important to the universities. University leaders may take a strategic view on support for USOs, particularly when they can see that USOs bring resources into the university that strengthen core activities. However, an important and often understated dimension in shaping stakeholder salience is the internal institutional configuration (Benneworth et al. 2015). USOs might also have strong supporters in formal governance bodies, whether as members of governing bodies, or as entrepreneurship or technology transfer committees. University units specifically responsible for supporting USOs (e.g. TTOs) may be perceived by managers as symbolically important despite their peripheral location within the university institutional structure (Benneworth et al. 2017). Faculties and research institutes typically witness the more problematic side of USOs, where good teachers and researchers are removed from these core duties (Slaughter and Leslie 1997), although benefits may come through contributing to teaching (e.g. through placements or guest lectures) and research (as users, co-researchers, funders). Other university structures may seemingly be unconcerned with USOs, but their attitudes may nevertheless influence university interest in supporting USOs: where promotions committees see entrepreneurial activity as appropriate for tenure or promotion, then academics are less discouraged from being entrepreneurial (Powell and Dayson 2013).

External stakeholders may also be influential here, particularly those with strong interests in university outcomes and resources (Benneworth et al. 2011). There are firms who are already engaged with the university around technology transfer, shareholders in USOs or partner companies, licensing university technologies or investors in those companies. Innovation support agencies are also stakeholders, as USOs represent potential clients for them, whilst regional and national policy-makers can use USOs to demonstrate their innovation policies success (McAdam et al. 2012). Research funders have in recent years become increasingly interested in using USOs to validate claims that research brings wider socio-economic benefits (Vincett 2010). At a national level, education ministries and university regulators may fund supporting instruments (Rasmussen and Rice 2012), and regulate universities' intellectual property strategies and hence their orientation to USOs. Financiers and property developers may invest in science parks and associated university real estate to make profits, whilst companies and services that provide USOs with services can benefit from the extra business. These effects where external stakeholders indirectly value USOs can be substantial: estimates show that about 13 per cent of UK universities' competitive research funding can be explained by their USO portfolio (Pitsakis et al. 2015).

CREATING SUPIEs TO PROMOTE USOs

We see the crux of the problem here, in that USOs are extremely unlikely to be strong direct stakeholders for universities, except the rare cases where they become highly profitable (Benneworth 2007). Although individual university activities may benefit from USOs (e.g. entrepreneurship education programmes), USOs are rarely able to make strong direct claims on substantive university resources. But this need not necessarily be true when considering indirect relationships, and the extent to which external stakeholders favour working with those universities that are supportive of USO creation. We contend that thinking of USOs in the context of SUPIEs provides a different perspective on USO salience (Crow and Bozeman 1987). These ecosystems make resources available to USOs and strengthen their competencies; they are supported by powerful (salient) external university stakeholders, and it is these ecosystems in aggregate that may become salient stakeholders for the universities. These ecosystems sustain the embeddedness of regional innovation activities and help to ensure that the bilateral relationships between university and USO help contribute to a more generally beneficial knowledge pool (Lawson, 1999).

We here specify SUPIEs as being constellations of support activities broader than individual projects, where universities in an interplay with other actors, create collective assets that add value to the USO but also are available potentially for other start-ups (McAdam et al. 2016). The university's contributions to such ecosystems are assembled in response to stakeholder pressures, therefore meet a wider set of stakeholder needs than just those of USOs and hence potentially have a wider effect on supporting innovation. But to achieve that desirable endpoint, it is necessary for support to fit with internal stakeholders' needs within the university, fitting both the universities' own governance style as well as supporting core activities around teaching and research.

The discussion so far sheds new light on how the interplay between external stakeholders, universities and USOs helps to create SUPIEs. Traditionally, university support to USOs has been seen as dyadic, where characteristics of the university and the USO are the main factors explaining a successful relationship and in which there is little consideration of potential positive externalities, despite positive externalities being one of the most important characteristics of knowledge capital (Berbegal-Mirabent et al. 2015; O'Shea et al. 2005). We infer that this approach has become dominant because of the differences of structures and main purpose of universities and new technology businesses, and considering these dyads introduces an already high degree of analytic complexity.

The transformation from academic research activities into commercial business activities poses challenges both for the university and the newly minted USO. We propose that the barriers to these interactions in real SUPIEs will not be resolved exclusively through the sum total of these dyadic relationships, but solutions will emerge via wider stakeholder networks that jointly build embedded regional innovation competence through the practices of providing support to USOs. Moreover, universities' motivation and ability to support USOs is clearly influenced by the network of external stakeholders. This leads us to propose the conceptual framework in Figure 23.1 consisting of the following elements. First, USOs are likely to achieve higher growth and impact when receiving support in developing entrepreneurial competencies from their parent

Start-up incubation ecosystem (SUPIE)

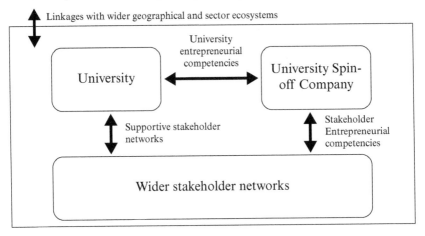

Figure 23.1 Conceptual model for a SUPIE supportive of USOs

university. This effect is likely to be strengthened when the university support is complemented by support from the university's wider stakeholder network. Moreover, the university is more likely to support USOs in developing entrepreneurial competencies when the university's wider stakeholder network is supportive. This reinforcing connection between the external stakeholders, the university and the USOs constitutes an ecosystem supportive of USO creation. However, to be effective in creating successful USOs this ecosystem needs to be linked with wider geographical and sectoral ecosystems that jointly constitute a SUPIE that determines the total level and success of USO creation from the university.

What is important in this heuristic is that the direct benefits that each party (notably universities) receives from co-operation do not compellingly explain why universities and USOs would work together. It is these wider stakeholder benefits that make the university–USO relationship valuable but at the same time contribute to the development of the collective assets. In Figure 23.1, university support for USOs involves building direct support activities that become embedded within dynamic SUPIEs that can meet wider entrepreneurial stakeholder networks' needs whilst simultaneously helping these USOs.

Our model implies that understanding university contributions to USO growth and impact requires looking more broadly than at just the dyadic university–USO relationships. Rather, we need to understand the way that universities are influenced by and engage with external stakeholders in providing SUPIEs with easier access to entrepreneurial competencies. USOs are companies created in positions of extreme uncertainty, and the competency approach highlights that universities can play a significant direct and indirect role in helping these firms develop their business opportunities, secure champions and access resources (Rasmussen et al. 2014). We highlight how actors outside the USO have relationships to these firms or see them as mechanisms to achieve their own goals (Fini et al. 2018). This can potentially facilitate the access to critical resources for the company, both from the knowledge and business ecosystems (Clarysse et al. 2014).

IMPLICATIONS FOR FUTURE RESEARCH, POLICY AND PRACTICE

The framework proposed in this chapter has clear implications for further research, policy and practice. If USOs are regarded as stakeholders, then further research should shift from the complex environment of the university to highlighting the role of USOs as stakeholders in their own right. This requires answering the questions of which stakeholder groups USOs are tied to, in particular internal university stakeholders. More attention is required for the topology of the stakeholder networks in which USOs access support, and how these network dynamics influence the ways in which USOs benefit from university support. The understanding of how universities promote USOs is fragmented and the effect of different policy initiatives is therefore highly uncertain (Mathisen and Rasmussen 2019). Hence, more research is needed to understand how SUPIEs can be nurtured, as well as how individual interventions shape the power relationships of stakeholders and USOs' positions in those ecosystems.

To succeed, USOs require access to resources to grow, but potential resource providers are often unable to judge whether USOs are going to succeed and hence be able to repay any invested resources. One element here is a lack of access to finance (the so-called 'Valley of Death'), that can be addressed by instruments such as subsidized venture capital seed funds (Munari et al. 2015). But USOs also can benefit from more tacit resources held by universities that require trust, collaboration and interaction to access (Rasmussen and Wright 2015): policy-makers can encourage universities to make resources available by signalling, for example, via research assessments and evaluations, that working with USOs is rewarded.

Although policy may seek to facilitate and improve university contributions to SUPIEs, improving ecosystem functioning can never be delivered exclusively by universities but rather requires a more subtle set of responsible nurturing practices by a variety of ecosystem actors. There can be a tension between universities seeking to providing general ecosystem benefits available to many firms and working with a more limited group to give private benefits, what Bozeman et al. (2013) refer to as 'public value failures'. If policy-makers do want to improve SUPIEs rather than simply create some successful USOs, they must ensure that the university–USO relationships can function as networks, and acquire 'ecosystemic' properties ensuring accessibility for all within the ecosystem (O'Kane et al. 2015; Rasmussen and Borch 2010). The question here is how existing academics and entrepreneurs can become useful to new start-ups through, for example, mentoring activities and signposting.

An entrepreneurial ecosystem for USOs is not necessarily a place where all actors are deliberately creating firms all the time but one that offers fertile niches where entrepreneurs can flourish, often as the by-product of other activities. Thus a critical issue for policy-makers is in supporting the 'fertility' of the underlying knowledge resources, to allow the spillover benefits to emerge from the university to lead to future firm creation, and to create effective SUPIEs. Although there may have been a need 25 years ago for policy-makers to shake up academia (Berman 2011), continuing exclusive emphasis on a primacy for entrepreneurship by university may be increasingly counter-productive (Philpott et al. 2011) by using resources in entrepreneurial ecosystems faster than they can be replaced.

Our framework also implies practical ways universities' stakeholder communities could support USO entrepreneurial activity in a way that is better aligned with their own institutional goals. University management can sustain a commitment to entrepreneurship and supporting USOs, creating institutional frameworks that give university employees real incentives to benefit from entrepreneurship (not exclusively financially). These institutional frameworks will be – in line with the institutional nature of universities – both formal regulations and structures alongside informal cultures and practices. Institutional leaders at all levels (institutional, faculty, research group) play a role here in reshaping the external environment (e.g. research assessment practices) to persuade external parties to value and/or reward the university for its pro-activity in stimulating USO support.

Universities can be motivated to support SUPIEs by explicitly acknowledging and championing the benefits working with USOs brings to the university (Pitsakis et al. 2015) and how working with USOs can benefit individual academics and research groups. This involves internal stakeholders regarding entrepreneurship as a legitimate pathway to fulfilling core academic tasks, for example, the degree to which tenure, promotion or sabbatical committees acknowledge work with USOs as being valid. A final associated element here is where universities persuade other external stakeholders to explicitly value universities' work for USOs, thereby creating external validation for these internal stakeholders that contributing to SUPIEs is a legitimate and desirable activity.

REFERENCES

Agrawal, A. (2006). Engaging the inventor: Exploring licensing strategies for university inventions and the role of latent knowledge. *Strategic Management Journal, 27*(1), 63–79.
Auerswald, P., and Branscomb, L. (2003). Valleys of Death and Darwinian Seas: Financing the invention to innovation transition in the United States. *Journal of Technology Transfer, 28*(3–4), 227–239.
Benneworth, P. (2007). Seven Samurai opening up the Ivory Tower? The construction of Newcastle as an Entrepreneurial University. *European Planning Studies, 15*(4), 487–509.
Benneworth, P. S., Pinheiro, R., and Karlsen, J. (2017). Strategic agency and institutional change: Investigating the role of universities in Regional Innovation Systems (RISs). *Regional Studies, 51*(2), 235–248.
Benneworth, P., de Boer, H., and Jongbloed, B. (2015). Between good intentions and urgent

stakeholder pressures: Institutionalizing the universities' third mission in the Swedish context. *European Journal of Higher Education*, 5(3), 280–296.

Benneworth, P., Hospers, G.-J., Jongbloed, B., Leiyste, L., and Zomer, A. (2011). The 'Science City' as a system coupler in fragmented strategic urban environments? *Built Environment*, 37(3), 317–335.

Berggren, E. and A. L. Dahlstrand 2009. Creating an entrepreneurial region: Two waves of academic spin-offs from Halmstad University. *European Planning Studies*, 17(8), 1171–1189.

Berbegal-Mirabent, J., Ribeiro-Soriano, D. E., and Sánchez García, J. L. (2015). Can a magic recipe foster university spin-off creation? *Journal of Business Research*, 68(11), 2272–2278.

Bercovitz, J., and Feldman, M. (2008). Academic entrepreneurs: Organizational change at the individual level. *Organization Science*, 19(1), 69–89.

Berman, E. P. (2011). *Creating the market university: How academic science became an economic engine*. Princeton: Princeton University Press.

Bjørkquist, C. (2009). Stakeholder Influence in Higher Education: Old Ideas in New Bottles? PhD thesis, Karlstad University, Karlstad, Sweden.

Bozeman, B., and Landsbergen, D. (1989). Truth and credibility in sincere policy analysis alternative approaches for the production of policy-relevant knowledge. *Evaluation Review*, 13(4), 355–379.

Bozeman, B., Fay, D., and Slade, C. (2013). Research collaboration in universities and academic entrepreneurship: The-state-of-the-art. *Journal of Technology Transfer*, 38(1), 1–67.

Breznitz, S. M., Clayton, P. A., Defazio, D., and Isett, K. R. (2018). Have you been served? The impact of university entrepreneurial support on start-ups' network formation. *Journal of Technology Transfer*, 43(2), 343–367.

Bruneel, J., D'Este, P., and Salter, A. (2010). Investigating the factors that diminish the barriers to university–industry collaboration. *Research Policy*, 39(7), 858–868.

Clark, B. R. (1998). *Creating entrepreneurial universities – organizational pathways of transformation*. Oxford: Elsevier Science Ltd.

Clarysse, B., Wright, M., and Van de Velde, E. (2011). Entrepreneurial origin, technological knowledge, and the growth of spin-off companies. *Journal of Management Studies*, 48(6), 1420–1442.

Clarysse, B., Wright, M., Bruneel, J., and Mahajan, A. (2014). Creating value in ecosystems: Crossing the chasm between knowledge and business ecosystems. *Research Policy*, 43(7), 1164–1176.

Colombo, M., Croce, A., and Murtinu, S. (2014). Ownership structure, horizontal agency costs and the performance of high-tech entrepreneurial firms. *Small Business Economics*, 42(2), 265–282.

Crow, M. M., and Bozeman, B. L. (1987). A new typology for R&D laboratories: Implications for policy analysts. *Journal of Policy Analysis and Management*, 6(3), 328–341.

D'Este, P., and Perkmann, M. (2011). Why do academics engage with industry? The entrepreneurial university and individual motivations. *Journal of Technology Transfer*, 36(3), 316–339.

Di Gregorio, D., and Shane, S. (2003). Why do some universities generate more start-ups than others? *Research Policy*, 32(2), 209–227.

Etzkowitz, H., and Klofsten, M. (2005). The innovating region: Toward a theory of knowledge-based regional development. *R&D Management*, 35(3), 243–255.

Fini, R., Fu, K., Mathisen, M. T., Rasmussen, E., and Wright, M. (2017). Institutional determinants of university spin-off quantity and quality: a longitudinal, multilevel, cross-country study. *Small Business Economics*, 48(2), 361–391.

Fini, R., Rasmussen, E., Siegel, D., and Wiklund, J. (2018). Rethinking the commercialization of public science: From entrepreneurial outcomes to societal impacts. *Academy of Management Perspectives*, 32(1), 4–20.

Foss, L., and Gibson, D. V. (2015). *The Entrepreneurial University: Context and Institutional Change*. Oxford: Routledge.

Freeman, R. E. (1984). *Strategic management: A stakeholder approach.* Boston: Pitman Publishing.

Garnsey, E., and P. Heffernan (2005). High-technology clustering through spin-out and attraction: The Cambridge case. *Regional Studies, 39*(8), 1127–1144.

Ghio, N., Guerini, M., and Rossi-Lamastra, C. (2016). University knowledge and the creation of innovative start-ups: An analysis of the Italian case. *Small Business Economics, 47*(2), 293–311.

Gruber, M., MacMillan, I. C., and Thompson, J. D. (2013). Escaping the prior knowledge corridor: What shapes the number and variety of market opportunities identified before market entry of technology start-ups? *Organization Science, 24*(1), 280–300.

Guerrero, M., and Urbano, D. (2012). The development of an entrepreneurial university. *Journal of Technology Transfer, 37*(1), 43–74.

Guerrero, M., Cunningham, J. A., and Urbano, D. (2015). Economic impact of entrepreneurial universities' activities: An exploratory study of the United Kingdom. *Research Policy, 44*(3), 748–764.

Harrison, R. T., and Leitch, C. (2010). Voodoo institution or entrepreneurial university? Spin-off companies, the entrepreneurial system and regional development in the UK. *Regional Studies, 44*(9), 1241–1262.

Hayter, C. S., Nelson, A. J., Zayed, S., and O'Connor, A. C. (2018). Conceptualizing academic entrepreneurship ecosystems: A review, analysis and extension of the literature. *Journal of Technology Transfer.* In press.

Hayter, C. S., Rasmussen, E., & Rooksby, J. H. (2018). Beyond formal university technology transfer: Innovative pathways for knowledge exchange. *Journal of Technology Transfer.* In press.

Henrekson, M., and Rosenberg, N. (2001). Designing efficient institutions for science-based entrepreneurship: Lessons from the US and Sweden. *Journal of Technology Transfer, 26*(1/2), 207–231.

Jongbloed, B., Enders, J., and Salerno, C. (2008). Higher education and its communities: Interconnections, interdependencies and a research agenda. *Higher Education, 56*(3), 303–324.

Lawson, C. (1999). Towards a competence theory of the region. *Cambridge Journal of Economics, 23*, 151–166.

Link, A. N., and Scott, J. T. (2003). US science parks: The diffusion of an innovation and its effects on the academic missions of universities. *International Journal of Industrial Organization, 21*(9), 1323–1356.

Mason, C., and Brown, R. (2013). Creating good public policy to support high-growth firms. *Small Business Economics, 40*(2), 211–225.

Mason, C., and Brown, R. (2014). Entrepreneurial ecosystems and growth oriented entrepreneurship. Final Report to OECD, Paris.

Mathisen, M.T., and Rasmussen, E. (2019). The development, growth and performance of university spin-offs: A critical review. *Journal of Technology Transfer.* In press.

McAdam, M., Miller, K., and McAdam, R. (2016). Situated regional university incubation: A multi-level stakeholder perspective. *Technovation, 50*, 69–78.

McAdam, R., Miller, K., McAdam, M., and Teague, S. (2012). The development of University Technology Transfer stakeholder relationships at a regional level: Lessons for the future. *Technovation, 32*(1), 57–67.

Mitchell, R. K., Agle, B. R., and Wood, D. J. (1997). Toward a theory of stakeholder identification and salience: Defining the principle of who and what really counts. *Academy of Management Review, 22*(4), 853–886.

Moray, N., and Clarysse, B. (2005). Institutional change and resource endowments to science-based entrepreneurial firms. *Research Policy, 34*(7), 1010–1027.

Mowery, D. C., and Sampat, B. N. (2005). The Bayh-Dole Act of 1980 and University-Industry Technology Transfer: A model for other OECD Governments? *Journal of Technology Transfer, 30*(1/2), 115–127.

Munari, F., Rasmussen, E., Toschi, L., and Villani, E. (2015). Determinants of the university technology transfer policy-mix: A cross-national analysis of gap-funding instruments. *Journal of Technology Transfer*, *41*(6), 1377–1405.

O'Kane, C., Mangematin, V., Geoghegan, W., and Fitzgerald, C. (2015). University technology transfer offices: The search for identity to build legitimacy. *Research Policy*, *44*(2), 421–437.

O'Shea, R. P., Allen, T. J., Chevalier, A., and Roche, F. (2005). Entrepreneurial orientation, technology transfer and spinoff performance of US universities. *Research Policy*, *34*(7), 994–1009.

Philpott, K., Dooley, L., O'Reilly, C., and Lupton, G. (2011). The entrepreneurial university: Examining the underlying academic tensions. *Technovation*, *31*(4), 161–170.

Pitsakis, K., Souitaris, V., and Nicolaou, N. (2015). The Peripheral Halo Effect: Do academic spinoffs influence universities' research income? *Journal of Management Studies*, *52*(3), 321–353.

Powell, J., and Dayson, K. (2013). Engagement and the idea of the civic university, in P. Benneworth, (ed.), *University Engagement With Socially Excluded Communities*. Dordrecht: Springer, pp. 143–162.

Rasmussen, E., and Borch, O. J. (2010). University capabilities in facilitating entrepreneurship: A longitudinal study of spin-off ventures at mid-range universities. *Research Policy*, *39*(5), 602–612.

Rasmussen, E., and Clausen, T. H. (2012). Openness and innovativeness within science-based entrepreneurial firms, in F. Welter, D. Smallbone, and A. V. Gils, (eds.), *Entrepreneurial Processes in a Changing Economy*. Cheltenham, UK: Edward Elgar, pp. 139–158.

Rasmussen, E., and Rice, M. P. (2012). A framework for government support mechanisms aimed at enhancing university technology transfer: The Norwegian case. *International Journal of Technology Transfer and Commercialisation*, *11*(1/2), 1–25.

Rasmussen, E., and Wright, M. (2015). How can universities facilitate academic spin-offs? An entrepreneurial competency perspective. *Journal of Technology Transfer*, *40*(5), 782–799.

Rasmussen, E., Borch, O. J., and Sørheim, R. (2008). University entrepreneurship and government support schemes, in A. Fayolle and P. Kyrö, (eds.), *The Dynamic between Entrepreneurship, Environment and Education*. Cheltenham: Edward Elgar, pp. 105–130.

Rasmussen, E., Mosey, S., and Wright, M. (2014). The influence of university departments on the evolution of entrepreneurial competencies in spin-off ventures. *Research Policy*, *43*(1), 92–106.

Schaeffer, V., and Matt, M. (2016). Development of academic entrepreneurship in a non-mature context: The role of the university as a hub-organisation. *Entrepreneurship & Regional Development*, *28*(9–10), 724–745.

Shane, S., and Stuart, T. (2002). Organizational endowments and the performance of university start-ups. *Management Science*, *48*(1), 154–170.

Slaughter, S., and Leslie, L. L. (1997). *Academic Capitalism: Politics, Policies, and the Entrepreneurial University*. Baltimore: Johns Hopkins University Press.

Smith, H. L., and Bagchi-Sen, S. (2012). The research university, entrepreneurship and regional development: Research propositions and current evidence. *Entrepreneurship & Regional Development*, *24*(5–6), 383–404.

Spigel, B. (2017). The relational organization of entrepreneurial ecosystems. *Entrepreneurship Theory and Practice*, *41*(1), 49–72.

Vanaelst, I., Clarysse, B., Wright, M., Lockett, A., Moray, N., and S'Jegers, R. (2006). Entrepreneurial team development in academic spinouts: An examination of team heterogeneity. *Entrepreneurship Theory and Practice*, *30*(2), 249–271.

Villani, E., Rasmussen, E., and Grimaldi, R. (2017). How intermediary organizations facilitate university–industry technology transfer: A proximity approach. *Technological Forecasting and Social Change*, 114, 86–102.

Vincett, P. S. (2010). The economic impacts of academic spin-off companies, and their implications for public policy. *Research Policy*, *39*(6), 736–747.

Vohora, A., Wright, M., and Lockett, A. (2004). Critical junctures in the development of university high-tech spinout companies. *Research Policy, 33*(1), 147–175.

Weick, K. E. (1976). Educational organizations as loosely coupled systems. *Administrative Science Quarterly, 21*(1), 1–19.

Zahra, S. A., Van de Velde, E., and Larraneta, B. (2007). Knowledge conversion capability and the performance of corporate and university spin-offs. *Industrial and Corporate Change, 16*(4), 569–608.

Zomer, A. H., Jongbloed, B. W. A., and Enders, J. (2010). Do spin-offs make the academics' heads spin? *Minerva, 48*(3), 331–353.

Index